Standard Functions

ABS (x)	FLOAT (x)	MIN (T)	SIZE (T)
CAP (ch)	HIGH (a)	ODD (x)	TRUN
CHR (x)	MAX (T)	ORD (x)	[illegible]

Standard Procedures

DEC (x)	EXCL (s, i)	INC (x)	(s, i)
DEC (x, n)	HALT	INC (x, n)	

Standard Types

BITSET	CHAR	LONGREAL
BOOLEAN	INTEGER	PROC
CARDINAL	LONGINT	REAL

Sample Type Declarations

```
TYPE Days = (Mon, Tue, Wed, Thu, Fri);          (* enumeration    *)
     Months = [1..12];                          (* subrange type  *)
     HourlyReading =
       ARRAY Days, [0..23] OF REAL;             (* array type     *)
     String10 = ARRAY [0..9] OF CHAR;           (* string type    *)
     Coordinate = RECORD
                    x, y: REAL                  (* record type    *)
                  END;
     Figure =
       RECORD
         location: Coordinate;
         CASE shape: (circle, rectangle) OF     (* record with a  *)
           circle:    radius: REAL |            (* variant part   *)
           rectangle: length, width: REAL
         END
       END;
     SetOfDays = SET OF Days;                   (* set type       *)
     FigurePtr = POINTER TO Figure;             (* pointer type   *)
     ConvFunc = PROCEDURE (INTEGER): REAL;      (* procedure type *)
```

Modula-2
A Complete Guide

K. N. King
Georgia State University

D. C. HEATH AND COMPANY
Lexington, Massachusetts Toronto

Published simultaneously in Canada.

Printed in the United States of America.

International Standard Book Number: 0-669-11091-4

Library of Congress Catalog Card Number: 87-81177

10 9 8 7 6 5 4 3

To my parents,
Paul and Marcelia King

Preface

Modula-2: A Complete Guide was written to serve two purposes. First, it is a complete reference to the Modula-2 language. The book has been organized by language feature, making it possible for the reader to find information quickly. Second, it can be used as a text for classroom instruction or for self-study. The features of the language are presented in a logical order so that the chapters may be read in order; extensive examples illustrate each language feature.

This book has a variety of uses:

- As a reference for computer science courses in which Modula-2 is used for programming assignments or project work. Modula-2 is particularly appropriate for courses where data abstraction and modular software development are taught (including data structures and software engineering) and courses that require low-level, machine-dependent programming (for example, compiler construction, operating systems, and computer graphics). Modula-2 is also an excellent choice for a course in comparative programming languages.
- As a text for teaching Modula-2 as a second programming language.
- As a self-study text for software professionals or knowledgeable hobbyists.

The reader is assumed to have written programs in a structured, high-level language such as Pascal, PL/I, Ada, or C. Chapters 11 and 12 require a rudimentary knowledge of computer organization, such as one might obtain from writing assembly language programs.

Although Modula-2 was designed for systems programming, it is a true general-purpose language. For this reason, I have avoided directing the book solely to systems programmers. The examples should be accessible to any programmer, not just one involved in systems development.

Organization

Organizing a book for both reference and tutorial use is not an easy task. I have tried to serve the former by confining the discussion of each language feature to a single chapter rather than spreading out coverage over several chapters. At the same time, I have organized the chapters so that they may be read in sequence.

Chapter 1 provides a history of Modula-2 and an overview of the language. The overview has two parts. The first part explains the basic features of Modula-2 by comparison with Pascal. The second part covers Modula-2's advanced features.

Chapters 2–5 cover the fundamentals of Modula-2. Chapter 2 describes Modula-2 both "bottom-up" (by explaining the rules for forming Modula-2 symbols) and "top-down" (by explaining the structure of a Modula-2 program). Chapter 3 presents Modula-2's numeric, character, and Boolean types and their use in forming expressions and declaring constants and variables. Chapter 4 discusses Modula-2's assignment statement and control structures. Chapter 5 covers procedures (and functions) and shows how procedure declarations affect the scope of entities in a program.

Chapters 6–8 describe Modula-2's mechanisms for creating new types. Chapter 6 covers unstructured types (enumeration and subrange types), Chapter 7 explains structured types (arrays, records, and sets), and Chapter 8 discusses pointer and procedure types. All these types — with the exception of procedure types — appear in Pascal.

Chapters 9 and 10 describe modules, the most important new feature of Modula-2. Chapter 9 covers the syntax and semantics of library modules and local modules; it also explains separate compilation of modules and the scope issues that arise from the use of modules. Chapter 10 provides module examples and guidelines for the proper use of modules, and introduces the object-oriented approach to program design.

Chapter 11 covers Modula-2's low-level features in considerable detail. It also shows how to use these low-level features to write generic procedures and modules. The examples in this chapter are for the IBM PC family, but most can be adapted to other machines without difficulty.

Chapter 12 describes Modula-2's support for coroutines and interrupt handling. The chapter also presents the `Processes` module and shows how to write alternative process-handling modules. Two implementations appear for one such module (`ScheduledProcesses`); the second implementation features interrupt-driven process scheduling.

Chapter 13 covers Niklaus Wirth's input/output modules: `Terminal`, `InOut`, `RealInOut`, and `FileSystem`. I/O is not a part of the Modula-2 language, nor is there a standard I/O library for Modula-2 at present. Several proposed standard libraries exist, but it would be premature to predict which one will become the final standard. In the meantime, the closest to standard are the modules described in Wirth's *Programming in Modula-2*. Because most Modula-2 systems supply Wirth's modules (although often in modified form), I have chosen to devote one chapter to them. Because some systems provide a different I/O library, however, I have postponed the discussion of Wirth's modules until the final chapter, which can be skipped without loss of continuity. The example programs in the first twelve chapters depend little on Wirth's modules; readers using a different I/O library should have no trouble modifying the programs.

Features

Program Examples The book contains over two dozen complete programs in addition to numerous procedures and modules. Lengthy examples are set off from the rest of the text by the heading "Example Program" (for a complete program) or "Example" (for a procedure or module example) to help separate reference material from tutorial material. Most of the example programs appear in Chapters 9–13, where they are needed to explain Modula-2 concepts that are not found in Pascal. I have tested all programs, and most smaller examples, using at least one Modula-2 system. (The example programs—including all library module examples—are available in source form for MS-DOS and PC-DOS computers. Send a check or money order for $10 to Dr. K. N. King, Department of Mathematics and Computer Science, Georgia State University, University Plaza, Atlanta, Georgia 30303.)

Optional Topics Several chapters contain optional sections that may be skipped on first reading. These sections cover advanced (or, in some cases, esoteric) topics that will interest the expert but not necessarily the casual reader.

Comparisons with Standard Pascal Chapters 2–8 provide detailed, point-by-point comparisons between Pascal and Modula-2. These comparisons are for the benefit of readers who are familiar with Pascal; other readers may skip them. The version of Pascal used for these comparisons is Standard Pascal, as defined by the International Standards Organization (ISO DP7185). (For a good description of Standard Pascal, consult Doug Cooper's *Standard Pascal User Reference Manual*, Norton, New York, 1983.) The U.S. standard for Pascal (ANSI/IEEE770X3.97-1983) is essentially equivalent to Level 0 of ISO Standard Pascal. Because most Pascal compilers support extensions to Standard Pascal, some versions of Pascal will resemble Modula-2 more closely than our comparisons might indicate.

Coverage of Both Major Versions of Modula-2 The version of Modula-2 covered in this book is the one described in Wirth's *Programming in Modula-2*, Third, Corrected Edition. Because there is no official standard for Modula-2 at present (an international standard is in preparation), Wirth's book serves as the *de facto* standard. Some older Modula-2 systems may be based on the Second Edition of Wirth's book, which describes a slightly different version of the language. Because a particular system may be based on either of these editions, or a hybrid of the two, I have indicated in the text the differences between the two editions. Appendix V contains a complete list of differences.

Appendices Because this book is meant to serve as a comprehensive reference on Modula-2, much effort was devoted to making the appendices as detailed and useful as possible. Appendix I lists all reserved words and standard identifiers in Modula-2, including standard procedures and functions. Appendix II contains a complete EBNF (Extended Backus-Naur Form) description of the syntax of Modula-2. Appendix III offers a complete set of syntax charts for the language. To ensure accuracy and consistency, these charts are the same as those in the Third Edition of *Programming in Modula-2*. Appendix IV contains descriptions of the most widely used modules in Wirth's library. Appendix V lists changes made to Modula-2 between the Second and Third Editions of *Programming in Modula-2*. Appendix VI provides a table of the ASCII character set.

Glossary An extensive glossary of Modula-2 terms follows the appendices.

Bibliography The bibliography lists books, articles, and technical reports about Modula-2 and related topics. A reader who needs additional information about a particular aspect of Modula-2 (for example, writing a Modula-2 compiler or using Modula-2 for writing operating systems) should find the bibliography a useful starting point.

Resources The resources section provides both a list of periodicals that cover Modula-2 and a list of Modula-2 systems.

Exercises Exercises appear at the end of each chapter; answers to most exercises appear at the end of the book. The exercises reinforce the topics covered in the chapter, as well as serving as a source of additional examples.

Index The index is one of the most important features of any book; this is doubly true for reference books. Much effort has been put into making the index as complete and accurate as possible.

Using This Book as a Tutorial

When using this book as a tutorial on Modula-2, read the chapters in the following order:

1. Read all of Chapter 1 for an overview of Modula-2.
2. Chapters 2–8 cover Modula-2's Pascal-like features. Readers who already know Pascal need only skim these chapters, paying particular attention to the comparison between Standard Pascal and Modula-2 at the end of each chapter.
3. Read Chapters 9 and 10. These chapters explain the module concept, which is central to Modula-2.
4. Read Chapter 11 if interested in Modula-2's features for low-level, machine-dependent programming. After reading Chapter 11, readers who want to learn about Modula-2's support for coroutines and interrupt handling should continue to Chapter 12.
5. Refer to Chapter 13 as needed; unlike the other chapters, Chapter 13 need not be read in sequence. However, portions of Section 13.3 require some knowledge of topics in Chapter 11.

Acknowledgments

I thank several of my friends and colleagues in the School of Information and Computer Science at the Georgia Institute of Technology, where this book was written. Partha Dasgupta made important contributions to Chapter 12. Jeff Offutt provided detailed comments on an early version of the manuscript. Tom Wilkes was helpful during the early stages of this project. Burt Leavenworth was a source of many useful conversations during the year that he visited at Georgia Tech. The first example program in Section 11.3 is based on his unpublished design. John Passafiume provided invaluable assistance with equipment for this project. I owe a special debt to Alex Fox, who checked the answers to the exercises.

Two individuals outside Georgia Tech also provided valuable assistance. Jeanette Symons supplied information about the proposed BSI standard library. I am also indebted to Jeff Brumfield of the University of Texas, whose ideas on the presentation of programming language syntax influenced Appendices II and III as well as the syntax diagrams on the inside front and back covers.

I thank the instructors who tested the manuscript in their classes. I also thank the hundreds of students in those classes for their patience while grappling with a manuscript in various stages of completion.

Thanks go to the following reviewers, who worked to make this a better book: Thomas J. Ahlborn, West Chester University; Gene Blanford, Raymond Walters Community College; Vern J. Crandall, Brigham Young University; Albert L. Crawford, Southern Illinois University, Carbondale; Susan Lilly; Prabhaker Mateti, Case Western Reserve University; Mike Michaelson, Palomar College; Larry Neal, East Tennessee State University; James F. Peters III, St. John's University; Lawrence L. Rose, University of Pittsburgh; Barbara Smith-Thomas, University of North Carolina at Greensboro; Henry Walker, Grinnell College; and Chip Weems, University of Massachusetts at Amherst.

The following reviewers deserve special thanks for their contributions to this book: Ronald S. Curtis, Canisius College; Stan Osborne, San Francisco State University; and Richard E. Pattis, University of Washington.

The following Modula-2 vendors provided technical assistance during this project: Echelon, Inc., Interface Technologies Corporation, Logitech, Inc., and PCollier Systems, Inc. Chris Cale of Logitech was particularly helpful.

I thank Springer-Verlag for permission to reprint reference material from *Programming in Modula-2*.

Special thanks go to my editor, Karin Ellison, whose enthusiasm for this book never flagged, and whose hard work on behalf of the project will never be forgotten. I also thank my production editor, Jill Hobbs, for her patience with an often recalcitrant author.

Finally, I thank my wife, Cindy, who endured with grace the long hours I spent on this book. Without her support, I couldn't have written it.

K. N. K.

Contents

1 An Overview of Modula-2

Designed by Niklaus Wirth of Pascal fame, Modula-2 has attracted wide attention since 1980, when a description of it was first published. From its obscure beginnings as the base language for Wirth's Lilith computer system, Modula-2 has gained widespread acceptance as an alternative to such languages as Pascal, C, and Ada.

It is difficult to discuss Modula-2 without mentioning Pascal, because many of Modula-2's features come directly from Pascal with little or no modification. Modula-2 retains the strengths of Pascal: strong typing, a rich variety of data types, and a powerful set of control statements. Like Pascal, Modula-2 is a simple language that is easy to learn, easy to compile, and capable of being translated into efficient object code.

Strong typing means that every variable and constant in a Modula-2 program has a fixed type that is checked during compilation to ensure that the item is used in a consistent manner. Consequently, many programming errors are detected during compilation, when they are easiest to locate and fix.

The wide selection of data structures — including arrays, records, and sets — that made Pascal such a popular language also appear in Modula-2. This variety makes the programmer's task easier: he or she can design data structures that closely reflect the real-world objects they model.

Pascal is famous for its control statements, which allow the construction of well-structured programs that contain few `goto` statements (often none). Modula-2 contains all of Pascal's structured control statements and more.

Wirth strongly believes that programming languages should be simple and easy to master. He has followed that principle in designing all of his languages, including Pascal and Modula-2. Wirth also believes that languages should allow efficient translation and execution. In designing Modula-2, Wirth included only features that he knew could be compiled into efficient object code. Many programming languages have been designed long before they were implemented; Modula-2, however, was developed at the same time that its first compiler was written, ensuring that hard-to-compile features would not creep into the language.

In addition to retaining the best features of Pascal, Modula-2 includes new features that make it applicable to a much broader range of applications than Pascal. These features include

open array parameters
procedure types
opaque types
modules
separate compilation (with type-checking across compilation unit boundaries)
features for low-level, machine-dependent programming
coroutines
interrupt handling

These new features make Modula-2 ideal for developing systems software: operating systems, compilers, editors, linkers, debuggers, and the like. But Modula-2's support for modular program development and object-oriented design make it suitable for writing almost any large software system. In addition, Modula-2's small size and efficient object code have made it popular for programming microcomputers.

This chapter provides both a brief history of Modula-2 (Section 1.1) and a comprehensive overview of the language (Sections 1.2 and 1.3). Section 1.2 describes the basic features of Modula-2—the features that have Pascal counterparts—while Section 1.3 explains the advanced features of the language. As we sketch the basic features of Modula-2, we will mention briefly how these features differ from Standard Pascal's. More detailed comparisons between Modula-2 and Standard Pascal appear at the ends of Chapters 2–8. (*Note:* Knowledge of Pascal is not a prerequisite for reading this book. Readers who are familiar with Pascal will learn Modula-2 more quickly by comparison with Pascal; readers not familiar with Pascal can skip comparisons with that language without loss.)

1.1 A Brief History of Modula-2

Although Modula-2 is a relatively new language, its origins can be traced back to the early programming language Algol 60—the forerunner of Pascal, Ada, Modula-2, and many other languages.

Algol 60: The Story Begins

Algol 60 was designed by an international committee during the late 1950s, at a time when few high-level programming languages existed. (Fortran, one of the first high-level languages, appeared in 1957.) Algol 60 featured numerous innovations in language design: it was the first block-structured language, the first language to have a formal syntactic definition, the first to allow value parameters, the first to distinguish between local and global variables, and the first to supply an `if-then-else` statement. Yet Algol 60 suffered from a lack of standard input/output procedures and was not supported by major U.S. computer manufacturers. Although it became popular in Europe, Algol 60 never posed a serious threat to Cobol and Fortran in the United States.

Despite its lack of commercial success, Algol 60 was widely admired for its ideas; in the years following its original definition, numerous attempts were made to create improved versions of the language. Niklaus Wirth of the Swiss Federal Institute of Technology was one of many computer scientists interested in developing an improved Algol. During the 1960s, he created several Algol-based languages, including Euler (1963) and Algol W (1966). He also served on an international committee that was designing the successor to Algol 60, although he eventually left the committee because he disagreed with the direction that the design of the new language was taking. Wirth believed that a programming language should be simple and its compilers efficient. The new language, now known as Algol 68, was elegant but difficult to understand and implement.

Pascal: Wirth's Answer to Algol 68

In reaction to the complexity of Algol 68, Wirth designed a new language, Pascal, which he announced in a 1971 report. He set several goals for Pascal. First and foremost, it was to be a simple language. In addition, Pascal was to provide support for systematic program development ("structured programming"). Wirth also wanted it to be possible to implement Pascal efficiently.

Pascal not only met Wirth's goals, but also became tremendously popular during the 1970s and early 1980s. Its popularity began in computer science departments, where it became a leading language of programming instruction, but later spread to industry, where Pascal is now widely used for commercial software development. Pascal is also a popular alternative to Basic as a language for programming microcomputers.

Modula: The Forerunner of Modula-2

As Pascal was gaining recognition, Wirth's increasing interest in multiprogramming (the concurrent execution of several tasks) led him to design Modula, a language similar to Pascal but with support for multiprogramming. Wirth described Modula (*Modu*lar *la*nguage) in a series of papers published in 1977. Although Modula attracted the attention of programming language specialists, it never advanced beyond the experimental stage.

During 1976–1977, Wirth visited the Xerox Palo Alto Research Center, where he became acquainted with the Xerox Alto, a powerful single-user computer system, and with Mesa, a Pascal-like language for large-scale system development. On returning to Switzerland, Wirth began to develop a single-user system similar to the Alto. This system, which he called Lilith, featured a high-performance processor, a bit-mapped display, a mouse, and a system architecture designed to support high-level language compilers. (Lilith was appropriately named. In Jewish mythology, Lilith is the name of a female demon who seduces men away from their wives and children.)

The Genesis of Modula-2

At the start of the Lilith project, Wirth decided that the machine would be designed to execute programs written in a single language. This language would be high-level, yet capable of expressing low-level operations — operations specific to the Lilith hardware. Pascal was inappropriate, because it contained no provision for programming at the machine level. The Modula language had one advantage over Pascal: Modula programs could be divided into "modules" — program units capable of hiding some of their entities (variables and procedures, for example) while making others visible to the rest of the program. Modules are particularly useful for a language that allows low-level programming, because machine dependencies can be confined to certain modules, not spread throughout an entire program. To design the language for Lilith, Wirth started with Pascal, added a few features — including the module concept from Modula (with some modifications inspired by Mesa) — and made some syntax changes. Since the new language was highly modular, he named it Modula-2.

After its creation in 1978, Modula-2 was quickly implemented (in 1979, on a DEC PDP-11). The first official description of the language appeared in 1980, as did the first publicly available compiler.

Modula-2 Today

Although the Lilith system itself has not caught on in the United States, Modula-2 attracted immediate interest. Modula-2 systems are now available for most popular microcomputers and some minicomputers and mainframes.

The only definitive description of Modula-2 is in Wirth's *Programming in Modula-2*, Third, Corrected Edition (New York: Springer-Verlag, 1985), which includes both the "Report on the Programming Language Modula-2" and a tutorial on the language. At present, no national or international standard exists for Modula-2, although a working group is currently preparing a definition of the language for submission to the International Standards Organization (ISO). In the absence of a precise definition of Modula-2, our discussion of the language must necessarily be based on *Programming in Modula-2*. Where Wirth's book lacks a complete discussion of a feature or is ambiguous, we rely on his published remarks or describe the feature the way it is implemented in typical Modula-2 systems (we will always point this out to the reader).

Almost all Modula-2 systems available at the time this book was written were based on either the Second or Third Edition of *Programming in Modula-2*. There are about two dozen minor differences between the version of the language described in the Second Edition and the version described in the Third; these differences are mentioned at relevant places throughout the book and collected in Appendix V. Traditionally, Modula-2 compilers have been "multi-pass": they perform several passes over a program during compilation. However, some recent compilers are one-pass, which allows faster compilation but requires a few small changes to the language definition; these changes are also mentioned in the book.

Much of Modula-2's power comes from its libraries, where reusable software components reside. Unfortunately, there is no standard set of library modules for Modula-2 at present, although a standard library is under preparation for ISO. The most standard are the library modules described in *Programming in Modula-2*, which are provided (although sometimes in modified form) by most Modula-2 systems. Therefore, our programming examples will use Wirth's library. It must be emphasized, however, that almost all of the examples use only the most rudimentary capabilities of this library and therefore can easily be adapted to another library.

1.2 Modula-2's Basic Features

This section sketches the basic features of Modula-2 and describes how they differ from the features of Standard Pascal.

In many respects, Modula-2 is a smaller language than Pascal. In particular, some of Pascal's standard features are provided in Modula-2 by library modules that are included as part of a Modula-2 system. For example, Modula-2 has no built-in procedures for input and output; these are supplied by library modules instead.

EXAMPLE PROGRAM

Integer Exponentiation

Before discussing the features of Modula-2, we present a simple program, `ComputePower`, that gives the flavor of the language. `ComputePower` will accept two nonnegative integers, `i` and `j`, from the user, compute `i` to the power `j`, and display the result on the user's screen.

```
MODULE ComputePower;
   (* reads a pair of nonnegative integers i and j and prints
      the result of raising i to the power j *)
```

```
  FROM InOut IMPORT ReadCard, WriteCard, WriteString, WriteLn;

  VAR i, j, power: CARDINAL;

  PROCEDURE IntExp(base, exponent: CARDINAL): CARDINAL;
    (* returns "base" raised to the power "exponent" *)
    VAR i, result: CARDINAL;
  BEGIN
    result := 1;
    FOR i := 1 TO exponent DO
      result := result * base
    END;
    RETURN result
  END IntExp;

BEGIN
  WriteString("This program computes i to the power j.");
  WriteLn;

    (* read values for i and j *)
  WriteString("Enter i: ");
  ReadCard(i);
  WriteLn;
  WriteString("Enter j: ");
  ReadCard(j);
  WriteLn;

    (* compute i to the power j *)
  power := IntExp(i, j);

    (* write the answer *)
  WriteString("i to the power j is: ");
  WriteCard(power, 1);
  WriteLn
END ComputePower.
```

At first glance, this program might appear to be written in Pascal. A closer look reveals some of the differences between Pascal and Modula-2:

- Modula-2 keywords, such as BEGIN, END, and FOR, must contain only uppercase letters. (In general, Modula-2 is sensitive to the case of letters.)

- A Modula-2 program begins with the reserved word MODULE, followed by the name of the program. This name must also appear at the end of the program, after the word END.

- Modula-2 supplies a new type, CARDINAL, whose values consist of the nonnegative integers (up to some limit).

- Modula-2 provides no standard procedures for input and output. Instead, I/O procedures are supplied by library modules that are furnished as part of a Modula-2 system. Because these procedures are not recognized by the compiler, they must be *imported* from a library module (`InOut` in the sample program) before they can be used. Each input or output procedure in `InOut` can read or write only a single value of a particular type. `ReadCard`, for example, will read a single `CARDINAL` value; it can't be used to read two `CARDINAL` values or values of another type. (By the way, "Card" is short for "Cardinal"—it doesn't indicate the input medium.) The `WriteLn` procedure writes the end-of-line character, marking the end of a line of output. The number `1` in `WriteCard(power, 1)` is analogous to the "field width" of Pascal's `write` and `writeln` procedures: it indicates that the value of `power` should be written in a field of size 1 (or more if necessary). Specifying a value of 1 causes `power` to be written without leading blanks.

- In Pascal, the body of the `FOR` statement would be enclosed between the words `begin` and `end`, because it consists of several statements. Modula-2 instead adopts the rule that the body of a `FOR` statement is always terminated by the word `END` (even if it consists of a single statement) but never preceded by the word `BEGIN`. The same rule applies to all of Modula-2's other structured statements as well.

Symbols

Modula-2's symbols can be divided into the following categories:

identifiers
reserved words
standard identifiers
numbers (integer and real literals)
strings
special symbols

In most respects, Modula-2's symbols resemble Pascal's; there are only a few major differences:

- Modula-2 is case-sensitive: it distinguishes between upper- and lowercase letters in identifiers (thus, `i` and `I` are treated as two different identifiers). Reserved words must contain only uppercase letters. Pascal is not case-sensitive.
- Modula-2 has more reserved words than Pascal, because of added features that do not appear in Pascal. Yet Modula-2 has fewer standard identifiers, because many procedures that are standard in Pascal are supplied by library modules in Modula-2.

- Modula-2 allows octal and hexadecimal integer literals; for example, the decimal value 100 can also be expressed as 144B (octal) or 64H (hexadecimal). Pascal integers must be expressed in decimal form only. Modula-2 also allows the use of an octal number, followed by the letter C, to represent a character; for example, 12C represents the ASCII line-feed character.
- In Modula-2, only the (* and *) symbols are allowed to delimit comments; comments can be nested. In Pascal, comments can be enclosed between either { and } or (* and *); comments cannot be nested.

Declarations

Modula-2 allows the declaration of

constants
types
variables
procedures (including functions)
modules

Pascal allows the declaration of labels, constants, types, variables, and procedures (and functions). Modula-2 does not provide label declarations, since there is no GOTO statement in the language (in Pascal, labels are used only as targets of goto statements).

Modula-2 allows the different kinds of declarations to appear in any order (constants need not be declared before types, for example). Furthermore, it is not necessary for all declarations of a particular kind to be grouped together; it is possible to declare several variables, then a few constants, then more variables, for example. Consequently, related declarations (of a type and variables of that type, say) may be grouped together. Pascal requires that declarations appear in a particular order: labels first, then constants, types, variables, and procedures. Like Pascal, Modula-2 forbids forward references in declarations (with the exception of pointer type declarations).

Types

Like Pascal, Modula-2 is a strongly typed language. Each variable and constant has a fixed type; when an operation is to be performed, its operands must have appropriate types. An attempt to perform an operation on operands of the wrong type (adding two characters, for example) will be detected by the compiler, resulting in an error message during compilation. Modula-2's rules for type-checking are even stricter than Pascal's. Integer and real numbers cannot be mixed in expressions—and integer values cannot be assigned to real variables—unless the programmer requests that an explicit conversion of type be performed. Because of its intended use as a systems programming language, Modula-2 allows type-checking to be disabled when necessary.

One of Modula-2's strengths is its rich variety of data types. Modula-2's types can be divided into four classes:

- unstructured types
  numeric (CARDINAL, INTEGER, LONGINT, REAL, LONGREAL)
  character (CHAR)
  Boolean (BOOLEAN)
  enumeration
  subrange
- structured types
  array
  record
  set
- pointer types
- procedure types

Modula-2 provides nine *standard* (predefined) types: CARDINAL, INTEGER, LONGINT, REAL, LONGREAL, CHAR, BOOLEAN, BITSET, and PROC. The CARDINAL, LONGINT, LONGREAL, BITSET, and PROC types are new in Modula-2; the other standard types appear in Pascal.

An *enumeration type* is a type whose values are specified (enumerated) by the programmer and represented by identifiers:

```
TYPE Days = (Sun, Mon, Tue, Wed, Thu, Fri, Sat);
```

The other way to create a new unstructured type is by selecting a range of consecutive values from an existing unstructured type:

```
TYPE Weekdays = [Mon..Fri];    (* subrange of Days *)
```

Weekdays is called a *subrange type*. Modula-2's enumeration and subrange types are almost identical to Pascal's. (Note, however, that a Modula-2 subrange type must be enclosed in brackets.)

Modula-2 provides three structured types: arrays, records, and sets. An *array* is a structure whose components all have the same type and are accessed by position. For example, suppose that the type Vector is defined as follows:

```
TYPE Vector = ARRAY [1..10] OF REAL;
```

A variable A of type Vector is a structure with 10 components, each of type REAL, named A[1], A[2], ..., A[10]. (In Modula-2, unlike Pascal, the index type of an array is not enclosed in brackets. The index type of the array `A` is the subrange `[1..10]`; the brackets belong to the subrange, not the array specification.) Character strings are represented by arrays whose components are of type `CHAR`:

```
TYPE String10 = ARRAY [0..9] OF CHAR;
```

By convention, Modula-2 strings have 0 as the lower index bound (Pascal requires a lower bound of 1). Pascal's strings must be packed arrays; Modula-2 does not allow arrays (or records or sets, for that matter) to be declared `packed`.

A *record* is a collection of values, possibly of different types, whose components are accessed by name:

```
TYPE CharCount = RECORD
                   ch: CHAR;
                   count: CARDINAL
                 END;
```

A variable `rec` of type `CharCount` is a structure with two components, one of type `CHAR` and one of type `CARDINAL`. The first component is named `rec.ch` and the second `rec.count`.

The third structured type is the *set*. A set is an unordered collection of values of the same type, with no duplicates. When declaring a set type, the programmer must specify the universe from which the elements of the set are chosen:

```
TYPE DigitSet = SET OF [0..9];
```

Values of type `DigitSet` include `DigitSet{0, 2, 3, 9}`, `DigitSet{1, 4}`, and `DigitSet{}` (the empty set). (In Pascal, set values are enclosed between [and] and do not include the name of the set type.)

In addition to structured and unstructured types, Modula-2 provides *pointer types* and *procedure types*. A value of a pointer type is a "pointer" or "reference" to an anonymous variable that has been created during program execution. Each pointer type is "bound" to some other type—its values can point only at anonymous variables of that type. For example, if `NodePtr` is defined as

```
TYPE NodePtr = POINTER TO Node;
```

then a value of type `NodePtr` is a pointer to an anonymous variable of type `Node`. (In Pascal, the ^ symbol would be used instead of the words `POINTER TO`.)

Pascal allows procedures to be supplied as parameters to other procedures as though they were data values. Modula-2 takes this concept a step further—it allows procedures to be assigned to variables (including array and record components). A variable to which a procedure is assigned must have a procedure type, such as

```
TYPE Comparison = PROCEDURE (REAL, REAL): BOOLEAN;
```

Variables of type `Comparison` can be assigned functions that have two parameters, both of type REAL, and return a value of type BOOLEAN.

Expressions

Modula-2's operators are almost identical to Pascal's. These operators fall into four classes:

arithmetic:	+ - * / DIV MOD
logical:	NOT ~ AND & OR
set:	+ - * /
relational:	= <> # < <= > >= IN

Three operators have alternate names: NOT can be written ~, AND can be written &, and <> can be written # (their names in Pascal are NOT, AND, and <>). The set operation / (symmetric difference) does not appear in Pascal.

Modula-2 performs "short-circuit" evaluation of Boolean expressions: a Boolean expression is evaluated from left to right only until the value of the expression can be determined. For example, the expression

```
(i <= length) & (A[i] # 0)
```

has the value FALSE if `i` is greater than `length`; the subexpression `(A[i] # 0)` is guaranteed not to be evaluated in this case. If A's upper bound is `length`, short-circuit evaluation avoids an index-out-of-range error. Pascal does not guarantee short-circuit evaluation of Boolean expressions.

Modula-2 allows a constant expression wherever a constant value is expected:

```
CONST pi = 3.14159;
      twoPi = 2.0 * pi;
      oneK = 1024;
TYPE Buffer = ARRAY [0..3*oneK-1] OF CHAR;
```

Pascal does not follow this rule.

Mathematical functions (with the exception of ABS) are not standard in Modula-2; they must be imported from a library module.

Statements

Modula-2 provides a small but powerful set of eleven statements:

assignment	CASE	LOOP	RETURN
procedure call	WHILE	FOR	WITH
IF	REPEAT	EXIT	

Almost all these statements are for the control of program flow (only the assignment and WITH statements do not affect the order in which statements are executed). Two statements (IF and CASE) allow a choice to be made among alternate control paths. The WHILE, REPEAT, LOOP, and FOR statements are used to repeatedly execute a group of statements. The LOOP statement allows a sequence of statements to be repeated indefinitely until an EXIT statement is executed. The RETURN statement allows a procedure to return before the end of its body is reached.

Modula-2's selection of control structures is so rich that virtually no situation requires a GOTO statement, a staple of many older programming languages. Consequently, there is no GOTO statement in Modula-2. In addition to the EXIT and RETURN statements, which are essentially restricted GOTO statements, Modula-2 supplies a HALT procedure, which terminates program execution. (Pascal has nothing comparable to EXIT, RETURN, or HALT; the programmer must use goto statements instead.)

In addition to the lack of a GOTO statement, Modula-2's statements differ from Pascal's in several other ways:

- Modula-2's CASE statement, unlike Pascal's, allows an ELSE clause, which is executed if the value of the case expression matches none of the case labels. Modula-2's CASE statement also allows ranges bounded by constant expressions as case labels.
- Pascal has no statement corresponding to Modula-2's LOOP statement. (The same effect can be achieved in other ways, however. For example, a LOOP statement can be simulated by a while statement that tests a condition that is always true, with goto statements instead of EXIT statements.)
- Modula-2's FOR statement includes an optional BY clause that allows the programmer to specify the step size as a constant expression; Pascal's for statement allows only +1 (to) and −1 (downto) as step sizes.

Modula-2's IF, WHILE, FOR, and WITH statements may contain statement sequences and always end with the reserved word END. Pascal's if, while, for, and with statements may contain only single statements, which may be compound (a compound statement is a sequence of statements bracketed by begin and end). For example, the body of a Modula-2 WHILE statement is a sequence of statements, followed by the word END; the body of a Pascal `while` statement is a single statement, which may be compound:

Modula-2	*Pascal*	

`WHILE` *Expression* `DO`
  StatementSequence
`END`
	`while` *Expression* `do`
	  Statement
		`while` *Expression* `do`
		  `begin`
		    StatementSequence
		  `end`

The net effect is that the body of a Modula-2 `WHILE` statement is always followed by the word END, but never preceded by the word `BEGIN`.

Procedures

Modula-2 allows the declaration of procedures (sometimes called *subprograms* or *subroutines* in other programming languages). In Modula-2, the term *procedure* includes functions (called *function procedures* in Modula-2) since declarations of both begin with the word PROCEDURE. (In Pascal, function declarations begin with the word `function`.) In Modula-2, a function returns a value by executing a RETURN statement that specifies the desired value. In Pascal, the value to be returned by a function is assigned to the function name as though it were a variable.

Like Pascal, Modula-2 offers two kinds of parameters: variable parameters and value parameters. Changes made to a variable parameter from within a procedure cause the corresponding actual parameter to change; changes made to a value parameter do not affect the actual parameter.

In most respects, Modula-2 procedures are virtually identical to Pascal procedures. However, Modula-2 has one important feature that is missing in Level 0 Standard Pascal: the *open array parameter*. For example, if `P` is declared as

```
PROCEDURE P(x: ARRAY OF REAL);
```

then the actual parameter supplied when `P` is called can be any one-dimensional array of `REAL` values. Level 1 Standard Pascal contains a feature (conformant array parameters) similar to Modula-2's open array parameters.

Input/Output

The Modula-2 language provides no input/output procedures. Instead, programs must use I/O procedures that are supplied by library modules. Two commonly available I/O modules are `InOut` and `RealInOut`, both of which appear in

Wirth's *Programming in Modula-2*. We use these modules in the program examples in this book, but they are not the only library modules that provide I/O procedures, nor must every Modula-2 system provide them. And, of course, programmers are free to write their own I/O libraries.

I/O procedures supplied by a library module are subject to the same rules as all Modula-2 procedures. In particular, each I/O procedure must have a fixed number of parameters and each parameter must have a fixed type. Consequently, I/O procedures normally allow only one value to be read or written at a time, as we saw in the sample program:

```
WriteString("i to the power j is: ");
WriteCard(power, 1);
WriteLn
```

Pascal's I/O procedures allow varying numbers of parameters of varying types; in Pascal, these three calls would be replaced by one call of `writeln`:

```
writeln("i to the power j is: ", power: 1);
```

Modula-2 has no special syntax for indicating to an output procedure how many characters should be written (the "field width," in Pascal terms); this value must be supplied to the procedure as a parameter (as in the call of `WriteCard`).

Unlike Pascal, the Modula-2 language does not provide `file` types. However, Modula-2 systems normally include a file-handling module (such as Wirth's `FileSystem` module) that supplies a file type and a collection of procedures that perform file operations.

1.3 Modula-2's Advanced Features

Although Modula-2 has much in common with Pascal, the former provides a number of important features not present in the latter. These features can be divided into the following categories:

modules
opaque types
separate compilation
low-level features
coroutines
interrupt handling

Modules, opaque types, and separate compilation constitute essential features of

Modula-2 with which every programmer must become familiar. Low-level features, coroutines, and interrupt handling are used mostly in systems programming.

Modules

The primary difference between Modula-2 and Pascal is the former's support for modules. In Pascal, a program is a single entity that is compiled as a whole (although many Pascal compilers allow some form of separate compilation). In Modula-2, however, a program consists of one or more modules. One of these (the *program module*) contains the main program; the others are called *library modules*.

Library modules serve as convenient repositories of related entities (constants, types, variables, and procedures). Not all of the entities defined in a module are available for use by other modules, however. Modules act as walls: Entities declared inside a module are not visible outside the module unless the module voluntarily *exports* them. In order for another module to gain access to any of these exported entities, the module must *import* the entity.

A program module may import from any number of library modules; these modules, in turn, may import from other library modules. Thus, a complete Modula-2 program consists of a set of interconnected modules, with one—the program module—serving as the main program. (In addition, modules may be declared inside other modules; a module nested inside another is called a *local module*.) Programs consisting of a single module are rare; most programs import input/output procedures from library modules, because the Modula-2 language provides no standard I/O procedures.

Library Modules

Library modules have two parts: a *definition part* and an *implementation part*. The definition part specifies the entities that the module exports; the implementation part gives the rest of the module. For example, if a procedure is exported by a library module, only the procedure heading appears in the definition part of the module; the implementation part contains the full declaration of the procedure. In other words, the definition part describes *what* the module does; the implementation part describes *how* it does it.

Consider the program `ComputePower` in Section 1.2. This program makes use of the (function) procedure `IntExp`, which returns `i` to the power `j` when given two `CARDINAL` numbers `i` and `j`. This procedure will be needed by many programs, because Modula-2 does not provide an exponentiation operator. To avoid having to redefine `IntExp` in these other programs, we could create a library module called `ExpLib` that would export `IntExp`; the `ComputePower` program could then import IntExp from ExpLib. We might wish to make ExpLib more useful by including other procedures besides IntExp. A logical choice would be RealExp, a procedure that computes x to the power y for REAL values x and y. The definition part of ExpLib might then look like this:

```
DEFINITION MODULE ExpLib;
  (* exports exponentiation functions *)

  PROCEDURE IntExp(base, exponent: CARDINAL): CARDINAL;
    (* returns "base" raised to the power "exponent" *)

  PROCEDURE RealExp(base, exponent: REAL): REAL;
    (* returns "base" raised to the power "exponent";
       terminates program if base is not positive *)

END ExpLib.
```

Note: Older Modula-2 compilers may require the line

```
EXPORT QUALIFIED IntExp, RealExp;
```

at the beginning of the definition module. This requirement was eliminated in the Third Edition of Wirth's *Programming in Modula-2*.

The definition part of ExpLib includes all the information that a programmer needs in order to use the procedures IntExp and RealExp. The procedure headings show how many parameters are expected, what their types are, and what type of result is returned. The comments that accompany each procedure indicate what it does and discuss any special constraints on the procedure's parameters. Information not needed in order to call the procedures (such as the algorithms used to perform exponentiation) is deliberately omitted from the definition part of the module.

Using just the definition part of ExpLib, we can rewrite ComputePower to import IntExp instead of declaring it. ComputePower will import IntExp from ExpLib in the same way that it imports procedures from InOut. The revised version of ComputePower would look like this:

```
MODULE ComputePower;
  (* reads a pair of nonnegative integers i and j and prints
     the result of raising i to the power j *)

  FROM InOut IMPORT ReadCard, WriteCard, WriteString, WriteLn;
  FROM ExpLib IMPORT IntExp;

  VAR i, j, power: CARDINAL;

BEGIN
  WriteString("This program computes i to the power j.");
  WriteLn;
```

```
    (* read values for i and j *)
  WriteString("Enter i: ");
  ReadCard(i);
  WriteLn;
  WriteString("Enter j: ");
  ReadCard(j);
  WriteLn;

    (* compute i to the power j *)
  power := IntExp(i, j);

    (* write the answer *)
  WriteString("i to the power j is: ");
  WriteCard(power, 1);
  WriteLn
END ComputePower.
```

The implementation part of a library module gives complete information about the entities listed in the definition part. When a procedure heading appears in the definition part, the implementation part must contain the full procedure declaration, including the heading (which must match the heading in the definition part). Because the definition part of `ExpLib` contains headings for `IntExp` and `RealExp`, the implementation part must include full declarations of `IntExp` and `RealExp`. The declaration of `IntExp` can be copied from the first version of `ComputePower`. To implement the procedure `RealExp`, we can use the formula

$$x^y = e^{y \cdot \ln(x)}$$

provided that $x > 0$. The implementation part of `ExpLib` follows:

```
IMPLEMENTATION MODULE ExpLib;

  FROM InOut IMPORT WriteString, WriteLn;
  FROM MathLib0 IMPORT exp, ln;

  PROCEDURE IntExp(base, exponent: CARDINAL): CARDINAL;
    (* returns "base" raised to the power "exponent" *)
    VAR i, result: CARDINAL;
  BEGIN
    result := 1;
    FOR i := 1 TO exponent DO
      result := result * base
    END;
    RETURN result
  END IntExp;

  PROCEDURE RealExp(base, exponent: REAL): REAL;
    (* returns "base" raised to the power "exponent";
       terminates program if base is not positive *)
```

```
    BEGIN
      IF base <= 0.0 THEN
        WriteString("Error:  RealExp called with illegal base");
        WriteLn;
        HALT
      END;
      RETURN exp(exponent * ln(base))
    END RealExp;

  END ExpLib.
```

The mathematical functions exp and ln are not standard in Modula-2, but must be imported from a library module such as Wirth's MathLib0 module.

We have seen one of the advantages of declaring IntExp in a library module rather than in ComputePower: IntExp can be shared with other programs. Another advantage is the ease with which IntExp can be modified. "Real-world" programs undergo frequent changes, not only to correct errors, but also to add new features or improve performance. When a program is divided into modules, many modifications affect only the implementation part of a single library module. For example, after using ExpLib for a while, we may notice that IntExp is too slow for large exponents, because it uses y multiplications to compute x^y. Fortunately, the number of multiplications can be reduced by using a better algorithm. For example, suppose that we factor x^{11} in the following way:

$$x^{11} = x^8 x^2 x$$

Only five multiplications are required to compute x^{11} using this formula (three multiplications to compute x^2, x^4, and x^8 by squaring, then two more to multiply x^8, x^2, and x). In general, x^n can be computed by the following method: compute x^2, x^4, x^8, and so forth, by repeated squaring, then multiply the appropriate powers of x to get the final result. Which powers of x should be multiplied can be found by examining the binary expansion of n; for example, 11 written in binary is 1011, indicating that we should multiply x^8, x^2, and x (but not x^4) to get x^{11}.

A new version of the implementation part of ExpLib follows; IntExp now uses the algorithm that we just described. The body of the LOOP statement in IntExp tests the rightmost bit of exponent; if it is 1, result is multiplied by the current value of base. IntExp then divides exponent by 2, in effect shifting the binary expansion of exponent one position to the right. IntExp also squares base each time through the loop.

```
IMPLEMENTATION MODULE ExpLib;

  FROM InOut IMPORT WriteString, WriteLn;
  FROM MathLib0 IMPORT exp, ln;

  PROCEDURE IntExp(base, exponent: CARDINAL): CARDINAL;
    (* returns "base" raised to the power "exponent" *)
```

```
  VAR result: CARDINAL;
BEGIN
  result := 1;
  LOOP
    IF ODD(exponent) THEN              (* rightmost bit is 1 *)
      result := result * base
    END;
    exponent := exponent DIV 2;
    IF exponent = 0 THEN EXIT END;
    base := base * base
  END;
  RETURN result
END IntExp;

PROCEDURE RealExp(base, exponent: REAL): REAL;
  (* returns "base" raised to the power "exponent";
     terminates program if base is not positive *)
BEGIN
  IF base <= 0.0 THEN
    WriteString("Error:  RealExp called with illegal base");
    WriteLn;
    HALT
  END;
  RETURN exp(exponent * ln(base))
END RealExp;

END ExpLib.
```

Two points about the new version of IntExp are worth mentioning. First, IntExp actually performs one more multiplication than strictly necessary, because the first multiplication of result by base takes place when result has the value 1. Second, a good compiler will implement the division by 2 as a shift — a much faster operation than division — making IntExp relatively efficient.

Because the change to IntExp does not affect the way in which the procedure is used, the definition part of ExpLib need not be modified nor must ComputePower be changed.

Opaque Types

The ExpLib module illustrates the usefulness of library modules for collecting frequently used procedures. Library modules have many other uses, as well. One of the most important features of Modula-2 is its provision for hiding the structure of a data type within a module. A type whose structure is hidden in this fashion is called an *opaque type*. The definition of an opaque type in the definition part of a library module is an abbreviated form of a normal type declaration; it consists only of the reserved word TYPE and the name of the type (the rest of the declaration is omitted).

For example, suppose that we are writing a program that requires a stack of characters. As we will see later, it can be advantageous to declare a stack type (which we will call CharStack) and hide the structure of this type in a library module. This module (call it CharacterStacks) must export procedures for manipulating variables of type CharStack, because no other module will know what the CharStack type really looks like. Here is the definition part of CharacterStacks:

```
DEFINITION MODULE CharacterStacks;
  (* exports type CharStack (stack of characters) and
     procedures for manipulating variables of type CharStack *)

  TYPE CharStack;    (* opaque export *)

  PROCEDURE Initialize(VAR s: CharStack);
    (* creates a stack s and makes it empty *)

  PROCEDURE Push(VAR s: CharStack; ch: CHAR);
    (* pushes ch onto stack s; terminates program if stack is
       full *)

  PROCEDURE Pop(VAR s: CharStack; VAR ch: CHAR);
    (* stores top element of stack s into ch, then pops s;
       terminates program if stack is empty *)

  PROCEDURE IsEmpty(s: CharStack): BOOLEAN;
    (* returns TRUE if s is empty, FALSE otherwise *)

END CharacterStacks.
```

The definition part of CharacterStacks gives no information about CharStack other than its name. Modules that import the CharStack type can use it to declare variables, but the only way to manipulate these variables is by calling the procedures Initialize, Push, Pop, and IsEmpty. Modula-2 requires that a full declaration of CharStack appear in the implementation part of CharacterStacks, along with full declarations of Initialize, Push, Pop, and IsEmpty. (The details are beyond the scope of this chapter; the implementation part of CharacterStacks appears in Section 9.1.)

Separate Compilation

Although separate compilation is not a required feature of Modula-2, virtually every Modula-2 system provides it. Program modules and the definition and implementation parts of library modules can be separately compiled, and hence are called *compilation units*. To emphasize that the definition part of a library module can be compiled separately from the implementation part, the former is called a *definition module* and the latter an *implementation module*.

Once the modules in a program have been compiled, they must be linked together before execution. Some Modula-2 systems require an explicit linking phase; others perform the linking automatically when the user requests that a program be executed.

There are many details of separate compilation and linking: file-naming conventions (in many systems each program module, definition module, and implementation module occupies a different file), order of compilation (for example, the definition part of a module must be compiled before the implementation part), mechanisms for version checking (to ensure that the interface between two modules is consistent even after one of the modules is changed), and so forth. Knowledge of these details is not necessary for writing simple programs, so we postpone a detailed discussion of separate compilation until Section 9.2.

For the time being, we will restrict our attention to programs that do not include any programmer-defined library modules. For these programs, it is only necessary to compile the program module and then link it with any system-provided library modules (such as `InOut` or `MathLib0`) that it may need. When a program is linked, most Modula-2 systems do not require the programmer to name all the modules to be linked. Instead, they ask only for the name of the program module; the linker then determines which modules need to be linked to the program module. These modules will include those from which the program module imported entities, modules from which those modules imported, and so forth. (For example, a request to link `ComputePower` will cause `ExpLib` to be linked also, because `ComputePower` imports from `ExpLib`. But `ExpLib` imports from `InOut` and `MathLib0`, so these modules must also be linked. `InOut` and `MathLib0` may import from still other modules, and so the process continues.) Because of such "hidden" imports, the linking process often causes a dramatic increase in the size of a program's object code.

Local Modules

Because local modules are declared inside compilation units, they cannot be separately compiled. Local modules are used for one purpose: to control the visibility of names within a program. A local module acts like a wall around the entities inside it. Entities visible outside the module are not visible inside it unless explicitly imported by the module; by the same token, entities visible inside the module are not visible outside unless exported by the module.

Consider the following program, named `PrintFibonacciNumbers`. This program prints the numbers in the sequence

$$1, 1, 2, 3, 5, 8, 13, \ldots$$

up to some predetermined limit. The Fibonacci numbers are generated by the `NextFibonacci` function. Each time it is called, `NextFibonacci` returns the next number in the sequence. In order to keep track of which number should be generated next, `NextFibonacci` needs two variables `fib1` and `fib2`. Because these variables are used only by `NextFibonacci`, they need not be visible throughout the rest of the program. Yet `fib1` and `fib2` cannot be declared local to `NextFibonacci`, because their values would be lost between calls of `NextFibonacci`. Declaring `fib1` and `fib2` in a local module along with `NextFibonacci`, but exporting only `NextFibonacci`, guarantees that `fib1` and `fib2` cannot be seen elsewhere in the program.

```
MODULE PrintFibonacciNumbers;
  (* prints Fibonacci numbers *)

  FROM InOut IMPORT WriteCard, WriteLn;

  CONST maxFib = 10000;    (* prints numbers up to this limit *)

  VAR fib: CARDINAL;

  MODULE FibonacciGenerator;
    (* exports NextFibonacci while hiding fib1 and fib2 *)

    EXPORT NextFibonacci;

    VAR fib1, fib2: CARDINAL;

    PROCEDURE NextFibonacci(): CARDINAL;
      (* returns the next Fibonacci number, in order, each time
         it is called; the first two calls return 1 *)
    BEGIN
      IF fib1 < fib2 THEN
        INC(fib1, fib2);
        RETURN fib2
      ELSE
        INC(fib2, fib1);
        RETURN fib1
      END
    END NextFibonacci;

  BEGIN
    fib1 := 0;
    fib2 := 1
  END FibonacciGenerator;

BEGIN
  LOOP
    fib := NextFibonacci();
    IF fib > maxFib THEN EXIT END;
    WriteCard(fib, 1);
    WriteLn
```

```
  END
END PrintFibonacciNumbers.
```

INC is a standard procedure in Modula-2; INC(i, n) is equivalent to the statement i := i + n.

Low-Level Features

In some applications, a program must be able to perform low-level, machine-dependent operations (examining the address of a variable or changing the contents of a machine register, for example)—operations that are normally not possible when using a high-level programming language. Modula-2 was designed for systems programming, so it provides special features for performing low-level operations.

The data type BITSET allows ready access to the individual bits of a word. For example, the BITSET value {0, 5, 8, 15} represents a word containing 1's in positions 0, 5, 8, and 15, and 0's in all other positions. By applying combinations of normal set operations to BITSET values, it is possible to perform any desired bit operation on a word.

The module SYSTEM is another source of support for low-level programming. SYSTEM supplies the programmer with system-dependent data types, such as ADDRESS and WORD, that have special properties. SYSTEM also provides procedures such as ADR, which allows a program to determine the run-time address of a variable:

```
VAR addr: ADDRESS;
          .
          .
          .
addr := ADR(x);     (* fetch address of variable x *)
```

Type transfer functions provide a way to circumvent Modula-2's normal type-checking mechanism. For example, if i is an INTEGER variable and b is a BITSET variable, the assignment

```
b := i;
```

is normally forbidden, because b and i have different types. However, using the type transfer function BITSET, we can write

```
b := BITSET(i);
```

The advantage of viewing i as a BITSET value is that its individual bits are now directly accessible. Type transfer can be used between any pair of types, either standard or programmer-defined, provided that the values of the two types occupy the same amount of storage. Thus, our example is valid only if INTEGER and BITSET values require the same amount of storage (which they normally do).

Finally, many Modula-2 systems provide a mechanism for specifying the run-time address of a variable. For example, Modula-2 systems for the IBM Personal Computer often allow the programmer to specify an address as a *segment:offset* pair. The declaration

```
VAR equipmentFlag [0:410H]: BITSET;
```

tells the compiler to locate the variable equipmentFlag at the address whose segment is 0 and whose offset is 410 (hex). The word located at this address can then be accessed through equipmentFlag. The ability to locate variables at specific addresses is not a required feature of Modula-2.

Coroutines

Coroutines are similar to procedures. However, coroutines do not use the call-and-return mechanism that procedures do. A coroutine begins execution when control is transferred to it; it ceases to execute when it transfers control to another coroutine. Should control ever be transferred to the coroutine again, it will not begin executing from the beginning, but will instead resume from where it left off. Thus, the state of a coroutine's computation is preserved when the coroutine is not executing.

Coroutines are particularly useful in the construction of operating systems and other programs in which processes must appear to operate concurrently. By switching among several coroutines at frequent intervals, a program can make it appear that the coroutines are executing simultaneously.

Modula-2 allows a program to create coroutines (by calling the procedure NEWPROCESS) and switch between them (by calling TRANSFER). Both NEWPROCESS and TRANSFER must be imported; neither is predefined.

Interrupt Handling

Systems programmers must often be concerned with interrupts (hardware-generated signals indicating that a particular event has occurred—the completion of an input/output operation, for example). Modula-2's support for coroutines allows the language to provide a simple method of writing interrupt handlers (routines that respond to interrupts). The programmer writes the interrupt handler as a coroutine, then causes the coroutine to be suspended until the desired interrupt occurs. (The suspension of the interrupt handler is done by a call of IOTRANSFER, which must be imported.) When the interrupt occurs, control is transferred to the interrupt handler, which then performs whatever processing is needed to respond to the interrupt. The handler then suspends itself until the next interrupt.

At times it is important to disable all or selected interrupts (for example, an interrupt handler should not be interrupted by the interrupt being serviced). Modula-2 provides a simple mechanism for inhibiting interrupts: the presence of a *priority* in the heading of a module indicates that interrupts of equal or lower priority are to be disabled when the module is being executed.

2 The Structure of a Modula-2 Program

Chapter 1 presented an overview of Modula-2. This chapter begins a detailed description of the language, starting with the symbols that make up a Modula-2 program (Section 2.1) and continuing with the overall structure of a Modula-2 main program (Section 2.2).

2.1 The Vocabulary of Modula-2

We begin our exploration of Modula-2 by explaining the rules for forming the symbols that can appear in Modula-2 programs. These symbols include

identifiers
reserved words
standard identifiers
numbers (integer and real)
strings
special symbols

We will also show how to include comments in a program.

Identifiers

Programmer-defined names are called *identifiers* in Modula-2. An identifier is a letter followed by zero or more letters and digits. We can show the syntax of an identifier more formally using a *syntax chart* (Figure 2.1). To determine the syntax of an identifier, start at the left edge of the chart and follow the arrows to the right edge. Each path through the chart yields a syntactically valid identifier. When a syntax chart contains a loop, the portion of the chart inside the loop can

Figure 2.1

Ident

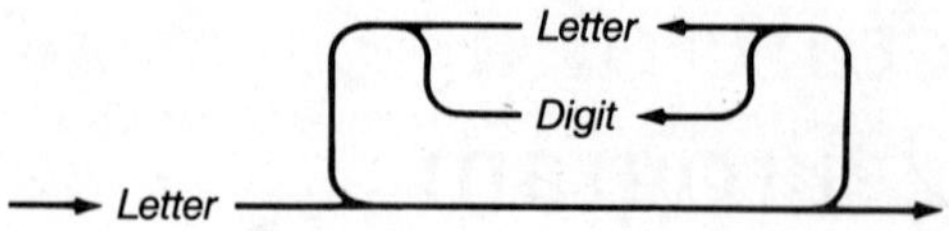

be repeated. For example, according to the chart in Figure 2.1, an identifier can contain as many letters and/or digits as desired, after the initial letter.

The following are all valid identifiers:

```
x  oldch  SortNumbers  DONE  String10
```

The following are *not* valid identifiers:

```
Get_Next_Character  <>  30X
```

The first two contain characters other than letters and digits; the third begins with a digit.

Modula-2 is a *case-sensitive* language: Two identifiers are the same only if both contain exactly the same characters in the same order; the uppercase and lowercase versions of a letter are not considered the same character. Thus, the following identifiers are all different:

```
oldch  OLDCH  OldCh  OLDch  oldCH  oLdCh
```

It is not a good idea for a program to contain two identifiers that are the same except for capitalization; a person reading the program (not to mention the original programmer) is likely to confuse the two.

Modula-2 imposes no limit on the length of an identifier; all characters in an identifier are significant. As a practical matter, however, some Modula-2 compilers may place a (large) limit on the length of identifiers.

Reserved Words

Modula-2 does not allow programmers to use the symbols in Table 2.1 (called *reserved words*) as identifiers. Six of these (AND, DIV, IN, MOD, NOT, and OR) are operators; the others are keywords that help Modula-2 compilers recognize language constructs. Reserved words must contain only uppercase letters.

Table 2.1 Reserved Words

AND	ELSIF	LOOP	REPEAT
ARRAY	END	MOD	RETURN
BEGIN	EXIT	MODULE	SET
BY	EXPORT	NOT	THEN
CASE	FOR	OF	TO
CONST	FROM	OR	TYPE
DEFINITION	IF	POINTER	UNTIL
DIV	IMPLEMENTATION	PROCEDURE	VAR
DO	IMPORT	QUALIFIED	WHILE
ELSE	IN	RECORD	WITH

Standard Identifiers

The Modula-2 identifiers in Table 2.2, called *standard identifiers*, have predefined meanings. These identifiers represent standard types (CARDINAL), standard constants (FALSE), and standard procedures (ODD). Standard identifiers marked with an asterisk appear in the Third Edition of Wirth's *Programming in Modula-2*, but not in the Second Edition, so older compilers may not recognize them. Also, NEW and DISPOSE are standard identifiers in the Second Edition, but not in the Third.

Table 2.2 Standard Identifiers

ABS	CHAR	FLOAT	INTEGER	NIL	SIZE*
BITSET	CHR	HALT	LONGINT*	ODD	TRUE
BOOLEAN	DEC	HIGH	LONGREAL*	ORD	TRUNC
CAP	EXCL	INC	MAX*	PROC	VAL
CARDINAL	FALSE	INCL	MIN*	REAL	

Do not confuse standard identifiers with reserved words. A program can declare a standard identifier to have a different meaning; reserved words cannot be redefined. Redefining a standard identifier is usually a poor idea, because this prevents using the identifier with its standard meaning and confuses anyone who is reading the program.

Standard identifiers, like reserved words, must contain only uppercase letters. (Some Modula-2 compilers allow the programmer to override the uppercase-only requirement for reserved words and standard identifiers.) Consequently, these symbols stand out in a program, making the structure of the program more apparent. Because all reserved words and standard identifiers in Modula-2 contain only capital letters, it is good practice to use lowercase or mixed uppercase and lowercase letters for programmer-defined identifiers. In identifiers that consist of more than one word, such as `TestForBlank`, it is good style to begin each word (except possibly for the first) with an uppercase letter. (Section 3.5 describes the capitalization convention followed in this book.)

Numbers

Two kinds of numbers (that is, numeric literals) may appear in Modula-2 programs: integers and real numbers (Figure 2.2). An integer is a sequence of digits:

```
0   231   32767
```

In Modula-2, integers are expressed in base 10, by default; the language also allows octal (base 8) and hexadecimal (base 16) literals. An octal integer is a sequence of octal digits (digits between `0` and `7`) followed by the letter `B`:

```
0B   347B   77777B
```

(The letter `B` is intended to suggest the numeral 8.) A hexadecimal integer is a sequence of hexadecimal digits (digits between `0` and `9`, plus the letters between `A` and `F`) followed by the letter `H`:

```
0H   0E7H   7FFFH
```

A hexadecimal number must always begin with a decimal digit. Without this rule, a hex number beginning with a letter (`E7H`, for example) would appear to be an identifier. Fortunately, adding the digit `0` to the beginning of the number (`0E7H`, in our example) will make it legal.

Figure 2.2

Number

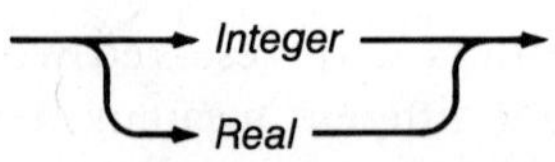

Figure 2.3 summarizes the possible forms of an integer. We have not shown the charts for *Digit*, *OctalDigit*, and *HexDigit*. The values of *Digit* are `0`, `1`, . . . , `9`, the values of *OctalDigit* are `0`, `1`, . . . , `7`, and the values of *HexDigit* are `0`, `1`, . . . , `9`, `A`, `B`, . . . , `F`.

Note that the chart in Figure 2.3 does not allow a Modula-2 integer to begin with a plus or minus sign. A programmer can still write `-231`, but this is considered an expression—the result of applying the unary - operator to the number 231—instead of a number.

Figure 2.3

Integer

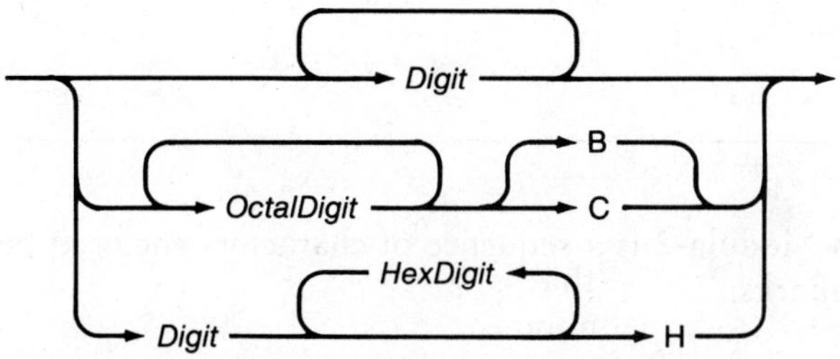

The chart in Figure 2.3 seems to show that an integer can be a sequence of octal digits followed by the letter C. In fact, this symbol represents a character (see Section 3.2). Its appearance in the *Integer* chart is an anomaly; apparently Wirth wanted to avoid having a separate syntax chart for this kind of symbol.

A real number must contain a decimal point preceded by at least one digit. No digits need follow the decimal point. The following are legal real numbers in Modula-2:

```
143.87   0.253   3902.
```

A real number may include a *scale factor*. A scale factor consists of the letter E (uppercase only), an optional sign, then one or more digits:

```
1.2944E10   3.E-8   15.0E+12
```

A number's scale factor indicates the power of 10 by which the number should be scaled. For example, 1.2944E10 (1.2944×10^{10} in scientific notation) represents the number 12,944,000,000.

Modula-2 makes no provision for real numbers to be expressed in bases other than 10.

Figures 2.4 and 2.5 show the *Real* and *ScaleFactor* syntax charts.

Figure 2.4

Real

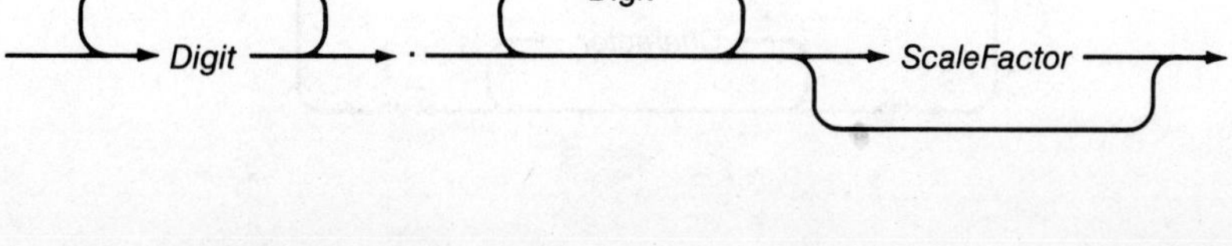

Figure 2.5 **ScaleFactor**

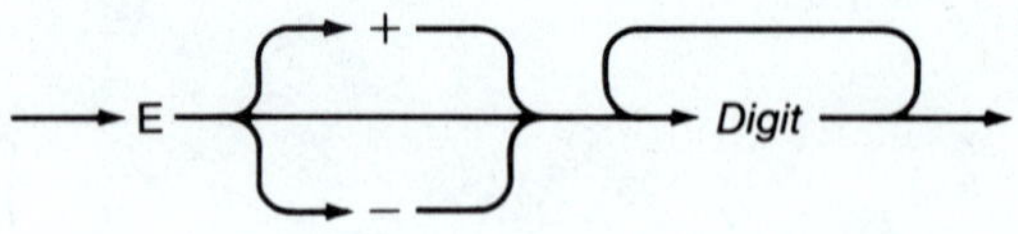

Strings

A *string* in Modula-2 is a sequence of characters enclosed between single or double quote marks:

```
'error 14'
"error 14"
```

The *String* syntax chart appears in Figure 2.6. As the chart shows, single and double quotes are not interchangeable; if a string begins with a single quote, it must end with a single quote (the same is true for double quotes).

If double quotes delimit a string, then the single quote mark may appear within the string. If single quotes delimit the string, then double quotes can appear inside the string:

```
"Madam, I'm Adam"
'Spell the word "obfuscation"'
```

A string cannot contain both single and double quotes:

```
"This string's not "legal""
```

Single-character strings obey the same rules as do longer strings. For example, both `'A'` and `"A"` represent the letter *A*.

Modula-2 provides no way to include nonprinting characters in a string. (However, the language does offer a special notation for representing a single nonprinting character; see Section 3.2.) Strings, like other symbols, cannot be split over two lines.

Figure 2.6 **String**

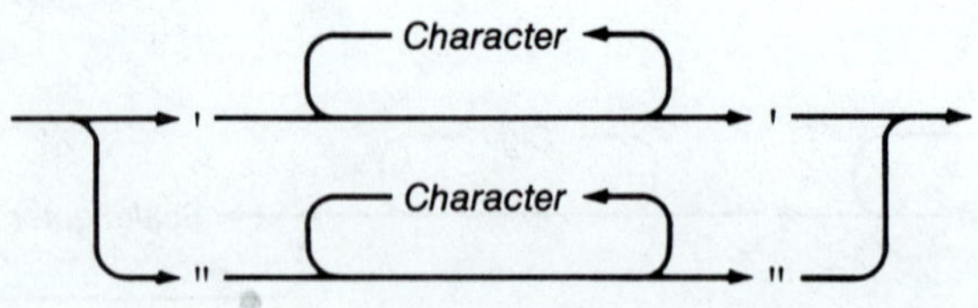

Special Symbols

Modula-2 uses the following special symbols:

+	addition, set union
-	subtraction, set difference
*	multiplication, set intersection
/	real division, symmetric set difference
&	logical conjunction
~	logical negation
=	equal
# <>	not equal
<	less than
<=	less than or equal to, set inclusion
>	greater than
>=	greater than or equal to, set inclusion
:=	assignment
( )	expressions; enumeration types; parameter lists
{ }	sets
[ ]	subrange types; array indexing; module priorities
(* *)	comments
^	pointer dereferencing
' "	strings
, ; : | . ..	punctuation

The symbol ~ appears in the Third Edition of *Programming in Modula-2*, but not in the Second Edition.

Comments

Any sequence of characters between the symbols `(*` and `*)` is a *comment*.

```
(* This is an example of a comment *)
```

Comments can appear anywhere in a program, either within a line or extending over many lines. Although comments usually occur between declarations or statements, they may appear between any two symbols:

```
CONST pi = (* to five decimal places *) 3.14159;
```

Comments may not divide a symbol, however:

```
CONST pi = 3.1415(* unsure about this digit *)9;    (* illegal*)
```

In general, Modula-2 compilers ignore comments (treat them as blanks); they serve only to document a program. Some compilers, however, allow comments to contain compiler directives. For example, the following comments signal the Logitech Modula-2/86 compiler to disable the test for arithmetic overflow for the duration of one statement:

```
(*$R-*)
i := j * k;
(*$R+*)
```

This feature is not standard.

Modula-2 allows the programer to nest comments. This ability is useful to temporarily take some portion of a program out of commission, perhaps during testing:

```
(**************************************************************
WriteString("The value of i is currently ");
WriteCard(i, 1); (* i should have the value 10 at this point *)
WriteLn;
**************************************************************)
```

The symbol `*)` after the word `point` ends only the comment begun on that line, not the comment begun two lines earlier. All the statements shown are within a comment, so none can be executed. (The lines of asterisks are to help readers locate the beginning and end of the comment, which may be many lines apart.)

The ability to nest comments provides a second benefit. If a programmer accidentally omits the closing symbol `*)` somewhere in a program, at the end of the program the compiler will detect a badly formed comment and will advise the programmer. In a language that does not allow nested comments, an omitted closing symbol will—without any indication to the programmer—cause the compiler to treat as a comment the portion of the program up to the next closing symbol.

Modula-2 Is Free-Format

Modula-2 programs are "free-format": they can be spread out over many lines or compressed into a few lines. Modula-2 compilers ignore blanks and ends of lines (allowing the programmer freedom to format the program for easier reading)—with two exceptions. First, a symbol cannot be split between two lines or divided by a blank or a comment. Second, the programmer must separate identifiers, reserved words, and numbers by at least one blank whenever ambiguity would result. In the statement

```
IF i > max THEN max := i END;
```

the blanks between `IF` and `i`, `max` and `THEN`, `THEN` and `max`, and `i` and `END` are all mandatory. If no blank appeared between `IF` and `i`, for example, a Modula-2 compiler would see a single identifier, `IFi`. The other blanks, such as those around the > operator, are not required.

2.2 Program Modules

A Modula-2 program consists of a *program module* and possibly one or more *library modules*. The program module serves as the "main program," while the library modules provide services to the program module (or to each other). For example, consider the following program, which writes the digits of a nonnegative integer in reverse order:

```
MODULE ReverseNumber;
  (* writes the digits of a nonnegative integer in reverse
     order *)

  FROM InOut IMPORT ReadCard, WriteCard, WriteString, WriteLn;

  VAR number: CARDINAL;

BEGIN
  WriteString("Enter number to be reversed: ");
  ReadCard(number);
  WriteLn;

  WriteString("The reversal is: ");
  REPEAT
    WriteCard(number MOD 10, 1);
    number := number DIV 10
  UNTIL number = 0;
  WriteLn
END ReverseNumber.
```

This module, together with the `InOut` library module (and any modules from which `InOut` imports) comprises a complete Modula-2 program. (`InOut` is one of Wirth's library modules; see Section 13.2.) In order to write small programs in

Modula-2, we need only know the rules for writing program modules and have some knowledge of I/O library modules. To write large programs, however, we need to know how to write library modules (Section 9.1).

Figure 2.7 shows the syntax of a program module. A program module begins with the reserved word MODULE, followed by an identifier (the program name). A *priority* may optionally follow the program name, specifying an interrupt priority level for the module. (We discuss interrupt handling in Chapter 12; until then, we always assume that the priority is omitted.) Next comes a semicolon, followed by the import lists—lists of entities to be imported from library modules. (Although Figure 2.7 shows that no import lists are necessary, most programs import input/output procedures from a library module.) After the import lists appears a block containing the module's declarations and statements, then the program name, and finally a period. The name at the end of a program module must be identical to the name that appears at the beginning; even the case of corresponding letters must be the same.

Notice that Modula-2 makes no provision for a program module to export entities—program modules are "consumers" of services provided by library modules, never "producers."

Figure 2.7

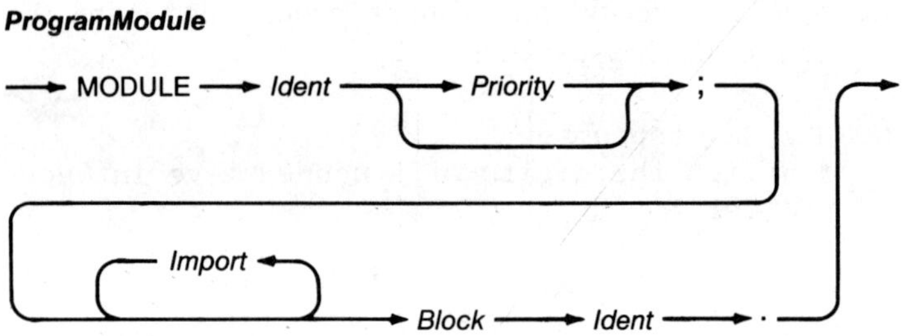

Having covered the overall structure of a program module, we now take a closer look at its parts.

Import Lists

The import lists at the beginning of a program module specify entities to be imported from library modules. For example, the import list

```
FROM InOut IMPORT ReadCard, WriteCard, WriteString, WriteLn;
```

in `ReverseNumber` indicates that the module needs the entities `ReadCard`, `WriteCard`, `WriteString`, and `WriteLn` exported by the `InOut` module.

When a Modula-2 compiler encounters an import list, it must fetch descriptions of the imported entities so that it can perform type-checking whenever the module references one of these entities. The source of these descriptions varies. Some Modula-2 systems require prior compilation of the definition part of a library module, causing a "symbol file" to be created; this file contains information about the entities that the module exports. Other systems do not require advance compilation; these systems compile the definition part of a library module every time the module is referenced in an import list.

Figures 2.8 and 2.9 show the general form of an import list. Notice that the programmer may omit the FROM part of an import list. When FROM is omitted, the identifiers following the word IMPORT must be module names; the effect is to import *all* identifiers that these modules export. For example, ReverseNumber could use the following import list:

```
IMPORT InOut;
```

This form of import makes available all the entities that InOut exports.

Figure 2.8

Import

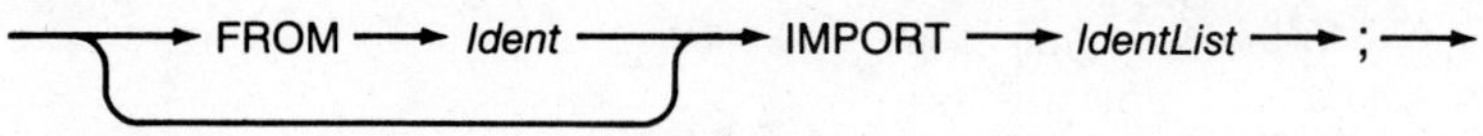

Figure 2.9

IdentList

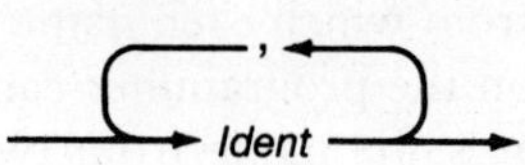

Although import lists in which FROM is omitted are simple, they have two disadvantages. First, such an import list gives no clue as to which entities exported by the library module are actually used in the program. Second, all references to entities that the module exports must be *qualified* (preceded by the name of the module). For example, if ReverseNumber were to import InOut without the FROM clause, it would appear as follows:

```
MODULE ReverseNumber;
  (* writes the digits of a nonnegative integer in reverse
     order *)

  IMPORT InOut;

  VAR number: CARDINAL;

BEGIN
  InOut.WriteString("Enter number to be reversed: ");
  InOut.ReadCard(number);
  InOut.WriteLn;
```

```
    InOut.WriteString("The reversal is: ");
    REPEAT
      InOut.WriteCard(number MOD 10, 1);
      number := number DIV 10
    UNTIL number = 0;
    InOut.WriteLn
  END ReverseNumber.
```

A name such as `InOut.WriteString` is a *qualified identifier*. In theory, qualified identifiers can consist of many identifiers strung together (see Figure 2.10), but in practice a qualified identifier is almost always just two identifiers separated by a period. The name preceding the period (the module name) is a *qualifying identifier*.

Figure 2.10 ***Qualident***

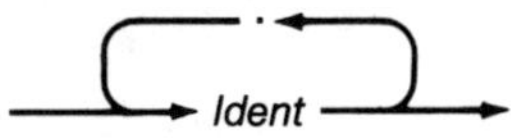

Because it is so cumbersome to write `InOut.WriteString` instead of just `WriteString`, programmers normally use the FROM option in import lists. (Some programmers prefer the qualified form when writing a module with many imported names, because the module from which each name was imported is then immediately apparent.) In one situation the programmer cannot use FROM, however: when importing entities with the same name from two different modules. For example, both of the modules `InOut` and `RealInOut` export a variable named Done (see Section 13.2). The following import lists are illegal:

```
FROM InOut IMPORT OpenInput, CloseInput, Done;
FROM RealInOut IMPORT ReadReal, WriteReal, Done;    (* illegal *)
```

A Modula-2 compiler cannot allow both import lists; if it did, a reference to Done later in the program would be ambiguous.

To resolve the problem of conflicting names, we can remove the FROM clause from one of the two import lists:

```
FROM InOut IMPORT OpenInput, OpenOutput, Done;
IMPORT RealInOut;
```

The names `OpenInput`, `OpenOutput`, and Done require no qualification. The entities `ReadReal`, `WriteReal`, and Done in `RealInOut` must be called `RealInOut.ReadReal`, `RealInOut.WriteReal`, and `RealInOut.Done`. Now the ambiguity is gone: the name Done refers to the entity Done in `InOut`, while the name `RealInOut.Done` refers to the entity Done in `RealInOut`.

This solution to the problem is somewhat unsatisfactory from the programmer's point of view, because ReadReal and WriteReal must be qualified even though the names of these entities are unambiguous. Fortunately, Modula-2 allows an improved solution:

```
FROM InOut IMPORT OpenInput, OpenOutput, Done;
IMPORT RealInOut;
FROM RealInOut IMPORT ReadReal, WriteReal;
```

(The order of the import lists is not significant.) Now we can use the names ReadReal and WriteReal without qualification. This collection of import lists may look illegal (because ReadReal and WriteReal are accessible both with and without qualification), but it is not.

A final note: Importing a name using the FROM option does not prevent qualification. If a program imports Done from InOut using the FROM option, it may reference the entity either as Done or InOut.Done.

Blocks

The heart of a program module is a *block*: a collection of declarations followed by a sequence of statements to be executed. Figure 2.11 shows the syntax of a block.

Figure 2.11

Block

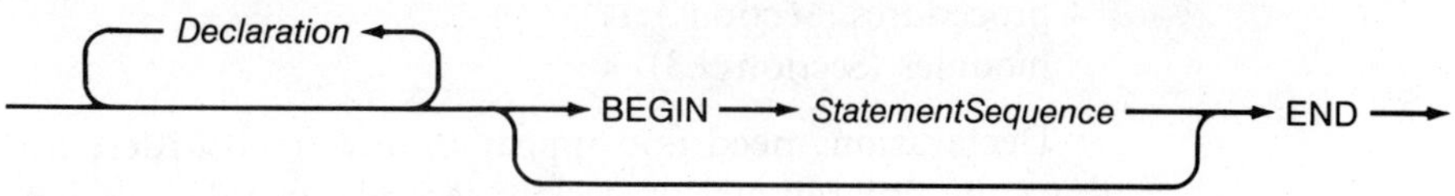

A block begins with an optional sequence of *declarations*. Declarations are mandatory in Modula-2: the programmer must declare all names used in a program (other than standard identifiers or imported names).

Modula-2 allows declarations of

constants
types
variables
procedures (including functions)
modules

We refer to these as *entities*. (Wirth uses the term *object* rather than *entity*, but we prefer to use *object* in the sense of "object-oriented"—see Chapter 10.) Although the five kinds of entities are very different, all have certain properties in common: all are represented by programmer-created identifiers, all must be declared, and all are subject to the scope rules of Modula-2.

Modula-2 allows a program to intermix declarations of different kinds of entities, as Figure 2.12 shows.

Figure 2.12 ***Declaration***

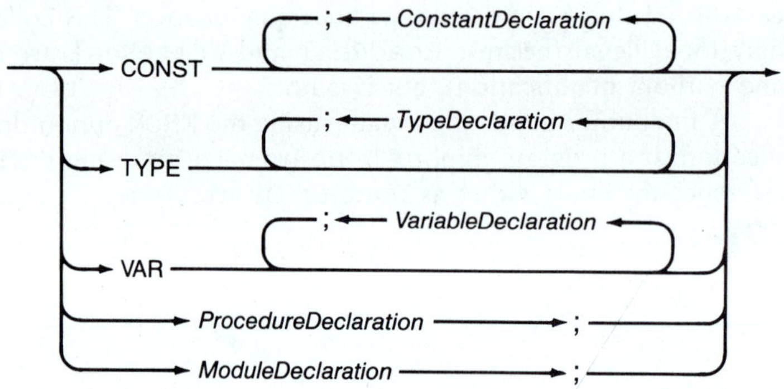

Discussions of the five kinds of declarations appear in the following sections:

constants (Section 3.5)
types (Section 6.1)
variables (Section 3.5)
procedures (Section 5.1)
modules (Section 9.3)

Declarations need not appear in any fixed order; for example, Modula-2 allows the programmer to declare several constants, then a module, then a type, then several variables, then more constants. However, a programmer cannot use one entity to declare another without first declaring the former. For example, before a constant can appear in a type declaration, the programmer must declare the constant. (This rule has one exception: The declaration of a pointer type may refer to a type not yet declared—see Section 8.1.)

Statements

After the declarations comes the body of the block: a statement sequence, preceded by the word BEGIN and followed by the word END. A *statement sequence* (Figure 2.13) consists of one or more statements, separated by semicolons.

Figure 2.13

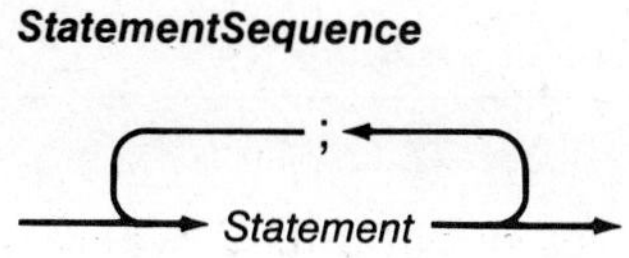

Modula-2 provides eleven kinds of statements, as Figure 2.14 shows. Discussions of these statements appear in the following sections:

assignment (Section 4.1)
procedure call (Section 5.1)
IF (Section 4.2)
CASE (Section 4.2)
WHILE (Section 4.3)
REPEAT (Section 4.3)
LOOP (Section 4.3)
FOR (Section 4.4)
WITH (Section 7.3)
EXIT (Section 4.3)
RETURN (Section 5.3)

Note also that the *Statement* chart (Figure 2.14) allows a statement to be *empty*—to contain no symbols.

Figure 2.14

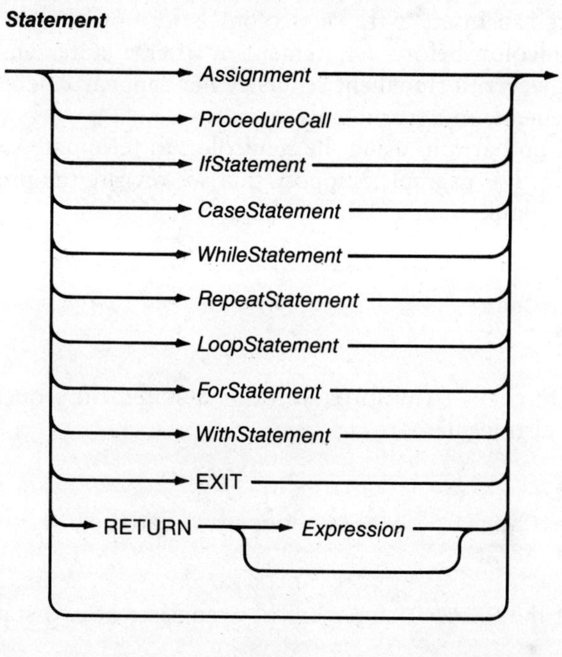

Statement Sequences and the Empty Statement

Blocks are just one of many places in Modula-2 where statement sequences appear. A general rule is that a statement sequence may appear wherever Modula-2 allows a single statement. This fact, together with the existence of the empty statement, has important consequences for Modula-2 programmers.

The *empty statement* contains no symbols and has no effect. Here is an example:

```
ReadCard(i); ; j := 3 * i + 4;
```

In this sequence of three statements, the middle statement is empty.

The empty statement has two primary uses. First, it allows a statement sequence to be empty (a statement sequence must always contain at least one statement, but that one statement can be empty). Consider the following WHILE statement:

```
WHILE GetChar() # ' ' DO
END;
```

The only purpose of the WHILE statement is to call the function GetChar repeatedly until it returns the blank character; consequently, the body of the WHILE statement is empty.

Second, the empty statement makes semicolon placement less critical. In fact, programmers can insert extra semicolons before or after any statement. Putting an extra semicolon before a statement or after a statement creates a statement sequence; however, a statement sequence may appear wherever Modula-2 allows a single statement, so no problems arise.

There is no harm in using the semicolon to terminate statements rather than separate them. For example, suppose that we rewrite the preceding WHILE statement to skip blanks rather than nonblanks:

```
REPEAT
  ch := GetChar()
UNTIL ch # ' ';
```

The statement ch := GetChar() forms a statement sequence of length 1. The following is also legal:

```
REPEAT
  ch := GetChar();    (* unnecessary semicolon *)
UNTIL ch # ' ';
```

The body of the REPEAT statement now consists of two statements, but the second is empty. Some programmers deliberately use the semicolon as a statement terminator, because this style makes programs easier to modify. In the example, we can insert a new statement after `ch := GetChar();` without making any other changes; if we had not already ended the statement with a semicolon, we would have had to add one.

Standard Pascal

1. Pascal is not case-sensitive; Pascal compilers do not distinguish between uppercase and lowercase letters when determining whether two identifiers are the same. For example, the identifiers `FirstNum` and `firstnum` are the same in Pascal. Programmers can write reserved words and standard identifiers using any combination of uppercase and/or lowercase letters.
2. The following Pascal reserved words do not appear in Modula-2: `downto`, `file`, `function`, `goto`, `label`, `nil`, `packed`, `program`. (`NIL` is a standard identifier in Modula-2, not a reserved word.)
3. The following Pascal standard identifiers do not appear in Modula-2: `arctan`, `cos`, `dispose`, `eof`, `eoln`, `exp`, `get`, `ln`, `new`, `pack`, `page`, `pred`, `put`, `read`, `readln`, `reset`, `rewrite`, `round`, `sin`, `sqr`, `sqrt`, `succ`, `text`, `unpack`, `write`, `writeln`.
4. Every special symbol in Pascal appears in Modula-2, with the exception of the alternative symbols @, ↑, `(.`, and `.)`. Both @ and ↑ are alternatives for ^, while `(.` and `.)` are alternatives for `[` and `]`, respectively.
5. Pascal numbers can begin with a sign (+ or -).
6. Pascal does not allow octal and hexadecimal numbers.
7. In a Pascal real number, at least one digit must appear after the decimal point; a programmer can omit the decimal point itself if the scale factor is present. The `E` at the beginning of the scale factor can be either uppercase or lowercase.

   Allowed: `13E2` and `13.0e2`

   Not allowed: `1300.` (no digit after decimal point)
8. A Pascal string must be enclosed in single quotes. A programmer can include a single quote in a string by preceding it with another single quote:

   ```
   'Can''t face the facts'
   ```

Modula-2

1. Modula-2 is case-sensitive. The case of a letter is significant when determining whether two identifiers are the same, hence the identifiers `FirstNum` and `firstnum` are different in Modula-2. Programmers must write reserved words and standard identifiers using only uppercase letters.

2. The following Modula-2 reserved words do not appear in Pascal: `BY`, `DEFINITION`, `ELSIF`, `EXIT`, `EXPORT`, `FROM`, `IMPLEMENTATION`, `IMPORT`, `LOOP`, `MODULE`, `POINTER`, `QUALIFIED`, `RETURN`.

3. The following Modula-2 standard identifiers do not appear in Pascal: `BITSET`, `CAP`, `CARDINAL`, `DEC`, `EXCL`, `FLOAT`, `HALT`, `HIGH`, `INC`, `INCL`, `LONGINT`, `LONGREAL`, `MAX`, `MIN`, `NIL`, `PROC`, `SIZE`, `VAL`. (`nil` is a reserved word in Pascal, not a standard identifier.)

4. The following Modula-2 special symbols do not appear in Pascal: &, ~, #, |.

5. When a + or - symbol precedes a Modula-2 number, the language does not consider the + or - to be the number's sign; instead, it views the symbol as a unary operator applied to the number. This rule is a mere technicality; it allows a simpler description of Modula-2's syntax without restricting the use of signed numbers.

6. Modula-2 allows both octal and hexadecimal numbers. An octal number is a sequence of octal digits followed by the letter `B`. A hexadecimal number is a sequence of hexadecimal digits followed by the letter `H`. A hexadecimal number may not begin with a letter.

   Octal number: `75732B`
   Hexadecimal number: `0A5FH`

7. A Modula-2 real number must contain a decimal point. At least one digit must precede the decimal point, but no digit need follow the decimal point. The `E` at the beginning of the scale factor must be uppercase.

   Allowed: `1300.`
   Not allowed: `13E2` (no decimal point) and `13.0e2` (lowercase `e`)

8. A Modula-2 string can be enclosed between either single or double quotes. If the programmer uses double quotes, the string may contain single quotes, and vice-versa:

   ```
   "Can't face the facts"
   '"Hello," he said.'
   ```

   A string cannot contain both single and double quotes.

Standard Pascal

9. In Pascal, the symbols { and } delimit comments; the language allows (* and *) as alternatives. Pascal does not permit nested comments.

```
{ This is a comment }
(* This is also a comment *)
```

10. Pascal does not allow division of a program into modules.

11. A Pascal program must begin with the word `program` and end with the word end, followed by a period:

```
program Sample;
        .
        .
        .
end.
```

12. In the heading of a Pascal program, a list of program parameters, representing external files, may follow the program name:

```
program Sample (input, output);
```

13. A Pascal program may declare labels, constants, types, variables, procedures, and functions.

14. Declarations in a Pascal block must occur in a fixed order: labels, constants, types, variables, and finally procedures and functions. The programmer must group together all declarations of a particular kind of entity (constants, say), with the identifying keyword (`const`) appearing only once.

```
const intVectorLength = 100;
      realVectorLength = 200;
type  IntVectorType = array [1..intVectorLength] of integer;
      RealVectorType = array [1..realVectorLength] of real;
var   intVector: IntVectorType;
      realVector: RealVectorType;
```

15. In a Pascal block, the word `begin` must always appear, even if the block contains no statements.

16. In addition to assignment, procedure call, `if`, `case`, `while`, `repeat`, `for`, and `with` statements, Pascal provides a `goto` statement and a compound statement.

Modula-2

9. In Modula-2, the symbols `(*` and `*)` delimit comments. (Modula-2 uses the symbols { and } to enclose set values.) Programmers may nest comments.

```
(* This is a comment (* This is a nested comment *) *)
```

10. A Modula-2 program consists of a program module and (optionally) one or more library modules. The program module establishes connections with the library modules by importing entities (constants, types, variables, or procedures) that the library modules export.

11. A Modula-2 program must begin with the word MODULE and end with the word END, followed by the name of the program and a period:

```
MODULE Sample;
      .
      .
      .
END Sample.
```

12. In the heading of a program module, Modula-2 does not allow a list of program parameters to follow the program name. However, a priority may follow the program name (as discussed in Chapter 12):

```
MODULE Sample [7];
```

13. In addition to constants, types, variables, procedures, and functions, Modula-2 allows the programmer to declare modules. Labels do not exist in Modula-2, because the language provides no GOTO statement.

14. Declarations in a Modula-2 block can appear in any order (for example, constant declarations need not precede type declarations). The programmer need not group together declarations of a particular kind of entity. As in Pascal, a programmer must first declare an entity before using it to declare another.

```
CONST intVectorLength = 100;
TYPE  IntVectorType = ARRAY [1..intVectorLength] of INTEGER;
VAR   intVector: IntVectorType;

CONST realVectorLength = 200;
TYPE  RealVectorType = ARRAY [1..realVectorLength] of REAL;
VAR   realVector: RealVectorType;
```

15. In a Modula-2 block, the word BEGIN need not appear if the block has no statements.

16. In addition to assignment, procedure call, IF, CASE, WHILE, REPEAT, FOR, and WITH statements, Modula-2 provides LOOP, EXIT, and RETURN statements, but not GOTO or compound statements. The EXIT and RETURN statements, together with the standard procedure HALT, remove the need for a

Standard Pascal

17. In Pascal, the semicolon is a statement separator. Pascal does not allow use of the semicolon as a statement terminator in all contexts.

GOTO statement. Compound statements are unnecessary because of Modula-2's general rule that a statement sequence may appear wherever the language allows a single statement.

17. In the formal syntax of Modula-2, the semicolon is a statement separator; however, programmers may use the semicolon as a statement terminator if desired.

EXERCISES

Section 2.1

1. Which of the following are legal Modula-2 identifiers? (Remember: Reserved words are not identifiers.)

(a) `PiTimes2`	(d) `Add-Columns`	(g) `Char_Buffer`
(b) `Begin`	(e) `PROCEDURE`	(h) `ERROR`
(c) `plus`	(f) `ReverseVideoOn`	(i) `40Lines`

2. Modula-2's case sensitivity has been criticized by some. What are the advantages and disadvantages of case sensitivity?

3. Which of the following are legal integers?

(a) `349`	(d) `12FH`	(g) `819B`
(b) `1AD`	(e) `40C`	(h) `001`
(c) `777B`	(f) `FFFH`	(i) `4B3GH`

4. Which of the following are legal real numbers?

(a) `3.33E-01`	(d) `10.E+10`	(g) `1.0000E8`
(b) `.998`	(e) `5.0E+10.0`	(h) `20202.3E`
(c) `0.02`	(f) `1E20`	(i) `144.`

5. Which of the following are legal strings?

(a) `" "`	(d) `"It's "done""`	(g) `"12C"`
(b) `'Hit "RETURN"'`	(e) `'Written by:'`	(h) `'isn''t it?'`
(c) `'Stop him!"`	(f) `'");'`	(i) `"ABC's"`

6. In the Ada programming language, comments begin with the symbol `--` and continue to the end of the line. Compare this method of indicating a comment with the method used by Modula-2. What are the advantages and disadvantages of each method?

Section 2.2

7. The Logitech Modula-2/86 system provides library modules named `FileSystem` (for file handling) and `Strings` (for string manipulation). Suppose that a program needs to import `Delete` and `Length` from `FileSystem` (to delete a file and determine the length of a file, respectively) and `Delete` and `Length` from `Strings` (to delete characters from a string and determine the length of a string). Write a sequence of import lists that will allow access to all four procedures; these lists should allow the programmer to reference `Delete` (in `FileSystem`) and `Length` (in `Strings`) without qualification.

8. (For Pascal programmers) Modula-2 (but not Pascal) allows programmers to use semicolons as statement terminators. Give an example showing how using semicolons in this fashion would yield an illegal Pascal program.

3 Basic Types

Modula-2 is a *strongly typed* language. Every variable in a Modula-2 program must have a *type* to indicate the range of values that the variable can assume; the compiler checks this type wherever an operation on the variable appears in the program.

Strong typing has several advantages. First, many programming errors result in type mismatches; with strong typing, it is possible to detect these errors during compilation, when they are easiest to fix. Second, types provide information that a Modula-2 compiler needs. In particular, the compiler can—from the type of a variable—deduce the amount of storage the variable requires. Third, the type of a variable serves as an important source of program documentation: by looking at the declaration of a variable, someone reading a program can quickly determine the range of values that the variable can assume.

Some types are *standard*; Modula-2 compilers recognize these types and hence the programmer need not declare them. Of Modula-2's standard types, the most important are the *basic* types, which consist of the numeric types (INTEGER, CARDINAL, REAL, and—in some implementations—LONGINT and LONGREAL), the character type (CHAR), and the Boolean type (BOOLEAN). Sections 3.1–3.3 discuss the seven basic types; Table 3.1 summarizes these types and indicates the section in which we explain each.

Table 3.1 Basic Types

Name	*Values*	*Section*
INTEGER	integers	3.1
CARDINAL	nonnegative integers	3.1
REAL	real numbers	3.1
LONGINT	integers (larger range than INTEGER)	3.1
LONGREAL	real numbers (greater precision and range than REAL)	3.1
CHAR	characters	3.2
BOOLEAN	Boolean values (TRUE and FALSE)	3.3

Section 3.4 introduces the general rules for forming expressions in Modula-2. Section 3.5 shows how to declare constants and variables.

3.1 Numeric Types

Every Modula-2 system must supply the three numeric types INTEGER, CARDINAL, and REAL. The INTEGER type consists of whole numbers, both positive and negative, in a system-defined range. The CARDINAL type is similar, but includes only 0 and a range of positive integers. REAL values represent real numbers, both positive and negative. Newer Modula-2 compilers may also supply the types LONGINT and LONGREAL.

The INTEGER Type

The range of INTEGER values varies from one Modula-2 system to another, but is usually the same as the range supported by the underlying computer. The standard functions MIN and MAX, when applied to the type INTEGER, yield the smallest and largest INTEGER values. For example, if INTEGER values have a 16-bit representation, MAX(INTEGER) is 32,767 and MIN(INTEGER) is usually −32,768. (*Note:* MIN and MAX appear in the Third Edition of *Programming in Modula-2*, but not in the Second, so older compilers may not supply these functions.)

Modula-2 supplies five binary operations for values of type INTEGER (see Table 3.2).

Table 3.2 INTEGER Operators

+	addition
-	subtraction
*	multiplication
DIV	quotient
MOD	remainder

The only operations that deserve special mention are DIV ("divide") and MOD ("modulus"). If i and j have type INTEGER, then i DIV j is the quotient obtained when i is divided by j (with the fractional portion dropped if the result is not an integer), and i MOD j is the remainder.

Expression	*Value*
`6 DIV 2`	3
`6 MOD 2`	0
`1 DIV 3`	0
`1 MOD 3`	1
`-3 DIV 2`	−1
`3 DIV -2`	−1

The value of `i MOD j` is defined only if `i` is nonnegative and `j` is positive; otherwise, the value of `i MOD j` depends on the underlying machine.

The operations `*`, `DIV`, and `MOD` take precedence over the operations `+` and `-`. Modula-2 performs operations at the same level of precedence from left to right:

Expression	*Value*
`1 - 6 - 4`	−9
`5 + 8 * 3`	29
`4 * 10 + 6 DIV 2`	43

The programmer can use parentheses to change the order of evaluation:

Expression	*Value*
`1 - (6 - 4)`	−1
`(5 + 8) * 3`	39
`4 * (10 + 6) DIV 2`	32

The symbols `+` and `-` represent unary operators as well as binary operators. However, Modula-2 forbids adjacent operators, so `+` and `-` can appear only at the beginning of an arithmetic expression or when preceded by a left parenthesis.

Expression	*Value*
`-9 + 4 DIV 2`	−7
`12 + -3`	not legal (`+` and `-` are adjacent)
`12 + (-3)`	9

The standard functions `ABS` and `ODD` can be applied to integers. `ABS(i)` is the absolute value of `i`. The value of `ODD(i)` is `TRUE` if `i` is odd, `FALSE` if `i` is even:

Expression	*Value*
`ABS(4)`	4
`ABS(-4)`	4
`ODD(2)`	`FALSE`
`ODD(-7)`	`TRUE`
`ODD(0)`	`FALSE`

Oddly enough, Modula-2 does not provide an EVEN function. To test whether i is even, use the expression NOT ODD(i).

The CARDINAL Type

CARDINAL is similar to INTEGER, except that CARDINAL includes only nonnegative integers. Most Modula-2 systems store values of type CARDINAL in the same amount of space as values of type INTEGER. The bit that normally indicates the sign of an INTEGER value can store part of the magnitude of a CARDINAL number; consequently, the largest CARDINAL is normally twice as large as the largest INTEGER, plus 1. The expression MAX(CARDINAL) gives the largest CARDINAL number; the smallest CARDINAL is always 0.

For example, suppose that a system represents INTEGER values using 16 bits. MAX(INTEGER) is 32,767 ($2^{15} - 1$), because the magnitude of an INTEGER value occupies 15 bits; the remaining bit indicates the number's sign. MAX(CARDINAL), however, is 65,535 ($2^{16} - 1$), because the system can use all 16 bits to store the magnitude of a CARDINAL.

All INTEGER operators are defined for CARDINAL operands as well (with the exception of the unary - operation), as is the standard function ODD. (ABS, however, is not useful, because the absolute value of a CARDINAL number is the number itself.)

The fact that the INTEGER and CARDINAL types overlap raises some intriguing questions. For example, what is the type of a number (numeric literal) such as 1, which could be either an INTEGER or a CARDINAL? When a Modula-2 compiler cannot determine the type of a number uniquely, the compiler treats the number as though it were both INTEGER and CARDINAL. Thus, the following table gives the type of a number *n*:

Value of n	*Type of* n
$0 \le n \le$ MAX(INTEGER)	INTEGER or CARDINAL
MAX(INTEGER) $< n \le$ MAX(CARDINAL)	CARDINAL

The type of a number is important to know, because—as we will see shortly—Modula-2 operators do not allow operands of different numeric types.

We gain several advantages by declaring a variable i to have type CARDINAL instead of type INTEGER if we know that i never takes on negative values. First, i can take on larger values without overflow. Second, arithmetic operations involving i may execute faster on some machines. Third, by declaring i to be of type CARDINAL, the programmer documents the fact that i should never be negative. Best of all, the program will terminate if i ever takes on a negative value, serving as an early signal that the program is not behaving as expected.

The CARDINAL type also has disadvantages. CARDINAL values cannot be mixed freely with INTEGER values in expressions, as we will see later in this section; combining CARDINAL and INTEGER values requires type conversion. Furthermore, the CARDINAL type requires careful handling; the programmer must ensure that CARDINAL expressions can never be negative. For example, suppose that i, j, and k are variables of type CARDINAL; one might expect the CARDINAL expression

```
i - j + k
```

to be legal provided that its value is not negative. Unfortunately, the expression is illegal if i is less than j, because the result of subtracting j from i is negative (and hence not a CARDINAL value). Another problem can occur when the control variable in a FOR statement is of type CARDINAL (see Section 4.4).

Because of these disadvantages, the CARDINAL type is not as useful as might appear at first. Still, it is important in systems programming, because here unsigned numbers are common and the arithmetic performed on them is simple (adding or subtracting 1, for example).

The REAL Type

Values of type REAL represent real (floating-point) numbers. Binary operations allowed for REAL values are shown in Table 3.3.

Table 3.3 REAL Operators

+	addition
-	subtraction
*	multiplication
/	division

The REAL operators are similar to the INTEGER and CARDINAL operators, except that / replaces DIV and MOD is absent. The different division symbol reminds us that dividing two REAL values does not produce a remainder; the quotient is as exact as the underlying hardware allows.

Modula-2 allows the use of unary + and - and the ABS function (but not ODD) with REAL numbers.

The LONGINT and LONGREAL Types

The Third Edition of *Programming in Modula-2* introduces two new numeric types, LONGINT and LONGREAL, that do not appear in the Second Edition. LONGINT includes a larger range of integers than INTEGER, while LONGREAL provides real numbers of greater precision (and possibly greater magnitude) than REAL. For example, if INTEGER values are 16 bits long, then LONGINT values are typically 32 bits long. If so, MAX(LONGINT) would be 2,147,483,647 and MIN(LONGINT) would usually be −2,147,483,648. Similarly, a LONGREAL value might occupy twice as many bits as a REAL value. The manual for a particular Modula-2 system should provide information about the representation of LONGINT and LONGREAL values.

Unfortunately, *Programming in Modula-2* gives virtually no information about how to use LONGINT and LONGREAL values; consequently, Modula-2 systems that provide these types are likely to be inconsistent. In particular, Wirth does not give a method for specifying that a literal has type LONGINT or LONGREAL, nor does he provide functions for converting to or from these types. Some systems use a trailing L to indicate a LONGINT number:

```
0L
65535L
```

In other systems, any integer literal whose value is greater than MAX(CARDINAL) but less than or equal to MAX(LONGINT) has type LONGINT. To indicate that a number between 0 and MAX(CARDINAL) has type LONGINT, the programmer can use the standard function VAL. For example, VAL(LONGINT, 10) is a LONGINT number whose value is 10.

In some systems, LONGREAL numbers have the same appearance as REAL numbers, but with D instead of E at the beginning of the scale factor:

```
0.0D0
52.94D10
```

Be aware that these conventions are not universal, however. (For example, at least one system requires the letter D instead of L at the end of a LONGINT number.) Similarly, functions for converting to or from LONGINT and LONGREAL vary from one system to another; consult the system manual for more information.

Some Modula-2 systems may also provide a LONGCARD type. Because the Third Edition of *Programming in Modula-2* does not list LONGCARD among the standard types of Modula-2, we must consider it an extension to the language.

Mixed Expressions

Modula-2 does not allow *mixed expressions*; values combined in an expression must have the same type. For example, the addition operator may not have one operand of type INTEGER and the other of type CARDINAL or REAL. (More precisely, operands in an expression must be *compatible*. The slightly weaker requirement of compatibility treats values of a subrange type as though they belong to the base type. We discuss compatibility in Section 6.4.)

When INTEGER, CARDINAL, and/or REAL values are mixed in an expression, the programmer must use conversion functions to convert the operands to the same type. Table 3.4 summarizes Modula-2's conversion functions.

Table 3.4 Conversion Between Arithmetic Types

Old Type	*New Type*	*Function Call*	*Source of Function*
INTEGER	CARDINAL	VAL(CARDINAL, i)	standard
CARDINAL	INTEGER	VAL(INTEGER, c)	standard
CARDINAL	REAL	FLOAT(c)	standard
REAL	CARDINAL	TRUNC(r)	standard
INTEGER	REAL	real(i)	import from MathLib0
REAL	INTEGER	entier(r)	import from MathLib0

For example, suppose that c, i, and r are variables of types CARDINAL, INTEGER, and REAL, respectively. The conversion functions in the table allow us to combine any two of these variables in an expression:

Expression	*Type*
c + VAL(CARDINAL, i)	CARDINAL
i + VAL(INTEGER, c)	INTEGER
r + FLOAT(c)	REAL
c + TRUNC(r)	CARDINAL
r + real(i)	REAL
i + entier(r)	INTEGER

An alternate (and more succinct) way to convert from INTEGER to CARDINAL is to use the standard function ORD. If i is an INTEGER value, ORD(i) is the corresponding CARDINAL value.

We run some risk in converting from CARDINAL to INTEGER, or vice-versa. An attempt to convert a negative INTEGER to CARDINAL is illegal, as is an attempt to convert a CARDINAL value larger than MAX(INTEGER) to INTEGER. In *Programming in Modula-2*, Wirth does not specify what ORD and VAL should do when asked to perform an illegal conversion. Implementers of Modula-2 seem to be reaching a consensus that ORD and VAL should check for illegal conversions and terminate the program. Be aware, however, that some Modula-2 systems do not test for legality.

Modula-2 provides yet another way to convert between INTEGER and CARDINAL, taking advantage of the fact that nonnegative INTEGER values normally have the same internal representation as the corresponding CARDINAL values. As part of its repertoire of low-level features, Modula-2 supplies a method called *type transfer* (Section 11.4). To perform a transfer from one type to another, we use the name of the latter type as though it were a function. For example, to add an INTEGER i and a CARDINAL c, we might choose to treat c as though it were of type INTEGER:

```
WriteInt(i + INTEGER(c), 1);    (* type transfer *)
```

When a Modula-2 compiler encounters such an expression, it generates an instruction to add i and c; it does not generate any code for type conversion. Using INTEGER as a type transfer function has no effect other than to force the compiler to accept c as an INTEGER value. The advantage of type transfer is that the compiler generates no code for type conversion, making the object program smaller and faster. The disadvantage of type transfer is that programs using it can be error-prone. If the value of c is greater than MAX(INTEGER), then i + INTEGER(c) will not produce a meaningful result, because the value of c—when viewed as an INTEGER—will appear to be a large negative number. Similarly, if i is negative, then CARDINAL(i) is a very large positive number.

In *Programming in Modula-2*, Wirth lists the CARDINAL and INTEGER functions as the primary way to convert between types CARDINAL and INTEGER. We recommend the use of ORD or VAL instead, because—on many systems—these functions perform error checking. Type transfer functions, by their very nature, cannot test for errors.

Unlike CARDINAL and INTEGER, the standard functions FLOAT and TRUNC cause a genuine conversion of type. FLOAT converts a CARDINAL number to the corresponding REAL value. (FLOAT can also convert a nonnegative INTEGER value to REAL.) TRUNC converts a REAL value to a CARDINAL value by dropping the REAL number's fractional part:

Expression	*Value*
TRUNC(6.05)	6
TRUNC(7.5)	7
TRUNC(8.9)	8

To round a REAL number r to the closest CARDINAL value, use the expression TRUNC(r + 0.5). (Modula-2 provides no standard rounding function.)

The real and entier functions are similar to FLOAT and TRUNC, but allow conversions between INTEGER and REAL values. Unlike FLOAT and TRUNC, real and entier are not standard functions; a program must import them from a library module. (In Wirth's library, this module is called MathLib0, but the name may vary from one Modula-2 system to another.) This anomaly (FLOAT and TRUNC are standard, while real and entier are not) stems from the fact that FLOAT and TRUNC are somewhat simpler than real and entier, as the former deal only with nonnegative numbers. Because of the simplicity of FLOAT and TRUNC, most Modula-2 systems replace calls of these functions by one (or a few) machine instructions; calls of real and entier are not expanded in this fashion.

Although explicit type conversions are a nuisance, programmers do not need them very often. Moreover, forcing the programmer to perform the conversion explicitly has certain advantages. The programmer thus becomes aware of type conversions; in other languages, many conversions occur without the programmer's knowledge, which leads to errors. Also, Modula-2 compilers can be smaller and faster if the programmer handles type conversions.

Wirth's `MathLib0` Module

We saw earlier in this section that Modula-2 provides the `ABS` (absolute value) function. No other mathematical functions are standard in Modula-2. Programs that need additional mathematical functions must import them from a library module. Wirth's `MathLib0` module provides most of the common mathematical functions, plus functions for converting `INTEGER` values to `REAL`, and vice-versa. Table 3.5 lists all the functions in `MathLib0`.

Table 3.5 Functions in `MathLib0`

Name	*Type of* `x`	*Type of Result*	*Function Performed*
`sqrt(x)`	REAL	REAL	square root
`exp(x)`	REAL	REAL	exponential (e^x)
`ln(x)`	REAL	REAL	natural logarithm
`sin(x)`	REAL	REAL	sine
`cos(x)`	REAL	REAL	cosine
`arctan(x)`	REAL	REAL	arctangent
`real(x)`	INTEGER	REAL	convert to real
`entier(x)`	REAL	INTEGER	convert to integer

The `sin` and `cos` functions expect values in radians, not degrees; the value that `arctan` returns is also in radians. The value of `entier(x)` is the greatest integer less than or equal to `x`:

Expression	*Value*
`entier(6.1)`	6
`entier(6.9)`	6
`entier(-6.1)`	−7

The word *entier* is French for "integer." The use of *entier* to name the "greatest integer" function is a tradition that dates back to Algol 60.

EXAMPLE PROGRAM **Converting a Fahrenheit Temperature to Celsius**

The following program, `ConvertToCelsius`, converts a Fahrenheit temperature to Celsius. Because we normally express temperatures as integers, the program reads the Fahrenheit temperature as an integer and prints the Celsius equivalent as an integer. Inside `ConvertToCelsius`, however, we use real arithmetic so that the result can be rounded to the nearest integer. Therefore, `ConvertToCelsius` uses the `real` function to convert the input value to type REAL and the `entier` function to convert the output back to type INTEGER.

```
MODULE ConvertToCelsius;
  (* converts a Fahrenheit temperature to Celsius *)

  FROM InOut IMPORT ReadInt, WriteInt, WriteString, WriteLn;
  FROM MathLib0 IMPORT real, entier;

  VAR fahrenheit: INTEGER;
      celsius: REAL;

BEGIN
  WriteString("Enter Fahrenheit temperature: ");
  ReadInt(fahrenheit);
  WriteLn;

  celsius := (real(fahrenheit) - 32.0) * 5.0 / 9.0;

  WriteString("Celsius equivalent is: ");
  WriteInt(entier(celsius + 0.5), 1);         (* round answer *)
  WriteLn
END ConvertToCelsius.
```

3.2 The CHAR Type

Values of type CHAR include letters, digits, punctuation marks, and nonprinting (control) characters. CHAR is not the same for all Modula-2 systems, because its values are the characters provided by the underlying hardware. We use the ASCII character set in our examples, because it is common in microcomputers and minicomputers, the machines for which Modula-2 is most widely available. Note, however, that Modula-2 systems are *not* required to support the ASCII character set.

In Modula-2, strings of length 1 represent CHAR values. Thus, the programmer can enclose a character between either single quotes (`'A'`, for example) or double quotes (`"A"`). The string `"'"` represents the character `'` and the string `'"'` represents the character `"`.

The values of type CHAR are ordered, but the ordering depends on the character set in use. Table 3.6 shows the ordering of the characters in the ASCII character set. The first column gives the *ordinal number* of each character in decimal, while the second column displays it in octal. Notice that the ordering of characters begins at 0 rather than 1.

Table 3.6 ASCII Character Set

Ordinal Number (Decimal)	*Ordinal Number (Octal)*	*Character*	*Ordinal Number (Decimal)*	*Ordinal Number (Octal)*	*Character*	*Ordinal Number (Decimal)*	*Ordinal Number (Octal)*	*Character*	*Ordinal Number (Decimal)*	*Ordinal Number (Octal)*	*Character*
0	000	nul	32	040		64	100	@	96	140	`
1	001	soh (^A)	33	041	!	65	101	A	97	141	a
2	002	stx (^B)	34	042	"	66	102	B	98	142	b
3	003	etx (^C)	35	043	#	67	103	C	99	143	c
4	004	eot (^D)	36	044	$	68	104	D	100	144	d
5	005	enq (^E)	37	045	%	69	105	E	101	145	e
6	006	ack (^F)	38	046	&	70	106	F	102	146	f
7	007	bel (^G)	39	047	'	71	107	G	103	147	g
8	010	bs (^H)	40	050	(	72	110	H	104	150	h
9	011	ht (^I)	41	051	)	73	111	I	105	151	i
10	012	lf (^J)	42	052	*	74	112	J	106	152	j
11	013	vt (^K)	43	053	+	75	113	K	107	153	k
12	014	ff (^L)	44	054	,	76	114	L	108	154	l
13	015	cr (^M)	45	055	-	77	115	M	109	155	m
14	016	so (^N)	46	056	.	78	116	N	110	156	n
15	017	si (^O)	47	057	/	79	117	O	111	157	o
16	020	dle (^P)	48	060	0	80	120	P	112	160	p
17	021	dc1 (^Q)	49	061	1	81	121	Q	113	161	q
18	022	dc2 (^R)	50	062	2	82	122	R	114	162	r
19	023	dc3 (^S)	51	063	3	83	123	S	115	163	s
20	024	dc4 (^T)	52	064	4	84	124	T	116	164	t
21	025	nak (^U)	53	065	5	85	125	U	117	165	u
22	026	syn (^V)	54	066	6	86	126	V	118	166	v
23	027	etb (^W)	55	067	7	87	127	W	119	167	w
24	030	can (^X)	56	070	8	88	130	X	120	170	x
25	031	em (^Y)	57	071	9	89	131	Y	121	171	y
26	032	sub (^Z)	58	072	:	90	132	Z	122	172	z
27	033	esc	59	073	;	91	133	[	123	173	{
28	034	fs	60	074	<	92	134	\	124	174	|
29	035	gs	61	075	=	93	135	]	125	175	}
30	036	rs	62	076	>	94	136	^	126	176	~
31	037	us	63	077	?	95	137	_	127	177	del

Representing Nonprinting Characters

The ASCII characters with ordinal numbers between 0 and 31 cannot be printed (nor can the character with ordinal number 127). The nonprinting characters include the control characters, ^A through ^Z, which we can generate at the keyboard by holding down the Control key and striking one of the letters between A and Z. Programmers cannot include nonprinting characters in programs using the normal single- or double-quote convention. In order to allow nonprinting characters to appear in programs, Modula-2 allows an alternate representation of a character: an octal number (the ordinal number of the character), followed by the letter C. For example, the following statement writes the line-feed character:

```
Write(12C);    (* write line-feed character *)
```

The second column of Table 3.6 is useful for writing characters using the C notation, because it gives ordinal numbers in octal rather than decimal. Here are the Modula-2 representations of some common nonprinting ASCII characters:

Modula-2 Symbol	*ASCII Character*
0C	null
7C	bell (^G)
10C	backspace (^H)
11C	horizontal tab (^I)
12C	line feed (^J)
15C	carriage return (^M)
33C	escape
177C	delete

The ORD and CHR Functions

The standard function ORD computes the ordinal number of a character. For example, if the character set is ASCII, then ORD('A') is 65 and ORD('a') is 97. The standard function CHR yields the inverse of ORD. Thus, CHR(65) is 'A' and CHR(97) is 'a'.

We can use the standard function VAL instead of CHR. VAL is a general-purpose function that returns a value of a specified type when given the ordinal number of the value. Thus, VAL(CHAR, i) returns the CHAR value whose ordinal number is i, which is exactly what CHR(i) returns. For obvious reasons, most programmers prefer to write CHR(i) instead of VAL(CHAR, i). VAL is most useful in conjunction with enumeration types (Section 6.2).

Modula-2 provides no operations for CHAR values other than the relational operations =, # (or <>), <, <=, >, and >= (Section 3.3). In particular, the arithmetic operators do not allow character operands. However, the programmer can use ORD and CHR to perform arithmetic on characters. For example, to compute the offset between the uppercase letters and the lowercase letters in ASCII, we could *not* use the expression

```
'a' - 'A'
```

That expression is illegal; instead, we would use

```
ORD('a') - ORD('A')
```

The CAP Function

Modula-2 provides a standard function called CAP that is often useful when dealing with character data. When given a lowercase letter, CAP returns the corresponding uppercase letter; when given an uppercase letter, CAP returns the same letter unchanged. Thus, CAP('a') is 'A' and CAP('A') is 'A'. In *Programming in Modula-2*, Wirth does not specify the value of CAP(ch) if ch is not a letter. On an ASCII machine, CAP(ch) is normally computed by clearing one bit in the binary representation of ch ('a' in binary is 1100001; 'A' is 1000001). Some implementations of CAP first check whether ch is a letter; others simply clear the bit without checking. To ensure portability, a program should test whether ch is a letter before applying CAP to it.

EXAMPLE PROGRAM

Encoding a Message

The program Encode encodes a message as it is typed at the keyboard. Encode uses a simple "rotation" scheme to perform the encoding: it replaces the letters from *A* through *M* by *N* through *Z*, respectively, and replaces the letters from *N* through *Z* by *A* through *M*. Characters that are not letters do not change. The program has two key statements. One converts an uppercase letter to its encoded version; the other encodes a lowercase letter. The following statement does the uppercase encoding:

```
ch := CHR((ORD(ch) - ORD('A') + 13) MOD 26 + ORD('A'));
```

The idea is to perform a "circular shift" of the letter ch by adding 13 to ORD(ch), taking the result modulo 26, then converting back to character form by using CHR. This operation will work only if the program first subtracts ORD('A') from ORD(ch)—to scale it into the range between 0 and 25—and adds it after performing the MOD operation. (This strategy assumes that the uppercase letters occupy contiguous positions in the underlying character set—as is true in ASCII, but not in every character set.)

Encode reads characters typed at the keyboard until the user presses the escape key (which generates the character 33C). The program uses the Read and Write procedures (imported from InOut) to read and write one character at a time. Because Read does not echo characters typed at the keyboard, the user sees only the encoded version of the message, not the original version.

```
MODULE Encode;
  (* encodes a message; assumes ASCII character set *)

  FROM InOut IMPORT Read, Write, WriteString, WriteLn;

  CONST esc = 33C;   (* escape key *)

  VAR ch: CHAR;

BEGIN
  WriteString("Enter message to be encoded.");
  WriteLn;
  WriteString("Indicate end of message by pressing Esc.");
  WriteLn;

  Read(ch);
  WHILE ch # esc DO
    IF ('A' <= ch) & (ch <= 'Z') THEN
      ch := CHR((ORD(ch) - ORD('A') + 13) MOD 26 + ORD('A'))
    ELSIF ('a' <= ch) & (ch <= 'z') THEN
      ch := CHR((ORD(ch) - ORD('a') + 13) MOD 26 + ORD('a'))
    END;
    Write(ch);
    Read(ch)
  END
END Encode.
```

One property of this code is that a second application of the encoding algorithm undoes the result of the first application. Consequently, we can also use Encode for decoding.

3.3 The BOOLEAN Type

The BOOLEAN type has only two values, denoted by the standard identifiers TRUE and FALSE. The *relational operators* (equal, not equal, less than, and so on) produce BOOLEAN values. The three *logical operators* (AND, OR, and NOT) require BOOLEAN operands and produce a BOOLEAN result.

Relational Operators

Modula-2 provides seven relational operators (Table 3.7).

Table 3.7 Relational Operators

=	equal
<> or #	not equal
<	less than
<=	less than or equal to
>	greater than
>=	greater than or equal to
IN	set membership

The symbols <> and # represent the "not equal" operator and are interchangeable. (The latter symbol is meant to suggest the ≠ relation of mathematics.)

We can use the relational operators (other than IN) to compare values of types INTEGER, CARDINAL, REAL, BOOLEAN, CHAR, or any enumeration type (Section 6.2) or subrange type (Section 6.3). (Presumably, the relational operators also allow operands of types LONGINT and LONGREAL, although Wirth does not mention this possibility in *Programming in Modula-2*.)

Modula-2 considers the BOOLEAN value FALSE to be less than the value TRUE. CHAR values are compared using their ordinal numbers:

Expression	*Value*
'a' < 'b'	TRUE (ORD('a') is 97 and ORD('b') is 98)
'a' < 'A'	FALSE (ORD('a') is 97 and ORD('A') is 65)

In order to compare two values using one of the operators =, <>, <, <=, >, or >=, the values must have compatible types (Section 6.4). In essence, the operands must have the same type—the only exception is for subrange types.

We can also use the operators = and <> to compare sets (Section 7.5) and pointers (Section 8.1). The relational operator IN is meaningful only in conjunction with sets. The operators <= and >= have a special meaning (set inclusion) when we use them to compare sets.

Logical Operators

Modula-2 provides three logical operators: AND, OR, and NOT. These operators require BOOLEAN operands and produce a BOOLEAN result. The symbol & is a synonym for AND; we can use the two interchangeably. Similarly, ~ is a synonym for NOT. (Note: The symbol ~ first appears in the Third Edition of *Programming in Modula-2*, so older compilers may not recognize it.) Table 3.8 summarizes the logical operators.

Table 3.8 Logical Operators

AND or &	logical conjunction
OR	logical disjunction
NOT or ~	logical negation

The following rules define the values of the expressions *p* AND *q*, *p* OR *q*, and NOT *p*:

Expression	*Has the Value* TRUE *If*
p AND *q*	both *p* and *q* are TRUE
p OR *q*	*p* or *q* (or both) is TRUE
NOT *p*	*p* is FALSE

The expressions are FALSE in all other cases.

Another way to specify the meaning of AND, OR, and NOT is by truth tables (see Tables 3.9, 3.10, and 3.11).

Table 3.9 Truth Table for AND

p	*q*	*p* AND *q*
FALSE	FALSE	FALSE
FALSE	TRUE	FALSE
TRUE	FALSE	FALSE
TRUE	TRUE	TRUE

Table 3.10 Truth Table for OR

p	*q*	*p* OR *q*
FALSE	FALSE	FALSE
FALSE	TRUE	TRUE
TRUE	FALSE	TRUE
TRUE	TRUE	TRUE

Table 3.11 Truth Table for NOT

p	NOT *p*
FALSE	TRUE
TRUE	FALSE

In expressions involving two or more logical operators, NOT takes precedence over AND, and AND takes precedence over OR. Both AND and OR are left-associative. Thus, the expression

p OR *q* AND NOT *r* OR *s*

is equivalent to

(*p* OR (*q* AND (NOT *r*))) OR *s*

Modula-2 requires "short-circuit" evaluation of the AND and OR operators. In the expression *p* AND *q*, the value of *p* is first checked; if it is FALSE, then the expression is automatically FALSE, so *q* is not evaluated. Similarly, *p* OR *q* has the value TRUE if *p* is TRUE; *q* is not evaluated. For example, consider the following expression:

```
(i < j) AND (j < k) OR (k < j) AND (j < i)
```

If `(i < j)` is FALSE, then `(j < k)` is not evaluated; if `(k < j)` is also FALSE, then `(j < i)` is not evaluated either. However, if `(i < j)` and `(j < k)` are both TRUE, then neither `(k < j)` nor `(j < i)` are evaluated.

Short-circuit evaluation of BOOLEAN expressions can be very useful. For example, in the expression

```
(x > 0.0) AND (y / x > 0.0)
```

the value of `y / x` will not be computed if `x` is less than or equal to zero, thus preventing a division by zero. Programmers often use this kind of expression to prevent an array index from going out of range or to test that a pointer is not `NIL` before dereferencing it. For example, if A is an array whose indices range from `low` to `high`, the following loop searches A for the value `x`:

```
i := low;
WHILE (i <= high) AND (A[i] # x) DO
  INC(i)
END;
```

If `x` does not appear in A, then `i` will eventually reach the value `high + 1`. At this point, the expression `(i <= high)` will be FALSE, so the loop will terminate; the expression `(A[i] # x)` will not be evaluated, thus avoiding an index out of range.

Although Modula-2 provides only three logical operators, it is possible to get the effect of several more by judiciously using relational operators. In particular, we can interpret the operators <=, =, and <>, when applied to BOOLEAN values, as implication (often written →), logical equivalence (written ≡), and exclusive OR, respectively:

Expression	*Has the Value* TRUE *If*
p <= *q*	*p* is FALSE or *q* is TRUE
p = *q*	*p* and *q* are both TRUE or both FALSE
p <> *q*	*p* or *q* is TRUE, but not both

The expressions are FALSE in all other cases.

3.4 Expressions

Having introduced Modula-2's basic types in Sections 3.1, 3.2, and 3.3, we can now give a complete description of the syntax of Modula-2 expressions. Formally, a Modula-2 expression (Figure 3.1) is either a simple expression or two simple expressions joined by a relational operator (Figure 3.2). For example, the expression `i + j * (k - 1) < 10 * n` contains two simple expressions, `i + j * (k - 1)` and `10 * n`.

Figure 3.1

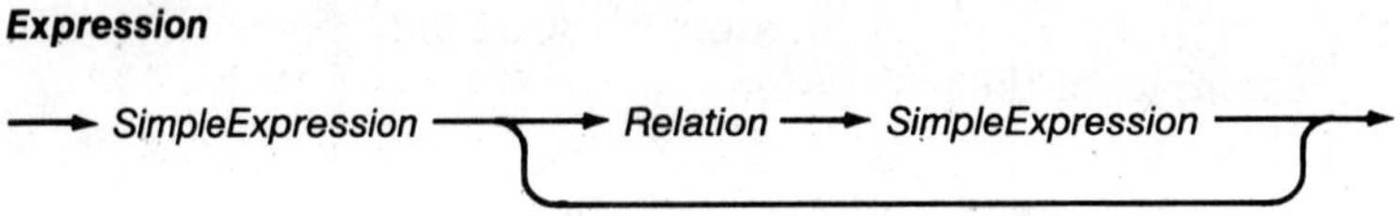

Figure 3.2

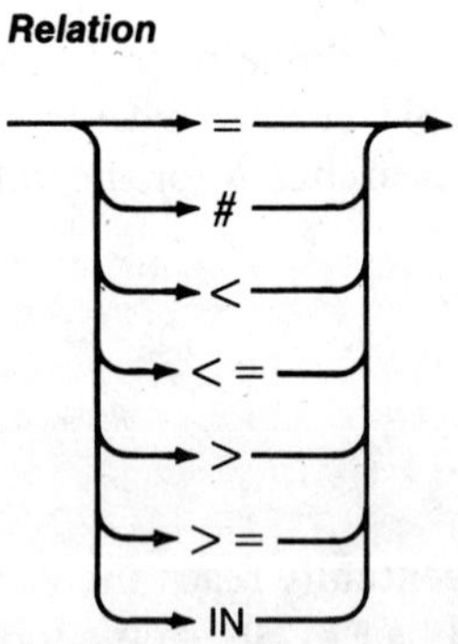

A simple expression (Figure 3.3) is one or more terms, separated by addition operators (Figure 3.4) and possibly preceded by a unary + or - operator. The simple expression `i + j * (k - 1)` contains the terms `i` and `j * (k - 1)`, while the simple expression `10 * n` is a single term.

Figure 3.3

SimpleExpression

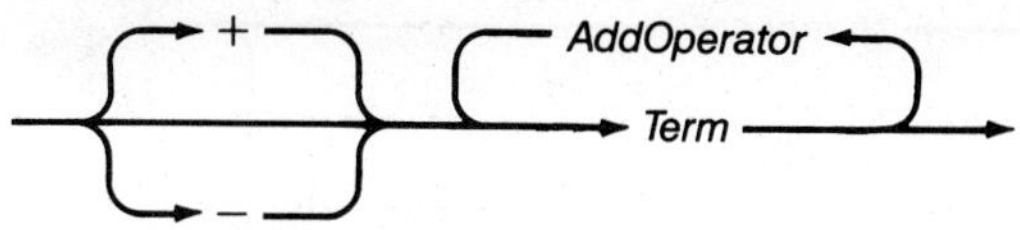

Figure 3.4

AddOperator

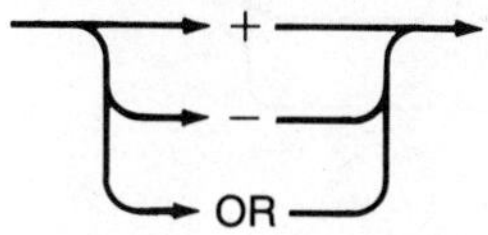

Each term (Figure 3.5) is one or more factors, separated by multiplication operators (Figure 3.6). The term `i` is a single factor, while the term `j * (k - 1)` contains the factors `j` and `(k - 1)` and the term `10 * n` contains the factors `10` and `n`.

Figure 3.5

Term

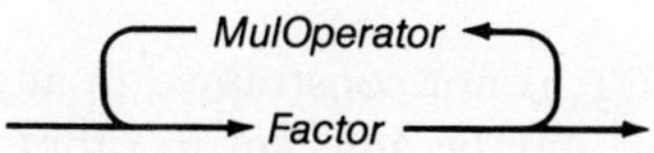

Figure 3.6

MulOperator

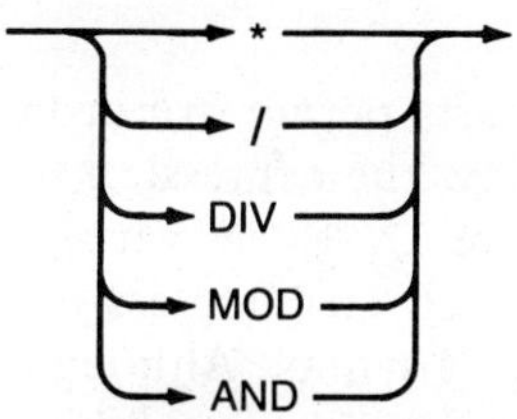

A factor (Figure 3.7) is either an indivisible operand (a number, string, set, or designator), or an expression enclosed in parentheses, or a factor preceded by the NOT operator. Designators include variables and functions, hence the factors `i`, `j`, and `n` are all designators. (We discuss designators in Section 7.3; for now, think of them as identifiers.) The factor `(k - 1)` is a parenthesized expression, and the factor `10` is a number.

Some implications of these charts are rather subtle. In particular, the *Simple-Expression* chart (Figure 3.3) severely restricts the use of the unary + and - operators by prohibiting them from being adjacent to any other arithmetic operator.

Figure 3.7 ***Factor***

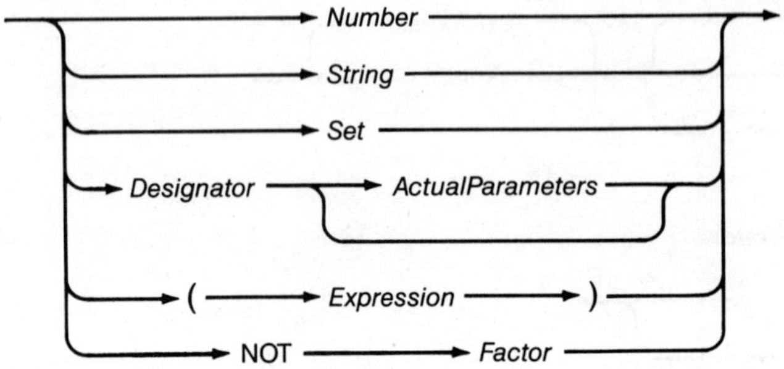

In general, unary + and - can appear only at the beginning of an expression, following a relational operator, or preceded by a left parenthesis:

Legal	*Illegal*
`-(-i)`	`--i`
`i + (-j)`	`i + -j`
`-i + j`	
`i > -j`	

The other unary operator, NOT, is not constrained in any way. In contrast to unary + and -, the NOT operator may be adjacent to other operators (including itself):

```
NOT NOT p
p AND NOT q
```

Many of the expressions these charts permit are in fact not meaningful in Modula-2. For example, the charts allow the expression `3 + 'A'` as well as the expression `i AND j`, where `i` and `j` are `INTEGER` variables. The designer of a programming language often allows such meaningless expressions in order to simplify the description of the language's syntax. Although such expressions are *syntactically* legal, the *semantics* of the language prohibits them. In the case of Modula-2, the expression `3 + 'A'` is illegal because the + operator does not allow operands of type `CHAR`, and `i AND j` is illegal because the `AND` operator allows only operands of type `BOOLEAN`.

Operator Precedence and Associativity

Modula-2's arithmetic, relational, and logical operators allow the construction of complicated expressions. To ensure that each expression has a unique meaning, Modula-2 provides rules for operator precedence and associativity. The syntax charts given earlier mirror Modula-2's rules for operator precedence. By dividing expressions into four categories (expressions, simple expressions, terms, and factors), the charts display Modula-2's four-level operator precedence hierarchy. The NOT operator has the highest precedence, followed by the multiplication operators, the addition operators, and finally the relational operators (see Table 3.12).

Table 3.12 Operator Precedence

NOT ~
* / DIV MOD AND &
+ - OR
= # <> < <= > >= IN

The charts do not show the rule for associativity, which is a simple one: All binary operators are left-associative. Thus, operations at the same level of precedence are performed from left to right.

The rules for precedence and associativity come into play whenever an expression contains more than one operator. If the expression contains operators at different levels of precedence, the program performs the operations in the order just described. If several operations are at the same precedence level, the associativity rule dictates performing them from left to right. For example,

Expression	*Order of Evaluation*
i * 3 - j DIV 2	(i * 3) - (j DIV 2)
i DIV j * k	(i DIV j) * k
-i - j - k	((-i) - j) - k
p OR q AND r	p OR (q AND r)
p AND q AND r	(p AND q) AND r
p AND NOT q OR r	(p AND (NOT q)) OR r
i + 2 * j < k + 1	(i + (2 * j)) < (k + 1)

Note, however, that in an expression such as

```
p AND NOT q
```

the expression p is evaluated before NOT q, even though NOT takes precedence over AND. Because Modula-2 requires "short-circuit" evaluation of BOOLEAN expressions, NOT q is not evaluated at all if p is FALSE.

We can use parentheses to change the order of evaluation within an expression. When in doubt, and particularly when expressions are complicated, use parentheses liberally.

The fact that the relational operators have lower precedence than the logical operators means that relational expressions must be enclosed in parentheses when combined using logical operators. For example, if `i`, `j`, and `k` are `INTEGER` variables, the expression

```
i < j AND j < k
```

is not legal in Modula-2; AND has higher precedence than <, so a Modula-2 compiler interprets the expression as `(i < (j AND j)) < k`. When parentheses enclose the relational expressions, the problem vanishes:

```
(i < j) AND (j < k)
```

Constant Expressions

In Modula-2, a *constant expression* may appear wherever the language allows a constant. As Figure 3.8 shows, a constant expression has the same syntax as an expression. Unlike an ordinary expression, however, a constant expression must contain only constant operands, never variables. Furthermore, a compiler must be able to evaluate a constant expression by a "mere textual scan without actually executing the program" (*Programming in Modula-2*, Third Edition). Therefore, constant expressions can include calls of standard functions such as `MAX` and `MIN`, but may not contain calls of user-defined functions. Wirth does not explicitly state which standard functions may appear in constant expressions; some compilers may allow all standard functions, while others prohibit certain standard functions. (In the Second Edition, constant expressions could not contain function calls at all.) The following are examples of constant expressions:

```
13.5 * 1.0567 / 4.0
(MAX(CARDINAL) - 1) DIV 2
('+' < '-') OR ('Z' >= 'z')
```

The only identifiers that may appear in constant expressions (other than the names of standard functions) are identifiers bound to constant values by means of constant declarations (Section 3.5).

Figure 3.8

ConstExpression

→ *Expression* →

3.5 Constant and Variable Declarations

Modula-2 provides two ways to associate an identifier with a data value: by a *constant declaration* or by a *variable declaration*. A constant declaration specifies an identifier and a constant value; the association between the identifier and the value is permanent and cannot be changed by assignment. A variable declaration specifies an identifier and a type. No fixed value is associated with the identifier; its value changes during program execution as the result of assignment.

Constant Declarations

A constant declaration binds an identifier to a constant value; each subsequent appearance of the identifier is equivalent to an appearance of the constant value that it represents. A constant declaration has the form shown in Figure 3.9. As the syntax chart for declarations (Figure 2.12) shows, the reserved word CONST must precede a sequence of constant declarations; also, a semicolon must terminate each declaration. Here are several constant declarations:

```
CONST speedOfLight = 1.86E5;          (* in miles per second *)
      absoluteZero = -273.1;          (* Celsius *)
      monthlySalesGoal = 1000;
      questionMark = '?';
      lineFeed = 12C;
      debugOption = TRUE;
      errorMessage = "END expected";
```

As the example shows, constants can represent numbers, strings, and values of types CHAR and BOOLEAN. Constants can also represent enumeration values (Section 6.2) and sets (Section 7.5).

Arbitrary constant expressions may appear to the right of the equals sign:

```
CONST pi = 3.14159;
      radius = 10.0;
      area = pi * radius * radius;
      first = 0;
      last = 99;
      length = last - first + 1;
```

The programmer must declare a constant before using it to declare other constants. For example, the declaration of `area` relies on the previously declared constants `pi` and `radius`. An attempt to declare `area` before `pi` and `radius` would be illegal:

```
CONST area = pi * radius * radius;    (* illegal *)
      pi = 3.14159;
      radius = 10.0;
```

Figure 3.9 ***ConstantDeclaration***

→ *Ident* → = → *ConstExpression* →

Giving a name to a constant value has several advantages:

- The name helps document the meaning of the constant value (`speed-OfLight` is more helpful to someone reading a program than `1.86E5` would be).
- To change the value of the constant, the programmer must change only the declaration of the constant, not every occurrence of the constant in the program. (`speedOfLight` is unlikely to change, but `monthlySalesGoal` probably will.)
- When the same constant value occurs more than once in a program, some of its appearances may be incorrect because of typographical errors. (Long numerical values such as `2.7182818284` are prone to this sort of error.) If an identifier replaces each occurrence of the value, the risk of error greatly diminishes, because the value itself appears only once in the program (in the constant declaration that binds the identifier to the value).

Variable Declarations

Modula-2 requires the programmer to declare every variable. A variable declaration consists of a list of identifiers and a type; the variables are permanently bound to that type and can be assigned only values belonging to the type. Figure 3.10 shows the syntax of a variable declaration. The reserved word VAR must precede a sequence of variable declarations, and a semicolon must terminate each declaration. For example, here is a group of three variable declarations:

```
VAR i1, i2, i3: INTEGER;
    epsilon: REAL;
    oldChar, newChar: CHAR;
```

Figure 3.10

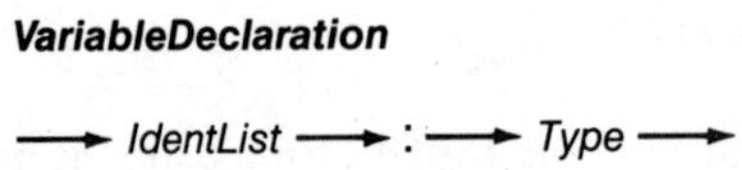

A Capitalization Convention

Because Modula-2 identifiers can contain only letters and digits, not underscores, programmers typically use uppercase letters to begin each word within an identifier (as we have done with `speedOfLight` and `monthlySalesGoal`) to make the identifier easier to read. It is not clear whether we should capitalize the first letter of an identifier—such capitalization apparently has little effect on program readability. In issue #0 of *Modula-2 News*, Jirka Hoppe has suggested that programmers capitalize the names of types, procedures, and modules, but *not* the names of constants, variables, and procedure parameters.* Constants, variables, and parameters represent data values; types, procedures, and modules do not.

Hoppe's convention is easy to remember and follow, yet provides useful information to anyone reading a program. For example, Hoppe's convention makes it easy to spot variables and constants in import lists.

I have found Hoppe's convention useful, so I have used it throughout this book. Be aware that it is not in universal use, however. Some programmers prefer other conventions (one that distinguishes between variables and constants, for example).

A few programmers use even more complicated schemes for creating identifiers. For example, the name of each variable might include a code indicating the variable's type. Although such a convention can help a programmer avoid errors when writing in a language that performs little or no type-checking, it is much less useful in a strongly typed language such as Modula-2.

EXAMPLE PROGRAM

Computing the Circumference and Area of a Circle

The following program computes the circumference and area of a circle. We declare the number 3.14159 as a constant, so it needs to appear only once in the program.

```
MODULE Circle;
  (* computes the circumference and area of a circle *)

  FROM InOut IMPORT WriteString, WriteLn;
  FROM RealInOut IMPORT ReadReal, WriteReal;

  CONST pi = 3.14159;
        twoTimesPi = 2.0 * pi;

  VAR radius: REAL;

BEGIN
  WriteString("Enter radius: ");
  ReadReal(radius);
  WriteLn;

  WriteString("Circumference is: ");
  WriteReal(twoTimesPi * radius, 10);
  WriteLn;

  WriteString("Area is: ");
  WriteReal(pi * radius * radius, 10);
  WriteLn
END Circle.
```

*Jirka Hoppe, "Some Problems with the Specification of Standard Modules," *Modula-2 News*, 0 (October 1984), 4–6.

Standard Pascal

1. Pascal provides two numeric types: `integer` and `real`.

2. In Pascal, the required identifier `maxint` represents the largest value of type `integer`. The expression `-maxint` gives the smallest `integer` value.

3. The value of the Pascal expression `i mod j` is defined for integers `i` and `j` if `j` is positive.

4. Pascal allows the use of the operator / with `integer` and/or `real` operands; the result is always of type `real`.

5. Pascal allows the programmer to mix `real` and `integer` values in expressions without explicit conversion of type. (When a `real` value is combined with an `integer` value, the latter is converted to type `real`.) For type conversion, Pascal provides the functions `trunc` and `round`. The former converts `real` values to `integer` values by truncation; the latter performs the conversion by rounding.

6. Pascal provides eight arithmetic functions: `abs`, `sqr`, `sqrt`, `exp`, `ln`, `sin`, `cos`, and `arctan`. All these functions allow both `integer` and `real` parameters.

7. In Pascal, programmers must enclose a character value in single quotes, with `''''` representing the character `'`. Although Pascal does not have a special convention for representing nonprinting characters, programmers can use the `chr` function for this purpose. For example, `chr(10)` represents the line-feed character.

8. Pascal has no function for converting lowercase letters to uppercase.

9. The symbol <> represents the "not equal" relational operator.

Modula-2

1. In addition to INTEGER and REAL, Modula-2 also provides CARDINAL, LONGINT, and LONGREAL. The type CARDINAL in Modula-2 consists of the integers between 0 and MAX(CARDINAL), where MAX(CARDINAL) is usually equal to 2 * MAX(INTEGER) + 1. LONGINT offers a larger range of integer values than INTEGER, and LONGREAL provides greater precision and allows larger magnitudes than REAL.
2. The Modula-2 functions MAX and MIN return the largest and smallest values in a type. Thus, MAX(INTEGER) is equivalent to Pascal's maxint.
3. The value of the Modula-2 expression i MOD j is defined only if i is nonnegative and j is positive.
4. Modula-2 allows the use of the operator / only with operands of type REAL.
5. Modula-2 does not allow mixing of real and integer values in expressions. Before performing an operation on operands of mixed types, a program must convert the type of one operand so that both operands have the same type. Modula-2 provides the standard functions FLOAT and TRUNC for this purpose. FLOAT converts CARDINAL values to REAL values; TRUNC converts REAL values to CARDINAL values by truncation. Modula-2 supplies no standard functions for conversion from INTEGER to REAL or REAL to INTEGER, although most Modula-2 systems include a library module that provides functions for this purpose (in Wirth's MathLib0 module, they are called real and entier). Modula-2 has no standard function analogous to Pascal's round.
6. The only standard arithmetic function in Modula-2 is ABS; library modules must provide other mathematical functions. In Wirth's library, the module MathLib0 provides the functions sqrt, exp, ln, sin, cos, and arctan, whose parameters must be of type REAL.
7. In Modula-2, either single or double quotes may enclose a character value. The single-quote character is written "'" and the double-quote character '"'. Alternatively, the programmer may write any character (nonprinting characters in particular) as an octal number (the ordinal number of the character) followed by the letter C. For example, 12C represents the line-feed character. Programmers can also use the CHR function as in Pascal.
8. The standard function CAP, when given a lowercase letter as its parameter, returns the corresponding uppercase letter. When given an uppercase letter, CAP returns the letter unchanged.
9. The symbols <> and #, which can be used interchangeably, represent the "not equal" relational operator.

Standard Pascal

10. The reserved word AND represents logical conjunction; NOT represents logical negation.

11. Pascal does not specify the evaluation order of expressions involving the and and or operators; the method of evaluation may vary from one Pascal implementation to another. For example, consider the following expression:

    ```
    (i < j) and (j < k)
    ```

    Some implementations may evaluate both `(i < j)` and `(j < k)`, then perform the and operation on the results. Other implementations may first evaluate `(i < j)`, and if it is false, skip the evaluation of `(j < k)`.

12. In a Pascal constant declaration, the value to the right of the equals sign must be a number, the name of a previously declared constant, or a string (including a single character). A + or - sign may precede a number or an identifier representing a number, but Pascal allows no other form of expression. For example, the following is permissible:

    ```
    const plus100  = 100;
          minus100 = -plus100;
    ```

    But not this:

    ```
    const pi    = 3.14159;
          twoPi = 2.0 * pi;
    ```

Modula-2

10. Both the reserved word AND and the symbol & represent logical conjunction; both NOT and ~ represent logical negation.

11. Modula-2 requires "short-circuit" evaluation of expressions involving AND and OR; evaluation of a BOOLEAN expression ceases as soon as the value of the expression can be determined. When the expression

```
(i < j) AND (j < k)
```

is evaluated, the subexpression `(j < k)` will not be evaluated if the value of `(i < j)` is FALSE.

12. In a Modula-2 constant declaration, the value to the right of the equals sign may be any *constant expression* (an expression whose operands are constants and that can be evaluated without executing the program). Thus, Modula-2 permits the following declaration:

```
CONST pi = 3.14159;
      twoPi = 2.0 * pi;
```

As a general rule, a constant expression may appear wherever the language allows a constant value.

EXERCISES

Section 3.1

1. Assume that INTEGER values are represented in two's-complement form using 16-bit words and that CARDINAL values are represented as unsigned 16-bit integers. If i is an INTEGER variable and c is a CARDINAL variable, what is the value of

   (a) CARDINAL(i), if i has the value 32,767?
   (b) CARDINAL(i), if i has the value −32,768?
   (c) INTEGER(c), if c has the value 32,767?
   (d) INTEGER(c), if c has the value 65,535?

2. Given the declarations

```
VAR c1, c2: CARDINAL;
    i1, i2: INTEGER;
    r1, r2: REAL;
```

   explain why each of the following is *not* a legal Modula-2 expression:

   (a) `1 - (c1 + 2)`
   (b) `c1 + i1`
   (c) `-c1 * c2`
   (d) `2.0 * i1 + 8`
   (e) `i1 / i2 - 1`
   (f) `-1 + TRUNC(r1)`
   (g) `(r1 + r2) / 2`
   (h) `i1 ** i2`
   (i) `r1 MOD r2`

3. Rewrite the following statement from the ConvertToCelsius program to postpone the conversion to type REAL as long as possible. (The statement should still have the same effect.)

```
celsius := (real(fahrenheit) - 32.0) * 5.0 / 9.0;
```

Section 3.2

4. List five ways that a printing character can appear in a Modula-2 program (calls of standard functions are allowed). List three ways that a nonprinting character can appear.

5. Suppose that the variable ch (of type CHAR) contains a digit. Give an expression involving ch whose value is the "complement" of ch, where the complement of '0' is '9', the complement of '1' is '8', and so on.

Section 3.3

6. The truth tables for AND and OR that appear in Section 3.3 are somewhat misleading: because of short-circuit evaluation, it is sometimes possible to determine the value of *p* AND *q* or *p* OR *q* even when *q* is undefined. For example, if *p* has the value TRUE, then *p* OR *q* is TRUE even when *q* has no defined value (because it causes a division by zero, say). Redo the truth tables for AND and OR, using the values FALSE, TRUE, and "undefined" for both *p* and *q* (the result of an operation will also be FALSE, TRUE, or "undefined").

7. Because of Modula-2's short-circuit evaluation of BOOLEAN expressions, it is often possible to determine the value of a BOOLEAN expression without evaluating all of its operands. Assume that *p*, *q*, *r*, and *s* are BOOLEAN expressions whose values are TRUE, FALSE, TRUE, and FALSE, respectively. For

each of the following expressions, indicate which of p, q, r, and s are evaluated during the evaluation of the expression:

(a) p AND q AND r
(b) p OR q AND r OR s
(c) NOT p AND NOT q
(d) (p OR q) OR (r OR s)
(e) NOT (p AND q) AND r
(f) p AND NOT q OR r

8. Assuming that p and q are BOOLEAN expressions, show how to write each of the following expressions using only the operators AND, OR, and NOT:

(a) $p < q$
(b) p <= q
(c) $p > q$
(d) p >= q
(e) $p = q$
(f) p # q

Section 3.4

9. What is the value of each of the following expressions? (Assume that CHAR is the ASCII character set.)

(a) `10 + 1 DIV 4`
(b) `8 * 25 MOD 10`
(c) `3.0 / 4.0 / 5.0`
(d) `1.5 + 3.1 * 2.0 - 1.0`
(e) `CHR(ORD('?') - 16B)`
(f) `ORD(CAP('z'))`
(g) `TRUNC(10.3 - 2.7) # TRUNC(10.3) - TRUNC(2.7)`
(h) `('A' < '[') AND ('[' < 'a')`

10. Write each of the following mathematical expressions as Modula-2 expressions.

(a) $(1/2\pi)\sqrt{k/\mu}$
(b) $(eh/2m)\sqrt{l(l+1)}B \cos\theta$
(c) $(1/2\pi)\sqrt{ke^2/mr^3}$
(d) $Ae^{-\varepsilon/kT}$

Section 3.5

11. Locate any errors in the following sequence of constant declarations.

```
CONST h = 6.62559E-34;
      H = h / (2.0 * pi);
      numWeeks = 10;
      numGames = numTeams DIV 2;
      numScores = numGames * numWeeks;
      numTeams = 200;
      lenTeamName = 30;
```

4 Statements

This chapter presents eight of Modula-2's eleven statements. Section 4.1 covers the assignment statement. We devote the remainder of the chapter to *control structures*, which control the order in which statements are executed. We can divide Modula-2's control structures into three groups. Statements in the first group are for *selection*: choosing between two or more computation paths. The other control structures provide ways to perform *iteration* or *looping* — the repeated execution of a sequence of statements. Some of these statements allow *indefinite iteration*, in which the loop executes an indefinite number of times (typically under the control of a BOOLEAN expression). One control structure (the FOR statement) provides *definite iteration*, in which we know the number of iterations before the loop executes.

Table 4.1 summarizes Modula-2's control structures and indicates the section in which we explain each.

Table 4.1 Control Structures

Name	*Use*	*Effect*	*Section*
IF	selection	choose among alternatives based on BOOLEAN expressions	4.2
CASE	selection	choose among alternatives based on the value of an expression	4.2
WHILE	indefinite iteration	repeat as long as a BOOLEAN expression remains TRUE	4.3
REPEAT	indefinite iteration	repeat until a BOOLEAN expression becomes FALSE	4.3
LOOP	indefinite iteration	repeat until an EXIT statement is executed	4.3
FOR	definite iteration	repeat as a control variable takes on a sequence of values	4.4

All the statements in Table 4.1 are *structured*: they contain other statements as components. (Modula-2 has one other structured statement, WITH, but it is not a control structure.) The structured statements all end with the reserved word END. For example, the WHILE statement has the form

```
WHILE Expression DO
  StatementSequence
END
```

When we write a structured statement, we always put each statement inside, as well as the terminating END, on a separate line. To make a structured statement easier to read, we align its final END with the first line of the statement and indent the statements inside two spaces. (Some programmers prefer to indent three or more spaces; some also indent the END the same number of spaces as the inner statements.)

Perhaps the most notable aspect of Modula-2, as far as statements are concerned, is the lack of a GOTO statement. Almost every programming language provides a GOTO statement; programmers find it virtually impossible to write programs in certain languages without using GOTO statements.

Modula-2 does not provide a GOTO statement for two reasons. First, programs containing GOTO statements can be difficult to read and modify. Second, if a Modula-2 compiler is to optimize the object code generated from a Modula-2 source program, certain kinds of optimization are simpler and faster to perform using the knowledge that the source program contained no GOTO statements.

Most programmers will hardly notice the lack of a GOTO statement. In many programming languages, some forms of selection and iteration require GOTO statements. Modula-2's wide variety of control structures renders unnecessary this use of the GOTO. (In theory, IF and WHILE statements alone are sufficient to write any program without using a GOTO; in practice, other control structures are necessary for program clarity.) Other common uses of the GOTO are to break out of a loop, return from a procedure prematurely, or terminate a program when an error is detected. Modula-2 provides three constructs to handle these situations:

the EXIT statement
the RETURN statement
the HALT procedure

We can view each of these as a restricted GOTO statement.

The EXIT statement can appear only inside LOOP statements. Executing an EXIT statement terminates execution of the LOOP statement in which the EXIT appears; thus, EXIT is effectively a GOTO statement whose target is the statement immediately following the LOOP statement.

The RETURN statement can appear in procedures and modules. Executing a RETURN statement terminates execution of the procedure or module in which the statement appears. A RETURN statement is effectively a GOTO statement whose target is the end of the enclosing procedure or module.

The standard procedure HALT causes the entire program to terminate, thus acting like a GOTO whose target is the end of the program module. Modula-2 systems usually regard HALT as causing abnormal termination; consequently, many systems print an error message after stopping the program.

Because EXIT, RETURN, and HALT can transfer control only in the forward direction, they are unlikely to cause the tangled flow of control that can result from the uncontrolled use of GOTO statements.

4.1 The Assignment Statement

The Modula-2 assignment statement has the form shown in Figure 4.1. The designator denotes a storage location—a place to store a value. Most of the time, a designator is just the name of a variable. A designator can also be

an array component (Section 7.1)
a record field (Section 7.3)
an anonymous variable named by dereferencing a pointer variable (Section 8.1)

When an assignment statement is executed, the expression to the right of the := symbol is evaluated and the result stored in the location indicated by the designator. The definition of Modula-2 does not specify the relative order in which the designator and the expression are evaluated.

Here are some examples of assignment statements:

```
VAR temperature: INTEGER;
    high, low, average: REAL;
    grade: CHAR;
    done, lessThan: BOOLEAN;
              .
              .
              .
temperature := -10;
low := 1.5;
high := 3.75;
average := (low + high) / 2.0;
grade := 'B';
done := FALSE;
lessThan := low < high;
```

Figure 4.1 ***Assignment***

→ *Designator* → := → *Expression* →

In general, the types of the designator and the expression in an assignment statement must be *assignment-compatible*. Assignment compatibility is somewhat weaker than requiring that the types be the same. In particular, INTEGER and CARDINAL are assignment-compatible, allowing assignment of an INTEGER value to a CARDINAL variable and vice-versa. Of course, such an assignment is illegal if the expression is negative and the designator has type CARDINAL or if the expression is a CARDINAL value greater than MAX(INTEGER) and the designator is INTEGER. (A Modula-2 compiler cannot usually catch such an error, which must be detected during program execution.) We define assignment compatibility more precisely in Section 6.4.

The rule of assignment compatibility has one exception: Modula-2 allows the assignment of a string literal to any string variable of equal or greater length (see Section 7.2).

The INC and DEC Procedures

Modula-2 furnishes two standard procedures, INC and DEC, that can often take the place of an assignment statement. When given a variable i of type INTEGER or CARDINAL, INC increments the value of i, while DEC decrements its value:

```
INC(i);          (* equivalent to i := i + 1 *)
DEC(i);          (* equivalent to i := i - 1 *)
```

Presumably, programmers can use INC and DEC with variables of type LONGINT as well, although Wirth does not mention this possibility in *Programming in Modula-2*.

INC and DEC allow an optional second parameter, which specifies the amount by which to increment or decrement the first parameter:

```
INC(i, n);       (* equivalent to i := i + n *)
DEC(i, n);       (* equivalent to i := i - n *)
```

INC and DEC can be used with variables of type CHAR:

```
INC(ch);         (* equivalent to ch := CHR(ORD(ch) + 1) *)
DEC(ch);         (* equivalent to ch := CHR(ORD(ch) - 1) *)
INC(ch, n);      (* equivalent to ch := CHR(ORD(ch) + n) *)
DEC(ch, n);      (* equivalent to ch := CHR(ORD(ch) - n) *)
```

INC(ch) replaces ch by the character next in the ordering of CHAR values. DEC(ch) replaces ch by the character prior to it in the ordering. Thus, if ch contains 'b' initially, then ch would have the value 'c' after INC(ch) and 'a' after DEC(ch). INC and DEC have a similar effect when used with variables of an enumeration type (Section 6.2).

In *Programming in Modula-2*, Wirth does not specify the type of the second parameter to INC or DEC. Modula-2 compilers usually allow either INTEGER or CARDINAL expressions, possibly subject to some restrictions; for example, some compilers prohibit negative increments if the first parameter has type CARDINAL.

INC and DEC are useful for at least three reasons. First, they provide a convenient way to step through values of type CHAR or an enumeration type. Second, some Modula-2 compilers may generate more efficient object code for a call of INC or DEC than for an ordinary assignment statement. Third, a call of INC or DEC is simpler than the corresponding assignment statement, particularly if the designator on the left side of the assignment is complicated.

4.2 The IF and CASE Statements

Modula-2 provides two control structures for selection: the IF statement and the CASE statement. The IF statement chooses among alternatives based on the value of one or more BOOLEAN expressions. The CASE statement makes its choice based on the value of a single *case expression*.

The IF Statement

In its basic form, the IF statement allows a program to choose between two alternatives based on the value of a BOOLEAN expression:

```
IF divisor # 0 THEN
  result := dividend DIV divisor
ELSE
  HALT
END;
```

If the condition divisor # 0 has the value TRUE, the statement between THEN and ELSE will be executed; if the condition is FALSE, the statement between ELSE and END is performed instead.

Programmers can omit the ELSE clause if no action is to be taken when the condition is false:

```
IF divisor = 0 THEN
  HALT
END;
result := dividend DIV divisor;
```

The word END must terminate every IF statement, no matter how simple.

Any number of statements can appear between THEN and ELSE and between ELSE and END:

```
IF divisor # 0 THEN
  result := dividend DIV divisor;
  remainder := dividend MOD divisor
ELSE
  WriteString("Error:  attempted division by zero");
  WriteLn;
  HALT
END;
```

In general, a statement sequence may appear wherever Modula-2 allows a single statement.

Programmers can nest IF statements. For example, the following IF statement will find the largest of the three numbers num1, num2, and num3:

```
IF num1 < num2 THEN
  IF num2 < num3 THEN
    largest := num3
  ELSE
    largest := num2
  END
ELSE
  IF num1 < num3 THEN
    largest := num3
  ELSE
    largest := num1
  END
END;
```

Programs often perform a series of tests, only one of which will succeed. For example, suppose we need to determine the sign of the value stored in the variable number. We could use nested IF statements for this purpose:

```
IF number < 0 THEN
  sign := -1
ELSE
  IF number > 0 THEN
    sign := +1
  ELSE
    sign := 0
  END
END;
```

However, Modula-2 provides a more concise way to express the same series of tests:

```
IF number < 0 THEN
  sign := -1
ELSIF number > 0 THEN
  sign := +1
ELSE
  sign := 0
END;
```

Using ELSIF avoids the many ENDs that would otherwise appear at the end of a deeply nested IF statement. ELSIF clauses also indicate that the IF statement has a simple structure: it merely evaluates a series of conditions until one of the conditions has the value TRUE.

Because of the possibility of ELSIF and ELSE clauses, the IF statement requires a relatively complicated syntax chart (Figure 4.2). An IF statement may have as many ELSIF clauses as desired (including none), but at most one ELSE clause. The expression following the words IF or ELSIF must be of type BOOLEAN.

Figure 4.2 ***IfStatement***

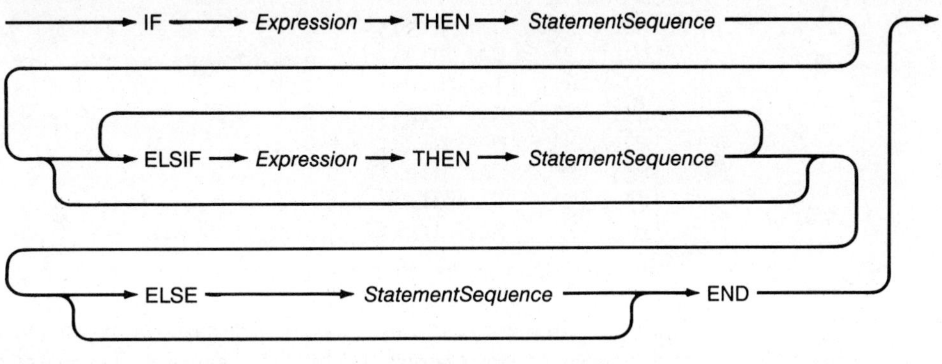

The CASE Statement

Consider the problem of translating a letter on a telephone dial or key to the corresponding digit. Assume that the variable `letter` stores a capital letter other than *Q* or *Z* (the letters *Q* and *Z* don't appear on a telephone dial). We must map the letter to one of eight digits, so we could use an IF statement controlled by eight BOOLEAN expressions:

```
IF (letter = 'A') OR (letter = 'B') OR (letter = 'C') THEN
  digit := 2
ELSIF (letter = 'D') OR (letter = 'E') OR (letter = 'F') THEN
  digit := 3
ELSIF (letter = 'G') OR (letter = 'H') OR (letter = 'I') THEN
  digit := 4
ELSIF (letter = 'J') OR (letter = 'K') OR (letter = 'L') THEN
  digit := 5
ELSIF (letter = 'M') OR (letter = 'N') OR (letter = 'O') THEN
  digit := 6
ELSIF (letter = 'P') OR (letter = 'R') OR (letter = 'S') THEN
  digit := 7
ELSIF (letter = 'T') OR (letter = 'U') OR (letter = 'V') THEN
  digit := 8
ELSIF (letter = 'W') OR (letter = 'X') OR (letter = 'Y') THEN
  digit := 9
END;
```

We can replace this rather lengthy IF statement with a much simpler CASE statement:

```
CASE letter OF
  'A', 'B', 'C': digit := 2 |
  'D', 'E', 'F': digit := 3 |
  'G', 'H', 'I': digit := 4 |
  'J', 'K', 'L': digit := 5 |
  'M', 'N', 'O': digit := 6 |
  'P', 'R', 'S': digit := 7 |
  'T', 'U', 'V': digit := 8 |
  'W', 'X', 'Y': digit := 9
END;
```

A CASE statement contains a *case expression* (between the words CASE and OF) and a series of *cases* separated by the | symbol. Each case consists of a series of values (*case labels*) followed by a statement sequence. When a CASE statement is executed, the value of the case expression is computed and compared to the case labels. If the value matches one of the labels, the corresponding statement sequence is executed. For example, if the value of `letter` matches either `'A'`, `'B'`, or `'C'`, the statement `digit := 2` will be executed.

If it is possible that the value of the case expression might not match any of the case labels, a CASE statement can include an ELSE clause. In our example, if `letter` might have a value other than the ones listed, the CASE statement should have an ELSE clause:

```
CASE letter OF
  'A', 'B', 'C': digit := 2 |
  'D', 'E', 'F': digit := 3 |
  'G', 'H', 'I': digit := 4 |
  'J', 'K', 'L': digit := 5 |
  'M', 'N', 'O': digit := 6 |
  'P', 'R', 'S': digit := 7 |
  'T', 'U', 'V': digit := 8 |
  'W', 'X', 'Y': digit := 9
ELSE
  WriteString("Error:  illegal character in CASE statement");
  WriteLn
END;
```

What happens if `letter` has the value `'Q'` and the CASE statement has no ELSE clause? In *Programming in Modula-2*, Wirth does not specify the action to be taken when the value of the case expression does not match any of the case labels. Many Modula-2 systems provide a choice (via a compile-time option): either a run-time error results and the program is terminated or the error is ignored (the effect on program flow is implementation-dependent). In either case, the programmer can always include an empty ELSE clause to ensure that missing cases will simply be ignored.

Figure 4.3 gives the full syntax of the CASE statement. The type of the case expression must be CARDINAL, INTEGER, LONGINT, CHAR, BOOLEAN, an enumeration type (Section 6.2), or a subrange type (Section 6.3). Some compilers do not allow case expressions of type LONGINT, however.

Figure 4.3

CaseStatement

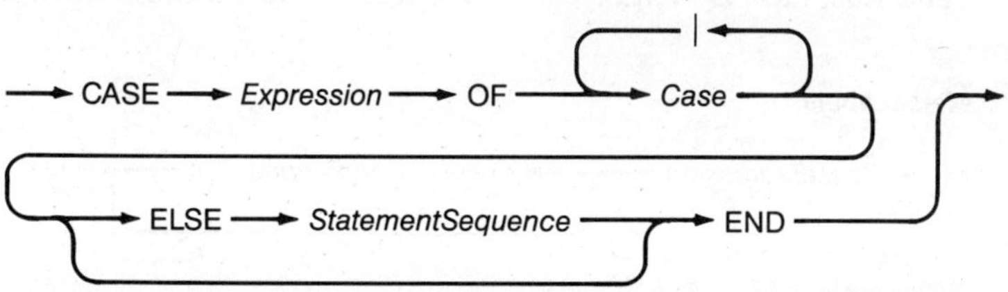

Figures 4.4 and 4.5 show the syntax of a case. Notice that a case may be empty. The Second Edition of *Programming in Modula-2* did not allow empty cases, but the Third Edition does. The existence of the empty case makes the placement of | symbols less critical (much as the existence of the empty statement makes the placement of semicolons less critical). More than one | symbol may separate cases, and extra | symbols may precede the first case or follow the last case.

Figure 4.4

Case

Figure 4.5

CaseLabelList

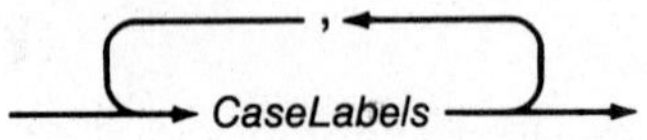

Case labels are most often just constants, but may be constant expressions. (Remember Modula-2's general rule: A constant expression may appear wherever the language allows a constant.) Programmers can abbreviate a sequence of consecutive case labels by writing the first and last label, separated by two periods:

```
CASE letter OF
  'A'..'C':       digit := 2 |
  'D'..'F':       digit := 3 |
  'G'..'I':       digit := 4 |
  'J'..'L':       digit := 5 |
  'M'..'O':       digit := 6 |
  'P', 'R'..'S': digit := 7 |
  'T'..'V':       digit := 8 |
  'W'..'Y':       digit := 9
END;
```

The *CaseLabels* syntax chart (Figure 4.6) takes these options into account.

Figure 4.6

CaseLabels

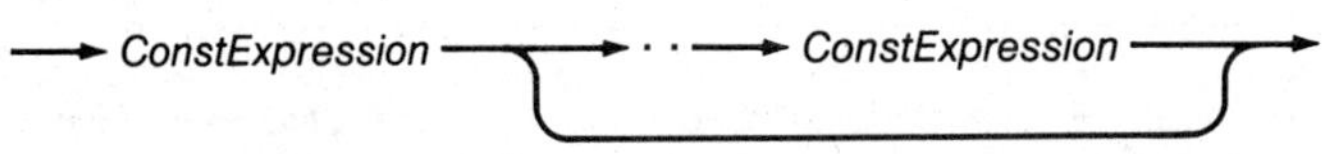

No label may appear more than once in a CASE statement. The type of each label must be compatible (Section 6.4) with the type of the case expression; hence, labels must have the same type as the case expression (or the same base type, if the case expression has a subrange type).

A style note: Some programmers prefer to put the | symbol to the left of each case:

```
CASE score OF
    90..100: letterGrade := 'A'
  | 80..89:  letterGrade := 'B'
```

```
  | 70..79:  letterGrade := 'C'
  | 60..69:  letterGrade := 'D'
  | 0..59:   letterGrade := 'F'
END;
```

In a large CASE statement, this style makes it easier to find the beginning of each case. It also makes CASE statements easier to modify, because the programmer need not move | symbols when adding statements to a case or deleting statements from a case.

In theory, CASE statements are unnecessary, because we can translate every CASE statement into an equivalent IF statement. In practice, however, a CASE statement is usually much simpler than the corresponding IF statement. Furthermore, the CASE statement is often more efficient, particularly if the number of case labels is large. However, the IF statement may be the better choice if the case labels are widely separated or if we expect the ELSE clause to be executed frequently. The manual for a particular Modula-2 system may give information about the relative efficiency of the IF and CASE statements.

4.3 The WHILE, REPEAT, and LOOP Statements

The WHILE, REPEAT, and LOOP statements are closely related; they all provide a means of indefinite iteration. The first two allow a sequence of statements (the *body* of the loop) to execute repeatedly under the control of a BOOLEAN expression, while the LOOP statement allows a statement sequence to execute repeatedly until an EXIT statement is reached.

The WHILE Statement

The WHILE statement allows a sequence of statements to execute repeatedly as long as a stated condition remains true. For example, suppose that we want to read a series of integers and find their sum, stopping when we read a negative value. Using a WHILE statement, we can write

```
sum := 0;
ReadInt(i);
WHILE i >= 0 DO
  sum := sum + i;
  ReadInt(i)
END;
```

When the WHILE statement is first reached, the expression `i >= 0` is evaluated. If its value is TRUE, then the body of the loop (the statements `sum := sum + i` and `ReadInt(i))` is executed and the expression is evaluated again. If the expression is again TRUE, then the body is executed once more. This process continues until the value of the expression is FALSE. At this point, the loop terminates and the statement following the WHILE statement will be executed next.

The most important fact to remember about the WHILE statement is that its termination condition is tested *before* the body of the loop is executed. If the condition is false when control reaches the WHILE statement, then the body is not executed at all. Note also that, if the condition is true initially, the WHILE statement will not terminate unless the statements in the body change the value of the condition.

Figure 4.7

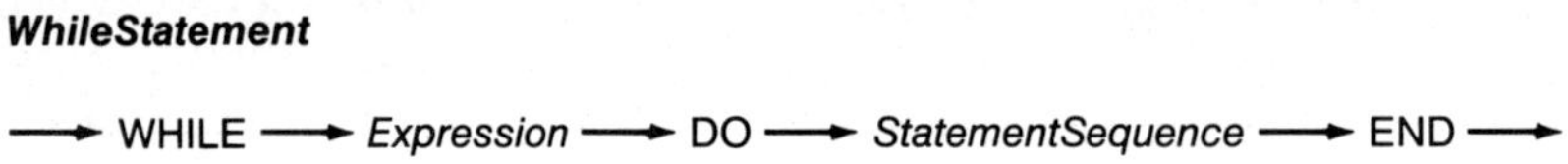

The REPEAT Statement

The REPEAT statement is similar to the WHILE statement, except that the body of the loop is executed *until* a stated condition becomes true; furthermore, the condition is tested *after* each execution of the loop body, not before. The body of a REPEAT statement is always executed at least once. The syntax of the REPEAT statement (Figure 4.8) mirrors the fact that the condition is tested after the body of the loop has been executed. The expression after the word UNTIL must be of type BOOLEAN.

Figure 4.8

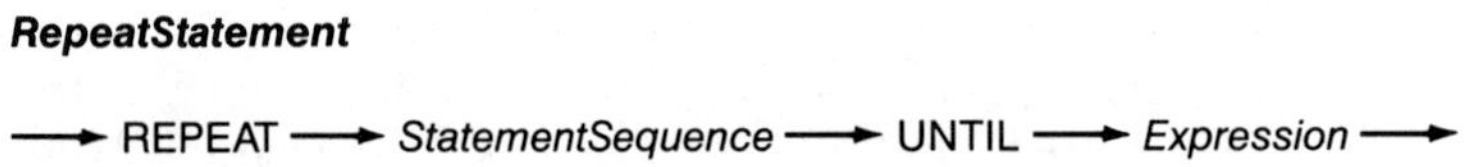

The REPEAT statement is useful when the first execution of the loop body establishes values that the termination condition is to test. For example, consider the problem of prompting the user to enter a value within a particular range (between 1 and 10, say). If the value typed by the user is invalid, the program should repeatedly prompt the user to enter valid input. Using the WHILE statement, we might write

```
WriteString("Enter a number between 1 and 10: ");
ReadCard(number);
WriteLn;
WHILE NOT ((1 <= number) AND (number <= 10)) DO
  WriteString("Enter a number between 1 and 10: ");
  ReadCard(number);
  WriteLn
END;
```

Unfortunately, the three statements in the body of the WHILE statement also appear before the WHILE statement to give number an initial value. We could eliminate them by giving number an initial value not between 1 and 10. A better solution is to use a REPEAT statement instead of a WHILE statement:

```
REPEAT
  WriteString("Enter a number between 1 and 10: ");
  ReadCard(number);
  WriteLn
UNTIL (1 <= number) AND (number <= 10);
```

The first execution of the loop gives number a value so that we need not initialize it above the loop.

The LOOP Statement

WHILE and REPEAT statements are natural for expressing most loops. Yet sometimes these statements are awkward to use:

- when the programmer wants an infinite loop
- when the condition for loop exit occurs in the middle of the loop, not at the beginning or end
- when the loop has more than one exit point

The LOOP statement (Figure 4.9) handles these situations.

Figure 4.9

LoopStatement

→ LOOP → *StatementSequence* → END →

A LOOP statement allows the statements in its body to execute indefinitely. Executing an EXIT statement causes the loop to terminate. (The loop can also be terminated in a more drastic fashion by executing a RETURN statement or calling the HALT procedure.)

Let's take a closer look at the three situations that call for a LOOP statement.

1. An Infinite Loop.

Although most programs eventually terminate, a few programs should never stop (for example, an operating system or a program that controls a digital clock). The heart of such a program is an infinite loop, which we express in Modula-2 as a LOOP statement whose body contains no EXIT statements.

2. An Exit from the Middle of a Loop.

Recall the example that we used earlier to illustrate the WHILE statement:

```
sum := 0;
ReadInt(i);
WHILE i >= 0 DO
  sum := sum + i;
  ReadInt(i)
END;
```

The statement `ReadInt(i)` appears twice: once before the loop (to read the first value of `i`) and once inside the loop (to read the next value of `i`). This duplication is typical of WHILE statements, because the test for termination must come at the beginning of the loop. By using a LOOP statement and moving the test for termination to the middle of the loop, we can eliminate the first call of `ReadInt`:

```
sum := 0;
LOOP
  ReadInt(i);
  IF i < 0 THEN EXIT END;
  sum := sum + i
END;
```

In this example, we gain little by using a LOOP statement instead of a WHILE statement. But if we can save several statements in this fashion, the program becomes easier to read and modify.

IF statements often control EXIT statements:

```
IF i < 0 THEN EXIT END;
```

When we use an IF statement in this fashion, we write the entire statement on a single line instead of three lines; this construct is so common that it is worth making an exception to our usual style.

3. Multiple Exit Points.

As before, suppose that we are reading integers and computing their sum. To this point, we have ignored the possibility that no more integers remain. If so, we want to exit the loop. We might also want to print a message indicating that the loop terminated abnormally. When using the InOut module, a successful read or write assigns the value TRUE to the variable Done (which we must import from InOut). Thus, if Done is FALSE after a call of ReadInt, we have read all the integers. Knowing this, we can write a LOOP statement with two exits:

```
sum := 0;
LOOP
  ReadInt(i);
  IF NOT Done THEN
    WriteString("No negative value was found");
    WriteLn;
    EXIT
  END;
  IF i < 0 THEN EXIT END;
  sum := sum + i
END;
```

Several points about the EXIT statement are worth mentioning:

- Modula-2 does not limit the number of EXIT statements that may appear in a LOOP statement.
- When an EXIT statement appears in a LOOP statement nested within another LOOP statement, executing the EXIT statement terminates only the inner loop.
- EXIT statements can appear only within LOOP statements.

We cannot use an EXIT statement to exit from a WHILE, REPEAT, or FOR statement, unless that statement appears within the body of a LOOP statement:

```
LOOP
  WHILE ··· DO
    .
    .
    .
    IF ··· THEN EXIT END;
    .
    .
    .
  END;
END;
```

When the EXIT statement is reached, control is transferred to the statement immediately following the LOOP statement; thus, the EXIT effectively terminates both the WHILE and LOOP statements.

Careful programmers use the LOOP statement sparingly. In most cases, it is best to formulate loops using WHILE or REPEAT statements. In particular, use a WHILE or REPEAT statement instead of a LOOP statement if the loop has a single exit point that falls at the beginning or end of the loop. Instead of

```
LOOP
  IF i > n THEN EXIT END;
  i := i * 2
END;
```

use the following WHILE statement:

```
WHILE i <= n DO
  i := i * 2
END;
```

EXAMPLE PROGRAM

Testing the MathLib0 Module

When using a library module, programmers sometimes find it helpful to have a program that tests the module's behavior. Such a program certainly aids the author of the module, who can use it to verify that the module works properly. However, the program can be useful to others as well.

A programmer who must use a library module that someone else has written needs to know in detail what the module does. If the module is not properly commented or lacks complete documentation, the programmer may need to test the module's behavior. (This situation arises more often than it should.) For example, someone using Wirth's MathLib0 module may not be sure whether sin expects a value expressed in degrees or radians (Wirth's comments don't say).

Other characteristics of a library module that may need testing include:

- *error handling*: what happens if we try to take the square root of a negative number?
- *performance*: how long does the sin function take to compute the sine of a number?
- *accuracy*: how accurate are the algorithms that the functions in MathLib0 use?

The TestMathLib0 program allows us to test six of the functions exported by MathLib0. The user of the program enters (1) a one-letter code indicating which function to test and (2) a real number to which the function should be applied; the program calls the selected function and prints the result. This sequence of events repeats indefinitely to allow the user to test more than one function or to test the same function on different values. The program terminates when the user presses the escape key.

The LOOP statement is ideal for this program because the test for termination (did the user press the escape key?) naturally falls in the middle of the loop. Nested inside the LOOP statement is a CASE statement that recognizes the six one-letter commands that the user may enter. The CASE statement's ELSE clause prints an error message when the user types a character other than one of the six allowable commands. Using CAP in the case expression allows the user to enter commands as either uppercase or lowercase letters.

```
MODULE TestMathLib0;
  (* tests the MathLib0 module *)

  FROM InOut IMPORT Read, Write, WriteString, WriteLn;
  FROM RealInOut IMPORT ReadReal, WriteReal;
  FROM MathLib0 IMPORT arctan, cos, exp, ln, sin, sqrt;

  CONST esc = 33C;

  VAR command: CHAR;
      realNum: REAL;

BEGIN
  WriteString("When prompted, enter a real number and a ");
  WriteString("one-letter command representing a");
  WriteLn;
  WriteString("mathematical function.  Legal commands ");
  WriteString("are:  a (arctan), c (cosine), e (exp),");
  WriteLn;
  WriteString("l (natural log), q (square root), and ");
  WriteString("s (sine).  Press Esc to exit.");
  WriteLn;
  WriteLn;

LOOP
  WriteString("Enter a one-letter command: ");
  Read(command);
  IF command = esc THEN EXIT END;
  Write(command);
  WriteLn;

  WriteString("Enter a real number: ");
  ReadReal(realNum);
  WriteLn;
```

```
    CASE CAP(command) OF
      'A': WriteReal(arctan(realNum), 15) |
      'C': WriteReal(cos(realNum), 15)    |
      'E': WriteReal(exp(realNum), 15)    |
      'L': WriteReal(ln(realNum), 15)     |
      'Q': WriteReal(sqrt(realNum), 15)   |
      'S': WriteReal(sin(realNum), 15)
    ELSE
      WriteString("Command not recognized.")
    END;
    WriteLn
  END
END TestMathLib0.
```

4.4 The FOR Statement

The FOR statement allows a sequence of statements to execute repeatedly as a progression of values is assigned to a certain variable. For example, to find the sum of the squares of the first 100 positive integers, we could write

```
sum := 0;
FOR i := 1 TO 100 DO
  sum := sum + i * i
END;
```

The statement `sum := sum + i * i` is executed 100 times, with `i` assuming the values 1, 2, ..., 100, in that order. The variable `i` is called the *control variable*, and the values 1 and 100 are called the *starting value* and *limit*, respectively.

The number of repetitions need not be a constant, as long as we can express it in terms of the values of program variables. A more general program would read a number n, then compute the sum of the squares of the first n positive integers:

```
sum := 0;
ReadCard(n);
FOR i := 1 TO n DO
  sum := sum + i * i
END;
```

We don't know in advance how many times the loop will be executed, but it is fixed once the program has read the value of n. This example illustrates the difference between the WHILE, REPEAT, and LOOP statements (which perform *indefinite* iteration) and the FOR statement (which performs *definite* iteration).

The number of times the body of a FOR statement is executed should not depend on the actions taking place inside the body; in general, this property does not hold for the WHILE, REPEAT, and LOOP statements.

As an option, a FOR statement may specify an *increment* for the control variable. For example, if we want to sum the squares of the odd positive integers up to n, we could write

```
sum := 0;
FOR i := 1 TO n BY 2 DO
  sum := sum + i * i
END;
```

Now i takes on the values 1, 3, 5, ..., n (or n - 1 if n is even). Thus, i is incremented by 2 each time through the loop, instead of 1. Modula-2 allows negative increments. If n is odd, the following FOR statement will give the same answer as the previous one:

```
FOR i := n TO 1 BY -2 DO
  sum := sum + i * i
END;
```

Figure 4.10 shows the syntax of the FOR statement. The semantics of the FOR statement can be expressed by showing an equivalent WHILE statement; the form of the WHILE statement depends on whether the increment is positive or negative.

FOR *Statement with Positive Increment*

```
FOR var := lower TO upper BY +inc DO
  StatementSequence
END
```

Equivalent WHILE *Statement*

```
var := lower;
WHILE var <= upper DO
  StatementSequence;
  INC (var, inc)
END
```

FOR *Statement with Negative Increment*

```
FOR var := upper TO lower BY -inc DO
  StatementSequence
END
```

Equivalent WHILE *Statement*

```
var := upper;
WHILE var >= lower DO
  StatementSequence;
  DEC (var, inc)
END
```

Figure 4.10 ***ForStatement***

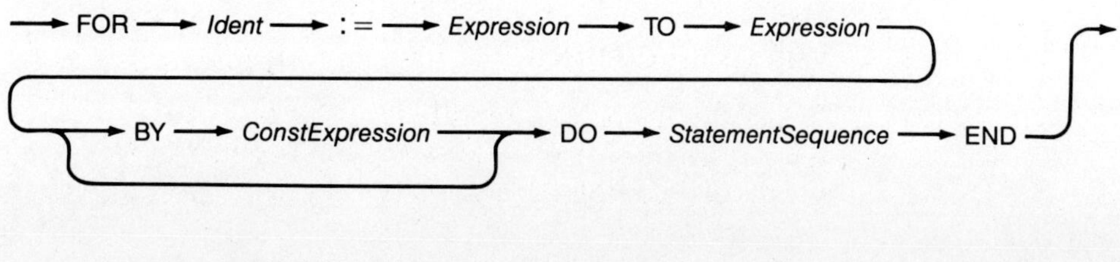

Modula-2 restricts the use of the FOR statement in a number of ways:

- The type of the control variable may not be REAL or LONGREAL; allowable types are CARDINAL, INTEGER, BOOLEAN, CHAR, an enumeration type (Section 6.2), or a subrange type (Section 6.3). (Some compilers may also allow the control variable to have type LONGINT.) For example, the following FOR statement prints a table showing the ordinal numbers of the characters between 'A' and 'Z':

```
FOR letter := 'A' TO 'Z' DO
  WriteCard(ORD(letter), 1);
  WriteString("  ");
  Write(letter);
  WriteLn
END;
```

- The increment, if present, must be a constant expression of type INTEGER or CARDINAL (regardless of the type of the control variable).
- The types of the starting value and limit must be compatible (Section 6.4) with the type of the control variable. (The Second Edition of *Programming in Modula-2* specified assignment compatibility; the Third Edition requires compatibility, a stronger condition.)
- The control variable cannot be

  a component of a structured variable (an array element or a record field)
  an anonymous variable named by dereferencing a pointer
  a variable imported from another module
  a formal parameter
- The body of a FOR statement should not change the control variable nor should it alter the starting value or limit. Modula-2 compilers cannot always detect errors of this kind; as a result, programs that violate these restrictions may behave unpredictably.
- Once a FOR statement has terminated, the value of its control variable is undefined. ("Undefined" means that the value varies from one Modula-2 system to another and cannot be depended on.)

If a FOR statement whose increment is positive has a starting value greater than its limit, the body of the loop is not executed even once. (The same is true if the increment is negative and the starting value is less than the limit.) Watch out for the following error, however:

```
VAR i, n: CARDINAL;
     .
     .
     .
```

```
FOR i := 0 TO n - 1 DO
      .
      .
      .
END;
```

Suppose that the value of n is 0 at the time program control reaches the FOR statement. Instead of the body of the FOR loop being skipped, a run-time error occurs: the expression n - 1 has type CARDINAL, but subtracting 1 from 0 gives a non-CARDINAL result. We can avoid the problem by declaring i and n to have type INTEGER or by putting the FOR statement inside an IF statement that tests whether n is greater than 0 before executing the FOR statement.

Standard Pascal

1. The only way for a Pascal program to terminate normally is for control to pass the final statement in the body of the program.

2. Pascal allows the assignment of an `integer` value to a `real` variable.

```
var r: real;
    i: integer;
       .
       .
       .
r := i;
```

3. Pascal provides no special procedures for incrementing and decrementing variables; programmers must use assignment statements. In the case of an `integer` variable, the assignment statement would simply add or subtract 1:

```
i := i + 1;      (* increment i *)
i := i - 1;      (* decrement i *)
```

   More generally, programmers can use the standard functions `succ` and `pred` to increment or decrement a variable of any ordinal type:

```
i := succ(i);    (* compute successor of i *)
i := pred(i);    (* compute predecessor of i *)
```

4. The `if` statement in Pascal has the form

   `if` *Expression* `then` *Statement* `else` *Statement*

   (the `else` clause is optional). No special symbol marks the end of an `if` statement. Single statements must follow the words `then` and `else`. To include a sequence of statements in either place, the programmer must create a compound statement by enclosing the statement sequence between `begin` and `end`.

```
if ('A' <= letterGrade) and (letterGrade <= 'D') then
  begin
    write('Passed');
    passing := passing + 1
  end
else if letterGrade = 'F' then
```

Modula-2

1. A Modula-2 program terminates when the last statement in the program module has been executed. A Modula-2 program also terminates if the program module executes a RETURN statement (normal termination) or if the standard procedure HALT is executed anywhere in the program (abnormal termination).

2. Modula-2 does not allow the assignment of an INTEGER or CARDINAL value to a REAL variable; the program must first convert the value to type REAL.

```
VAR r: REAL;
    i: INTEGER;
    c: CARDINAL;
     .
     .
     .
r := real(i);    (* exported by Wirth's MathLib0 module *)
r := FLOAT(c);
```

3. Modula-2 provides standard INC and DEC procedures for incrementing and decrementing variables. INC(i, n) adds n to the variable i; DEC(i, n) subtracts n from i. If the programmer omits the second parameter, the increment (or decrement) is 1:

```
INC(i);    (* increment i *)
DEC(i);    (* decrement i *)
```

4. The Modula-2 IF statement has the form

IF *Expression* THEN
  StatementSequence
ELSIF *Expression* THEN
  StatementSequence
ELSE
  StatementSequence
END

The ELSIF clause is optional and may be repeated as many times as desired. The ELSE clause is optional.

```
IF ('A' <= letterGrade) AND (letterGrade <= 'D') THEN
  WriteString("Passed");
  INC(passing)
```

Standard Pascal

```
  write('Failed')
else if letterGrade = 'W' then
  write('Withdrew')
else
  write('Unknown grade');
```

5. The Pascal `case` statement has the form

```
case Expression of
  CaseConstantList : Statement ;
      .
      .
      .
  CaseConstantList : Statement
end
```

Each case consists of a list of constants (Pascal does not allow constant expressions or ranges of values) followed by a single statement (which may be compound). Semicolons separate cases. The `case` statement has no `else` clause.

```
case letterGrade of
  'A', 'B', 'C', 'D':
      begin
        write('Passed');
        passing := passing + 1
      end;
  'F': write('Failed');
  'W': write('Withdrew')
end;
```

6. The body of a Pascal `while` or `for` statement must be a single (possibly compound) statement; no special symbol marks the end of a `while` or `for` statement.

```
while sum <= n do
  begin
    i := i + 1;
    sum := sum + 2 * i + 1
  end;
```

7. Pascal does not provide a `loop` statement or an `exit` statement, although programmers can achieve the same effect in other ways. For example, a `while` statement controlled by the constant `true` can simulate a `loop` statement, with `goto` statements instead of `exit` statements:

Modula-2

```
ELSIF letterGrade = 'F' THEN
  WriteString("Failed")
ELSIF letterGrade = 'W' THEN
  WriteString("Withdrew")
ELSE
  WriteString("Unknown grade")
END;
```

5. The Modula-2 CASE statement has the form

```
CASE Expression OF
  CaseLabelList : StatementSequence |
        .
        .
        .
  CaseLabelList : StatementSequence
ELSE
  StatementSequence
END
```

A list of case labels consists of individual values or ranges of values (an initial value, two periods, and a final value), separated by commas. Case labels may be constant expressions. The | character separates cases. The ELSE clause is optional.

```
CASE letterGrade OF
  'A'..'D': WriteString("Passed");
            INC(passing) |
  'F':      WriteString("Failed") |
  'W':      WriteString("Withdrew")
ELSE
  WriteString("Unknown grade")
END;
```

6. The word END must terminate Modula-2 WHILE and FOR statements. The body of a WHILE or FOR statement is a sequence of statements.

```
WHILE sum <= n DO
  i := i + 1;
  sum := sum + 2 * i + 1
END;
```

7. Modula-2's LOOP statement allows a sequence of statements to execute indefinitely. The EXIT statement (which may only appear inside LOOP statements) terminates execution of the loop.

Standard Pascal

```
while true do
  begin
    read(i);
    if i < 0 then goto 10;
    sum := sum + 1
  end;
10:
```

8. In a Pascal `for` statement, the loop increment must be either 1 (by default) or −1 (by using the word `downto` instead of `to`):

```
for i := n downto 1 do
  writeln('T minus ', i:1, ' and counting');
```

9. The control variable in a Pascal `for` statement may not be a formal parameter, an anonymous variable accessed through a pointer, or a component of a structured variable. The control variable must be declared in the block that contains the `for` statement.

Modula-2

```
LOOP
  ReadInt(i);
  If i < 0 THEN EXIT END;
  sum := sum + i
END;
```

8. In a Modula-2 FOR statement, an optional BY clause permits the programmer to use an arbitrary constant expression as the increment.

```
FOR i := n TO 1 BY -1 DO
  WriteString("T minus ");
  WriteCard(i, 1);
  WriteString(" and counting");
  WriteLn
END;
```

9. The control variable in a Modula-2 FOR statement may not be a formal parameter, an anonymous variable, or a component of a structured variable, nor may it be imported from another module. No rule requires the control variable to be local to the block in which the FOR statement appears.

EXERCISES

Section 4.2

1. The CASE statement in Section 4.2 that computes the digit corresponding to a letter on a telephone dial does not take advantage of the structure of the numbering system (the only nonregularity is the absence of the letter *Q*). Write an equivalent `IF` statement that exploits this structure. Include an ELSE clause to detect illegal characters. (Hint: Use the `ORD` function.)

2. An `IF` statement with `ELSIF` clauses is essentially a generalized `CASE` statement. Demonstrate this point by translating the `CASE` statement in the `TestMathLib0` program (Section 4.3) into an `IF` statement.

3. (For Pascal programmers) Why does the Modula-2 `IF` statement allow the use of `ELSIF` but the Pascal `if` statement does not?

4. (For Pascal programmers) One problem with the Pascal `if` statement is the apparent ambiguity of certain nested `if` statements. For example, consider the following statement:

   `if` p `then if` q `then` S_1 `else` S_2

   It is not immediately clear to which `if` statement the `else` S_2 clause belongs. Pascal resolves the ambiguity of such a statement by the rule that an `else` clause matches the nearest previous unmatched `then`. Does this problem exist in Modula-2? If so, how does the language resolve it?

5. Suppose that the variables `day`, `month`, and `year` (of type `CARDINAL`) collectively represent a date. Write one or more statements whose effect is to advance the date by one day.

Section 4.3

6. The `exp` function that `MathLib0` supplies can be computed using the following series:

   $$e^x = 1 + x + x^2/2! + x^3/3! + x^4/4! + \cdots$$

   Use a `WHILE` or `REPEAT` statement to evaluate this formula; have the loop terminate when the value of the most recently computed term ($x^n/n!$) becomes less than 0.001. Hint: Don't compute $n!$; the factorial function grows so rapidly that it may cause arithmetic overflow. Instead, compute the nth term from the previous term by multiplying by x and dividing by n.

7. Suppose that we are writing a program that must read from a file of character data in which the end of a line is indicated in one of three ways: by a carriage return (`15C`), by a line feed (`12C`), or by a carriage return immediately followed by a line feed. Write a `LOOP` statement that skips to the beginning of the next line; that is, the body of the `LOOP` statement calls the `Read` procedure (from `InOut`) until a carriage return, line feed, or carriage-return/line-feed pair is read. On exit from the `LOOP` statement, the variable `ch` should contain the first character on the next line.

8. Modify `TestMathLib0` to test the validity of the command entered by the user *before* prompting the user to enter a real number.

9. Show how to rewrite any `WHILE` statement as a `REPEAT` statement.

10. Show how to rewrite any `WHILE` statement as a `LOOP` statement.

11. Show how to rewrite any `REPEAT` statement as a `WHILE` statement.

12. Show how to rewrite any `REPEAT` statement as a `LOOP` statement.

Section 4.4

13. Use a `WHILE` statement to write the first `n` values in the sequence 1, 4, 13, 40, 121, ... (each value is 3 times the previous value plus 1). Redo your solution three times, using a `REPEAT`, `LOOP`, and `FOR` statement instead of a `WHILE` statement.

14. Show how to rewrite any `FOR` statement as a `LOOP` statement.

15. Section 4.4 contains a `FOR` statement that prints the ordinal numbers of the characters between `'A'` and `'Z'`. Rewrite this statement so that the ordinal number of the character, not the character itself, controls the statement. Which is better, the original `FOR` statement or the revised version?

16. The control variable in a `FOR` statement must not be of type `REAL` or `LONGREAL`. What is the reason for this restriction?

17. The body of a `FOR` statement must not change the value of the control variable. Why is it difficult for a Modula-2 compiler to test for this condition?

5 Procedures

A *procedure* is an entity that a program can call (activate) to perform a computation. We can divide procedures into two groups: (1) *functions*, which compute a single value and whose calls appear in expressions; and (2) *proper procedures*, whose calls are statements.

In earlier chapters we used standard procedures and procedures imported from library modules. The standard procedure ABS, for example, is a function. When given a number x, ABS computes the absolute value of x; a call of ABS appears in an expression, representing the value that ABS computes. The standard procedure INC, however, is a proper procedure. A call of INC is a statement; executing INC changes the value stored in a variable.

Procedures are one of the most important features provided by Modula-2 (or by almost any programming language, for that matter). Using procedures benefits both the original (source) program and the object program that a compiler produces:

- *Programs are easier to write*. Procedures save time during program development, because a programmer need only write a procedure once, but can use it many times. Procedures greatly simplify the task of writing certain recursive algorithms. Procedures provide a way to manage the complexity of a large program by breaking it into smaller parts. (Procedures are particularly useful in conjunction with top-down design. A programmer can divide a task into smaller parts, each accomplished by a procedure. The task each procedure performs is then further divided, creating still more procedures.) Procedures provide a form of *abstraction*: calling a procedure requires only that the programmer know what the procedure is to accomplish, not the details of how the procedure works.
- *Programs are easier to read*. Procedures can make programs shorter, hence easier to read, by replacing long sequences of statements with procedure calls. The procedure names themselves, if well chosen, help document a program; their nesting helps explain its structure.

- *Programs are easier to modify*. When repeated actions are replaced with procedure calls, a program becomes easier to modify; many changes affect only the procedure itself, not its calls. Programs are also easier to change if they use procedures to access data structures, rather than accessing the data structures directly. Changes that affect the way in which the program stores data require only that the programmer change the access procedures; the changes do not affect the rest of the program. (This concept is important in Modula-2, where programmers can hide data structures in modules and access them through procedures. We discuss this point in detail in Chapters 9 and 10.)
- *Programs take less time to compile*. Replacing a sequence of statements with a procedure call usually reduces compilation time if the program contains more than one call of the procedure.
- *Object programs require less memory*. Procedures decrease the amount of memory needed for an object program in two ways. First, they reduce code duplication because the procedure's code appears only once in the object program. Second, procedures allow more efficient storage of data, because storage for a procedure's variables is allocated when the procedure is called and deallocated when it returns.

Procedures have one disadvantage: Executing a procedure requires extra time because of the additional work that must be done when the procedure is called and when it returns. Most of the time, however, the advantages of procedures far outweigh the overhead of procedure calls.

The rest of this chapter discusses Modula-2's rules for using procedures. Section 5.1 presents an overview of how programmers declare and call procedures, and discusses the differences between local and global entities. Section 5.2 shows how to write procedures with parameters, while Section 5.3 covers functions. Section 5.4 explains how procedure declarations affect the scope of entities in a Modula-2 program (the *scope* of an entity is the region of the program where references to the entity are legal).

5.1 Procedure Declarations

Procedures, like other entities in a Modula-2 program, must be declared. A *procedure declaration* specifies

the name of the procedure
information about the procedure's parameters
the type of value that the procedure returns (if it is a function)
declarations of entities that belong to the procedure
a sequence of statements to be executed when the procedure is called

The simplest procedures require no parameters. For example, the following declaration is for a procedure that a program can call when it encounters a fatal error:

```
PROCEDURE FatalError;
  (* writes an error message and terminates program *)
BEGIN
  WriteString("Fatal error; abandoning program.");
  WriteLn;
  HALT
END FatalError;
```

More often, however, a procedure has one or more parameters. The following procedure exchanges the contents of two INTEGER variables supplied as parameters:

```
PROCEDURE Swap(VAR i, j: INTEGER);
  (* exchanges the contents of i and j *)
  VAR temp: INTEGER;
BEGIN
  temp := i;
  i := j;
  j := temp
END Swap;
```

The word VAR preceding the parameters i and j indicates that i and j represent variables (not expressions) to supply when calling Swap. Swap contains a declaration of a variable called temp that the procedure uses for temporary storage during the exchange of i and j.

Both FatalError and Swap are proper procedures, not functions. We discuss functions in Section 5.3; however, much information in this section pertains to functions as well as to proper procedures.

Figure 5.1 shows the syntax chart for a procedure declaration. A procedure declaration has two parts: (1) the *procedure heading*, which gives information necessary to call the procedure, and (2) the *procedure body*. A procedure body, which must be a block (Section 2.2), contains declarations of entities belonging to the procedure and statements to be executed when the procedure is called. The reserved word BEGIN precedes the statements; the reserved word END follows them.

Figure 5.1

ProcedureDeclaration

The heading of a procedure (Figure 5.2) consists of the reserved word PROCEDURE, the name of the procedure, and (optionally) a list of formal parameters. Formal parameters are identifiers that represent variables or expressions to supply when calling the procedure.

Figure 5.2

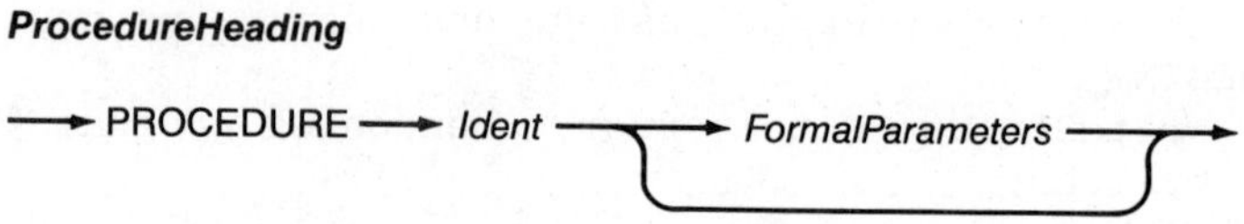

The name of a procedure must appear twice in its declaration: (1) in the heading (after the word PROCEDURE) and (2) at the end (after the word END). The requirement that the name appear at the end of the declaration helps make programs more readable, because the name clearly marks the end of a procedure declaration and makes it easy to find. This rule also enables a Modula-2 compiler to recover from an error caused by an unpaired BEGIN or END.

Procedure Calls

A *procedure call* consists of a procedure name and (if the procedure has parameters) a list of *actual parameters*. The call of a proper procedure is a statement. (Function calls are expressions; see Section 5.3.) For example, a call of Swap looks like this:

```
Swap(lower, upper);
```

When program control reaches this statement, Swap begins to execute. When the last statement in the body of Swap has been executed, the procedure *returns*; the next statement to be executed is the statement after the call of Swap.

A call of a proper procedure with no parameters consists of the procedure name alone:

```
FatalError;
```

The programmer may put a pair of empty parentheses after the name, if desired:

```
FatalError();
```

Figure 5.3 shows the syntax chart for a procedure call. Notice that the *ProcedureCall* chart does not require the programmer to use an identifier to specify the

Figure 5.3

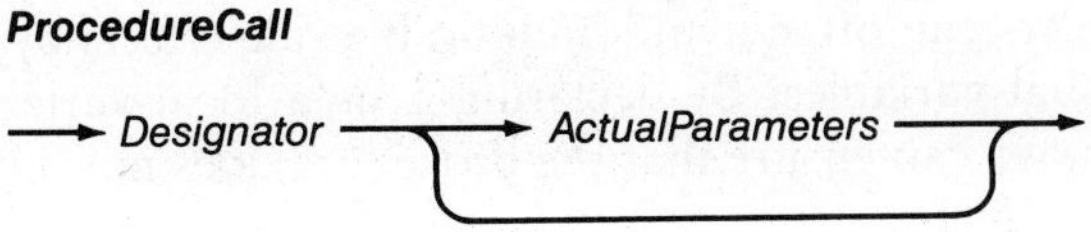

procedure being called. Instead, it allows a *designator* (Section 7.3), which includes not only qualified identifiers but also record fields, array elements, and anonymous variables referenced through pointers. The reason for allowing a designator is that Modula-2 allows programs to treat procedures as data values; for example, a program can store a procedure in a record or an array and later call it. We discuss procedure types in Section 8.2.

Declarations of Local Entities

A procedure declaration can itself include declarations. Typically, these declarations are of constants, types, or variables, but they can also be declarations of procedures (see Section 5.4) or even modules (Section 9.3). Entities declared within a procedure are *local* to the procedure: they exist only when the procedure is being executed and their names are visible only inside the procedure. Entities referenced in a procedure but not declared in the procedure are *global* to the procedure.

To see the difference, consider the following procedure:

```
PROCEDURE WriteLines(n: CARDINAL);
  (* writes n blank lines *)
BEGIN
  FOR i := 1 TO n DO
    WriteLn
  END
END WriteLines;
```

Because `i` is not declared in `WriteLines`, it is global to the procedure. Each call of `WriteLines` changes the value of `i`, overwriting the value stored in `i` prior to the call. We call this change to the value of `i` a *side effect*. A side effect is a hidden—and possibly unintentional—effect that results from a procedure call.

Side effects are usually unwanted. A programmer using `WriteLines` has no reason to suspect that it does anything but write blank lines; the change to `i` will come as a surprise. The programmer should be able to view `WriteLines` as an abstraction; it should not be necessary to read the statements inside procedure `WriteLines` in order to use it.

Programmers can often avoid undesirable side effects by using local variables instead of global variables. By declaring `i` as a local variable within procedure `WriteLines`, we can ensure that the procedure does not modify any global variables as a side effect:

```
PROCEDURE WriteLines(n: CARDINAL);
  (* writes n blank lines *)
  VAR i: CARDINAL;
BEGIN
  FOR i := 1 TO n DO
    WriteLn
  END
END WriteLines;
```

Storage for a procedure's local variables is allocated (on a run-time stack) when the procedure is called. When the procedure returns, this storage is released (by popping the stack), thereby becoming available for subsequent procedure calls. Consequently, the values of its local variables are lost between calls of the procedure.

The limited lifetime of local variables has advantages and disadvantages. The chief advantage is that procedures allow efficient use of storage; by making variables local instead of global wherever possible, a programmer can minimize the amount of data storage that a program needs. The primary disadvantage is that programs cannot have variables that are local to a procedure yet retain their values between calls of the procedure (these are often called "own" variables, a term from Algol 60). If a program needs to save the value of a local variable between calls of a procedure, the programmer must declare the variable global to the procedure or supply it as a parameter to the procedure. In either case, however, the variable is visible outside the procedure. One use of local modules (Section 9.3) is for hiding a procedure's "own" variables from the rest of the program.

The RETURN Statement

A proper procedure returns when the last statement in its body has been executed. A procedure may terminate prematurely by executing a RETURN statement. For example, the following procedure searches a line of input for a particular character; when it finds the character, the procedure immediately returns.

```
PROCEDURE SearchForChar(ch: CHAR);
  (* read characters until ch is found or end of line is
     reached; issue an error message in the latter case *)
  VAR inputChar: CHAR;
```

```
BEGIN
  REPEAT
    Read(inputChar);
    IF inputChar = ch THEN RETURN END
  UNTIL inputChar = EOL;
  WriteString("Search failed; character not found");
  WriteLn
END SearchForChar;
```

If a RETURN statement is the only statement appearing inside an IF statement, we usually write the IF statement on a single line; we adopted a similar convention for the EXIT statement.

In a function, the RETURN statement serves a second purpose: In addition to causing the function to terminate, a RETURN statement indicates the value that the function should return. In a function, an expression (the value to return) must follow the word RETURN; in a proper procedure, an expression must *not* follow the word RETURN. It is an error for a function to "fall through" without executing a RETURN statement; in a proper procedure, using RETURN statements is optional.

Order of Procedure Declarations

According to *Programming in Modula-2* (in both Second and Third Editions), procedure declarations may occur in any order; thus, a program may call a procedure before its declaration has appeared. However, a number of recent Modula-2 compilers make only one pass over a program; as a result, they do not allow a procedure call to precede the declaration of the procedure.

When using a one-pass compiler, it is best to arrange procedures to avoid forward references. Such an arrangement is not always possible, however, when using *recursive* procedures. A procedure P can be recursive in two ways: (1) the body of P may contain a call of P (*direct recursion*), or (2) P may call Q, which calls R, and so on, until P is called (*indirect recursion*). For example, the following procedures exhibit a simple form of indirect recursion:

```
PROCEDURE P;
BEGIN
  (* body contains a call of Q *)
END P;

PROCEDURE Q;
BEGIN
  (* body contains a call of P *)
END Q;
```

Direct recursion causes no problems for a one-pass compiler, but indirect recursion does. In the example, the call of Q (in the body of P) precedes the declaration of Q. But if we declare Q first, then the call of P precedes the declaration of P. To resolve this problem, one-pass compilers usually provide a special form of procedure declaration in which the word FORWARD replaces the body of the procedure (the full heading must appear, however). This declaration signals the compiler that a complete declaration of the procedure appears later in the same block; in the meantime, this "preliminary" declaration provides information that the compiler needs to process calls of the procedure. The following declarations could handle our example of indirect recursion:

```
PROCEDURE Q; FORWARD;

PROCEDURE P;
BEGIN
  (* body contains a call of Q *)
END P;

PROCEDURE Q;
BEGIN
  (* body contains a call of P *)
END Q;
```

One-pass compilers usually require that the full declaration repeat the procedure's parameter list and—if it is a function—the result type.

5.2 Parameters

Most procedures depend on data that varies from one call to the next. For this reason, Modula-2 allows a procedure heading to include a list of identifiers that represent variables or expressions to supply when calling the procedure. The programmer can use these identifiers, known as *formal parameters*, in the body of the procedure in the same fashion as ordinary variables.

The procedure SolveQuadratic demonstrates the usefulness of parameters. SolveQuadratic computes the roots of the equation

$$ax^2 + bx + c = 0$$

assuming that $a \neq 0$ (otherwise there is only one root) and $b^2 - 4ac \geq 0$ (otherwise the roots are imaginary). SolveQuadratic needs five parameters: three for input (a, b, and c) and two for output (root1 and root2).

```
PROCEDURE SolveQuadratic(a, b, c: REAL;
                         VAR root1, root2: REAL);
  (* finds both roots of the quadratic equation
     ax2 + bx + c = 0, assuming that a <> 0 and
     b2 - 4ac >= 0 *)
  VAR squareRoot, denominator: REAL;
BEGIN
  squareRoot := sqrt(b * b - 4.0 * a * c);
  denominator := 2.0 * a;
  root1 := (-b + squareRoot) / denominator;
  root2 := (-b - squareRoot) / denominator
END SolveQuadratic;
```

A call of a procedure with parameters must include a list of *actual parameters*. The number of actual parameters must be the same as the number of formal parameters. Correspondence between actual and formal parameters is by position: the first actual parameter corresponds to the first formal parameter, the second actual parameter to the second formal parameter, and so on. The type of each actual parameter must match the type of the corresponding formal parameter (the meaning of "match" depends on whether the formal parameter is a variable parameter or a value parameter, as we will see later). A call of SolveQuadratic might look like this:

```
SolveQuadratic(1.0, -8.0, 15.0, r1, r2);
```

The actual parameters are the expressions 1.0, -8.0, and 15.0 and the variables r1 and r2; they match the formal parameters a, b, c, root1, and root2, in that order.

Modula-2 provides two kinds of formal parameters: *variable parameters* and *value parameters*. In a procedure heading, if the reserved word VAR precedes a formal parameter, then it is a variable parameter; otherwise, it is a value parameter. Any changes made to a variable parameter within the body of the procedure also affect the corresponding actual parameter, which must be a variable (more precisely, a designator). However, if a formal parameter is a value parameter, the corresponding actual parameter—which may be any form of expression—is protected against change. Variable parameters allow information to flow into and/or out of a procedure; value parameters allow information to flow into a procedure, but not out of the procedure.

In the procedure SolveQuadratic, we made a, b, and c value parameters, because the procedure needs only the values of the actual parameters. We could have declared a, b, and c to be variable parameters instead, because SolveQuadratic does not change their values. Making them value parameters is preferable, because doing so documents the fact that SolveQuadratic needs only the values of the matching actual parameters. Furthermore, making a, b, and `c` variable parameters would prove too restrictive, because the corresponding actual parameters would have to be variables; we could not use the expressions `1.0`, `-8.0`, and `15.0` as actual parameters.

We have declared `root1` and `root2` to be variable parameters, however. By assigning values to `root1` and `root2`, `SolveQuadratic` can change the values of the corresponding actual parameters; these values are then available for use after the procedure returns. For example, after the call of `SolveQuadratic` shown earlier, the values of `r1` and `r2` are 5 and 3, respectively. Declaring `root1` and `root2` to be value parameters would be a mistake, because assignments to `root1` and `root2` would not affect `r1` and `r2`.

Figure 5.4 shows the syntax of a formal parameter list. The list of formal parameters is enclosed in parentheses and may be followed by a colon and the name of a type. (The colon and type name are present only in the declaration of a *function*—see Section 5.3.) The list of formal parameters, if not empty, consists of sections (Figure 5.5); each section is a list of parameters of the same type. Each section may optionally begin with the reserved word VAR, to indicate that the parameters in the section are variable parameters. If VAR is missing, all the parameters in the section are value parameters.

Figure 5.4

FormalParameters

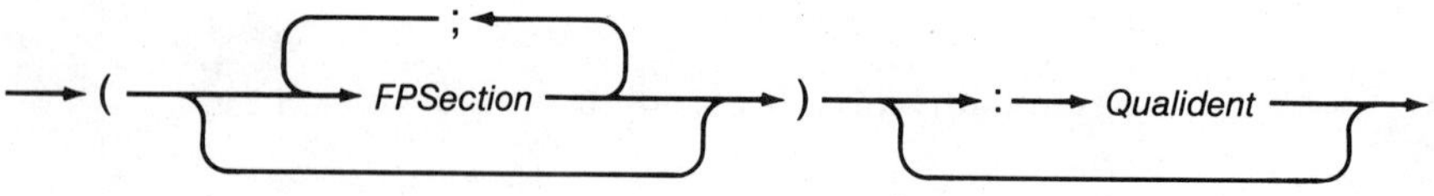

Figure 5.5

FPSection

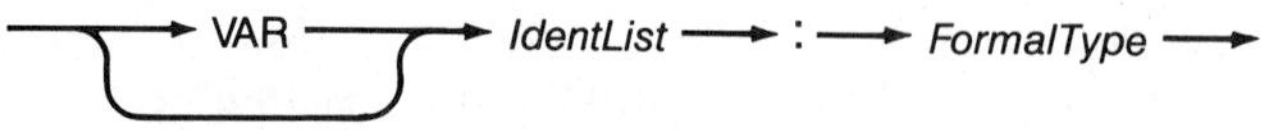

When declaring a procedure with no parameters, the programmer may either omit the parameter list:

```
PROCEDURE P;
```

or include an empty parameter list (a pair of empty parentheses):

```
PROCEDURE P();
```

The type of a formal parameter is usually given as a qualified identifier (the name of a type). If the words ARRAY OF precede the type name (see Figure 5.6),

Figure 5.6 **FormalType**

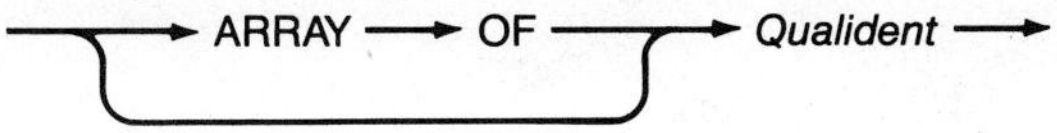

the parameter is an *open array parameter*. If a procedure has an open array parameter, the corresponding actual parameter can be an array of any length, provided that its component type matches the type appearing after the words ARRAY OF. We consider open array parameters in Section 7.1.

A list of actual parameters consists of zero or more expressions, separated by commas and enclosed in parentheses, as Figures 5.7 and 5.8 show.

Figure 5.7 **ActualParameters**

Figure 5.8 **ExpList**

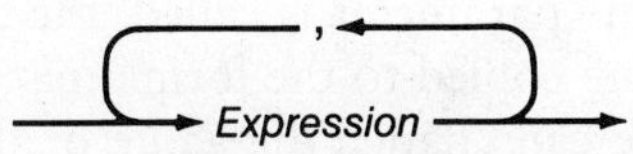

Variable Parameters

The actual parameter corresponding to a variable parameter must be a variable, an array component (Section 7.1), a record component (Section 7.3), or an anonymous variable accessed through a pointer (Section 8.1). It cannot be a constant or any other form of expression, even if no assignments to the formal parameter appear in the procedure body.

The Third Edition of *Programming in Modula-2* requires that a variable parameter and each corresponding actual parameter have the same type. (The Second Edition specified a weaker condition: the types needed only be compatible.) Modula-2 allows exceptions to this rule for parameters of types `WORD` and ADDRESS (Section 11.2).

When a procedure has a variable parameter and the corresponding actual parameter is an array component, the index expression that selects the component is evaluated at the time the procedure is called; subsequent changes to the index do not affect the selection of the array component. For example, suppose that the call `SumArray(component, lower, upper, sum)` sums the values of component as the value of the global variable i varies from lower to upper. The call

```
SumArray(A[i], 1, 10, sum);
```

will not sum A[1] through A[10]; the reference to A[i] is fixed at the time of the call and changes to i do not affect it.

Value Parameters

The actual parameter corresponding to a value parameter can be any kind of expression (including, but not limited to, constants and variables). The type of the actual parameter must be assignment-compatible (Section 6.4) with the type of the value parameter, unless the value parameter has type WORD or ADDRESS (Section 11.2), in which case special rules apply. The assignment compatibility requirement allows the types of formal and actual parameters to differ in some cases; in particular, a formal parameter may have type INTEGER while the matching actual parameter has type CARDINAL, or vice-versa.

When a procedure with a value parameter is called, the corresponding actual parameter is evaluated and its value copied to the formal parameter, which serves as a local variable. The procedure can change the value of the formal parameter by assignment, but any change will not affect the actual parameter, even if it is a variable. For example, suppose that we rewrite the procedure WriteLines of Section 5.1 to use a WHILE statement instead of a FOR statement:

```
PROCEDURE WriteLines(n: CARDINAL);
  (* writes n blank lines *)
BEGIN
  WHILE n > 0 DO
    WriteLn;
    DEC(n)
  END
END WriteLines;
```

WriteLines changes the value of n by decrementing it each time through the body of the WHILE statement. But because n is a value parameter, only the procedure's local copy of n changes; the actual parameter does not. A value parameter behaves exactly like a local variable; the only difference between the two is that a value parameter has an initial value (the value of the matching actual parameter).

So that changes to a value parameter will not affect the corresponding actual parameter, a Modula-2 system must copy the actual parameter each time the procedure is called. If the actual parameter requires a large amount of storage (for example, if it is a large array), this copying can be expensive in terms of both time and space. Variable parameters incur no such penalty.

At least two other factors also affect the choice between variable and value parameters. First, if the actual parameter should reflect changes to the formal parameter, the latter must be a variable parameter. Second, if the actual parameter will be an expression other than a variable, we must use a value parameter. If neither condition holds, a value parameter is probably the best choice, unless efficiency dictates using a variable parameter.

5.3 Functions

Every Modula-2 procedure is either a *function procedure* or a *proper procedure* (the terminology is Wirth's). A function procedure computes a single value; furthermore, calls of the function procedure may appear in expressions. For example, the expression on the right side of the following assignment contains calls of the `sin` and `cos` function procedures:

```
tanx = sin(x) / cos(x);
```

A call of a proper procedure, however, is a statement. A proper procedure must store its results into actual parameters or global variables; a call of a proper procedure cannot appear in an expression.

We will use the simpler term *function* rather than "function procedure." We use the word *procedure* to mean a function procedure or a proper procedure.

A function declaration differs only slightly from the declaration of a proper procedure. First, the function's heading must specify the type of value it returns. Second, the body of the function must include a RETURN statement that, when executed, indicates the value that the function returns. The following declaration of the `SquareRoot` function illustrates these differences:

```
PROCEDURE SquareRoot(n: CARDINAL): CARDINAL;
  (* returns the greatest integer whose square is less than
     or equal to n *)
  VAR root: CARDINAL;
BEGIN
  root := 1;
  WHILE root * root <= n DO
    INC(root)
  END;
  RETURN root - 1
END SquareRoot;
```

The appearance of a colon following `SquareRoot`'s parameter list indicates that `SquareRoot` is a function rather than a proper procedure; the type name `CARDINAL` after the colon specifies that `SquareRoot` returns a value of type `CARDINAL`. The `RETURN` statement indicates that `SquareRoot` returns the final value of the expression `root - 1`.

Any expression can appear after the word `RETURN`, provided that its type is assignment-compatible (Section 6.4) with the type specified in the heading of the function (`CARDINAL`, in this case). The body of a function may contain more than one `RETURN` statement; the first one encountered during the execution of the function causes it to return. Reaching the end of a function body without executing a `RETURN` statement is an error; the effect of so doing depends on the particular Modula-2 system (most systems terminate the program). Attempting to compile a function that does not contain at least one `RETURN` statement is not a good idea, even if the function is never called; some Modula-2 systems do not check for the presence of a `RETURN` statement during compilation, but others report the lack of a `RETURN` statement as an error.

A function call consists of a designator followed by a list of actual parameters enclosed in parentheses:

```
SquareRoot(a * a + b * b)
```

No separate chart describes the syntax of a function call; instead, a function call appears as one alternative in the *Factor* chart (Figure 3.7). A proper procedure call is a statement, but a function call is an expression of the type specified in the function heading. Consequently, a function call can appear wherever a value of that type can (only calls of standard functions may appear in constant expressions, however). Some examples:

```
VAR i, j, sum: CARDINAL;
      .
      .
      .
sum := SquareRoot(i) + SquareRoot(j);
WriteCard(SquareRoot(i + j), 1);
```

Although Modula-2 allows functions to have side effects, it is usually best to avoid this practice. The reader of a program does not expect a function to have any effect other than computing a single value; it is easy to overlook changes made to parameters or global variables. If a function may have side effects, it is usually better to write the function as a proper procedure instead. (Wirth could have written several procedures exported by the `InOut` module as functions, including `Read` and `ReadCard`, but did not for this reason.)

Functions can return values of any unstructured type (see Section 6.1), including all the basic types. In the Third Edition of *Programming in Modula-2*, Wirth states unequivocally that "the result of a function procedure cannot be structured," thus ruling out arrays (Section 7.1), records (Section 7.3), and sets (Section 7.5). Since the Third Edition appeared, Wirth has softened this stance by stating that Modula-2 systems are free to allow functions to return values of any type. The manual for a particular system should state what restrictions the compiler places on types returned by functions.

The syntax of Modula-2 prohibits using the value returned by a function as a designator. Thus a program cannot

select a component of an array or record result
dereference a pointer result
call a procedure result

This restriction should cause no problems: a program can store the value returned by a function in a variable, then select, dereference, or call the variable.

Functions, like proper procedures, can be recursive. The following function computes the *greatest common divisor* of two `CARDINAL` values `i` and `j`: the largest integer that divides both `i` and `j` evenly.

```
PROCEDURE GCD(i, j: CARDINAL): CARDINAL;
  (* returns the greatest common divisor of i and j *)
BEGIN
  IF j = 0 THEN
    RETURN i
  ELSE
    RETURN GCD(j, i MOD j)
  END
END GCD;
```

A function must always have a parameter list, but the list may be empty. Although functions with no parameters are not common, they are occasionally useful. For example, we may need a function that will generate a sequence of pseudorandom `CARDINAL` numbers $c_1, c_2, \ldots$ using the linear congruence method. In this method, we generate the $(i+1)st$ number in the sequence from the ith number by the formula

$$c_{i+1} = (multiplier \cdot c_i + increment) \bmod modulus$$

where *multiplier*, *increment*, and *modulus* are appropriate constants. Each call of `Random` returns the next number in the sequence. `Random` also saves this number in a global variable `randomCardinal` so that it can generate the next number in the sequence at the next call of `Random`. Because the value returned by `Random` depends only on the value stored in randomCardinal, Random does not need any parameters:

```
PROCEDURE Random(): CARDINAL;
  (* returns a pseudorandom number between 0 and modulus - 1;
     modifies the variable randomCardinal *)
BEGIN
  randomCardinal := (multiplier * randomCardinal + increment)
                    MOD modulus;
  RETURN randomCardinal
END Random;
```

The value returned by Random can be divided by modulus to give a pseudorandom real number between 0 and 1.

In a call of a function with no parameters, an empty list of actual parameters must follow the name of the function:

```
rand := Random();
```

Modula-2 requires the empty parentheses because the language allows procedures to be treated as data (see Section 8.2). A Modula-2 compiler would interpret the statement

```
rand := Random;
```

as an assignment of the Random function itself to the variable rand.

5.4 Scope and Visibility

When a program contains procedures, the same identifier may appear in different places in the program representing different entities. We need rules to determine the meaning of each occurrence of an identifier, as the following example illustrates:

```
MODULE Mod;
  VAR i: INTEGER;

  PROCEDURE Proc;
    VAR i: CARDINAL;
  BEGIN
    i := 0
  END Proc;

END Mod.
```

Does the assignment to `i` in the body of `Proc` refer to the variable declared in `Proc`, or to the one declared in `Mod`?

The problem of determining the meaning of an identifier is complicated by the fact that a procedure declaration may contain other procedure declarations. (In theory, this nesting can be arbitrarily deep; in practice, programmers rarely nest procedures more than two deep.)

Determining the Scope of an Entity

Each entity (constant, type, variable, procedure, or module) in a Modula-2 program has a *scope*—the region of the program in which references to the entity may appear; we say that the entity is *visible* in this region. (Some authors distinguish between scope and visibility; following Wirth, I do not.) The scope of an entity `x` declared in a program module or procedure `Outer` is the entirety of `Outer`, with the possible exception of procedures or modules declared in `Outer`:

If a procedure `Inner` declares a parameter or local entity whose name is `x`, the scope of the original entity `x` does not include the declaration of `Inner`. The original `x` is not visible within the declaration of `Inner`; Modula-2 interprets all references to `x` within `Inner` as references to the local entity named `x`.

`x` is not visible in a local module unless the module explicitly imports `x`.

A discussion of the effect of local modules (and library modules) on the scope of entities appears in Chapter 9.

Consider the module `M` (Figure 5.9), which contains the declaration of a procedure `P`. We have enclosed `M` and `P` in boxes to emphasize that each serves to define the scope of the entities declared inside it. Comments show what variables and constants are visible in each region of the program. The scope of the variables `a` and `d` declared in `P` is the entire declaration of `P` (the inner box). The scope of the variables `a`, `b`, and `c` declared in `M` is the entire module (the outer box), except for the variable `a` of type `CARDINAL`; this variable is not visible in `P`, because `P` contains a declaration of another entity with the same name.

As the example illustrates, entities declared in a procedure are not visible outside the procedure. Entities declared outside a procedure *are* visible inside the procedure, provided that no entity declared within the procedure has the same name.

In general, we can determine the meaning of a reference to an entity `x` as follows: Search the declarations belonging to the procedure in which the reference to `x` occurs. If `x` is not declared in this procedure, search the declarations of the enclosing procedure (or program module). Repeat until a declaration of `x` is found.

Figure 5.9
Module M Containing the Declaration of Procedure P

```
MODULE M;
  VAR a: CARDINAL;
      b: REAL;
  CONST c = 100;

  PROCEDURE P;
    VAR a: CHAR;
        d: INTEGER;
    (* visible: a (in P), b (in M),
                c (in M), d (in P)   *)
  END P;

    (* visible: a (in M), b (in M),
                c (in M)             *)
END M.
```

Figure 5.10
Module M with Procedure Q Nested Inside Procedure P

```
MODULE M;
  VAR a: CARDINAL;
      b: REAL;
  CONST c = 100;

  PROCEDURE P;
    VAR a: CHAR;
        d: INTEGER;

    PROCEDURE Q;
      CONST b = 25.0;
      VAR d: CARDINAL;
          e: BOOLEAN;
    (* visible: a (in P), b (in Q),
                c (in M), d (in Q),
                e (in Q)             *)
    END Q;

    (* visible: a (in P), b (in M),
                c (in M), d (in P)   *)
  END P;

    (* visible: a (in M), b (in M),
                c (in M)             *)
END M.
```

Returning to our previous example, let's add a procedure declaration nested inside the declaration of P (Figure 5.10). The scope of the CHAR variable a is still the entire declaration of P (including the declaration of Q), but we have reduced the scope of the INTEGER variable d—it does not include Q, because Q declares another entity with the same name. Similarly, the scope of the constant c is still the entire program, but the scope of the REAL variable b does not include the declaration of Q, because Q declares a constant named b.

The relative position of its declaration within its defining procedure (or module) does not affect the scope of an entity. In other words, reordering the declarations within a procedure does not affect the scope of the declared entities. Consider the following example:

```
PROCEDURE Proc1;
  CONST length = 100;

  PROCEDURE Proc2;
    CONST upperBound = length - 1;
          length = 200;
  END Proc2;

END Proc1;
```

The scope of both upperbound and length (the one declared in Proc2) is the entire declaration of Proc2. Consequently, the declaration of upperBound contains an illegal forward reference (a constant declaration may not reference a constant declared later in the program). In order to define upperBound in terms of the value of length in Proc1, we should delete the declaration of length in Proc2:

```
PROCEDURE Proc1;
  CONST length = 100;

  PROCEDURE Proc2;
    CONST upperBound = length - 1;
  END Proc2;

END Proc1;
```

If upperBound is to use the value of length in Proc2, we must switch the declarations of length and upperBound to avoid a forward reference:

```
PROCEDURE Proc1;
  CONST length = 100;

  PROCEDURE Proc2;
    CONST length = 200;
          upperBound = length - 1;
  END Proc2;

END Proc1;
```

The formal parameters of a procedure have the same scope as entities declared local to the procedure. Consequently, none of a procedure's local entities may have the same name as any of its parameters. Furthermore, a parameter may hide the name of a global entity. In the following example, the parameter `i` hides the variable `i` declared in `Mod`.

```
MODULE Mod;
  VAR i:  INTEGER;

  PROCEDURE Proc(VAR i:  CARDINAL);
  BEGIN
    i := 0    (* refers to the parameter i *)
  END Proc;

END Mod.
```

The Scope of Procedure Names

Procedure names are subject to the same scope rules as are other entities. The scope of a procedure name P extends over the procedure or module in which it is declared, unless another entity with the name P is declared in a procedure nested inside this region. Note that the scope of P is larger than the scope of its local entities: these entities are visible only *inside* P, while P itself is visible throughout the procedure or module in which P is declared.

Figure 5.11 illustrates the scope of procedure names. A comment in each region shows what procedure names are visible in that region.

Why would a programmer want to nest procedures in this fashion? One reason is that entities declared in a procedure are not visible outside the procedure. If a procedure P2 needs access to a variable declared in another procedure P1, the programmer either must declare P2 inside P1 (as in Figure 5.11) or must supply the variable to P2 as a parameter.

It is sometimes advantageous to nest a procedure Q inside a procedure P even though Q does not require access to any of P's local entities. As we have just seen, the scope of a procedure name is the procedure (or module) in which it is declared. Thus, if we declare Q inside P, then Q is not visible outside P. By "hiding" a procedure in this way, we can prevent errors that could arise from an accidental call of the procedure in another part of the program. We can also avoid name conflicts: in a large program, it is easy to inadvertently give the same name to two procedures, particularly if more than one programmer is working on the program.

Figure 5.11

The Scope of Procedure Names

```
MODULE M;
  PROCEDURE P1;
    PROCEDURE P2;
    (* visible: P1, P2, P3 *)
    END P2;

    (* visible: P1, P2, P3 *)
  END P1;

  PROCEDURE P3;
    PROCEDURE P4;
    (* visible: P1, P3, P4 *)
    END P4;

    (* visible: P1, P3, P4 *)
  END P3;

  (* visible: P1, P3      *)
END M.
```

Procedure nesting often arises from the program design technique known as "top-down design" or "stepwise refinement," in which the programmer divides a large task into smaller tasks, and then divides these tasks further, and so on. If we write the original task as a procedure P, we can then write a subtask as a procedure Q nested inside P. When we divide the subtask, we declare another set of procedures within Q.

Visibility of Standard Identifiers

Standard identifiers (such as INTEGER, TRUE, and ABS) are automatically visible throughout a program (in Wirth's terminology, they are *pervasive*), except in regions where another entity is represented by the same identifier. For example, the following function Larger declares a variable with the name MAX, hence the standard function MAX is not visible within Larger:

```
PROCEDURE Larger(i, j: CARDINAL): CARDINAL;
  VAR MAX: CARDINAL;
```

```
BEGIN
  IF i > j THEN
    MAX := i
  ELSE
    MAX := j
  END;
  RETURN MAX
END Larger;
```

Needless to say, redefining standard identifiers can make a program difficult to read and is therefore not recommended.

EXAMPLE PROGRAM

Counting Words and Sentences in a Text File

To show how nested procedures arise naturally from top-down design, let's write a program called `CountWords` to count the number of words and sentences in a file of English text.

First we notice that `CountWords` has two main tasks—counting the words and sentences (while reading the input file) and printing the statistics thereby accumulated—so we decide to write two procedures, `CollectStatistics` and `PrintStatistics`. The body of `CountWords` will open the input file, call `CollectStatistics` and `PrintStatistics`, then close the input file.

`PrintStatistics` consists of calls of output procedures, so it needs no further decomposition into procedures. We next decide on a strategy for `CollectStatistics`: it will read characters one at a time from the input file, incrementing the appropriate count when it encounters a word or sentence boundary. We delegate these subtasks—detecting a word boundary and detecting a sentence boundary—to the procedures `IncWordCount` and `IncSentenceCount`. Because these procedures are needed by `CollectStatistics` but not by `PrintStatistics`, we nest them inside the declaration of the former procedure.

`IncWordCount` can detect the beginning of a word by looking for a whitespace character followed by a nonwhitespace character. (A *whitespace* character is a character that appears as white space when printed, such as blank, tab, line feed, and carriage return.) `IncSentenceCount` can detect the end of a sentence by looking for a period, question mark, or exclamation mark, followed by a whitespace character or right parenthesis.

Both `IncWordCount` and `IncSentenceCount` need to be able to detect whitespace characters, so we decide to add the function `IsWhiteSpace`. `IsWhiteSpace` tests whether its parameter is less than or equal to the blank character; if so, it must be a blank or nonprinting character (in ASCII, at least). Because both `IncWordCount` and `IncSentenceCount` need `IsWhiteSpace`, we nest it inside CollectStatistics, where it will be visible to both procedures. Figure 5.12 shows the final structure of CountWords.

Figure 5.12

The Structure of the CountWords Program

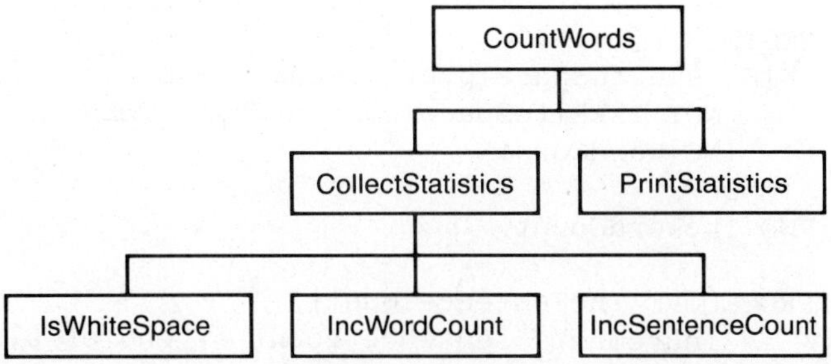

Unlike our example programs in previous chapters, CountWords must read from a file. One advantage of the InOut module is that reading from a file is just as easy as accepting input from a terminal. A program uses the same procedures to read from a file; the only difference is that the program must call OpenInput before reading from the file and CloseInput when it no longer needs the file. A call of OpenInput takes one parameter: a string representing a default extension. When OpenInput is called, it prompts the user to enter the name of a file; if the file name typed by the user does not have an extension, OpenInput will append the default extension. (Section 13.2 explains OpenInput and CloseInput in more detail.)

```
MODULE CountWords;
  (* counts the number of words and sentences in a text file *)

  FROM InOut IMPORT OpenInput, CloseInput, Read, Done,
                    WriteCard, WriteString, WriteLn;

  VAR numWords, numSentences: CARDINAL;

  PROCEDURE CollectStatistics(VAR wordCount,
                                  sentenceCount: CARDINAL);
    (* reads characters from input file, computing word count
       and sentence count *)

    VAR previousChar, currentChar: CHAR;

    PROCEDURE IsWhiteSpace(ch: CHAR): BOOLEAN;
      (* returns TRUE if ch is a whitespace character;
         assumes ASCII character set *)
```

```
    BEGIN
      RETURN ch <= ' '
    END IsWhiteSpace;

    PROCEDURE IncWordCount;
      (* increments word count at beginning of a word *)
    BEGIN
      IF IsWhiteSpace(previousChar) AND
         NOT IsWhiteSpace(currentChar) THEN
        INC(wordCount)
      END
    END IncWordCount;

    PROCEDURE IncSentenceCount;
      (* increments sentence count at end of a sentence *)
    BEGIN
      IF ((previousChar = '.') OR (previousChar = '?') OR
          (previousChar = '!')) AND
         (IsWhiteSpace(currentChar) OR (currentChar = ')'))
      THEN
        INC(sentenceCount)
      END
    END IncSentenceCount;

  BEGIN  (* CollectStatistics *)
    wordCount := 0;
    sentenceCount := 0;
    previousChar := ' ';
    Read(currentChar);
    WHILE Done DO
      IncWordCount;
      IncSentenceCount;
      previousChar := currentChar;
      Read(currentChar)
    END
  END CollectStatistics;

  PROCEDURE PrintStatistics(wordCount, sentenceCount:
                                 CARDINAL);
    (* prints the word count and sentence count with
       appropriate captions *)
  BEGIN
    WriteString("Number of words: ");
    WriteCard(wordCount, 1);
    WriteLn;
    WriteString("Number of sentences: ");
    WriteCard(sentenceCount, 1);
    WriteLn
  END PrintStatistics;
```

```
BEGIN
  WriteString("Enter name of input file.");
  WriteLn;
  OpenInput("TXT");
  WriteLn;
  CollectStatistics(numWords, numSentences);
  PrintStatistics(numWords, numSentences);
  CloseInput
END CountWords.
```

In addition to serving as a simple example of top-down design, the CountWords program illustrates several other points discussed in Sections 5.1–5.4:

- The nesting of IncWordCount and IncSentenceCount inside CollectStatistics—a consequence of the top-down design of the program—is necessary to give these procedures access to wordCount and sentenceCount (the formal parameters of CollectStatistics), as well as to previousChar and currentChar, which are local to CollectStatistics.
- To avoid potential problems, we were careful to declare IsWhiteSpace before IncWordCount and IncSentenceCount, which call IsWhiteSpace. Although most older Modula-2 compilers are not sensitive to the order of procedure declarations, the newer one-pass compilers are.
- CollectStatistics transmits values to PrintStatistics through the variables numWords and numSentences, which appear as parameters in the calls of both procedures. CollectStatistics modifies these variables (hence the wordCount and sentenceCount parameters of CollectStatistics must be variable parameters) and then PrintStatistics accesses them (allowing wordCount and sentenceCount to be value parameters in PrintStatistics). We could have written CollectStatistics and PrintStatistics without parameters; they would instead communicate directly through numWords and numSentences.

Standard Pascal

1. In Pascal, the name of a procedure (or function) does not appear at the end of the procedure's declaration:

```
procedure P;
      .
      .
      .
 end;
```

2. In the declaration of a Pascal procedure without parameters, no parentheses follow the procedure name; each call of the procedure must also omit the parentheses.

```
procedure RequestInput;
begin
  writeln('Enter a real number');
  write('> ')
end;
      .
      .
      .
RequestInput;
```

3. Pascal has no `return` statement. The only way to return from a procedure (or function) is to "fall through" the end of the procedure body. Returning from the middle of a procedure or function requires a `goto` statement:

```
procedure AddToBuffer(ch: char);
  label 1;
begin
  if bufferFull then goto 1;
  (* add ch to buffer *)
1:
end;
```

4. Pascal requires that the declaration of a procedure (or function) precede all calls of the procedure. To allow mutually recursive procedures, Pascal permits a procedure declaration in which the word `forward` replaces the body of the procedure. A full declaration of the procedure must appear later in the same block. The parameter list (and result type, in the case of a function) appears only in the original declaration (the one using `forward`), not in the second declaration.

```
procedure Q; forward;

procedure P;
```

Modula-2

1. In Modula-2, the name of a procedure must appear at the end of the procedure's declaration, after the reserved word END:

```
PROCEDURE P;
    .
    .
    .
END P;
```

2. In the declaration of a Modula-2 proper procedure without parameters, parentheses may or may not follow the procedure name. Regardless of whether parentheses appear in the declaration, each call of the procedure may either include or omit the parentheses.

```
PROCEDURE RequestInput();    (* parentheses may be omitted *)
BEGIN
  WriteString("Enter a real number");
  WriteLn;
  WriteString("> ")
END RequestInput;
    .
    .
    .
RequestInput();    (* parentheses may be omitted *)
```

3. Modula-2 provides a RETURN statement to allow a premature return from a procedure:

```
PROCEDURE AddToBuffer(ch: CHAR);
BEGIN
  IF bufferFull THEN RETURN END;
  (* add ch to buffer *)
END AddToBuffer;
```

4. Modula-2 does not restrict the order of procedure declarations:

```
PROCEDURE P;
BEGIN
  Q;  (* Q has not yet been declared, but there's no
       problem *)
END P;

PROCEDURE Q;
BEGIN
  P;
END Q;
```

Standard Pascal

```
begin
  Q;   (* the earlier declaration of Q makes this possible *)
end;

procedure Q;
begin
  P;
end;
```

5. In Pascal, a function declaration begins with the word `function`.
6. Within the body of a Pascal function, the value to be returned is assigned to the function name as though it were a variable:

```
function Cube(n: integer): integer;
begin
  Cube := n * n * n
end;
```

7. In a declaration or call of a Pascal function with no parameters, parentheses must not follow the function name:

```
function NextNonblank: char;
  var ch: char;
begin
  repeat
    read(ch)
  until ch <> ' ';
  NextNonblank := ch
end;
     .
     .
     .
currentChar := NextNonblank;
```

Modula-2

Some recent Modula-2 compilers are one-pass; such compilers require the programmer to use FORWARD in the same manner as Pascal. (These compilers generally require that the parameter list—and result type, in the case of a function—appear in the full declaration of the procedure.)

5. In Modula-2, a function declaration begins with the word PROCEDURE.
6. In Modula-2, a RETURN statement specifies the value that a function returns:

```
PROCEDURE Cube(n: INTEGER): INTEGER;
BEGIN
  RETURN n * n * n
END Cube;
```

7. In a declaration or call of a Modula-2 function with no parameters, empty parentheses must always follow the name of the function:

```
PROCEDURE NextNonblank(): CHAR;
  VAR ch: CHAR;
BEGIN
  REPEAT
    Read(ch)
  UNTIL ch <> ' ';
  RETURN ch
END NextNonblank;
          .
          .
          .
currentChar := NextNonblank();
```

EXERCISES

Section 5.1

1. Write a procedure called `ListPrimes` that, when given a `CARDINAL` number `n` as a parameter, writes the first `n` prime numbers.

Section 5.2

2. Write a procedure called `ComplexMult` that multiplies two complex numbers. A complex number consists of two `REAL` values (the real and imaginary parts of the number), so `ComplexMult` will need six parameters: four for input and two for output.

3. Write a procedure called `ConvertToScientific` that, when given a positive real number, determines how to express the number in scientific notation as a mantissa and a (base 10) exponent. `ConvertToScientific` should have three parameters: the real number (input), the mantissa (output), and the exponent (output). The mantissa should be greater than or equal to 1 but less than 10. For example, the number 294.03 would have a mantissa of 2.9403 and an exponent of 2.

4. In the Ada programming language, programmers can declare formal parameters as `in`, `out`, or `in out`. An `in` parameter can only transmit information into a procedure (assignment to an `in` parameter is forbidden). An `out` parameter can only transmit data out of a procedure. An `in out` parameter can transmit data in both directions. How do Ada's parameters compare with Modula-2's variable and value parameters? What are the advantages and disadvantages of each language's approach?

Section 5.3

5. Rewrite the function `GCD` so that it is not recursive.

6. Modify the function `Random` to return a `REAL` number between 0 and 1.

7. Write a function called `Reverse` that, when given a `CARDINAL` number `n`, returns the number whose digits are the reverse of the digits of `n`. For example, the value of `Reverse(5429)` should be 9245.

8. Write a function called `IsFibonacci` that, when given a `CARDINAL` number `n`, returns `TRUE` if `n` is a Fibonacci number and `FALSE` otherwise. The Fibonacci numbers are the numbers in the sequence

   $$1, 1, 2, 3, 5, 8, 13, 21, \ldots$$

   where each number after the first two is the sum of the two preceding numbers.

9. The standard function `CAP`, when given a letter as a parameter, returns the letter unchanged if it is an uppercase letter; if the letter is lowercase, `CAP` returns the corresponding uppercase letter. Write a declaration for `CAP` (assume that `CAP` returns its parameter unchanged if it is not a letter).

10. (For Pascal programmers) In Pascal, the value to be returned by a function is assigned to the name of the function as though it were a variable; in Modula-2, a RETURN statement specifies the value. What are the advantages and disadvantages of each method?

11. In a call of a function with no parameters, empty parentheses must follow the function name, yet a proper procedure with no parameters does not need the empty parentheses. What is the reason for this discrepancy?

Section 5.4

12. For each region in the following program, indicate which entities (including procedures) are visible in that region.

```
MODULE M;
  VAR a: BOOLEAN;
      d: REAL;
      e: CHAR;

  PROCEDURE P;
    VAR c: CHAR;
        d: INTEGER;
  END P;

  PROCEDURE Q;
    VAR a: CHAR;
        b: INTEGER;
        c: CARDINAL;

    PROCEDURE R;
      VAR b: CARDINAL;
          d: BOOLEAN;
          f: REAL;
    END R;

  END Q;

END M.
```

13. Is the following procedure declaration legal? If not, why not?

```
PROCEDURE Confused;
  CONST TRUE = FALSE;
        FALSE = TRUE;
END Confused;
```

6 Enumeration and Subrange Types

Chapter 3 described the basic types of Modula-2. This chapter and the next two show how to augment this collection by defining new types. Section 6.1 provides an overview of Modula-2's mechanisms for defining new types. Sections 6.2 and 6.3 then explain the rules for defining enumeration and subrange types. Finally, Section 6.4 presents Modula-2's type-checking rules. Chapters 7 and 8 describe other methods for specifying new types.

6.1 Programmer-defined Types

Some Modula-2 types are predefined; a Modula-2 compiler recognizes these *standard types* without the programmer having to define them. The basic types (Chapter 3) are all standard; the only other standard types are PROC (Section 8.2) and BITSET (Section 11.1). In addition to using standard types, Modula-2 programmers can create new types.

Every Modula-2 type, whether standard or not, falls into one of four categories; it is either an *unstructured*, *structured*, *pointer*, or *procedure* type.

A value of an unstructured type is a single, indivisible item of data, such as a number or character. The basic types are all unstructured. Modula-2 also allows programmers to create new unstructured types in two ways: (1) by listing (enumerating) the values of the new type or (2) by selecting a sequence of consecutive values from a previously defined unstructured type. We call these *enumeration types* and *subrange types*, respectively.

A value of a structured type is a collection of data items. The only standard structured type is BITSET; the programmer must define all other structured types. Structured types are of three kinds: *array types*, *record types*, and *set types*. When creating a new structured type, the programmer must specify how many components a value of the type will contain, what the types of these components will be, and how to access the components. Chapter 7 discusses structured types.

Pointer and procedure types are special-purpose types that share few properties of the other types. A value of a pointer type is a reference to another data value; a value of a procedure type is a reference to a procedure. Chapter 8 discusses pointer and procedure types.

Modula-2 types, both standard and programmer-defined, can be summarized as follows:

- unstructured types
  - standard (CARDINAL, INTEGER, LONGINT, REAL, LONGREAL, BOOLEAN, CHAR)
  - enumeration
  - subrange
- structured types
  - array
  - record
  - set (including the standard type BITSET)
- pointer types
- procedure types (including the standard type PROC)

The syntax charts in Figures 6.1 and 6.2 summarize Modula-2's types. The *Qualident* option in Figure 6.2 represents the name of a type (standard or programmer-defined).

Figure 6.1

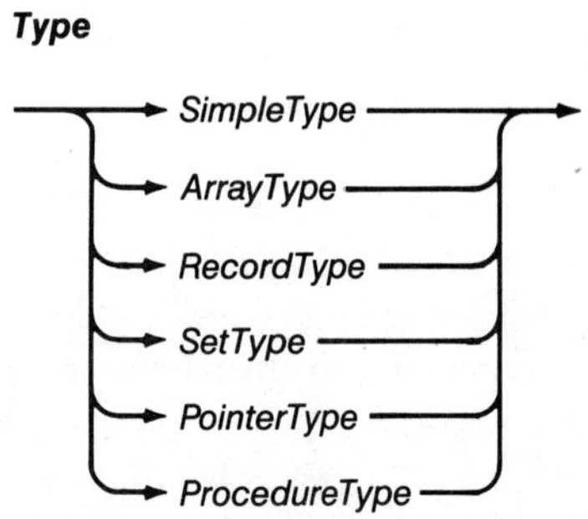

Figure 6.2

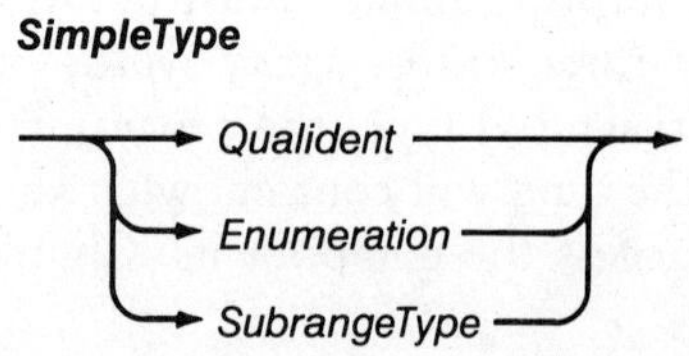

Type Specifications

A *type specification* is a description of a new type. A type specification must contain enough information for a Modula-2 compiler to determine what values belong to the type.

To illustrate simple forms of type specification, we will use enumeration and subrange types (the subjects of this chapter). An enumeration type is an ordered sequence of values represented by identifiers. The specification of an enumeration type is a list of identifiers enclosed in parentheses:

```
(small, medium, large)
```

A subrange type is a sequence of consecutive values chosen from an existing unstructured type. The specification of a subrange type is a pair of constant expressions separated by two periods and enclosed in brackets:

```
[32..212]
```

Both forms of specification inform the compiler what the values of the new type are. The first specification indicates that the type contains three (and only three) values, represented by the identifiers `small`, `medium`, and `large`. The second specification defines a type with 181 values (the integers 32, 33, 34, . . ., 212).

Type specifications can appear in two places: variable declarations and type declarations. In a variable declaration, a type specification can appear in place of a type name:

```
VAR shirtSize: (small, medium, large);
```

When a type specification appears in a variable declaration, the variable's type is *anonymous*, because the programmer has created a new type without naming it. The type of the variable `shirtSize` is anonymous.

Type Declarations

A programmer can name a new type by using a *type declaration*, then use the name in the same way as the name of a standard type. For example, instead of using a type specification to declare the variable `shirtSize`, we could first declare a type `Sizes`, then use `Sizes` to declare `shirtSize`:

```
TYPE Sizes = (small, medium, large);
VAR shirtSize: Sizes;
```

The name of a new type may appear in any number of variable declarations:

```
VAR hatSize: Sizes;
    coatSize: Sizes;
```

Figure 6.3 shows the syntax of a type declaration. The identifier on the left of the equals sign is the name of the new type; the specification of the new type appears on the right. Type declarations appear in sequences of one or more. The reserved word TYPE must precede the first type declaration in a sequence; in addition, a semicolon must terminate every type declaration:

```
TYPE Sizes = (small, medium, large);
     Temperatures = [32..212];
```

Once we have declared a new type, we can use it to declare other types:

```
TYPE Days = (Sun, Mon, Tue, Wed, Thu, Fri, Sat);
     Weekdays = [Mon..Fri];
```

The type `Weekdays` is a subrange of the `Days` type. The order of these two type declarations is important, because Modula-2 does not allow forward references in declarations. (This rule has one exception: the specification of a pointer type may refer to a type whose declaration has not yet appeared.)

Figure 6.3

TypeDeclaration

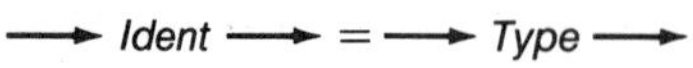

When creating a new type, the programmer must decide whether to give the type a name (using a type declaration) or to leave it anonymous. The former is usually preferable, for several reasons:

- A type name can appear many times in a program, simplifying the program and providing a form of documentation—as long as the type name is meaningful. Furthermore, the program is easier to modify. (Suppose, for example, that we decide to change the lower or upper bound of the `Temperatures` subrange. We need only modify the declaration of `Temperatures`, not the declarations of variables of type `Temperatures`.)
- An anonymous type differs from all other types (either named or anonymous) in a program. Consequently, Modula-2's type-checking rules severely limit the usefulness of a variable whose type is anonymous, as we will see in Section 6.4.
- The programmer must use a name—not a specification—to declare the type of a formal parameter.

6.2 Enumeration Types

Often a programmer faces the need to declare a variable that will take on one of a small set of values. For example, a program to process astronomical observations might require a variable whose values represent the nine planets in the solar system. One possibility is to declare the variable to be of type CARDINAL and to use a code for each planet:

```
CONST Mercury = 0;
      Venus   = 1;
      Earth   = 2;
      Mars    = 3;
      Jupiter = 4;
      Saturn  = 5;
      Uranus  = 6;
      Neptune = 7;
      Pluto   = 8;
VAR planet1, planet2: CARDINAL;
CONST closestToEarth = Venus;
```

Modula-2 provides a better alternative: to declare an *enumeration type* with nine values, representing the nine planets.

```
TYPE Planets = (Mercury, Venus, Earth, Mars, Jupiter, Saturn,
                Uranus, Neptune, Pluto);
VAR planet1, planet2: Planets;
CONST closestToEarth = Venus;
```

Creating an enumeration type rather than using a code has several advantages. First, an enumeration type is easier to declare than the values of a code. Second, defining an enumeration type avoids the risk that two code names might accidentally be given the same value. Most importantly, when the programmer uses code values (of type CARDINAL, say), the compiler cannot check that values are assigned only to variables of the right type. For example, suppose that values of type CARDINAL represent the planets, as sketched earlier. After the declarations

```
CONST Sun = 0;
            .
            .
            .
      Sat = 6;
VAR Day: CARDINAL;   (* value should be one of Sun, ..., Sat *)
```

the programmer might forget the name of the constant representing the planet Saturn and write

```
planet1 := Sat;
```

This statement is perfectly legal from Modula-2's point of view; only when the program produces the wrong results will the programmer become aware of any problem. Trying to track down an error of this nature can be difficult; using enumeration types allows the compiler to detect the error.

To define an enumeration type, the programmer simply invents names for the values of the type, then encloses a list of these names in parentheses (Figure 6.4).

Figure 6.4

Enumeration

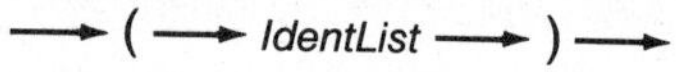

The names in the list must all be different; furthermore, no name may be the same as the name of another entity declared in the same block. If two enumeration types are declared in the same block, no value belonging to both can have the same name. The following declarations are illegal, because the identifiers `red` and `blue` appear in two enumeration types:

```
TYPE FlagColors    = (red, white, blue);
     PrimaryColors = (blue, red, yellow);     (* illegal *)
```

The basic type BOOLEAN is essentially an enumeration type defined as:

```
TYPE BOOLEAN = (FALSE, TRUE);
```

BOOLEAN has special properties not shared by programmer-defined enumeration types, however.

Enumeration types have numerous uses. The type of a tag field in a record with a variant part (Section 7.4) is often an enumeration. Enumeration types are useful for defining "state" variables—variables that record the current state of a program. For example, the following variable allows a program to keep track of whether it is adding entries to a table or retrieving them from the table:

```
VAR mode: (enterMode, fetchMode);
```

Enumeration types are also useful for expressing a result computed by a function:

```
TYPE CompareResult = (less, equal, greater);
PROCEDURE CompareWord(w1, w2: Word): CompareResult;
```

or supplying information to a procedure:

```
TYPE EchoMode = (echo, noEcho);
PROCEDURE ReadChar(VAR ch: CHAR; mode: EchoMode);
```

This use deserves special mention. Many procedures have parameters that can take on only two values; the programmer may feel tempted to declare such a parameter to have type BOOLEAN. However, using a two-valued enumeration type provides better program documentation. The call

```
ReadChar(ch, noEcho);
```

is much more understandable than the call

```
ReadChar(ch, FALSE);
```

which would occur if the second parameter were of type BOOLEAN.

The ORD and VAL Functions

In the specification of an enumeration type, the order in which the identifiers (enumeration values) appear is important. Each value has an *ordinal number* representing its position in the list. The first value in a list has ordinal number 0, the second has ordinal number 1, and so forth. The standard function ORD returns the ordinal number of an enumeration value:

Expression	*Value*
ORD(Mercury)	0
ORD(Mars)	3
ORD(Pluto)	8

The standard function VAL serves as an inverse to ORD. VAL requires two parameters, a type name T and a CARDINAL number i, and returns the value of type T whose ordinal number is i.

Expression	*Value*
VAL(Planets, 0)	Mercury
VAL(Planets, 3)	Mars
VAL(Planets, 8)	Pluto

Modula-2 provides no operations for enumeration types other than assignment and the relational operations:

```
planet2 := planet1;
planet1 := Mars;
IF planet2 < Earth THEN
  WriteString("Planet 2 is closer to the sun than Earth")
END;
```

Comparisons between values of an enumeration type depend on their ordinal numbers; for example, `Venus` is less than `Earth` because `ORD(Venus)` is less than `ORD(Earth)`.

The INC and DEC Procedures

Because no arithmetic operations are defined for enumeration types, a program cannot increment a variable of an enumeration type by an assignment statement of the following form:

```
planet1 := planet1 + 1;    (* illegal *)
```

Using ORD and VAL yields a somewhat complicated assignment:

```
planet1 := VAL(Planets, ORD(planet1) + 1);
```

Fortunately, the standard procedures INC and DEC allow parameters of an enumeration type:

```
INC(planet1);
```

INC and DEC permit a second parameter that serves as an increment (or decrement). Thus, after the statements

```
planet1 := Earth;
DEC(planet1, 2);
```

are executed, the value of `planet1` is `Mercury`.

INC and DEC provide a convenient way to loop over all the values of an enumeration type (or a range thereof):

```
planet1 := Mercury;
WHILE planet1 <= Pluto DO
        .
        .
        .
  INC(planet1)
END;
```

Alternatively, we can use a FOR statement for this purpose:

```
FOR planet1 := Mercury TO Pluto DO
        .
        .
        .
END;
```

Calls of INC and DEC may produce undefined results: `INC(planet1)` is illegal if the value of `planet1` is `Pluto`; similarly, `DEC(planet1)` is illegal if the value of `planet1` is `Mercury`. Because some Modula-2 systems may not detect such errors, a program must ensure (by testing the variable beforehand) that a call of INC or DEC will produce a valid result.

EXAMPLE **Writing Values of an Enumeration Type**

Because the programmer creates enumeration types, the programmer is also responsible for providing procedures to read and write enumeration values. Fortunately, few programs need to perform input and output of enumeration types; in any event, I/O procedures for enumeration types are relatively easy to write.

To write enumeration values in human-readable form, a program may use a CASE statement to select a string representing a particular value. For example, the following procedure writes values of type `Planets`.

```
PROCEDURE WritePlanet(planet: Planets);
  (* writes the name of a value of type Planets *)
BEGIN
  CASE planet OF
    Mercury: WriteString("Mercury") |
    Venus:   WriteString("Venus")   |
    Earth:   WriteString("Earth")   |
    Mars:    WriteString("Mars")    |
    Jupiter: WriteString("Jupiter") |
    Saturn:  WriteString("Saturn")  |
    Uranus:  WriteString("Uranus")  |
    Neptune: WriteString("Neptune") |
    Pluto:   WriteString("Pluto")
  END
END WritePlanet;
```

As this example shows, CASE statements are ideal for choosing among the values of an enumeration type.

Alternatively, a program may need to write enumeration values to a file where another program will read them later. In this case, it is more efficient to write a code (typically the ordinal number of the enumeration value) rather than a string.

6.3 Subrange Types

Often the programmer knows in advance that a variable will assume values in a limited range within a particular type. For example, the variable age, representing a person's age, must have a value between 0 and 150, say. We can indicate these bounds by declaring the type of age to be a *subrange* of the type CARDINAL:

```
TYPE AgeRange = [0..150];     (* subrange of CARDINAL *)
VAR age: AgeRange;
```

There are three advantages to declaring age in this fashion instead of declaring it to be of type CARDINAL. First, the declaration helps a reader of the program understand what age represents and what values it can assume. Second, the declaration may allow the compiler to reduce the amount of storage allocated for age. Third, the declaration allows the value of age to be checked as the program is executed: if an assignment to age would cause its value to be outside the specified range (indicating a programming error), the program will be terminated with an error message. (Most compilers allow this feature to be deactivated—either for an entire compilation unit or just selected regions—thereby increasing the speed of program execution by a small amount, at the expense of reduced ability to detect errors.)

The values of a subrange type must be a range of consecutive values selected from a previously defined unstructured type, called the *base type*. The base type for a subrange must be CARDINAL, INTEGER, LONGINT, CHAR, or any enumeration type. (The base type could also be BOOLEAN, but this choice wouldn't be very useful.) Some compilers do not allow LONGINT to be the base type of a subrange.

Here are several subrange types:

```
TYPE UpperCase = ['A'..'Z'];          (* subrange of CHAR     *)
     LowerCase = ['a'..'z'];          (* subrange of CHAR     *)
     VHFChannels = [2..13];           (* subrange of CARDINAL *)
     CloseToSun = [Mercury..Mars];    (* subrange of Planets  *)
```

The base type of a subrange is determined by the types of its bounds. Thus, the base type for `UpperCase` and `LowerCase` is `CHAR`, and the base type for `CloseToSun` is `Planets` (defined in Section 6.2). When the bounds are both integers, as is the case with `VHFChannels`, the base type is `INTEGER` if the smaller bound is negative and `CARDINAL` otherwise.

The specification of a subrange type consists of a pair of constant expressions, separated by the `..` symbol and enclosed in brackets. (In Modula-2, the `..` symbol separates the lower and upper limits of a range of values. We saw this use in the `CASE` statement.) The value of the first expression must be less than or equal to the value of the second (that is, the type must have at least one possible value). Optionally, a type name may precede the specification to indicate the base type of the subrange (see Figure 6.5). The option of specifying the base type of a subrange first appeared in the Third Edition of *Programming in Modula-2*. In the Second Edition, a type name could not precede a subrange type specification; the base type was always inferred from the types of the bounds.

Figure 6.5

SubrangeType

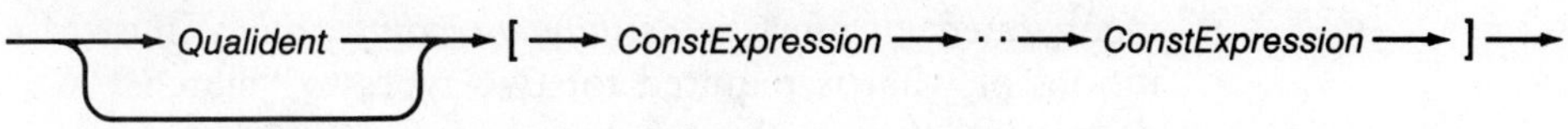

The ability to specify the base type of a subrange is useful when the base type would be `CARDINAL` by default but the programmer wants it to be `INTEGER` instead:

```
TYPE WaterTemperatures = INTEGER[32..212];
```

If the programmer omitted the type name `INTEGER`, the base type of `WaterTemperatures` would be `CARDINAL`. The choice of `INTEGER` rather than `CARDINAL` as the base type for `WaterTemperatures` is only important in situations where `WaterTemperatures` must be *compatible* with `INTEGER`. We return to this point in Section 6.4.

A subrange type inherits all the operations of its base type. For example, all the operations legal for `CARDINAL` values also apply to values of type `AgeRange`, because `AgeRange` is a subrange of `CARDINAL`. If `age1`, `age2`, and `ageDifference` are variables of type `AgeRange`, then Modula-2 allows the assignment

```
ageDifference := age1 - age2;
```

provided that the value of `age1 - age2` is not negative. In addition, Modula-2 allows the programmer to combine values of type `AgeRange` with values of type `CARDINAL` or another subrange of `CARDINAL`:

```
age1 := age2 + 10;
```

In general, Modula-2's operators require that their operands be *compatible* (Section 6.4). For purposes of type compatibility, Modula-2 treats a value of a subrange type as though it belonged to the base type. (In the preceding statement, for example, the variable age2 is treated as having type CARDINAL.) An arithmetic operation performed when either operand has a subrange type produces a value of the base type. Thus, the type of age2 + 10 is CARDINAL.

6.4 Compatibility and Assignment Compatibility

Because Modula-2 is a strongly typed language, compilers must check the types of values appearing in Modula-2 expressions and statements. The kind of check performed varies, depending on the context. When a procedure is called, the type of each variable parameter must be the *same* as the type of the matching actual parameter. The types of the operands in an expression need not be the same, but must be *compatible*, and the types of the variable and expression in an assignment statement must be *assignment-compatible*. Thus, Modula-2 has three definitions of what is required for two types to "match." We can now give precise definitions of these three terms.

Type Equivalence

Two types are the *same* if they have the same name or if they were derived—directly or indirectly—from the same type name. Thus, the following types are all the same:

```
TYPE Length = REAL;
     Distance = Length;
     Mileage = Length;
     Mass = REAL;
```

For example, we can trace both Distance and REAL back to the type name REAL; we can trace Distance and Mileage back to Length (or REAL).

Types that merely have the same structure are *not* the same:

```
TYPE WorkDays = [Mon..Fri];
     SchoolDays = [Mon..Fri];
```

WorkDays and SchoolDays have the same base type and the same values, but we cannot trace them back to the same type name.

An anonymous type, by definition, cannot be the same as any other type. However, two variables with anonymous types can have the same type:

```
VAR day1, day2: [Mon..Fri];
```

Although both day1 and day2 have an anonymous type, their types are the same, because they appear in the same declaration. However, no other variables have the same type as day1 and day2. If we declare day3 as

```
VAR day3: [Mon..Fri];
```

then day3's type is different from that of day1 and day2.

In only one context must types be the same, not merely compatible or assignment-compatible: The type of a variable parameter must be the same as the type of a corresponding actual parameter. For example, if we declare the variable small as

```
VAR small: [0..99];
```

then the following procedure call is illegal:

```
ReadCard(small);    (* illegal *)
```

ReadCard allows only parameters of type CARDINAL (or any type declared to be the same as CARDINAL); subranges do not qualify.

Compatibility

Two types T_1 and T_2 are *compatible* if they are the same, or if one is a subrange of the other, or if both are subranges with the same base type. Consider the following types:

```
TYPE SmallCards = [0..999];
     LargeCards = [100..9999];
```

SmallCards and CARDINAL are compatible, because the former is a subrange of the latter. LargeCards is compatible with CARDINAL for the same reason. Also, SmallCards and LargeCards are compatible, because both are subranges of CARDINAL.

Modula-2 requires compatibility for

the operands in an arithmetic expression

the operands in a relational expression

the case labels and case expression in a CASE statement

the starting value, limit, and control variable in a FOR statement

We now see the advantage of specifying a base type of INTEGER in the declaration

```
TYPE WaterTemperatures = INTEGER[32..212];
```

This declaration ensures that WaterTemperatures is compatible with INTEGER and all subranges of INTEGER (rather than compatible with CARDINAL and its subranges). Thus, WaterTemperatures values can be combined with other temperatures that may be negative:

```
VAR outsideTemperature: INTEGER;
    lakeTemperature: WaterTemperatures;
            .
            .
            .
IF outsideTemperature >= lakeTemperature THEN
  WriteInt(outsideTemperature - lakeTemperature, 1);
  WriteLn
END;
```

If WaterTemperatures were a subrange of CARDINAL, it would be illegal to compare outsideTemperature and lakeTemperature or to compute their difference.

Assignment Compatibility

Assignment statements require an even weaker compatibility condition. Two types are *assignment-compatible* if they are compatible or if both are INTEGER or CARDINAL or subranges with base types INTEGER or CARDINAL. Thus, the following types are assignment-compatible with each other and with INTEGER and CARDINAL:

```
TYPE SmallCards = [0..999];
     LargeCards = [100..9999];
     SmallInts = [-999..999];
```

Modula-2 requires assignment compatibility for:

the designator and expression in an assignment statement (with the exception of the assignment of a string literal to a string variable or variable of type CHAR—see Section 7.2)

an array's index type and an expression used as an index (see Section 7.1)

a value parameter and each corresponding actual parameter

the type of result to be returned by a function and the expression in a RETURN statement in the body of the function

Assignment compatibility does not guarantee the validity of an operation. If the variables `small` and `large` have types `SmallInts` and `LargeCards`, respectively, then the assignment

```
small := large;
```

is legal only when the value of `large` is between 100 and 999; this condition cannot be tested until the program is executed.

Summary

We can summarize Modula-2's three forms of type compatibility as follows:

- Types T_1 and T_2 are the *same*
  if T_1 and T_2 have the same name
  or if both types have been derived from the same type name by type declarations.
- Types T_1 and T_2 are *compatible*
  if T_1 and T_2 are the same
  or if one is a subrange of the other
  or if both are subranges with the same base type
- Types T_1 and T_2 are *assignment-compatible*
  if T_1 and T_2 are compatible
  or if one is CARDINAL (or a subrange thereof) and the other is INTEGER (or a subrange thereof)

We have arranged these conditions in order of decreasing strength. Requiring compatibility is weaker than requiring types to be the same, because it allows a subrange to be treated (for type-checking purposes) as though it belonged to the base type. Assignment compatibility is even weaker, because it blurs the distinction between INTEGER and CARDINAL.

Standard Pascal

1. Pascal supplies two standard functions, `succ` and `pred`, that map a value of an enumerated type to its successor or predecessor in the enumeration:

```
type Days = (Sun, Mon, Tue, Wed, Thu, Fri, Sat);
var today: Days;
        .
        .
        .
today := Sun;
today := succ(today);     (* today is now Mon *)
today := pred(today);     (* today is now Sun *)
today := succ(Wed);       (* today is now Thu *)
```

2. Pascal provides no inverse to the `ord` function (except for type `char`, where `chr` serves as the inverse).

3. In Pascal, the specification of a subrange type is a pair of constants separated by two periods:

```
type Months = 1..12;
```

The bounds of a subrange must be single (constant) values, not expressions.

4. Pascal's rules for determining whether two types are the same, compatible, or assignment-compatible are the same as Modula-2's rules, with a few added cases. In Pascal, two set types are compatible (and assignment-compatible) if

Modula-2

1. The `succ` and `pred` functions do not exist in Modula-2; the standard procedures `INC` and `DEC` take their place. Programmers can use `INC` and `DEC` to increment or decrement a variable of an enumeration type.

```
TYPE Days = (Sun, Mon, Tue, Wed, Thu, Fri, Sat);
VAR today: Days;
        .
        .
        .
today := Sun;
INC(today);       (* today is now Mon *)
DEC(today);       (* today is now Sun *)
```

   `INC` and `DEC` are proper procedures, not functions like `succ` and `pred`. Unlike `succ` and `pred`, which return a value, `INC` and `DEC` modify the actual parameter. This parameter must be a variable; thus, `INC(Wed)` is illegal.

   `INC` and `DEC` allow a second parameter, which indicates the amount by which to increment or decrement the first parameter:

```
today := Sun;
INC(today, 3);    (* today is now Wed *)
DEC(today, 2);    (* today is now Mon *)
```

2. In Modula-2, the standard function `VAL` serves as an inverse to `ORD`. If `T` is one of the standard identifiers `CHAR`, `INTEGER`, `CARDINAL`, or the name of an enumeration type, and `i` has type `CARDINAL`, then `VAL(T, i)` is the value of type `T` whose ordinal number is `i`. For example, `VAL(Days, 0)` is `Sun`.

3. In Modula-2, the programmer must enclose a subrange specification in brackets:

```
TYPE Months = [1..12];
```

   The bounds of a subrange can be constant expressions:

```
CONST maxTableSize = 1000;
TYPE TableIndex = [0..maxTableSize-1];
```

   Optionally, a type name may precede a subrange specification, to indicate the base type of the subrange:

```
TYPE Months = INTEGER[1..12];
```

4. Modula-2's rules for determining whether two types are the same, compatible, or assignment-compatible are the same as Pascal's rules, with a few exceptions. In Modula-2, two set types must be the same if they are to be

Standard Pascal

their base types are compatible and either both types or neither are packed. Two string types are compatible (and asssignment-compatible) if both have the same number of components. The types `real` and `integer` are assignment-compatible (in one direction only: the programmer may assign an `integer` value to a `real` variable).

Modula-2

compatible or assignment-compatible. The same is true for strings: two string types are compatible or assignment-compatible only if the types are the same. In Modula-2, REAL is not assignment-compatible with INTEGER (or CARDINAL).

EXERCISES

Section 6.2

1. What is wrong with the following type declaration?

```
TYPE Scale = (do, re, mi, fa, so, la, ti, do);
```

2. Write a procedure called `NextDay` to increment a variable of type `Days`. `NextDay` should "wrap around" at the end of the week; if the value of the actual parameter is `Sat` before a call of `NextDay`, it should have the value `Sun` when `NextDay` returns.

3. Write a procedure called `ReadDay` to read a value of type `Days` typed by the user. When called, `ReadDay` should prompt the user to enter 0 for `Sun`, 1 for `Mon`, etc. If the value entered is illegal, `ReadDay` should ask the user to try again.

4. (For Pascal programmers) Unlike Pascal, Modula-2 does not supply `succ` and `pred` functions for computing the successor and predecessor of an enumeration value. Show how to write these functions in Modula-2 for a particular enumeration type.

Section 6.4

5. Assume that we have declared the types `Grades`, `Range`, `Scores`, and `Change` as follows:

```
TYPE Grades = [0..100];
     Range = [-99..99];
     Scores = CARDINAL;
     Change = INTEGER;
```

For each of the following pairs of types, indicate whether the types are the same, compatible, or assignment-compatible (mention all that apply).

(a) `INTEGER, Grades`
(b) `INTEGER, Range`
(c) `INTEGER, Scores`
(d) `INTEGER, Change`
(e) `CARDINAL, Grades`
(f) `CARDINAL, Range`
(g) `CARDINAL, Scores`
(h) `CARDINAL, Change`
(i) `Grades, Range`
(j) `Grades, Scores`
(k) `Grades, Change`
(l) `Range, Scores`
(m) `Range, Change`
(n) `Scores, Change`

6. Modula-2's rule for determining the equivalence of types is a weak form of *name equivalence*. In strict name equivalence, which Ada requires, types are not the same unless they have the same name. What are the advantages and disadvantages of Modula-2's form of name equivalence as opposed to Ada's?

7. Some early Pascal compilers used the rule of *structural equivalence*. In structural equivalence, two types are the same if they have the same structure. Under the rule of structural equivalence, the following variables have the same type:

```
VAR day1: [Mon..Fri];
    day2: [Mon..Fri];
```

What are the advantages and disadvantages of structural equivalence as opposed to Modula-2's form of name equivalence?

7 Array, Record, and Set Types

Chapter 6 showed how a programmer can create new unstructured types in Modula-2. Chapter 7 shows how to define new *structured* types—arrays, records, and sets. Section 7.1 covers both array types and the related topic of open array parameters, which make it possible to write procedures that can accept arrays of different sizes. Section 7.2 shows how to define and use string types; in Modula-2, strings are just one-dimensional arrays of characters. Section 7.3 discusses record types and the `WITH` statement, which simplifies the task of accessing fields in a record. The treatment of record types continues in Section 7.4, which describes records with variant parts. Section 7.5 covers set types and the operations that Modula-2 provides for sets.

7.1 Array Types

An *array* is a structure containing a fixed number of values, all of the same type, that can be selected by position. The values stored in an array are the *components* of the array; their type is the *component type*. The values that indicate the positions of components are *indices*; their type is the *index type*. For example, consider the following declarations:

```
TYPE ArrayType = ARRAY [1..10] OF INTEGER;
VAR A: ArrayType;
```

The component type of A is INTEGER, and the index type is `[1..10]` (a subrange of CARDINAL). We can visualize A as follows:

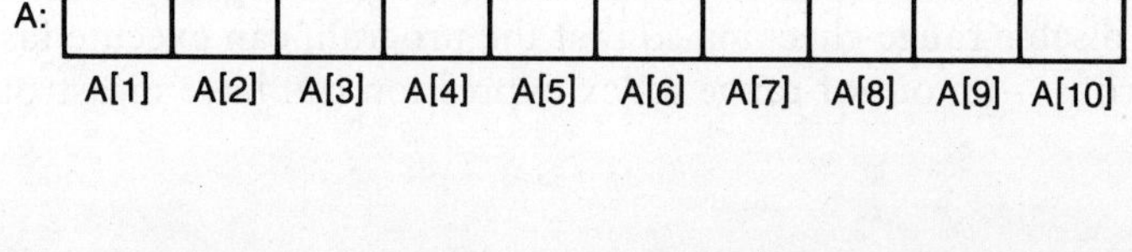

The name A refers to the array as a whole; the expressions A[1], A[2], ..., A[10] select individual components of A.

The components of an array may be of any type. The index type, however, must be CHAR, BOOLEAN, or an enumeration or subrange type. (Although CARDINAL and INTEGER are not legal index types, the programmer can overcome this restriction by using equivalent subranges. Instead of CARDINAL, for example, the programmer can use the subrange 0..MAX(CARDINAL).) The following are all legal array types:

```
TYPE BitVector = ARRAY [0..255] OF BOOLEAN;
     CharCounts = ARRAY CHAR OF CARDINAL;
     LetterCounts = ARRAY ['a'..'z'] OF CARDINAL;
     PlanetValues = ARRAY Planets OF REAL;
                    (* Planets was defined in Section 6.2 *)
```

The bounds of a subrange may be constant expressions, so type declarations such as the following are legal:

```
CONST range = 100;
TYPE Measurements = ARRAY [-(range-1)..range-1] OF REAL;
```

To select an array component, the programmer writes an expression in brackets after the name of the array. For example, if A is the array declared earlier, we can access the fifth component of A by writing any of the following: A[5], A[i] (if i has the value 5), or A[1 + 2 * j] (if j has the value 2). Each of these is a *designator*; the expression inside the brackets is the *selector* or *index expression*. A designator of an array component has most of the properties of a variable; in particular, it can appear on the left side of an assignment statement:

```
FOR i := 1 TO 10 DO
  A[i] := 0    (* assign 0 to each component of A *)
END;
```

In an array designator, the type of the index expression must be assignment-compatible with the array's index type. (In the case of the array A, an index expression may have type INTEGER, CARDINAL, or any subrange of INTEGER or CARDINAL.) Furthermore, if the index type is a subrange, the value of the index expression must lie within the bounds of the subrange. Unless the index expression is constant, a Modula-2 compiler cannot check this condition; instead, most Modula-2 systems perform the test as the program executes, terminating the program if the expression is out of range. (Some compilers allow the programmer to disable range-checking so that the program can execute faster. Doing so is dangerous—an out-of-range index expression can have disastrous results. For example, an assignment to `A[i]` when the value of `i` is 11 will change the value of whatever variable happens to be stored after `A` in memory, causing the program to behave unpredictably.)

Modula-2 allows references to whole arrays (as opposed to array components) in only two contexts. First, an array name (representing a whole array) may appear on either side of an assignment statement:

```
A := B;
```

Such an assignment copies each component of `B` to the corresponding component of `A`. Second, the programmer may supply an array name as an actual parameter in a procedure call:

```
Sort(A);
```

In either case, the usual rules of type compatibility apply. For a programmer to assign one array to another, the arrays must have the same type. An array used as an actual parameter must have the same type as the corresponding formal parameter. (In the case of array types, the distinction between *same*, *compatible*, and *assignment-compatible* does not exist; all three terms are equivalent.)

Using a type specification rather than a type name to declare an array limits the use of the array as a whole. For example, suppose that we use an array type specification to declare the variables `A` and `B`:

```
VAR A, B: ARRAY [1..10] OF INTEGER;
```

`A` and `B` have the same anonymous type. No other arrays can have the same type, so `A` and `B` can appear only in assignment statements in which one array is assigned to the other. `A` and `B` cannot appear as parameters in procedure calls (unless the corresponding formal parameter is an open array parameter, as we will see later). This form of declaration does not limit access to the components of `A` and `B`, however; the programmer can use them as `INTEGER` variables.

Multidimensional Arrays

In Modula-2, programmers create multidimensional arrays by nesting one-dimensional arrays. For example, the following declaration creates a 50-by-100 matrix type:

```
TYPE Matrix = ARRAY [1..50] OF ARRAY [1..100] OF INTEGER;
```

Because this sort of type declaration can be unwieldy, Modula-2 allows the equivalent declaration

```
TYPE Matrix = ARRAY [1..50], [1..100] OF INTEGER;
```

The syntax chart for an array specification (Figure 7.1) shows the possibility of multiple index types. In general, the specification

$$\text{ARRAY } T_1 , T_2 , \ldots, T_n \text{ OF } T$$

is an abbreviation for

$$\text{ARRAY } T_1 \text{ OF ARRAY } T_2 \text{ OF} \ldots \text{ ARRAY } T_n \text{ OF } T$$

Modula-2 places no limit on the number of dimensions in an array.

Figure 7.1

ArrayType

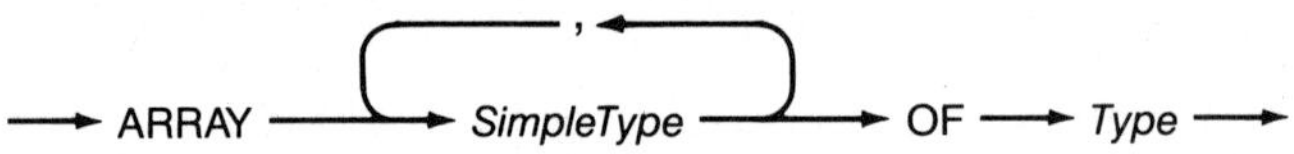

If M is a variable of type Matrix, we can access the component in row i and column j of M by writing either M[i][j] or M[i, j]. The first form emphasizes the fact that M is a one-dimensional array whose components are one-dimensional arrays. The index i selects a value of type ARRAY [1..100] OF INTEGER; the index j selects a component from this array. The other form, M[i, j], is shorter and more closely resembles array access in other programming languages.

Because each row of M is an array, rows can appear in assignment statements as whole arrays:

```
M[1] := M[2];
```

Rows of M cannot appear in assignment statements with other variables, however, because the type of a row is anonymous. If access to the rows of M is important, we can name the type of the rows. The following procedure, which interchanges rows i and j of a matrix, shows how to do so:

```
TYPE Row = ARRAY [1..100] OF INTEGER;
     Matrix = ARRAY [1..50] OF Row;

PROCEDURE ExchangeRows(VAR M: Matrix; i, j: CARDINAL);
  (* exchanges rows i and j of M *)
  VAR temp: Row;
```

```
BEGIN
  temp := M[i];
  M[i] := M[j];
  M[j] := temp
END ExchangeRows;
```

Because temp, M[i], and M[j] each has type Row, assignments involving any two are legal. This definition of Matrix does not affect access to the components of M; they can be accessed by writing either M[i, j] or M[i][j].

Open Array Parameters

Modula-2 provides two ways of supplying an array parameter to a procedure. In one method, the programmer declares the array type outside the procedure, and then declares the formal parameter and each actual parameter to have this type. Consider the FindMax function, which finds the largest component in an array of type CardArray:

```
CONST arrayLength = 100;
TYPE CardArray = ARRAY [1..arrayLength] OF CARDINAL;

PROCEDURE FindMax(A: CardArray): CARDINAL;
  (* returns the largest component of A *)
  VAR i, max: CARDINAL;
BEGIN
  max := 0;
  FOR i := 1 TO arrayLength DO
    IF A[i] > max THEN
      max := A[i]
    END
  END;
  RETURN max
END FindMax;
```

The only problem with FindMax is that it accepts only arrays of type CardArray, and all such arrays must have exactly 100 components. If we wanted to find the largest component in arrays of lengths 200, 300, and 400 as well, we would need three more procedures, each identical to FindMax except for the type of the parameter A.

Modula-2 therefore provides a second way to specify the type of an array parameter. Instead of using a type name to specify the type of the formal parameter, the programmer declares it to have type

```
ARRAY OF T
```

where T is a type name. We call a formal parameter declared in this fashion an *open array parameter*. Note: The programmer may use an ARRAY OF T type specification only to declare the type of a formal parameter in a procedure heading, not in ordinary variable or type declarations.

No index type is specified for an open array parameter, thus allowing the programmer to supply as an actual parameter any array whose components are of type T. The index type of an open array parameter is always a subrange of CARDINAL whose lower bound is 0. The upper bound varies, depending on the length of the array that the programmer has supplied as an actual parameter. If A is an open array parameter, the upper bound of A's index type is HIGH(A). (HIGH is a standard function.) Because A's lower index bound is 0, the number of components in the actual parameter is not HIGH(A), but HIGH(A) plus 1.

In FindMax, if we make A an open array parameter, then we can supply as an actual parameter any one-dimensional array whose components have type CARDINAL.

```
PROCEDURE FindMax(A: ARRAY OF CARDINAL): CARDINAL;
  (* returns the largest component of A *)
  VAR i, max: CARDINAL;
BEGIN
  max := 0;
  FOR i := 0 TO HIGH(A) DO
    IF A[i] > max THEN
      max := A[i]
    END
  END;
  RETURN max
END FindMax;
```

When two or more parameters are open arrays, the actual parameters need not have the same length. For example, consider the procedure InnerProduct, which computes the inner (or "dot") product of two vectors.

```
PROCEDURE InnerProduct(v, w: ARRAY OF REAL): REAL;
  (* returns the inner product of vectors v and w *)
  VAR i: CARDINAL;
      sum: REAL;
BEGIN
  IF HIGH(v) # HIGH(w) THEN
    WriteString("Length error in InnerProduct");
    WriteLn;
    HALT
  END;
  sum := 0.0;
  FOR i := 0 TO HIGH(v) DO
    sum := sum + v[i] * w[i]
```

```
  END;
  RETURN sum
END InnerProduct;
```

The actual parameters in a call of `InnerProduct` may not have the same length, so `InnerProduct` tests whether the lengths match, terminating the program if they do not.

We can use individual components of an open array in the same manner as we use components of ordinary arrays. Modula-2 allows only one operation for whole open arrays, however: The name of an open array may appear as an actual parameter in a procedure call (the corresponding formal parameter must also be an open array parameter). The language does not allow whole array assignment for open array parameters.

Open array parameters, useful as they are, have two problems. First, open arrays cannot be multidimensional (although standards groups are considering adding this feature to Modula-2). More precisely, an open array parameter can have more than one dimension, but only the first dimension is flexible. For example, the following procedure operates on two-dimensional arrays; the number of rows in the arrays may vary, but the number of columns is fixed.

```
CONST rowLength = 100;
TYPE Row = ARRAY [1..rowLength] OF CARDINAL;

PROCEDURE MatrixAdd(A, B: ARRAY OF Row; VAR C: ARRAY OF Row);
  (* computes the matrix sum of A and B and stores it in C;
     A, B, and C must have the same number of rows *)
  VAR i, j: CARDINAL;
BEGIN
  IF (HIGH(A) # HIGH(B)) OR (HIGH(A) # HIGH(C)) THEN
    WriteString("Length error in MatrixAdd");
    WriteLn;
    HALT
  END;
  FOR i := 0 TO HIGH(A) DO
    FOR j := 1 TO rowLength DO
      C[i, j] := A[i, j] + B[i, j]
    END
  END
END MatrixAdd;
```

Another problem with open array parameters stems from the fact that the index bounds of the actual parameter are lost. When we use an array of length 10 as an actual parameter and the corresponding formal parameter is an open array, the array's index range appears to be `[0..9]`, even though it may actually be `[1..10]` or `[11..20]` or even `['A'..'J']`. Most of the time, the actual index type of the array is irrelevant; only the length of the array matters. In some cases, however, the actual bounds are important. The function FindIndexOfMax illustrates one of these cases. FindIndexOfMax returns not the *value* of the largest component in an array, but its *position*. Because FindIndexOfMax has no knowledge of the bounds of the actual parameter, it has no choice but to return a value between 0 and HIGH(A), where A is the open array parameter.

```
PROCEDURE FindIndexOfMax(A: ARRAY OF CARDINAL): CARDINAL;
  (* returns the index of the largest component in A; the value
     returned falls between 0 and HIGH(A) *)
  VAR i, maxPos: CARDINAL;
BEGIN
  maxPos := 0;
  FOR i := 1 TO HIGH(A) DO
    IF A[i] > A[maxPos] THEN
      maxPos := i
    END
  END;
  RETURN maxPos
END FindIndexOfMax;
```

We must adjust the value that FindIndexOfMax returns by adding the lower bound of the actual parameter's index range.

EXAMPLE PROGRAM

Sorting Using the Quicksort Algorithm

The Quicksort algorithm, because of its simplicity and efficiency, is one of the most popular sorting methods. When expressed in recursive fashion, Quicksort has a remarkably concise description:

1. Given a collection of keys to sort, remove one of the keys (call this the "partitioning element"). Then partition the remaining keys into two groups so that one group contains only keys that are less than or equal to the partitioning element and the other group contains only keys that are greater than or equal to the partitioning element.
2. Sort each group, using the same method recursively.
3. Create the final sorted list by joining the two sorted lists created in Step 2, separated by the partitioning element.

A Quicksort program is easy to write if we store the keys in a one-dimensional array. During partitioning, we rearrange keys within the array so that all "small" keys (those less than or equal to the partitioning element) occupy the left portion of the array and all "large" keys occupy the right portion. We do the partitioning by using two variables, L and R, as "fingers" to select components of the array. Initially, we position L at the left end of the array and R at the right end. Then we choose one array component (the one selected by L, say) to serve as the partitioning element. We copy this component to a variable, leaving a "hole" in the array at the left end. While L remains stationary, marking the location of the hole, R sweeps across the array from right to left until it selects an array component that is smaller than the partitioning element; we copy this component to the location marked by L. R now points to a hole, so L sweeps across the array until it selects a component that is larger than the partitioning element; we copy this component to the hole marked by R. L and R continue alternating in this fashion until they meet somewhere in the middle of the array. When they meet, both L and R point to a hole; we copy the partitioning element into the hole.

For example, suppose that we begin with an array containing six numbers to sort. Before partitioning, L points to the leftmost array component and R to the rightmost component:

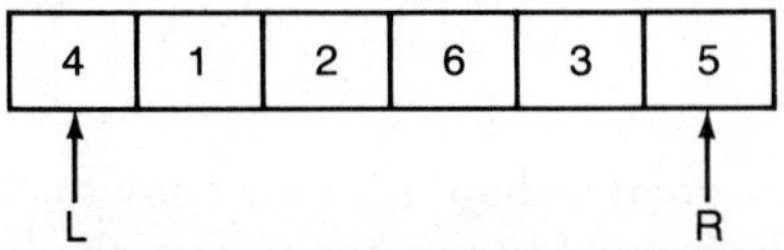

We begin by copying the partitioning element (selected by L) to a variable, leaving a hole at the left end of the array:

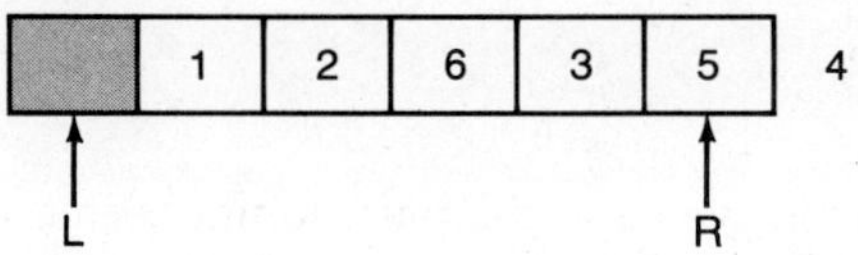

We then move R to the left until it selects an array component less than the partitioning element. Because 5 is not less than 4, we move R one position to the left:

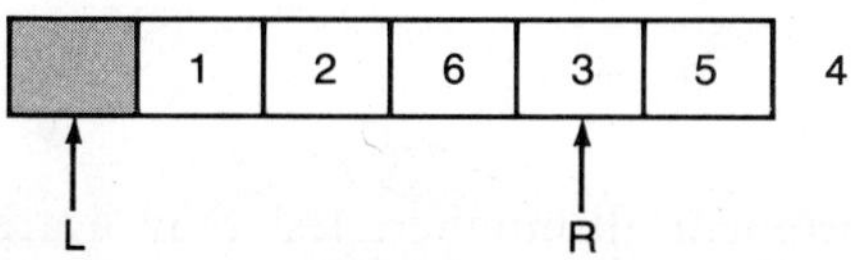

The element selected by R is now less than 4, so we copy it to the hole marked by L and move L one position to the right:

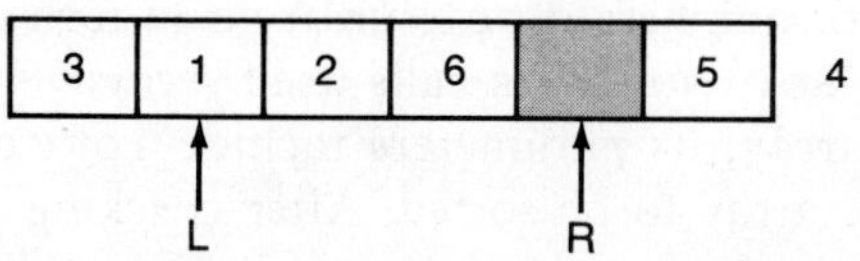

The number selected by L is less than 4, so we continue to move L:

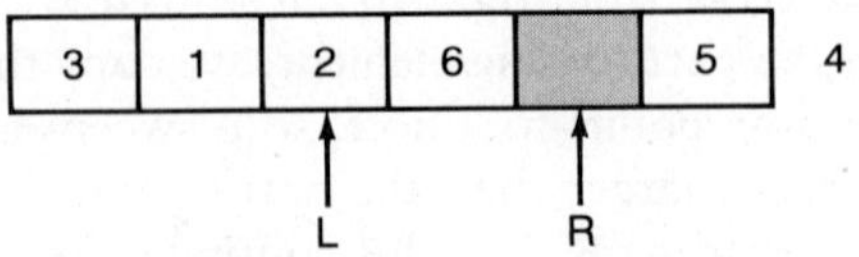

Again the number selected by L is less than 4, so we move L once more:

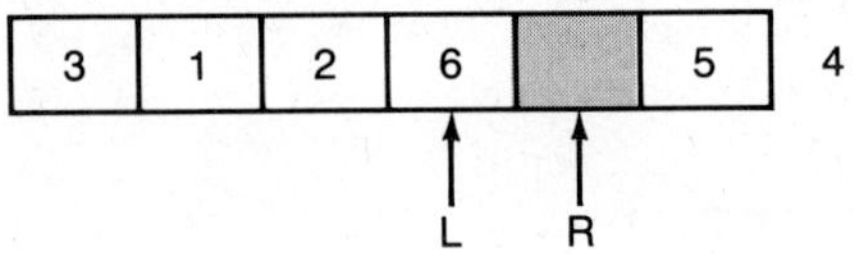

This time L selects a number greater than 4, so we copy the number selected by L to the hole marked by R, then move R one position to the left:

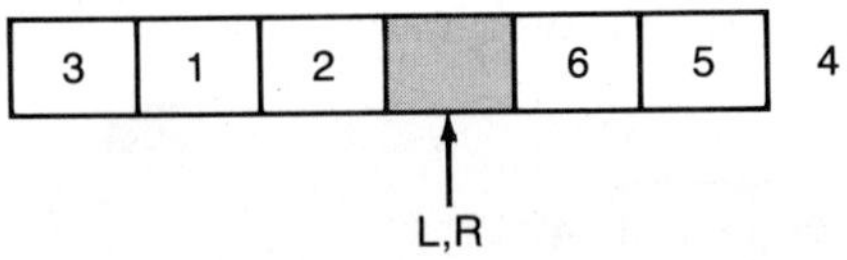

Because L and R have met, we copy the partitioning element back into the array at the position selected by L and R:

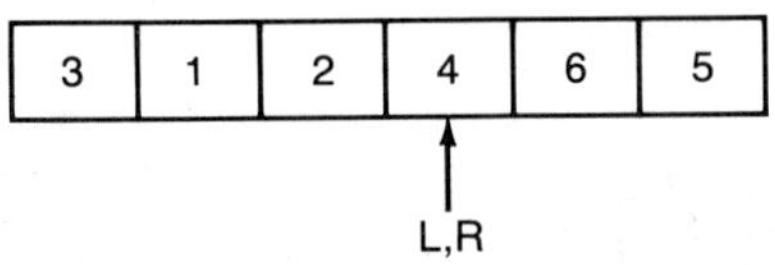

The array is now partitioned: all numbers less than 4 are left of the position marked by L and R, and all numbers greater than 4 are right of this position. We can now complete the sort by two recursive applications of Quicksort: one to sort the first three positions of the array and one to sort the last two positions.

The following `Quicksort` program uses two procedures, `SortNumbers` and `Split`, to implement the Quicksort algorithm. `Quicksort` calls `SortNumbers` to sort an array of numbers; `SortNumbers` in turn calls `Split` to partition the array. Because `SortNumbers` calls itself recursively to sort increasingly small portions of the array, its parameters include `lower` and `upper`, which define the region of the array to be sorted. After checking that the region to be sorted is not empty, SortNumbers calls Split to partition the region. Split returns a value (through the parameter middle) indicating the position of the partitioning element; SortNumbers then calls itself recursively to sort the lower part of the region (from lower to middle - 1) and the upper part of the region (from middle + 1 to upper).

```
MODULE Quicksort;
  (* uses Quicksort to sort a file of CARDINAL numbers *)

  FROM InOut IMPORT OpenInput, CloseInput, OpenOutput,
                    CloseOutput, WriteString, WriteLn,
                    ReadCard, Done, WriteCard;

  CONST maxLen = 1000;

  VAR array: ARRAY [0..maxLen-1] OF CARDINAL;
      actualLen: CARDINAL;

  PROCEDURE ReadNumbers(VAR array: ARRAY OF CARDINAL;
                        VAR numberRead: CARDINAL);
    (* reads CARDINAL numbers from a file and stores into
       array; numberRead indicates how many numbers were
       read *)
    VAR number: CARDINAL;
  BEGIN
    WriteString("Enter name of file to be sorted");
    WriteLn;
    OpenInput("NUM");
    numberRead := 0;
    LOOP
      ReadCard(number);
      IF NOT Done THEN EXIT END;
      IF numberRead > HIGH(array) THEN
        WriteString("Array overflow in ReadNumbers");
        WriteLn;
        HALT
      END;
      array[numberRead] := number;
      INC(numberRead)
    END;
    CloseInput
  END ReadNumbers;

  PROCEDURE Split(VAR array: ARRAY OF CARDINAL;
                  L, R: INTEGER; VAR middle: INTEGER);
    (* partitions region of array between L and R so that
       all values to the left of "middle" are less than or
       equal to all values to its right *)
```

```
  VAR middleNumber: CARDINAL;
BEGIN
  middleNumber := array[L];

  LOOP
    WHILE (L < R) & (middleNumber <= array[R]) DO
      DEC(R)
    END;
    IF L >= R THEN EXIT END;
    array[L] := array[R];
    INC(L);

    WHILE (L < R) & (array[L] <= middleNumber) DO
      INC(L)
    END;
    IF L >= R THEN EXIT END;
    array[R] := array[L];
    DEC(R)
  END;

  array[R] := middleNumber;
  middle := R
END Split;

PROCEDURE SortNumbers(VAR array: ARRAY OF CARDINAL;
                      lower, upper: INTEGER);
  (* sorts portion of array between lower and upper *)
  VAR middle: INTEGER;
BEGIN
  IF lower >= upper THEN RETURN END;
  Split(array, lower, upper, middle);
  SortNumbers(array, lower, middle - 1);
  SortNumbers(array, middle + 1, upper)
END SortNumbers;

PROCEDURE WriteNumbers(VAR array: ARRAY OF CARDINAL;
                       length: CARDINAL);
  (* copies CARDINAL numbers from array to a file; "length"
     indicates length of array *)
  VAR i: CARDINAL;
BEGIN
  WriteString("Enter name of output file");
  WriteLn;
  OpenOutput("NUM");
  FOR i := 0 TO length - 1 DO
    WriteCard(array[i], 1);
    WriteLn
  END;
  CloseOutput
END WriteNumbers;
```

```
BEGIN
  ReadNumbers(array, actualLen);
  SortNumbers(array, 0, actualLen - 1);
  WriteNumbers(array, actualLen)
END Quicksort.
```

Notice the use of open array parameters in the `ReadNumbers`, `Split`, `SortNumbers`, and `WriteNumbers` procedures. Alternatively, we could have allowed these procedures to access the variable `array` as a global variable.-

Multidimensional Open Arrays (OPTIONAL)

The Third Edition of *Programming in Modula-2* allows only one-dimensional open array parameters. Since the publication of the Third Edition, Wirth has stated that he is considering extending Modula-2 to allow multidimensional open arrays. His proposed extension would allow formal parameters of type

```
ARRAY OF ... ARRAY OF T
```

where the programmer may repeat the words `ARRAY OF` any number of times to indicate the number of dimensions.

Modula-2 compilers that allow this extension must provide a way to determine the actual parameter's length in each dimension. The British Standards Institution's Modula-2 Working Group has proposed one possibility based on the observation that multidimensional arrays are simply nested one-dimensional arrays. Therefore, if `A` is a multidimensional open array, the upper bound for the first dimension of `A` is `HIGH(A)`, the upper bound for the second dimension is `HIGH(A[0])`, the upper bound for the third dimension is `HIGH(A[0, 0])`, and so on. Using this convention, we would write the `MatrixAdd` procedure that appears earlier in this section as follows:

```
PROCEDURE MatrixAdd(A, B:  ARRAY OF ARRAY OF CARDINAL;
                    VAR C: ARRAY OF ARRAY OF CARDINAL);
  (* computes the matrix sum of A and B and stores it in C;
     A, B, and C must be the same size *)
  VAR i, j: CARDINAL;
BEGIN
  IF (HIGH(A) # HIGH(B)) OR (HIGH(A) # HIGH(C)) OR
     (HIGH(A[0]) # HIGH(B[0])) OR (HIGH(A[0]) # HIGH(C[0]))
  THEN
    WriteString("Length error in MatrixAdd");
    WriteLn;
    HALT
  END;
  FOR i := 0 TO HIGH(A) DO
```

```
    FOR j := 0 TO HIGH(A[0]) DO
      C[i, j] := A[i, j] + B[i, j]
    END
  END
END MatrixAdd;
```

7.2 String Types

A *string type* is any type of the form

```
ARRAY [0..n] OF CHAR
```

for n greater than or equal to 0. A *string variable* is any variable of a string type. In the following example, ShortString and LongString are string types; firstName and bookTitle are string variables:

```
TYPE ShortString = ARRAY [0..9] OF CHAR;
     LongString = ARRAY [0..49] OF CHAR;
VAR  firstName: ShortString;
     bookTitle: LongString;
```

Although *Programming in Modula-2* states that string types have a lower index bound of 0, Wirth does not make it clear whether this bound is a requirement of the language or merely a convention. Some Modula-2 compilers may allow other lower bounds without ill effects. Be aware, however, that string-handling procedures imported from a library module usually assume a lower bound of 0.

In previous chapters, we have used the term *string* to mean a sequence of characters enclosed between single or double quotes, such as

```
"Hello, how are you?"
```

For the remainder of this section, we will call this a *string literal*. "Strings" will include both string literals and string variables. The type of a string literal of length n is

```
ARRAY [0..n-1] OF CHAR
```

Thus, the type of "Hello, how are you?" is

```
ARRAY [0..18] OF CHAR
```

The quotation marks surrounding a string literal are not part of the string; we do not include them when computing its length.

Strictly speaking, the type of a one-character string literal ("A", for example) is ARRAY [0..0] OF CHAR, rather than CHAR. The distinction is purely academic, because the Third Edition of *Programming in Modula-2* states that a one-character string literal is compatible with type CHAR, effectively allowing "A" to be treated as being of either type CHAR or type ARRAY [0..0] OF CHAR as needed. (According to the Second Edition, a one-character string literal has type CHAR; this edition gives no special compatibility rule for one-character strings. Consequently, older compilers may not allow "A" as an actual parameter if the formal parameter has type ARRAY OF CHAR.)

Because string variables are arrays, Modula-2 allows all the usual array operations for strings: selecting a character in a string variable (by indexing), assigning one string to another (provided that the strings have the same type), and supplying a string as a parameter in a procedure call (if the types of actual and formal parameters are the same or if the formal parameter is an open array parameter). The only operation Modula-2 defines for string variables but not for arrays in general is the assignment of a string literal to a string variable. This operation has a special property that has important consequences for string manipulation.

When we assign a string literal to a string variable, the length of the literal need not match the length of the variable, provided that the variable is at least as long as the literal. If the literal fails to fill the entire variable, it is copied into the variable starting at the leftmost position and followed by a special terminator, the character 0C. The remaining characters in the variable have undefined values. For example, consider the assignment of the string "Modula-2" to two variables, one of the right length and one too long:

```
VAR short:  ARRAY [0..7] OF CHAR;
    long:   ARRAY [0..13] OF CHAR;
     .
     .
     .
short := "Modula-2";    (* the string fills the array *)
long  := "Modula-2";    (* the string fills positions 0 through
                           7; 0C occupies position 8 *)
```

After the two assignments, short and long look like this:

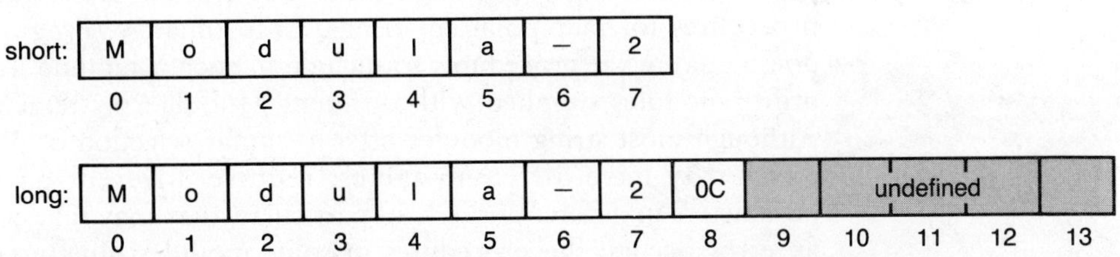

This special rule does not extend to the assignment of one string variable to another; the types of the two variables must be the same. Thus, the assignment `long := short` is illegal, even though `long` is large enough to hold the contents of `short`, because `short` and `long` do not have the same type.

A Modula-2 string variable, like any array, has a fixed length. However, Modula-2's convention of including a terminating character when a short string literal is assigned to a longer string variable allows the programmer to simulate variable-length strings. If a program needs strings whose lengths will vary as the program runs, but which will never exceed 80 characters, say, the programmer can declare a string type of length 80 and use this type to declare all the variables:

```
TYPE String80 = ARRAY [0..79] OF CHAR;
VAR string1, string2, string3: String80;
```

Whenever a program assigns a string literal to one of these variables, the character `0C` automatically terminates the string (unless it fills the variable). When the program copies one of the variables to another, the `0C` will also be copied. Thus, the `0C` character always marks the end of the variable-length string stored inside the fixed-length array.

Some Modula-2 systems require that the character `0C` terminate every string. These systems regard the string `"Modula-2"` as having length 9, rather than 8, because of the implicit `0C` character at the end of the string. As a result, the assignment

```
short := "Modula-2";
```

is illegal, because `short` has no room for the `0C` character.

A final note: Although the normal Modula-2 convention is to terminate a string with the `0C` character when it does not fill a string variable, programmers need not follow this convention. The Exercises explore one popular alternative for indicating the length of a string.

A String-handling Module

Because Modula-2 supplies no operations on strings, most Modula-2 systems provide a library module, often called `Strings` or `String`, that contains useful procedures for manipulating strings. Unfortunately, *Programming in Modula-2* doesn't say what procedures to include in such a module. As a result, the string utility modules supplied with different Modula-2 systems are rarely the same. Although most string modules offer a similar selection of procedures, the procedures may have different names, require different parameters, or expect parameters in different orders. In particular, they may take different actions when an error occurs: the procedures in some modules quietly return when an error occurs, while others terminate the program.

If the string-handling module that a Modula-2 system supplies is not satisfactory (or if the system supplies none at all), the programmer can easily write one. Modula-2's open array parameters, together with the special properties of string assignment, make it easy to write general-purpose string-handling procedures.

Section 10.2 contains both the definition and implementation parts of a library module called `String`. `String` has one distinguishing characteristic: most of its procedures have a "success" parameter indicating whether or not the procedure could perform the desired operation. After a procedure returns, the program can test this value and decide whether to continue execution or abort. All the procedures exported by `String` assume the usual Modula-2 convention: If the string stored in a variable does not fill the variable, the character 0C terminates the string.

`String` exports the following eight procedures:

- `PROCEDURE Length(str: ARRAY OF CHAR): CARDINAL;`

`Length` computes the length of the string `str`, which may be either a string literal or a string variable. If the actual parameter is a string literal or a string variable not containing the character 0C, `Length` returns `HIGH(str)` plus 1. If the actual parameter is a string variable containing a 0C character, `Length` returns the index of the leftmost 0C character.

- ```
  PROCEDURE Assign(source: ARRAY OF CHAR;
                   VAR dest: ARRAY OF CHAR;
                   VAR success: BOOLEAN);
  ```

`Assign` copies a string from `source` to `dest`. This procedure is needed when the programmer wants to copy a string from one string variable to another of a different length. (Because string variables are arrays, Modula-2 only allows assignment when the variables have the same type.) If the destination variable is not long enough to hold the source string, `Assign` copies as much of the string as possible and sets `success` to FALSE.

- ```
  PROCEDURE Insert(source: ARRAY OF CHAR;
                   VAR dest: ARRAY OF CHAR;
                   index: CARDINAL;
                   VAR success: BOOLEAN);
  ```

`Insert` inserts `source` into `dest` before the position `index`. If the value of `index` exceeds the upper index of the string stored in `dest`, then `dest` does not change and the procedure sets `success` to FALSE. If `dest` is not large enough to hold the result of the insertion, `Insert` truncates the result and stores it into `dest`, and sets `success` to FALSE.

- PROCEDURE Delete(VAR str: ARRAY OF CHAR;
                   index: CARDINAL;
                   len: CARDINAL;
                   VAR success: BOOLEAN);

  Delete removes len characters from string str starting at position index. Delete does not change str and sets success to FALSE if index lies outside the bounds of the string stored in str, or if index + len is larger than HIGH(str) + 1.

- PROCEDURE Position(pattern: ARRAY OF CHAR;
                     source: ARRAY OF CHAR;
                     VAR index: CARDINAL;
                     VAR found: BOOLEAN);

  Position searches source for an occurrence of pattern. If the search succeeds, Position sets found to TRUE and index indicates the position where the first character of pattern occurs in source. If the search does not succeed, found is FALSE and index is undefined.

- PROCEDURE Substring(source: ARRAY OF CHAR;
                      index: CARDINAL;
                      len: CARDINAL;
                      VAR dest: ARRAY OF CHAR;
                      VAR success: BOOLEAN);

  Substring attempts to copy a substring of source of length len, starting at index, to the variable dest. Substring does not change dest and sets success to FALSE if index lies outside the bounds of the string stored in source or if len is larger than HIGH(dest) + 1. If neither case holds, but index + len is larger than HIGH(source) + 1, then Substring copies as many characters as possible to dest, but sets success to FALSE.

- PROCEDURE Concat(source1: ARRAY OF CHAR;
                   source2: ARRAY OF CHAR;
                   VAR dest: ARRAY OF CHAR;
                   VAR success: BOOLEAN);

  Concat concatenates the strings source1 and source2 and puts the result in the variable dest. If the resulting string is too large to fit in dest, Concat truncates it and sets success to FALSE.

- PROCEDURE Compare(string1: ARRAY OF CHAR;
                    string2: ARRAY OF CHAR): CompareResult;

The `Compare` function compares `string1` and `string2`, returning a value of type `CompareResult`, which has the following definition:

```
TYPE CompareResult = (less, equal, greater);
```

`Compare` compares the strings from left to right until it finds one string to be less than the other or until the procedure reaches the end of either string.

EXAMPLE PROGRAM

Replacing a String in a Text File

When given two strings (the "pattern" and "replacement" strings) and a file of text, the `ReplaceString` program deletes the first occurrence of the pattern string on each line of the file and puts the replacement string in its place. Lines not containing the pattern string do not change.

`ReplaceString` performs the following actions for each line of text in the input file. First, `ReplaceString` calls `ReadLine` to read a line into a string variable named `line`. (`ReadLine` reads characters one by one from the input file until it finds an end-of-line character, represented by the constant `EOL`.) `ReplaceString` then calls the `Replace` procedure to search the line for the pattern and, if it finds the pattern, to substitute the replacement string. A call of `WriteString` then writes the line to an output file.

`Replace` uses four of the procedures `String` exports: `Length`, `Insert`, `Delete`, and `Position`. `Position` determines whether the pattern string occurs in the text line and, if so, where. If the pattern is present, `Replace` calls `Delete` to delete it (using `Length` to determine how many characters to delete) and then calls `Insert` to insert the replacement string.

`ReplaceString` depends heavily on Modula-2's convention of using the `0C` character to mark the end of a string. `ReadLine` puts the `0C` character into the `line` array. The `Length`, `Insert`, `Delete`, and `Position` procedures all assume that the marker is present. `WriteString` also uses the `0C` to determine how much of `line` to write.

```
MODULE ReplaceString;
  (* prompts for pattern and replacement strings, then copies
     input file to output file, replacing the first occurrence
     of the pattern on each line by the replacement string *)

  FROM InOut IMPORT OpenInput, CloseInput, OpenOutput,
                    CloseOutput, Read, ReadString, WriteString,
                    WriteLn, Done, EOL;

  FROM String IMPORT Length, Insert, Delete, Position;

  CONST maxLineLen = 80;
```

```
TYPE LineBuffer = ARRAY [0..maxLineLen-1] OF CHAR;

VAR line, pattern, replacement: LineBuffer;
    endOfFile: BOOLEAN;

PROCEDURE Error(message: ARRAY OF CHAR);
  (* prints an error message and terminates the program *)
BEGIN
  CloseInput;
  CloseOutput;
  WriteString(message);
  WriteLn;
  HALT
END Error;

PROCEDURE ReadLine(VAR string: ARRAY OF CHAR;
                   VAR endOfFile: BOOLEAN);
  (* reads a line of text from the input; sets endOfFile
     to TRUE if the end of the file is encountered during
     reading *)
  VAR pos: CARDINAL;
      ch: CHAR;
BEGIN
  endOfFile := FALSE;
  pos := 0;
  REPEAT
    Read(ch);
    IF NOT Done THEN
      endOfFile := TRUE
    ELSIF pos > HIGH(string) THEN
      Error("Buffer overflow in ReadLine")
    ELSE
      string[pos] := ch;
      INC(pos)
    END
  UNTIL endOfFile OR (ch = EOL);
  IF pos <= HIGH(string) THEN
    string[pos] := 0C
  END
END ReadLine;

PROCEDURE Replace(VAR source: ARRAY OF CHAR;
                  pattern, replacement: ARRAY OF CHAR);
  (* replaces the first occurrence of pattern in source by
     replacement *)
  VAR index: CARDINAL;
      found, success: BOOLEAN;
```

```
    BEGIN
      Position(pattern, source, index, found);
      IF found THEN
        Delete(source, index, Length(pattern), success);
        Insert(replacement, source, index, success);
        IF NOT success THEN
          Error("Buffer overflow in Replace")
        END
      END
    END Replace;

  BEGIN
    WriteString("Enter pattern> ");
    ReadString(pattern);
    WriteLn;
    WriteString("Enter replacement> ");
    ReadString(replacement);
    WriteLn;
    WriteString("Enter name of input file.");
    WriteLn;
    OpenInput("TXT");
    WriteString("Enter name of output file.");
    WriteLn;
    OpenOutput("TXT");

    REPEAT
      ReadLine(line, endOfFile);
      Replace(line, pattern, replacement);
      WriteString(line);
    UNTIL endOfFile;

    CloseInput;
    CloseOutput
  END ReplaceString.
```

7.3 Record Types

A *record* is a structure whose components, which may be of different types, are selected by names created by the programmer. To declare a record type, a program must list each of the components (*fields*) in the record, giving each a name and a type. For example, suppose we need to represent information about items of merchandise that a store carries. The information for a single item consists of several pieces of data of different types, so it is convenient to collect the information about the item into a record. This information might include an identifying number, a description of the item, the price of the item, and the quantity on hand:

```
TYPE StringType = ARRAY [0..19] OF CHAR;
     Item = RECORD
                number: CARDINAL;
                description: StringType;
                price: REAL;
                onHand: INTEGER
            END;
```

Figures 7.2 and 7.3 show the syntax of a record specification. The *FieldList* syntax chart is rather complicated because a record may contain a variant part. For now, we assume that a field list is a list of identifiers, followed by a colon, followed by a type; the *FieldList* syntax chart appears in Section 7.4.

Figure 7.2

RecordType

Figure 7.3

FieldListSequence

The fields of a record may be of any type, including array and record types. The `Item` type, for example, contains a field (`description`) of an array type. In a similar fashion, a record may contain another record:

```
TYPE NameString = ARRAY [0..14] OF CHAR;
     NameRecord = RECORD
                    lastName, firstName: NameString;
                    middleInitial: CHAR
                  END;
     PersonnelRecord = RECORD
                         number: [0..9999];   (* employee no. *)
                         name: NameRecord;
                       END;
```

We could have avoided declaring the `NameRecord` type, instead declaring the `name` field using the specification of `NameRecord`.

The names of record fields are local to a particular record type; they do not conflict with any other names in a program. In particular, we may use the same identifier to name fields in more than one record type. Thus, the same program may declare both the `Item` and `PersonnelRecord` types, even though they both contain a field named number. The same field name cannot appear twice in the same record, however, except within a nested record. For example, it would be legal to add a field named number to NameRecord, but not to PersonnelRecord.

One advantage of records is the increased flexibility they offer for handling a collection of related data values. Much of the time, a program will access individual fields in a record; at other times, it is more convenient to work with the record as a whole. Modula-2 allows both forms of access.

A reference to a record field consists of a record name and a field name, separated by a period. For example, suppose that we declare the variables item1 and item2 as

```
VAR item1, item2: Item;
```

To reference the number field in item1, we would write

```
item1.number
```

This notation is the same that we use for qualified identifiers (Section 2.2). Little chance of confusion arises, however, because the first identifier in a qualified identifier is a module name, not a record name.

One way to change the value of a record variable is to assign values to its fields:

```
item1.number := 143;
item1.description := "Men's black umbrella";
item1.price := 9.99;
item1.onHand := 10;
```

In general, a record field of type T has the same properties as a variable of type T; it can appear in expressions, on the left side of an assignment, and so on.

Whole records may appear in assignment statements and as parameters in procedure calls; Modula-2 allows no other whole-record operations. Instead of assigning values piecemeal to the fields of a record, a program may instead change all its fields by whole-record assignment:

```
item1 := item2;
```

This assignment statement copies item2.number to item1.number, item2.description to item1.description, and so on. Assigning one record to another requires that the types of the records be the same. (As with arrays, the terms *same*, *compatible*, and *assignment-compatible* have the same meaning.) Similarly, when we supply a record as a parameter in a procedure call, the record's type must be the same as the type of the corresponding formal parameter. To be the same, two record types must have the same name or be derived from the same type name (see Section 6.4). It is not enough for the record types to have fields with the same names and types.

EXAMPLE Updating Inventory Records

Although grouping related variables into a single record is of some value, the most important advantage of record types is their usefulness in creating other types. For example, we can use the `Item` type as the component type for an array; this structure could store information about many items of merchandise. We might also create a pointer type (Section 8.1) whose values are pointers to records of type `Item`; a program could use this type to dynamically create as many `Item` records as needed.

For example, if we assume that a store stocks no more than 1,000 different items, we could represent its entire inventory by an array of 1,000 records of type `Item`:

```
CONST maxInventory = 1000;
VAR inventory: ARRAY [1..maxInventory] OF Item;
    lastItem: [0..maxInventory];
      (* marks position of last item in inventory array *)
```

One operation that we might perform on such an array is to change the number of items on hand to reflect sales and incoming shipments. The following procedure performs this operation:

```
PROCEDURE UpdateInventory(itemNum: CARDINAL; change: INTEGER;
                          VAR found: BOOLEAN);
  (* updates inventory record for itemNum to reflect change in
     number on hand; sets found to TRUE if record is found,
     FALSE otherwise *)
  VAR currentPos: CARDINAL;
BEGIN
  currentPos := 1;
  LOOP
    IF currentPos > lastItem THEN
      found := FALSE;
      EXIT
    ELSIF itemNum = inventory[currentPos].number THEN
      INC(inventory[currentPos].onHand, change);
      found := TRUE;
      EXIT
    END;
    INC(currentPos)
  END
END UpdateInventory;
```

Designators

The `UpdateInventory` procedure uses expressions such as `inventory[currentPos].number` and `inventory[currentPos].onHand` in which an index selects an array component and then a field identifier selects a field within the component (because the array components are records). We call such an expression a *designator*. A designator is an identifier (perhaps qualified), possibly followed by any combination of the following:

a list of index expressions in brackets
a period, then a field identifier
the ^ symbol (for dereferencing a pointer—see Section 8.1)

Figure 7.4 shows the syntax of a designator.

Figure 7.4 ***Designator***

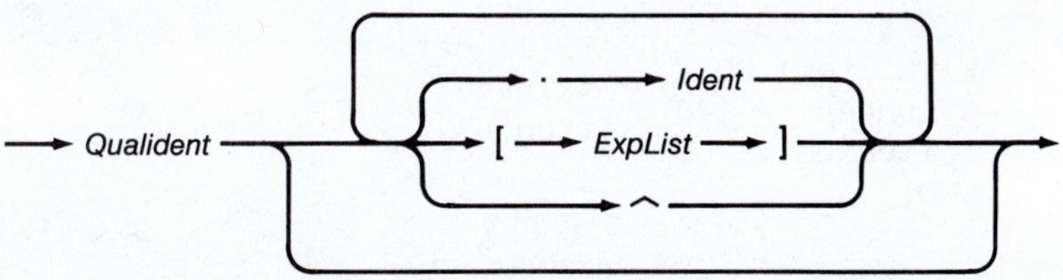

Modula-2 allows arbitrary nesting of structured types, so designators may become quite complex:

```
inventory[currentPos].description[0]
```

Designators may appear in expressions and on the left sides of assignment statements. In fact, a designator can appear wherever Modula-2 allows a variable, with one exception: The control variable in a `FOR` statement must be an identifier, not a designator.

The `WITH` Statement

Normally, a programmer refers to a record field by giving a designator for the field, consisting of a designator for the record itself, followed by a period and the name of the field. Because designators can be very long (`inventory[currentPos].number`, for example), Modula-2 supplies the `WITH` statement. When part of a program repeatedly refers to fields in the same record, the `WITH` statement allows the program to access the fields without having to name the record every time.

One common use of the WITH statement is to surround a sequence of assignments to the fields of a record:

```
WITH item1 DO
  number := 143;
  description := "Men's black umbrella";
  price := 9.99;
  onHand := 10
END;
```

When it encounters a WITH statement, a Modula-2 compiler tries to interpret each identifier mentioned inside the statement as a field in the specified record (item1 in this case). If the attempt fails, the identifier has its usual meaning. Thus, if a program contains the statement

```
WITH item1 DO
  number := 143;
  itemNum := 59
END;
```

the compiler interprets number as item1.number, but because itemNum is not the name of a field in item1, the compiler treats it as though it were not inside the WITH statement.

Figure 7.5 shows the syntax of the WITH statement. The designator that appears between WITH and DO must represent a record. Between the words DO and END, we can access fields within this record by their names alone.

Figure 7.5

WithStatement

→ WITH → *Designator* → DO → *StatementSequence* → END →

WITH statements can simplify a program and make its structure more apparent. WITH statements can also—in some cases—make a program more efficient. Consider the effect of replacing

```
inventory[currentPos].number := 143;
inventory[currentPos].description := "Men's black umbrella";
inventory[currentPos].price := 9.99;
inventory[currentPos].onHand := 10;
```

by the following:

```
WITH inventory[currentPos] DO
  number := 143;
  description := "Men's black umbrella";
  price := 9.99;
  onHand := 10
END;
```

The `WITH` statement allows the compiler to avoid repeatedly producing object code to evaluate `inventory[currentPos]`, thus making the object program smaller and faster. (Some compilers perform this optimization even when the programmer does not use the `WITH` statement.)

Modula-2 places one important restriction on the `WITH` statement: A program should not try to change the designator from within the body of a `WITH` statement. We can illustrate this point using the `LOOP` statement from the procedure `UpdateInventory`. Within the body of the loop are references to fields `inventory[currentPos].number` and `inventory[currentPos].onHand`. To avoid having to include `inventory[currentPos]` in these designators, we could enclose the `IF` statement in a `WITH` statement:

```
LOOP
  WITH inventory[currentPos] DO
    IF currentPos > lastItem THEN
      found := FALSE;
      EXIT
    ELSIF itemNum = number THEN
      INC(onHand, change);
      found := TRUE;
      EXIT
    END
  END;
  INC(currentPos)
END;
```

Modula-2 evaluates the designator `inventory[currentPos]` only when control enters the `WITH` statement. Because `currentPos` does not change inside the `WITH` statement, this version of the loop will work correctly. In contrast, consider the following version of the loop, in which the scope of the `WITH` statement has expanded to include the entire `LOOP` statement:

```
WITH inventory[currentPos] DO         (* incorrect use of WITH *)
  LOOP
    IF currentPos > lastItem THEN
      found := FALSE;
      EXIT
```

```
      ELSIF itemNum = number THEN
        INC(onHand, change);
        found := TRUE;
        EXIT
      END;
      INC(currentPos)        (* does not have the desired effect *)
    END
  END;
```

This version will not work properly. The WITH statement is entered only once, immediately after currentPos is assigned the value 1. Consequently, the designator inventory[currentPos] *always* refers to inventory[1], and the identifiers number and onHand always refer to inventory[1].number and inventory[1].onHand. As a result, the search for the item number always fails, except when the desired number is in inventory[1].number.

In general, Modula-2 compilers cannot detect this kind of error, so the programmer must write WITH statements carefully. Because of this problem, and because WITH statements can make a program difficult to understand, use them sparingly.

7.4 Records with Variant Parts

Suppose that we want to write a program to keep track of a computer store's inventory. We decide to use records to store information about each major component of a computer system, such as a system unit, monitor, or printer. However, we want a single record type, because we plan to create an array of such records. The problem is that the information we want to store for a given component depends on what kind of component it is. Each item has a manufacturer, a model, and a price, for example, but other information varies. A record that represents a printer should have a field that can hold the printing speed of the device, but this piece of information is irrelevant for other components.

This kind of problem arises so often that Modula-2 allows a record type to have a *variant part*; different records of that type can have different combinations of fields. The word CASE marks the beginning of the variant part:

```
TYPE ComponentType = (systemUnit, monitor, printer);
     StringType = ARRAY [0..19] OF CHAR;
     MechanismType = (dotMatrix, daisyWheel, laser);
     SystemComponent =
       RECORD
         manufacturer: StringType;
         model: StringType;
```

```
  CASE kind: ComponentType OF
    systemUnit: memory: CARDINAL;    (* in units of 1K *)
                numDiskDrives: CARDINAL;
                hardDisk: BOOLEAN |
    monitor:    color: BOOLEAN;
                numLines, numColumns: CARDINAL |
    printer:    mechanism: MechanismType;
                speed: CARDINAL  (* characters/second *)
  END;
  price: REAL
END;
```

Every record of type `SystemComponent` has fields named `manufacturer`, `model`, `kind`, and `price`. The `kind` field is a *tag field*: its value indicates whether the record represents a system unit, a monitor, or a printer. The value of the tag field selects a particular group of fields, called a *variant*. In the example, if the value of `kind` is `systemUnit`, the record has additional fields named `memory`, `numDiskDrives`, and `hardDisk`. The values `monitor` and `printer` select the other two variants. Thus, the record has three possible appearances, depending on the value of the `kind` field (see Figure 7.6).

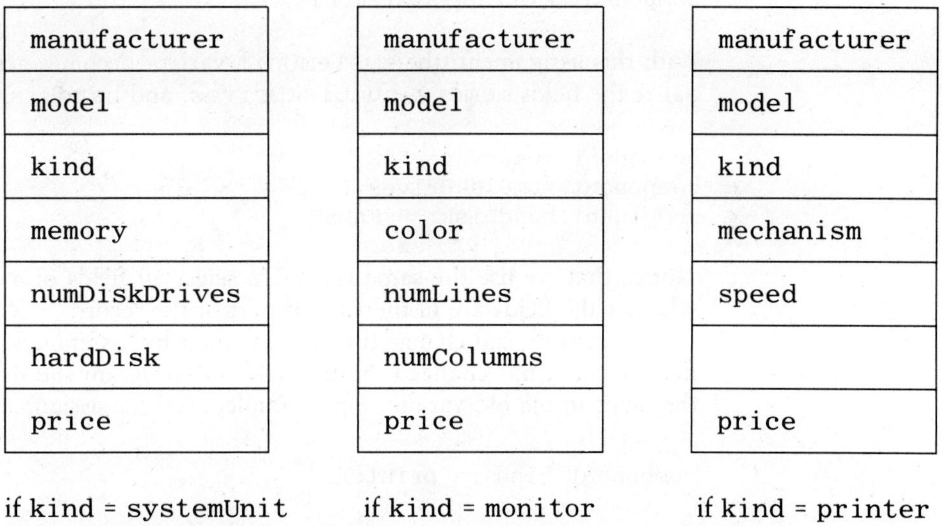

Figure 7.6
The Three Forms of a SystemComponent Record

Because the fields in one variant are never in use at the same time as the fields in the other variants, Modula-2 compilers typically save space by overlaying variants in memory, as Figure 7.6 suggests. (This figure does not show the exact overlay, which depends on the amount of storage required for each field, among other factors.) When the variants require different amounts of space, a compiler allocates enough space for the largest variant. Thus, when `kind` has the value printer, some space within the record remains unused (hence the blank space in the third diagram).

A program should not reference the fields within the variant part of a record until the program has assigned a value to the tag field. When a program assigns the tag field a value, the variant with a case label corresponding to that value becomes *active*; then the program may legally refer to the fields listed within that variant. Suppose, for example, that we have declared the variable component as follows:

```
VAR component: SystemComponent;
```

We can immediately initialize the fields manufacturer, model, and price, which are not in the variant part of the record:

```
component.manufacturer := "IBM";
component.model := "Personal Computer";
component.price := 1000.00;
```

We cannot reference the other fields in the record until we have given the tag field a value. We might choose to initialize the tag field to systemUnit:

```
component.kind := systemUnit;
```

With this assignment, the systemUnit variant becomes active, and we can initialize the fields memory, numDiskDrives, and hardDisk:

```
component.memory := 512;
component.numDiskDrives := 2;
component.hardDisk := FALSE;
```

Notice that we use the same syntax to select all fields of a record, regardless of whether the fields are in the variant part of the record.

A program can change the active variant by assigning a new value to the tag field. Once it has changed the tag field, the program should no longer reference the fields in the old variant. For example, after the assignment

```
component.kind := printer;
```

the printer variant becomes active. References to the fields mechanism and speed are now legal, but references to memory, numDiskDrives, and hard-Disk are not.

What happens if a program attempts to reference a field in a variant that is not active? For example, what if the statement

```
WriteCard(component.speed, 1);
```

is executed when the `systemUnit` variant is active? In theory, a Modula-2 system could check the value of the `kind` field before each reference to a field in the variant part of the record. Unfortunately, this test must be performed during program execution, not during compilation. Because this test can noticeably increase a program's execution time, most systems don't perform it. Without the check, the call of `WriteCard` produces a meaningless number. This example illustrates the danger of using records with variant parts: A reference to an inactive variant generally does not terminate the program, but does result in erroneous operation; unfortunately, this kind of programming error is hardest to fix. To prevent incorrect use of a record with a variant part, a program should always use an `IF` or CASE statement to check the value of the tag field if any doubt exists about which variant is active. For example, we can ensure that the call of `WriteCard` is valid by using an `IF` statement to check the value of the `kind` field:

```
IF component.kind = printer THEN
  WriteCard(component.speed, 1)
ELSE
  WriteString("Illegal reference to speed field");
  WriteLn;
  HALT
END;
```

Having seen records with variant parts, we can now give the syntax chart for a field list. A field list can have three possible forms, of which we have seen two:

a list of field names followed by a type
a variant part, beginning with the word CASE and containing several variants

A third possibility is that a field list may be empty. The *FieldList* syntax chart (Figure 7.7) shows all three options.

Figure 7.7 ***FieldList***

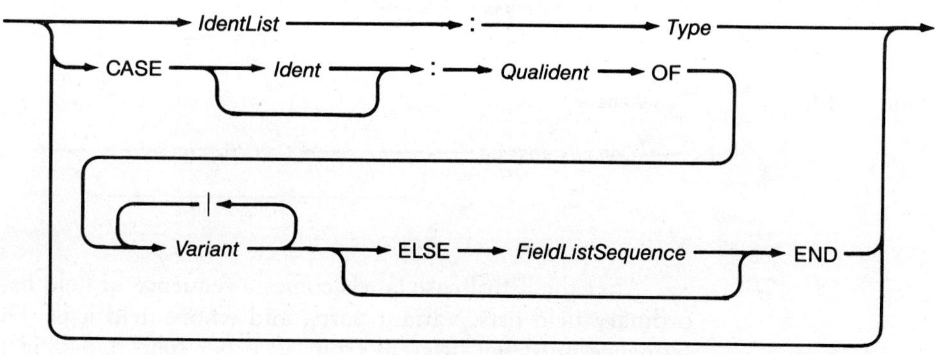

A variant part of a record resembles a CASE statement. The | symbol separates the cases in a CASE statement, as well as the variants in a variant part.

(Consequently, programmers tend to format variants in much the same way as cases in a CASE statement. In particular, some programmers prefer to put the | symbol at the beginning of each variant, rather than at the end. See Section 4.2 for an example of this style.) In a CASE statement, the value of the case expression indicates which one of several statement sequences will be executed; in a record with a variant part, the value of the tag field indicates which variant is currently active. Furthermore, the syntax chart for a variant (Figure 7.8) closely resembles the chart for a case.

Figure 7.8

Variant

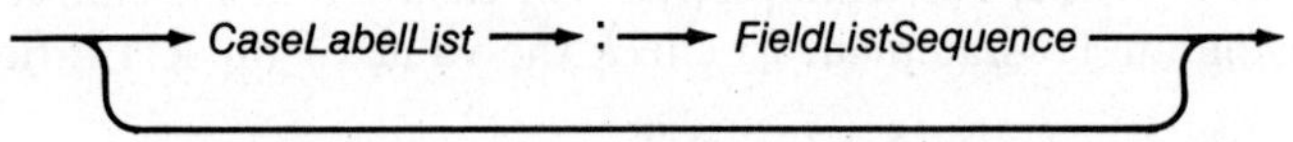

Each variant begins with a list of *case labels*: constant expressions of the same type as the tag field. (In *Programming in Modula-2*, Wirth does not mention any restrictions on the type of the tag field. However, because of the similarity between variant parts and CASE statements, it is reasonable to assume that a tag field is subject to the same restrictions as a case expression, which must be of a basic type—other than REAL or LONGREAL—or an enumeration or subrange type. Some compilers may prohibit tag fields of type LONGINT.) No case label can appear in two different variants. The *CaseLabelList* and *CaseLabels* syntax charts (Figures 7.9 and 7.10) are the same ones used in defining the syntax of the CASE statement.

Figure 7.9

CaseLabelList

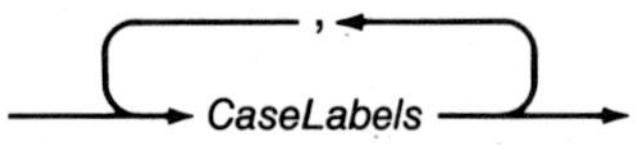

Figure 7.10

CaseLabels

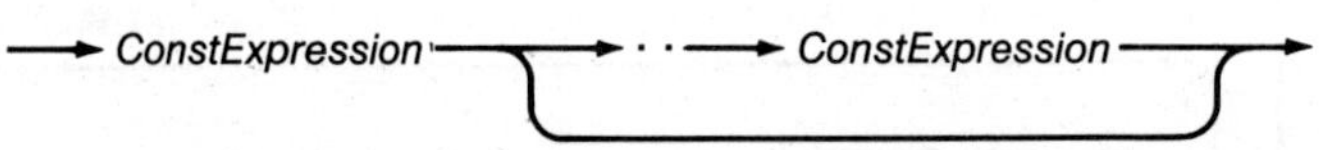

After the list of case labels comes a sequence of field lists, which may include ordinary field lists, variant parts, and empty field lists. The field names in this sequence must be different from all other field names in the record, including those belonging to fields outside the variant part, fields in other variants, and the tag field itself.

If we carefully examine these syntax charts, we see that Modula-2 allows great flexibility in declaring records with variant parts:

The Tag Field of a Variant Part May Be Omitted.

Consider the following example:

```
TYPE ClothingType = (shirt, pants);
     MensClothing =
       RECORD
         CASE : ClothingType OF
           shirt: neckSize: REAL;
                  sleeveLength: CARDINAL |
           pants: waist, inseam: CARDINAL
         END
       END;
```

(According to the Third Edition of *Programming in Modula-2*, the colon that normally follows the name of the tag field must be present even if the programmer omits the name itself; the presence of the colon clearly shows that what remains is the *type* of the tag field. The Second Edition states that the colon must be omitted if the name of the tag field is.) A record of type `MensClothing` has two possible appearances:

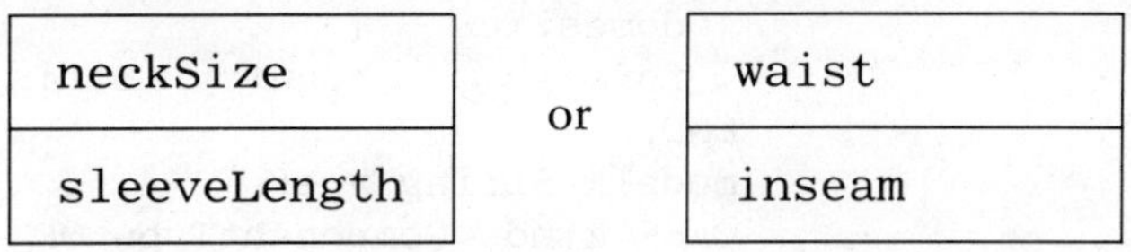

No tag field distinguishes between the two variants, so the program is responsible for remembering which variant is active.

Because omitting the tag field makes it more difficult to check that the program is using variants properly, programmers almost always include the tag field. The only reason for omitting it is to save space. (Modula-2 compilers normally do not allocate memory for a missing tag field. When the programmer omits the tag field, the specification of the tag field type serves only as a form of documentation.)

A Variant May Be Empty.

This possibility first appears in the Third Edition of *Programming in Modula-2*; the Second Edition does not allow empty variants. The change makes the placement of | symbols less critical: at least one | must separate two variants, but additional | symbols may occur before the first variant, after the last variant, or between variants. In particular, the programmer is free to use | as a variant terminator rather than a separator:

```
TYPE MensClothing =
       RECORD
         CASE : ClothingType OF
           shirt: neckSize: REAL;
                  sleeveLength: CARDINAL |
           pants: waist, inseam: CARDINAL |     (* terminator *)
         END
       END;
```

A Record May Have More Than One Variant Part.

For example, we might revise the SystemComponent type to include the country in which a component is manufactured:

```
TYPE OriginType = (domestic, foreign);
     SystemComponent =
       RECORD
         manufacturer: StringType;
         CASE origin: OriginType OF
           domestic:    |
           foreign:     country: StringType
         END;
         model: StringType;
         CASE kind: ComponentType OF
           systemUnit: memory: CARDINAL;     (* in units of 1K *)
                       numDiskDrives: CARDINAL;
                       hardDisk: BOOLEAN |
           monitor:    color: BOOLEAN;
                       numLines, numColumns: CARDINAL |
           printer:    mechanism: MechanismType;
                       speed: CARDINAL  (* characters/second *)
         END;
         price: REAL
       END;
```

A record of type SystemComponent now has two tag fields: origin and kind. If origin has the value foreign, then the field country will give the name of the country of origin, but if origin has the value domestic, we need no other field. (Modula-2 does not require that a variant actually contain any fields; this ability can be useful, as the example shows.)

A Variant Part of a Record May Itself Contain a Variant Part.

The following revised declaration of `SystemComponent` allows us to specify the color of a monochrome monitor:

```
TYPE SystemComponent =
       RECORD
         manufacturer: StringType;
         model: StringType;
         CASE kind: ComponentType OF
           systemUnit: memory: CARDINAL;     (* in units of 1K *)
                       numDiskDrives: CARDINAL;
                       hardDisk: BOOLEAN |
           monitor:    CASE color: BOOLEAN OF
                         FALSE: screenColor: (amber, green) |
                         TRUE:
                       END;
                       numLines, numColumns: CARDINAL |
           printer:    mechanism: MechanismType;
                       speed: CARDINAL  (* characters/second *)
         END;
         price: REAL
       END;
```

A Variant Part May Contain an ELSE *Clause.*

If an ELSE clause is present, it must follow the last variant, but precede the END that closes the variant part. We can reference the fields listed in the ELSE clause only when the current value of the tag field does not match any of the case labels (hence none of the variants are active). Returning to the `MensClothing` example, suppose that we enlarge the `ClothingType` enumeration to include other types of clothing, all of which require only a single size. The only change we need make is to add an ELSE clause to `MensClothing`:

```
TYPE ClothingType = (shirt, pants, hat, belt, socks, shoes);
     MensClothing =
       RECORD
         CASE : ClothingType OF
           shirt: neckSize: REAL;
                  sleeveLength: CARDINAL |
           pants: waist, inseam: CARDINAL
         ELSE
           size: REAL   (* others require only one size *)
         END
       END;
```

An ELSE clause can be particularly useful if listing all values of the tag field, either individually or in ranges, would be inconvenient (as might be the case if the tag field were to have type INTEGER, for example).

7.5 Set Types

In mathematics, a *set* is an unordered collection of elements without duplicates. The elements of a set come from a universe of possible values. For example, if the universe is

{violet, blue, green, yellow, orange, red}

then sets over this universe include

{blue, yellow}
{red, blue, green}
{}

({} is the empty set—the set with no elements.) Because sets are unordered, the sets

{blue, yellow}
{yellow, blue}

are the same. Duplicate elements do not change the value of a set, so the following sets are the same:

{orange, red}
{orange, red, orange, red}
{red, orange, red, red}

Sets appear in Modula-2 in almost exactly the same form as in mathematics. To declare a set type whose values are sets of colors, we could use the following type declarations:

```
TYPE Colors = (violet, blue, green, yellow, orange, red);
     SetOfColors = SET OF Colors;
```

Colors is the *base type* of SetOfColors: the universe from which the elements of a `SetOfColors` value come. A total of 64 (2^6) sets are possible using the six values in `Colors`, so `SetOfColors` has 64 values.

Figure 7.11

SetType

To specify a new set type, the programmer need only give the base type (see Figure 7.11). The base type must be either an enumeration type (or a subrange of an enumeration type) or a subrange of `CARDINAL`. In the former case, the enumeration type must have at most `N` values, and in the latter case, the upper bound of the subrange must be at most `N - 1`, where `N` is a constant that will vary from one Modula-2 system to another. According to Wirth, `N` will be the number of bits in a word on the computer on which the Modula-2 system is running or "a small multiple thereof." This restriction allows Modula-2 compilers to represent sets using only one word (or a few words) of memory, thus saving both space and execution time (most operations on single-word sets require only a single machine instruction). Common values of `N` are 16 and 32. Our examples assume that `N` is 16, in which case the following are both legal set types:

```
TYPE SetOfChannels = SET OF [2..13];
     YellowRedSet = SET OF [yellow..red];
```

The following set types are *illegal* if `N` is 16:

```
TYPE IntSet = SET OF [-1..10];   (* subrange of INTEGER *)
     CardSet = SET OF [1..16];   (* upper bound exceeds N - 1 *)
     CharSet = SET OF CHAR;      (* illegal base type *)
```

Some compilers allow much larger sets. When the base type is a subrange, some compilers limit the extent of the subrange, not its upper bound. Some compilers allow the base type to be `CHAR` or even a subrange of `LONGINT`.

Modula-2 has one standard set type, called `BITSET`. If it were not a standard type, we could define `BITSET` as follows:

```
TYPE BITSET = SET OF [0..W-1];
```

where `W` is implementation-dependent (but usually the computer's word length). The elements of a `BITSET` value normally correspond to the bits in one word of memory. The BITSET type is useful primarily for low-level (machine-dependent) programming; we discuss it in more detail in Section 11.1.

Although we consider sets to be structured values, they actually have little in common with arrays and records. We have already seen two important differences. First, the elements of a set must be CARDINAL or enumeration values; the components of an array or record can be of any type. Second, a set value occupies a fixed amount of memory, typically only a single word; arrays and records can be arbitrarily large. Later in the section we point out other ways in which sets differ from arrays and records.

Constructing Set Values

Modula-2 allows the programmer to write an expression that constructs a set value from its elements. The language does not provide this ability for the other structured types. The programmer cannot construct an array or record from its components (except for a string, which is an array constructed from individual characters).

To construct a set, the programmer specifies the name of the set type and the elements to include in the set:

```
SetOfColors{red, blue, green, yellow}
```

We separate the elements of a set with commas, enclose them between the symbols { and }, and precede the entire expression by a (possibly qualified) identifier, which must be the name of a set type (see Figure 7.12).

Figure 7.12 ***Set***

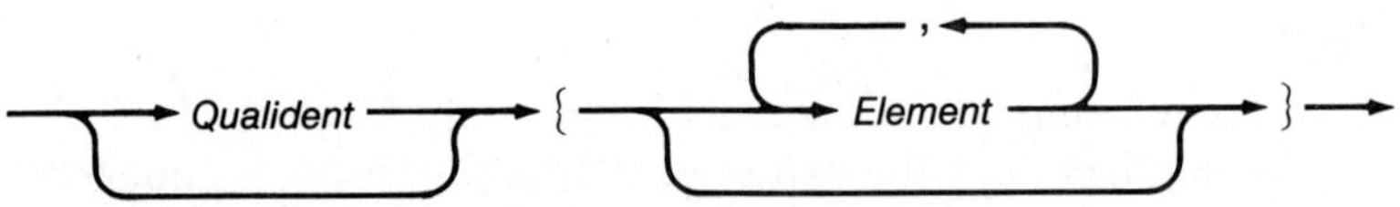

Including the name of the set type allows a Modula-2 compiler to perform type-checking (notice that a compiler cannot usually deduce the type of a set from its elements). If we omit the name of the set type, the type of the set is BITSET by default. If no elements appear between the { and } symbols, the set is empty:

```
SetOfColors{}
```

We can use either individual expressions or ranges to specify set elements (see Figure 7.13). Thus, we could write the set containing `red`, `blue`, `green`, and `yellow` as

```
SetOfColors{red, blue..yellow}
```

Figure 7.13

Element

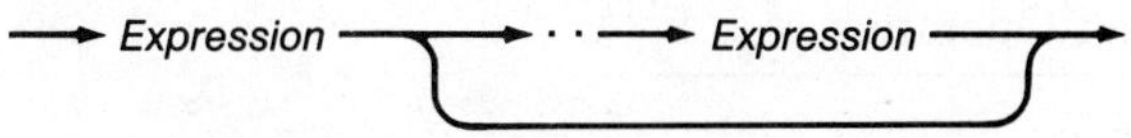

Set elements are often constants, but in general may be expressions. For example, the following set contains one element, the color whose ordinal number is `i`:

```
SetOfColors{VAL(Colors, i)}
```

The Second Edition of *Programming in Modula-2* allowed programmers to use only constant expressions (and ranges bounded by constant expressions) to specify set elements; the Third Edition allows arbitrary expressions.

Set Assignment

A program may assign a set value to a variable of a set type. For example, after the declaration

```
VAR set1, set2, set3: SetOfColors;
```

the following assignment stores the set `{red, blue, green, yellow}` in the variable `set1`:

```
set1 := SetOfColors{red, blue, green, yellow};
```

As usual, the type of the designator on the left side of an assignment must be assignment-compatible with the type of the expression on the right side. For set types, as with arrays and records, the terms *same*, *compatible*, and *assignment-compatible* are synonymous.

Set Operators

The existence of set operators and set expressions is another feature that distinguishes sets from arrays and records. The same symbols that represent the four arithmetic operators for REAL numbers also represent the four set operators (see Table 7.1).

Table 7.1 Set Operators

+	union
-	difference
*	intersection
/	symmetric difference

If A and B are sets, then:

The *union* of A and B is the set of elements belonging to A or B (or both).
The *difference* of A and B is the set of elements belonging to A but not to B.
The *intersection* of A and B is the set of elements belonging to both A and B.
The *symmetric difference* of A and B is the set of elements belonging either to A or to B, but not both.

We can use Venn diagrams to visualize the four set operations. In each of the diagrams in Figure 7.14, the circles marked A and B represent the sets A and B; the shaded portion represents the result of the operation shown underneath the diagram.

Figure 7.14
Venn Diagrams of Set Operations

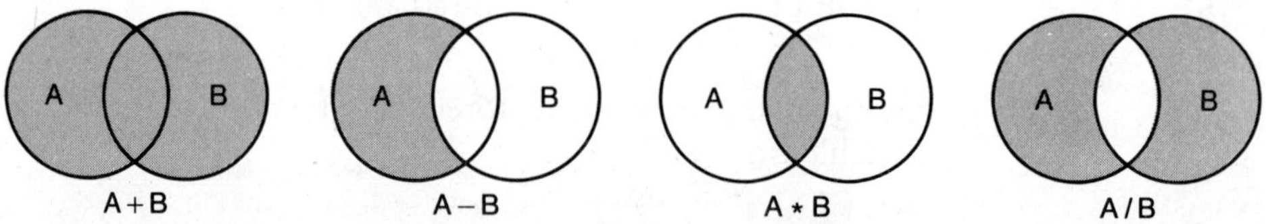

After the assignments

```
set1 := SetOfColors{red, blue, yellow};
set2 := SetOfColors{green, red, orange};
```

the following expressions have the indicated values:

Expression	*Value*
`set1 + set2`	`{red, green, blue, yellow, orange}`
`set1 - set2`	`{blue, yellow}`
`set1 * set2`	`{red}`
`set1 / set2`	`{blue, yellow, green, orange}`

The four set operators require that their operands be of the same set type; the result is always of this type.

Set Constants

Modula-2 does not permit record constants, and strings are the only array constants allowed. The existence of set expressions, however, makes possible the declaration of set constants:

```
CONST NoColors = SetOfColors{};
      BlueOnly = SetOfColors{blue};
      RedOnly = SetOfColors{red};
      RedAndBlue = BlueOnly + RedOnly;
```

The declaration of a set constant is no different from the declaration of any other kind of constant. We can use any (constant) set expression to declare a set constant. We must have previously declared a set type (such as `SetOfColors`) that appears in a constant declaration.

Relational Operators

Table 7.2 shows the five relational operators for sets.

Table 7.2 Relational Operators for Sets

=	equal
<> or #	not equal
<=	subset of
>=	superset of
IN	member of

Each of these produces a BOOLEAN result. As usual, the symbols <> and # are interchangeable. Notice that the relational operators for sets do not include the < and > symbols.

The IN operator tests whether a given value belongs to a set. After the assignment

```
set1 := SetOfColors{blue, green, yellow};
```

the following expressions have the values shown:

Expression	*Value*
green IN set1	TRUE
orange IN set1	FALSE

In an expression of the form *e* IN *s*, the type of *e* must be compatible with the base type of *s*.

The operators = and # (or <>) test whether two sets are equal or not equal. Two sets are equal if they have the same elements. After the assignments

```
set1 := SetOfColors{violet, blue, green, yellow};
set2 := SetOfColors{blue, yellow, green, violet};
set3 := SetOfColors{blue, yellow, violet};
```

the following expressions have the values shown:

Expression	*Value*
set1 = set2	TRUE
set1 = set3	FALSE
set2 # set3	TRUE

When applied to sets, the operators <= and >= test the subset and superset relations, respectively. If A and B are sets, A is a *subset* of B if every element of A is also an element of B; A is a *superset* of B if every element of B is an element of A. After the assignments

```
set1 := SetOfColors{yellow, orange};
set2 := SetOfColors{green, orange, yellow};
set3 := SetOfColors{yellow, green, orange};
```

the following expressions have the indicated values:

Expression	*Value*
`set1 <= set2`	TRUE
`set1 >= set2`	FALSE
`set2 <= set3`	TRUE
`set2 >= set3`	TRUE

The operators =, <>, #, <=, and >= require operands of the same set type.

Note that `set1 <= set2` has the value TRUE if `set1` and `set2` are equal; we say that `set1` is an *improper* subset of `set2` in this case. To test whether `set1` is a *proper* subset of `set2`, the programmer must use the expression

```
(set1 <= set2) & (set1 # set2)
```

Similar remarks apply to the >= operator; to test whether `set1` is a proper superset of `set2`, use the expression

```
(set1 >= set2) & (set1 # set2)
```

The INCL and EXCL Procedures

Modula-2 provides two standard procedures, INCL ("include") and EXCL ("exclude"), for updating the value of a set. INCL adds an element to a set (if it is not already there). EXCL removes an element from a set; it has no effect if the element does not belong to the set.

```
set1 := SetOfColors{orange, blue};
INCL(set1, green);        (* set1 is now {orange, blue, green} *)
INCL(set1, orange);       (* no change *)
EXCL(set1, blue);         (* set1 is now {orange, green} *)
EXCL(set1, yellow);       (* no change *)
```

If `s` is a variable of type `SetType`, the call

```
INCL(s, x);
```

is equivalent to the statement

```
s := s + SetType{x};
```

and the call

```
EXCL(s, x);
```

is equivalent to

```
s := s - SetType{x};
```

where `x` is any expression belonging to the base type of `SetType`.

`INCL` and `EXCL` are similar to the standard procedures `INC` and `DEC`. We use the `INCL` and `EXCL` procedures, like `INC` and `DEC`, to make incremental changes to a variable. As with `INC` and `DEC`, a Modula-2 compiler may generate more efficient object code for a call of `INCL` or `EXCL` than for a corresponding assignment statement; furthermore, a call of `INCL` or `EXCL` is often simpler than an assignment statement.

EXAMPLE Checking Weekly Schedules

Suppose that a store employs two part-time workers, each of whom works only a few days a week. We can represent each employee's weekly schedule as a value of type `SetOfDays`, where `SetOfDays` is the following set type:

```
TYPE Days = (Sun, Mon, Tue, Wed, Thu, Fri, Sat);
     SetOfDays = SET OF Days;
```

Assume that the store is open seven days a week, and that it needs at least one worker each day, and needs both on Saturday. The following procedure checks the workers' schedules to ensure that at least one person works each day and that both work on Saturday.

```
PROCEDURE CheckSchedule(sched1, sched2: SetOfDays);
  (* checks that every day of the week is included on at
     least one schedule and that Saturday is on both *)
  VAR daysCovered: SetOfDays;
      day: Days;
BEGIN
  daysCovered := sched1 + sched2;
  FOR day := Sun TO Sat DO
    IF NOT (day IN daysCovered) THEN
      WriteDay(day);
      WriteString(" is not covered");
      WriteLn
    END
  END;
  IF NOT (Sat IN sched1 * sched2) THEN
    WriteString("Fewer than two workers on Saturday");
    WriteLn
  END
END CheckSchedule;
```

`CheckSchedule` calls a procedure `WriteDay` to write the name of a `Days` value. Although we do not give `WriteDay` here, it is similar to the `WritePlanet` procedure in Section 6.2.

Standard Pascal

1. In Pascal array specifications, brackets always enclose index types:

```
array [char] of integer
array [1..10] of char
array [1..10, 1..10] of real
```

2. In Level 0 of Standard Pascal, a formal parameter of an array type must have a fixed size:

```
const low = 1;
      high = 100;
type ArrayOfReal = array [low..high] of real;

procedure Square(var A: ArrayOfReal);
  var i: integer;
begin
  for i := low to high do
    A[i] := A[i] * A[i]
end;
```

Level 1 also allows conformant array parameters:

```
procedure Square(var A: array [low..high: integer] of real);
  var i: integer;
begin
  for i := low to high do
    A[i] := A[i] * A[i]
end;
```

Here `low` and `high` are not constants, but *bound identifiers* whose values change to conform to the bounds of the actual parameter. Conformant array parameters may be multidimensional.

3. A Pascal string type is a one-dimensional packed array of characters whose index type is an integer subrange with a lower bound of 1:

```
type String10 = packed array [1..10] of char;
```

4. Pascal allows string comparison using the relational operators =, <>, <, <=, >, and >=.

Modula-2

1. In Modula-2 array specifications, brackets do *not* enclose index types:

   ```
   ARRAY CHAR OF INTEGER
   ARRAY [1..10] OF CHAR
   ARRAY [1..10], [1..10] OF REAL
   ```

   The brackets in the second and third examples belong to the subrange type `[1..10]`.

2. A Modula-2 array parameter may be fixed in size or may be *open*. The declaration of a fixed-size array parameter is the same as in Pascal:

   ```
   CONST low = 1;
         high = 100;
   TYPE ArrayOfReal = ARRAY [low..high] OF REAL;

   PROCEDURE Square(VAR A: ArrayOfReal);
     VAR i: CARDINAL;
   BEGIN
     FOR i := low TO high DO
       A[i] := A[i] * A[i]
     END
   END Square;
   ```

   An open array parameter has type `ARRAY OF T`, where `T` is a type name. If a formal parameter has type `ARRAY OF T`, then a corresponding actual parameter can be an array of any length, provided that its components have type `T`. Within the body of the procedure, the index type of the formal parameter is a subrange of `CARDINAL` whose lower bound is 0 and whose upper bound is the value of the standard function `HIGH` when applied to the name of the formal parameter.

   ```
   PROCEDURE Square(VAR A: ARRAY OF REAL);
     VAR i: CARDINAL;
   BEGIN
     FOR i := 0 TO HIGH(A) DO
       A[i] := A[i] * A[i]
     END
   END Square;
   ```

   Only the first dimension of a multidimensional array parameter may be open.

3. A Modula-2 string type is a one-dimensional array of characters whose index type is a `CARDINAL` subrange with a lower bound of 0:

   ```
   TYPE String10 = ARRAY [0..9] OF CHAR;
   ```

4. Modula-2 does not allow use of the relational operations with strings. However, most Modula-2 systems provide a library module for string manipulation; this module usually contains a procedure for comparing strings.

Standard Pascal

5. In Pascal, assignment of a string literal to a string variable is legal only if both have the same length:

```
var str: String10;
  .
  .
  .
str := 'TooShort  ';   (* blanks are needed to pad string *)
```

6. In a Pascal record specification, no field list may be empty. Exactly one semicolon must separate adjacent field lists. A semicolon may follow the last field list, but Pascal allows no other superfluous semicolons.

```
type Coordinate = record
                      x, y: real
                    end;
     Circle = record
                 center: Coordinate;
                 radius: real;      (* superfluous semicolon *)
               end;
```

7. In Pascal's `with` statement, a single statement (which may be compound) follows the word do. Between the words `with` and do, Pascal allows a list of record variables, separated by commas. (A `with` statement with multiple record variables is equivalent to nested `with` statements involving single record variables.)

```
with circ, center do   (* circ is a variable of type Circle *)
  begin
    x := 3.5;           (* circ.center.x := 3.5   *)
    y := -10.0;         (* circ.center.y := -10.0 *)
    radius := 5.0       (* circ.radius   := 5.0   *)
  end;
```

8. In Pascal, the variant part of a record must come at the end of the record. A record can have only one variant part (although the variant part may itself have a variant part). Parentheses must enclose each field list within a variant; semicolons separate variants. A variant must not be empty.

```
type Shape = (circle, rectangle);
     Figure = record
                 location: Coordinate;
                 case tag: Shape of
                   circle:     (radius: real);
```

Modula-2

5. Modula-2 allows the assignment of a string literal to any string variable of equal or greater length:

```
VAR str: String10;
        .
        .
        .
str := "TooShort";     (* no padding needed *)
```

When the string literal is too short to fill the variable, it is copied left-justified and terminated by the character 0C.

6. In a Modula-2 record specification, field lists may be empty. This rule allows the programmer to insert extra semicolons before the first field list, after the last field list, and between field lists.

```
TYPE Coordinate = RECORD;            (* superfluous semicolon *)
                     x, y: REAL
                   END;
     Circle =  RECORD
                  center: Coordinate; ;
                                       (* superfluous semicolon *)
                  radius: REAL;        (* superfluous semicolon *)
               END;
```

7. Modula-2's WITH statement requires a statement sequence after the word DO; the word END must follow the statement sequence. Only a single record variable may appear between the words WITH and DO; however, Modula-2 allows nested WITH statements.

```
WITH circ DO              (* circ is a variable of type Circle *)
  WITH center DO
    x := 3.5;             (* circ.center.x := 3.5   *)
    y := -10.0            (* circ.center.y := -10.0 *)
  END;
  radius := 5.0           (* circ.radius   := 5.0   *)
END;
```

8. In Modula-2, the variant part of a record need not come at the end of the record. A record can have more than one variant part. Because variant parts may occur anywhere in a record, the word END must terminate each variant part. Parentheses do not enclose field lists within a variant part; the | symbol separates variants. Variants can be empty, allowing superfluous | symbols.

```
TYPE Shape = (circle, rectangle);
     Figure = RECORD
                 location: Coordinate;
                 CASE tag: Shape OF
```

Standard Pascal

```
                rectangle: (length, width: real)
            end;
```

9. In the variant part of a Pascal record, each variant begins with a list of constant values.

```
type Planets = (Mercury, Venus, Earth, Mars, Jupiter, Saturn,
                Uranus, Neptune, Pluto);
     PlanetData = record
                    distanceFromSun: real;
                    case tag: Planets of
                      Mercury, Venus, Mars, Jupiter, Saturn,
                      Uranus, Neptune, Pluto:
                        (distanceFromEarth: real);
                      Earth: ();
                  end;
```

All values of the tag field must appear in one of these lists.

10. If the tag field is omitted in a variant part, the colon that normally follows the tag field is also omitted.

```
type Figure = record
                location: Coordinate;
                case: Shape of
                  circle:    (radius: real);
                  rectangle: (length, width: real)
              end;
```

11. The base type of a Pascal set can be any ordinal type (`boolean`, `char`, `integer`, or an enumerated or subrange type), although Pascal allows implementations to restrict the number of values in the base type.

```
                circle:     radius: REAL |
                rectangle: length, width: REAL
              END
            END;
```

9. A Modula-2 variant begins with a list of case labels, specified either as constant expressions or as ranges (two constant expressions separated by the .. symbol).

```
TYPE Planets = (Mercury, Venus, Earth, Mars, Jupiter, Saturn,
                Uranus, Neptune, Pluto);
     PlanetData = RECORD
                    distanceFromSun: REAL;
                    CASE tag: Planets OF
                      Mercury, Venus, Mars..Pluto:
                        distanceFromEarth: REAL |
                      Earth:
                    END
                  END;
```

A variant part may include an ELSE clause; fields listed in this clause are active whenever the value of the tag field fails to match any of the case labels.

```
TYPE PlanetData = RECORD
                    distanceFromSun: REAL;
                    CASE tag: Planets OF
                      Earth:
                    ELSE
                      distanceFromEarth: REAL
                    END
                  END;
```

10. If the tag field is omitted in a variant part, the colon that normally follows the tag field remains.

```
TYPE Figure = RECORD
                location: Coordinate;
                CASE : Shape OF
                  circle:     radius: REAL |
                  rectangle: length, width: REAL
                END
              END;
```

11. The base type of a Modula-2 set must be either an enumeration type (or a subrange thereof) with at most N values or a subrange of CARDINAL whose upper bound is at most N - 1, where N is system-defined. N is usually the word length or a small multiple of the word length.

Standard Pascal

12. Pascal provides no predefined set types.

13. Brackets enclose Pascal set values:

```
type Days = (Sun, Mon, Tue, Wed, Thu, Fri, Sat);
     SetOfDays = set of Days;
var daySet: SetOfDays;
        .
        .
        .
daySet := [Sun, Tue..Sat];
```

14. The only set operations defined in Pascal are + (union), - (difference), and * (intersection).

15. Pascal has a number of fairly complicated compatibility rules for sets; these rules stem from the fact that a compiler cannot always determine the type of a set expression. Pascal requires assignment compatibility for assignment statements. Operands in a set expression must belong to the same canonical set-of-T; furthermore, either both operands or neither must be packed. (The canonical set-of-T is the "apparent" type of a set. For example, the value `[1..10]` belongs to the canonical set of `integer`). All the relational operators except `in` require that their operands belong to the same canonical set-of-T and that either both or neither be packed. In the expression *e* `in` *s*, if *e* belongs to the type `T1`, then *s* must belong to the canonical set-of-`T1`.

16. Pascal does not allow the definition of set constants.

17. Pascal provides no procedures for adding an element to a set or removing an element from a set; programmers must use the union and difference operators:

```
daySet := daySet + [Wed];
daySet := daySet - [Thu];
```

18. Pascal provides four structured types: arrays, records, sets, and files.

Modula-2

12. Modula-2 provides one standard set type, BITSET, which has the following definition:

```
TYPE BITSET = SET OF [0..W-1];
```

The value of W, although system-dependent, is usually the length of a word.

13. Modula-2 set values are enclosed in braces and preceded by the name of the set type:

```
TYPE Days = (Sun, Mon, Tue, Wed, Thu, Fri, Sat);
     SetOfDays = SET OF Days;
VAR daySet: SetOfDays;
          .
          .
          .
daySet := SetOfDays{Sun, Tue..Sat};
```

If the programmer omits the type name, the set is of type BITSET by default.

14. In addition to the set operations of Pascal, Modula-2 also provides the operator / (symmetric difference). The symmetric difference of sets A and B is the set of elements that are in either A or B but not in both.

15. Modula-2 requires that the designator and expression in a set assignment have the same type. Operands in a set expression must have the same type. All the relational operators except IN require operands of the same set type. In the expression *e* IN *s*, the type of *e* must be compatible with the base type of *s*.

16. Modula-2 allows the declaration of set constants:

```
CONST weekdays = SetOfDays{Mon..Fri};
```

17. Modula-2 provides two standard procedures, INCL and EXCL, for set manipulation. INCL adds an element to a set, while EXCL removes an element from a set:

```
INCL(daySet, Wed);     (* daySet := daySet + SetOfDays{Wed} *)
EXCL(daySet, Thu);     (* daySet := daySet - SetOfDays{Thu} *)
```

18. Modula-2 does not provide file types. Programs manipulate files through library modules such as FileSystem (Section 13.3).

Standard Pascal

19. In Pascal, any of the four structured types (arrays, records, sets, or files) can be declared `packed`, thereby instructing the compiler to minimize the storage allocated to a value of the type (at the expense of increasing the time to access a component of the structure). Pascal also provides two procedures called `pack` and `unpack` for converting a structure from an unpacked representation to a packed one and vice-versa.

Modula-2

19. Modula-2 does not provide a method to declare that the values of a structured type are to be packed, nor does it furnish procedures for packing and unpacking. Programmers can use Modula-2's low-level features (Chapter 11) to achieve the effect of packing.

EXERCISES

Section 7.1

1. Write a program that computes the frequency of letters in a file of text. The output of the program should look as follows:

```
A  101
B   12
C    5
D    8
     .
     .
     .
```

   The count for a letter should include the number of times the letter appears in either uppercase or lowercase form. Hint: Keep the frequency counts in an array of type `ARRAY['A'..'Z'] OF CARDINAL`. Use `OpenInput` to open the file and `CloseInput` to close it.

2. Write a procedure that searches a 10 x 10 array for a number n. The heading of the procedure should be

```
PROCEDURE SearchArray (A: SquareArray; n: CARDINAL;
                       VAR i, j: CARDINAL;
                       VAR found: BOOLEAN);
```

   where `SquareArray` has the following declaration:

```
TYPE SquareArray = ARRAY [1..10], [1..10] OF CARDINAL;
```

   If `SearchArray` finds `n`, it should give `found` the value `TRUE` and set the values of `i` and `j` to indicate the row and column in which `n` was found. If it does not find `n`, `SearchArray` should set `found` to `FALSE`.

3. Assume that the array `A` in exercise 2 is sorted by both row and column (that is, the numbers in each row and column increase or stay the same when going from left to right or top to bottom). Use this information to make `SearchArray` more efficient. Hint: `SearchArray` need never examine more than 19 components of `A`.

4. Write a procedure called `ReverseVector` that, when given a one-dimensional array of `REAL` values, rearranges the components of the array so that the last component is first, the next-to-last is second, and so on. Use an open array parameter.

5. Write a function that evaluates a polynomial of the form

$$p(x) = a_n x^n + a_{n-1} x^{n-1} + \ldots + a_1 x + a_0$$

   The heading of the function should be

```
PROCEDURE EvaluatePoly(a: ARRAY OF REAL; x: REAL): REAL;
```

The values `a[0]`, `a[1]`, ..., `a[HIGH(a)]` contain the coefficients a_0, a_1, ..., a_n, respectively. Hint: A polynomial can be evaluated efficiently using Horner's rule:

$$p(x) = ((((a_n x + a_{n-1})x + a_{n-2})x + \ldots)x + a_1)x + a_0$$

6. Revise the function `FindIndexOfMax` so that it accepts a second parameter, `lowerBound`, indicating the true lower bound of the actual parameter corresponding to `A`. Using `lowerBound`, `FindIndexOfMax` should adjust the value that it returns to reflect the true index bounds of the array supplied to it. What are the advantages and disadvantages of this method?

7. Show how the value returned by `FindIndexOfMax` would be adjusted if the index range of the actual parameter is `['A'..'J']`.

Section 7.2

8. The usual Modula-2 rule for indicating the end of a string (termination with the `0C` character) is not the only convention possible. A popular alternative is to store the length of a string variable in its first component (whose index is 0). For example, suppose that `str` is a variable of type `ARRAY [0..255] OF CHAR`. After an assignment of the string `"Modula-2"` to `str`, it would have the following appearance:

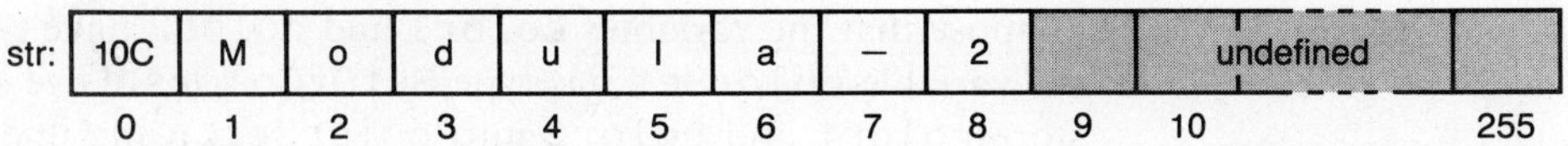

The character `10C` stored in component 0 of `str` indicates the length of the string that follows (the ordinal number of `10C` is 8, the length of `"Modula-2"`). Components 1 through 8 of `str` contain the characters in `"Modula-2"`. With this convention, a program cannot use a normal Modula-2 assignment statement to assign a string literal to a string variable. Instead, the program must call a procedure, perhaps named `AssignLiteral`. Write this procedure.

9. Write the `Assign` procedure of the `String` module using the convention of exercise 8.

10. Write the `Length` procedure of the `String` module using the convention of exercise 8.

11. What are the advantages and disadvantages of the convention described in exercise 8, as compared to the usual Modula-2 convention?

12. The procedures exported by the `String` module contain many parameters of type `ARRAY OF CHAR`. The designers of this module used variable parameters only when absolutely necessary; most parameters are value

parameters. What would be some of the advantages and disadvantages of using variable parameters for all ARRAY OF CHAR parameters belonging to these procedures?

13. Rewrite the `Replace` procedure in the `ReplaceString` program so that it replaces *all* occurrences of the pattern string, not just the first occurrence.

Section 7.4

14. Write a declaration of a record type called `Publication` whose values represent citations of articles and books. `Publication` should contain a variant part with two variants, one for articles and one for books. The variant for an article should include the name of the magazine, the volume and issue number, and the starting and ending page numbers of the article. The variant for a book should include the publisher's name, city, and state. The fixed part of the record should contain the author's name, the title of the article or book, and the year of publication.

15. Write a procedure that, when supplied with a record of type `SystemComponent`, will print the values of the fields in the record (with suitable captions). Use a CASE statement to determine which variant is active.

16. Section 7.4 stated that, if a variant part of a record has no tag field, "the program is responsible for remembering which variant is active." Describe at least two ways that a program could do so.

Section 7.5

17. Suppose that the variables `color1` and `color2` have type `Colors` and that the variable `colorSet` has type `SetOfColors`. Give at least three ways to store `color1` and `color2` into `colorSet`, using one or more statements. (For example, if `color1` has the value `blue` and `color2` has the value `yellow`, `colorSet` should have the value `{blue, yellow}`.)

18. Show two ways in which to express the / (symmetric difference) set operator in terms of the other three set operations.

19. Write a procedure named `WriteSetOfColors` capable of writing a value of type `SetOfColors`. For example, the output produced by the call

```
WriteSetOfColors(SetOfColors{red, yellow, green});
```

might be

```
{green, yellow, red}
```

The procedure need not display the elements of the set in any particular order.

8 Pointer and Procedure Types

Chapters 6 and 7 covered Modula-2's unstructured and structured types. Pointer and procedure types, the only Modula-2 types not discussed in previous chapters, are the subject of Chapter 8.

Section 8.1 explains pointer types and dynamic storage allocation. A pointer value "points to" an anonymous variable created during program execution. Pointers often point to records that themselves contain pointers. This combination of record and pointer types allows the construction of linked data structures, including lists, trees, and graphs.

Section 8.2 presents procedure types, whose values are procedures. Procedure types make possible the declaration of procedure variables. A program can assign a procedure to a procedure variable and later activate it by a "call" of the variable. A programmer can also use procedure types to write procedures that accept other procedures as parameters and functions that return procedures.

Pointer types and procedure types have little in common with Modula-2's other types. Pointer values and procedure values are not "data" in the traditional sense. Both are indirect references—to anonymous variables in the case of pointer types, and to procedures in the case of procedure types. A program must "dereference" a pointer value to access the anonymous variable to which it points; a program must "call" a procedure value. Unlike the values of other Modula-2 types, neither pointers nor procedure values are human-readable.

We can think of both pointer values and procedure values as machine-level addresses. A pointer value is the address of an anonymous variable; consequently, we can use pointers as addresses when we do low-level programming (Chapter 11). Many Modula-2 systems represent a procedure value as an address (the address of the procedure's object code), although the language does not require such representation.

8.1 Pointer Types

Some programs are difficult to write using data structures of fixed sizes. For example, consider a program that maintains a list of names and telephone numbers, allowing the user to add new names at any time and to delete old names. Because the program does not know the maximum number of names in advance, it cannot store the names and numbers in an array. In such a program, *dynamic storage allocation* (and deallocation) is useful. Dynamic storage allocation is the allocation of storage during the execution of a program, in response to requests by the program. The program just described would perform both dynamic allocation and deallocation. When the user wants to add a new name to the list of names and numbers, the program requests enough space to store the name and associated phone number. When the user removes a name from the list, the program can release the space used for that name and phone number and can then use it for a new name (or for some other purpose). The space occupied by names and phone numbers will vary during the execution of the program, increasing when the user adds a name to the list and decreasing when the user deletes one.

In Modula-2, variables may be created dynamically as a program executes. Because these variables are not declared in the program, they have no names; they are *anonymous*. A language that allows anonymous variables must provide some way to refer to these variables so that we can assign values to them and later retrieve the values. Modula-2 provides *pointers* for this purpose. A pointer is a reference to an anonymous variable.

Defining Pointer Types

A pointer variable is not free to point to any anonymous variable; it must point only to anonymous variables of a single type. (Despite not having a name, each anonymous variable has a type.) We must include this type in the specification of the pointer type.

For example, suppose that a program is to dynamically allocate anonymous variables of type `Complex`:

```
TYPE Complex = RECORD
                  realPart, imagPart: REAL
               END;
```

The following declaration creates a type whose values are pointers to records of type `Complex`:

```
TYPE PtrToComplex = POINTER TO Complex;
```

We can then use `PtrToComplex` to declare pointer variables:

```
VAR ptr1, ptr2: PtrToComplex;
```

The variables `ptr1` and `ptr2` do not take on `Complex` values; instead, the value of each is a pointer to an anonymous variable of type `Complex`. Modula-2 does not allow ptr1 and ptr2 to point to ordinary program variables; they can point only to anonymous (dynamically allocated) variables. Furthermore, ptr1 and ptr2 are *bound* to a single type (Complex, in our example)—they cannot point at anonymous variables of other types. (We can circumvent these restrictions when we use pointers for low-level programming; see Chapter 11.)

The syntax chart for a pointer type (Figure 8.1) is simple. The type pointed to

Figure 8.1 ***PointerType***

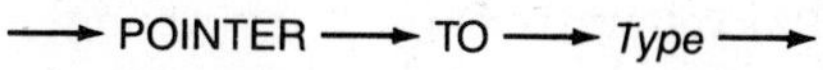

can be any standard or programmer-defined type; in practice, it is usually a record type. We can even use an anonymous type to define a pointer type:

```
TYPE PtrToCoordinate = POINTER TO
                           RECORD
                             x, y: REAL
                           END;
```

Creating Anonymous Variables

We can draw the pointer variable ptr1 as a box containing a pointer to an anonymous variable. Before we have assigned ptr1 a value, it is undefined:

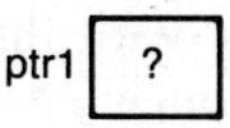

In Modula-2, pointer variables (like variables in general) are not guaranteed any particular initial value. Programs that fail to initialize pointer variables may produce the wrong results or fail during execution.

To create an anonymous variable, a program must call a storage allocation procedure. Modula-2 provides no standard procedure for this purpose. A programmer can either use an allocation procedure imported from a library module (normally provided as part of a Modula-2 system) or write a customized allocation procedure. In Wirth's library, the Storage module exports an allocation procedure named ALLOCATE. ALLOCATE requires two parameters: a pointer variable p and a CARDINAL value n. ALLOCATE creates an anonymous variable using n units of storage (usually words or bytes, depending on the system) and modifies p to point to this new variable. The programmer need not know the value of n; Modula-2 supplies a standard function SIZE that will compute it. If T is a type name, SIZE(T) is the amount of storage required to hold a value of type T. (The programmer can also apply SIZE to a variable to determine the amount of storage required for the variable.) In our example, ptr1 is to point to a variable of type Complex, so our call to ALLOCATE contains SIZE(Complex) as the second parameter:

```
ALLOCATE(ptr1, SIZE(Complex));
```

Warning: Be careful to apply SIZE to the type of the anonymous variable, not to the pointer type itself:

```
ALLOCATE(ptr1, SIZE(PtrToComplex));     (* wrong! *)
```

Using the name of the pointer type will probably cause the program to allocate the wrong amount of space for the anonymous variable, causing subtle errors during program execution. (Most of the time, the amount of storage required for an anonymous variable is greater than the amount required for a pointer value. When the program allocates too little space for the anonymous variable, it will appear to overlap another anonymous variable; changes to one of the two variables will affect the other in unpredictable ways.) A Modula-2 compiler cannot detect this error, because ALLOCATE is a low-level procedure that accepts any CARDINAL value as its second parameter.

The Second Edition of *Programming in Modula-2* specifies a different method of creating anonymous variables. Compilers that conform to this edition provide a standard procedure called NEW. Such compilers translate the call

```
NEW(ptr1);
```

into a call of ALLOCATE. The programmer must import ALLOCATE from a library module (or otherwise provide a procedure with this name). The SIZE function is not standard in the Second Edition, although a program may import it from the SYSTEM module. (The meaning of SIZE is also somewhat different in the Second Edition. See Section 11.2 for a discussion of SIZE and the related function TSIZE.) Some compilers that conform to the Third Edition of Wirth's book may still offer NEW as a standard procedure.

If a call of ALLOCATE fails because of insufficient storage, it terminates the program. For most programs, termination is proper, because the program could not continue without the requested storage. Some programs, however, may wish to recover and continue execution. For this reason, Wirth's Storage module provides the Available procedure:

```
PROCEDURE Available(size: CARDINAL): BOOLEAN;
```

By calling Available, a program can determine—before calling ALLOCATE—whether the desired amount of storage is available:

```
IF Available(SIZE(Complex)) THEN
  ALLOCATE(ptr1, SIZE(Complex))
```

```
ELSE
    (* attempt to recover *)
END;
```

Pointer Operations: Dereferencing, Assignment, and Comparison

After the call of ALLOCATE given earlier, ptr1 has a value: it points to a newly created (anonymous) variable of type Complex:

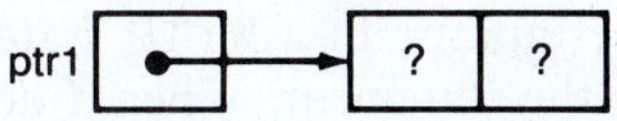

The new variable has no value, however. The programmer can assign it one in the following way:

```
ptr1^.realPart := 5.0;
ptr1^.imagPart := 1.2;
```

The expression ptr1^ serves as a name for the record that ptr1 points to; the programmer can reference fields within this record by using the field names as selectors. After the assignment to the fields of ptr1^, it has the following appearance:

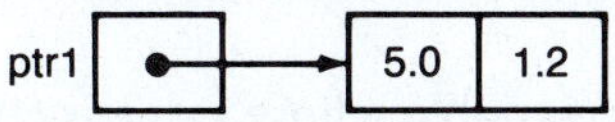

The process of forming a name for an anonymous variable by appending the symbol ^ to a pointer variable is called *dereferencing*. Dereferencing is one of the three operations that we can use to form a designator (Section 7.3). We can combine it freely with the other two operations: selecting an array component and selecting a record field. If p is of type POINTER TO T, we can use the designator p^ in exactly the same way as any variable of type T (with one exception: p^ may not be the control variable in a FOR statement).

It is normally an error to dereference a pointer variable whose value is undefined. However, a pointer variable—regardless of its value—may be dereferenced without error if the function SIZE is applied to the result. Consider the type PtrToCoordinate, whose values are pointers to records of an anonymous type. If ptr is a variable of type PtrToCoordinate, we must allocate space for an anonymous variable by the call

```
ALLOCATE(ptr, SIZE(ptr^));
```

The type to which ptr points has no name, so SIZE must have ptr^ as its parameter (recall that SIZE allows either a type name or a variable as its parameter). Because SIZE is evaluated during program compilation rather than during program execution, the value of ptr is irrelevant.

If a pointer variable points to a record, the dereferenced variable can appear as the designator in a WITH statement to allow easy access to the record's fields:

```
WITH ptr1^ DO
  realPart := 5.0;
  imagPart := 1.2
END;
```

As we saw in Section 7.3, the designator in a WITH statement should not be changed from within the body of the statement. When a dereferenced pointer is used as the designator, the pointer should not be altered inside the body of the WITH statement.

A program can assign the value NIL to a pointer variable to indicate that it does not currently point to an anonymous variable:

```
ptr1 := NIL;
```

NIL is a Modula-2 standard identifier that represents the "empty pointer." Modula-2 considers NIL to belong to every pointer type, so we may assign it to any pointer variable. After assigning NIL to ptr1, we draw ptr1 as follows:

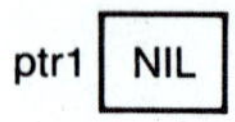

It is illegal to dereference a pointer variable whose value is NIL. The manual for a particular Modula-2 system will specify the effect of dereferencing a NIL pointer. Typically, a test is made before each pointer reference to ensure that the pointer is not NIL; if it is, a run-time error results. Some systems allow the programmer to disable this check in order to improve the program's execution speed; this is not recommended, particularly during program development.

We may assign the value of one pointer variable to another pointer variable:

```
ptr2 := ptr1;
```

The types of the two variables must be the same; in the case of pointer types, *same*, *compatible*, and *assignment-compatible* have the same meaning. If ptr1 has a non-NIL value, the assignment makes ptr2 point to the same anonymous variable as ptr1:

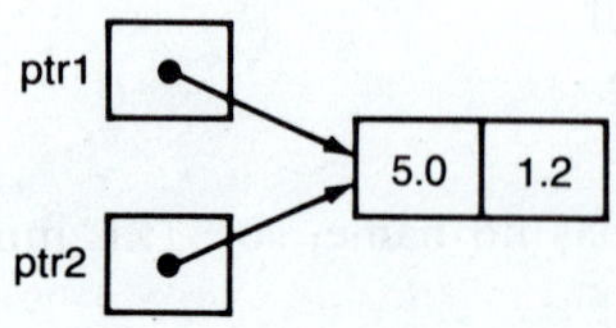

The similar-looking assignment

```
ptr2^ := ptr1^;
```

has a completely different effect: it copies the contents of the anonymous variable `ptr1^` to the anonymous variable `ptr2^`. For example, if `ptr1` and `ptr2` point to different anonymous variables before the assignment, then `ptr1` and `ptr2` have the following appearance afterward:

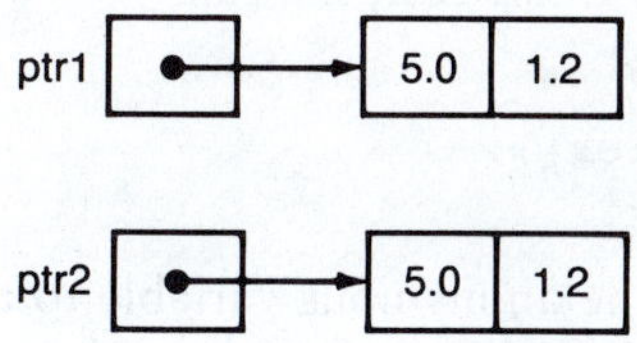

This assignment is legal only if `ptr1` and `ptr2` contain valid pointer values.

Functions may return pointer values:

```
PROCEDURE MakeComplex(realPart, imagPart: REAL): PtrToComplex;
  (* creates an anonymous variable of type Complex and returns
     a pointer to it *)
  VAR temp: PtrToComplex;
BEGIN
  ALLOCATE(temp, SIZE(Complex));
  temp^.realPart := realPart;
  temp^.imagPart := imagPart;
  RETURN temp
END MakeComplex;
```

A call of such a function may appear on the right side of an assignment:

```
ptr1 := MakeComplex(5.0, 1.2);
```

The only relational operations allowed on pointer values are tests for equality and inequality. Two pointer values are equal only if both point to the same anonymous variable or if both are `NIL`. Pointers being tested for equality or inequality must have the same type; however, we can compare any pointer for equality or inequality with `NIL`.

Disposing of Anonymous Variables

What happens to an anonymous variable when the variable that points to it is assigned a new value? If another pointer variable does not point to the anonymous variable, it becomes *garbage*—we have no way to access it. Losing anonymous variables this way is not necessarily a problem; however, if a program loses too many, it may eventually exhaust the pool of storage from which it obtains anonymous variables. Fortunately, the same library module that exports a procedure for dynamic storage allocation normally also exports a deallocation procedure. In Wirth's `Storage` module, this procedure is called DEALLOCATE. Once a program has deallocated an anonymous variable, the space that it occupied can be reused when the program requests a new anonymous variable. The parameters for DEALLOCATE are the same as the parameters for ALLOCATE. If `ptr1` points to an anonymous variable of type `Complex`, the call

```
DEALLOCATE(ptr1, SIZE(Complex));
```

returns the storage allocated for the anonymous variable to the pool of available storage. The value of `ptr1` after the call is system-dependent, although many versions of DEALLOCATE set `ptr1` to NIL.

The Second Edition of *Programming in Modula-2* specified that Modula-2 systems must provide a standard procedure called `DISPOSE` for disposing of anonymous variables. A call of `DISPOSE` looks like this:

```
DISPOSE(ptr1);
```

The compiler translates each call of `DISPOSE` into a call of DEALLOCATE, so the programmer must import DEALLOCATE from a library module or provide it in the program. The `DISPOSE` procedure is not standard in the Third Edition, although systems can still provide it.

DEALLOCATE, like ALLOCATE, can be dangerous to use. One danger is that the size given when a program deallocates an anonymous variable may not match the size specified when the variable was allocated. Deallocating less than the full size results only in a loss of space, but deallocating too much space may cause subtle errors.

Another danger of using DEALLOCATE occurs when two or more pointers point to the same anonymous variable. If both `ptr1` and `ptr2` point to the same variable, then disposing of the variable via `ptr1` leaves `ptr2` pointing to a variable that no longer exists (we say that `ptr2` is a *dangling pointer*). Any subsequent use of `ptr2` may have disastrous effects; worse still, the error can be extremely difficult to find. The following example illustrates the problem:

```
ALLOCATE(ptr1, SIZE(Complex));
ptr1^.realPart := 5.0;
ptr1^.imagPart := 1.2;
         .
         .
         .
```

```
ptr2 := ptr1;
      .
      .
      .
 DEALLOCATE(ptr1, SIZE(Complex));
      .
      .
      .
WriteReal(ptr2^.realPart, 10);
   (* error: ptr2 points to a variable that no longer exists *)
```

The error is easy to spot in this example; however, if these statements were spread over a large program, we would find it difficult to detect—at the call of `WriteReal`—that `ptr2` is dangling.

EXAMPLE

Using Pointers to Construct Linked Lists

Pointers and dynamic storage allocation support the construction of linked structures. A linked structure is a collection of *nodes*, each of which contains one or more pointers to other nodes. A node is just a record in which one or more fields are pointers.

The simplest linked structure is the *linked list*. A linked list consists of a number of nodes, each of which contains one or more pieces of data plus a pointer; the pointers cause the nodes to form a chain:

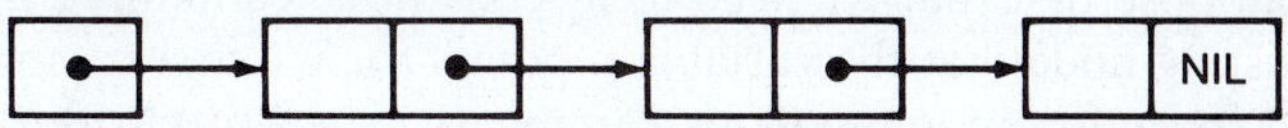

A pointer variable points to the first node in the list, the first node points to the second node, and so forth. The last node contains `NIL` in its pointer field.

To illustrate linked lists, we show how to define and manipulate a linked list whose nodes contain single characters. First, we must declare two types: `CharNode`, the type of a node in the list, and `CharList`, the type of a pointer to one of these nodes. A value of type `CharNode` will be a record with two fields: `char` (the character stored in the node) and `next` (a pointer to the next node in the list).

```
TYPE CharList = POINTER TO CharNode;
     CharNode = RECORD
                  char: CHAR;
                  next: CharList   (* points to the next node *)
                END;
```

The declaration of `CharList` contains a forward reference to `CharNode`. In general, the declaration of a pointer type may refer to a type not yet declared;

without this capability, we could not create linked data structures. The appearance of a forward reference in a pointer type specification is the only exception to the general Modula-2 rule that a program must declare an entity before using it in another declaration.

We can draw a value of type CharNode as a box with two cells named char and next:

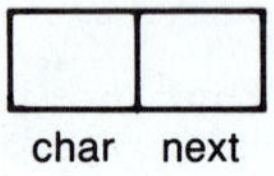

Using this notation, a list of characters would look like this:

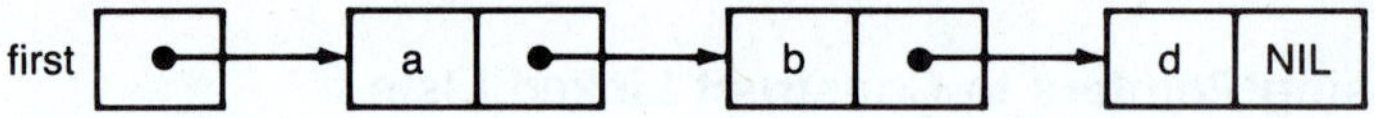

The variable first (of type CharList) points to the first node on the list (of type CharNode). The list is empty (has no nodes) if the value of first is NIL.

We can modify the structure of a linked list in two ways: (1) by inserting a new node into the list and (2) by deleting a node from the list. We now look at each of these operations in turn.

The task of inserting a node can be separated into two cases, depending on whether or not we intend to insert the node after an existing node or at the beginning of the list (so that it becomes the first node).

Suppose first that we need to insert a node containing the character ch after an existing node that the variable p points to. We first create a new node by allocating space for an anonymous variable of type CharNode:

```
ALLOCATE(new, SIZE(CharNode));
```

We then store the desired character in the node:

```
new^.char := ch;
```

We next set the pointer in the new node to point to the node following p^:

```
new^.next := p^.next;
```

Finally, we set the pointer in p^ to point to the new node.

```
p^.next := new;
```

Figure 8.2 shows the result when we insert a node containing 'c' into a list that contains 'a', 'b', and 'd'. We insert the new node immediately after the node containing 'b'.

Figure 8.2
Insertion of a Node into a List

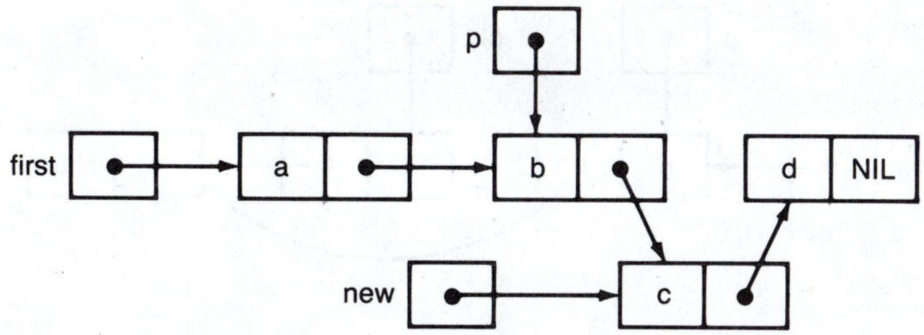

The procedure `InsertAfter` performs the operation just described.

```
PROCEDURE InsertAfter(p: CharList; ch: CHAR);
  (* creates a node containing ch and adds it to the list just
     after the node pointed to by p; p must be non-NIL *)
  VAR new: CharList;
BEGIN
  ALLOCATE(new, SIZE(CharNode));
  new^.char := ch;
  new^.next := p^.next;
  p^.next := new
END InsertAfter;
```

The operation of inserting a node at the beginning of a list is only slightly different. After creating the new node and storing the desired data in it, we make the new node point to the first node on the list, then make `first` point to the new node, as the following procedure shows.

```
PROCEDURE InsertAtFront(VAR first: CharList; ch: CHAR);
  (* creates a node containing ch and adds it to the front of
     the list pointed to by first; first may be NIL *)
  VAR new: CharList;
BEGIN
  ALLOCATE(new, SIZE(CharNode));
  new^.char := ch;
  new^.next := first;     (* make new node point to first node *)
  first := new            (* make first point to new node *)
END InsertAtFront;
```

We can also divide into two cases the operation of deleting a node from a list, depending on whether or not another node precedes the node we want to delete. In the first case, suppose that p points to the node preceding the one we want to delete. We first set a temporary pointer (stored in the variable `old`) to point to the node to be deleted. We then alter the pointer in `p^` to point to the node following `old^`. Finally, we dispose of the deleted node by calling DEALLOCATE. For example, suppose that we delete the second node from a list containing the characters `'a'`, `'b'`, and `'c'`. Figure 8.3 shows the appearance of the list immediately before we destroy `old^`.

Figure 8.3
Deletion of a Node from a List

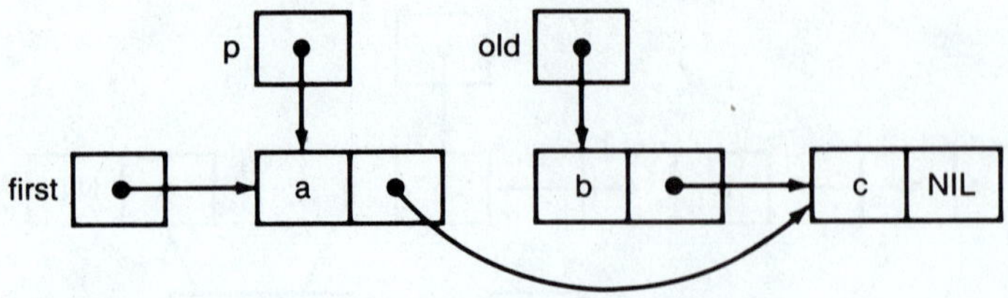

The procedure `DeleteAfter` performs the operation just described.

```
PROCEDURE DeleteAfter(p: CharList);
  (* deletes the node immediately following p; p must be
     non-NIL *)
  VAR old: CharList;
BEGIN
  old := p^.next;
  p^.next := old^.next;
  DEALLOCATE(old, SIZE(CharNode))
END DeleteAfter;
```

The operation of deleting the first node on the list is similar:

```
PROCEDURE DeleteAtFront(VAR first: CharList);
  (* deletes the first node; first must be non-NIL *)
  VAR old: CharList;
BEGIN
  old := first;
  first := first^.next;
  DEALLOCATE(old, SIZE(CharNode))
END DeleteAtFront;
```

Before deleting a node, both `DeleteAfter` and `DeleteAtFront` are careful to save a pointer to the next node in the list. Consider what would happen if `DeleteAtFront` tried to delete the first node without saving a reference to the second node:

```
DEALLOCATE(first, SIZE(CharNode));
first := first^.next;
```

Because DEALLOCATE may have changed the value of `first` (setting it to NIL, for example), the second statement may not have the desired effect.

For examples of how to use the procedures `InsertAfter`, `InsertAtFront`, `DeleteAfter`, and `DeleteAtFront`, see Section 10.3, where we use them to build a module that exports a "set of characters" type.

EXAMPLE **Using Pointers to Construct Binary Trees**

Perhaps the most common linked structure, other than the linked list, is the *binary tree*. Each node in a binary tree contains one or more data fields plus two pointer fields. (Our examples assume one data field containing a CARDINAL number.) The two pointers point to the *left descendant* and *right descendant* of the node. In the following tree, for example, the left descendant of the node labeled 31 is the node labeled 21 and the right descendant is the node labeled 40:

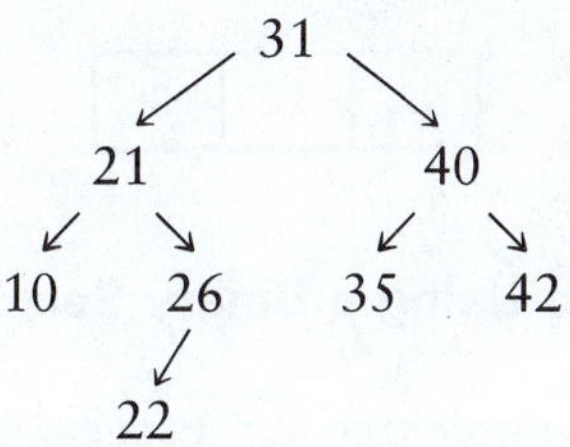

Each tree has only one node that no other node points to; this node is called the *root* of the tree. A subtree of a binary tree consists of any node in the tree and all nodes that we can reach from that node by following pointers; the node from which the process starts is the root of the subtree. Each node in the tree has a *left subtree* (the subtree whose root is the node's left descendant) and a *right subtree* (the subtree whose root is the node's right descendant). Either subtree may be empty.

Two types are necessary for the construction of a binary tree: one for nodes and one for pointers to nodes.

```
TYPE BinTree = POINTER TO TreeNode;
     TreeNode = RECORD
                  left: BinTree;
                  value: CARDINAL;
                  right: BinTree
                END;
```

The `left` field contains a pointer to the left descendant of the node; `right` contains a pointer to the right descendant. We will draw a value of type `TreeNode` as a box with three cells:

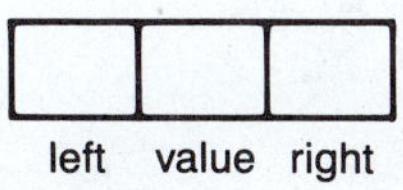

Figure 8.4 shows how we would represent the tree given earlier using `TreeNode` records. A pointer variable would point to the root node of the tree. If the value of this variable is NIL, the tree contains no nodes.

Figure 8.4
A Modula-2 Representation of a Binary Tree

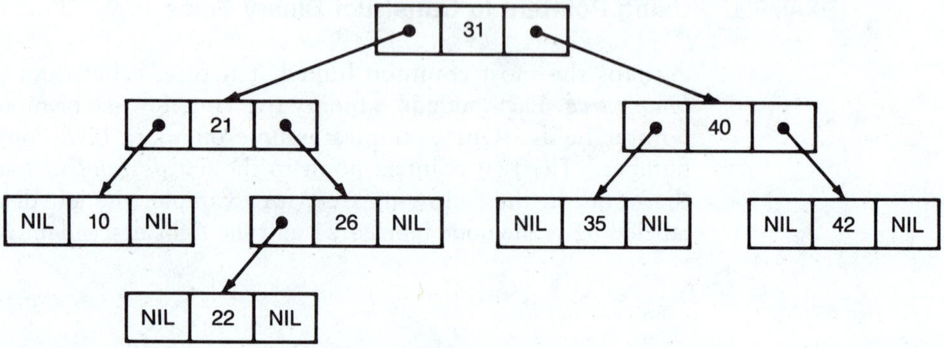

EXAMPLE PROGRAM

Sorting Using a Binary Search Tree

Our example tree has a special property: The value stored in each node of the tree is greater than or equal to the values stored in its left subtree, and less than or equal to the values stored in its right subtree. We call a binary tree with this property a *binary search tree*. As the name implies, it is easy to write a procedure (call it `FindNumber`) to search such a tree to see if it contains a particular number. To see if a number `n` is in a binary search tree, we call `FindNumber` with a pointer to the root of the tree as a parameter. `FindNumber` compares `n` to the value stored at the root node. If the numbers match, `FindNumber` returns. If `n` is less than the root value, then `n` must occur in the left subtree (if it is in the tree at all), so `FindNumber` calls itself recursively with a pointer to the left descendant of the root as a parameter. Similarly, if `n` is greater than the root value, `FindNumber` calls itself recursively with a pointer to the root's right descendant as a parameter.

```
PROCEDURE FindNumber(tree: BinTree; n: CARDINAL): BinTree;
  (* returns a pointer to a node containing n; if no node
     contains n, returns NIL *)
BEGIN
  IF (tree = NIL) OR (n = tree^.value) THEN
    RETURN tree
  ELSIF n < tree^.value THEN
    RETURN FindNumber(tree^.left, n);
  ELSE
    RETURN FindNumber(tree^.right, n)
  END
END FindNumber;
```

As an example of how to use binary trees, we will develop a program called `TreeSort` that sorts a file of `CARDINAL` numbers. `TreeSort` reads the numbers from the input file and uses them to build a binary search tree. `TreeSort` then traverses the tree, writing the numbers to an output file as it encounters them.

The algorithm for adding numbers to the tree is similar to that used by the `FindNumber` procedure. Suppose we want to sort the numbers 22, 15, 33, 20, and 17. The tree is empty, initially. `TreeSort` first reads the number 22 and adds a node containing 22 to the tree:

`TreeSort` then reads the number 15. Because 15 is less than 22, it examines the left subtree. The left subtree is empty, so `TreeSort` creates a node containing 15 and makes it the left descendant of the root node:

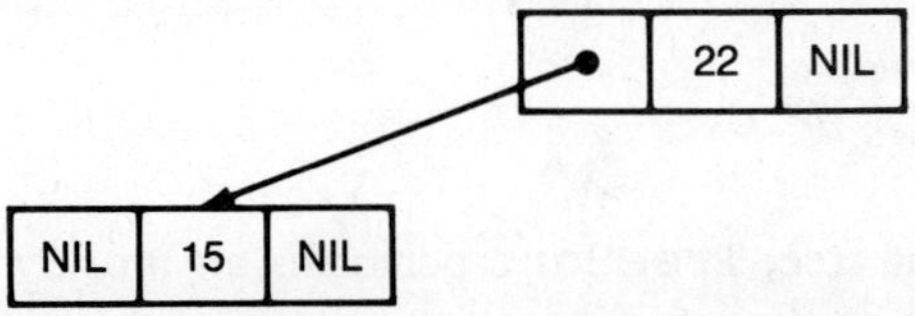

`TreeSort` next reads the number 33. Because 33 is greater than 22, it checks the right subtree of the root. This subtree is empty, so `TreeSort` creates a node to hold 33 and makes it the right descendant of the root:

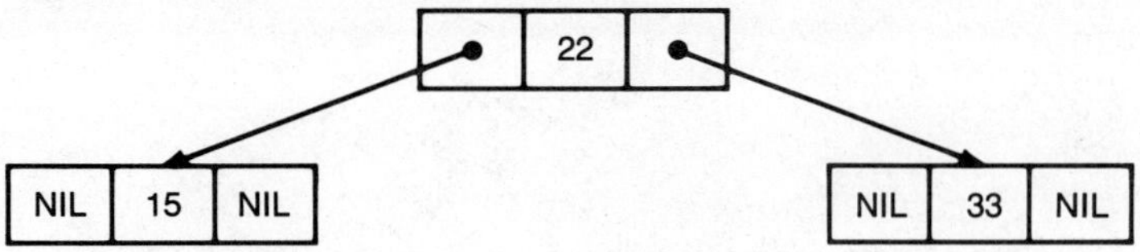

The next number read is 20. `TreeSort` first compares 20 with 22. Because 20 is smaller, `TreeSort` next compares it with 15. This time 20 is greater. No further comparisons are possible, so `TreeSort` creates a node containing 20 and makes it the right descendant of the node containing 15:

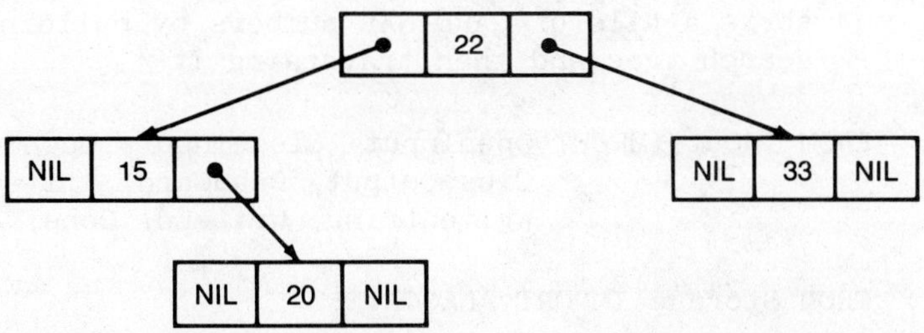

The final number is 17. Because 17 is less than 22, greater than 15, and less than 20, `TreeSort` adds it to the tree as the left descendant of 20:

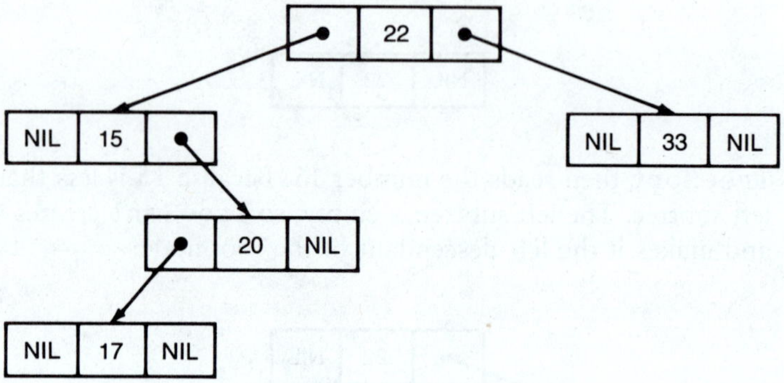

After building the tree, `TreeSort` performs an *inorder* traversal of the tree: First it visits all nodes in the left subtree, then it visits the root, and finally it visits all nodes in the right subtree. (`TreeSort` traverses the left and right subtrees by using the same method recursively.) When `TreeSort` traverses the tree and prints the number stored in each node, it produces the following output:

```
15
17
20
22
33
```

`TreeSort` relies on three procedures. `BuildTree` reads the numbers and builds the binary search tree. `BuildTree` calls the recursive procedure `InsertNumber`, which inserts a new number into the tree. The third procedure, `PrintTree`, performs an inorder traversal of the binary search tree, writing the values of the nodes as it visits them.

```
MODULE TreeSort;
  (* sorts a file of CARDINAL numbers by building a binary
     search tree and then traversing it *)

  FROM InOut IMPORT OpenInput, CloseInput, OpenOutput,
                    CloseOutput, ReadCard, WriteCard,
                    WriteString, WriteLn, Done;

  FROM Storage IMPORT ALLOCATE;
```

```
TYPE BinTree = POINTER TO TreeNode;
     TreeNode = RECORD
                  left: BinTree;
                  value: CARDINAL;
                  right: BinTree
                END;

VAR tree: BinTree;

PROCEDURE InsertNumber(VAR tree: BinTree; n: CARDINAL);
  (* inserts the number n into its proper place in a binary
     search tree *)
BEGIN
  IF tree # NIL THEN
    IF n < tree^.value THEN
      InsertNumber(tree^.left, n)
                                   (* insert in left subtree *)
    ELSE
      InsertNumber(tree^.right, n)
                                   (* insert in right subtree *)
    END
  ELSE     (* create a node and insert in the proper place *)
    ALLOCATE(tree, SIZE(TreeNode));
    tree^.value := n;
    tree^.left := NIL;
    tree^.right := NIL
  END
END InsertNumber;

PROCEDURE BuildTree(VAR tree: BinTree);
  (* reads CARDINAL numbers and uses them to create a binary
     search tree *)
  VAR n: CARDINAL;
BEGIN
  tree := NIL;
  ReadCard(n);
  WHILE Done DO
    InsertNumber(tree, n);
    ReadCard(n)
  END;
END BuildTree;

PROCEDURE PrintTree(tree: BinTree);
  (* traverses a binary search tree in inorder, printing the
     values stored in the nodes *)
BEGIN
  IF tree # NIL THEN
    PrintTree(tree^.left);        (* print left subtree  *)
    WriteCard(tree^.value, 1);    (* print root value    *)
```

```
      WriteLn;
      PrintTree(tree^.right)        (* print right subtree *)
    END
  END PrintTree;

BEGIN
  WriteString("Enter name of file to be sorted.");
  WriteLn;
  OpenInput("NUM");
  WriteLn;
  BuildTree(tree);
  CloseInput;

  WriteString("Enter name of output file.");
  WriteLn;
  OpenOutput("NUM");
  WriteLn;
  PrintTree(tree);
  CloseOutput
END TreeSort.
```

8.2 Procedure Types

Modula-2 allows the creation of *procedure types*, whose values are procedures (or, more precisely, references to procedures). Procedure types have much in common with pointer types. In particular, the operations allowed for procedure values correspond closely to the operations defined for pointers:

A program can assign a procedure value to a procedure variable.
A program can supply a procedure value or variable as a parameter in a procedure call.
A function can return a procedure value.
A program can call a procedure variable (just as it can dereference a pointer variable).

(*Programming in Modula-2* does not state whether or not it is legal to compare procedures for equality or inequality in the same fashion as pointer values. As a result, some Modula-2 compilers allow equality and inequality tests while others do not. For program portability, it is best to avoid such comparisons.)

Although procedure types may seem esoteric, they are surprisingly useful. Uses of procedure types include

using a procedure variable as a method of choosing among several alternative procedures
"installing" a procedure in a module
constructing "generic" modules
storing a procedure in a record field

Examples of the first two uses appear in this section; examples of the other two appear in Section 11.3.

Defining Procedure Types

The specification of a procedure type (Figures 8.5 and 8.6) resembles a procedure heading; it gives full information about the procedures that belong to the type:

the number of parameters and the type of each parameter
whether each parameter is a value parameter or a variable parameter
the type of value returned by procedures belonging to the type (if they are functions)

We can assign to a variable of this type only procedures that match the specification completely. For example, if we declare ProcType as

```
TYPE ProcType = PROCEDURE (REAL, VAR INTEGER);
```

then a variable of type ProcType can store only procedures with two parameters, where the first is a value parameter of type REAL and the second a variable parameter of type INTEGER. If we declare FuncType as

```
TYPE FuncType = PROCEDURE (CARDINAL): CARDINAL;
```

then a variable of type FuncType can store any function that has one value parameter of type CARDINAL and returns a result of type CARDINAL.

Figure 8.5 ***ProcedureType***

Figure 8.6 ***FormalTypeList***

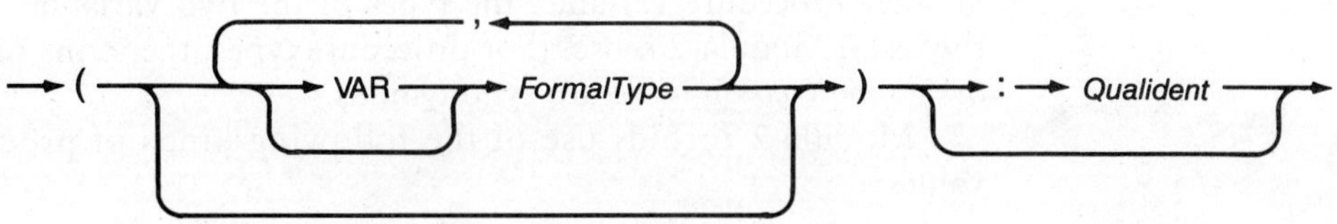

Modula-2 provides one standard procedure type, PROC, which has the following definition:

```
TYPE PROC = PROCEDURE;
```

Any proper procedure that has no parameters is of type PROC. (Incidentally, the specifications PROCEDURE and PROCEDURE () are equivalent.) PROC simplifies library modules that export procedures with procedure parameters. For example, the procedure NEWPROCESS (Section 12.1) requires that its first parameter have type PROC.

Procedure Assignment

We can give a value to a procedure variable by assignment. The right side of the assignment may be either a procedure name, a procedure variable, or a call of a function that returns a procedure value. For example, suppose that func1 and func2 are variables of type BinaryOp:

```
TYPE BinaryOp = PROCEDURE (CARDINAL, CARDINAL): CARDINAL;
VAR func1, func2: BinaryOp;
```

If the function IntExp has the heading

```
PROCEDURE IntExp(base, exponent: CARDINAL): CARDINAL;
```

we can assign it to func1:

```
func1 := IntExp;
```

(The absence of parentheses following the name IntExp signals the compiler that IntExp itself—not the value returned by a call of IntExp—is to be assigned to func1.) We can also copy the procedure reference stored in func1 to func2:

```
func2 := func1;
```

When the name of a procedure appears on the right side of an assignment to a procedure variable, the heading of the procedure must match the specification of the variable's type in every detail. When we assign a procedure variable to another procedure variable, the types of the two variables must be the same, in the usual Modula-2 sense. (For procedure types, the terms *same*, *compatible*, and *assignment-compatible* are synonymous.)

Modula-2 forbids use of the following kinds of procedures as procedure values:

standard procedures (such as ABS and INC)
procedures that are local to other procedures

These procedures cannot be assigned to procedure variables, used as parameters, or returned by functions; Modula-2 compilers will detect violations of this rule.

Note that procedures exported by library modules do not fall into either of these categories.

Calling a Procedure Variable

We can call a procedure variable, once it has a value, in the same way as an ordinary procedure (or function). Thus, after the assignments to `func1` and `func2`, the following statements are equivalent:

```
WriteCard(IntExp(i, j), 1);
WriteCard(func1(i, j), 1);
WriteCard(func2(i, j), 1);
```

The first statement calls `IntExp` directly. The second calls `IntExp` indirectly through the variable `func1`, which contains a reference to `IntExp`. And, because the value of `func1` was copied to `func2`, the call of `func2` in the third statement is also a call of `IntExp`. A procedure variable has no particular initial value; attempting to call a procedure variable before we have assigned it a value will have unpredictable results.

Procedures Used as Parameters

Procedure types make it possible to supply a procedure as a parameter to a call of another procedure. For example, the following function, when we give it a function `f` as a parameter, finds the smallest nonnegative integer `n` for which `f(n)` is 0. The parameter `f` must be a function that has a single value parameter of type `INTEGER` and produces an `INTEGER` result.

```
TYPE IntToInt = PROCEDURE (INTEGER): INTEGER;

PROCEDURE FindZero(f: IntToInt): INTEGER;
  (* returns the smallest nonnegative integer n for which
     f(n) = 0; does not terminate if f(n) is never 0 *)
  VAR n: INTEGER;
BEGIN
  n := 0;
  WHILE f(n) # 0 DO
    INC(n)
  END;
  RETURN n
END FindZero;
```

If Poly is the following function:

```
PROCEDURE Poly(i: INTEGER): INTEGER;
BEGIN
  RETURN i * i + i - 12
END Poly;
```

then the call

```
WriteCard(FindZero(Poly), 1);
```

writes the number 3, because Poly(0) is −12, Poly(1) is −10, Poly(2) is −6, and Poly(3) is 0.

Functions That Return Procedure Values

Modula-2 functions may return values of a procedure type. The following function, when given one of the characters '+', '-', '*', or '/', returns a function to perform the corresponding arithmetic operation.

```
TYPE ArithmeticOp = PROCEDURE (REAL, REAL): REAL;

PROCEDURE FindOp(operator: CHAR): ArithmeticOp;
  (* returns a function corresponding to a one-character
     operator; character must be one of +, -, *, or / *)
BEGIN
  CASE operator OF
    '+': RETURN Add       |
    '-': RETURN Subtract  |
    '*': RETURN Multiply  |
    '/': RETURN Divide
  END
END FindOp;
```

Add, Subtract, Multiply, and Divide are programmer-defined functions of type ArithmeticOp.

EXAMPLE PROGRAM

Displaying a File in Decimal, Hex, or Octal

Some programs need to choose a procedure to call from a group of several alternatives. One way to do so is to use a variable of an unstructured type to keep track of which procedure to call. For example, suppose that we are writing a program that will display the ordinal numbers of the characters in a file in either base

8, base 10, or base 16. The program prompts the user to enter a letter *d*, *h*, or *o* to indicate a decimal, hexadecimal, or octal format. Each time it writes a character, the program uses an IF or CASE statement to determine the output format:

```
CASE CAP(base) OF
  'D': WriteCard(ORD(buffer[i]), 7) |     (* decimal *)
  'H': WriteHex(ORD(buffer[i]), 7)  |     (* hex     *)
  'O': WriteOct(ORD(buffer[i]), 7)        (* octal   *)
END;
```

(WriteOct and WriteHex are similar to WriteCard, but they write CARDINAL values in octal and hexadecimal, respectively. Wirth's InOut module exports both procedures.)

After the initial assignment to base, its value does not change during the execution of the program; consequently, the program wastes some time by repeatedly testing the value of CAP(base) against 'D', 'H', and 'O'. By using a procedure variable, the program can avoid making this test. We first observe that WriteCard, WriteHex, and WriteOct are all compatible with the following type:

```
TYPE WriteProcedure = PROCEDURE (CARDINAL, CARDINAL);
```

Therefore, we can declare a variable capable of storing either WriteCard, WriteHex, or WriteOct:

```
VAR writeNumber: WriteProcedure;
```

Once the user has selected decimal, hex, or octal, a CASE statement stores either WriteCard, WriteHex, or WriteOct in writeNumber. When the time comes to write the ordinal number of a character, the statement

```
writeNumber(ORD(buffer[i]), 7);
```

will call either WriteCard, WriteHex, or WriteOct.

The DisplayFile program does what we have just described. After asking the user for a base (decimal, hex, or octal) and a file name, DisplayFile reads the file into an array of characters (the variable buffer), then writes the ordinal numbers of the characters to the screen. Each screenful contains 24 rows, with 10 numbers per row; the program suspends output after each screenful until the user types a character.

DisplayFile uses a buffer rather than printing the characters as they are read because the InOut module does not allow simultaneous reading from the keyboard and from a file. We do not need the buffer if we use Wirth's FileSystem module (Section 13.3) to read from the file.

```
MODULE DisplayFile;
  (* displays the contents of a file in either decimal, hex,
     or octal *)

  FROM InOut IMPORT OpenInput, CloseInput, Read, Done, Write,
                    WriteString, WriteLn, WriteCard, WriteOct,
                    WriteHex;

  CONST maxBufferSize = 32767;

  VAR   buffer: ARRAY [1..maxBufferSize] OF CHAR;
        bufferSize: CARDINAL;

  TYPE WriteProcedure = PROCEDURE (CARDINAL, CARDINAL);

  VAR writeNumber: WriteProcedure;

  PROCEDURE AskForBase(VAR writeNumber: WriteProcedure);
    (* ask user for base in which to display file *)
    VAR base: CHAR;
  BEGIN
    WriteString("Display file in decimal, hex, or octal?");
    WriteLn;
    WriteString("Enter d, h, or o: ");
    Read(base);
    Write(base);
    WriteLn;

    CASE CAP(base) OF
      'D': writeNumber := WriteCard |
      'H': writeNumber := WriteHex  |
      'O': writeNumber := WriteOct
    ELSE
      WriteString("Base not recognized; using decimal.");
      WriteLn;
      writeNumber := WriteCard
    END
  END AskForBase;

  PROCEDURE ReadFile(VAR buffer: ARRAY OF CHAR;
                     VAR length: CARDINAL);
    (* read contents of file into buffer and determine length
       of file *)
    VAR ch: CHAR;
  BEGIN
    WriteString("Enter name of input file.");
    WriteLn;
    OpenInput("DAT");
```

```
    WriteLn;
    length := 0;
    LOOP
      Read(ch);
      IF NOT Done THEN EXIT END;
      INC(length);
      IF length > bufferSize THEN
        WriteString("Buffer overflow in ReadFile");
        WriteLn;
        HALT
      END;
      buffer[length] := ch
    END;
    CloseInput
  END ReadFile;

  PROCEDURE WriteBuffer(VAR buffer: ARRAY OF CHAR;
                        length: CARDINAL;
                        writeNumber: WriteProcedure);
    (* display contents of buffer, one screenful at a time;
       call writeNumber procedure to display ordinal number
       of each character *)
    CONST numbersPerLine = 10;
          linesPerScreen = 25;
          numbersPerScreen = numbersPerLine *
                                  (linesPerScreen - 1);
    VAR i: CARDINAL;
        ch: CHAR;
  BEGIN
    FOR i := 1 TO length DO
      writeNumber(ORD(buffer[i]), 7);
            (* calls either WriteCard, WriteHex, or WriteOct *)
      IF i MOD numbersPerLine = 0 THEN
        WriteLn
      END;
      IF i MOD numbersPerScreen = 0 THEN
        WriteString("Type any character to continue...");
        Read(ch);
        WriteLn
      END
    END
  END WriteBuffer;

BEGIN
  AskForBase(writeNumber);
  ReadFile(buffer, bufferSize);
  WriteBuffer(buffer, bufferSize, writeNumber)
END DisplayFile.
```

Storing a procedure in a variable works well in `DisplayFile` because the variable does not change after its initial assignment. In a program that calls one of several procedures inside a loop, using a procedure variable saves no time, because the program would still need an `IF` or `CASE` statement. In such situations—when a program must choose among a group of procedures based on the value of a variable `i`—we may find it worthwhile to store the procedures in an array and use `i` as an index to select the appropriate procedure.

Procedure Types and Modules (OPTIONAL)

One of the most important uses of procedure types (and undoubtedly a major reason for their inclusion in Modula-2) is to supply a procedure to a module so that the module can store it for later use. The module may either save the procedure in a procedure variable or store it as part of a larger structure, often a record.

Consider the `DisplayFile` program. Instead of storing `WriteCard`, `WriteHex`, or `WriteOct` in a variable, `DisplayFile` could have "installed" it in a library module. The definition part of this module might have the following appearance:

```
DEFINITION MODULE CardinalOut;
  (* write CARDINAL values in various formats *)

  TYPE WriteProcedure = PROCEDURE (CARDINAL, CARDINAL);

  PROCEDURE InstallWriteProc(writeProc: WriteProcedure);
    (* "install" a procedure to be called whenever a CARDINAL
       number is to be written *)

  PROCEDURE WriteCardinal(x, n: CARDINAL);
    (* call the installed procedure to write the number x,
       using at least n characters *)

END CardinalOut.
```

The implementation part of `CardinalOut` hides the variable in which the procedure is stored:

```
IMPLEMENTATION MODULE CardinalOut;

  VAR writeNumber: WriteProcedure;

  PROCEDURE InstallWriteProc(writeProc: WriteProcedure);
    (* "install" a procedure to be called whenever a CARDINAL
       number is to be written *)
  BEGIN
    writeNumber := writeProc    (* store for later use *)
  END InstallWriteProc;
```

```
  PROCEDURE WriteCardinal(x, n: CARDINAL);
    (* call the installed procedure to write the number x,
       using at least n characters *)
  BEGIN
    writeNumber(x, n)    (* call stored procedure *)
  END WriteCardinal;

END CardinalOut.
```

This example—despite being artificial—helps explain why procedure variables are more important in a modular language such as Modula-2 than in a language without modules. In Pascal, for example, every procedure (except for procedures nested inside other procedures) is visible throughout the entire program. If a Pascal program needs to "remember" which procedure to call later, it can always store a value in an ordinary variable, and then test the variable later using an `if` or `case` statement. In Modula-2, a procedure is only visible in a portion of a program—the module in which its declaration appears—unless exported to other modules. In particular, procedures declared in a program module cannot be made visible in a library module. Thus, `CardinalOut` does not have the option of using an `IF` or `CASE` statement to determine which procedure to call; it has no choice but to store the procedure itself in a local variable, where it can be saved until needed.

The `CardinalOut` module, although it shows how to "install" a procedure in a module, does not illustrate the power of this concept. For more realistic examples, we need only turn to the library modules provided with several popular Modula-2 systems.

Wirth's `Windows` *Module*

The `Windows` module allows a program to manipulate multiple windows on a display. To open a new window, the program calls the procedure `OpenWindow`:

```
PROCEDURE OpenWindow(VAR u: Window; x, y, w, h: CARDINAL;
                     Repaint: RestoreProc; VAR done: BOOLEAN);
```

The values `x` and `y` indicate the position of the window on the screen, while `w` and `h` indicate the width and height of the window. The `Repaint` parameter is a procedure of type `RestoreProc`:

```
TYPE RestoreProc = PROCEDURE (Window);
```

The program calls `Repaint` to restore the contents of the window whenever it is subsequently moved or changed in size. The `Window` parameter to `Repaint` tells it which window to restore; this parameter allows the program to use the same procedure as the `Repaint` procedure for several windows.

The Turbo Modula-2 Texts *Module*

The Texts module exports procedures for input and output using either the user's terminal or a text file. The procedures that Texts exports resemble those in Wirth's InOut module, but have an additional parameter of type TEXT to indicate the input or output medium. For example, the call

```
WriteString(output, "Processing completed.");
```

writes a string to the medium selected by the variable output. To allow input and output using devices other than the terminal or a file, the Texts module allows a program to "connect" an I/O procedure to a particular TEXT value. The I/O procedure must have two parameters, one of type TEXT and the other of type CHAR:

```
TYPE TextDriver = PROCEDURE (TEXT, VAR CHAR);
```

A call of ConnectDriver creates a connection between a procedure and a TEXT variable:

```
PROCEDURE ConnectDriver(VAR t: TEXT; p: TextDriver);
```

Any subsequent I/O operations on this TEXT use the driver supplied by the program instead of the normal driver. For example, we might install a procedure called NewDriver as the driver for device1:

```
ConnectDriver(device1, NewDriver);
```

If we were to call WriteString with device1 as its first parameter, WriteString would call NewDriver repeatedly to write the individual characters in the string. Similarly, if we called WriteCard to write a number i, WriteCard would convert i to a character string, then call NewDriver for each character in the string.

The Volition Systems Files *Module*

The Files module uses procedure variables as a means of handling errors. Files (which resembles Wirth's FileSystem module) exports a type FILE and a collection of procedures for manipulating variables of that type. The Files module also exports the following procedure type:

```
TYPE FileHandler = PROCEDURE (FileState);
```

FileState is an enumeration type whose values indicate the possible states of a file. The value FileOK indicates that the file is in a correct state; other values of FileState represent various errors that can occur while a program is using a file. The procedure `SetFileHandler` allows a program to associate a procedure `handler` with a file `f`:

```
PROCEDURE SetFileHandler(f: FILE; handler: FileHandler);
```

After a call of `SetFileHandler`, any file operation that detects an error (that is, any operation that sets `f`'s state to a value other than `FileOK`) calls `handler`. The state of the file is supplied to `handler` as a parameter; `handler` can use the file state to decide what action to take (terminate the program or close the file and try to recover).

Standard Pascal

1. The specification of a pointer type in Pascal consists of a type name prefixed by the symbol ^.

```
type String = ^StringRec;
     StringRec = record
                   length: 0..80;
                   string: packed array [1..80] of char
                 end;
```

2. The procedures new and dispose allocate and deallocate storage for anonymous variables.

```
var str: String;
        .
        .
        .
new(str);
dispose(str);
```

If p is a pointer variable, the amount of storage that new(p) allocates (or dispose(p) deallocates) is the amount required to store a value of the type that p points to.

3. Pascal allows programmers to use procedures and functions as parameters, known as "procedural" and "functional" parameters, respectively. The specification of a procedural (functional) parameter in a parameter list is identical to a procedure (function) heading:

```
function FindZero(function f(i: integer): integer): integer;
```

Programmers may not use required (predefined) procedures and functions as actual parameters. Pascal does not provide procedure variables, nor may functions return procedure values.

Modula-2

1. In Modula-2, the specification of a pointer type begins with the words POINTER TO.

```
TYPE String = POINTER TO StringRec;
     StringRec = RECORD
                    length:  [0..80];
                    string: ARRAY [1..80] OF CHAR
                 END;
```

A type name or a type specification may follow the words POINTER TO.

```
TYPE String = POINTER TO
                 RECORD
                   length:  [0..80];
                   string:  ARRAY [1..80] OF CHAR
                 END;
```

2. A program may allocate and deallocate storage for anonymous variables using procedures imported from a library module or included in the program. In Wirth's library, the Storage module exports procedures ALLOCATE and DEALLOCATE. These procedures require two parameters: a pointer variable (to point to the anonymous variable being created or destroyed) and a CARDINAL number (representing the size of the anonymous variable).

```
VAR str: String;
      .
      .
      .
ALLOCATE(str, SIZE(StringRec));
DEALLOCATE(str, SIZE(StringRec));
```

When given a type name T as a parameter, the standard function SIZE returns a number representing the amount of space (usually measured in words or bytes) required to store a value of type T. A program can also apply SIZE to a variable to determine the amount of space that the variable occupies.

3. Instead of procedural and functional parameters, Modula-2 provides a more general feature: procedure types. By using procedure types, a program can manipulate procedures as data values. The declaration of a procedure type has the following appearance:

```
TYPE WriteProc = PROCEDURE (CARDINAL, CARDINAL);
```

The programmer can use a procedure type to declare variables:

```
VAR writeNumber: WriteProc;
```

Standard Pascal

Modula-2

A program can assign a procedure to a variable; once a procedure variable has a value, the program can call the variable, thereby activating the procedure stored in it:

```
writeNumber := WriteCard;
writeNumber(n, 1);            (* WriteCard is called *)
writeNumber := WriteHex;
writeNumber(n, 1);            (* WriteHex is called  *)
```

A formal parameter of a procedure type is equivalent to a Pascal procedural or functional parameter:

```
TYPE IntToInt = PROCEDURE (INTEGER): INTEGER;

PROCEDURE FindZero(f: IntToInt): INTEGER;
```

Functions may return procedure values:

```
PROCEDURE FindWriteProc(hexFlag: BOOLEAN): WriteProc;
BEGIN
  IF hexFlag THEN
    RETURN WriteHex
  ELSE
    RETURN WriteCard
  END
END FindWriteProc;
```

A standard procedure or a procedure declared within another procedure cannot be assigned to a procedure variable, used as an actual parameter, or returned by a function.

EXERCISES

Section 8.1

1. Some programming languages do not require pointers to point only to anonymous variables of a particular type; they may point at named variables or virtually anywhere in a program. What are the advantages and disadvantages of Modula-2's restrictions on pointers?

2. If two pointers p and q are equal, are p^ and q^ sometimes, always, or never equal? If p and q are unequal, are p^ and q^ sometimes, always, or never equal?

3. The following declarations allow the construction of a linked list of records, each containing a name and telephone number:

```
TYPE String30 = ARRAY [0..29] OF CHAR;
     PhonePtr = POINTER TO PhoneRecord;
     PhoneRecord = RECORD
                     name, number: String30;
                     next: PhonePtr
                   END;

VAR phoneList: PhonePtr;
```

   The variable `phoneList` points to the first record on the list; `phoneList` has the value `NIL` if the list is empty. Write the following procedure:

```
PROCEDURE Insert(name, number: ARRAY OF CHAR);
  (* inserts a new name and phone number; if name matches an
     existing name, updates phone number *)
```

4. Assuming the declarations of exercise 3, write the following procedure:

```
PROCEDURE Delete(prefix: ARRAY OF CHAR);
  (* deletes names beginning with the given prefix; if prefix
     is empty, deletes all names *)
```

5. Assuming the declarations of exercise 3, write the following procedure:

```
PROCEDURE Print(prefix: ARRAY OF CHAR);
  (* for all names beginning with the given prefix, prints
     both the name and phone number; if prefix is empty,
     prints all names and numbers *)
```

6. If a Modula-2 system does not provide `NEW` and `DISPOSE`, could the programmer write them? If so, write `NEW` and `DISPOSE`. If not, explain why.

Section 8.2

7. Let `RealFunction` be the following type:

```
TYPE RealFunction = PROCEDURE (REAL): REAL;
```

   Write a procedure called `Tabulate` that prints a table showing the values of a function of type `RealFunction`. `Tabulate`'s parameters should include the starting and ending values and increment to use in the tabulation. Each line of output should consist of a pair of numbers: a REAL number x and the value of the function when applied to x.

8. Write the following procedure:

```
PROCEDURE ApplyToAll(f: RealFunction; VAR v: ARRAY OF REAL);
  (* applies the function f to every component of v *)
```

(Exercise 7 defines RealFunction.) For example, if f is a function that computes the square of its parameter, ApplyToAll will square every component of v.

9. Write the following function:

```
TYPE ArithmeticOp = PROCEDURE (REAL, REAL): REAL;

PROCEDURE Reduction(f: ArithmeticOp; v: ARRAY OF REAL): REAL;
```

Reduction should apply f to v[0] and v[1], then use f again to combine the result with v[2], then combine that result with v[3], and so forth; the final result is the value returned by Reduction. If v has only one component, Reduction should return that component. (The name of this function comes from the APL programming language, which supplies a similar function.)

10. Use the Reduction function of exercise 9 to do the following:
    (a) Compute the sum of the components in a vector.
    (b) Compute the product of the components in a vector.
    (c) Find the largest component in a vector.
    (d) Find the smallest component in a vector.

11. Write the following function:

```
TYPE Filter = PROCEDURE (CARDINAL): BOOLEAN;

PROCEDURE Sum(low, high: CARDINAL; f: Filter): CARDINAL;
  (* sums the integers between low and high (inclusive) for
     which f returns TRUE *)
```

12. Use the Sum function of exercise 11 to do the following:
    (a) Sum the odd numbers between 1 and 100.
    (b) Sum the prime numbers between 100 and 1000.
    (c) Sum the powers of 2 between 1 and 1024.

13. Why does Modula-2 not allow a program to assign a standard procedure to a procedure variable? Why does it prohibit the assignment of a procedure that is local to another procedure?

9 Modules

A Modula-2 program consists of a program module (the main program) and any number of *library modules* from which the program module imports entities (constants, types, variables, and procedures). These library modules may in turn import from other library modules, which are also considered part of the program. Each Modula-2 system provides a basic collection of library modules; the programmer is free to write additional library modules to use in a single program or in many programs. Program modules and library modules may contain smaller, nested modules hidden from the rest of the program; these are called *local modules*.

Modules serve as convenient repositories of related entities. Not all the entities that belong to a module are available for use by other modules, however. Modules act as walls: entities declared inside a module are not visible outside the module unless the module *exports* them.

Writing a program as a collection of modules — rather than as a single unit — offers many advantages:

- *Modules are a powerful tool for creating large programs*. A programmer can design a large program as a collection of modules connected through clearly defined interfaces. Writing and testing the program is simpler because the programmer can work on one module at a time, using the services provided by other modules but ignoring the details of how those modules work (the principle of *abstraction*). Modular design is particularly useful when a team of programmers develops a program. Each module can be assigned to a single member of the team, who writes and tests the module knowing only the specifications of that module and others in the program.

- *Modules help make programs easier to modify*. Modules make *information hiding* possible: a programmer can change details that are hidden inside a module without affecting the rest of the program, provided that the module's specifications remain the same. For example, when a module exports a procedure, the programmer can modify the body of the procedure to correct an error or to take advantage of a better algorithm. Similarly, the programmer can hide the representation of a data structure in a module and change it without affecting other modules in the program.

- *Modules help make programs more portable.* A programmer can hide machine-dependent portions of a program in a module (or a few modules). When transporting the program to another computer, the programmer need only change this module to account for machine differences.
- *Modules make separate compilation possible.* Modules provide a natural way of dividing a program into pieces that a compiler can process separately. Although Wirth does not require Modula-2 systems to provide separate compilation, most do. When separate compilation is available, a change to one module requires recompilation of only that module, not of the entire program, provided that the module's interface with the rest of the program did not change. (The programmer may need to relink the modules, however.) In Modula-2, separate compilation involves no loss of safety, because compilers perform full type-checking across module boundaries.
- *Modules enable programmers to develop libraries of reusable code.* If a library module developed for one program is written in a general fashion, programmers can reuse the module in other programs. Reusable modules not only save programming time, but also contribute to program reliability because they have undergone testing in previous programs.

Although the programs in Chapters 1–8 used library modules, these chapters did not discuss how to write and compile library modules, nor did the programs in those chapters use local modules. Library modules and local modules are the subject of Chapter 9. Section 9.1 explains how to write library modules. Section 9.2 shows how to compile library modules separately and then link them with a program module to form a complete program. Section 9.3 describes local modules. Finally, Section 9.4 discusses how modules affect the visibility of entities in a program.

9.1 Library Modules

A library module has two parts: the *definition part* and the *implementation part*. The definition part contains only definitions of entities (constants, types, variables, and procedures) that the module exports; it defines the interface of the library module with the rest of the program. The implementation part describes how to implement the services listed in the definition part. To emphasize that the definition and implementation parts of a library module are themselves complete program units, the first is often called a *definition module* and the second an *implementation module*. Most Modula-2 systems require programmers to keep definition modules and implementation modules in separate files and compile them separately.

A definition module contains *definitions*, not declarations. Definitions resemble declarations, but in some cases provide less information. The definition of a procedure consists of the procedure heading only, not the body of the procedure. The definition of a type may omit the specification of the type, giving only the name of the type.

The parameters of the trigonometric functions in Wirth's `MathLib0` module must be expressed in radians, not in degrees. Programs that measure angles in degrees need functions to convert from degrees to radians and vice-versa (call these functions `DegreesToRadians` and `RadiansToDegrees`). Because these functions are useful in more than one program, it makes sense to create a library module called `AngleConversions` that exports the two functions. Once written and tested, the module becomes a reusable tool that any number of programs can use. The definition part of `AngleConversions` might look as follows:

```
DEFINITION MODULE AngleConversions;
  (* exports procedures for converting between degrees and
     radians *)

  PROCEDURE DegreesToRadians(degrees: REAL): REAL;
    (* converts angle in degrees to radians *)

  PROCEDURE RadiansToDegrees(radians: REAL): REAL;
    (* converts angle in radians to degrees *)

END AngleConversions.
```

The definition part of a library module specifies what services the module provides. The definition part of `AngleConversions` gives only the headings of `DegreesToRadians` and `RadiansToDegrees`; a comment accompanying each function describes what it does. The implementation part hides the internal details of the module (here, the bodies of the functions).

A module that imports an entity exported by a library module is said to be a *client* of the library module. The following module, `ComputeThirdSide`, is a client of the library module `AngleConversions`, from which it imports the function `DegreesToRadians` (`ComputeThirdSide` is also a client of the library modules `InOut`, `RealInOut`, and `MathLib0`):

```
MODULE ComputeThirdSide;
  (* computes the length of the third side of a triangle from
     the lengths of the other two sides and the angle between
     the sides *)

  FROM InOut IMPORT WriteString, WriteLn;
  FROM RealInOut IMPORT ReadReal, WriteReal;
  FROM MathLib0 IMPORT sqrt, cos;
  FROM AngleConversions IMPORT DegreesToRadians;

  VAR side1, side2, side3, angle: REAL;
```

```
BEGIN
  WriteString("Enter length of one side: ");
  ReadReal(side1);
  WriteLn;
  WriteString("Enter length of other side: ");
  ReadReal(side2);
  WriteLn;
  WriteString("Enter angle between sides (in degrees): ");
  ReadReal(angle);
  WriteLn;

  side3 := sqrt(side1 * side1 + side2 * side2 -
             2.0 * side1 * side2 * cos(DegreesToRadians(angle)));
    (* law of cosines *)

  WriteString("The length of the third side is: ");
  WriteReal(side3, 15);
  WriteLn
END ComputeThirdSide.
```

Notice that `ComputeThirdSide` knows nothing of how `DegreesToRadians` works; in fact, we can compile `ComputeThirdSide` before we write the implementation part of `AngleConversions`.

The implementation part of a library module "fills in the blanks" left by the definition part—it supplies all information missing from the definition part. Procedures whose headings appear in the definition part must have complete declarations in the implementation part. If we have omitted the specification of a type in the definition part, we must declare it in full in the implementation part.

The implementation part of a library module begins with the words `IMPLEMENTATION MODULE`, followed by the module name (which must match the name given in the definition part of the module). Here is the implementation part of `AngleConversions`:

```
IMPLEMENTATION MODULE AngleConversions;

  CONST twoPi = 2.0 * 3.14159265;

  PROCEDURE DegreesToRadians(degrees: REAL): REAL;
    (* converts angle in degrees to radians *)
  BEGIN
    RETURN (twoPi * degrees) / 360.0
  END DegreesToRadians;

  PROCEDURE RadiansToDegrees(radians: REAL): REAL;
    (* converts angle in radians to degrees *)
  BEGIN
    RETURN (360.0 * radians) / twoPi
  END RadiansToDegrees;

END AngleConversions.
```

In addition to supplying information missing in the definition part of the module (in the case of `AngleConversions`, complete declarations of the procedures `DegreesToRadians` and `RadiansToDegrees`), the implementation part may declare entities not mentioned in the definition part. These entities (such as the constant `twoPi` in `AngleConversions`) are local to the implementation module: they are not visible elsewhere in the program. The implementation part of a module may have a body (the word BEGIN, followed by a sequence of statements), which typically serves to initialize the module's variables. (`AngleConversions` has no variables, so its body is empty. When the body of a module is empty, we may omit the word BEGIN.)

A Modula-2 compiler uses the information in the definition part of `AngleConversions` to check for proper use of the procedures it exports (for example, that they are called with parameters of correct number and appropriate types). When we later compile the implementation part of `AngleConversions`, the compiler will check that it is consistent with the definition part (for example, that procedure headings match). In this way, a Modula-2 system can perform type-checking across module boundaries.

Definition Modules

Figure 9.1 shows the syntax of a definition module. A definition module contains *definitions* of constants, types, variables, and procedures. Definitions are similar to declarations, but may provide less information.

Figure 9.1 ***DefinitionModule***

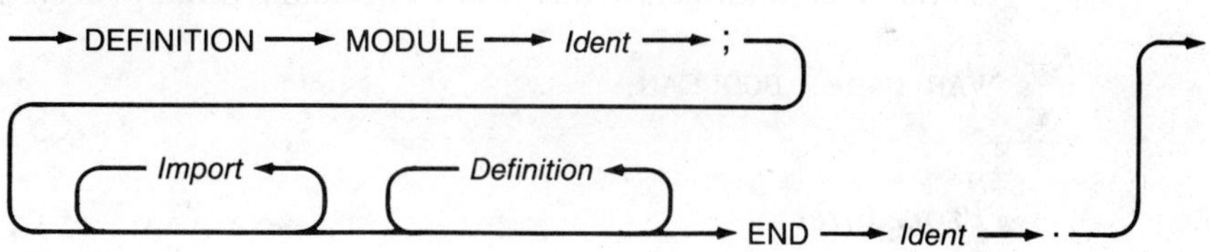

Constants

Constant definitions are identical to normal constant declarations:

```
CONST EOL = 36C;    (* end of line character *)
```

Types

We can define types in two ways. One possibility is to use a normal type declaration:

```
TYPE Complex = RECORD
                   realPart, imagPart: REAL
               END;
```

A type whose full declaration appears in a definition module is subject to *transparent export*; the structure of the type is visible to client modules. Transparent export of a record type causes the names of the record's fields to be exported; a module that imports `Complex` automatically imports the field names `realPart` and `imagPart`. Similarly, the transparent export of an enumeration type causes the export of the names of the enumeration constants as well. For example, if a definition module contains the definition

```
TYPE Scale = (do, re, mi, fa, so, la, ti);
```

then the module exports the names `do`, `re`, `mi`, `fa`, `so`, `la`, and `ti` along with `Scale`.

Alternatively, we can omit the equals sign and type specification in a type definition:

```
TYPE Complex;
```

We call a type defined in this fashion an *opaque type*, because client modules do not know its structure. A full declaration of an opaque type must appear in the matching implementation module. We will see later that a value of an opaque type must be a pointer; thus, a Modula-2 compiler always knows how much space to allocate for a variable of an opaque type.

Variables

Variable definitions are identical to ordinary variable declarations:

```
VAR Done: BOOLEAN;
```

Procedures

The definition of a procedure consists of just the heading of the procedure:

```
PROCEDURE Add(c1, c2: Complex): Complex;
```

A full declaration of the procedure (including both the heading and body) must appear in the matching implementation module.

Figure 9.2 summarizes the possible forms of a definition.

A definition module may include import lists. Import lists are not mandatory, and in fact many definition modules do not contain any. Because the sole purpose of the definition part of a library module is to supply definitions of the entities that the module exports, the only entities it might need to import are constants and types, which can be used to define other entities. A definition module might

Figure 9.2 ***Definition***

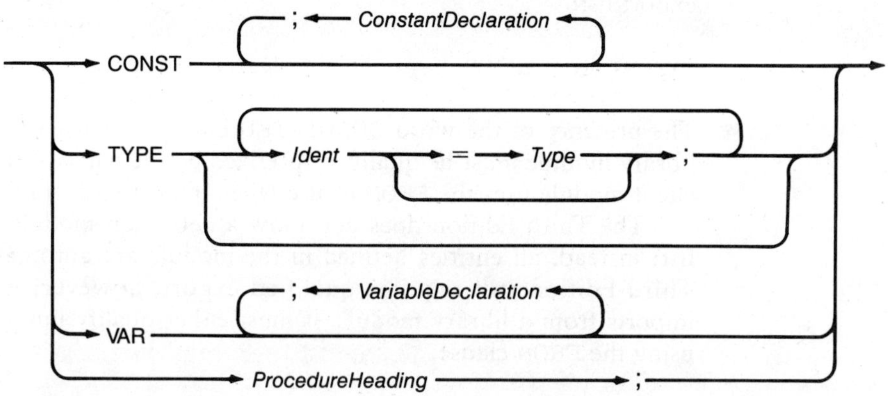

import a constant that it needs in order to declare an array type, or it might import a type to declare another type or to specify the type of a procedure parameter. For example, the following definition module, which exports procedures for file manipulation, imports a file type to use in declaring the procedures' parameters:

```
DEFINITION MODULE FileOperations;
    (* exports procedures for performing file operations *)

    FROM FileSystem IMPORT File;

    PROCEDURE Copy(VAR f1, f2: File);
      (* copies f1 to f2 *)

    PROCEDURE Compare(VAR f1, f2: File): BOOLEAN;
      (* returns TRUE if the contents of f1 and f2 are the same,
         FALSE otherwise *)

END FileOperations.
```

The definition part of a library module should import only those constants and types needed for its definitions; the implementation part should be responsible for importing all other entities needed by the module. In general, programs are easier to modify if modules are as independent of each other as possible.

The Second Edition of *Programming in Modula-2* requires that a definition module explicitly state what entities it is exporting by including an *export list* between the import lists and the definitions. An export list has the form

EXPORT QUALIFIED *IdentList* ;

where *IdentList* is a list of identifiers separated by commas. For example, the definition part of AngleConversions would need to begin with the following export list:

```
EXPORT QUALIFIED DegreesToRadians, RadiansToDegrees;
```

The presence of the word QUALIFIED indicates that entities imported from the library module must be qualified (prefixed by the name of the module), unless the client module uses the FROM clause when importing from the library module.

The Third Edition does not allow a definition module to contain an export list; instead, all entities defined in the module are automatically exported. The Third Edition still requires qualified export, however; when a client module imports from a library module, it must either qualify imported names or import using the FROM clause.

EXAMPLE The Definition Part of a Stack Module

Suppose that we are writing a program called Reverse that will read a character string and print its reversal. Reverse is easy to write if we use a stack to store the string. As Reverse reads characters, it pushes them onto the stack, stopping when it reaches the end of the string. Reverse then pops characters from the stack until it is empty, writing each character as it is popped.

We could either declare the stack within Reverse or place it in a module of its own (called CharStackModule, say). The latter approach offers several advantages:

- Reverse becomes simpler and easier to understand, because it contains only natural stack operations such as Push and Pop.
- Reverse cannot affect correct functioning of the stack, because we can hide the variables that make up the stack within CharStackModule, limiting access to these variables to the procedures exported by CharStackModule. Reverse cannot corrupt the stack, say by accidentally changing the value of a variable that marks the top of the stack.
- We can change the implementation of the stack later without changing Reverse. For example, if we use an array to represent the stack, stack overflow may occur too often. If so, we might switch to a dynamic data structure (a linked list, for example) to implement the stack.
- Other programs could use CharStackModule.

Our informal description of Reverse reveals that we need three stack operations: (1) push a character onto the stack, (2) pop a character off the stack, and (3) test whether the stack is empty. (The implementation part of CharStackModule will handle stack initialization.) Therefore, CharStackModule exports the three procedures Push, Pop, and IsEmpty:

```
DEFINITION MODULE CharStackModule;
  (* exports procedures for manipulating a hidden stack of
     characters *)
```

```
  PROCEDURE Push(ch: CHAR);
    (* pushes ch onto the stack; terminates program if stack
       is full *)

  PROCEDURE Pop(VAR ch: CHAR);
    (* stores the top element of the stack into ch, then pops
       the stack; terminates program if stack is empty *)

  PROCEDURE IsEmpty(): BOOLEAN;
    (* returns TRUE if the stack is empty, FALSE otherwise *)

END CharStackModule.
```

The definition part of CharStackModule furnishes all the information that Reverse needs to know about Push, Pop, and IsEmpty. Reverse does not need to know the details of how Push, Pop, and IsEmpty work, nor does it need to know the representation of the stack. As a matter of style, Modula-2 programmers customarily accompany each definition in a definition module with a comment explaining the entity being defined. These comments must be complete and accurate, particularly when other programmers must use the module.

We can write Reverse using our knowledge of the definition part of CharStackModule; we need not worry about the implementation part of the module (which appears later in this section). Reverse imports Push, Pop, and IsEmpty from CharStackModule in the same way that it imports from InOut.

```
MODULE Reverse;
  (* reverses a string typed by the user *)

  FROM InOut IMPORT Read, Write, WriteLn, EOL, WriteString;
  FROM CharStackModule IMPORT Push, Pop, IsEmpty;

  VAR ch: CHAR;

BEGIN
  WriteString("Enter string: ");
  Read(ch);
  WHILE ch # EOL DO
    Write(ch);   (* echo character read *)
    Push(ch);
    Read(ch)
  END;
  WriteLn;

  WriteString("The reversal is: ");
  WHILE NOT IsEmpty() DO
    Pop(ch);
    Write(ch)
  END;
  WriteLn
END Reverse.
```

Implementation Modules

An implementation module has exactly the same syntax as a program module, except that the former begins with the words IMPLEMENTATION MODULE instead of MODULE (Figure 9.3). The three paths through the chart in Figure 9.3 reflect the three kinds of *compilation units*: definition modules, implementation modules, and program modules.

Figure 9.3 ***CompilationUnit***

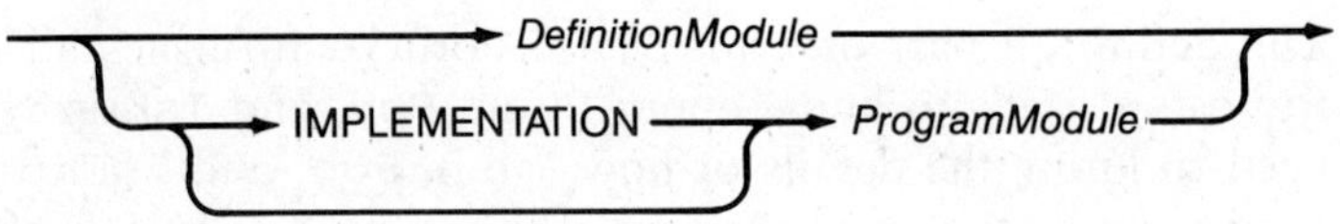

Implementation modules, like program modules, may contain both import lists and declarations. Import lists allow an implementation module to import entities from other library modules. Declarations serve two purposes: (1) to fill in details missing from the matching definition module and (2) to declare entities that are strictly local to the implementation module.

Any entities *defined* in the definition part of a library module are visible in the implementation part as well. For example, the following definition module defines two entities, the type NameString and the array charNames:

```
DEFINITION MODULE ControlChars;
  (* exports an array containing names of ASCII control
     characters *)

  TYPE NameString = ARRAY [0..2] OF CHAR;

  VAR charNames: ARRAY [0C..37C] OF NameString;

END ControlChars.
```

Both NameString and charNames are visible in the corresponding implementation module (although it does not use NameString):

```
IMPLEMENTATION MODULE ControlChars;
BEGIN
  charNames[0C] := "nul";
  charNames[1C] := "soh";
        .
        .
        .
  charNames[36C] := "rs";
  charNames[37C] := "us"
END ControlChars.
```

However, entities *imported* into the definition part of a module are not automatically visible in the implementation part; if both the definition and implementation parts need the same entity, both must import it. For example, the implementation part of `FileOperations` needs to import the `File` type, even though the definition part (shown earlier in this section) imports it:

```
IMPLEMENTATION MODULE FileOperations;
  FROM FileSystem IMPORT File;
    (* required even though imported by definition module *)
      .
      .
      .
END FileOperations.
```

An implementation module may contain declarations of all five kinds of Modula-2 entities:

- *Constants*. Constants defined in the definition part of a module are automatically visible in the implementation part. Any constants declared in an implementation module are local to the implementation module; they are not visible outside the implementation module.
- *Types*. Types defined in the definition part of a module are automatically visible in the implementation part. If the specification of the type appears in the definition part, a declaration of the type must *not* appear in the implementation part. However, if the definition part omits the type specification, a full declaration of the type must appear in the implementation part. The implementation part may also declare new types not mentioned in the definition part; these are local to the implementation module.
- *Variables*. Variables defined in the definition part of a module may not be declared in the implementation part, because they are automatically visible there. All variables declared in an implementation module are local to the module.
- *Procedures*. The implementation part of a module must contain a full declaration of every procedure whose heading appears in the definition part. (The full declaration must agree in every detail with the heading given in the definition part; in particular, parameters must have the same names and types and appear in the same order.) In addition, an implementation module may declare other procedures that are local to the module.
- *Modules*. An implementation module may have modules declared inside it. These *local modules* are discussed in Section 9.3.

All variables declared at the outermost level of a library module (that is, not nested inside a procedure), whether declared in the definition part or the implementation part, are *static*: they retain their values throughout the lifetime of the program. (In contrast, variables declared in a procedure lose their values whenever the procedure returns.) Consequently, we need initialize the variables belonging to a library module only once—when the program begins execution.

So that a library module can initialize its variables, Modula-2 allows the implementation part of the module to have a body; the statements in the body are executed at the beginning of program execution, before the body of the program module is executed.

EXAMPLE The Implementation Part of a Stack Module

Before we write the implementation part of `CharStackModule`, we must decide how it will represent a stack of characters. We have many choices; for simplicity, we use a one-dimensional array of characters called `stackArray` together with a variable `topOfStack` indicating the top of the stack. In addition to declarations of the procedures listed in the definition part of `CharStackModule`, the implementation part will contain declarations of `stackArray`, `topOfStack`, and a constant (`stackSize`) used to specify the stack's maximum size. These entities are strictly local to the implementation part of `CharStackModule`.

Before a client module can call the procedures `Push`, `Pop`, and `IsEmpty`, `CharStackModule` must initialize the stack by assigning the value 0 to `topOfStack`; the body of the module performs this assignment.

```
IMPLEMENTATION MODULE CharStackModule;

  FROM InOut IMPORT WriteString, WriteLn;

  CONST stackSize = 100;   (* maximum size of stack *)

  VAR stackArray: ARRAY [1..stackSize] OF CHAR;
      topOfStack: [0..stackSize+1];

  PROCEDURE Push(ch: CHAR);
    (* pushes ch onto the stack; terminates program if stack
       is full *)
  BEGIN
    INC(topOfStack);
    IF topOfStack > stackSize THEN
      WriteString("Stack overflow in CharStackModule.Push");
      WriteLn;
      HALT
    END;
    stackArray[topOfStack] := ch
  END Push;

  PROCEDURE Pop(VAR ch: CHAR);
    (* stores the top element of the stack into ch, then pops
       the stack; terminates program if stack is empty *)
  BEGIN
    IF topOfStack = 0 THEN
      WriteString("Stack underflow in CharStackModule.Pop");
```

```
      WriteLn;
      HALT
    END;
    ch := stackArray[topOfStack];
    DEC(topOfStack)
  END Pop;

  PROCEDURE IsEmpty(): BOOLEAN;
    (* returns TRUE if the stack is empty, FALSE otherwise *)
  BEGIN
    RETURN topOfStack = 0
  END IsEmpty;

BEGIN
  topOfStack := 0
END CharStackModule.
```

The body of `CharStackModule` will be executed before the body of `Reverse`, ensuring proper initialization of the stack before `Reverse` performs any operations on it.

`CharStackModule` reacts to stack overflow or underflow by writing an error message and terminating the program. A better version of `CharStackModule` would signal the error to the client module, allowing it to decide whether to terminate the program or continue execution. Section 10.4 discusses several ways in which a library module can inform a client that an error has occurred.

Order of Module Initialization

Because a program may contain any number of library modules, each of which may have a body, we need to know the order of module initialization. The Second Edition of *Programming in Modula-2* did not specify the order of initialization. The Third Edition states that the bodies of all imported modules must be executed before the body of a client module can be executed. (This order ensures proper initialization of each library module before a client performs any operations on it.) When the client module imports from several modules, they are initialized in the order they are imported. The program module is always executed last, after the bodies of all imported modules have been executed.

For example, suppose that a program module `M1` imports from a library module `M2`, whose implementation part imports from another library module `M3`. Graphically, we can represent this relationship as

$$M1 \leftarrow M2 \leftarrow M3$$

`M1` is a client of `M2`, so `M2` must be initialized before the body of `M1` can be executed. But `M2` is a client of `M3`, so `M3` must be initialized before `M2` can execute. Thus, the order of initialization will be `M3` first, `M2` second, and `M1` last.

A more interesting case occurs when M1 imports from both M2 and M3, which in turn import from M4:

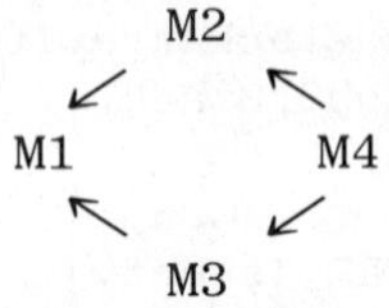

The order of initialization depends on the order of the import lists in M1. Assuming that the import list for M2 precedes the list for M3, the order of initialization will be M4, M2, M3, then M1.

The order of initialization is undefined if the pattern of importation among two or more implementation modules forms a circle:

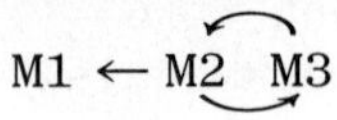

In this case, the Modula-2 system chooses the order in which M2 and M3 are initialized. If this choice does not correspond to what the programmer had in mind, the program will not function properly. For example, consider the modules M2 and M3 in Figure 9.4. If the body of M3 is executed first, setting j to 0, then M2 will set i to 0. But if the body of M2 is executed first, then i will receive an undefined value.

Figure 9.4
Mutually Importing Implementation Modules

```
DEFINITION MODULE M2;
  VAR i: CARDINAL;
END M2.
```

```
DEFINITION MODULE M3;
  VAR j: CARDINAL;
END M3.
```

```
IMPLEMENTATION MODULE M2;
  FROM M3 IMPORT j;
BEGIN
  i := j;
END M2.
```

```
IMPLEMENTATION MODULE M3;
  FROM M2 IMPORT i;
BEGIN
  j := 0;
END M3.
```

The programmer should try to avoid creating such loops. If a loop is unavoidable, the programmer must ensure that the initialization of each module in the loop does not depend on the initialization of any other module in the loop.

Opaque Types

A definition module can export a type whose structure is unknown, by defining just the name of the type. For example, the definition part of a library module called ComplexNumbers might contain the following definition:

```
TYPE Complex;
```

A type declared in this fashion is subject to *opaque export*, because client modules have no knowledge of the type's structure. We call the type itself an *opaque type*.

A client module that imports an opaque type may use it in the same fashion as any Modula-2 type; in particular, the module may use the type to declare variables. Because client modules do not know the structure of the type, the only operations they may perform on variables of the type are assignment and tests for equality and inequality. (The Third Edition of *Programming in Modula-2* requires these operations. The Second Edition does not specify what operations on opaque types, if any, are allowed.) The module that exports the opaque type must supply procedures to perform all other operations that clients may need. Because these procedures are declared in the same implementation module as the opaque type, they have access to the structure of the type.

When the definition part of a library module defines an opaque type, the implementation part of the module must include a full declaration of the type. According to the Third Edition of *Programming in Modula-2*, the full declaration of an opaque type must specify it to be a pointer type. Thus, the implementation part of the ComplexNumbers module might contain the following declaration:

```
TYPE Complex = POINTER TO RECORD
                           realPart, imagPart: REAL
                         END;
```

In the Second Edition of *Programming in Modula-2*, Wirth specified that an opaque type could be either a pointer type or a subrange of a standard type. The Third Edition does not mention the latter possibility.

The restriction of opaque types to pointers is a consequence of the separation of the definition and implementation parts of a library module. Suppose that a program module P imports an opaque type T from a library module M (see Figure 9.5). When we compile P, the compiler must know how much storage to allocate for the variable x. We have hidden the specification of T in the implementation part of M, however, which is not accessible during the compilation of P. The requirement that T be a pointer type solves the problem, because all pointer types—in a particular system—require the same amount of storage.

Figure 9.5
Importing an Opaque Type

```
MODULE P;
  FROM M IMPORT T;
  VAR x: T;
END P.
```

```
DEFINITION MODULE M;
  TYPE T;

END M.
```

Requiring values of an opaque type to be pointers is not nearly as harsh as it may seem. In fact, it is hardly a restriction at all, because we can define an opaque type as a pointer to a record type with as many fields as we want. Many opaque types represent linked structures (stacks, queues, or trees, for example) and therefore would be pointer types in any event. Using a pointer type as an opaque type can even be advantageous. Because values of the opaque type are pointers to anonymous variables, we can export procedures to create and destroy these variables, allowing better management of space. Also, we can write functions that return a value of an opaque type (most Modula-2 systems do not allow functions to return arrays and records).

Client modules may not take advantage of the fact that values of an opaque type are pointers. Writing a client module that tries to use a variable of an opaque type as though it were a pointer (by dereferencing it, for example) is one of the most common mistakes that beginning Modula-2 programmers make.

However, client modules cannot completely ignore the fact that values of an opaque type are pointers. In some (but not all) cases, it is incorrect to rely on Modula-2's built-in capability to test whether two variables of an opaque type are equal. Because this test simply compares two pointers, not the anonymous variables to which they point, it may not always give the desired result. For example, if `c1` and `c2` are variables of type `Complex`, the expression `c1 = c2` has the value `TRUE` if `c1` and `c2` point to the same anonymous variable. If `c1` and `c2` point to different anonymous variables, the result is `FALSE` even if the anonymous variables have the same real and imaginary parts. A similar problem arises when variables of an opaque type appear in assignment statements. The assignment `c1 := c2` causes `c1` to point to the same anonymous variable as `c2`; a subsequent change to the real part of `c2` would cause the real part of `c1` to change as well. To avoid these problems, a module that exports an opaque type can export procedures that perform assignment and equality tests. The assignment procedure can change the fields in an anonymous variable, while the equality procedure can compare the values of anonymous variables, not the pointers to them.

EXAMPLE A Module That Exports an Opaque Stack Type

The module `CharStackModule` is fine for a program that needs only one stack of characters, but is useless if we need two or more stacks. We can increase the value of this module by having it export a `CharStack` type and a collection of procedures that operate on `CharStack` variables. A client module can then import `CharStack` and use it to declare any number of stacks.

Starting with `CharStackModule`, we will create a new module called `CharacterStacks` that exports type `CharStack` and procedures `Push`, `Pop`, and `IsEmpty`. Each procedure must now have an additional parameter of type `CharStack`, so that a call of the procedure can specify which variable of type `CharStack` to use for the operation. As a first attempt at writing the definition part of `CharacterStacks`, we will declare `CharStack` to be a record containing a stack array and a top-of-stack index.

```
DEFINITION MODULE CharacterStacks;
 (* exports type CharStack (stack of characters) and
    procedures for manipulating variables of type CharStack *)

  CONST stackSize = 100;   (* maximum size of a CharStack *)

  TYPE CharStack = RECORD
                     stackArray: ARRAY [1..stackSize] OF CHAR;
                     topOfStack: [0..stackSize+1]
                   END;
    (* transparent export of CharStack *)

  PROCEDURE Push(VAR s: CharStack; ch: CHAR);
    (* pushes ch onto stack s; terminates program if stack is
       full *)

  PROCEDURE Pop(VAR s: CharStack; VAR ch: CHAR);
    (* stores top element of stack s into ch, then pops s;
       terminates program if stack is empty *)

  PROCEDURE IsEmpty(s: CharStack): BOOLEAN;
    (* returns TRUE if s is empty, FALSE otherwise *)

END CharacterStacks.
```

This module is perfectly legal in Modula-2, but leaves much to be desired. If we decide to increase the maximum stack size, we must recompile all modules that import from `CharacterStacks`. We must also recompile if the representation of `CharStack` ever changes. Furthermore, by revealing the representation of a character stack, the definition part of `CharacterStacks` allows client modules to directly access the components of the stack (`stackArray` and `topOfStack`). Changing the representation of `CharStack` would be difficult, because we would have to carefully inspect and modify all client modules. Other problems arise as well. The client module is responsible for initializing `topOfStack` to 0 before using the stack; this step is easy to overlook. Once it is initialized, we cannot guarantee the correct functioning of a `CharStack` variable, because the client module may modify `stackArray` or `topOfStack` in such a way as to corrupt the stack. (For example, suppose that the client accidentally increments `topOfStack` without storing a value in `stackArray`. The next call of `Pop` will fetch a meaningless character.)

We can improve `CharacterStacks` by making `CharStack` an opaque type, allowing `CharacterStacks` to export `CharStack` without providing any information to client modules about the actual structure of a `CharStack` variable. This approach solves our problems: we can change the representation of `CharStack` at any time without changing client modules, and we ensure that clients cannot modify `CharStack` variables except through procedures exported by `CharacterStacks`.

An improved version of the definition part of CharacterStacks follows, this time with CharStack defined as an opaque type. Note that CharacterStacks must export a procedure capable of initializing a stack; a client module has no direct way to initialize a CharStack variable, because the module cannot see the structure of the variable.

```
DEFINITION MODULE CharacterStacks;
  (* exports type CharStack (stack of characters) and
     procedures for manipulating variables of type CharStack *)

  TYPE CharStack;   (* opaque export *)

  PROCEDURE Initialize(VAR s: CharStack);
    (* creates a stack s and makes it empty *)

  PROCEDURE Push(VAR s: CharStack; ch: CHAR);
    (* pushes ch onto stack s; terminates program if stack is
       full *)

  PROCEDURE Pop(VAR s: CharStack; VAR ch: CHAR);
    (* stores top element of stack s into ch, then pops s;
       terminates program if stack is empty *)

  PROCEDURE IsEmpty(s: CharStack): BOOLEAN;
    (* returns TRUE if s is empty, FALSE otherwise *)

END CharacterStacks.
```

The definition part of CharacterStacks gives no information about CharStack other than its name. Modules that import CharStack can declare variables of type CharStack, but the only way to manipulate these variables is through the procedures Initialize, Push, Pop, and IsEmpty.

To show how a client module uses CharacterStacks, we will modify Reverse to use CharacterStacks instead of CharStackModule. Reverse must declare a variable s of type CharStack, initialize it by calling Initialize, and include s as a parameter when calling Push, Pop, and IsEmpty.

```
MODULE Reverse;
  (* reverses a string typed by the user *)

  FROM InOut IMPORT Read, Write, WriteLn, EOL, WriteString;
  FROM CharacterStacks IMPORT CharStack, Initialize, Push, Pop,
                              IsEmpty;

  VAR s: CharStack;
      ch: CHAR;

BEGIN
  Initialize(s);    (* make stack s empty *)
```

```
  WriteString("Enter string: ");
  Read(ch);
  WHILE ch # EOL DO
    Write(ch);    (* echo character read *)
    Push(s, ch);
    Read(ch)
  END;
  WriteLn;

  WriteString("The reversal is: ");
  WHILE NOT IsEmpty(s) DO
    Pop(s, ch);
    Write(ch)
  END;
  WriteLn
END Reverse.
```

The call of `Initialize` is critical. Attempting to call `Push`, `Pop`, or `IsEmpty` before initializing `s` will have unpredictable results.

The full specification of the `CharStack` type must appear in the implementation part of `CharacterStacks`. Because `CharStack` must be a pointer type, we declare it to be a pointer to a record containing fields `stackArray` and `topOfStack`. The `Initialize` procedure allocates space for one of these records, then sets the `topOfStack` field to 0. Here is the implementation part of `CharacterStacks`:

```
IMPLEMENTATION MODULE CharacterStacks;

  FROM Storage IMPORT ALLOCATE;

  FROM InOut IMPORT WriteString, WriteLn;

  CONST stackSize = 100;  (* maximum size of a CharStack *)

  TYPE StackRecord =
         RECORD
           stackArray: ARRAY [1..stackSize] OF CHAR;
           topOfStack: [0..stackSize+1]
         END;
       CharStack = POINTER TO StackRecord;

  PROCEDURE Initialize(VAR s: CharStack);
    (* creates a stack s and makes it empty *)
  BEGIN
    ALLOCATE(s, SIZE(StackRecord));
    s^.topOfStack := 0
  END Initialize;

  PROCEDURE Push(VAR s: CharStack; ch: CHAR);
    (* pushes ch onto stack s; terminates program if stack is
       full *)
```

```
  BEGIN
    INC(s^.topOfStack);
    IF s^.topOfStack > stackSize THEN
      WriteString("Stack overflow in CharacterStacks.Push");
      WriteLn;
      HALT
    END;
    s^.stackArray[s^.topOfStack] := ch
  END Push;

  PROCEDURE Pop(VAR s: CharStack; VAR ch: CHAR);
    (* stores top element of stack s into ch, then pops s;
       terminates program if stack is empty *)
  BEGIN
    IF s^.topOfStack = 0 THEN
      WriteString("Stack underflow in CharacterStacks.Pop");
      WriteLn;
      HALT
    END;
    ch := s^.stackArray[s^.topOfStack];
    DEC(s^.topOfStack)
  END Pop;

  PROCEDURE IsEmpty(s: CharStack): BOOLEAN;
    (* returns TRUE if s is empty, FALSE otherwise *)
  BEGIN
    RETURN s^.topOfStack = 0
  END IsEmpty;

END CharacterStacks.
```

The implementation part of `CharacterStacks` points out a minor problem caused by the rule that opaque types must be pointer types—the annoyance of having to dereference a pointer in order to access a value of an opaque type. Fortunately, the `WITH` statement can make dereferencing less painful. For example, the `Push` procedure can use a `WITH` statement to avoid having to mention `s^` every time it accesses `stackArray` or `topOfStack`:

```
PROCEDURE Push(VAR s: CharStack; ch: CHAR);
  (* pushes ch onto stack s; terminates program if stack is
     full *)
BEGIN
  WITH s^ DO
    INC(topOfStack);
    IF topOfStack > stackSize THEN
      WriteString("Stack overflow in CharacterStacks.Push");
      WriteLn;
      HALT
```

```
    END;
    stackArray[topOfStack] := ch
  END
END Push;
```

9.2 Separate Compilation

Modula-2 supports *separate compilation*; we can compile each compilation unit (program module, definition module, or implementation module) separately from the other compilation units in a program. Separate compilation in Modula-2 differs from the *independent compilation* that some programming languages allow, where each program unit is compiled without knowledge of the other units. In Modula-2, the compiler checks that each entity imported from a library module is used in a manner consistent with its definition in the module. (The compiler performs this check using the information in the definition part of the library module; the implementation part of the library module plays no role.) When the implementation part of a library module is compiled, the compiler checks that it is consistent with the definition part of the module.

Separate compilation is a boon to the programmer: when we change a program, we only need to recompile the affected modules, not every module in the program. Both separate and independent compilation have this property, but with separate compilation the compiler performs the same kind of type-checking among modules that it would do within a single module. These checks may reveal errors that would otherwise be difficult to find.

The remainder of this section discusses the method of separate compilation that the Logitech Modula-2/86 system (Version 3.0) uses. Although this method is typical of many existing Modula-2 systems, it is not the only one in use. Later in this section we point out some differences between Logitech's method of separate compilation and that used by other systems. For more information, consult the manual for a particular Modula-2 system.

Compilation Order

The Logitech system assumes that each program module and implementation module is in a separate file with a .MOD extension and that each definition module is in a file with a .DEF extension. We must compile each of these modules separately. The order in which we compile the modules is important: *A definition module must be compiled* before *all modules that import from it and before its matching implementation module*. The motivation for this rule is simple. Since the entities defined in a definition part of a module are visible in the implementation part as well, we must compile the definition part first to allow the compiler to process the definitions. Because the clients of a library module depend on the information in the definition part of the module, not the implementation part, we must compile the definition part before the client modules.

To illustrate this rule, suppose that we need to compile a program consisting of the modules `Upper`, `Search`, and `Keywords`, where `Upper` is the program module. These modules will reside in five files:

UPPER.MOD
SEARCH.DEF
SEARCH.MOD
KEYWORDS.DEF
KEYWORDS.MOD

Suppose that `Upper` imports from `Search` and `Keywords`, while the implementation part of `Search` imports from `Keywords`. The dependency diagram in Figure 9.6 shows the five files; an arrow from one file to another means that the former file must wait for the latter file to be compiled. We cannot compile any of the .MOD files first, because UPPER.MOD and SEARCH.MOD must wait for SEARCH.DEF and KEYWORDS.DEF to be compiled, and KEYWORDS.MOD must wait for KEYWORDS.DEF. Thus, only the following compilation orders are possible (we may compile files listed on the same line in any order):

1. SEARCH.DEF, KEYWORDS.DEF
2. UPPER.MOD, SEARCH.MOD, KEYWORDS.MOD

or

1. KEYWORDS.DEF
2. KEYWORDS.MOD
3. SEARCH.DEF
4. UPPER.MOD, SEARCH.MOD

A quick count reveals a total of eight different compilation orders. To avoid confusion, it is a good idea to compile all .DEF files before compiling any .MOD files.

Figure 9.6
A Dependency Diagram for a Modula-2 Program

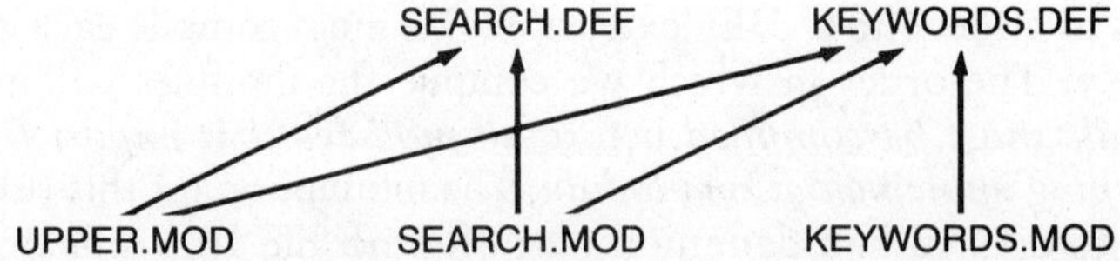

When the definition modules in a program do not import from each other, we can compile them in any order. If imports exist among definition modules, the rule given earlier constrains the order in which we may compile them. In our example, if KEYWORDS.DEF were to import from SEARCH.DEF, only three compilation orders would be possible:

1. SEARCH.DEF
2. KEYWORDS.DEF
3. UPPER.MOD, SEARCH.MOD, KEYWORDS.MOD

Figure 9.7
Mutually Importing Definition Modules

```
DEFINITION MODULE M1;
  FROM M2 IMPORT j;
  VAR i: CARDINAL;
END M1.
```

```
DEFINITION MODULE M2;
  FROM M1 IMPORT i;
  VAR j: CARDINAL;
END M2.
```

If a program contains two or more definition modules whose import lists form a circle, then the program cannot be compiled. Consider the pair of definition modules shown in Figure 9.7. `M1` imports from `M2`, so we must compile M2.DEF before M1.DEF; however, `M2` imports from `M1`, so we must compile M1.DEF before M2.DEF. Solutions to this problem include

merging the two modules into one
creating a third module that exports the entities common to both `M1` and `M2`
rewriting one of the library modules so that its implementation part imports from the other module, not its definition part

When we change a program module, we only need to recompile that one module (and relink the entire program). Likewise, if we change the implementation part of a library module, and the changes do not affect the definition part, then we only need to recompile the implementation part. If we change the definition part of a module, however, we must recompile first it, and then the implementation part and all modules that import from the library module. (If any of the affected modules is a definition module, we must recompile its clients as well.) In our example, if we change KEYWORDS.DEF, then we must recompile the following modules (in the order shown):

1. KEYWORDS.DEF
2. UPPER.MOD, SEARCH.MOD, KEYWORDS.MOD

Notice that we must recompile KEYWORDS.MOD regardless of whether we changed it. Recompilation allows the compiler to check that the definitions in KEYWORDS.DEF are still consistent with KEYWORDS.MOD.

Compilation

In the Logitech system, the compilation of a definition module produces a .SYM (symbol) file containing information about the entities exported by the module (see Figure 9.8).* (The compiler and linker produce additional files not shown in Figures 9.8–9.10; these files are not relevant to our discussion.)

Figure 9.8
Compiling a Definition Module

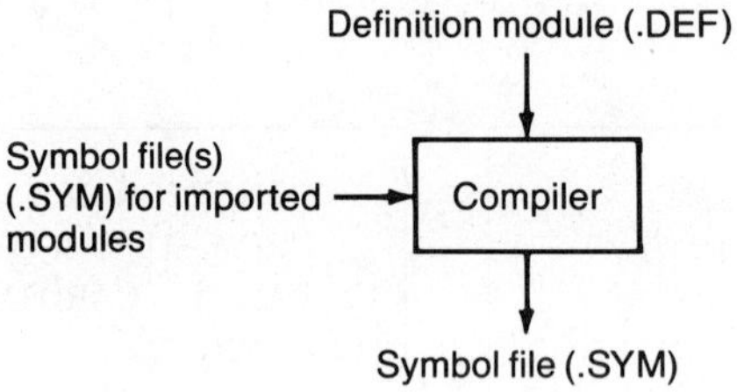

When it compiles an implementation module, the Logitech compiler consults the symbol file for the corresponding definition module plus symbol files for all imported modules; it produces an .OBJ file containing the object code for the module, as well as other information needed for linking (Figure 9.9).†

Figure 9.9
Compiling an Implementation Module

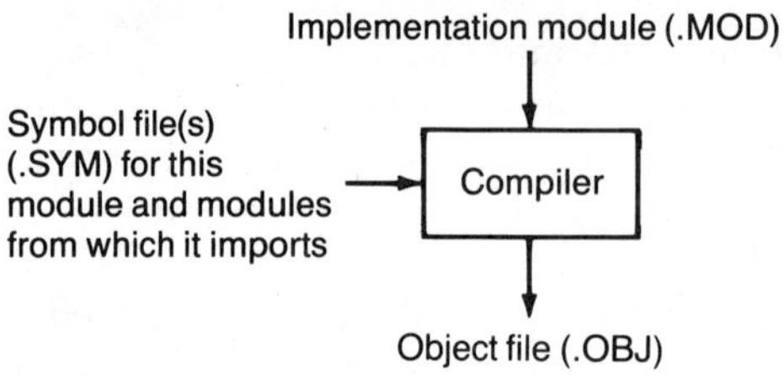

Linking

To link a Modula-2 program, a programmer need only invoke the Logitech linker and specify the name of the program module. The linker determines which modules to link to this module to complete the program. For example, when we link the program `Upper`, the linker will link UPPER.OBJ with SEARCH.OBJ and KEYWORDS.OBJ. In general, the modules to be linked include not only modules from which the program module imports, but also modules imported by these modules, and so forth. The output of the Logitech linker is an .EXE (executable)

*Adapted from illustration in *LOGITECH Modula-2* from LOGITECH, Inc., 1987.

†Adapted from illustration in *LOGITECH Modula-2* from LOGITECH, Inc., 1987.

file. Figure 9.10 summarizes the process of compiling and linking a program module.* Notice that the object code for modules supplied by the Logitech system resides in .LIB (library) files, not object files.

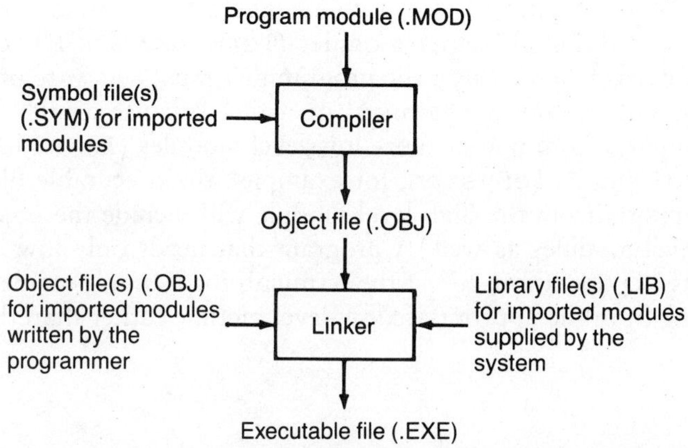

Figure 9.10
Compiling and Linking a Program Module

Several facts about linking are not obvious:

- *Only one copy of a module's object code is linked.* Regardless of how many other modules import from a library module, the executable file that the linker produces contains only one copy of the module's object code. For example, although both `Upper` and `Search` import from `Keywords`, only one copy of the object code for `Keywords` is linked, not two.
- *Modules are usually linked in their entirety.* The Logitech linker normally links all the object code for a module, no matter how many or how few entities the other modules in the program actually import. Thus, when a program module imports `WriteString` from `InOut`, the linker includes the code for all the other procedures in `InOut`, even though the program never calls these procedures. On request, the Logitech linker will omit the object code for all procedures that cannot be called.
- *"Hidden" imports may cause large executable files.* When asked to link a program, the linker uses not only the object code for the program module and modules that it imports from, but also the code for modules that these modules import from, and so forth, for as many levels as needed. Thus, the executable file includes code for every module of which the program module is a direct or indirect client.

  If space is a problem, the programmer can often minimize the effect of hidden imports by choosing library modules carefully. For example, consider

*Adapted from illustration in *LOGITECH Modula-2* from LOGITECH, Inc., 1987.

the problem of choosing a library module from which to import procedures for input and output. Most libraries provide more than one I/O module. Some I/O modules (`InOut` in Wirth's library) provide a high-level view of I/O, in which the program can easily manipulate input and output streams without having to worry about whether the streams represent files or the user's terminal. Other modules (`Terminal` and `FileSystem`) provide a low-level view of I/O; the programmer must be aware of whether an input or output stream is a terminal or a file. Because a high-level module usually imports from one or more low-level modules (`InOut` imports from `Terminal` and `FileSystem`, for example), the executable file for a program that imports from the high-level module will include the object code for the low-level modules as well. A program that needs only low-level I/O (because all its I/O operations affect the terminal, for example) can save space by importing from the appropriate low-level module rather than the high-level module.

Version Checking

Modula-2 systems that allow separate compilation must take steps to ensure that the interfaces between modules are consistent even though the modules are compiled separately. Usually such systems employ a simple version-checking mechanism such as that used by the Logitech system.

When we compile a definition module—say M1.DEF—the compiler assigns a *module key* to the resulting symbol file, M1.SYM. (This key is unique—if we were to recompile M1.DEF, the compiler would generate a different key.) Suppose that M2.MOD imports from `M1`. When we compile M2.MOD, the compiler will use M1.SYM to get information about the entities imported from `M1`. At this time, the compiler copies the key from M1.SYM to M2.OBJ. When we compile `M1`'s implementation module, M1.MOD, the compiler also copies the key to M1.OBJ. At linking time, the linker compares the keys stored in M1.OBJ and M2.OBJ; if they don't match, linking cannot proceed.

The purpose of this mechanism is to ensure that the code in M1.OBJ and M2.OBJ is consistent. For example, each call in `M2` of a procedure imported from `M1` should be consistent with the procedure declaration in `M1`. An inconsistency would arise if we changed and recompiled M1.DEF and M1.MOD without recompiling M2.MOD. The compiler would generate a new key for M1.SYM, and then copy it into M1.OBJ. M2.OBJ would still contain the old key, so M1.OBJ and M2.OBJ could not be linked. A mismatch of keys also occurs if we change and recompile M1.DEF and M2.MOD without recompiling M1.MOD.

The Logitech system also uses module keys to detect inconsistencies among definition modules. When one definition module imports from another, the compiler copies the key from the latter's symbol file into the former's symbol file. To see how this action is useful, consider the following example. Suppose that a program module M1 imports from modules M2 and M3, and both M2 and M3 import from another module M4. Here is one sequence that might take place when a programmer compiles this program:

M4.DEF is compiled; the compiler generates a module key, k_1, and stores it in M4.SYM.
M2.DEF is compiled; the compiler copies k_1 into M2.SYM.
The programmer changes M4.DEF.
M4.DEF is recompiled; the compiler generates a new module key, k_2, and stores it in M4.SYM.
M3.DEF is compiled; the compiler copies k_2 into M3.SYM.
M1.MOD is compiled.

The compilation of M1.MOD poses a problem: M1 depends on M2 and M3, which import from different versions of M4. M2 imports from a version of M4 that no longer exists, which will make it impossible to link the program later. The Logitech compiler can detect the inconsistency during the compilation of M1.MOD by comparing the module keys for M4 stored in M2.SYM and M3.SYM. In our example, the two keys are different, forcing the programmer to recompile M2.DEF before again attempting to compile M1.MOD.

A final comment on version checking: Although the module key mechanism ensures a consistent interface, it does not ensure an up-to-date interface. If we change and recompile a definition module, but not its matching implementation module or its clients, then the module key stored in the implementation module's object file will still match the key stored in the clients' object files. The interface between the implementation module and the client modules is still consistent, although it is no longer the interface specified by the definition module.

Separate Compilation Under Other Systems

The following is a partial list of ways in which Modula-2 systems may differ from the Logitech system in their handling of separate compilation.

- *Different file-naming conventions*. The use of the extensions .DEF (for definition modules) and .MOD (for program and implementation modules) is fairly common, but other extensions vary considerably from one system to another. For example, some systems use the extension .SBL instead of .SYM for symbol files, or one of the extensions .LNK, .MCD, .SMR, .OJM, or .O instead of .OBJ for object (link) files.
- *No compilation of definition modules*. Some Modula-2 systems do not require the programmer to compile definition modules. During the compilation of a program module or implementation module, the compiler reads from the .DEF file for each imported library module.

- *Dynamic linking*. The Logitech system requires an explicit linking phase prior to program execution. Some systems instead perform linking as the program is loaded into memory for execution. This method is often called *dynamic linking* or *load-time linking*.
- *Creation of load files*. Some linkers produce a load file, not an executable file. To execute a program, the user invokes a run-time system, which then loads the program and executes it. (Note, however, that these systems may provide a program for converting a load file to executable format.)

Subprogram Modules (OPTIONAL)

Most Modula-2 systems allow a program to "call" a program module as though it were a procedure. We call a module used in this way a *subprogram module* (or *subprogram*). The mechanism for calling a subprogram is not part of Modula-2 itself, but must be provided by a procedure in a library module. In many Modula-2 systems, the procedure has the name `Call` and can be imported from the module `Program`. The exact parameters to `Call` vary, but usually include the name of the subprogram to be called and a status variable that `Call` changes to indicate whether the subprogram terminated normally.

There is no way to supply parameters to a subprogram. Instead, the main program must communicate with a subprogram through a module from which both import. For example, if the main program wants to supply a value to a subprogram, it can store the value into a variable exported by the shared module. The subprogram can later access that variable to retrieve the value.

The primary reason for using subprograms is to reduce the amount of memory required to execute a program. If a program is too large to fit into memory, the programmer can often identify one or more modules that need not exist simultaneously. The main program can call these modules as subprograms when needed. Once a subprogram has completed execution, it returns control to the main program, which can then call another subprogram. All subprograms can share the same region of memory, because only one is resident at a time. (In other words, subprograms provide code overlays.) Some Modula-2 compilers are themselves organized as subprograms; each pass of the compiler is loaded into memory, executed, and then is overlaid by the next pass.

9.3 Local Modules

A program module, implementation module, or procedure, in addition to declaring constants, types, variables, and procedures, can declare modules as well. A module declared inside another module or procedure is called a *local module*. Declarations of local modules appear in the same place as declarations of the other entities; programmers can intermix the different kinds of declarations freely.

Local modules have properties similar to library modules, including the ability to import and export entities. Although separate compilation of local modules is not possible, they retain the other advantage of library modules: Entities within a local module that are not exported are not visible to the rest of the program. In particular, variables declared in a local module but not exported are protected against change. A programmer can hide a data structure inside a local module, providing access to the structure through procedures that the module exports. Local modules cannot hide the structure of a type, however, because they are incapable of opaque export.

Programming situations in which local modules are useful arise more often than one might expect. For example, consider the function Random (Section 5.3), which generates a sequence of pseudorandom CARDINAL numbers. We must save the value that Random computes, so that the next call of Random can use it. We cannot store this value in a variable local to Random, because then it would be lost when Random returns. Storing it in a variable randomCardinal that is global to Random leads to the version of Random given in Section 5.3:

```
PROCEDURE Random(): CARDINAL;
  (* returns a pseudorandom number between 0 and modulus - 1;
     modifies the variable randomCardinal *)
BEGIN
  randomCardinal := (multiplier * randomCardinal + increment)
                    MOD modulus;
  RETURN randomCardinal
END Random;
```

A potential problem appears here: The variable randomCardinal, because it is visible outside Random, is vulnerable to accidental change. By declaring a local module that contains both randomCardinal and Random, we can protect randomCardinal:

```
MODULE RandomNumberGenerator;
  (* exports modulus and Random; Random returns a pseudorandom
     CARDINAL number between 0 and modulus - 1 *)

  IMPORT seed;

  EXPORT modulus, Random;

  CONST multiplier = 40;
        increment = 3641;
        modulus = 729;

  VAR randomCardinal: CARDINAL;
```

```
  PROCEDURE Random(): CARDINAL;
    (* returns a pseudorandom number between 0 and modulus - 1;
       modifies the variable randomCardinal *)
  BEGIN
    randomCardinal := (multiplier * randomCardinal + increment)
                          MOD modulus;
    RETURN randomCardinal
  END Random;

BEGIN
  randomCardinal := seed
END RandomNumberGenerator;
```

The declaration of RandomNumberGenerator would appear in a program in place of the declaration of Random; we cannot compile RandomNumberGenerator separately. RandomNumberGenerator declares five entities: multiplier, increment, modulus, randomCardinal, and Random. Of these, only two—modulus and Random—are visible outside the module. (RandomNumberGenerator must export modulus to allow scaling of the value returned by Random into a desired range: 0.0 to 1.0 or 0 to 9, for example.) The other entities are not exported and are not visible outside RandomNumberGenerator. In particular, randomCardinal cannot be changed outside the module.

One problem with RandomNumberGenerator remains, however. RandomNumberGenerator imports the initial ("seed") value of randomCardinal and assigns it to randomCardinal in the body of the module. This method of initialization makes it difficult to restart the process of random number generation using a new seed value. To solve this problem, we add an initialization procedure to RandomNumberGenerator. This procedure must be exported to make it visible outside the module:

```
MODULE RandomNumberGenerator;
  (* exports modulus and Random; Random returns a pseudorandom
     CARDINAL number between 0 and modulus - 1 *)

  EXPORT modulus, Random, InitializeSeed;

  CONST multiplier = 40;
        increment = 3641;
        modulus = 729;

  VAR randomCardinal: CARDINAL;

  PROCEDURE Random(): CARDINAL;
    (* returns a pseudorandom number between 0 and modulus - 1;
       modifies the variable randomCardinal *)
```

```
  BEGIN
    randomCardinal := (multiplier * randomCardinal + increment)
                        MOD modulus;
    RETURN randomCardinal
  END Random;

  PROCEDURE InitializeSeed(seed: CARDINAL);
  BEGIN
    randomCardinal := seed
  END InitializeSeed;

END RandomNumberGenerator;
```

The module (or procedure) in which `RandomNumberGenerator` is declared can call `InitializeSeed` to restart random number generation with a different seed.

Local modules are particularly useful in conjunction with coroutines and interrupt handling, as we will see in Chapter 12. Local modules can hide variables shared by coroutines (examples appear in Sections 12.1, 12.2, and 12.3). Local modules can also be used to disable interrupts within selected regions of a program (see Section 12.4).

Local Module Declarations

A local module looks exactly like a program module, with two exceptions:

A local module may contain an export list. If present, this must appear immediately after the import lists.

A semicolon, not a period, follows the declaration of a local module.

The *ModuleDeclaration* syntax chart (Figure 9.11) is almost identical to the *ProgramModule* syntax chart.

Figure 9.11 ***ModuleDeclaration***

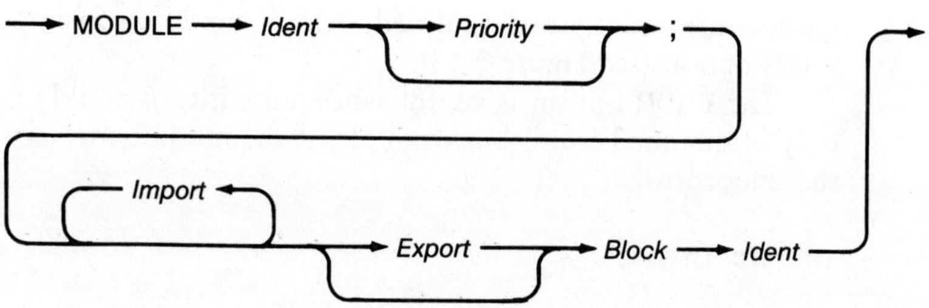

By default, all entities declared in a local module are visible only within the module itself; entities visible in the enclosing block (module or procedure) are not visible in the module. In Figure 9.12, the variable x is visible throughout the Outer module but not in the Inner local module. The variable y is visible only inside Inner, not in Outer.

Figure 9.12
A Local Module with No Import or Export Lists

```
MODULE Outer;
  VAR x: REAL;

  MODULE Inner;
    VAR y: REAL;
  (* only y is visible *)
  END Inner;

  (* only x is visible *)
END Outer.
```

The only connection between a local module and its surrounding environment is through the module's import lists and export list. An import list specifies that one or more entities visible in the enclosing block are to be visible in the module. An export list specifies that entities visible in the module are to be visible in the enclosing block as well. A local module acts as a wall through which entities can pass only by appearing in an import or export list.

Import into a Local Module

An import list in a local module has the same form as an import list in a program module or implementation module (see Section 2.2). However, importing using the FROM option, which is common in program and implementation modules, is rare in local modules. Because identifiers visible in the block surrounding a local module are usually not qualified, a local module can import them without the FROM option (see Figure 9.13).

The FROM option is useful when an entity is visible in the enclosing block only in qualified form. For example, if the module Outer imports InOut using the import list

```
IMPORT InOut;
```

all the entities exported by InOut are visible in Outer in qualified fashion. If the local module Inner needs to import the procedure WriteString, it has two options: (1) import InOut as a whole (Figure 9.14) or (2) import WriteString alone using an import list with a FROM clause (Figure 9.15). The first option makes all the entities exported by `InOut` visible in `Inner` (qualification is required, however). The second option makes only `WriteString` visible in `Inner`; no qualification is necessary. It is not legal to import `WriteString` into `Inner` using the import list

```
IMPORT InOut.WriteString;    (* illegal *)
```

because an import list may contain only identifiers, not qualified identifiers.

Figure 9.13
Importing without the FROM Option

```
MODULE Outer;
  VAR x: REAL;

  MODULE Inner;
    IMPORT x;
    VAR y: REAL;
  (* both x and y are
     visible *)
  END Inner;

  (* only x is visible *)
END Outer.
```

Figure 9.14, left
Importing a Module as a Whole

Figure 9.15, right
Importing with the FROM Option

```
MODULE Outer;
  IMPORT InOut;

  MODULE Inner;
    IMPORT InOut;

  END Inner;

END Outer.
```

```
MODULE Outer;
  IMPORT InOut;

  MODULE Inner;
    FROM InOut IMPORT
      WriteString;
  END Inner;

END Outer.
```

Export from a Local Module

Figure 9.16 shows the syntax of the export list in a local module. If the word `QUALIFIED` appears in a module's export list, we must use the name of the module to qualify the names of the exported entities (Figure 9.17). If we omit the word QUALIFIED, then we may reference exported entities outside the module by using their names alone. (Modula-2 still allows qualification when we omit QUALIFIED, however.) Figure 9.18 shows the export of a variable without the QUALIFIED option.

Figure 9.16

Export

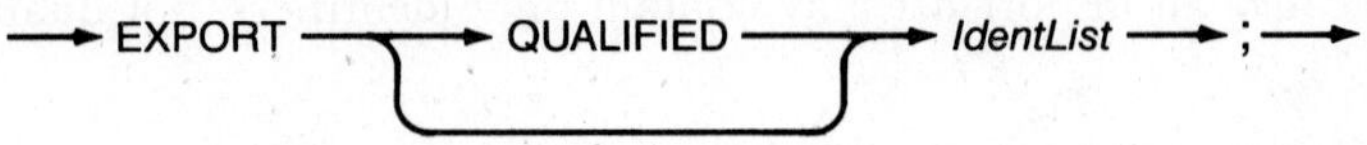

Figure 9.17
Exporting with the QUALIFIED Option

```
MODULE Outer;
  VAR x: REAL;

  MODULE Inner;
    EXPORT QUALIFIED y;
    VAR y: REAL;
  (* only y is visible *)
  END Inner;

(* both x and Inner.y are
   visible *)
END Outer.
```

Figure 9.18
Exporting without the QUALIFIED Option

```
MODULE Outer;
  VAR x: REAL;

  MODULE Inner;
    EXPORT y;
    VAR y: REAL;
  (* only y is visible *)
  END Inner;

(* both x and y are
   visible; y may also be
   referenced as Inner.y *)
END Outer.
```

We must use the QUALIFIED option when exporting a name would cause a conflict with another name visible in the enclosing block. In Figure 9.19, it would be illegal for the module Inner to export x without the QUALIFIED option, because another entity named x is already visible in Outer. The QUALIFIED option makes possible the export of x.

Figure 9.19
Exporting with the QUALIFIED Option to Avoid a Name Conflict

```
MODULE Outer;
  VAR x: REAL;

  MODULE Inner;
    EXPORT QUALIFIED x;
    VAR x: REAL;
  END Inner;

  (* x refers to the variable
     declared in Outer;
     Inner.x refers to the
     variable in Inner *)
END Outer.
```

Because a local module may have only one export list, the QUALIFIED option—if used—applies to all entities that the module exports.

Import and Export of Enumeration and Record Types

In two cases, exporting a name causes the automatic export of other names. First, if a local module exports an enumeration type, then the module automatically exports the identifiers that represent values of the enumeration type. (Alternatively, the module may export individual enumeration constants without exporting the type itself.) Second, exporting a record type causes the export of the names of its fields. The field names are not directly visible in the enclosing block; we can use them only to select fields in a record of that type. The module DateTypes illustrates these two cases.

```
MODULE SetDate;
  (* sets current date *)

  MODULE DateTypes;
    (* exports Month and Date types *)
```

```
    EXPORT Months, Date;

    TYPE Months = (Jan, Feb, Mar, Apr, May, Jun, Jul, Aug, Sep,
                   Oct, Nov, Dec);
         Date = RECORD
                  month: Months;
                  day: [1..31];
                  year: CARDINAL
                END;

  END DateTypes;

  VAR currentDate: Date;

BEGIN
  currentDate.month := Nov;
  currentDate.day := 13;
  currentDate.year := 1986
END SetDate.
```

The assignments to the fields of `currentDate` are legal because the field names `month`, `day`, and `year` were exported along with `Date`. The use of `Nov` on the right side of the first assignment is legal because `Nov` was exported along with `Months`.

The special rules for exporting enumeration and record types apply to importing as well. Importing an enumeration type causes automatic import of the identifiers representing its values; importing a record type automatically imports its field names.

Module Initialization

A local module may have a *body*: a sequence of statements most often used to initialize the module's variables. In Figure 9.20, the body of the local module `Inner` initializes the variable `y`. A program cannot "call" a local module in the way that it can call a procedure; instead, the body of a local module is executed automatically when the enclosing module or procedure is executed. The order of execution is important: The body of a local module is always executed immediately *before* the body of the enclosing module or procedure. In Figure 9.20, the body of `Inner` will be executed before the body of `Outer`; thus, `y` has the value 1.0 when the body of `Outer` is executed. If several local modules are nested inside the same module or procedure, their bodies are executed in the order of the module declarations (but all are executed before the body of the enclosing module or procedure).

Figure 9.20
Initialization of a Local Module

```
MODULE Outer;
  VAR x: REAL;

  MODULE Inner;
    EXPORT y;
    VAR y: REAL;
  BEGIN
    y := 1.0
  END Inner;

BEGIN
  x := 2.0 * y + 1.0
END Outer.
```

The body of a local module may contain a RETURN statement. The effect of executing a RETURN statement is to terminate execution of the module body. Execution continues with the body of the module or procedure that would normally be executed next according to the rules just described.

The body of a local module declared in a program module or implementation module will be executed only once (because the body of the enclosing module is executed once). Variables in the local module are *static*: they retain their values throughout the execution of the program. However, the body of a local module declared in a procedure will be executed every time the procedure is called. In this case, the variables of the local module have the same lifetime as the variables of the procedure; the values of both are lost whenever the procedure returns. In general, variables in a local module have the same lifetime as variables in the enclosing block; thus, a local module restricts the visibility of variables without affecting their lifetime.

EXAMPLE PROGRAM

Counting Words and Sentences in a Text File

To see how local modules are used, we will revise the program `CountWords` of Section 5.4 so that it contains a local module. Recall that `CountWords` counts the number of words and sentences in a file of English text. The program stores these counts in the variables `numWords` and `numSentences`, which are visible throughout `CountWords`.

We will revise `CountWords` to include a local module, called `Counts`, which hides `numWords` and `numSentences`. `Counts` communicates with the rest of `CountWords` only through the procedures `UpdateCounts` and `FetchCounts`. `CollectStatistics` calls `UpdateCounts` each time it reads a character from the file; `UpdateCounts` then updates the values of `numWords` and numSentences. When CollectStatistics reaches the end of the file, PrintStatistics calls FetchCounts to fetch the final values of numWords and numSentences.

One advantage of this version of CountWords is a clearer division between the portion of the program that deals with input and output (CollectStatistics and PrintStatistics and the body of the program module) and the portion that counts words and sentences (the Counts module). In general, such a division makes a program easier to modify.

```
MODULE CountWords;
  (* counts the number of words and sentences in a text file *)

  FROM InOut IMPORT OpenInput, CloseInput, Read, Done,
                    WriteCard, WriteString, WriteLn;

  MODULE Counts;
    (* maintains word and sentence counts *)

    EXPORT UpdateCounts, FetchCounts;

    VAR numWords, numSentences: CARDINAL;
        previousChar: CHAR;

    PROCEDURE UpdateCounts(currentChar: CHAR);
      (* updates word and sentence counts to reflect
         currentChar *)

      PROCEDURE IsWhiteSpace(ch: CHAR): BOOLEAN;
        (* returns TRUE if ch is a whitespace character;
           assumes ASCII character set *)
      BEGIN
        RETURN ch <= ' '
      END IsWhiteSpace;

      PROCEDURE IncWordCount;
        (* increments word count at beginning of a word *)
      BEGIN
        IF IsWhiteSpace(previousChar) AND
           NOT IsWhiteSpace(currentChar) THEN
          INC(numWords)
        END
      END IncWordCount;

      PROCEDURE IncSentenceCount;
        (* increments sentence count at end of a sentence *)
      BEGIN
        IF ((previousChar = '.') OR (previousChar = '?') OR
            (previousChar = '!')) AND
           (IsWhiteSpace(currentChar) OR (currentChar = ')'))
```

```
        THEN
          INC(numSentences)
        END
      END IncSentenceCount;

    BEGIN  (* UpdateCounts *)
      IncWordCount;
      IncSentenceCount;
      previousChar := currentChar
    END UpdateCounts;

    PROCEDURE FetchCounts(VAR wordCount,
                              sentenceCount: CARDINAL);
      (* fetches current word and sentence counts *)
    BEGIN
      wordCount := numWords;
      sentenceCount := numSentences
    END FetchCounts;

  BEGIN  (* Counts *)
    numWords := 0;
    numSentences := 0;
    previousChar := ' '
  END Counts;

  PROCEDURE CollectStatistics;
    (* reads characters from input file, computing word count
       and sentence count *)
    VAR currentChar: CHAR;
  BEGIN
    Read(currentChar);
    WHILE Done DO
      UpdateCounts(currentChar);
      Read(currentChar)
    END
  END CollectStatistics;


  PROCEDURE PrintStatistics;
    (* prints the word count and sentence count with
       appropriate captions *)
    VAR wordCount, sentenceCount: CARDINAL;
  BEGIN
    FetchCounts(wordCount, sentenceCount);
    WriteString("Number of words: ");
    WriteCard(wordCount, 1);
    WriteLn;
    WriteString("Number of sentences: ");
    WriteCard(sentenceCount, 1);
    WriteLn
  END PrintStatistics;
```

```
BEGIN
  WriteString("Enter name of input file.");
  WriteLn;
  OpenInput("TXT");
  WriteLn;
  CollectStatistics;
  PrintStatistics;
  CloseInput
END CountWords.
```

The `Counts` module exports two entities: the procedures `UpdateCounts` and `FetchCounts`. If the export list had contained the word `QUALIFIED`, then we would refer to the entities as `Counts.UpdateCounts` and `Counts.FetchCounts` in the enclosing module. Because the export list does not contain the word `QUALIFIED`, we can use the names `UpdateCounts` and `FetchCounts` outside the `Counts` module without qualification. The other entities declared in `Counts` (the variables `numWords`, `numSentences`, and `previousChar`) are not visible in the rest of `CountWords`.

Import and Export of Modules (OPTIONAL)

Modula-2 allows local modules to import and export other local modules (modules, after all, are entities). In Figure 9.21, the module M2 exports the module M3, which is then imported by M4.

Figure 9.21
Exporting a Local Module

```
MODULE M1;

  MODULE M2;
    EXPORT M3;

    MODULE M3;
      EXPORT x;
      VAR x: REAL;
    END M3;

  END M2;

  MODULE M4;
    IMPORT M3;
  END M4;

END M1.
```

The Second Edition of *Programming in Modula-2* contains the following sentence: "If a module identifier is exported, then all identifiers occurring in that module's export list are also exported." A *literal* reading of this sentence would indicate that x is visible not only in M3 and M2, but also in M1, because M2 exports M3 and M3 exports x. Some compilers based on the Second Edition assume this interpretation. However, Wirth has since explained that if a module M is exported, the names that M exports become visible only if qualified by M; this rule remains true regardless of whether or not the word QUALIFIED appears in M's export list. (Thus, the import and export of local modules closely resembles the import and export of record types.) For example, M3.x is visible in both M1 and M4. The sentence just quoted does not appear in the Third Edition.

9.4 Scope and Visibility

Section 5.4 showed how procedures affect the visibility of names in a program. We must extend the scope rules presented in that section to account for library modules and local modules. In this section, we first show how to determine the visibility of entities in a module, then discuss the effect of nesting modules and procedures.

The rules for determining which entities are visible in a given module (program, definition, implementation, or local) are simple. An entity x is visible in a module M

if x is declared at the outermost level of M
or if x is imported into M
or if x is exported by a local module declared at the outermost level of M

If M is an implementation module, entities defined in the matching definition module are also visible in M.

Figure 9.22 shows a program with a complex structure that includes a library module and nested local modules. A comment in each module shows what variables are visible in that module. (Although our examples show only variables, the same scope rules apply to all other entities as well.)

This example illustrates an important point about local modules: We must import and export one level at a time. Module M3, for example, cannot import the variable c directly from M4, where it is declared. Instead, M1 must first import c, then M2 must import c. Only then can M3 import c.

The scope rules for modules allow an entity to be exported from one local module and imported into another (see Figure 9.23). Because M2 exports x, it is visible in M1. But because x is visible in M1, M3 can import it. A local module can import any entity that is visible in the enclosing block, whether or not the entity is actually declared in that block.

Figure 9.22
Visibility of Names in a Program Containing a Library Module and Local Modules

```
MODULE M1;
  FROM M4 IMPORT c, d;
  VAR a, b: CARDINAL;

  MODULE M2;
    IMPORT a, c;
    EXPORT e, f;
    VAR e: REAL;

    MODULE M3;
      IMPORT c, e;
      EXPORT f;
      VAR f: BOOLEAN;
    (* visible:
               c, e, f *)
    END M3;

  (* visible:
             a, c, e, f *)
  END M2;

(* visible:
        a, b, c, d, e, f *)
END M1.
```

```
DEFINITION MODULE M4;
  VAR c: CARDINAL;
      d: BOOLEAN;
(* visible:
                c, d *)
END M4.
```

```
IMPLEMENTATION MODULE M4;
  VAR g: CHAR;
      h: REAL;

  MODULE M5;
    IMPORT c, g;
    EXPORT i;
    VAR i: CARDINAL;
  (* visible:
              c, g, i *)
  END M5;

(* visible:
          c, d, g, h, i *)
END M4.
```

Figure 9.23
Exporting an Entity from One Local Module and Importing It into Another

```
MODULE M1;

  MODULE M2;
    EXPORT x;
    VAR x: REAL;
  END M2;

  MODULE M3;
    IMPORT x;
  END M3;

END M1.
```

When a local module exports an entity, the scope of that entity expands over the enclosing block. Thus, the preceding program would still be legal if we declared `M3` before `M2`. (Some one-pass compilers do not observe this rule, however, and require that an entity be defined prior to being imported into a local module.)

Exporting an entity from a local module and then importing it into another local module is like exporting an entity from a definition module and importing it into a program module or implementation module. Think of a Modula-2 system as a single, huge module surrounding all program, definition, and implementation modules. Figure 9.24 shows a program module `M1` importing an entity `x` from the definition module `M2`. When `M2` exports `x`, the name `M2.x` becomes visible in the surrounding environment (in this case, the entire system). When `M1` imports `x`, the `FROM` clause makes `x` visible in `M1` without qualification. The process of exporting to an enclosing environment, then importing into another module, is exactly the same as in our previous example. This figure shows why we must qualify the name of an entity exported from a definition module; if Modula-2 allowed unqualified export of entities from definition modules, to avoid conflicts the programmer would have to know the names of all entities exported by all definition modules in the Modula-2 system.

Figure 9.24
Visibility of Names in a Modula-2 System

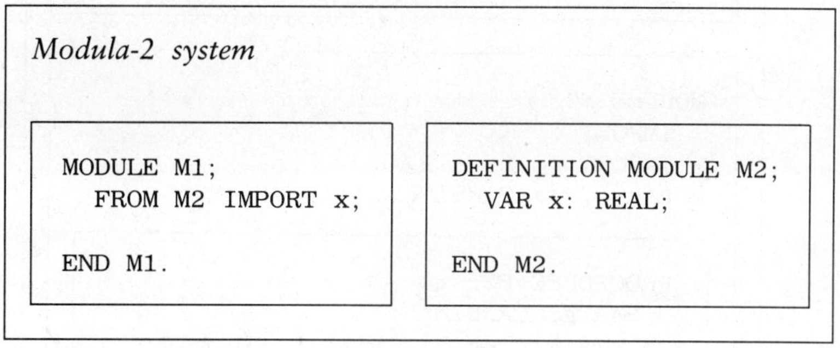

Scope Rules for Nested Procedures and Modules

Modula-2 allows nested procedure declarations and nested module declarations. But Modula-2 also allows programmers to declare procedures within modules, and modules within procedures. So, in fact, we can nest procedure and module declarations in any conceivable combination. (In practice, programmers rarely nest local modules inside procedures; nesting procedures inside local modules is more common.) Fortunately, it is not hard to determine the visibility of names provided that we remember the differences between the scope rules for procedures and the scope rules for modules.

In Section 5.4, we discussed Modula-2's scope rules for procedures. Names visible in the block surrounding a procedure are automatically visible inside the

Figure 9.25
Visibility of Names in a Program Containing Procedures and Local Modules

```
MODULE M1;
  VAR a, b, c: CARDINAL;

  PROCEDURE P1;
    VAR a: CARDINAL;

    MODULE M2;
      IMPORT a, b, f;
      EXPORT d;
      VAR d: CARDINAL;
     (* visible: a (in P1), b (in M1),
                 d (in M2), f (in M3)    *)
    END M2;

    (* visible: a (in P1), b (in M1),
                c (in M1), d (in M2),
                e (in M3), f (in M3),
                M2, M3, P1               *)
  END P1;

  MODULE M3;
    IMPORT c;
    EXPORT e, f;
    VAR e, f: CARDINAL;

    PROCEDURE P2;
      VAR g: CARDINAL;
     (* visible: c (in M1), e (in M3),
                 f (in M3), g (in P2),
                 P2                      *)
    END P2;

    (* visible: c (in M1), e (in M3),
                f (in M3), P2            *)
  END M3;

  (* visible: a (in M1), b (in M1),
              c (in M1), e (in M3),
              f (in M3), M3, P1          *)
END M1.
```

procedure unless it declares an entity of the same name. However, entities declared in a procedure are not visible outside the procedure. Because names in the block surrounding a procedure are automatically visible in the procedure, we say that a procedure declaration defines an *open scope*.

A module defines a *closed scope*. Entities declared in the block surrounding a module are not automatically visible within the module, although they become visible if the module imports them. Likewise, entities declared inside a module are visible in the surrounding block only if the module exports them.

Figure 9.25 demonstrates the effects of combining open and closed scopes. This diagram shows the visibility of procedure and module names, not just variable names, because the same scope rules apply to all entities in a program. The visibility of procedure names is important because a call of a procedure is possible only where the procedure name is visible. The importance of module name visibility is not immediately clear, because we cannot "call" a module. In fact, the only use for a module name is to qualify the name of an entity that it exports.

Visibility of Standard Identifiers

The Third Edition of *Programming in Modula-2* states that standard identifiers (such as `INTEGER`, `TRUE`, and `ABS`) may be redefined within a module. For example, a module could declare `INTEGER` to be the name of a variable. Any standard identifiers not otherwise visible in a module are automatically imported with their usual meanings. In other words, a Modula-2 compiler always attempts to determine the meaning of an identifier using the normal scope rules for procedures and modules. If the identifier is not visible using these rules, the compiler then checks to see if it is a standard identifier.

The Second Edition stated that standard identifiers were automatically imported by all modules and therefore could not be redefined in modules (although this edition allowed redefinition in procedures).

EXERCISES

Section 9.1

1. Write both the definition and implementation parts of a library module called `ErrorMessages` that exports two procedures, `FatalError` and `Diagnostic`. Both procedures expect a single parameter, named `message`, of type `ARRAY OF CHAR`. When called, `FatalError` writes

   `Fatal error:` *message*

   where *message* is the value of the string `message`, and then terminates the program. `Diagnostic` writes

   `Diagnostic:` *message*

   and then returns.

2. Revise the `ErrorMessages` module of exercise 1 so that the implementation part of the module hides a variable called `diagnosticCount`, which it increments at each call of `Diagnostic`. `ErrorMessages` should export a procedure named `FetchDiagnosticCount` that retrieves the current value of `diagnosticCount`.

3. Write the definition part of a library module named `PolyArithmetic` that performs arithmetic on polynomials. `PolyArithmetic` should export an opaque type named `Polynomial` and procedures to perform the following operations on polynomials:

   create a polynomial from its coefficients
   destroy a polynomial
   test whether two polynomials are equal
   compute the degree of a polynomial
   extract the *i*th coefficient from a polynomial
   evaluate a polynomial
   add two polynomials
   subtract two polynomials
   multiply two polynomials
   divide two polynomials (yielding both a quotient and remainder)

4. Rewrite the implementation part of `CharacterStacks` to implement `CharStack` using a linked list rather than an array. The definition part of `CharacterStacks` should not change.

5. Write the implementation part of the library module `ComplexNumbers`, given the following definition part:

```
DEFINITION MODULE ComplexNumbers;
  (* exports type Complex and procedures for manipulating
     complex numbers *)

  TYPE Complex;

  PROCEDURE Create(realPart, imagPart: REAL): Complex;
    (* creates a complex number from its real and imaginary
       parts *)

  PROCEDURE Assign(c1: Complex; VAR c2: Complex);
    (* copies the value of c1 to c2 *)

  PROCEDURE Equal(c1, c2: Complex): BOOLEAN;
    (* returns TRUE if c1 and c2 have the same real and
       imaginary parts, FALSE otherwise *)

  PROCEDURE RealPart(c: Complex): REAL;
    (* returns the real part of a complex number *)
```

```
    PROCEDURE ImagPart(c: Complex): REAL;
      (* returns the imaginary part of a complex number *)

    PROCEDURE Add(c1, c2: Complex; VAR c3: Complex);
      (* adds c1 and c2 and stores the result in c3 *)

    PROCEDURE Subtract(c1, c2: Complex; VAR c3: Complex);
      (* subtracts c2 from c1 and stores the result in c3 *)

    PROCEDURE Multiply(c1, c2: Complex; VAR c3: Complex);
      (* multiplies c1 and c2 and stores the result in c3 *)

    PROCEDURE Divide(c1, c2: Complex; VAR c3: Complex);
      (* divides c1 by c2 and stores the result in c3 *)

END ComplexNumbers.
```

6. We could have written the procedures `Add`, `Subtract`, `Multiply`, and `Divide` in exercise 5 as functions instead. For example, Add would have the following heading:

```
PROCEDURE Add(c1, c2: Complex): Complex;
  (* returns the sum of c1 and c2 *)
```

What would be the advantages and disadvantages of writing these as functions?

Section 9.2

7. Suppose that a program consists of the following modules:

M1.MOD—imports from `M2`, `M3`, `M4`
M2.DEF —imports from `M3`
M2.MOD—imports from `M4`
M3.DEF
M3.MOD—imports from `M2`
M4.DEF —imports from `M2`
M4.MOD

Assuming that definition modules must be compiled, give one compilation order for this program.

8. In the program of exercise 7, how many different compilation orders are possible?

9. In the program of exercise 7, if M2.DEF changes, what other modules must we recompile?

10. In the program of exercise 7, in what order will the bodies of `M1`, `M2`, `M3`, and `M4` be executed?

11. Is it possible to write a program consisting of a program module and one or more library modules in such a way that the program has only one possible compilation order? If so, sketch the program; if not, explain why not.

12. Some Modula-2 systems require compilation of definition modules; others do not. What are the advantages and disadvantages of each approach?

13. Some Modula-2 systems require a separate linking phase prior to program execution; other systems perform linking when a program is loaded for execution. What are the advantages and disadvantages of each approach?

Section 9.3

14. The first version of the `RandomNumberGenerator` module imports an entity called `seed`. The body of `RandomNumberGenerator` will be executed before the body of the enclosing block, so it would seem that `seed` must be a constant rather than a variable, because the enclosing block cannot initialize it. Are there any circumstances in which `seed` could be a variable?

15. Write a local module called `Time` that allows a program to keep track of the current time of day. `Time` should export the following procedures:

```
PROCEDURE SetTime(hour, minute, second: CARDINAL);
  (* sets the current time *)

PROCEDURE AddSecond;
  (* adds one second to the current time *)

PROCEDURE GetTime(VAR hour, minute, second: CARDINAL);
  (* fetches the current time *)
```

Store the current time in one or more variables declared in `Time` but not exported.

16. True or false: A local module with no import or export lists can have no effect on the behavior of a program. Explain your answer.

Section 9.4 17. For each region (module or procedure) in the following program, indicate which entities (including modules and procedures) are visible in that region:

```
MODULE M1;
  IMPORT MathLib0;
  FROM MathLib0 IMPORT sqrt;
  VAR a: CARDINAL;
      b: REAL;

  PROCEDURE P1;
    VAR c: INTEGER;

    MODULE M2;
      FROM MathLib0 IMPORT exp;
      IMPORT a;
      EXPORT d;
      VAR c, d: CHAR;
    END M2;

  END P1;

  MODULE M3;
    IMPORT b, sqrt;
    EXPORT e;
    VAR e: BOOLEAN;

    PROCEDURE P2;
      VAR b: CHAR;
    END P2;

  END M3;

END M1.
```

18. In what order will the bodies of the modules in Figure 9.22 be executed?

19. In what order will the bodies of the modules in Figure 9.25 be executed?

10 Program Design Using Modules

When designing a program, the programmer faces the difficult task of deciding how many modules to divide the program into and what to put into each module. Chapter 10 supplies guidelines for designing library modules and for dividing a program into modules. In addition, Chapter 10 provides a number of example modules. Unlike the other chapters in this book, Chapter 10 does not introduce any features of Modula-2.

Section 10.1 discusses four useful groupings of entities into library modules. Section 10.2 describes a library module for handling strings, while Section 10.3 presents a library module that exports an opaque type whose values are sets of characters. These modules illustrate the groupings that Section 10.1 discusses; they are also useful additions to a programmer's toolkit. Section 10.4 goes a step further than Section 10.1: It describes a design methodology (called *object-oriented design*) that allows a programmer to proceed from an informal description of a program to a formal design of the modules in the program. Section 10.5 presents several ways in which a library module can signal a client module that an error has occurred.

10.1 A Classification of Library Modules

Although a library module can export any mixture of constants, types, variables, and procedures, the following kinds of modules have proved particularly useful:

- modules that export related procedures (the module hides only the details of how it implements the procedures)
- modules that export related constants and/or types (the module hides nothing)
- modules that export procedures operating on a data structure hidden within the implementation part of the module

modules that export an opaque type and a collection of procedures that operate on values of that type (the implementation part of the module hides the representation of the type)

Notice that none of these modules export variables. Although Modula-2 allows library modules to export variables, doing so can be dangerous; one module might incorrectly alter a variable that belongs to another module, causing errors in the latter's operation. It is safer for modules to communicate through procedures rather than by directly examining and changing each other's variables.

Modules That Export Related Procedures

We have seen several examples of modules that export collections of related procedures:

`ExpLib` (Section 1.3)
Wirth's `MathLib0` module (Section 3.1)
`AngleConversions` (Section 9.1)

Another example (the `String` module) appears in Section 10.2. Wirth's `InOut` module, which exports input/output procedures, might seem to fall in this category but in fact does not. Hidden in the implementation part of `InOut` are variables that keep track of the current input and output streams.

Sometimes a module whose main purpose is the export of related procedures may also need to export other entities. A case in point is the following module, which exports a `Vector` type and a collection of procedures that perform common vector operations.

```
DEFINITION MODULE VectorOperations;
  (* exports type Vector and procedures for performing
     operations on vectors *)

  TYPE Vector = ARRAY [1..3] OF REAL;

  PROCEDURE Add(v, w: Vector; VAR sum: Vector);
    (* adds v and w, storing the result in sum *)

  PROCEDURE Subtract(v, w: Vector; VAR difference: Vector);
    (* subtracts w from v, storing the result in difference *)

  PROCEDURE Scale(r: REAL; v: Vector; VAR w: Vector);
    (* multiplies v by the scalar r, storing the result in w *)

  PROCEDURE InnerProduct(v, w: Vector): REAL;
    (* returns the inner product of v and w *)
```

```
  PROCEDURE CrossProduct(v, w: Vector; VAR product: Vector);
    (* computes the cross product of v and w, storing the
       result in product *)

END VectorOperations.
```

Although VectorOperations exports a type, its primary purpose is to export a collection of related procedures. The type is merely a convenient way to ensure that the vector parameters to the procedures are one-dimensional REAL arrays of length 3. Because Vector is not an opaque type, the implementation part of VectorOperations hides nothing but procedure bodies. If Vector were an opaque type, the VectorOperations module would fall in a different category, because the implementation part of the module would hide the representation of Vector. (Notice, by the way, that we would gain little by making Vector an opaque type. The natural representation of a vector as a one-dimensional array with three components is natural, efficient, and unlikely to change.)

Modules That Export Related Constants or Types

A library module can serve to collect related constants:

```
DEFINITION MODULE LengthConversions;
  (* exports constants used in converting from U.S. to metric
     lengths; to convert, multiply by the number shown *)

  CONST feetToMeters = 0.3048;
        inchesToCentimeters = 2.54;
        milesToKilometers = 1.6093;
        yardsToMeters = 0.9144;

END LengthConversions.
```

Client modules can simply import the names of the various constants from LengthConversions without having to define their values. A module that exports constants is not only a convenience for the programmer but also helps prevent inconsistencies caused by two modules using different values for the same constant (a common error, particularly when the value of the constant is a multi-digit number). Furthermore, should we have to modify the value of a constant, we need perform the change only in one place: in the definition part of the module that exports the constant.

A module that exports related constants is often useful in more than one program. For example, some Modula-2 systems provide a library module called ASCII, which contains declarations of constants representing nonprinting ASCII characters (nul represents 0C, bel represents 7C, etc.).

It can sometimes be convenient to collect related types in a module:

```
DEFINITION MODULE AstronomicalTypes;
  (* exports types useful for astronomical programs *)

  TYPE Planets = (Mercury, Venus, Earth, Mars, Jupiter, Saturn,
                  Uranus, Neptune, Pluto);
       BrightestStars = (Sirius, Canopus, AlphaCentauri, Vega,
                         Capella, Arcturus, Rigel, Procyon);

END AstronomicalTypes.
```

A module that exports types provides the same advantages as a module that exports constants. In fact, it is not unusual for library modules to export both constants and types. For example, the module AstronomicalTypes might be more useful if it also exported common astronomical constants.

A final note: When a definition module defines only constants and/or types, the matching implementation module is normally empty:

```
IMPLEMENTATION MODULE LengthConversions;
  (* empty *)
END LengthConversions.
```

Even though such an implementation module may seem unnecessary, many Modula-2 systems require that the programmer compile and link it along with the other modules in a program.

Modules That Hide an Object

We use the term *object* to describe a data structure hidden in the implementation part of a library module. A client of the library module can access and modify the object only by calling procedures that the module exports; these procedures, because they are declared in the same implementation module as the object, can see the object's internal structure. Client modules, however, see only the procedures that the module exports. Clients can neither see nor take advantage of the object's internal structure.

The library module CharStackModule of Section 9.1 is an example of a module that hides an object (a stack, in this case). CharStackModule exports procedures that operate on the stack, but the stack itself is not visible to client modules.

Another example, the SymbolTable module, hides a symbol table of the kind a two-pass assembler uses to keep track of labels in an assembly language program. During its first pass over a program, the assembler enters labels into the table; with each label, it enters the object code address corresponding to the label. During the second pass, the assembler looks up each label used as an operand to obtain the corresponding address. Here is the definition part of SymbolTable:

```
DEFINITION MODULE SymbolTable;
  (* exports procedures for manipulating a hidden symbol
     table used by a two-pass assembler *)

  PROCEDURE EnterLabel(label: ARRAY OF CHAR; addr: CARDINAL;
                       VAR duplicate: BOOLEAN);
    (* enters label and addr into symbol table; sets duplicate
       to TRUE if the label is already in the table, FALSE
       otherwise *)

  PROCEDURE FindLabel(label: ARRAY OF CHAR; VAR addr: CARDINAL;
                      VAR found: BOOLEAN);
    (* looks up a label in the symbol table and stores its
       address into addr; sets found to TRUE if label is found,
       FALSE otherwise *)

END SymbolTable.
```

This definition module offers no clue as to how the symbol table is represented; it could be an array, a hash table, a binary search tree, or any other appropriate data structure.

Modules That Hide the Structure of a Type

A module that exports an opaque type and a collection of procedures that operate on values of that type is said to implement an *abstract data type*. Character-Stacks (Section 9.1) is an example of such a module. CharacterStacks exports an opaque type (CharStack), hiding the representation of the type inside the implementation part of the module. Clients of CharacterStacks may declare variables of type CharStack and operate on these variables using procedures that CharacterStacks exports; clients do not have access to the representation of CharStack, however.

The module Matrices, whose definition part follows, is another example of a module that implements an abstract data type:

```
DEFINITION MODULE Matrices;
  (* exports type Matrix and procedures for operating on values
     of this type *)

  TYPE Matrix;
```

```
    PROCEDURE Create(VAR m: Matrix; firstRow, lastRow,
                     firstcolumn, lastColumn: INTEGER);
      (* creates a matrix with the specified bounds and
         initializes all components to 0.0 *)

    PROCEDURE Destroy(VAR m: Matrix);
      (* destroys m, releasing the space that it occupies *)

    PROCEDURE Store(VAR m: Matrix; row, column: INTEGER;
                    component: REAL);
      (* stores a component into m in the specified row and
         column; attempting to store outside the bounds of the
         matrix causes program termination *)

    PROCEDURE Fetch(m: Matrix; row, column: INTEGER): REAL;
      (* returns the component of m in the specified row and
         column; attempting to fetch outside the bounds of the
         matrix causes program termination *)

    PROCEDURE Add(m1, m2: Matrix; VAR m3: Matrix);
      (* adds m1 and m2, storing the result in m3; if m1, m2,
         and m3 do not have the same size, the program is
         terminated *)

    PROCEDURE Multiply(m1, m2: Matrix; VAR m3: Matrix);
      (* multiplies m1 and m2, storing the result in m3; if the
         sizes of m1, m2, and m3 are not appropriate for
         multiplication, the program is terminated *)

END Matrices.
```

The `Matrices` module is designed to support the use of matrices too large to represent in the normal fashion (as two-dimensional arrays). Because `Matrix` is an opaque type, the implementation part of `Matrices` need not use the normal representation for variables of type `Matrix`; in particular, the implementation part may use sparse matrix techniques to allow the client to create very large matrices. (Note that calling these procedures involves little overhead, regardless of how large the matrices are, because values of type `Matrix` must be pointers.)

Choosing Between Objects and Opaque Types

Objects are closely related to opaque types. A value of an opaque type (`CharStack`, say) is an object (a stack) whose internal representation is hidden and that a client module can manipulate only by a specific set of procedures (`Initialize`, `Push`, `Pop`, and `IsEmpty`, in this case). Conversely, a module

(`CharStackModule`) that hides an object, exporting only procedures that manipulate the object, can be modified to export an opaque type (`CharStack`) instead, where each value of the opaque type is an object identical in structure to the original object.

A programmer who wants to write a library module to hide the representation of a data structure must decide whether the module will treat the data structure as (1) an object (the module exports only procedures that operate on the data structure) or as (2) an instance of an opaque type (the module exports an opaque type as well as a collection of procedures). Several factors influence this decision. The main advantage of objects is their simplicity. Procedures that manipulate an object do not need a parameter to indicate *which* object, because there is only one; procedures that manipulate variables of an opaque type must have an additional parameter to indicate the variable involved in the operation. An object does not need an initialization procedure, because the body of the implementation module can initialize the object. With an opaque type, an initialization procedure is mandatory, because many variables of that type may exist. Furthermore, we always run the risk that a program will fail to initialize one of these variables, with unpredictable consequences; objects can be initialized automatically, so no such danger exists. The primary advantage of exporting an opaque type is that client modules may use the type to declare any number of variables; this ability makes the module more general and increases the chance that we can reuse it in later programs. The export of an opaque type also makes it more apparent to clients that the procedures exported by the library module operate on a data structure. When a library module hides an object, clients may not always realize that the procedures exported by the module affect hidden variables.

The `SymbolTable` module in this section is an example of a data structure that is best written as an object. The client (the assembler) needs only one such table, so nothing is gained by having the module export an opaque type. The `Matrices` module, however, must export an opaque type to be of much use.

10.2 A String-handling Module

This section presents the definition and implementation parts of a string-handling module called `String`. In 1984 a group of Modula-2 experts prepared a collection of library modules to present to the British Standards Institution for possible standardization; `String` was one of these modules.* We devote a section to this module for several reasons. First, it serves as another example of a library module that exports only procedures and does not hide variables in its implementation

*R. Bush, "Modula-2 Library Draft," *Modula-2 News*, No. 1 (January 1985), pp. 22–37.

part. Second, the String module illustrates how string-handling procedures use open array parameters and the 0C terminator. Third, the module is a useful addition to a programmer's collection of general-purpose library modules.

The Definition Part of the String Module

In the definition part of String, a description of the procedure and examples of its use follow each procedure heading:

```
DEFINITION MODULE String;
  (*  Exports procedures for performing operations on strings.
   *  The examples assume the following declarations:
   *
   *  VAR str10: ARRAY [0..9] OF CHAR;
   *      str20: ARRAY [0..19] OF CHAR;
   *      i: CARDINAL;
   *      found, success: BOOLEAN;
   *)

  PROCEDURE Length(str: ARRAY OF CHAR): CARDINAL;
  (*  Returns the length of str.  If the actual parameter is a
   *  string variable containing a 0C character, returns the
   *  index of the first 0C character.
   *
   *  Length("ABCDEF") is 6
   *  If str10 has been assigned the value "ABCDEFGH",
   *    Length(str10) is 8
   *)

  PROCEDURE Assign(source: ARRAY OF CHAR;
                   VAR dest: ARRAY OF CHAR;
                   VAR success: BOOLEAN);
  (*  Copies a string from source to dest.  If dest is not long
   *  enough to hold the contents of source, Assign copies as
   *  much as possible and sets success to FALSE.
   *
   *  str10 := "ABCDEFGH";
   *  Assign(str10, str20, success);
   *    (* str20 now holds "ABCDEFGH"; success is TRUE *)
   *  str20 := "ABCDEFGHIJK";
   *  Assign(str20, str10, success);
   *    (* str10 now holds "ABCDEFGHIJ"; success is FALSE *)
   *)
```

```
PROCEDURE Insert(source: ARRAY OF CHAR;
                 VAR dest: ARRAY OF CHAR;
                 index: CARDINAL;
                 VAR success: BOOLEAN);
(*  Inserts source into dest before the position index.  If
 *  the value of index is greater than the upper index of
 *  the string stored in dest, then dest is not altered and
 *  success is set to FALSE.  If dest is not large enough to
 *  hold the result of the insertion, the result is truncated
 *  and stored into dest and success is set to FALSE.
 *
 *  str10 := "ABCJKL";
 *  Insert("DEF", str10, 3, success);
 *    (* str10 is now "ABCDEFJKL"; success is TRUE *)
 *  Insert("GHI", str10, 6, success);
 *    (* str10 is now "ABCDEFGHIJ"; success is FALSE *)
 *)


PROCEDURE Delete(VAR str: ARRAY OF CHAR;
                 index: CARDINAL;
                 len: CARDINAL;
                 VAR success: BOOLEAN);
(*  Removes len characters from string str starting at
 *  position index.  str is not changed and success is set to
 *  FALSE if index is outside the bounds of the string stored
 *  in str or if index + len is larger than HIGH(str) + 1.
 *
 *  str10 := "ABCDEFGHIJ";
 *  Delete(str10, 2, 4, success);
 *    (* str10 is now "ABGHIJ"; success is TRUE *)
 *  Delete(str10, 5, 6, success);
 *    (* str10 remains "ABGHIJ"; success is FALSE *)
 *)


PROCEDURE Position(pattern: ARRAY OF CHAR;
                   source: ARRAY OF CHAR;
                   VAR index: CARDINAL;
                   VAR found: BOOLEAN);
(*  Searches source for an occurrence of pattern.  If the
 *  search is successful, found is set to TRUE and index
 *  indicates the position where the first character of
 *  pattern occurs in source.  If the search is
 *  unsuccessful, found is FALSE and index is undefined.
 *
 *  Position("DEFG", "ABCDEFGHIJ", i, found);
 *    (* i is now 3; found is TRUE *)
 *  Position("DFG", "ABCDEFGHIJ", i, found);
 *    (* i is undefined; found is FALSE *)
 *)
```

```
PROCEDURE Substring(source: ARRAY OF CHAR;
                    index: CARDINAL;
                    len: CARDINAL;
                    VAR dest: ARRAY OF CHAR;
                    VAR success: BOOLEAN);
(* Attempts to copy a substring of source of length len,
 * starting at index, to dest. dest is not changed and
 * success is FALSE if index is outside the bounds of the
 * string stored in source or if len is larger than
 * HIGH(dest) + 1. If neither of these cases holds, but
 * index + len is larger than HIGH(source) + 1, then as
 * many characters as possible will be copied to dest, but
 * success will be set to FALSE.
 *
 * Substring("ABCDEFGHI", 1, 5, str10, success);
 *   (* str10 is now "BCDEF"; success is TRUE *)
 * Substring("ABCDEFGHI", 6, 5, str10, success);
 *   (* str10 is now "GHI"; success is FALSE *)
 *)

PROCEDURE Concat(source1: ARRAY OF CHAR;
                 source2: ARRAY OF CHAR;
                 VAR dest: ARRAY OF CHAR;
                 VAR success: BOOLEAN);
(* Concatenates the strings source1 and source2, putting the
 * result in dest. If the resulting string is too large to
 * fit in dest, it will be truncated and success set to
 * FALSE.
 *
 * Concat("ABCDE", "FGHIJ", str10, success);
 *   (* str10 is now "ABCDEFGHIJ"; success is TRUE *)
 * Concat("ABCDEF", "GHIJK", str10, success);
 *   (* str10 is now "ABCDEFGHIJ"; success is FALSE *)
 *)

TYPE CompareResult = (less, equal, greater);

PROCEDURE Compare(string1: ARRAY OF CHAR;
                  string2: ARRAY OF CHAR): CompareResult;
(* Compares string1 and string2 from left to right until
 * one is found to be less than the other or the end of
 * either string is reached; returns either less, equal, or
 * greater.
 *
 * Compare("ABCD", "ABD")  returns less
 * Compare("ABC", "ABCD")  returns less
 * Compare("ABCD", "ABAD") returns greater
 *)

END String.
```

The Implementation Part of the `String` Module

The implementation part of `String` follows. To save space, we have not repeated the comments that accompany each procedure in the definition module. The implementation part of `String` is somewhat more complicated than one might expect. Much of the complexity stems from the fact that the end of a string variable is marked either by the first `0C` character or, if the variable does not contain a `0C` character, by the end of the array itself.

```
IMPLEMENTATION MODULE String;

  PROCEDURE Length(str: ARRAY OF CHAR): CARDINAL;
    VAR i: CARDINAL;
  BEGIN
    i := 0;
    WHILE (i <= HIGH(str)) & (str[i] # 0C) DO
      INC(i)
    END;
    RETURN i
  END Length;


  PROCEDURE Assign(source: ARRAY OF CHAR;
                   VAR dest: ARRAY OF CHAR;
                   VAR success: BOOLEAN);
    VAR i: CARDINAL;
  BEGIN
    i := 0;
    WHILE (i <= HIGH(source)) & (source[i] # 0C) DO
      IF i > HIGH(dest) THEN   (* end of dest reached *)
        success := FALSE;
        RETURN
      END;
      dest[i] := source[i];
      INC(i)
    END;
    IF i <= HIGH(dest) THEN
      dest[i] := 0C
    END;
    success := TRUE
  END Assign;


  PROCEDURE Insert(source: ARRAY OF CHAR;
                   VAR dest: ARRAY OF CHAR;
                   index: CARDINAL;
                   VAR success: BOOLEAN);
    VAR sourceLen, destLen, i: CARDINAL;
```

```
BEGIN
  success := TRUE;
  sourceLen := Length(source);
  destLen := Length(dest);

  IF index >= destLen THEN    (* illegal index in dest *)
    success := FALSE;
    RETURN
  ELSIF sourceLen = 0 THEN    (* nothing to insert *)
    RETURN
  ELSIF sourceLen + destLen > HIGH(dest) + 1 THEN
      (* not enough room to insert all of source *)
    success := FALSE;
      (* adjust destLen and possibly sourceLen so that a
         partial insertion can be done *)
    IF sourceLen + index > HIGH(dest) + 1 THEN
      destLen := index;
      sourceLen := HIGH(dest) + 1 - index
    ELSE
      destLen := HIGH(dest) + 1 - sourceLen
    END
  END;

    (* make room to insert source *)
  FOR i := destLen - 1 TO index BY -1 DO
    dest[i + sourceLen] := dest[i]
  END;

    (* copy source into dest *)
  FOR i := 0 TO sourceLen - 1 DO
    dest[i + index] := source[i]
  END;

    (* if dest is not full, add 0C terminator *)
  IF destLen + sourceLen <= HIGH(dest) THEN
    dest[destLen + sourceLen] := 0C
  END
END Insert;

PROCEDURE Delete(VAR str: ARRAY OF CHAR;
                 index: CARDINAL;
                 len: CARDINAL;
                 VAR success: BOOLEAN);
  VAR strLen, i: CARDINAL;
BEGIN
  success := TRUE;
  strLen := Length(str);

  IF (index >= strLen) OR (index + len > HIGH(str) + 1) THEN
    success := FALSE;
    RETURN
```

```
  ELSIF len = 0 THEN   (* nothing to delete *)
    RETURN
  END;

    (* shift contents of str to the left len positions,
       starting at index *)
  FOR i := index + len TO strLen - 1 DO
    str[i - len] := str[i]
  END;

    (* put a 0C terminator at the end of str *)
  IF index + len >= strLen THEN
    str[index] := 0C
  ELSE
    str[strLen - len] := 0C
  END
END Delete;


PROCEDURE Position(pattern: ARRAY OF CHAR;
                   source: ARRAY OF CHAR;
                   VAR index: CARDINAL;
                   VAR found: BOOLEAN);
 VAR patternLen, sourceLen,
     sourceIndex, patternIndex, i: CARDINAL;
BEGIN
  found := FALSE;
  patternLen := Length(pattern);
  sourceLen := Length(source);

  IF patternLen > sourceLen THEN   (* pattern too long *)
    RETURN
  ELSIF patternLen = 0 THEN
    index := 0;
    found := TRUE;
    RETURN
  END;

    (* try to match pattern against source starting at each
       position between 0 and sourceLen - patternLen *)
  FOR i := 0 TO sourceLen - patternLen DO
    sourceIndex := i;
    patternIndex := 0;

      (* do character-by-character comparison of pattern
         with substring of source *)
    WHILE (patternIndex <= patternLen - 1) &
          (source[sourceIndex] = pattern[patternIndex]) DO
      INC(sourceIndex);
      INC(patternIndex)
    END;
```

```
        (* match was completed successfully *)
      IF patternIndex = patternLen THEN
        index := i;
        found := TRUE;
        RETURN
      END
    END
  END Position;

  PROCEDURE Substring(source: ARRAY OF CHAR;
                      index: CARDINAL;
                      len: CARDINAL;
                      VAR dest: ARRAY OF CHAR;
                      VAR success: BOOLEAN);
    VAR i: CARDINAL;
  BEGIN
    success := FALSE;

    IF (index >= Length(source)) OR (len > HIGH(dest) + 1) THEN
      RETURN
    END;

      (* copy characters from source to dest, starting at
         position index in source *)
    i := 0;
    WHILE (i < len) & (index + i <= HIGH(source)) DO
      dest[i] := source[index + i];
      INC(i)
    END;

    IF i = len THEN
      success := TRUE   (* successful copy of len characters *)
    END;

      (* if dest is not full, add 0C terminator *)
    IF i <= HIGH(dest) THEN
      dest[i] := 0C
    END
  END Substring;

  PROCEDURE Concat(source1: ARRAY OF CHAR;
                   source2: ARRAY OF CHAR;
                   VAR dest: ARRAY OF CHAR;
                   VAR success: BOOLEAN);
    VAR i, j: CARDINAL;
  BEGIN
    success := FALSE;

      (* copy source1 to dest *)
    i := 0;
    WHILE (i <= HIGH(source1)) & (source1[i] # 0C) DO
```

```
      IF i > HIGH(dest) THEN RETURN END;    (* end of dest *)
      dest[i] := source1[i];
      INC(i)
    END;

      (* copy source2 to dest *)
    j := 0;
    WHILE (j <= HIGH(source2)) & (source2[j] # 0C) DO
      IF i > HIGH(dest) THEN RETURN END;    (* end of dest *)
      dest[i] := source2[j];
      INC(i);
      INC(j)
    END;

      (* if dest is not full, add 0C terminator *)
    IF i <= HIGH(dest) THEN
      dest[i] := 0C
    END;
    success := TRUE
  END Concat;

  PROCEDURE Compare(string1: ARRAY OF CHAR;
                    string2: ARRAY OF CHAR): CompareResult;
    VAR c1, c2: CHAR;
        i: CARDINAL;
  BEGIN
    i := 0;

    LOOP
        (* fetch character from string1 (0C if end reached) *)
      IF i > HIGH(string1) THEN
        c1 := 0C
      ELSE
        c1 := string1[i]
      END;

        (* fetch character from string2 (0C if end reached) *)
      IF i > HIGH(string2) THEN
        c2 := 0C
      ELSE
        c2 := string2[i]
      END;

        (* compare characters from string1 and string2 *)
      IF c1 < c2 THEN
        RETURN less
      ELSIF c1 > c2 THEN
        RETURN greater
      ELSIF c1 = 0C THEN    (* both c1 and c2 are 0C *)
        RETURN equal
      END;
```

```
        INC(i)
      END
    END Compare;

  END String.
```

10.3 A Character Set Module

Recall from Section 7.5 that the base type of a Modula-2 set must be an enumeration type or a subrange of CARDINAL. As a result, the following type declaration is illegal:

```
TYPE SetOfChar = SET OF CHAR;    (* illegal base type *)
```

Although a few Modula-2 systems provide SET OF CHAR as an extension to the language, most do not. Programmers often find the lack of SET OF CHAR to be a problem, particularly when writing programs that perform a significant amount of character manipulation. The solution is to choose a different representation for the type SetOfChar rather than relying on a Modula-2 set type. The library module CharSet described in this section exports an opaque type named SetOfChar and a collection of procedures that operate on SetOfChar values. Any program that needs to use sets of characters can simply import SetOfChar and related procedures from CharSet.

In addition to its value as a library module, CharSet serves as another example of a module that exports an opaque type and a collection of procedures that operate on values of that type. And, because CharSet implements values of type SetOfChar as linked lists, the implementation part of CharSet provides many examples of list-handling techniques. Programmers can also use CharSet as a model for constructing other modules that export set types, because its implementation part does not depend heavily on the fact that set elements are characters. (In the Exercises we discuss alternate representations for SetOfChar; these do not generalize as well to other kinds of sets.)

The Definition Part of the CharSet Module

The procedures exported by the module CharSet perform most of the operations that Modula-2 normally provides for sets:

set operations (union, intersection, difference)
relational operations (equality, subset, membership)
inclusion and exclusion

Several set operations are missing, however. We leave symmetric difference as an exercise. Inequality is unnecessary as long as `CharSet` provides equality. Similarly, superset is unnecessary because `CharSet` provides subset.

`CharSet` also exports procedures for initializing a set, testing whether a set is empty, copying one set to another, and deleting all the elements in a set.

```
DEFINITION MODULE CharSet;
 (* exports type SetOfChar (set of characters) and procedures
    for operating on values of this type *)

  TYPE SetOfChar;

  PROCEDURE Initialize(VAR s: SetOfChar);
    (* initializes s to the empty set *)

  PROCEDURE IsEmpty(s: SetOfChar): BOOLEAN;
    (* returns TRUE if s is the empty set, FALSE otherwise *)

  PROCEDURE MakeEmpty(VAR s: SetOfChar);
    (* makes s empty by deleting all of its elements *)

  PROCEDURE CopySet(s1: SetOfChar; VAR s2: SetOfChar);
    (* copies set s1 to set s2 *)

  PROCEDURE Include(VAR s: SetOfChar; ch: CHAR);
    (* adds ch to set s; does nothing if ch is already in s *)

  PROCEDURE Exclude(VAR s: SetOfChar; ch: CHAR);
    (* removes ch from set s; does nothing if ch is not in s *)

  PROCEDURE IsMember(s: SetOfChar; ch: CHAR): BOOLEAN;
    (* returns TRUE if ch is a member of the set s, FALSE
       otherwise *)

  PROCEDURE IsEqual(s1, s2: SetOfChar): BOOLEAN;
    (* returns TRUE if s1 and s2 contain the same elements,
       FALSE otherwise *)

  PROCEDURE IsSubset(s1, s2: SetOfChar): BOOLEAN;
    (* returns TRUE if every element of s1 is in s2, FALSE
       otherwise *)

  PROCEDURE Union(s1, s2: SetOfChar; VAR s3: SetOfChar);
    (* computes the union of the sets s1 and s2 and stores the
       result in s3 *)

  PROCEDURE Intersection(s1, s2: SetOfChar; VAR s3: SetOfChar);
    (* computes the intersection of the sets s1 and s2 and
       stores the result in s3 *)
```

```
    PROCEDURE Difference(s1, s2: SetOfChar; VAR s3: SetOfChar);
      (* computes the difference of the sets s1 and s2 and stores
         the result in s3 *)

END CharSet.
```

Implementing CharSet Using Linked Lists

There are many ways to represent a set of characters. We will use a linked list, a simple and general (but sometimes inefficient) method. A list of nodes, each containing one character, will represent a set of characters. For example, if the variable s (of type SetOfChar) has the value {b, f, a}, s actually points to a linked list containing 'a', 'b', and 'f', in that order:

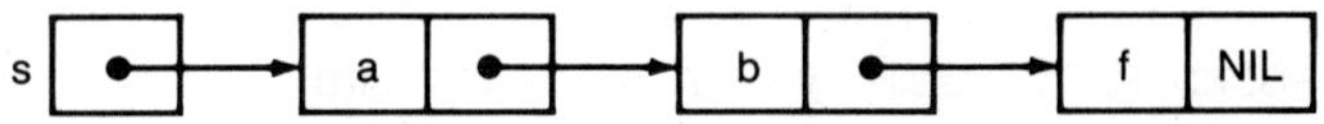

We will always store the elements of a set in sorted order to make some of the procedures in CharSet more efficient. To specify that a SetOfChar value is a pointer to a linked list of nodes containing characters, the implementation part of CharSet contains the following type declarations:

```
TYPE SetOfChar = POINTER TO CharNode;
     CharNode = RECORD
                  char: CHAR;
                  next: SetOfChar (* points to the next node *)
                END;
```

The implementation part of CharSet contains several utility procedures that the module does not export. Section 8.1 described four of these (InsertAfter, InsertAtFront, DeleteAfter, and DeleteAtFront). The fifth, named FindNode, searches a list p for a character ch:

```
PROCEDURE FindNode(p: SetOfChar; ch: CHAR;
                   VAR previous, current: SetOfChar);
```

When FindNode returns, current will point to the first node that contains ch or a character greater than ch, while previous points to the previous node (previous is NIL if there is no previous node). If the search fails, current will have the value NIL and previous will point to the last node on the list (previous is NIL if the list is empty).

We now describe briefly how we will implement each procedure in CharSet:

- Initialize(s) CharSet represents the empty set by the empty pointer, NIL, so Initialize need only assign the value NIL to s.
- IsEmpty(s) To test whether s is empty, IsEmpty compares it to NIL.
- MakeEmpty(s) To make an existing set empty, a client module could use the Initialize procedure. However, assigning NIL to s would cause the nodes to which s formerly pointed to become garbage—they would no longer be accessible. MakeEmpty uses a better method; it traverses the list to which s points, deleting nodes one by one and calling DEALLOCATE to recycle the space used by these nodes.
- CopySet(s1, s2) CopySet first sets s2 to NIL, then traverses s1, adding nodes to the end of the s2 list; when CopySet returns, s2 points to a new list identical to the list that s1 points to.
- Include(s, ch) Include takes advantage of the fact that CharSet stores the elements of s in order. To add the character ch to the set s, Include calls FindNode to search s for the place where ch should be added. If ch is already in s, Include does nothing. Otherwise, it calls InsertAtFront or InsertAfter to insert ch into the list.
- Exclude(s, ch) Exclude is similar to Include. Exclude calls FindNode to determine where in the list ch should appear. If it is not present, no further action is required. If a node containing the character is in the list, then Exclude calls either DeleteAtFront or DeleteAfter to remove it.
- IsMember(s, ch) IsMember calls FindNode to locate the first node containing a character greater than or equal to ch, then tests whether the node actually contains ch.
- IsEqual(s1, s2) To test whether s1 and s2 are equal, IsEqual need only check whether the two lists are identical (taking advantage of the fact that s1 and s2 are sorted) by traversing them simultaneously.
- IsSubset(s1, s2) Testing whether s1 is a subset of s2 requires a slightly tricky algorithm. IsSubset traverses the s2 list looking for the first element of s1. If IsSubset does not find it, then s1 is not a subset of s2. If it does appear, then IsSubset looks for the second element of s1 in s2, continuing from where the previous search ended. (This method works because CharSet stores the elements of s1 and s2 in order.) The process continues until IsSubset reaches the end of s1 or s2. If the end of s1 is reached first, then s1 is a subset of s2.
- Union(s1, s2, s3) The procedures Union, Intersection, and Difference are similar. All three traverse s1 and s2 simultaneously while adding nodes to s3. These procedures take advantage of the fact that the lists are sorted, so that only a single traversal of each list is necessary.

`Union` examines the first character on each list; if one character is less than the other, the procedure copies the former character to `s3` and adjusts the list it came from so that the next node is visible. If both characters are the same, `Union` copies that character to `s3` and adjusts both `s1` and `s2` so that the next node is visible. When the procedure reaches the end of one of the two lists, it copies the remaining characters in the other list to `s3`. A pointer called `last` keeps track of the last node on the list that `s3` points to; the procedure adds nodes at the end of `s3` rather than at the beginning so that the characters in `s3` will appear in order. We have simplified `Union` by having it create a dummy node initially and add the node to `s3`. This step ensures that `s3` is always nonempty, so that `Union` can use `InsertAfter` to add subsequent nodes. Before `Union` returns, it removes the dummy node.

- `Intersection(s1, s2, s3)` `Union` and `Intersection` differ in two ways. First, `Intersection` adds characters to `s3` only if they occur on both `s1` and `s2`. Second, when it reaches the end of `s1` or `s2`, `Intersection` does not add leftover nodes from the other list to `s3`.
- `Difference(s1, s2, s3)` `Difference` is also similar to `Union`. However, during the traversal of `s1` and `s2`, `Difference` copies a character to `s3` only if it is currently at the front of `s1` and the character at the front of `s2` is greater. (Because the lists are sorted, this rule guarantees that the character is not on the `s2` list.) If the procedure exhausts `s1` first, it adds no further nodes to `s3`. If it exhausts `s2` first, however, then it copies the remaining characters on `s1` to `s3`.

The Implementation Part of the `CharSet` Module

The implementation part of `CharSet` follows. For clarity, the utility procedures appear first, followed by the exported procedures.

```
IMPLEMENTATION MODULE CharSet;

  FROM Storage IMPORT ALLOCATE, DEALLOCATE;

  TYPE SetOfChar = POINTER TO CharNode;  (* NIL for empty set *)
       CharNode = RECORD
                    char: CHAR;
                    next: SetOfChar
                  END;

(******************* UTILITY PROCEDURES ********************)

  PROCEDURE InsertAfter(p: SetOfChar; ch: CHAR);
    (* creates a node containing ch and adds it to the list
```

```
      just after the node pointed to by p; p must be
      non-NIL *)
  VAR new: SetOfChar;
BEGIN
  ALLOCATE(new, SIZE(CharNode));
  new^.char := ch;
  new^.next := p^.next;
  p^.next := new
END InsertAfter;


PROCEDURE InsertAtFront(VAR first: SetOfChar; ch: CHAR);
  (* creates a node containing ch and adds it to the front of
     the list pointed to by first; first may be NIL *)
  VAR new: SetOfChar;
BEGIN
  ALLOCATE(new, SIZE(CharNode));
  new^.char := ch;
  new^.next := first;
  first := new
END InsertAtFront;


PROCEDURE DeleteAfter(p: SetOfChar);
  (* deletes the node immediately following p; p must be
     non-NIL *)
  VAR old: SetOfChar;
BEGIN
  old := p^.next;
  p^.next := old^.next;
  DEALLOCATE(old, SIZE(CharNode))
END DeleteAfter;


PROCEDURE DeleteAtFront(VAR first: SetOfChar);
  (* deletes the first node; first must be non-NIL *)
  VAR old: SetOfChar;
BEGIN
  old := first;
  first := first^.next;
  DEALLOCATE(old, SIZE(CharNode))
END DeleteAtFront;


PROCEDURE FindNode(p: SetOfChar; ch: CHAR;
                   VAR previous, current: SetOfChar);
  (* Searches p for the first character greater than or equal
     to ch.  If successful, current points to the node
     containing this character and previous points to the
```

```
        previous node (previous is NIL if there is no previous
        node).  If unsuccessful, current is NIL and previous
        points to the last node on the list (previous is NIL if
        list is empty). *)
  BEGIN
    current := p;
    previous := NIL;
    WHILE (current # NIL) & (current^.char < ch) DO
      previous := current;
      current := current^.next
    END
  END FindNode;

(******************* EXPORTED PROCEDURES *******************)

  PROCEDURE Initialize(VAR s: SetOfChar);
    (* initializes s to the empty set *)
  BEGIN
    s := NIL
  END Initialize;


  PROCEDURE IsEmpty(s: SetOfChar): BOOLEAN;
    (* returns TRUE if s is the empty set, FALSE otherwise *)
  BEGIN
    RETURN s = NIL
  END IsEmpty;


  PROCEDURE MakeEmpty(VAR s: SetOfChar);
    (* makes s empty by deleting all of its elements *)
    VAR old: SetOfChar;
  BEGIN
    WHILE s # NIL DO
      old := s;
      s := s^.next;
      DEALLOCATE(old, SIZE(CharNode))
    END
  END MakeEmpty;


  PROCEDURE CopySet(s1: SetOfChar; VAR s2: SetOfChar);
    (* copies set s1 to set s2 *)
    VAR last: SetOfChar;
  BEGIN
    s2 := NIL;
    IF s1 = NIL THEN RETURN END;
    InsertAtFront(s2, s1^.char);
    last := s2;
```

```
  s1 := s1^.next;
  WHILE s1 # NIL DO
    InsertAfter(last, s1^.char);
    last := last^.next;
    s1 := s1^.next
  END
END CopySet;


PROCEDURE Include(VAR s: SetOfChar; ch: CHAR);
  (* adds ch to set s; does nothing if ch is already in s *)
  VAR previous, current: SetOfChar;
BEGIN
  FindNode(s, ch, previous, current);
  IF (current # NIL) & (current^.char = ch) THEN RETURN END;
  IF previous = NIL THEN
    InsertAtFront(s, ch)
  ELSE
    InsertAfter(previous, ch)
  END
END Include;


PROCEDURE Exclude(VAR s: SetOfChar; ch: CHAR);
  (* removes ch from set s; does nothing if ch is not in s *)
  VAR previous, current: SetOfChar;
BEGIN
  FindNode(s, ch, previous, current);
  IF (current = NIL) OR (current^.char # ch) THEN RETURN END;
  IF previous = NIL THEN
    DeleteAtFront(s)
  ELSE
    DeleteAfter(previous)
  END
END Exclude;


PROCEDURE IsMember(s: SetOfChar; ch: CHAR): BOOLEAN;
  (* returns TRUE if ch is a member of the set s, FALSE
     otherwise *)
  VAR previous, current: SetOfChar;
BEGIN
  FindNode(s, ch, previous, current);
  RETURN (current # NIL) & (current^.char = ch)
END IsMember;


PROCEDURE IsEqual(s1, s2: SetOfChar): BOOLEAN;
  (* returns TRUE if s1 and s2 contain the same elements,
     FALSE otherwise *)
```

```
BEGIN
  WHILE (s1 # NIL) & (s2 # NIL) DO
    IF s1^.char # s2^.char THEN RETURN FALSE END;
    s1 := s1^.next;
    s2 := s2^.next
  END;
  RETURN (s1 = NIL) & (s2 = NIL)
END IsEqual;


PROCEDURE IsSubset(s1, s2: SetOfChar): BOOLEAN;
  (* returns TRUE if every element of s1 is in s2, FALSE
     otherwise *)
BEGIN
  WHILE s1 # NIL DO
    WHILE (s2 # NIL) & (s1^.char # s2^.char) DO
      s2 := s2^.next
    END;
    IF s2 = NIL THEN RETURN FALSE END;
    s1 := s1^.next;
    s2 := s2^.next
  END;
  RETURN TRUE
END IsSubset;


PROCEDURE Union(s1, s2: SetOfChar; VAR s3: SetOfChar);
  (* computes the union of the sets s1 and s2 and stores the
     result in s3 *)
  VAR last, leftOver: SetOfChar;
BEGIN
  ALLOCATE(s3, SIZE(CharNode));    (* create a dummy node *)
  s3^.next := NIL;
  last := s3;

    (* copy to s3 as long as elements remain in s1 and s2 *)
  WHILE (s1 # NIL) & (s2 # NIL) DO
    IF s1^.char < s2^.char THEN
      InsertAfter(last, s1^.char);
      s1 := s1^.next
    ELSIF s1^.char > s2^.char THEN
      InsertAfter(last, s2^.char);
      s2 := s2^.next
    ELSE
      InsertAfter(last, s1^.char);
      s1 := s1^.next;
      s2 := s2^.next
    END;
    last := last^.next
  END;
```

```
      (* determine whether any elements remain in s1 or s2 *)
    IF s1 # NIL THEN
      leftOver := s1
    ELSIF s2 # NIL THEN
      leftOver := s2
    ELSE
      leftOver := NIL
    END;

      (* copy remaining elements to s3 *)
    WHILE leftOver # NIL DO
      InsertAfter(last, leftOver^.char);
      last := last^.next;
      leftOver := leftOver^.next
    END;

    DeleteAtFront(s3)    (* remove dummy node *)
  END Union;


  PROCEDURE Intersection(s1, s2: SetOfChar; VAR s3: SetOfChar);
    (* computes the intersection of the sets s1 and s2 and
       stores the result in s3 *)
    VAR last: SetOfChar;
  BEGIN
    ALLOCATE(s3, SIZE(CharNode));    (* create a dummy node *)
    s3^.next := NIL;
    last := s3;

      (* copy elements to s3 that appear on both s1 and s2 *)
    WHILE (s1 # NIL) & (s2 # NIL) DO
      IF s1^.char < s2^.char THEN
        s1 := s1^.next
      ELSIF s1^.char > s2^.char THEN
        s2 := s2^.next
      ELSE
        InsertAfter(last, s1^.char);
        last := last^.next;
        s1 := s1^.next;
        s2 := s2^.next
      END
    END;

    DeleteAtFront(s3)    (* remove dummy node *)
  END Intersection;


  PROCEDURE Difference(s1, s2: SetOfChar; VAR s3: SetOfChar);
    (* computes the difference of the sets s1 and s2 and stores
       the result in s3 *)
```

```
    VAR last: SetOfChar;
  BEGIN
    ALLOCATE(s3, SIZE(CharNode));   (* create a dummy node *)
    s3^.next := NIL;
    last := s3;

      (* copy elements from s1 to s3 if not in s2 until end
         of s1 or s2 reached *)
    WHILE (s1 # NIL) & (s2 # NIL) DO
      IF s1^.char < s2^.char THEN
        InsertAfter(last, s1^.char);
        last := last^.next;
        s1 := s1^.next
      ELSIF s1^.char > s2^.char THEN
        s2 := s2^.next
      ELSE
        s1 := s1^.next;
        s2 := s2^.next
      END
    END;

      (* copy remaining elements from s1 to s3 *)
    WHILE s1 # NIL DO
      InsertAfter(last, s1^.char);
      last := last^.next;
      s1 := s1^.next
    END;

    DeleteAtFront(s3)     (* remove dummy node *)
  END Difference;

END CharSet.
```

10.4 Object-oriented Design

When writing a program of any appreciable size, a programmer should carefully design the program before beginning the actual coding. If using Modula-2, the programmer should—as part of the design—decide what modules the program will consist of and what entities each module will export. The task of designing a program is easier (and the design is often much better) if the programmer follows a design methodology.

We will briefly describe one popular methodology for designing programs to be written in modern languages, such as Modula-2 and Ada, that provide modules and support for abstract data types. The key feature of this methodology is the identification of objects, so it is known as *object-oriented design*. We saw in Section 10.1 that we can implement objects in two ways. We can hide the object in the implementation part of a module (such as `CharStackModule`) and export procedures that manipulate the hidden object. Or we can write a module (such as `CharacterStacks`) that exports an opaque type and a collection of procedures that operate on values of that type. In object-oriented design, the programmer identifies (1) the objects in a program and (2) the operations required for each object.

The idea of object-oriented *programming* has been around for many years; it is central to the Smalltalk programming language, for example. (Objects themselves can be traced back even further, to the language Simula.) By object-oriented *design*, however, we mean the particular design methodology formulated by Abbott and popularized by Booch.* Our presentation follows Booch closely. Readers may wish to consult one of these sources for more examples of object-oriented design.

Object-oriented design is based on the idea that programmers can represent "real-world" objects and operations by program objects and operations. Designing a program requires the programmer to identify these objects and operations. Booch's formulation of object-oriented design involves three steps:

1. *Define the problem*. It is difficult to design a program without a clear understanding of what the program is intended to do. Therefore, the first step in design is to define the problem, using terminology from the "problem space." For example, if the problem is to print weekly paychecks, the description of the problem will use words such as *employee*, *salary*, and *check*.
2. *Develop an informal strategy*. The next step is to write an informal prose description of a method that will solve the problem. This description again uses terminology from the problem space.
3. *Formalize the strategy*. This step has several parts:
   - Examine the description of the informal strategy developed in step 2, listing the *objects* mentioned in the strategy. We can easily spot them, because they are represented by English nouns.
   - Examine the description again, this time looking for verbs that describe *operations* to perform on the objects.
   - Group together in a library module each object and the operations to perform on it. If the strategy requires only one instance of an object, we can hide the object in a module that exports procedures representing allowable operations on the object. However, if the strategy calls for more than one instance of an object, we must hide the object's structure in a module that exports (1) an opaque type and (2) a collection of procedures representing

*R. J. Abbott, "Program Design by Informal English Descriptions," *Communications of the ACM*, Vol. 26, No. 11 (November 1983), pp. 882–894, and G. Booch, *Software Engineering with Ada*, Menlo Park, Calif.: Benjamin/Cummings, 1983.

operations on objects of that type. Client modules can then import the type and use it to declare as many objects as the strategy requires. This step produces a collection of definition modules, one for each object or opaque type.

- Finally, write the main program and implement the operations by writing the implementation parts of the library modules. As we write the implementation modules, we may discover that the set of operations for a particular object is insufficient. When this happens, we must add the missing operations to the object's definition module.

In many cases, we must go through the design process more than once. As we prepare to write a procedure in an implementation module, we face a new problem. This problem, if sufficiently complex, may require a fresh application of the object-oriented design methodology. This design will reveal new objects and operations and thus require us to create still more modules. We can often make these modules local to the implementation module we are writing.

EXAMPLE PROGRAM

Counting Occurrences of Words in a Text File

To illustrate object-oriented design, we will use it to develop a program for counting how many times words occur in a file of English text. We will follow Booch's steps in order, from problem definition to implementation.

1. Define the Problem

Our task is to write a program that prints a list of the words appearing in a file of English text. The program should print each word on a separate line, in all uppercase letters, followed by an integer indicating the number of times the word occurs in the file. The list should be sorted, first by number of occurrences (most frequently occurring words at the beginning), and then into alphabetical order.

A word is any string of characters that contains only letters and digits and, under certain circumstances, single quotes and hyphens. The program should treat single quotes as delimiters if they occur at the beginning or end of a word but not if they occur within words (as apostrophes). Words may contain single hyphens, but the program should treat double hyphens (dashes) as delimiters.

The program should treat all letters in the input file as though they were uppercase; it should ignore the case of letters when determining whether two words are the same.

We assume that the input file contains no words longer than 20 characters. If the program encounters a longer word, it should truncate the word by taking only the first 20 characters. We also assume that the file contains no more than 1,000 occurrences of the same word.

Here is an example of the program's input and output. (The input is a quotation from *Gödel, Escher, Bach: An Eternal Golden Braid*, by Douglas R. Hofstadter.)

Sample Input:

```
In our century the time was ripe for computers--computers
beyond the wildest dreams of Pascal, Leibniz, Babbage, or Lady
Lovelace.  In the 1930's and 1940's, the first "giant
electronic brains" were designed and built.  They catalyzed
the convergence of three previously disparate areas:  the
theory of axiomatic reasoning, the study of mechanical
computation, and the psychology of intelligence.
```

Sample Output:

```
THE 8
OF 5
AND 3
COMPUTERS 2
IN 2
1930'S 1
1940'S 1
AREAS 1
AXIOMATIC 1
BABBAGE 1
BEYOND 1
BRAINS 1
BUILT 1
CATALYZED 1
CENTURY 1
COMPUTATION 1
CONVERGENCE 1
DESIGNED 1
DISPARATE 1
DREAMS 1
ELECTRONIC 1
FIRST 1
FOR 1
GIANT 1
INTELLIGENCE 1
LADY 1
LEIBNIZ 1
LOVELACE 1
MECHANICAL 1
OR 1
OUR 1
PASCAL 1
PREVIOUSLY 1
PSYCHOLOGY 1
REASONING 1
RIPE 1
```

```
STUDY 1
THEORY 1
THEY 1
THREE 1
TIME 1
WAS 1
WERE 1
WILDEST 1
```

2. Develop an Informal Strategy

There are many ways to approach this problem. The following strategy is simple, yet relatively efficient, even when the input file is quite large:

1. Read a word from the input file and store it in a table that contains words and, for each word, the number of times it has been entered in the table; repeat until all words have been read.
2. Create an empty list for each possible number of word occurrences between 1 and 1,000.
3. From the table, fetch the largest word that has not previously been fetched, together with a count of how many times the word was entered in the table. Add this word to the beginning of the list of words that have the same number of occurrences. Repeat this step until every word in the table has been fetched.
4. Remove a word from the front of the list of words that have occurred 1,000 times and print the word, followed by its number of occurrences; repeat until the list is empty. Repeat this step, using the list of words that have occurred 999 times, and so on, until all the lists have been printed.

By "largest word," we mean the word that would appear last in a sorted list of all words in the table. Because we fetch words from the table in reverse alphabetical order, each list of words will be in alphabetical order.

3. Formalize the Strategy

A close reading of the informal strategy reveals three objects—`Word`, `WordTable`, and `WordList`—and several operations on each:

`Word`

`ReadWord` ("read a word")
`WriteWord` ("print [a] word")

`WordTable`

`EnterWord` ("store [a word] in [the] table")
`FetchLargestWord` ("fetch the largest word that has not previously been fetched")

`WordList`

`MakeListEmpty` ("create an empty list")
`AddWord` ("add [a] word to the beginning of [a] list")
`RemoveWord` ("remove a word from the front of [a] list")

We must next design the definition modules in the program by grouping objects and operations into modules. Because many words and many lists may exist, but only one table, we decide to make `Word` and `WordList` opaque types and `WordTable` a module.

The `Words` module will export the type `Word` and the operations `ReadWord` and `WriteWord`. Here is the definition part of `Words`:

```
DEFINITION MODULE Words;
  (* exports type Word and procedures for operating on values
     of this type *)

  FROM String IMPORT CompareResult;     (* Section 10.2 *)

  TYPE Word;

  PROCEDURE ReadWord(VAR w: Word; VAR success: BOOLEAN);
    (* reads a word from the input file; success is set to
       TRUE if word could be read, FALSE if end of file was
       encountered *)

  PROCEDURE WriteWord(w: Word);
    (* writes a word to the output file *)

  PROCEDURE CompareWords(w1, w2: Word): CompareResult;
    (* compares words w1 and w2; returns either "less",
       "equal", or "greater" *)

END Words.
```

A third operation, `CompareWords`, appears in the definition part of `Words`; the need for this operation arises later, during the implementation of the `WordTable` module. Because the parameters of `CompareWords` are of type `Word`, it must be exported by `Words`, which is the only module that knows the internal representation of the `Word` type.

Because the purpose of `WordTable` is to hide the table of words, it will not export any types; `WordTable` exports only the operations `EnterWord` and `FetchLargestWord`.

```
DEFINITION MODULE WordTable;
  (* exports procedures for manipulating a hidden table of
     words *)
```

```
    FROM Words IMPORT Word;

    PROCEDURE EnterWord(w: Word);
      (* enters a word into the table; all calls of EnterWord
         must precede the first call of FetchLargestWord *)

    PROCEDURE FetchLargestWord(VAR w: Word; VAR count: CARDINAL;
                               VAR success: BOOLEAN);
      (* fetches the largest word not previously fetched and a
         count of how many times it has been entered in the
         table; success is set to TRUE if a word was fetched,
         FALSE if all words have been fetched previously *)

END WordTable.
```

The constraint on `EnterWord`—that all calls of `EnterWord` must precede the first call of `FetchLargestWord`—stems from the informal strategy. Although we could implement `WordTable` without this constraint, we include it because of the possibility that we can implement `WordTable` more efficiently using this information about `EnterWord` and `FetchLargestWord`.

The module `WordLists` provides the type `WordList` and the operations `MakeListEmpty`, `AddWord`, and `RemoveWord`:

```
DEFINITION MODULE WordLists;
  (* exports type WordList and procedures for operating on
     values of this type *)

  FROM Words IMPORT Word;

  TYPE WordList;

  PROCEDURE MakeListEmpty(VAR list: WordList);
    (* initializes a list by making it empty *)

  PROCEDURE AddWord(w: Word; VAR list: WordList);
    (* adds w to the beginning of the list *)

  PROCEDURE RemoveWord(VAR w: Word; VAR list: WordList;
                       VAR success: BOOLEAN);
    (* fetches the first word on the list and removes it from
       the list; success is set to TRUE if the list is not
       empty, FALSE otherwise *)

END WordLists.
```

Having written the definition modules that the program requires, we can write the main program and implementation modules. Writing the main program is a simple matter of translating the informal strategy into Modula-2 statements, using the objects and operations provided by the Words, WordTable, and WordLists modules.

```
MODULE WordFrequencies;
  (* Creates a list of all words appearing in a text file.
     The list is sorted by number of occurrences; the most
     frequently occurring word appears first.  Words occurring
     the same number of times appear in alphabetical order. *)

  FROM InOut IMPORT OpenInput, CloseInput, OpenOutput,
                    CloseOutput, WriteString, WriteLn,
                    WriteCard;
  FROM Words IMPORT Word, ReadWord, WriteWord;
  FROM WordTable IMPORT EnterWord, FetchLargestWord;
  FROM WordLists IMPORT WordList, MakeListEmpty, AddWord,
                        RemoveWord;

  CONST maxCount = 1000;    (* maximum number of times a single
                               word may occur in a file *)

  VAR count: CARDINAL;
      w: Word;
      success: BOOLEAN;
      wordListArray: ARRAY [1..maxCount] OF WordList;

BEGIN
    (* read words and store in table *)
  WriteString("Enter name of input file.");
  WriteLn;
  OpenInput("TXT");
  ReadWord(w, success);
  WHILE success DO
    EnterWord(w);
    ReadWord(w, success)
  END;
  CloseInput;

    (* move words from table to sorted lists *)
  WriteString("Enter name of output file.");
  WriteLn;
  OpenOutput("TXT");
  FOR count := 1 TO maxCount DO
    MakeListEmpty(wordListArray[count])
  END;
  FetchLargestWord(w, count, success);
  WHILE success DO
    IF count > maxCount THEN
      WriteString("maxCount exceeded for word ");
      WriteWord(w);
```

```
        WriteString(".  Count was ");
        WriteCard(count, 1);
        WriteLn
      ELSE
        AddWord(w, wordListArray[count])
      END;
      FetchLargestWord(w, count, success)
    END;

      (* print contents of lists *)
    FOR count := maxCount TO 1 BY -1 DO
      RemoveWord(w, wordListArray[count], success);
      WHILE success DO
        WriteWord(w);
        WriteString(" ");
        WriteCard(count, 1);
        WriteLn;
        RemoveWord(w, wordListArray[count], success)
      END
    END;
    CloseOutput

END WordFrequencies.
```

If any word occurs more than 1,000 times in the input file, `WordFrequencies` prints an error message that gives the word and its count; the word does not appear in the normal list of words and counts.

Before we write the implementation part of the `Words` module, we must decide how to represent the type `Word`. We will use a simple representation: A value of type `Word` is a pointer to an array of characters. When a word fails to fill the array, the character `0C` terminates it. The rest of the module is easy to write, using the rules that the problem definition gives for recognizing words.

```
IMPLEMENTATION MODULE Words;

  FROM InOut IMPORT Read, Done, WriteString;
  FROM String IMPORT CompareResult, Compare;     (* Section 10.2 *)
  FROM Storage IMPORT ALLOCATE;

  CONST maxWordLen = 20;    (* maximum length of a word *)

  TYPE Word = POINTER TO String;
       String = ARRAY [0..maxWordLen-1] OF CHAR;

  PROCEDURE ReadWord(VAR w: Word; VAR success: BOOLEAN);
    (* reads a word from the input file; success is set to
       TRUE if word could be read, FALSE if end of file was
       encountered *)
```

```
    VAR ch, oldch: CHAR;
        i: CARDINAL;

    PROCEDURE IsDelim(ch: CHAR): BOOLEAN;
      (* returns TRUE if ch is a delimiter, FALSE otherwise *)
    BEGIN
      RETURN NOT (('A' <= CAP(ch)) & (CAP(ch) <= 'Z') OR
                  ('0' <= ch) & (ch <= '9') OR
                  (ch = "'") OR (ch = '-'))
    END IsDelim;

    PROCEDURE AddToWord(ch: CHAR);
      (* adds ch to the word being read, converting it to
         uppercase if it is a letter; ignores ch if adding it
         would cause w to overflow *)
    BEGIN
      IF i < maxWordLen THEN
        w^[i] := CAP(ch);
        INC(i)
      END
    END AddToWord;

  BEGIN  (* ReadWord *)
      (* skip delimiters *)
    REPEAT
      Read(ch);
      IF NOT Done THEN
        success := FALSE;
        RETURN
      END
    UNTIL NOT IsDelim(ch) & (ch # "'") & (ch # '-');

      (* read characters until a delimiter is reached, calling
         AddToWord to accumulate characters *)
    success := TRUE;
    ALLOCATE(w, SIZE(String));
    i := 0;
    LOOP
      AddToWord(ch);
      Read(ch);
      IF NOT Done OR IsDelim(ch) THEN
        EXIT
      ELSIF (ch = "'") OR (ch = '-') THEN
        oldch := ch;
        Read(ch);
        IF IsDelim(ch) OR (ch = "'") OR (ch = '-') THEN
          EXIT
        END;
        AddToWord(oldch)
      END
    END;
```

```
      (* add 0C terminator if room remains *)
    IF i < maxWordLen THEN
      w^[i] := 0C
    END
  END ReadWord;

  PROCEDURE WriteWord(w: Word);
    (* writes a word to the output file *)
  BEGIN
    WriteString(w^)
  END WriteWord;

  PROCEDURE CompareWords(w1, w2: Word): CompareResult;
    (* compares words w1 and w2; returns either "less",
       "equal", or "greater" *)
  BEGIN
    RETURN Compare(w1^, w2^)
  END CompareWords;

END Words.
```

There are many ways to implement the table of words. Because we must be able to fetch the largest word in the table, we need a data structure that allows us to implement this operation efficiently. The binary search tree (see Section 8.1) is suitable for this purpose. Because we know in advance that the program will enter all words into the table before fetching any, we will build the table to have two modes: "enter" and "fetch." The variable `mode` stores the mode. When the value of `mode` is `enterMode`, we can enter words; when it is `fetchMode`, we can fetch words but not enter them. The value of `mode` is `enterMode` initially; the first call of `FetchLargestWord` changes the value of `mode` to `fetchMode`, where it remains for the rest of the program. Including a mode in the module allows fast word fetching. The first call of `FetchLargestWord` begins an inorder traversal of the binary tree; subsequent calls of `FetchLargestWord` continue the traversal from where it left off. We cannot do the traversal recursively, as in Section 8.1, because we have no way to preserve the "state" of the traversal between calls of `FetchLargestWord`. Instead, we perform the traversal using a stack. (We have essentially performed another level of object-oriented design. The informal strategy for this level uses a stack object.) We need only one stack, so we can create a module `Stack` that exports the operations `Push`, `Pop`, and `IsEmpty` while hiding the stack's representation. Because only the module `WordTable` uses the stack, we make `Stack` a local module within `WordTable`.

```
IMPLEMENTATION MODULE WordTable;

  FROM Words IMPORT Word, CompareWords;
  FROM String IMPORT CompareResult;    (* Section 10.2 *)
```

```
FROM Storage IMPORT ALLOCATE;
FROM InOut IMPORT WriteString, WriteLn;

TYPE BinTree = POINTER TO TreeNode;
     TreeNode = RECORD
                  left: BinTree;
                  word: Word;
                  count: CARDINAL;
                  right: BinTree
                END;

VAR root: BinTree;
    mode: (enterMode, fetchMode);

MODULE Stack;
  (* local module that exports procedures for manipulating a
     hidden stack of binary trees *)

  IMPORT BinTree;
  IMPORT WriteString, WriteLn;

  EXPORT Push, Pop, IsEmpty;

  CONST stackSize = 100;   (* maximum size of stack *)

  VAR stackArray: ARRAY [1..stackSize] OF BinTree;
      topOfStack: [0..stackSize+1];

  PROCEDURE Push(t: BinTree);
    (* pushes t onto the stack; terminates program if stack
       is full *)
  BEGIN
    INC(topOfStack);
    IF topOfStack > stackSize THEN
      WriteString("Stack overflow in Stack.Push");
      WriteLn;
      HALT
    END;
    stackArray[topOfStack] := t
  END Push;

  PROCEDURE Pop(VAR t: BinTree);
    (* stores the top element of the stack into t, then pops
       the stack; terminates program if stack is empty *)
  BEGIN
    IF topOfStack = 0 THEN
      WriteString("Stack underflow in Stack.Pop");
      WriteLn;
      HALT
    END;
```

```
      t := stackArray[topOfStack];
      DEC(topOfStack)
    END Pop;

    PROCEDURE IsEmpty(): BOOLEAN;
      (* returns TRUE if the stack is empty, FALSE otherwise *)
    BEGIN
      RETURN topOfStack = 0
    END IsEmpty;

  BEGIN
    topOfStack := 0
  END Stack;

  PROCEDURE InsertInTree(VAR t: BinTree; w: Word);
    (* inserts the word w into its proper place in the binary
       search tree t; inserts words greater than the root into
       the left subtree and inserts words less than the root
       into the right subtree *)
  BEGIN
    IF t # NIL THEN
      CASE CompareWords(w, t^.word) OF
        less:    InsertInTree(t^.right, w) |
        equal:   INC(t^.count) |
        greater: InsertInTree(t^.left, w)
      END
    ELSE
      ALLOCATE(t, SIZE(TreeNode));
      t^.word := w;
      t^.count := 1;
      t^.left := NIL;
      t^.right := NIL
    END
  END InsertInTree;

  PROCEDURE EnterWord(w: Word);
    (* enters a word into the table; all calls of EnterWord
       must precede the first call of FetchLargestWord *)
  BEGIN
    IF mode = fetchMode THEN
      WriteString("fetchMode error in WordTable.EnterWord");
      WriteLn;
      HALT
    END;
    InsertInTree(root, w)
  END EnterWord;

  PROCEDURE FetchLargestWord(VAR w: Word; VAR count: CARDINAL;
                             VAR success: BOOLEAN);
```

```
    (* fetches the largest word not previously fetched and a
       count of how many times it has been entered in the
       table; success is set to TRUE if a word was fetched,
       FALSE if all words have been fetched previously *)
    VAR top: BinTree;
  BEGIN
      (* if first call of FetchLargestWord, initialize stack *)
    IF mode = enterMode THEN
      mode := fetchMode;
      IF root # NIL THEN
        Push(root);
        top := root;
        WHILE top^.left # NIL DO
          Push(top^.left);
          top := top^.left
        END
      END
    END;

      (* fetch word on top of stack, then prepare for next
         call of FetchLargestWord *)
    success := NOT IsEmpty();
    IF success THEN
      Pop(top);
      w := top^.word;
      count := top^.count;
      IF top^.right # NIL THEN
        Push(top^.right);
        top := top^.right;
        WHILE top^.left # NIL DO
          Push(top^.left);
          top := top^.left
        END
      END
    END
  END FetchLargestWord;

BEGIN
  root := NIL;
  mode := enterMode
END WordTable.
```

Our strategy for implementing `WordTable` reveals the need for another operation on values of type `Word`: Given two words `w1` and `w2`, determine whether `w1` is less than, equal to, or greater than `w2`. The procedure `CompareWords` in the module `Words` implements this operation.

Our final task is to write the implementation part of `WordLists`. There are several reasonable ways to represent an ordered list of words; here we use a linked list.

```
IMPLEMENTATION MODULE WordLists;

  FROM Words IMPORT Word;
  FROM Storage IMPORT ALLOCATE;

  TYPE WordList = POINTER TO ListElement;
       ListElement = RECORD
                       word: Word;
                       next: WordList
                     END;

  PROCEDURE MakeListEmpty(VAR list: WordList);
    (* initializes a list by making it empty *)
  BEGIN
    list := NIL
  END MakeListEmpty;

  PROCEDURE AddWord(w: Word; VAR list: WordList);
    (* adds w to the beginning of the list *)
    VAR new: WordList;
  BEGIN
      ALLOCATE(new, SIZE(ListElement));
      new^.word := w;
      new^.next := list;
      list := new
  END AddWord;

  PROCEDURE RemoveWord(VAR w: Word; VAR list: WordList;
                       VAR success: BOOLEAN);
    (* fetches the first word on the list and removes it from
       the list; success is set to TRUE if the list is not
       empty, FALSE otherwise *)
  BEGIN
    success := list # NIL;
    IF success THEN
      w := list^.word;
      list := list^.next
    END
  END RemoveWord;

END WordLists.
```

10.5 Error-handling in Library Modules

A procedure exported by a library module must be capable of handling errors that might occur when a client module calls the procedure (for example, the client may have supplied the procedure with invalid parameters or asked it to perform an illegal operation on a data structure). When it detects an error, the procedure has several choices: (1) ignore the error, (2) attempt to recover from the error itself, (3) print an error message and terminate the program, or (4) notify the client that an error has occurred. Ignoring errors is usually the worst option; it forces clients to take complete responsibility for detecting errors. Attempting to recover from an error is not usually possible. Printing an error message and terminating is acceptable for errors that prevent further execution of a program. In most cases, however, it is best to notify the client of the error, thus allowing the client to decide what action to take. This alternative requires some extra overhead for both the client and the library module; the latter must somehow signal that an error has occurred, while the former must detect the signal and take appropriate action.

A library module has at least five ways to notify a client of an error:

through an exported status variable
through an exported status procedure
through a status parameter supplied with each procedure
through a status value returned by each procedure
through an error-handling procedure "installed" by the client module

We now describe each of these methods and use the `CharStackModule` library module of Section 9.1 to illustrate. In addition, we briefly discuss the advantages and disadvantages of each method. The criteria for evaluating these methods include efficiency, ease of use, adherence to good programming practice, and ability to ignore errors (when the client can guarantee that errors will not occur).

- *Through an exported status variable*. A procedure changes the value of the variable when it detects an error; the client can test the variable after the procedure returns to see if an error occurred. There may be one status variable or several; the type of a status variable is usually BOOLEAN or an enumeration type.

  Only two errors are possible in the use of `CharStackModule`: (1) overflow (attempting to push a value onto the stack when it is full) and (2) underflow (attempting to pop the stack when it is empty). Therefore, `CharStackModule` could export either two BOOLEAN status variables (`overflow` and `underflow`) or a single status variable with three values: `normal`, `overflow`, and `underflow`. In the latter case, the definition part of `CharStackModule` would look like this:

```
DEFINITION MODULE CharStackModule;
  (* exports procedures for manipulating a hidden stack of
     characters *)

  TYPE StatusValues = (normal, overflow, underflow);

  VAR stackStatus: StatusValues;
    (* usually has the value "normal" *);
```

```
  PROCEDURE Push(ch: CHAR);
    (* pushes ch onto the stack; sets stackStatus to
       "overflow" if stack overflow occurs *)

  PROCEDURE Pop(VAR ch: CHAR);
    (* stores the top element of the stack into ch, then pops
       the stack; sets stackStatus to "underflow" if stack
       underflow occurs *)

  PROCEDURE IsEmpty(): BOOLEAN;
    (* returns TRUE if the stack is empty, FALSE otherwise *)

END CharStackModule.
```

Note that we could replace stackStatus by a BOOLEAN variable stackError that CharStackModule sets to TRUE when overflow or underflow occurs; because overflow is possible only during a call of Push and underflow only during a call of Pop, the client can always tell which error occurred.

Status variables are efficient, easy to use, and can be ignored if the client module wishes. The only potential problem with status variables is their vulnerability to change from outside the module; Modula-2 provides no way to make an exported variable "read-only." The vulnerability of a status variable may not be a problem, however, provided that each procedure exported by the library module ignores the value of the variable (because it may have been changed by a client) and always sets it before returning (so that the value of the variable is valid when control leaves the module).

- *Through an exported status procedure*. Such a procedure supplies status information when called. In its simplest form, a status procedure is a function with no parameters that returns a BOOLEAN or enumeration value.

```
DEFINITION MODULE CharStackModule;
  (* exports procedures for manipulating a hidden stack of
     characters *)

  TYPE StatusValues = (normal, overflow, underflow);

  PROCEDURE StackStatus(): StatusValues;
    (* returns current status of stack *)

  PROCEDURE Push(ch: CHAR);
    (* pushes ch onto the stack; sets status of stack to
       "overflow" if stack overflow occurs *)

  PROCEDURE Pop(VAR ch: CHAR);
    (* stores the top element of the stack into ch, then
       pops the stack; sets status of stack to "underflow"
       if stack underflow occurs *)
```

```
  PROCEDURE IsEmpty(): BOOLEAN;
    (* returns TRUE if the stack is empty, FALSE otherwise *)

END CharStackModule.
```

This method is similar to the previous one; the only difference is that the status variable is now hidden inside the implementation part of the library module and accessed through a procedure (in effect, the status variable becomes "read-only"). Status procedures are easy to use, can be ignored if desired, and follow good programming practice (because clients cannot alter the value of the status variable). Their disadvantage is the extra time required to perform a procedure call whenever the client wants status information.

- *Through a status parameter supplied with each procedure*. The procedure modifies the status parameter to indicate whether an error occurred, and then the client tests it when the procedure returns.

```
DEFINITION MODULE CharStackModule;
  (* exports procedures for manipulating a hidden stack of
     characters *)

  PROCEDURE Push(ch: CHAR; VAR overflow: BOOLEAN);
    (* pushes ch onto the stack; sets overflow to TRUE if
       stack overflow occurs, FALSE otherwise *)

  PROCEDURE Pop(VAR ch: CHAR; VAR underflow: BOOLEAN);
    (* stores the top element of the stack into ch, then pops
       the stack; sets underflow to TRUE if stack underflow
       occurs, FALSE otherwise *)

  PROCEDURE IsEmpty(): BOOLEAN;
    (* returns TRUE if the stack is empty, FALSE otherwise *)

END CharStackModule.
```

Alternatively, we could replace the parameters `overflow` and `underflow` by a parameter called `success` whose value after a call or `Push` or `Pop` is TRUE if an error did not occur.

This method is not as easy to use as the others (procedure calls become more complicated) and cannot be ignored (the client module must supply a status variable as a parameter even if the client never checks the variable's value afterward). It is relatively efficient, however, and does conform to good programming practice.

- *Through a status value returned by each procedure*. If a procedure might detect an error, we write it as a function rather than as a proper procedure. The value returned by the function indicates whether the operation was successful or whether an error occurred.

```
DEFINITION MODULE CharStackModule;
  (* exports procedures for manipulating a hidden stack of
     characters *)

  PROCEDURE Push(ch: CHAR): BOOLEAN;
    (* pushes ch onto the stack; returns TRUE if operation
       was successful, FALSE if overflow occurred *)

  PROCEDURE Pop(VAR ch: CHAR): BOOLEAN;
    (* stores the top element of the stack into ch, then pops
       the stack; returns TRUE if operation was successful,
       FALSE if underflow occurred *)

  PROCEDURE IsEmpty(): BOOLEAN;
    (* returns TRUE if the stack is empty, FALSE otherwise *)

END CharStackModule.
```

This method is easy to use and efficient. A client module cannot ignore it, however, because the client must deal with the return value somehow. Furthermore, this method violates the principle that functions should not have side effects.

- *Through an error-handling procedure "installed" by the client module*. The library module exports an installation procedure; a client module can call this procedure to "install" an error-handling procedure (that is, to store a reference to this procedure in a variable). When a procedure exported by the library module detects an error, it calls the error-handling procedure. Typically, the error-handling procedure has a parameter whose value indicates which error occurred.

```
DEFINITION MODULE CharStackModule;
  (* exports procedures for manipulating a hidden stack of
     characters *)

  TYPE StackErrors = (overflow, underflow);
       ErrorHandler = PROCEDURE (StackErrors);

  PROCEDURE InstallErrorHandler(handler: ErrorHandler);
    (* installs an error-handling procedure *)

  PROCEDURE Push(ch: CHAR);
    (* pushes ch onto the stack; the error handler is called
       if overflow occurs *)

  PROCEDURE Pop(VAR ch: CHAR);
    (* stores the top element of the stack into ch, then pops
       the stack; the error handler is called if underflow
       occurs *)
```

```
    PROCEDURE IsEmpty(): BOOLEAN;
      (* returns TRUE if the stack is empty, FALSE otherwise *)

  END CharStackModule.
```

This method is the most complicated of those we have presented, yet it allows clients to ignore errors and conforms to good programming practice. It is also the most efficient method, because client modules do not spend time checking for errors. The only real problem with this method is that the error-handling procedure may lack information about the context in which the error occurred.

We cannot say that a particular method is "best"; each has its advantages and disadvantages. In fact, each method has been used in the library modules supplied with at least one commercially available Modula-2 system.

A few Modula-2 systems provide a language feature known as *exceptions*. Exceptions allow the direct transfer of control from the point at which a program detects an error to another part of the program where the error can be handled. Because exceptions are not a standard feature of Modula-2, we will not discuss them further.

EXERCISES

Section 10.1

1. Write the implementation part of the `VectorOperations` module.
2. Modify the definition part of the `VectorOperations` module to make `Vector` an opaque type. This change requires the module to export additional procedures.
3. Write the implementation part of the `VectorOperations` module, assuming that the definition part has been modified as described in exercise 2.
4. Write the implementation part of the `SymbolTable` module.
5. Modify the definition part of the `SymbolTable` module so that it exports an opaque type called `SymTab`. Modify the procedures exported by `SymbolTable` to operate on variables of this type and add any additional procedures that may be needed.
6. Write the implementation part of the `SymbolTable` module, assuming that the definition part has been modified as described in exercise 5.

Section 10.2

7. The last `IF` statement in the `Compare` procedure is reasonably efficient when the strings being compared begin with different characters or begin with the same character but differ on the second. Show how to make the `IF` statement more efficient if the strings are expected to have several characters in common.

8. Rewrite the implementation part of the String module, assuming that the 0C character terminates every string.

9. Rewrite the implementation part of the String module, assuming that the first character of each string stores its length (see exercise 8 in Chapter 7).

Section 10.3

10. The CharSet module exports procedures for computing the union, intersection, and difference of two values of type SetOfChar. Write a procedure for computing the symmetric difference.

11. Assume that we have added a parameter of type ARRAY OF CHAR to the Initialize procedure exported by CharSet. A call of Initialize now creates a set containing the characters in the string. For example, the call

```
Initialize(s, "abcd");
```

would initialize the set s to have the value {a, b, c, d}. The characters in the string need not appear in any order, a character may appear more than once, and the string may be empty. Write the new version of Initialize.

12. Instead of using a linked list to represent a set of characters, we could instead use an array of BOOLEAN values:

```
TYPE SetOfChar = POINTER TO BooleanArray;
     BooleanArray = ARRAY CHAR OF BOOLEAN;
```

If s is a variable of type SetOfChar, s^[ch] will have the value TRUE if ch is an element of s. Rewrite the implementation part of CharSet using this representation for SetOfChar. (We can represent SetOfChar in a similar—but more compact—fashion as an array of BITSET values; see the Exercises at the end of Chapter 11.)

13. What are the advantages and disadvantages of using a linked list to represent a character set, as opposed to using an array of BOOLEAN values (as in exercise 12)?

Section 10.4

14. Redo the object-oriented design of Section 10.4, using a different informal strategy as a starting point.

15. Assume that the program of Section 10.4 must also compute the number of characters, lines, words, and sentences in the input file. Modify the informal strategy to reflect this requirement, and redo the object-oriented design.

Section 10.5

16. One alternative explored in Section 10.5 was to write each procedure that might detect an error as a function returning a status value. The client must then somehow use the value returned by the function. Is it true that the client must assign the return value to a variable (which it then ignores), or is there a more convenient way for it to ignore the return value?

17. Write the implementation part of the final version of CharStackModule (the version that exports InstallErrorHandler).

18. Section 10.5 presented five methods by which a library module can allow a client to detect and respond to errors. Show how to generalize these methods to library modules that export an opaque type.

11 Low-Level Programming

The first ten chapters of this book describe the high-level, machine-independent features of Modula-2. Although these features are adequate for most applications, some programs require machine-level operations not normally supported by high-level programming languages. In particular, systems programs — assemblers, loaders, compilers, operating systems, and the like — must be able to

- fetch and store data using machine addresses
- access bits, bit fields, and bytes — units of storage that are not meaningful in most high-level languages
- perform machine-level operations (such as bitwise Boolean operations and shifting)
- access registers and buffers belonging to input/output devices

These "low-level" operations can be useful in programs for which fast execution or efficient use of space is critical. Programmers also need them for writing certain kinds of reusable software components, including *generic* procedures and modules. A procedure is generic if it can accept parameters of more than one type. (The standard procedure ABS is generic: it allows parameters of any numeric type.) A generic module hides a data structure with components of an unspecified type (for example, a stack whose component type is not fixed, but may be selected by a client module) or exports a type representing such a generic data structure.

Most high-level programming languages do not provide direct support for low-level programming. Instead, programmers must use "tricks" to accomplish the desired effect. (In Pascal, for example, programmers often use a record with a variant part to trick the compiler into thinking that a value of one type actually belongs to another type.) Wirth designed Modula-2 for systems programming, however, so it provides a rich assortment of low-level features:

- The BITSET type allows access to individual bits in a word.
- The SYSTEM module provides low-level types, including WORD and ADDRESS, and procedures such as ADR, which computes the address of a variable.

Type transfer functions allow a program to treat a value of one type as though it belonged to another type.

The ability to locate a variable at a particular (absolute) address allows a program to access special memory locations (not all Modula-2 systems support this feature).

We describe these four features in Sections 11.1, 11.2, 11.4, and 11.5, respectively. Section 11.3 shows how to use the features `SYSTEM` provides to write generic procedures and modules.

Low-level programming has drawbacks. One problem, of course, is loss of portability. To achieve portability, programmers normally try to avoid features that depend on a particular computer or Modula-2 system. Low-level programming precludes complete portability. The other problem is the increased probability of errors. Operations on low-level values — words and addresses — are inherently error-prone; for example, storing a word into memory at the wrong address is an ever-present danger.

Careful use of Modula-2's low-level features can minimize the problems of low-level programming, however. Consider first the problem of transporting a program to a different environment (either a different computer, or a different Modula-2 system running on the same computer). The person transporting the program must locate any system or machine dependencies in the program and must modify them to fit the new environment. Modula-2 provides help for this task in two ways. First, the language's support for modules makes it easy for the original programmer to confine the use of low-level features to a few modules. Second, Wirth designed Modula-2 so that the reader of a program can easily determine where the original programmer used low-level features.

Programming at the machine level is normally done without types and therefore without the protection that type-checking provides. At the machine level, we have only bit patterns, which can be interpreted as numbers, characters, or other data values. The lack of types is one reason that programmers find it difficult to debug programs written in an assembly language. Modula-2 tries to solve this problem by enforcing normal type-checking throughout a program, requiring that the programmer explicitly inform the compiler at each point where it is necessary to suppress type-checking. Modula-2 compilers perform type-checking even for such low-level types as `WORD` and `ADDRESS`. Consider the type `WORD`, for example. Normally, no operations are defined for `WORD` values (other than assignment), so it is impossible to add `WORD` values, compare `WORD` values, and so forth. At the programmer's request, the compiler will treat a value of type `WORD` as though it were of another type, provided that values of that type occupy one word of memory. For example, suppose that `CARDINAL` values require one word. By requesting that the compiler treat two `WORD` values as `CARDINAL` numbers, it becomes possible to add the values or perform other arithmetic operations on them. Because Modula-2 requires type-checking even for low-level types, a Modula-2 compiler can detect errors during compilation that would go undetected if the program had been written in assembly language or most other systems programming languages.

Note: Unless otherwise indicated, I have tested all examples in this chapter on an IBM Personal Computer using the Logitech Modula-2/86 system. Although I have made every effort to make the examples independent of this environment, some examples will require modification for other computers or Modula-2 systems. No previous knowledge of the IBM PC is necessary to understand the examples. Readers who want more information about the IBM PC can consult *The Peter Norton Programmer's Guide to the IBM PC* (Bellevue, Washington: Microsoft Press, 1985).

11.1 The BITSET Type

BITSET is the only standard (predefined) structured type in Modula-2; it has the following definition:

```
TYPE BITSET = SET OF [0..W-1];
```

According to Wirth's *Programming in Modula-2*, the value of W may vary from one Modula-2 system to another, but is usually the number of bits in one word of memory.

At first glance, BITSET appears to be simply a particular set type. However, an important difference separates BITSET from programmer-defined set types. Recall from Section 7.5 that the base type for a programmer-defined set type can have at most N values, where N depends on the particular system, but is normally the number of bits in one word "or a small multiple thereof" (Wirth). Consequently, N need not be equal to W, but may be a multiple of it.

BITSET has one other property that distinguishes it from other set types: The word BITSET need not precede a value of type BITSET that appears in a program. Thus, the set value

```
{0, 8..15}
```

is the same as

```
BITSET{0, 8..15}
```

To make it easier to locate BITSET values in a program, the latter form is usually preferable.

BITSET is in the odd position of being a high-level type that is used primarily for low-level programming. By performing operations on a BITSET value, a program can examine and change the individual bits of a word. Most Modula-2 systems store a BITSET value in a single word (as Wirth's definition of BITSET suggests), where bit i of the word is 1 if i is a member of the set, and 0 if not a member. For example, suppose that words are 16 bits long and that a system numbers the bits in a word from 15 (most significant) to 0 (least significant). (Warning: Some Modula-2 systems number the bits in the opposite direction.) The BITSET value {0, 2..4, 8} would look like this:

15	14	13	12	11	10	9	8	7	6	5	4	3	2	1	0
0	0	0	0	0	0	0	1	0	0	0	1	1	1	0	1

This compact representation allows efficient storage and assignment of BITSET values. It also makes set operations easy to perform. For example, the set operation + (union) on two BITSET values corresponds to computing the bitwise OR of the two words that represent the sets. The other set operations also correspond to the bitwise Boolean instructions available on virtually all computers.

Knowing how a system represents BITSET values, the programmer can perform various low-level operations on words by treating them as BITSET values. Table 11.1 shows how we can interpret Modula-2's set operations—when applied to BITSET values—as operations on words. Sections 11.4 and 11.5 contain several examples that use BITSET operations in this fashion.

Table 11.1 BITSET Operations Interpreted as Operations on Words

w1 + w2	bitwise OR of words w1 and w2
w1 - w2	bitwise AND of w1 with complement of w2
w1 * w2	bitwise AND of words w1 and w2
w1 / w2	bitwise exclusive OR of words w1 and w2
{0..15} - w	bitwise complement of word w
i IN w	TRUE if bit i is set in word w
INCL(w, i)	set bit i in word w
EXCL(w, i)	clear bit i in word w

EXAMPLE PROGRAM

Sorting a File of CARDINAL Numbers

It is sometimes possible to write efficient sorting programs that use a one-dimensional array of BOOLEAN values. For example, consider the problem of sorting a file of CARDINAL numbers in which no duplicates appear. If we declare the variable bitVector as

```
VAR bitVector: ARRAY [0..MAX(CARDINAL)] OF BOOLEAN;
```

then we can sort the file in the following way:

1. Set all components of bitVector to FALSE.

2. Read a number i, set bitVector[i] to TRUE, and repeat until the end of the file is reached.
3. Examine each component of bitVector, from first to last; if bitVector[i] is TRUE, write i to the output file.

If CARDINAL values are 16 bits long (thereby limiting bitVector to 65,536 components) and if the file of numbers we want to sort is large, this technique is often faster than conventional sorting methods. (Not counting the time taken to initialize bitVector and compare each component with TRUE, we can sort a file of N numbers in time proportional to N; the best conventional methods require time proportional to $N \log N$.) The reason for its speed lies in the special characteristics of the file to be sorted: The values in the file come from a relatively small set (the CARDINAL numbers), there are no duplicate values, and no information is associated with each value (in most sorting applications, the sorting key is part of a record).

One problem with this algorithm is that the bitVector array occupies a great deal of space. For example, when using the Logitech Modula-2/86 system on the IBM Personal Computer, MAX(CARDINAL) is 65,535 and BOOLEAN values each occupy one byte, so the array requires 65,536 (64K) bytes.

To save space, we can pack 16 Boolean values into each word; bitVector then requires only 4,096 (4K) words (8K bytes). Because we need to access the individual bits in each word, we should declare bitVector to be an array of BITSET values:

```
CONST bitsPerWord = 16;
      vectorLength = MAX(CARDINAL) DIV bitsPerWord + 1;
VAR bitVector: ARRAY [0..vectorLength-1] OF BITSET;
```

Our sorting program needs to perform three operations on bitVector: set bit i (where i is a number between 0 and 65,535), test whether bit i is set, and clear the entire vector. The procedures SetBit, TestBit, and ClearVector, respectively, perform these operations. SetBit and TestBit both use the fact that bit i of bitVector occurs in position i MOD 16 of the component whose index is i DIV 16. ClearVector assigns the empty set to each component of bitVector. The full program follows.

```
MODULE SortCardinals;
  (* sorts a file of CARDINAL numbers; duplicate numbers are
     ignored *)

  FROM InOut IMPORT OpenInput, CloseInput, OpenOutput,
                    CloseOutput, ReadCard, Done, WriteCard,
                    WriteString, WriteLn;

  CONST bitsPerWord = 16;    (* IBM PC *)
        vectorLength = MAX(CARDINAL) DIV bitsPerWord + 1;
```

```
VAR bitVector: ARRAY [0..vectorLength-1] OF BITSET;
    i: CARDINAL;

PROCEDURE SetBit(i: CARDINAL);
  (* sets bit i in bitVector *)
BEGIN
  INCL(bitVector[i DIV bitsPerWord], i MOD bitsPerWord)
END SetBit;

PROCEDURE TestBit(i: CARDINAL): BOOLEAN;
  (* returns TRUE if bit i in bitVector is set *)
BEGIN
  RETURN (i MOD bitsPerWord) IN bitVector[i DIV bitsPerWord]
END TestBit;

PROCEDURE ClearVector;
  (* clears every bit in bitVector *)
  VAR i: CARDINAL;
BEGIN
  FOR i := 0 TO vectorLength - 1 DO
    bitVector[i] := BITSET{}
  END
END ClearVector;

BEGIN
    (* read numbers and set corresponding bits in bitVector *)
  WriteString("Enter name of file to be sorted.");
  WriteLn;
  OpenInput("NUM");
  ClearVector;
  ReadCard(i);
  WHILE Done DO
    SetBit(i);
    ReadCard(i)
  END;
  CloseInput;

    (* write the index of each 1 bit in bitVector *)
  WriteString("Enter name of output file.");
  WriteLn;
  OpenOutput("NUM");
  FOR i := 0 TO MAX(CARDINAL) DO
    IF TestBit(i) THEN
      WriteCard(i, 1);
      WriteLn
    END
  END;
  CloseOutput
END SortCardinals.
```

11.2 The SYSTEM Module

Every Modula-2 system must supply a module called SYSTEM that exports types and procedures that are useful for low-level programming. The exact contents of SYSTEM vary from one system to another, although SYSTEM always exports at least the entities shown in Table 11.2.

Table 11.2 Minimum Contents of SYSTEM Module

WORD	type	values are single words of memory
ADDRESS	type	values are machine addresses
ADR	function	returns the address of a variable
TSIZE	function	returns a number indicating the amount of space required to store a value of a given type

The required contents of SYSTEM changed between the Second and Third Editions of *Programming in Modula-2*:

The Second Edition required SYSTEM to export the function SIZE. In the Third Edition, SIZE is a standard function; in addition, the definition of SIZE changed slightly (as we will see later).

The Second Edition required that SYSTEM export the type PROCESS. PROCESS does not appear in the Third Edition; procedures that formerly took PROCESS parameters now expect parameters of type ADDRESS.

The Second Edition required SYSTEM to export the procedures NEWPROCESS and TRANSFER. (The procedure IOTRANSFER, if a particular Modula-2 system supplied it, was also required to be in SYSTEM.) The Third Edition allows SYSTEM or some other library module to export NEWPROCESS and TRANSFER. SYSTEM or some other module may export IOTRANSFER, if provided.

Chapter 12 discusses PROCESS, NEWPROCESS, TRANSFER, and IOTRANSFER in more detail.

We must emphasize that the entities shown in the table are the *minimum* contents of SYSTEM. Many Modula-2 systems provide a much richer version of SYSTEM, including

- storage types in addition to WORD (BYTE, for example)
- procedures for fetching or altering the contents of a machine register
- procedures for inserting machine instructions into a Modula-2 program
- procedures that invoke operating system functions
- procedures that communicate directly with input/output devices
- procedures that enable or disable interrupts, install an interrupt handler, change the priority of a process, or generate an interrupt (see Chapter 12)

The manual for a particular Modula-2 system should include a complete list of the entities its version of SYSTEM exports.

Some entities exported by SYSTEM have special properties a normal definition module cannot express. The parameter to the TSIZE function, for example, is a type name, an entity that cannot normally serve as a parameter. Because it is impossible to write a definition module for SYSTEM, we call it a *pseudomodule*. SYSTEM does not reside in files, like a normal library module; instead, Modula-2 compilers recognize the entities that SYSTEM exports. (Some systems provide a file containing a description of SYSTEM written in the form of a definition module; this file is for documentation purposes only and should not be compiled.)

Despite the fact that SYSTEM is really part of a Modula-2 compiler, programs must explicitly import any entities needed from SYSTEM. Although this requirement may seem odd, it has two advantages. First, the entities in SYSTEM are normally hidden from the programmer, thus preventing accidental use. (Improperly or accidentally using SYSTEM can produce hard-to-find errors.) Second, requiring the programmer to import entities from SYSTEM makes it easy to determine which modules use low-level, system-dependent features. This information is very helpful during program maintenance. When modifying a program to run in a different environment, the programmer must know which modules use Modula-2's low-level features; often the programmer only needs to glance at the beginning of each module to see if it imports from SYSTEM. (Some programmers go a step further and always qualify entities imported from SYSTEM; for example, they write SYSTEM.WORD instead of just WORD. This practice makes it easy to locate all uses of entities imported from SYSTEM.)

The WORD Type

Values of type WORD represent single words of computer memory. On the IBM Personal Computer, a value of type WORD contains 16 bits of information, as is typical of many microcomputers. On larger computers, 32 bits is a common word length.

The programmer may use WORD values as parameters and functions may return a result of type WORD. The only operation defined for type WORD is assignment. Modula-2 allows no other operations, including arithmetic and relational operations. However, type transfer functions make it possible to perform these operations on WORD values. (Section 11.4 explains type transfer and shows several examples of type transfer applied to values of type WORD.)

The primary usefulness of WORD lies in its special properties when used to declare formal parameters. If a formal parameter has type WORD, then the actual parameter can be of any type that occupies one word. (The list of allowable types varies from one system to another; in the Logitech Modula-2/86 system, values of type CARDINAL, INTEGER, and BITSET occupy one word.) For example, we can use the following procedure to copy any one-word value to any one-word variable:

```
PROCEDURE CopyWord(source: WORD; VAR dest: WORD);
  (* copies any one-word value *)
BEGIN
  dest := source
END CopyWord;
```

Thus, if b and i are variables of types BITSET and INTEGER, respectively, the call

```
CopyWord(b, i);
```

will copy the contents of b to i, despite the fact that the variables have different types.

A formal parameter of type ARRAY OF WORD matches an actual parameter of *any* type, even an array or record type. An ARRAY OF WORD formal parameter allows us to treat the actual parameter as a block (array) of words; we can access individual words by indexing the formal parameter in normal array fashion. This feature of Modula-2 allows the programmer to write procedures of great generality. An example of such a procedure appears in Section 11.3.

In some Modula-2 systems, SYSTEM provides the type BYTE in addition to WORD. A value of type BYTE normally consists of eight bits of information. The properties of the BYTE type resemble those of WORD; typically, these properties include the following:

The only allowable operation for values of type BYTE is assignment.

If a formal parameter has type BYTE, the corresponding actual parameter can be any value that occupies one byte of storage. (Allowable types might include CHAR, BOOLEAN, and enumeration types, for example.)

If a formal parameter has type ARRAY OF BYTE, a matching actual parameter can be of any type. Because some systems disallow the use of ARRAY OF WORD with actual parameters that occupy one byte, ARRAY OF BYTE may offer greater flexibility.

When a Modula-2 system does not provide BYTE, the programmer can often substitute CHAR. Of course, CHAR has none of the special properties of BYTE.

The ADDRESS Type

A value of type ADDRESS is the address of a word in main memory. ADDRESS behaves as though it had the following declaration:

```
TYPE ADDRESS = POINTER TO WORD;
```

All the operations that Modula-2 allows for normal pointer values—assignment, comparison, and dereferencing—are also defined for values of type ADDRESS. For example, if we declare addr as

```
VAR addr: ADDRESS;
```

then addr^ is the word in memory to which addr currently points.

ADDRESS also has special properties that other pointer types do not share. In particular, ADDRESS is compatible with any pointer type. Thus, if we declare ptr as

```
VAR ptr: POINTER TO T;    (* T can be any type *)
```

Modula-2 allows both of the following assignments:

```
ptr := addr;
addr := ptr;
```

Nevertheless, ptr and addr still point to values of different types: ptr^ has type T, while addr^ has type WORD. The compatibility of ADDRESS with all pointer types is particularly useful when we are writing procedures, because a formal parameter of type ADDRESS will match an actual parameter of any pointer type.

According to the Third Edition of *Programming in Modula-2*, the ADDRESS type is compatible with some arithmetic type, such as CARDINAL, INTEGER, or LONGINT, depending on the system; the Second Edition required compatibility with CARDINAL. Both editions specify that "all operators for integer arithmetic apply" to ADDRESS values. Modula-2 compilers vary considerably in interpreting this property, however. Many compilers restrict arithmetic operations on ADDRESS values, because some operations (division, for example) are rarely meaningful for ADDRESS values. Allowable operations usually include—as a minimum—adding a number to an ADDRESS value and subtracting a number from an ADDRESS value. Compilers often allow the programmer to use the INC and DEC procedures with variables of type ADDRESS, as well.

The ADR, SIZE, and TSIZE Functions

If x is a variable, ADR(x) returns a value of type ADDRESS representing the address of x during program execution.

We first encountered the standard function SIZE in Section 8.1. If x is the name of a variable, the value of SIZE(x) is the number of storage units required to store x; furthermore, if T is the name of a type (either standard or programmer-defined), then SIZE(T) is the number of storage units required to store a value of type T. The function TSIZE, which SYSTEM exports, is similar to

SIZE but allows only a type name, not a variable name, as its parameter. The reason for the existence of TSIZE is historical. The version of SYSTEM described in the Second Edition of *Programming in Modula-2* specified that SYSTEM exported both SIZE and TSIZE; programmers could apply SIZE only to variables, and TSIZE only to types. In the Third Edition, SIZE became a standard function applicable to both variables and types, removing the need for TSIZE. However, Wirth retained TSIZE so that programmers would not need to change programs that used TSIZE.

The meaning of "storage unit" varies from one Modula-2 system to another. Normally, a storage unit is the smallest addressable unit of storage on a given computer. For some machines, a storage unit is a word; for others, it is a byte. Not all Modula-2 systems follow this convention, however; at least one system measures storage in bits. The manual for a particular system will specify the meaning of the number returned by SIZE and TSIZE. (In the Logitech Modula-2/86 system, SIZE and TSIZE measure sizes in bytes.)

The Second Edition of *Programming in Modula-2* states that TSIZE returns a value of type CARDINAL, but the Third Edition says only that TSIZE must return a value of an arithmetic type (allowing TSIZE to return a value of type LONGINT, say). Again, the manual will indicate the type of the value that TSIZE returns.

Although the programmer cannot always avoid machine dependencies when using Modula-2's low-level features, careful use of SIZE or TSIZE can help. For example, instead of declaring

```
CONST intLength = 2;  (* an INTEGER value occupies two bytes *)
```

it is better to use the declaration

```
CONST intLength = SIZE(INTEGER);
```

We would have to change the former declaration—but not the latter—if we transported the program to a machine on which SIZE(INTEGER) is not 2.

EXAMPLE **Copying a Block of Words**

As an example of the kind of low-level programming made possible by the SYSTEM module, consider the problem of writing a procedure to copy a block of words of arbitrary length from one address to any another address. We could not write this procedure using only the high-level features of Modula-2. If we use WORD and ADDRESS, however, the procedure is straightforward:

```
PROCEDURE CopyWords(source, dest: ADDRESS; length: CARDINAL);
  (* copies a block of words of the specified length from
     source address to dest address *)
  VAR i: CARDINAL;
```

```
BEGIN
  FOR i := 1 TO length DO
    dest^ := source^;        (* dest^ and source^ have type WORD *)
    INC(source, SIZE(WORD));
    INC(dest, SIZE(WORD))
  END
END CopyWords;
```

Instead of adding 1 to `source` and `dest`, `CopyWords` adds `SIZE(WORD)`. Using `SIZE` makes the procedure less machine-dependent—if it simply added 1, `CopyWords` would not work on machines where words are not the smallest addressable units of storage.

Suppose that a program needs to copy a block of memory starting at address `addr` into the variable `buffer` (an array or record) for subsequent processing. The following call of `CopyWords` will perform the copy:

```
CopyWords(addr, ADR(buffer), SIZE(buffer) DIV SIZE(WORD));
```

The call of `ADR` returns the starting address of the variable `buffer`. The expression `SIZE(buffer) DIV SIZE(WORD)` computes the number of words that `buffer` occupies; it should give the correct value regardless of what storage units `SIZE` uses.

Inserting Machine Code into a Modula-2 Program (OPTIONAL)

The only problem with the `CopyWords` procedure is that it is slower than necessary, particularly when a program uses it to copy a large block of words. Many computers include a block transfer operation in their instruction sets. If we could get a Modula-2 compiler to generate this instruction, we could make `CopyWords` execute more quickly. Similarly, a program could perform the `ShiftLeft` and `ShiftRight` operations (Section 11.4) much faster using machine instructions for shifting. Because of such situations, some Modula-2 systems provide the programmer with a mechanism for writing part of a Modula-2 program in machine code or assembly language.

In the Logitech Modula-2/86 system, the `CODE` procedure (which must be imported from `SYSTEM`) allows us to insert machine instructions into a Modula-2 program. A call of `CODE` has the form

CODE(c_1, . . . , c_n);

where c_1 through c_n are `CARDINAL` constants between 0 and 255 (representing values of type `BYTE`) and n is any number. `CODE` is not a true procedure; when the Logitech compiler encounters a call of `CODE`, it simply inserts the values c_1 through c_n into the object program as executable instructions. (*Note:* The `CODE` procedure is not a standard feature of Modula-2, nor does Wirth mention it in *Programming in Modula-2*.)

Needless to say, the CODE procedure is a last resort, for use only when absolutely necessary. Uses of the CODE procedure include

speeding up program execution by inserting more efficient instructions than the compiler normally produces

inserting unusual instructions that the compiler does not usually generate

performing machine-level manipulations that are difficult to do in a high-level language (for example, rotate or shift operations)

Although not all systems supply the CODE procedure in the form described here, many provide similar methods for inserting machine instructions into a Modula-2 program. Some systems may also allow the linking of assembly language programs to a Modula-2 program. In addition to enabling programmers to use existing code that is written in assembly language, this feature also allows programmers to rewrite a critical portion of a Modula-2 program in assembly language to achieve greater speed.

11.3 Generics

A procedure is *generic* if different calls of the procedure can supply parameters of different types. Several of Modula-2's standard procedures are generic, including ABS, ORD, INC, and DEC. A call of ABS, for example, may supply an actual parameter of any numeric type. If these standard procedures were not generic, Modula-2 compilers would have to supply a different procedure for each combination of parameter types—considerably complicating the language.

Some programming languages (notably Ada) provide a high-level mechanism that allows programmers to write their own generic procedures; Modula-2 does not. The lack of such a mechanism explains why the InOut library module exports WriteCard, WriteInt, WriteString, and so forth, rather than a single generic procedure capable of writing a value of any type.

Despite Modula-2's lack of direct support for generics, programmers can use the low-level features of the language to get a similar effect. In this section, we first show how to write generic procedures in Modula-2. We then give two methods (one high-level and one low-level) for constructing a module that implements a generic abstract data type.

EXAMPLE **A Generic Swap Procedure**

Consider the problem of writing a procedure called GenericSwap that is capable of interchanging the contents of any two variables, provided that the variables have the same type. We could not write such a procedure in Modula-2, because we have no way to specify that two parameters have an unknown—but identical—type. In order to write GenericSwap, we must weaken its error-checking ability slightly: instead of swapping two variables of the same type, it will swap any two variables of equal size.

So that the actual parameters of GenericSwap can be variables of arbitrary types, its formal parameters will be of type ARRAY OF WORD. GenericSwap first checks that the sizes of the actual parameters are the same (using HIGH), and then interchanges the corresponding components of the two arrays:

```
PROCEDURE GenericSwap(VAR x, y: ARRAY OF WORD);
  (* swaps contents of two variables of the same size *)
  VAR i: CARDINAL;
      temp: WORD;
BEGIN
  IF HIGH(x) # HIGH(y) THEN
    WriteString("Size error in GenericSwap");
    WriteLn;
    HALT
  END;

  FOR i := 0 TO HIGH(x) DO
    temp := x[i];
    x[i] := y[i];
    y[i] := temp
  END
END GenericSwap;
```

When using low-level features such as ARRAY OF WORD, normal type-checking is not possible. The only error-checking that GenericSwap can do is to check that HIGH(x) equals HIGH(y). This test is not a perfect substitute for type-checking, of course; checking that the sizes of x and y match does not guarantee that x and y have the same type. Furthermore, the test that GenericSwap performs takes place during program execution, not during compilation, so it affects the program's execution speed.

Generic procedures such as GenericSwap are convenient when we need to use the same algorithm to process data of more than one type. In this situation, we gain several advantages by writing a generic procedure:

Development time is less. We need write and test only one procedure, instead of several almost identical procedures.

The program is shorter. A shorter program is easier to understand and maintain, and produces less object code.

Less chance of error exists. Having multiple versions of a procedure risks inconsistency.

The program is easier to change. If a change becomes necessary, we must modify only one procedure.

Generic Modules

It is also useful to be able to write generic modules that hide the structure of an object or export an opaque type. Section 9.1, for example, showed how to define a stack of characters as an object or an opaque type. If another program required a stack of integers or a stack of records instead, it would be convenient to reuse the previous stack module. After all, the operations performed on a stack do not depend on the type of values stored in the stack.

We will concentrate on writing generic modules that export an opaque type and procedures that operate on values of that type (that is, modules that implement a generic abstract data type). We can also use the same techniques to write generic modules that hide an object.

Before giving examples of generic modules, we first discuss two methods for writing the generic procedures that these modules will export. Although there are many ways to write generic procedures, we will examine only two: the "high-level" and the "low-level" methods.

In the high-level method, we declare each generic formal parameter to be of an opaque type (call it `GenericType`). Elsewhere we declare `GenericType` as a pointer to a record with a variant part; the variants reflect the types of values that we can supply to the procedure. For example, if the procedure must handle parameters of types CARDINAL and REAL, we define `GenericType` as follows:

```
TYPE TagType = (cardinalType, realType);
     GenericRecord = RECORD
                         CASE tag: TagType OF
                           cardinalType: cardinal: CARDINAL |
                           realType:     real:     REAL
                         END
                       END;
     GenericType = POINTER TO GenericRecord;
```

A value of type `GenericType` points to a record containing either a CARDINAL number or a REAL number (the tag field allows us to determine which). Informally, we can think of a `GenericType` value as simply a value that can be either CARDINAL or REAL.

In the low-level method, we declare the formal parameter to have type ARRAY OF WORD (or ARRAY OF BYTE, if provided) or ADDRESS. The procedure `GenericSwap` is an example of a procedure with formal parameters of type ARRAY OF WORD. An alternative approach is to use type ADDRESS, supplying the address of the actual parameter when calling the procedure (we can supply the length of the actual parameter as an additional parameter). The procedure `CopyWords` (Section 11.2) is essentially a generic copying procedure; its formal parameters are of type ADDRESS.

The high-level and low-level methods have one obvious difference: The high-level method is more restrictive, because the low-level method allows us to supply a value of any type as a parameter, while the high-level method allows only the types listed as variants in GenericRecord (although we can always add new types to GenericRecord as needed). The methods also have other differences, as we will see later.

The rest of this section presents a pair of example programs that contain generic modules. Both programs are modifications of the TreeSort program of Section 8.1, which uses a binary search tree to sort a file of CARDINAL numbers. Both programs include a module that exports a generic binary search tree; however, one module demonstrates the high-level method of writing generic procedures, while the other demonstrates the low-level method.

EXAMPLE PROGRAM

Using a High-Level Generic Binary Search Tree for Sorting

The module GenericTree1 exports the opaque type BinTree (whose values are binary search trees) and procedures that operate on values of type BinTree. The values stored in the tree nodes belong to the type GenericType, which GenericTree1 imports from a module called GenericTypeModule. To keep the program a manageable size, we have provided only three operations on BinTree values: InitializeTree, InsertValue, and PrintTree. These operations are the only ones we need for sorting; however, for GenericTree1 to be useful in other programs, we would need to augment this collection of operations.

```
DEFINITION MODULE GenericTree1;
  (* exports type BinTree (generic binary search tree) and
     procedures for operating on values of this type *)

  FROM GenericTypeModule IMPORT GenericType;

  TYPE BinTree;    (* generic binary search tree *)

  PROCEDURE InitializeTree(VAR t: BinTree);
    (* initializes the tree t by making it empty *)

  PROCEDURE InsertValue(VAR t: BinTree; x: GenericType);
    (* inserts the value x into its proper place in the
       tree t *)

  PROCEDURE PrintTree(t: BinTree);
    (* traverses the tree t in inorder, printing the values
       stored in the nodes, one per line *)

END GenericTree1.
```

The module GenericTypeModule exports GenericType and procedures that operate on values of this type. These operations include

converting to and from GenericType

comparing GenericType values

printing a GenericType value

The module must provide even operations as simple as comparing two GenericType values, because no other module in the program knows the representation of GenericType values. For simplicity, this version of GenericTypeModule allows a GenericType value to be a CARDINAL or REAL number; it is easy to modify GenericTypeModule to allow other types as well.

```
DEFINITION MODULE GenericTypeModule;
  (* exports type GenericType and procedures for operating
     on values of this type; used for constructing generic
     procedures and data structures *)

  TYPE GenericType;

  PROCEDURE CardToGeneric(c: CARDINAL; VAR x: GenericType);
    (* converts CARDINAL number to GenericType value *)

  PROCEDURE RealToGeneric(r: REAL; VAR x: GenericType);
    (* converts REAL number to GenericType value *)

  PROCEDURE GenericToCard(x: GenericType; VAR c: CARDINAL);
    (* converts GenericType value to CARDINAL number;
       terminates program if x is not a CARDINAL number *)

  PROCEDURE GenericToReal(x: GenericType; VAR r: REAL);
    (* converts GenericType value to REAL number; terminates
       program if x is not a REAL number *)

  PROCEDURE Equal(x, y: GenericType): BOOLEAN;
    (* returns TRUE if numerical values of x and y are equal,
       FALSE otherwise; terminates program if x and y are not
       both CARDINAL or both REAL *)

  PROCEDURE LessThan(x, y: GenericType): BOOLEAN;
    (* returns TRUE if numerical value of x is less than value
       of y, FALSE otherwise; terminates program if x and y are
       not both CARDINAL or both REAL *)

  PROCEDURE Print(x: GenericType);
    (* writes numerical value of x *)

END GenericTypeModule.
```

The program module, TreeSort1, is a rewritten version of TreeSort. It imports from both GenericTree1 and GenericTypeModule. Notice that the program first converts CARDINAL numbers to type GenericType before it supplies them to the procedure InsertValue.

```
MODULE TreeSort1;
  (* sorts a file of CARDINAL numbers by building a binary
     search tree and then traversing it *)

  FROM InOut IMPORT OpenInput, CloseInput, OpenOutput,
                    CloseOutput, ReadCard, Done, WriteString,
                    WriteLn;
  FROM GenericTree1 IMPORT BinTree, InitializeTree,
                           InsertValue, PrintTree;
  FROM GenericTypeModule IMPORT GenericType, CardToGeneric;

  VAR tree: BinTree;
      card: CARDINAL;
      genericValue: GenericType;
BEGIN
  InitializeTree(tree);

    (* read numbers and store in tree *)
  WriteString("Enter name of file to be sorted.");
  WriteLn;
  OpenInput("NUM");
  ReadCard(card);
  WHILE Done DO
    CardToGeneric(card, genericValue);
    InsertValue(tree, genericValue);
    ReadCard(card)
  END;
  CloseInput;

    (* traverse tree and print numbers in order encountered *)
  WriteString("Enter name of output file.");
  WriteLn;
  OpenOutput("NUM");
  PrintTree(tree);
  CloseOutput
END TreeSort1.
```

The implementation part of GenericTree1 is straightforward. Note that it imports LessThan and Print from GenericTypeModule.

```
IMPLEMENTATION MODULE GenericTree1;

  FROM InOut IMPORT WriteLn;
  FROM GenericTypeModule IMPORT GenericType, LessThan, Print;
  FROM Storage IMPORT ALLOCATE;
```

```
TYPE BinTree = POINTER TO TreeNode;
     TreeNode = RECORD
                   left: BinTree;
                    value: GenericType;
                    right: BinTree
                 END;

PROCEDURE InitializeTree(VAR t: BinTree);
  (* initializes the tree t by making it empty *)
BEGIN
  t := NIL
END InitializeTree;

PROCEDURE InsertValue(VAR t: BinTree; x: GenericType);
  (* inserts the value x into its proper place in the
     tree t *)
BEGIN
  IF t # NIL THEN
    IF LessThan(x, t^.value) THEN
      InsertValue(t^.left, x)
    ELSE
      InsertValue(t^.right, x)
    END
  ELSE
    ALLOCATE(t, SIZE(TreeNode));
    t^.value := x;
    t^.left := NIL;
    t^.right := NIL
  END
END InsertValue;

PROCEDURE PrintTree(t: BinTree);
  (* traverses the tree t in inorder, printing the values
     stored in the nodes, one per line *)
BEGIN
  IF t # NIL THEN
    PrintTree(t^.left);
    Print(t^.value);
    WriteLn;
    PrintTree(t^.right)
  END
END PrintTree;

END GenericTree1.
```

The implementation part of GenericTypeModule hides the actual representation of GenericType as a pointer to a record with a variant part. Note that the procedures that GenericTypeModule exports perform full type-checking on values of type GenericType, using the tag field of GenericRecord.

```
IMPLEMENTATION MODULE GenericTypeModule;

  FROM InOut IMPORT WriteString, WriteCard, WriteLn;
  FROM RealInOut IMPORT WriteReal;
  FROM Storage IMPORT ALLOCATE;

TYPE TagType = (cardinalType, realType);
     GenericRecord = RECORD
                       CASE tag: TagType OF
                         cardinalType: cardinal: CARDINAL |
                         realType:     real:     REAL
                       END
                     END;
     GenericType = POINTER TO GenericRecord;

PROCEDURE Error(message: ARRAY OF CHAR);
  (* prints message and terminates program *)
BEGIN
  WriteString(message);
  WriteLn;
  HALT
END Error;

PROCEDURE CardToGeneric(c: CARDINAL; VAR x: GenericType);
  (* converts CARDINAL number to GenericType value *)
BEGIN
  ALLOCATE(x, SIZE(GenericRecord));
  x^.tag := cardinalType;
  x^.cardinal := c
END CardToGeneric;

PROCEDURE RealToGeneric(r: REAL; VAR x: GenericType);
  (* converts REAL number to GenericType value *)
BEGIN
  ALLOCATE(x, SIZE(GenericRecord));
  x^.tag := realType;
  x^.real := r
END RealToGeneric;

PROCEDURE GenericToCard(x: GenericType; VAR c: CARDINAL);
  (* converts GenericType value to CARDINAL number;
     terminates program if x is not a CARDINAL number *)
BEGIN
  CASE x^.tag OF
    cardinalType: c := x^.cardinal |
    realType:     Error("Type mismatch in GenericToCard")
  END
END GenericToCard;
```

```
PROCEDURE GenericToReal(x: GenericType; VAR r: REAL);
  (* converts GenericType value to REAL number; terminates
     program if x is not a REAL number *)
BEGIN
  CASE x^.tag OF
    cardinalType: Error("Type mismatch in GenericToReal") |
    realType:     r := x^.real
  END
END GenericToReal;

PROCEDURE Equal(x, y: GenericType): BOOLEAN;
  (* returns TRUE if numerical values of x and y are equal,
     FALSE otherwise; terminates program if x and y are not
     both CARDINAL or both REAL *)
BEGIN
  IF x^.tag # y^.tag THEN
    Error("Type mismatch in Equal")
  END;
  CASE x^.tag OF
    cardinalType: RETURN x^.cardinal = y^.cardinal |
    realType:     RETURN x^.real = y^.real
  END
END Equal;

PROCEDURE LessThan(x, y: GenericType): BOOLEAN;
  (* returns TRUE if numerical value of x is less than value
     of y, FALSE otherwise; terminates program if x and y are
     not both CARDINAL or both REAL *)
BEGIN
  IF x^.tag # y^.tag THEN
    Error("Type mismatch in LessThan")
  END;
  CASE x^.tag OF
    cardinalType: RETURN x^.cardinal < y^.cardinal |
    realType:     RETURN x^.real < y^.real
  END
END LessThan;

PROCEDURE Print(x: GenericType);
  (* writes numerical value of x *)
BEGIN
  CASE x^.tag OF
    cardinalType: WriteCard(x^.cardinal, 1) |
    realType:     WriteReal(x^.real, 1)
  END
END Print;

END GenericTypeModule.
```

The high-level approach, as this program demonstrates, has a number of advantages:

- GenericTypeModule does full type-checking on GenericType values.
- GenericTree1 imports procedures for manipulating generic values (LessThan and Print) from GenericTypeModule; the client module (TreeSort1) does not need to bother with this detail.
- GenericTypeModule is not specific to binary search trees; we can use it to build other kinds of generic modules.
- A program can contain many trees of type BinTree, and each tree can have a different node type. In fact, a single tree can even contain values of different types. (If we want such a tree, however, we must modify the declaration of LessThan to allow comparison of values of different types.)

But the high-level approach also has disadvantages:

- GenericType values are limited to a small set of types (CARDINAL and REAL in our example); adding additional types requires us to recompile GenericTypeModule and its clients.
- GenericType values require extra space (because of the tag field). In addition, GenericType contains a variant part, which must be large enough to hold the largest variant.
- Conversion to and from GenericType values is required, thus slowing down program execution. Procedures that access GenericType values always check the type of the value, also slowing execution.

EXAMPLE PROGRAM

Using a Low-Level Generic Binary Search Tree for Sorting

The low-level module GenericTree2 exports the same entities as GenericTree1: the type BinTree and the procedures InitializeTree, InsertValue, and PrintTree. However, the second parameter to InsertValue (the value we want to insert) now has type ADDRESS instead of GenericType. Also, InitializeTree now has four parameters instead of one. The additional parameters depend on the kind of values the tree will contain:

valueSize (the amount of space required to store a node value)

lessThan (a procedure that determines whether one node value is less than another)

print (a procedure that prints a node value)

The definition part of GenericTree2 follows.

```
DEFINITION MODULE GenericTree2;
  (* exports type BinTree (generic binary search tree) and
     procedures for operating on values of this type *)

  FROM SYSTEM IMPORT ADDRESS;
```

```
    TYPE BinTree;    (* generic binary search tree *)
         ComparisonProc = PROCEDURE (ADDRESS, ADDRESS): BOOLEAN;
         PrintProc = PROCEDURE (ADDRESS);

    PROCEDURE InitializeTree(VAR t: BinTree;
                                  valueSize: CARDINAL;
                                  lessThan: ComparisonProc;
                                  print: PrintProc);
      (* initializes a tree t whose node values have size
         valueSize; installs procedures for comparing two node
         values and printing a node value *)

    PROCEDURE InsertValue(VAR t: BinTree; addr: ADDRESS);
      (* inserts the value at address addr into its proper place
         in the tree t *)

    PROCEDURE PrintTree(t: BinTree);
      (* traverses the tree t in inorder, printing the values
         stored in the nodes, one per line *)

  END GenericTree2.
```

The program module, TreeSort2, is similar to TreeSort1, except that it declares two procedures, LessThan and PrintCard, which it supplies to InitializeTree. (Both LessThan and PrintCard use the CARDINAL type transfer function to view WORD values as though they were of type CARDINAL. Section 11.4 discusses type transfer in more detail.)

```
MODULE TreeSort2;
  (* sorts a file of CARDINAL numbers by building a binary
     search tree and then traversing it *)

  FROM SYSTEM IMPORT ADDRESS, ADR;
  FROM InOut IMPORT OpenInput, CloseInput, OpenOutput,
                    CloseOutput, ReadCard, WriteCard, Done,
                    WriteString, WriteLn;
  FROM GenericTree2 IMPORT BinTree, InitializeTree,
                           InsertValue, PrintTree;

  VAR tree: BinTree;
      card: CARDINAL;

  PROCEDURE LessThan(addr1, addr2: ADDRESS): BOOLEAN;
    (* returns TRUE if CARDINAL value at address addr1 is less
       than CARDINAL value at address addr2, FALSE otherwise *)
  BEGIN
    RETURN CARDINAL(addr1^) < CARDINAL(addr2^)
  END LessThan;

  PROCEDURE PrintCard(addr: ADDRESS);
    (* writes CARDINAL value at address addr *)
```

```
  BEGIN
    WriteCard(CARDINAL(addr^), 1)
  END PrintCard;

BEGIN
  InitializeTree(tree, SIZE(CARDINAL), LessThan, PrintCard);

    (* read numbers and store in tree *)
  WriteString("Enter name of file to be sorted.");
  WriteLn;
  OpenInput("NUM");
  ReadCard(card);
  WHILE Done DO
    InsertValue(tree, ADR(card));
    ReadCard(card)
  END;
  CloseInput;

    (* traverse tree and print numbers in order encountered *)
  WriteString("Enter name of output file.");
  WriteLn;
  OpenOutput("NUM");
  PrintTree(tree);
  CloseOutput
END TreeSort2.
```

The implementation part of `GenericTree2` is more complicated than the implementation part of `GenericTree1`. In fact, the tree itself is more complicated; it begins with a special header node that contains four fields:

- `tree` (a pointer to the root of the binary search tree)
- `valueSize` (the size of each value in the tree)
- `lessThan` (a procedure that determines whether one node value is less than another)
- `print` (a procedure that prints a node value)

The last three fields contain the parameters supplied to `InitializeTree`.

```
IMPLEMENTATION MODULE GenericTree2;

  FROM SYSTEM IMPORT ADDRESS, WORD;
  FROM InOut IMPORT WriteLn;
  FROM Storage IMPORT ALLOCATE;

  TYPE BinaryTree = POINTER TO TreeNode;
       TreeNode = RECORD
                    left: BinaryTree;
```

```
                    value: ADDRESS;
                    right: BinaryTree
                  END;
      BinTree = POINTER TO HeaderNode;
      HeaderNode = RECORD
                     tree: BinaryTree;
                     valueSize: CARDINAL;
                     lessThan: ComparisonProc;
                     print: PrintProc
                   END;

PROCEDURE CopyWords(source, dest: ADDRESS; length: CARDINAL);
  (* copies a block of words of the specified length from
     source address to dest address *)
  VAR i: CARDINAL;
BEGIN
  FOR i := 1 TO length DO
    dest^ := source^;
    INC(source, SIZE(WORD));
    INC(dest, SIZE(WORD))
  END
END CopyWords;

PROCEDURE InitializeTree(VAR t: BinTree;
                             valueSize: CARDINAL;
                             lessThan: ComparisonProc;
                             print: PrintProc);
  (* initializes a tree t whose node values have size
     valueSize; installs procedures for comparing two node
     values and printing a node value *)
BEGIN
  ALLOCATE(t, SIZE(HeaderNode));
  t^.tree := NIL;
  t^.valueSize := valueSize;
  t^.lessThan := lessThan;
  t^.print := print
END InitializeTree;

PROCEDURE InsertValue(VAR t: BinTree; addr: ADDRESS);
  (* inserts the value at address addr into its proper place
     in the tree t *)

  PROCEDURE Insert(VAR tree: BinaryTree; addr: ADDRESS);
    (* recursively inserts the value at address addr into the
       tree *)
  BEGIN
    IF tree # NIL THEN
      IF t^.lessThan(addr, tree^.value) THEN
        Insert(tree^.left, addr)
```

```
          ELSE
            Insert(tree^.right, addr)
          END
        ELSE
          ALLOCATE(tree, SIZE(TreeNode));
          ALLOCATE(tree^.value, t^.valueSize);
          CopyWords(addr, tree^.value,
                    t^.valueSize DIV SIZE(WORD));
          tree^.left := NIL;
          tree^.right := NIL
        END
      END Insert;

    BEGIN  (* InsertValue *)
      Insert(t^.tree, addr)
    END InsertValue;

    PROCEDURE PrintTree(t: BinTree);
      (* traverses the tree t in inorder, printing the values
         stored in the nodes, one per line *)

      PROCEDURE Print(tree: BinaryTree);
        (* recursively traverses the tree in inorder, printing
           the values stored in the nodes, one per line  *)
      BEGIN
        IF tree # NIL THEN
          Print(tree^.left);
          t^.print(tree^.value);
          WriteLn;
          Print(tree^.right)
        END
      END Print;

    BEGIN  (* PrintTree *)
      Print(t^.tree)
    END PrintTree;

  END GenericTree2.
```

The low-level approach has several advantages:

- We may store a value of any type in a tree node. Allowing more types does not require recompilation.
- Many trees of type `BinTree` may exist simultaneously, each with a different node type.
- Access to values stored in tree nodes is efficient. We do not need to convert to a generic type; no type-checking is performed during program execution.
- We waste no space in storing generic values.

The disadvantages of the low-level approach are as follows:

- Because no type-checking is performed when node values are accessed, usage errors are possible. For example, the client module could accidentally retrieve — as a REAL number — a number stored as a CARDINAL.
- No more than one node type can exist in the same tree, because we would have no way to determine the type of the value stored in a particular node.
- The client module must supply lessThan and print procedures as parameters to InitializeTree. This requirement forces the client (TreeSort2 in our example) to declare these procedures (or possibly import them from another module). In the high-level approach, such details do not concern the client module.

These two approaches are not the only ones possible. In fact, they lie at opposite ends of a spectrum of methods for writing generic modules. We can weaken the high-level approach (for example, by omitting the tag field in GenericRecord and relying on the client module to remember what type of values are stored in a tree) or we can strengthen the low-level method (for example, by declaring the second parameter to InsertValue to be of type ARRAY OF WORD and by checking the size of the actual parameter against the valueSize field in the header node).

The programmer might find it worthwhile to use a high-level generic module during program development, when errors in module usage are likely, and then switch to a low-level generic module later. Or the programmer could use generic modules (either high-level or low-level) to build a prototype for a new program, and replace them with custom-tailored modules while developing the final program.

11.4 Type Transfer Functions

By using types that the SYSTEM module provides, we can treat any data value as an array of words (or bytes) and any pointer as an address. Modula-2 has a more general feature that allows us to treat a value of one type as though it were of another type, provided that the latter type has a name (call it T) and provided that values of the two types occupy the same amount of storage. We do so by using T as a function; a type name used in this fashion is called a *type transfer function*. For example, to treat a value of type INTEGER as though it had type BITSET, we can use the name BITSET as a function:

```
VAR i: INTEGER;
    s: BITSET;
        .
        .
        .
s := BITSET(i);    (* view i as a BITSET *)
```

A call of a type transfer function has the same syntax as any function call; because it is an expression, not a designator, it can appear only where Modula-2 allows an expression. In particular, a call of a type transfer function cannot appear on the left side of an assignment statement.

A type transfer function does not actually transform its parameter. In our example, suppose that i has the value 89. Stored as a 16-bit word, i would look like this:

15	14	13	12	11	10	9	8	7	6	5	4	3	2	1	0
0	0	0	0	0	0	0	0	0	1	0	1	1	0	0	1

Assuming that BITSET values are stored as Section 11.1 describes, then the value of i, interpreted as a BITSET, is {0, 3, 4, 6}. We did not alter the representation of i in any way, but simply interpreted it as a value of a different type. Clearly, proper use of type transfer functions requires knowledge of how a particular Modula-2 system represents values of different types. This information should be available in the system manual.

We first came across type transfer in Section 3.1, which showed how to use CARDINAL and INTEGER as type transfer functions. Such usage is dangerous, because there is no check that the result is meaningful. For example, on a 16-bit machine, the following bit pattern represents the CARDINAL number 65,535:

1	1	1	1	1	1	1	1	1	1	1	1	1	1	1	1

The result of applying INTEGER to this number as a type transfer function is −1 (assuming two's-complement arithmetic). Likewise, any negative INTEGER value becomes a positive CARDINAL value when we use CARDINAL to perform type transfer. For this reason, it is better to use VAL for conversion from INTEGER to CARDINAL or vice-versa, because many Modula-2 systems test the validity of conversions performed using VAL.

Modula-2 does not restrict type transfer to standard types; we may also use the names of programmer-defined types as type transfer functions. Furthermore, a type name used for type transfer need not represent an unstructured type; type transfer is legal for all types, including array and record types. Consider the following arrays; because they have different types, we cannot normally assign one to the other:

```
TYPE RealArray100 = ARRAY [1..100] OF REAL;
      RealArray101 = ARRAY [2..101] OF REAL;
VAR array100: RealArray100;
    array101: RealArray101;
```

Type transfer allows us to make the assignment, however, because the arrays require the same amount of storage:

```
array100 := RealArray100(array101);
```

The only requirement for applying a type name to an expression is that the value of the expression occupies the same amount of storage as do values of the type. This requirement, of course, is system-dependent; one compiler may reject a type transfer that another compiler allows.

We must be careful to distinguish between type conversion and type transfer. Type *conversion* has the following characteristics:

- The data value we are converting may undergo an actual transformation; the bit pattern that results from the conversion usually differs from the original bit pattern.
- Type conversion often produces a value that occupies a different amount of storage (for example, a one-word INTEGER value may become a two- or four-word REAL value).
- Type conversions are normally checked for validity during program execution; an error occurs if the conversion would not produce a meaningful result.
- Type conversion is machine-independent. When we recompile a program on a different system, the compiler automatically supplies the correct algorithm for conversion; the programmer need not be aware of how the system represents data values.

Type conversion is performed by standard functions such as FLOAT and TRUNC, which convert between types CARDINAL and REAL, and `real` and `entier` (exported by `MathLib0`), which convert between INTEGER and REAL. Type *transfer* has entirely different properties:

- Type transfer never causes a change in data representation.
- The result of a type transfer occupies the same amount of storage as the original value (it must, because the resulting bit pattern is identical to the original bit pattern).
- No check is performed to see if the result of a type transfer is meaningful; the programmer is responsible for using the result properly.
- Type transfer is system-dependent. When using type transfer, the programmer must know how a particular Modula-2 system, running on a particular computer, represents data values. Programs that use type transfer usually require modification before they can be compiled and executed in a different environment.

Using a type transfer function is just a way of circumventing Modula-2's normal type-checking mechanism. Using type transfer is therefore dangerous, because it allows programming errors that a Modula-2 compiler would normally detect. However, because the transfer is explicit, a programmer can easily determine where type-checking has been disabled. Some programming languages allow type transfer without any explicit action on the part of the programmer, which can result in errors that are extremely difficult to find.

Type transfer is one of Modula-2's most powerful tools for low-level programming. The degree to which type transfer is useful may not be apparent at first; we devote the remainder of this section to examples that show a few of the many uses of type transfer.

EXAMPLE Low-Level Operations on Words

Recall from Section 11.2 that the only operation defined for values of type WORD is assignment. In order to perform any other operation, we must use type transfer to make the WORD value seem to be a CARDINAL, INTEGER, BITSET, or other value that occupies one word of memory (the list of one-word types varies from one system to another, of course). For example, suppose we want to compute the bitwise logical OR of two words. By using type transfer to make the words appear to be of type BITSET, we can use the set operator + (see Section 11.1):

```
PROCEDURE BitwiseOR(w1, w2: WORD): WORD;
  (* returns the bitwise OR of the words w1 and w2 *)
BEGIN
  RETURN WORD(BITSET(w1) + BITSET(w2))
END BitwiseOR;
```

`BitwiseOR` uses type transfer to make `w1` and `w2` seem to be of type `BITSET`; after computing the union of the sets, the procedure uses type transfer once more to make the result appear to be of type WORD. This procedure is very fast, because no genuine type conversion takes place.

Another common operation on words is shifting. The following procedure, `ShiftRight`, shifts a WORD value to the right by using BITSET operations. `ShiftRight` first clears all bits in the variable `result`, then copies bits from the parameter w to `result` (using type transfer to view w as a BITSET), moving the bits n positions to the right in the process. Before returning, `ShiftRight` uses type transfer to make `result` appear to be of type WORD.

```
PROCEDURE ShiftRight(w: WORD; n: CARDINAL): WORD;
  (* returns contents of w shifted right n positions,
     left-filled with zeros *)
```

```
  VAR bit: CARDINAL;
      result: BITSET;
BEGIN
  result := BITSET{};                           (* clear all bits *)
  FOR bit := n TO bitsPerWord - 1 DO
    IF bit IN BITSET(w) THEN                    (* type transfer   *)
      INCL(result, bit - n)
    END
  END;
  RETURN WORD(result)                           (* type transfer   *)
END ShiftRight;
```

(We assume that `bitsPerWord` is declared outside the procedure and that the most significant bit has the number `bitsPerWord - 1`.) Shifting left is similar:

```
PROCEDURE ShiftLeft(w: WORD; n: CARDINAL): WORD;
  (* returns contents of w shifted left n positions,
     right-filled with zeros *)
  VAR bit: CARDINAL;
      result: BITSET;
BEGIN
  result := BITSET{};                           (* clear all bits *)
  FOR bit := 0 TO bitsPerWord - n - 1 DO
    IF bit IN BITSET(w) THEN                    (* type transfer   *)
      INCL(result, bit + n)
    END
  END;
  RETURN WORD(result)                           (* type transfer   *)
END ShiftLeft;
```

`BITSET` manipulation is not the only way to perform shifting. Other methods include multiplication or division by 2 (see the Exercises) and use of the CODE procedure (Section 11.2).

EXAMPLE

Converting from Bytes to Words

Although the standard functions ORD and CHR are not type transfer functions in the sense described earlier, they serve much the same purpose. Recall that `ORD(ch)` returns the ordinal number of the character `ch`, and `CHR(i)` returns the character whose ordinal number is `i`. Assuming that a character requires one byte of storage and a `CARDINAL` number requires two bytes, the following byte would represent the character `'a'`:

0	1	1	0	0	0	0	1

and the following word would represent ORD('a'):

0	0	0	0	0	0	0	0	0	1	1	0	0	0	0	1

Strictly speaking, ORD is not a type transfer function, because the value that it returns occupies more memory than does its parameter. However, ORD is very close to being a type transfer function, because the transformation it performs (adding a zero byte) is trivial. Similar remarks apply to CHR.

ORD is useful in low-level programming because it can extend a byte value to the size of a word:

```
PROCEDURE ByteToWord(b: BYTE): WORD;
  (* extends a byte to word size by adding a high-order zero
     byte *)
BEGIN
  RETURN WORD(ORD(CHAR(b)))
END ByteToWord;
```

EXAMPLE

Accessing Bits, Bit Fields, and Bytes

Low-level programming requires the ability to access small units of memory—individual bits, fields that are several bits long, and bytes—not just entire words. Type transfer is convenient for this purpose.

Access to a single bit in a word requires only that we apply the BITSET transfer function to the word. To test whether bit i is set in word w, a program can use the expression

```
i IN BITSET(w)
```

which has the value TRUE if the bit is set. We can set or clear a bit using INCL or EXCL, respectively.

We can also access bit fields of any length by using type transfer to BITSET. The following procedure shows one method for accessing a bit field:

```
PROCEDURE GetBitField(w: WORD; highBit, lowBit: CARDINAL): WORD;
  (* returns the contents of the bit field between highBit
     and lowBit (inclusive); returns 0 if lowBit is
     greater than highBit *)
  VAR bit: CARDINAL;
      result: BITSET;
BEGIN
  result := BITSET{};
  FOR bit := lowBit TO highBit DO
```

```
    IF bit IN BITSET(w) THEN
      INCL(result, bit - lowBit)
    END
  END;
  RETURN WORD(result)
END GetBitField;
```

GetBitField is similar to the ShiftRight procedure given earlier.

When a bit field has a fixed length and position, faster access is possible using "mask and shift" operations. For example, suppose we need to access bits 9 through 11 in a variable. We can construct a "mask" (a BITSET value) containing 1's in positions 9, 10, and 11, use a bitwise AND operation (set intersection) to select these bits, then shift the result to the right (by dividing by 2^9).

```
CONST mask    = BITSET{9..11};
      divisor = 512;    (* 2 ** 9 *)
VAR word: WORD;
    bitField: CARDINAL;
          .
          .
          .
bitField := CARDINAL(BITSET(word) * mask) DIV divisor;
```

This method is quite efficient, requiring only a single bitwise AND instruction and a single division. (Some compilers even replace the division by a shift.) Alternatively, we can replace the BITSET computation by an application of MOD. In the example, we can divide by 2^9, then take the result modulo 2^3 to obtain the desired three bits:

```
CONST modulus = 8;    (* 2 ** 3 *)
          .
          .
          .
bitField := CARDINAL(word) DIV divisor MOD modulus;
```

Using a BITSET mask seems to be slightly preferable, because it makes clear which bits we are extracting.

Although we can extract whole bytes by calling GetBitField or using mask and shift operations, simpler methods are available. For example, suppose that we have declared the record type TwoBytes as follows:

```
TYPE TwoBytes = RECORD
                   lowByte, highByte: BYTE
                END;
```

The Logitech Modula-2/86 compiler allocates two bytes of storage for values of type TwoBytes. Because words are two bytes long, we can apply type transfer to a value of type WORD to make it appear to be of type TwoBytes, and then extract the low-order byte by referencing the field lowByte. (Note: In IBM PC memory, the low-order byte of a word is stored before the high-order byte.)

```
PROCEDURE LowByte(w: WORD): BYTE;
  (* returns the low-order byte of w *)
  VAR temp: TwoBytes;
BEGIN
  temp := TwoBytes(w);
  RETURN temp.lowByte
END LowByte;
```

The variable temp is a necessity; it would be illegal to write

```
RETURN TwoBytes(w).lowByte;     (* illegal *)
```

because Modula-2 prohibits the use of a field name to select a field in a result returned by a function.

We can extract the high-order byte in a similar fashion:

```
PROCEDURE HighByte(w: WORD): BYTE;
  (* returns the high-order byte of w *)
  VAR temp: TwoBytes;
BEGIN
  temp := TwoBytes(w);
  RETURN temp.highByte
END HighByte;
```

We can also use the TwoBytes type to put two bytes together to form a word:

```
PROCEDURE BytesToWord(highByte, lowByte: BYTE): WORD;
  (* returns a word with the specified high and low bytes *)
  VAR temp: TwoBytes;
BEGIN
  temp.highByte := highByte;
  temp.lowByte := lowByte;
  RETURN WORD(temp)
END BytesToWord;
```

EXAMPLE PROGRAM

Solving the Knapsack Problem

A common real-life problem is that of filling a bag or box to its maximum capacity. When phrased in mathematical terms, this is called the *knapsack problem*: Given a collection of n objects of sizes $s_1, \ldots, s_n$ and a knapsack of capacity C, determine whether there is a subset of the objects that exactly fills the knapsack. (For simplicity, we will assume that $s_1, \ldots, s_n$ and C are positive integers.)

The simplest way to solve this problem is by brute force: Generate each possible subset of the objects, add the sizes of the objects, and compare the result to *C*. Assuming that there are no more than 16 objects, we can use a value of type BITSET to represent a subset of the objects. We can then generate all possible subsets by incrementing a CARDINAL variable i from 0 to MAX(CARDINAL) and viewing each value of i as a BITSET value. The following program uses this method:

```
MODULE SolveKnapsack;
  (* solves the knapsack problem for up to 16 objects *)

  FROM InOut IMPORT ReadCard, WriteCard, WriteString, WriteLn,
                    Done;

  CONST bitsPerWord = 16;   (* IBM PC *)

  VAR i, capacity: CARDINAL;
      size: ARRAY [0..bitsPerWord-1] OF CARDINAL;

  PROCEDURE ReadValidCard(VAR n: CARDINAL);
    (* attempts to read a CARDINAL number; repeats prompt
       until user enters a valid number *)
  BEGIN
    LOOP
      ReadCard(n);
      WriteLn;
      IF Done THEN EXIT END;
      WriteString("Not a valid number.  Try again: ")
    END
  END ReadValidCard;

  PROCEDURE Sum(subset: BITSET): CARDINAL;
    (* sums the sizes of objects in a particular subset *)
    VAR i, sum: CARDINAL;
  BEGIN
    sum := 0;
    FOR i := 0 TO bitsPerWord - 1 DO
      IF i IN subset THEN
        INC(sum, size[i])
      END
    END;
    RETURN sum
  END Sum;

  PROCEDURE WriteAnswer(subset: BITSET);
    (* writes the sizes of objects that exactly fill the
       knapsack *)
    VAR i: CARDINAL;
```

```
  BEGIN
    WriteString("A solution is: ");
    FOR i := 0 TO bitsPerWord - 1 DO
      IF i IN subset THEN
        WriteCard(size[i], 1);
        WriteString(" ")
      END
    END;
    WriteLn
  END WriteAnswer;

BEGIN
  WriteString("This program solves the knapsack problem ");
  WriteString("for up to ");
  WriteCard(bitsPerWord, 1);
  WriteString(" objects.");
  WriteLn;
  WriteString("Enter the object sizes as positive integers.");
  WriteString("  Enter 0 to terminate input.");
  WriteLn;
  WriteLn;

    (* read object sizes and store in size array *)
  i := 0;
  LOOP
    IF i = bitsPerWord THEN EXIT END;
    WriteString("Enter size: ");
    ReadValidCard(size[i]);
    IF size[i] = 0 THEN EXIT END;
    INC(i)
  END;

    (* set remaining sizes to 0 *)
  WHILE i <= bitsPerWord - 1 DO
    size[i] := 0;
    INC(i)
  END;

  WriteLn;
  WriteString("Enter capacity of knapsack: ");
  ReadValidCard(capacity);
  WriteLn;

    (* cycle through all possible subsets of objects; if the
       objects in a subset exactly fill the knapsack, then
       call WriteAnswer *)
  i := 0;
  LOOP
    IF Sum(BITSET(i)) = capacity THEN     (* type transfer *)
      WriteAnswer(BITSET(i));             (* type transfer *)
```

```
      EXIT
    ELSIF i = MAX(CARDINAL) THEN
      WriteString("There is no solution.");
      WriteLn;
      EXIT
    END;
    INC(i)
  END
END SolveKnapsack.
```

11.5 Absolute Addresses

In some computers, certain memory locations have special meanings; for example, they may represent registers used to control input/output devices. Consequently, many Modula-2 compilers allow the programmer to specify that a variable must be located at a particular memory address, thus making it easier to access and/or modify the value stored at this address.

Consider the problem of writing an interface to the system keyboard on a DEC PDP-11 (an example that originally appeared in *Programming in Modula-2*). The keyboard status register has address 777560 (octal), and the keyboard buffer register has address 777562. Locating a variable at each of these addresses provides easy access to the registers. To inform the compiler that it should locate a variable at a particular address, we enclose the address in brackets and include it in the declaration of the variable:

```
VAR keyboardStatus [777560B]: BITSET;
    keyboardBuffer [777562B]: CHAR;
```

We may locate a variable of any type at an absolute address. We declared `keyboardStatus` to have type `BITSET` to make it easier to test or set bits in the keyboard status register. For example, clearing bit 6 enables interrupts from the keyboard:

```
EXCL(keyboardStatus, 6);    (* enable interrupts *)
```

This mechanism for specifying the address of a variable is not a standard feature of Modula-2. Wirth mentions the mechanism only briefly in *Programming in Modula-2* and provides no syntax chart for it, although he does specify that the absolute address should be a constant integer expression enclosed in brackets and should appear immediately after the variable.

If a particular compiler does not allow the placement of variables at absolute addresses, a program can still access and modify the information at these addresses by using type transfer. For example, instead of locating `keyboard-`

Status at address 777560B, we could create a pointer variable called keyboardStatusAddr whose value is 777560B:

```
TYPE BitsetAddr = POINTER TO BITSET;
VAR keyboardStatusAddr: BitsetAddr;

          .
          .
          .

keyboardStatusAddr := BitsetAddr(777560B);   (* type transfer *)
```

Subsequent references to keyboardStatusAddr^ are equivalent to references to keyboardStatus. For example, the following is equivalent to the call of EXCL given earlier:

```
EXCL(keyboardStatusAddr^, 6);
```

When a Modula-2 system does allow the specification of absolute addresses, the form of the address may vary. On the IBM Personal Computer, for example, an address consists of two 16-bit quantities: a *segment* and an *offset*. For this reason, the Logitech Modula-2/86 system requires that an absolute address be specified by two CARDINAL numbers—the segment and offset, in that order—separated by a colon.

Programmers should use the absolute address mechanism only for gaining access to memory locations with special meanings. Using it for other purposes (such as forcing variables to share memory locations) can make programs difficult to debug.

EXAMPLE PROGRAM

Showing the Hardware Configuration of an IBM PC

Certain locations in the memory of an IBM Personal Computer contain information about the system's configuration. The *equipment flag*, stored at address 0:410H, contains the following bit fields (among others):

Bit Field	*Contents*
15–14	number of parallel ports
11–9	number of serial ports
7–6	if bit 0 is set, number of diskette drives minus 1
5–4	initial video mode (01 = 40 × 25 color, 10 = 80 × 25 color, 11 = 80 × 25 monochrome)
0	set if system has diskette drives

(We assume that the most significant bit is numbered 15 and the least significant is numbered 0.) The word located at address 0:413H contains the total size of main memory (in units of 1K).

The program ShowConfiguration, which follows, prints a summary of the information stored at addresses 0:410H and 0:413H. To gain access to these memory locations, ShowConfiguration declares two variables, equipFlag and memorySize, and instructs the compiler to locate them at addresses 0:410H and 0:413H, respectively:

```
VAR equipFlag [0:410H]: BITSET;
    memorySize [0:413H]: CARDINAL;
```

ShowConfiguration declares equipFlag to be a BITSET variable to allow access to individual bits in the word stored at address 0:410H; the program declares memorySize to have type CARDINAL, however, because ShowConfiguration displays the contents of the word at address 0:413H as an integer.

```
MODULE ShowConfiguration;
  (* displays information about the hardware configuration of
     an IBM Personal Computer *)

  FROM InOut IMPORT WriteString, WriteCard, WriteLn;

  CONST parMask   = BITSET{14..15};    (* parallel ports       *)
        parDiv    = 16384;             (* 2 ** 14              *)
        serMask   = BITSET{9..11};     (* serial ports         *)
        serDiv    = 512;               (* 2 ** 9               *)
        diskMask  = BITSET{6..7};      (* diskette drives - 1  *)
        diskDiv   = 64;                (* 2 ** 6               *)
        videoMask = BITSET{4..5};      (* initial video mode   *)
        videoDiv  = 16;                (* 2 ** 4               *)
        driveBit  = 0;                 (* set if system has    *)
                                       (* diskette drives      *)

  VAR equipFlag [0:410H]: BITSET;
      memorySize [0:413H]: CARDINAL;
      drives: CARDINAL;

BEGIN
  WriteString("Number of parallel ports: ");
  WriteCard(CARDINAL(equipFlag * parMask) DIV parDiv, 1);
  WriteLn;

  WriteString("Number of serial ports: ");
  WriteCard(CARDINAL(equipFlag * serMask) DIV serDiv, 1);
  WriteLn;

  drives := 0;
  IF driveBit IN equipFlag THEN
    drives := CARDINAL(equipFlag * diskMask) DIV diskDiv + 1
  END;
  WriteString("Number of diskette drives: ");
  WriteCard(drives, 1);
```

```
  WriteLn;

  WriteString("Initial video mode: ");
  CASE CARDINAL(equipFlag * videoMask) DIV videoDiv OF
    1: WriteString("40 x 25 color") |
    2: WriteString("80 x 25 color") |
    3: WriteString("80 x 25 monochrome")
  END;
  WriteLn;

  WriteString("Amount of memory installed: ");
  WriteCard(memorySize, 1);
  WriteString("K");
  WriteLn
END ShowConfiguration.
```

EXAMPLE **A Module for Accessing IBM PC Screen Memory**

Some computers provide access to the user's screen through a buffer stored in memory. The image displayed on the screen always matches the contents of this buffer; therefore, we can change the image by storing characters into the buffer. To access the display buffer from within a Modula-2 program, we can simply declare an array variable that extends over the region of memory occupied by the buffer. We can then alter the screen image by storing characters into components of the array.

To illustrate how to access a display buffer in Modula-2, we will develop a simplified screen-handling module. This module is specific to the IBM Personal Computer with a monochrome monitor, although we could easily adapt it for use with a color monitor.

The display buffer for the IBM PC with monochrome monitor starts at address `0B000H:0`. Because the monochrome monitor can display 25 lines of 80 characters each, 2,000 bytes are enough to contain all the characters on the screen. However, because each character is followed by an attribute byte containing information about how the character is displayed (normal display, reverse video, underlined, blinking, high intensity), the total size of the display buffer is actually 4,000 bytes. We can think of the buffer as an array with 25 rows and 80 columns; each element of the array consists of a character byte and an attribute byte:

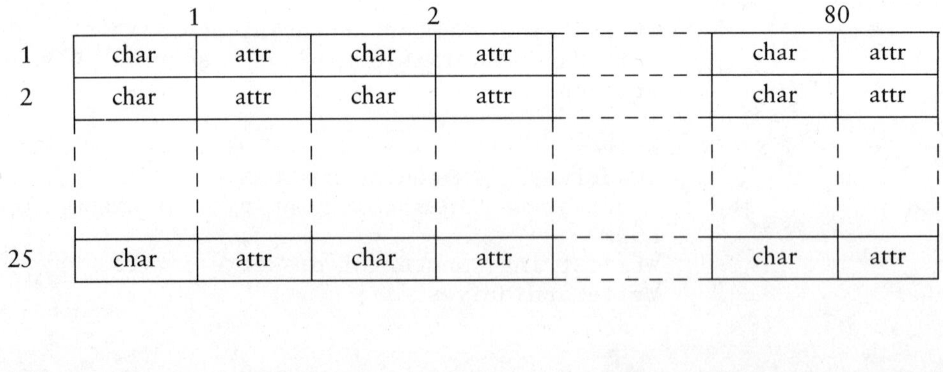

Storage of this array is by rows: The first 160 bytes of the display buffer contain the first row, the next 160 bytes contain the second row, and so on.

Our library module, `Screen`, provides useful constants and screen-handling procedures. It exports constants indicating the number of rows and number of columns on the screen, as well as constants representing the attribute bytes for normal display and reverse video (we could easily add constants that represent the other attributes). The procedure `ClearScreen` clears the screen and sets the attribute byte for each character to indicate normal display. `GotoXY` causes the cursor to move to a specified position on the screen. The parameters `x` and `y` represent the horizontal and vertical coordinates of the cursor; the coordinates of the upper left corner are (1, 1) and the coordinates of the lower right corner are (80, 25). The cursor is invisible—to display a visible cursor, a client module can call `WriteChar`, which writes a character on the screen at the current location of the cursor (the cursor does not move after the character is written). The client can access the attributes of the character at the current cursor position by calling `ReadAttr`, and it can change them by calling `WriteAttr`.

```
DEFINITION MODULE Screen;
  (* exports screen-handling procedures for the IBM PC with
     monochrome monitor *)

  CONST numRows = 25;
        numColumns = 80;
        normal = 7C;           (* normal attributes *)
        reverse = 160C;        (* reverse video attribute *)

  PROCEDURE ClearScreen;
    (* clears screen and sets all attributes to "normal" *)

  PROCEDURE GotoXY(x, y: CARDINAL);
    (* moves cursor to position x, y *)

  PROCEDURE WriteChar(char: CHAR);
    (* writes a character at cursor position *)

  PROCEDURE WriteAttr(attr: CHAR);
    (* changes attributes of character at cursor position *)

  PROCEDURE ReadAttr(VAR attr: CHAR);
    (* fetches attributes of character at cursor position *)

END Screen.
```

The key feature of the implementation part of `Screen` is a variable called `screen`, which is a 25-by-80 array of records; each record has two one-byte fields named `char` and `attr`. By specifying the address of this array to be `0B000H:0`, we make it occupy the same memory locations as the monochrome display buffer. The only other variables in the module are xPos and yPos, which mark the current position of the cursor. The rest of the module is straightforward.

```
IMPLEMENTATION MODULE Screen;

  VAR screen [0B000H:0]:          (* address of display buffer  *)
        ARRAY [1..numRows], [1..numColumns] OF
          RECORD
            char: CHAR;           (* character to be displayed  *)
            attr: CHAR            (* attributes of character    *)
          END;
      xPos, yPos: CARDINAL;       (* current position of cursor *)

  PROCEDURE ClearScreen;
    (* clears screen and sets all attributes to "normal" *)
    VAR x, y: CARDINAL;
  BEGIN
    FOR y := 1 TO numRows DO
      FOR x := 1 TO numColumns DO
        screen[y, x].char := ' ';
        screen[y, x].attr := normal
      END
    END
  END ClearScreen;

  PROCEDURE GotoXY(x, y: CARDINAL);
    (* moves cursor to position x, y *)
  BEGIN
    xPos := x;
    yPos := y
  END GotoXY;

  PROCEDURE WriteChar(char: CHAR);
    (* writes a character at cursor position *)
  BEGIN
    screen[yPos, xPos].char := char
  END WriteChar;

  PROCEDURE WriteAttr(attr: CHAR);
    (* changes attributes of character at cursor position *)
  BEGIN
    screen[yPos, xPos].attr := attr
  END WriteAttr;

  PROCEDURE ReadAttr(VAR attr: CHAR);
    (* fetches attributes of character at cursor position *)
  BEGIN
    attr := screen[yPos, xPos].attr
```

```
  END ReadAttr;

END Screen.
```

The `Screen` module is admittedly rather limited in its capabilities; it offers the operations we need for the following example program, but it is too primitive for most other applications. However, `Screen` can be used as a starting point for developing a more sophisticated screen-handling module. Some Modula-2 systems even include such a module in their libraries.

EXAMPLE PROGRAM

Playing the Game of Life

To show how `Screen` might be used by a client module, we will use it to develop a program that plays the game of Life. Invented by mathematician John H. Conway, Life models the birth and death of simple organisms. Life is played on a (potentially infinite) board ruled into squares, each representing a cell. Each cell is either *live* or *dead*. The initial configuration (the "first generation" of cells) is arbitrary; there may be any number of live cells, arranged in any pattern. The second generation depends on the first generation according to two simple rules:

A live cell survives to the next generation only if two or three of its eight neighbors are live during the current generation.

A dead cell becomes live during the next generation if exactly three of its neighbors are live during the current generation.

Subsequent generations follow the same rules.

The screen of a monochrome monitor makes an ideal playing field for Life. Each character on the screen represents a cell; a blank character in normal display mode indicates a dead cell, while a blank character in reverse video mode (displayed as a bright rectangle) indicates a live cell.

The following program allows the user to enter the first generation of cells; the program then computes and displays subsequent generations until the user stops it. Notice that the program stores the current generation only in the display buffer. The program computes the next generation by scanning the buffer, computing and storing neighbor counts in an array called `nextGeneration`. The program then updates the screen by a scan of `nextGeneration`.

After displaying each generation, the program tests whether the user has typed a character; if so, the program terminates. Because the `InOut` module provides no way of testing whether or not a character has been typed, the program imports its I/O procedures from `Terminal` (Section 13.1) instead. `Terminal` exports a procedure called `BusyRead` that stores the value `0C` into its parameter if no character is waiting to be read. (*Note:* In many Modula-2 systems, `BusyRead` either is not provided or produces a value other than `0C` if no character has been typed. When a system does not supply `BusyRead`, `Terminal` usually exports an alternative procedure. For example, the Logitech version of `Terminal` provides a procedure called `KeyPressed` that returns the value

TRUE if a character is waiting to be read. The program was actually tested using `KeyPressed` instead of `BusyRead`.)

```
MODULE Life;
  (* plays the game of Life *)

  FROM Terminal IMPORT Read, Write, WriteString, WriteLn,
                       BusyRead;
  FROM Screen IMPORT numRows, numColumns, normal, reverse,
                     ClearScreen, GotoXY, WriteChar, WriteAttr,
                     ReadAttr;

  VAR ch: CHAR;

  PROCEDURE EnterInitialPattern;
    (* allows the user to enter the initial pattern from the
       keyboard *)
    CONST cursor = '*';
          bel = 7C;
    VAR ch: CHAR;
        x, y: CARDINAL;    (* current position of cursor *)

    PROCEDURE MoveCursor(newX, newY: INTEGER);
      (* moves the cursor to a new position; does nothing if
         new position is off the screen *)
    BEGIN
      IF (1 <= newX) & (newX <= numColumns) &
         (1 <= newY) & (newY <= numRows) THEN
        WriteChar(' ');       (* erase cursor *)
        x := newX;
        y := newY;
        GotoXY(x, y);         (* move to new cursor position *)
        WriteChar(cursor)     (* display cursor *)
      END
    END MoveCursor;

  BEGIN  (* EnterInitialPattern *)
    x := numColumns DIV 2 + 1;
    y := numRows DIV 2 + 1;
    GotoXY(x, y);
    WriteChar(cursor);
    LOOP
      Read(ch);
      CASE CAP(ch) OF
        'H': MoveCursor(x - 1, y) |   (* move left    *)
        'J': MoveCursor(x, y + 1) |   (* move down    *)
        'K': MoveCursor(x, y - 1) |   (* move up      *)
        'L': MoveCursor(x + 1, y) |   (* move right   *)
```

```
      ' ': WriteAttr(normal)     |    (* erase cell    *)
      '.': WriteAttr(reverse)    |    (* mark cell     *)
      'Q': WriteChar(' ');            (* erase cursor *)
           EXIT
    ELSE
      Write(bel)                      (* illegal key   *)
    END
  END
END EnterInitialPattern;

PROCEDURE GenerateNextPattern;
  (* generates and displays the next generation of cells *)
  VAR x, y: CARDINAL;
      nextGeneration:
        ARRAY [1..numRows], [1..numColumns] OF CARDINAL;
      attr: CHAR;

  PROCEDURE Increment(x, y: CARDINAL);
    (* increments next generation count for square x, y *)
  BEGIN
    IF (1 <= x) & (x <= numColumns) &
       (1 <= y) & (y <= numRows) THEN
      INC(nextGeneration[y, x])
    END
  END Increment;

BEGIN  (* GenerateNextPattern *)

    (* initialize nextGeneration array *)
  FOR y := 1 TO numRows DO
    FOR x := 1 TO numColumns DO
      nextGeneration[y, x] := 0
    END
  END;

   (* increment count of each neighbor of a live cell *)
  FOR y := 1 TO numRows DO
    FOR x := 1 TO numColumns DO
      GotoXY(x, y);
      ReadAttr(attr);
      IF attr = reverse THEN
        Increment(x - 1, y - 1);
        Increment(x - 1, y    );
        Increment(x - 1, y + 1);
        Increment(x,     y - 1);
        Increment(x,     y + 1);
        Increment(x + 1, y - 1);
        Increment(x + 1, y    );
        Increment(x + 1, y + 1)
      END
```

```
      END
    END;

      (* update display to show next generation *)
    FOR y := 1 TO numRows DO
      FOR x := 1 TO numColumns DO
        GotoXY(x, y);
        ReadAttr(attr);
        IF attr = reverse THEN
          IF (nextGeneration[y, x] < 2) OR
            (nextGeneration[y, x] > 3) THEN   (* cell dies *)
            WriteAttr(normal)
          END
        ELSIF nextGeneration[y, x] = 3 THEN   (* cell is born *)
          WriteAttr(reverse)
        END
      END
    END
  END GenerateNextPattern;


BEGIN
  WriteString("Welcome to the game of Life.  To mark a ");
  WriteString("cell, move the cursor to the desired");
  WriteLn;
  WriteString("position and type a period.  The cursor ");
  WriteString("can be moved by typing h (move left), ");
  WriteLn;
  WriteString("j (move down), k (move up), or l (move ");
  WriteString("right).  To erase a cell, just type a ");
  WriteLn;
  WriteString("space.  When the pattern is complete, ");
  WriteString("type q to begin the game.  Once the ");
  WriteLn;
  WriteString("pattern has been entered, the game can ");
  WriteString("be stopped by typing any character.");
  WriteLn;
  WriteLn;
  WriteString("Type any character to start.");
  WriteLn;
  Read(ch);    (* wait for user to type a character *)

  ClearScreen;
  EnterInitialPattern;
  REPEAT
    GenerateNextPattern;
    BusyRead(ch)    (* returns 0C if no character was typed *)
  UNTIL ch # 0C
END Life.
```

Here are a few initial configurations of particular interest:

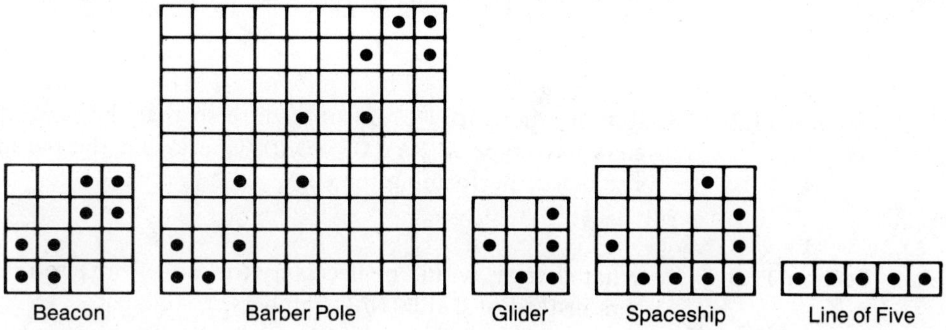

Other entertaining configurations can be formed by joining Lines of Five, such as

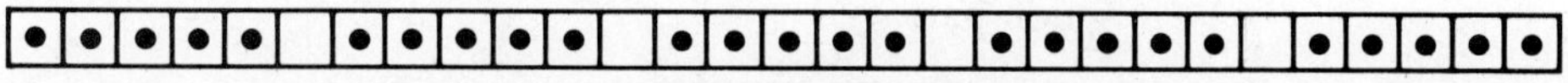

Note: We have shown live cells as circles for clarity; however, on the screen the cells appear as solid rectangles. For example, the Glider has the following appearance:

For more configurations and a thorough discussion of Life, consult Volume 2 of *Winning Ways*, by E. R. Berlekamp, J. H. Conway, and R. K. Guy (London: Academic Press, 1982).

EXERCISES

In the following Exercises, assume that words are 16 bits long and that bits are numbered from 15 (most significant) to 0 (least significant). Assume that the character set is ASCII.

Section 11.1

1. Rewrite the implementation part of the `CharSet` module (Section 10.3) using an array of eight `BITSET` values to represent a set of characters.

2. Compare (with respect to both space and time) the representation of `SetOfChar` described in exercise 1 with the linked list representation used in Section 10.3 and the BOOLEAN array representation of exercise 12 in Chapter 10.

Section 11.2

3. Rewrite the `CopyWords` procedure so that the `source` and `dest` parameters have type ARRAY OF WORD. Check that the parameters have the same size before performing the copy.

Section 11.3

4. What changes would be necessary to `TreeSort1` to make it sort REAL numbers instead of CARDINAL numbers?

5. What changes would we need to make in `TreeSort2` to make it sort REAL numbers instead of CARDINAL numbers?

6. Here is the definition part of a generic stack module; write the implementation part:

```
DEFINITION MODULE GenericStacks;
  (* exports type Stack (generic stack) and procedures for
     operating on values of this type *)

  FROM SYSTEM IMPORT WORD;

  TYPE Stack;

  PROCEDURE Initialize(VAR s: Stack; elementSize: CARDINAL);
    (* creates a stack s whose elements have size
       elementSize and makes it empty *)

  PROCEDURE Push(VAR s: Stack; element: ARRAY OF WORD);
    (* pushes element onto stack s; terminates program if
       stack is full or element has the wrong size *)

  PROCEDURE Pop(VAR s: Stack; VAR element: ARRAY OF WORD);
    (* stores top of stack s into element, then pops s;
       terminates program if stack is empty or element has
       the wrong size *)

  PROCEDURE IsEmpty(s: Stack): BOOLEAN;
    (* returns TRUE if s is empty, FALSE otherwise *)

END GenericStacks.
```

7. Modify the program `Reverse` of Section 9.1 to use the `GenericStacks` module instead of `CharacterStacks`.

8. Here is the definition part of a generic sorting module; write the implementation part:

```
DEFINITION MODULE GenericSorting;
  (* exports a generic sorting procedure *)

  FROM SYSTEM IMPORT ADDRESS;

  TYPE ComparisonProc = PROCEDURE (ADDRESS, ADDRESS):
                          BOOLEAN;

  PROCEDURE GenericSort(firstComp, lastComp: ADDRESS;
                          lessThan: ComparisonProc;
                          componentSize: CARDINAL);
    (* sorts the array whose first component begins at
       address firstComp, whose last component begins at
       address lastComp, and whose components have size
       componentSize; when given the addresses of two array
       components, lessThan returns TRUE if the first is
       less than the second, FALSE otherwise *)

END GenericSorting.
```

9. Show how to use `GenericSort` to sort the `inventory` array of Section 7.3. Sort only the components between 1 and `lastItem`, not all the components in the array. The sorting key should be the field `number`.

Section 11.4

10. Write the following procedure:

```
PROCEDURE Complement(w: WORD): WORD;
  (* returns the bitwise complement of w *)
```

11. Write the following procedure:

```
PROCEDURE WriteBits(w: WORD);
  (* writes the contents of w as a string of 0's and 1's;
     the most significant bit is written first *)
```

12. Rewrite the `ShiftRight` function to use division by 2 instead of `BITSET` operations.

13. Rewrite the `ShiftLeft` function to use multiplication by 2 instead of `BITSET` operations. Watch out for arithmetic overflow. (One way to avoid overflow is to clear the most significant bit before each multiplication by 2.)

14. Write the following procedure:

```
PROCEDURE CircularShift(w: WORD; n: CARDINAL): WORD;
  (* returns contents of w shifted right n positions; bits
     shifted off the right end are replaced at the left *)
```

15. What is wrong with the following procedure?

```
PROCEDURE WordToByte(w: WORD): BYTE;
  (* truncates a word to byte size by extracting its
     low-order byte *)
BEGIN
  RETURN BYTE(CHR(CARDINAL(w)))
END WordToByte;
```

16. The PC-DOS operating system stores the date of a disk file in one 16-bit word, using the following format:

15	14	13	12	11	10	9	8	7	6	5	4	3	2	1	0
y	y	y	y	y	y	y	m	m	m	m	d	d	d	d	d

The year is stored relative to 1980; for example, the bit pattern 0000111 represents the year 1987. Write the following procedure:

```
PROCEDURE PrintDate(date: WORD);
  (* prints the date of a PC-DOS file in mm-dd-yy format *)
```

17. Write the following procedure:

```
PROCEDURE SetBitField(VAR w: WORD;
                      highBit, lowBit: CARDINAL;
                      newField: WORD);
  (* modifies the contents of w by replacing the bit field
     between highBit and lowBit (inclusive) by the low-order
     bits of newField *)
```

18. Rewrite the `LowByte` and `HighByte` functions to use `ShiftRight` and `ShiftLeft` instead of type transfer. (Modify `LowByte` and `HighByte` to return values of type `WORD` instead of type `BYTE`.)

19. Write the following procedure:

```
PROCEDURE SwapBytes(w: WORD): WORD;
  (* returns a word identical to w with its high and low
     bytes interchanged *)
```

20. Write the following procedure:

```
PROCEDURE WriteHex(w: WORD);
  (* writes the contents of w as four hex characters *)
```

21. Write the following procedure:

```
PROCEDURE DisplayMemory(addr: ADDRESS; numWords: CARDINAL);
  (* displays the contents of memory (in hexadecimal)
     between the addresses addr and addr + numWords - 1;
     pauses after each screenful until user types a
     character *)
```

22. (For Pascal programmers) Show how to achieve the effect of type transfer in Pascal by using a record with a variant part. Why is Modula-2's method better?

23. One problem with Modula-2's type transfer mechanism is the difficulty of determining whether or not a module uses type transfer and, if so, where. How could we change the language to make the use of type transfer more visible?

Section 11.5

24. In the IBM Personal Computer, the address of the display buffer for a color monitor is `0B800H:0` (the address of the monochrome display buffer is `0B000H:0`). Modify the implementation part of the `Screen` module so that it can automatically adapt to either a color or monochrome monitor. During its initialization, `Screen` should test the equipment flag to see if the system has a color monitor or a monochrome monitor. In the former case, it will use the block of memory starting at address `0B800H:0`; in the latter case, it will use the block of memory starting at address `0B000H:0`. (No other changes to `Screen` should be necessary; in particular, `normal` and `reverse` can be left unchanged.)

12 Coroutines and Interrupt Handling

Wirth designed Modula-2 to be a systems programming language; he intended to use Modula-2 to write the operating system (and all the other software, for that matter) for his Lilith computer. Consequently, Modula-2 supports the creation of programs (including—but not limited to—operating systems) that manage processes and respond to interrupts.

Modula-2's support for processes and interrupt handling is based on the concept of the *coroutine*. We can simulate concurrent processes by using coroutines that transfer control among themselves, either directly or through a scheduling mechanism. We can also install coroutines as interrupt handlers; when an interrupt occurs, the appropriate coroutine services the interrupt, then suspends itself until the next interrupt occurs.

Section 12.1 introduces the coroutine concept and discusses Modula-2's features for creating coroutines and transferring control from one coroutine to another. Section 12.2 describes Wirth's `Processes` module, which provides features for the creation and synchronization of processes. Section 12.3 shows how programmers can create their own modules for process management and develops the `ScheduledProcesses` module as an example. Section 12.4 shows how to define interrupt handlers in Modula-2. Finally, Section 12.5 gives an implementation of the `ScheduledProcesses` module that performs interrupt-driven process scheduling.

The features Chapter 12 describes are useful for many kinds of programs, not just operating systems, so the chapter does not require any previous knowledge of operating system principles. The chapter does introduce a few concepts related to operating systems (and to concurrent programming in general). For more details about these topics, consult a book such as J. L. Peterson and A. Silberschatz, *Operating System Concepts*, Second Edition (Reading, Mass.: Addison-Wesley, 1985).

12.1 Coroutines

Although every programmer is familiar with *subroutines* (*procedures* in Modula-2), *coroutines* may be less familiar. Like a procedure, a coroutine contains both data (local variables) and code (statements). A procedure call activates a procedure; when the procedure returns control to its caller, the values of its local variables are lost. At the next call of the procedure, it begins to execute at the first statement in its body. We can activate a coroutine in much the same way we activate a procedure (we *transfer* control to the coroutine, however, rather than *call* it). When control leaves the coroutine, the values of its local variables are preserved. And, when we next activate the coroutine, it resumes execution at the statement immediately after the one that caused it to suspend execution earlier. In other words, the system preserves the state of the coroutine's computation so that it resumes execution from where it left off.

Suppose that P and Q are coroutines, and a program transfers control to P for the first time. After executing for a while, P may transfer control to Q, which then begins executing. Q may subsequently transfer control back to P, which resumes executing where it left off earlier. (So far, P and Q have behaved no differently than if they were procedures.) If P later transfers control to Q, then Q resumes executing from the point at which it had transferred control to P; Q does not start at the beginning of its body. Figure 12.1 shows the flow of control between P and Q.

Figure 12.1
Flow of Control between Coroutines P and Q

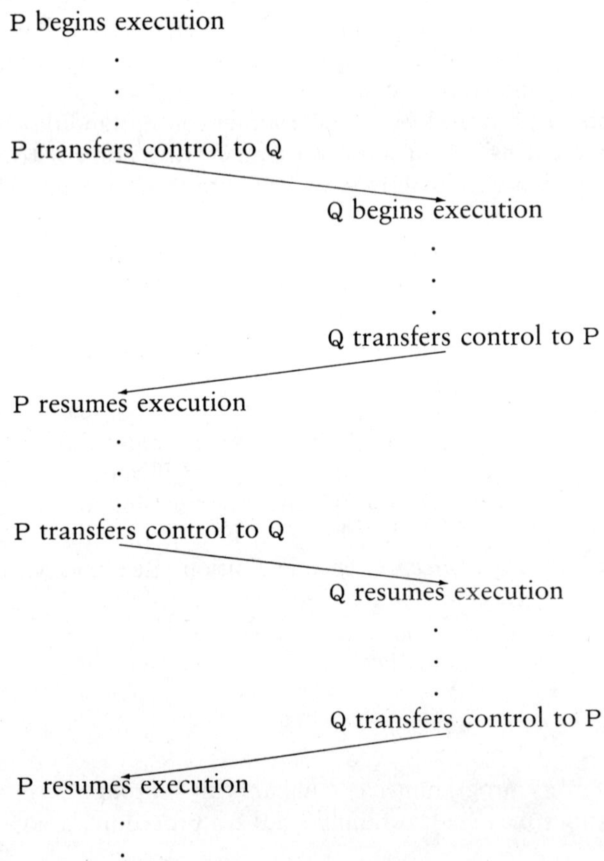

This example shows why we call P and Q *co*routines: they are equal in status; neither is subordinate to the other. By comparison, if P and Q are procedures and P calls Q, then P cannot resume until Q has completed execution; here Q is subordinate to P.

A program may have two, three, or more coroutines. Each coroutine may transfer control to any of the other coroutines. It is not possible to have just one coroutine. When a program first transfers control to a coroutine, the program itself becomes—in effect—a coroutine; the program and the coroutine coexist on an equal basis thereafter, with each capable of transferring control to the other.

Coroutines are useful in the following kinds of programs, among others:

- *Programs that consist of several components of equal status cooperating toward a common goal*. If no component is subordinate to the others, it may be easier to write the components as coroutines rather than procedures. For example, most compilers consist of several loosely connected components (lexical analyzer, parser, code generator, and so forth); it is natural to view these components as coroutines.
- *The kernel of an operating system*. One function of an operating system is to share the processor (or processors, in some computer systems) among many processes. The *kernel* performs this function by switching rapidly among different processes, allowing one to execute for a brief period before switching to another. The processes are essentially coroutines, because only one actually executes at a time. Furthermore, the state of each process is preserved while it is not executing. (Note, however, that processes—unlike coroutines in general—may be suspended involuntarily so that other processes have a chance to execute.)
- *Programs that must respond to events occurring outside the program*. Events may be internal to the system (a tick of the system clock, for example) or external (a keystroke generated at the system keyboard). Both cause an *interrupt*—a hardware signal that a particular event has occurred. As Section 12.4 shows, many Modula-2 systems allow a program to install a coroutine as an interrupt handler; the coroutine is activated automatically when the interrupt occurs, allowing the program to respond quickly to the event that caused the interrupt.
- *Programs that simulate discrete systems*. The programmer models each activity in a discrete system as a coroutine; by transferring control among the coroutines, the activities appear to progress in time.

Coroutine Creation

In Modula-2, we do not *declare* a coroutine; instead, we *create* it from a procedure. To create a coroutine, we call the NEWPROCESS procedure. (In the early development of Modula-2, Wirth used the term *process* instead of *coroutine*.)

Coroutines in Modula-2 are inherently low-level—they require programs to manipulate ADDRESS values—so we must import NEWPROCESS from a low-level module (usually the SYSTEM module).

A call of NEWPROCESS must specify not only the procedure from which the coroutine is to be created, but also a *workspace* (a block of memory) in which to store the state of the coroutine:

```
PROCEDURE NEWPROCESS(P: PROC; A: ADDRESS; n: CARDINAL;
                     VAR p1: ADDRESS);
```

The parameter P represents the procedure from which NEWPROCESS will create the coroutine. The parameters A and n indicate the address and size of the workspace. The fourth parameter, p1, must be a variable of type ADDRESS; NEWPROCESS changes the value of this variable to reference the new coroutine. The program will use the variable when the time comes for transferring control to the coroutine.

Modula-2 places two restrictions on the procedure P from which we create a coroutine. First, because P must be of type PROC, it cannot have parameters and cannot be a function. (Parameters are not as useful for coroutines as they are for procedures, because a coroutine does not begin executing from the beginning each time control is transferred to it. Instead, coroutines typically communicate through global variables.) Second, P must not be local to any other procedure. No other restrictions apply to P. In particular, P may contain local modules and may call procedures, including itself. (A coroutine that contains procedure calls may need a larger workspace than one that does not; we will return to this point at the end of the section.)

Before calling NEWPROCESS to create a coroutine, a program must allocate memory for the coroutine's workspace. A workspace is a region of memory that contains the local variables of the coroutine and the coroutine's stack, as well as other information. The simplest way to create a workspace is to declare an array of words:

```
CONST wkspSize = 1000;
VAR wksp: ARRAY [1..wkspSize] OF WORD;
```

Calculating an appropriate size for a workspace is difficult. We will sidestep the issue here, and will always use workspaces of 1,000 words. A more detailed discussion of workspaces appears at the end of this section.

Before calling NEWPROCESS, a program must also declare an ADDRESS variable to reference the new coroutine:

```
VAR cor: ADDRESS;    (* coroutine reference *)
```

A call of NEWPROCESS would then look like this:

```
NEWPROCESS(P, ADR(wksp), SIZE(wksp), cor);
```

Calling NEWPROCESS changes the value of cor to reference the new coroutine. Because ADDRESS values represent coroutines, programs do not depend on the actual representation of a coroutine, which may vary from one Modula-2 system to another.

We can create many identical coroutines from the same procedure. The procedure serves as a "template" for the coroutines we create from it; each of these coroutines executes the same statements and has local variables with the same names. However, each coroutine uses different memory locations for its local variables. The local variables belonging to a coroutine are stored in its workspace, and each coroutine has a different workspace.

Coroutine Transfer

The TRANSFER procedure allows one coroutine to transfer control to another:

```
PROCEDURE TRANSFER(VAR p1, p2: ADDRESS);
```

TRANSFER suspends the current coroutine (the one that called TRANSFER), stores a reference to it in p1, and resumes the coroutine that p2 identifies (hence p2 must have a value before we call TRANSFER, but p1 need not). Like NEWPROCESS, TRANSFER must be imported (usually from SYSTEM).

TRANSFER serves two purposes. First, it causes a newly created coroutine to begin executing:

```
NEWPROCESS(P, ADR(wksp), SIZE(wksp), new);
TRANSFER(old, new);
```

The call of TRANSFER is necessary because NEWPROCESS never causes a coroutine to begin executing—it only prepares the coroutine to execute. Second, TRANSFER allows a previously suspended coroutine to resume executing. For example, to transfer control back to the coroutine that was executing before the call of TRANSFER just given, we would use the call

```
TRANSFER(new, old);
```

When a Modula-2 program calls TRANSFER for the first time, it essentially becomes a coroutine. Suppose that the first call of TRANSFER is

```
TRANSFER(main, cor);
```

where a call of NEWPROCESS has previously initialized cor. The main program is suspended, and the coroutine that cor identifies begins to execute. The coroutine executes until it calls TRANSFER or terminates. If it calls TRANSFER, it may choose to resume the main program (by supplying main as the second parameter to TRANSFER) or transfer control to some other coroutine. Once suspended, the main program is treated like any other coroutine—it remains suspended until another coroutine allows it to resume execution.

TRANSFER allows two coroutines to transfer control back and forth using a single ADDRESS variable. For example, suppose that the variable previous identifies a coroutine that is not currently executing. The call

```
TRANSFER(previous, previous);
```

suspends the currently executing coroutine and stores a reference to it in previous while allowing the previously executing coroutine to resume execution. This technique works because TRANSFER *first* examines previous to determine which coroutine to resume, *then* changes previous to reference the newly suspended coroutine.

Coroutine Termination

If a coroutine ever reaches the end of its associated procedure (the point at which the procedure would normally return), the entire program—not just the coroutine—terminates, because the system cannot determine which coroutine should execute next. Therefore, procedures from which programs will create coroutines normally either contain an infinite loop (ensuring that the end of the procedure is never reached) or end with a call of TRANSFER:

```
PROCEDURE P;    (* to be used to create a coroutine *)
         .
         .
         .
BEGIN
         .
         .
         .
  TRANSFER(current, main); (* return control to main program *)
END P;
```

Of course, if the coroutine is ever resumed after this final transfer, it will reach the end of the procedure and the entire program will halt.

A coroutine is not an *entity*, because it is not declared and does not have a name. A coroutine is more like an anonymous variable—it is created dynamically and is "pointed to" by a variable. No mechanism exists for "disposing of" a coroutine (we can dispose of an anonymous variable by calling DEALLOCATE). However, deallocating the coroutine's workspace essentially destroys the coroutine as well. Attempting to transfer control to a coroutine whose workspace no longer exists will have unpredictable effects.

Changes Since the Second Edition

In the Second Edition of *Programming in Modula-2*, Wirth specified that the SYSTEM module would export a PROCESS type. Programs could use this type to declare coroutine variables:

```
VAR old, new: PROCESS;
```

In the Second Edition, the procedures NEWPROCESS and TRANSFER required parameters of type PROCESS:

```
PROCEDURE NEWPROCESS(P: PROC; A: ADDRESS; n: CARDINAL;
                     VAR p1: PROCESS);
PROCEDURE TRANSFER(VAR p1, p2: PROCESS);
```

The Third Edition does not mention PROCESS; instead, NEWPROCESS and TRANSFER require that p1 and p2 have type ADDRESS. (*Note:* Some Modula-2 systems that otherwise conform to the Third Edition continue to use the PROCESS type.)

Another difference between the Second and Third Editions of *Programming in Modula-2* concerns the location of the NEWPROCESS and TRANSFER procedures. The Second Edition requires the SYSTEM module to export these procedures. The Third Edition removes this requirement. Consequently, in some Modula-2 systems, a library module—not SYSTEM—may export NEWPROCESS and TRANSFER.

EXAMPLE PROGRAM

Printing Fibonacci Numbers

Our first example of how to use coroutines is a simple program called `PrintFibonacciNumbers` that prints all Fibonacci numbers up to some predetermined limit. (A similar program—without coroutines—appears in Section 1.3.)

`PrintFibonacciNumbers` uses two variables, `fib1` and `fib2`, to keep track of the last Fibonacci number printed and the one to print next. Two coroutines share the tasks of printing numbers and updating `fib1` and `fib2`. When `fib1` contains the next Fibonacci number, one coroutine prints `fib1`, adds `fib1` to `fib2` (so that `fib2` contains the next Fibonacci number), then transfers control to the other coroutine, which is identical except that it reverses the roles of `fib1` and `fib2`.

The two coroutines appear in the program as procedures named `IncFib1` and `IncFib2`. The body of `PrintFibonacciNumbers` creates coroutines from `IncFib1` and `IncFib2`, using the following calls of NEWPROCESS:

```
NEWPROCESS(IncFib1, ADR(wksp1), SIZE(wksp1), cor1);
NEWPROCESS(IncFib2, ADR(wksp2), SIZE(wksp2), cor2);
```

The variables `cor1` and `cor2` now contain references to the coroutines created from `IncFib1` and `IncFib2`, respectively. `PrintFibonacciNumbers` next transfers control to `IncFib1`:

```
TRANSFER(main, cor1);
```

TRANSFER saves a reference to the main program in the variable `main` before it transfers control to `IncFib1`. The following actions then take place:

1. `IncFib1` begins to execute. It writes 1 (the value of `fib2`), adds `fib2` to `fib1` (`fib1` is now 1), then transfers control to `IncFib2`, using the reference in `cor2`.
2. `IncFib2` begins to execute. After writing 1 (the value of `fib1`), it adds `fib1` to `fib2` (`fib2` is now 2), then transfers control to `IncFib1`, using the reference in `cor1`.
3. `IncFib1` resumes execution. It writes 2 (the value of `fib2`), adds `fib2` to `fib1` (`fib1` is now 3), then transfers control to `IncFib2`.
4. `IncFib2` resumes execution. After writing 3 (the value of `fib1`), it adds `fib1` to `fib2` (`fib2` is now 5), then transfers control to `IncFib1`.

Execution continues this way, with control alternating between `IncFib1` and `IncFib2`, until one of the coroutines detects that the value it was about to print exceeds `maxFib`. It then transfers control back to the main program, using the reference stored in the variable `main`.

`PrintFibonacciNumbers` looks like this:

```
MODULE PrintFibonacciNumbers;
  (* prints Fibonacci numbers using coroutines *)

  FROM SYSTEM IMPORT WORD, ADDRESS, NEWPROCESS, TRANSFER, ADR;
  FROM InOut IMPORT WriteCard, WriteLn;

  CONST wkspSize = 1000;
        maxFib = 10000;    (* prints numbers up to this limit *)

  VAR wksp1, wksp2: ARRAY [1..wkspSize] OF WORD;
      main, cor1, cor2: ADDRESS;    (* coroutines *)
      fib1, fib2: CARDINAL;

  PROCEDURE IncFib1;
    (* prints fib2, then adds fib2 to fib1 *)
  BEGIN
    WHILE fib2 <= maxFib DO
      WriteCard(fib2, 1);
      WriteLn;
      INC(fib1, fib2);
      TRANSFER(cor1, cor2)
    END;
    TRANSFER(cor1, main)
  END IncFib1;
```

```
  PROCEDURE IncFib2;
    (* prints fib1, then adds fib1 to fib2 *)
  BEGIN
    WHILE fib1 <= maxFib DO
      WriteCard(fib1, 1);
      WriteLn;
      INC(fib2, fib1);
      TRANSFER(cor2, cor1)
    END;
    TRANSFER(cor2, main)
  END IncFib2;

BEGIN
  fib1 := 0;
  fib2 := 1;
  NEWPROCESS(IncFib1, ADR(wksp1), SIZE(wksp1), cor1);
  NEWPROCESS(IncFib2, ADR(wksp2), SIZE(wksp2), cor2);
  TRANSFER(main, cor1)
END PrintFibonacciNumbers.
```

EXAMPLE PROGRAM

Sorting Using Coroutines

Our second coroutine example is a modification of the `Quicksort` program of Section 7.1. The key to `Quicksort` was the following procedure:

```
PROCEDURE Split(VAR array: ARRAY OF CARDINAL;
                L, R: INTEGER; VAR middle: INTEGER);
  (* partitions region of array between L and R so that
     all values to the left of "middle" are less than or
     equal to all values to its right *)
  VAR middleNumber: CARDINAL;
BEGIN
  middleNumber := array[L];

  LOOP
    WHILE (L < R) & (middleNumber <= array[R]) DO
      DEC(R)
    END;
    IF L >= R THEN EXIT END;
    array[L] := array[R];
    INC(L);

    WHILE (L < R) & (array[L] <= middleNumber) DO
      INC(L)
    END;
    IF L >= R THEN EXIT END;
    array[R] := array[L];
    DEC(R)
  END;
```

```
    array[R] := middleNumber;
    middle := R
END Split;
```

Split uses two "fingers," L and R, to mark positions in the array. Split moves R to the left until it points to a value less than middleNumber, then copies array[R] to array[L]. Split next moves L to the right until it points to a value greater than middleNumber, then copies array[L] to array[R]. Split continues in this manner, alternating between moving R and moving L, until it has partitioned the array. (Section 7.1 describes Split in more detail and illustrates it with figures.)

The alternating movement of L and R suggests that our program contain two coroutines: one to move L to the right, and one to move R to the left. We will write these coroutines as procedures named MoveL and MoveR, respectively, and reference them through coroutine variables named moveL and moveR. When MoveL and MoveR have completed the partitioning, they transfer control back to Split, which we reference as a coroutine through a variable named split.

MoveR tests whether the array component that R selects is less than middleNumber. If so, it copies the array component to the position marked by L, then transfers control to MoveL. When control eventually returns to MoveR, it moves R to the left, checks whether L and R have met, then repeats its earlier actions, starting with the test of whether the array component that R selects is less than middleNumber. When L and R meet, MoveR transfers control to Split, because partitioning is complete.

```
PROCEDURE MoveR;
  (* moves R to the left *)
BEGIN
  WHILE L < R DO
    IF middleNumber > array[R] THEN
      array[L] := array[R];
      TRANSFER(moveR, moveL)
    END;
    DEC(R)
  END;
  TRANSFER(moveR, split)
END MoveR;
```

MoveL is similar:

```
PROCEDURE MoveL;
  (* moves L to the right *)
BEGIN
  INC(L);
  WHILE L < R DO
    IF array[L] > middleNumber THEN
      array[R] := array[L];
      TRANSFER(moveL, moveR)
```

```
    END;
    INC(L)
  END;
  TRANSFER(moveL, split)
END MoveL;
```

MoveL and MoveR are not completely symmetrical. For example, MoveL increments L before entering the WHILE loop, while MoveR does not perform a similar action. The asymmetry is unavoidable, because L—not R—initially points to a "hole" in the array.

When called, Split copies the partitioning element to the variable middleNumber, creates coroutines from the procedures MoveL and MoveR, then transfers control to the one created from MoveR. MoveR and MoveL transfer control back and forth until they have completely partitioned the array, when control returns to Split. Split replaces the partitioning element before returning.

```
PROCEDURE Split(lower, upper: INTEGER; VAR middle: INTEGER);
  (* partitions region of array between lower and upper so
     that all values to the left of "middle" are less than
     or equal to all values to its right *)
BEGIN
  middleNumber := array[lower];
  L := lower;
  R := upper;
  NEWPROCESS(MoveL, ADR(wksp1), SIZE(wksp1), moveL);
  NEWPROCESS(MoveR, ADR(wksp2), SIZE(wksp2), moveR);
  TRANSFER(split, moveR);
  array[R] := middleNumber;
  middle := R
END Split;
```

Notice that array, L, R, and middleNumber must be global variables so that they will be visible in MoveL and MoveR. (In the original program, the first three were parameters, while middleNumber was local to Split.)

Here is the full version of Quicksort, using coroutines to perform partitioning:

```
MODULE Quicksort;
  (* uses Quicksort to sort a file of CARDINAL numbers;
     partitioning is done using coroutines *)

  IMPORT SYSTEM;
  FROM InOut IMPORT OpenInput, CloseInput, OpenOutput,
                    CloseOutput, WriteString, WriteLn,
                    ReadCard, Done, WriteCard;

  CONST maxLen = 1000;
```

```
VAR array: ARRAY [0..maxLen-1] OF CARDINAL;
    actualLen: CARDINAL;

PROCEDURE ReadNumbers(VAR array: ARRAY OF CARDINAL;
                      VAR numberRead: CARDINAL);
  (* reads CARDINAL numbers from a file and stores into
     array; numberRead indicates how many numbers were
     read *)
  VAR number: CARDINAL;
BEGIN
  WriteString("Enter name of file to be sorted");
  WriteLn;
  OpenInput("NUM");
  numberRead := 0;
  LOOP
    ReadCard(number);
    IF NOT Done THEN EXIT END;
    IF numberRead > HIGH(array) THEN
      WriteString("Array overflow in ReadNumbers");
      WriteLn;
      HALT
    END;
    array[numberRead] := number;
    INC(numberRead)
  END;
  CloseInput
END ReadNumbers;

MODULE Partition;
  (* exports Split procedure *)

  FROM SYSTEM IMPORT WORD, ADDRESS, NEWPROCESS, TRANSFER,
                     ADR;
  IMPORT array;

  EXPORT Split;

  CONST wkspSize = 1000;

  VAR wksp1, wksp2: ARRAY [1..wkspSize] OF WORD;
      split, moveL, moveR: ADDRESS;   (* coroutines *)
      middleNumber: CARDINAL;
      L, R: INTEGER;

  PROCEDURE MoveR;
    (* moves R to the left *)
  BEGIN
    WHILE L < R DO
      IF middleNumber > array[R] THEN
        array[L] := array[R];
        TRANSFER(moveR, moveL)
```

```
      END;
      DEC(R)
    END;
    TRANSFER(moveR, split)
  END MoveR;

  PROCEDURE MoveL;
    (* moves L to the right *)
  BEGIN
    INC(L);
    WHILE L < R DO
      IF array[L] > middleNumber THEN
        array[R] := array[L];
        TRANSFER(moveL, moveR)
      END;
      INC(L)
    END;
    TRANSFER(moveL, split)
  END MoveL;

  PROCEDURE Split(lower, upper: INTEGER;
                  VAR middle: INTEGER);
    (* partitions region of array between lower and upper so
       that all values to the left of "middle" are less than
       or equal to all values to its right *)
  BEGIN
    middleNumber := array[lower];
    L := lower;
    R := upper;
    NEWPROCESS(MoveL, ADR(wksp1), SIZE(wksp1), moveL);
    NEWPROCESS(MoveR, ADR(wksp2), SIZE(wksp2), moveR);
    TRANSFER(split, moveR);
    array[R] := middleNumber;
    middle := R
  END Split;

END Partition;

PROCEDURE SortNumbers(VAR array: ARRAY OF CARDINAL;
                      lower, upper: INTEGER);
  (* sorts portion of array between lower and upper *)
  VAR middle: INTEGER;
BEGIN
  IF lower >= upper THEN RETURN END;
  Split(lower, upper, middle);
  SortNumbers(array, lower, middle - 1);
  SortNumbers(array, middle + 1, upper)
END SortNumbers;

PROCEDURE WriteNumbers(VAR array: ARRAY OF CARDINAL;
                       length: CARDINAL);
```

```
    (* copies CARDINAL numbers from array to a file; "length"
       indicates length of array *)
    VAR i: CARDINAL;
  BEGIN
    WriteString("Enter name of output file");
    WriteLn;
    OpenOutput("NUM");
    FOR i := 0 TO length - 1 DO
      WriteCard(array[i], 1);
      WriteLn
    END;
    CloseOutput
  END WriteNumbers;

BEGIN
  ReadNumbers(array, actualLen);
  SortNumbers(array, 0, actualLen - 1);
  WriteNumbers(array, actualLen)
END Quicksort.
```

We would have preferred to nest the procedures `MoveL` and `MoveR` inside `Split`, along with the variables that they share. We could not do so because a coroutine must be created from a procedure that is not nested inside another procedure. However, we achieved much the same effect by placing `Split`, `MoveL`, and `MoveR` in a local module called `Partition` that hides all but `Split` from the rest of the program. `Partition` imports `array` and declares `L`, `R`, and `middleNumber`, so all four variables are accessible to `MoveL` and `MoveR` as well as to `Split`.

Note: TRANSFER is an expensive operation, because it involves saving the entire state of the current coroutine (which may include the contents of all machine registers), then restoring the state of the coroutine to be executed next. Consequently, using coroutines to implement the partitioning phase of `Quicksort` yields an unacceptably slow program. The purpose of the example is to illustrate the use of coroutines in a familiar setting, not to suggest that programmers should use coroutines in everyday programs.

Workspaces (OPTIONAL)

Our examples have ignored two important questions about coroutine workspaces: how large should a workspace be, and where should we locate it?

To answer the first question, we need to know what a workspace contains. Although the exact contents vary from one Modula-2 system to another, a workspace usually includes the following:

a fixed-size area in which to save the state of the coroutine when the coroutine is suspended the coroutine's local variables

the coroutine's stack (used for procedure calls performed while the coroutine is executing)

Some systems also include a heap in each workspace (used for dynamic storage allocation performed while the coroutine is executing).

The manual for a particular Modula-2 system should give the minimum size of a workspace. A coroutine may need a larger workspace if it calls procedures, because storage for procedure calls is allocated on the coroutine's stack. A coroutine may also need a larger workspace if it performs dynamic storage allocation (assuming that the workspace contains the coroutine's heap).

We can put a workspace in one of three possible places:

in the space allocated for global variables

on the system stack, which contains space for local variables belonging to procedures

in the system heap, which contains space for anonymous, dynamically allocated variables

Which location we use depends on the lifetime of the coroutine. If a coroutine will have the same lifetime as the program itself, then we should store its workspace with the program's global variables:

```
MODULE M;
  CONST wkspSize = 1000;
  VAR workspace: ARRAY [1..wkspSize] OF WORD;
     .
     .
     .
END M.
```

If a coroutine exists only while a certain procedure is active, then it makes sense to store the workspace with that procedure's local variables. In this way, the workspace only occupies space while the procedure is executing.

```
PROCEDURE P;
  CONST wkspSize = 1000;
  VAR workspace: ARRAY [1..wkspSize] OF WORD;
     .
     .
     .
END P;
```

The third possibility is that we will be creating and destroying coroutines in a fairly arbitrary fashion. It is then best to store workspaces in the system heap, because space in the heap can be allocated and deallocated under program control.

```
VAR workspace: ADDRESS;
        .
        .
        .
ALLOCATE(workspace, wkspSize);
```

When using stack or heap storage for a workspace, the programmer must ensure that the workspace remains in existence throughout the coroutine's lifetime. Deallocating the workspace while the coroutine still exists will have unpredictable (and usually disastrous) effects.

Another factor that affects workspace placement is whether the number of coroutines that a program will create is fixed or will vary from one execution of the program to another. If the number can vary, then the program must either declare workspaces as local variables in a recursive procedure (each recursive call of the procedure allocates room for one or more new workspaces) or—more often—allocate them dynamically in the heap.

12.2 Wirth's `Processes` Module

Although coroutines are useful for some kinds of programs, many programs are easier to write and understand if we write them using *processes* instead. The process concept comes from the field of operating systems, where a process is often defined as a "program in execution." This definition acknowledges that, in a computer system, many programs may be currently executing. If the system has multiple processors, the processes may be able to execute *concurrently*. If the system has only a single processor, the processes execute *quasi-concurrently*—processor time is divided among the processes so that they *appear* to execute concurrently. Processes created by a Modula-2 program have similar properties. A multiple-processor machine may execute them in true concurrent fashion; more often, a single processor will execute the processes quasi-concurrently.

Although Modula-2 provides no direct support for processes, we can write library modules that allow process manipulation. *Programming in Modula-2* describes one such module, called `Processes`. The `Processes` module allows a program to create processes and also provides a mechanism (signals) for synchronizing processes. The definition part of `Processes`, which follows, gives no clue as to whether the processes will execute concurrently or quasi-concurrently; the choice depends on the underlying environment and on the implementation of the module. (Coroutines provide a natural mechanism for implementing processes on a single-processor machine.)

```
DEFINITION MODULE Processes;
  (* allows the creation and synchronization of processes *)
```

```
  TYPE SIGNAL;

  PROCEDURE StartProcess(P: PROC; n: CARDINAL);
    (* starts a process created from P with a workspace of
       size n *)

  PROCEDURE SEND(VAR s: SIGNAL);
    (* allows one process waiting for s to resume execution *)

  PROCEDURE WAIT(VAR s: SIGNAL);
    (* waits until another process performs a SEND on s *)

  PROCEDURE Awaited(s: SIGNAL): BOOLEAN;
    (* returns TRUE if at least one process is waiting for s,
       FALSE otherwise *)

  PROCEDURE Init(VAR s: SIGNAL);
    (* initializes s *)

END Processes.
```

A call of `StartProcess` requires two parameters: (1) a procedure `P` with no parameters, and (2) a number `n` indicating the amount of space to set aside for the process's workspace. `StartProcess` dynamically allocates the workspace and allows the process to begin executing. By repeatedly calling `StartProcess`, a program can create any number of processes.

A module that allows the creation of processes must furnish a mechanism for these processes to synchronize with one another; the `Processes` module provides *signals*. `Processes` exports a `SIGNAL` type and the procedures `Init`, `SEND`, `WAIT`, and `Awaited`, which operate on `SIGNAL` variables.

When a process executes a `WAIT` operation on a signal `s`, the process is suspended and must wait for some other process to perform a `SEND` operation on `s`. Because more than one process can perform a `WAIT` operation on the same signal, several processes may be suspended, all waiting for the same signal. These processes normally are kept in a queue (a first-in, first-out data structure) to ensure that the first process to be suspended will be the first to be resumed when a `SEND` operation is performed. A call of `SEND` allows at most one process to resume execution.

Signals are useful when a process must temporarily suspend its normal operation until a certain condition is satisfied. For example, one process may be placing characters into a buffer while another reads characters from the buffer (call these the "producer" and "consumer" processes). The producer can proceed independently of the consumer until the buffer is full, at which point the producer must wait for the consumer to read at least one character. We can handle this situation nicely by introducing a `SIGNAL` variable:

```
VAR nonfull: SIGNAL;
```

When the buffer becomes full, the producer performs a `WAIT` operation on the `nonfull` signal:

```
IF (* buffer full *) THEN
  WAIT(nonfull)
END;
```

When the consumer has fetched a character, it performs a `SEND` operation to notify the producer that space is now available in the buffer:

```
SEND(nonfull);
```

We must initialize variables of type `SIGNAL` by calling the `Init` procedure. The `Awaited` function allows a program to determine whether any processes are currently waiting for a particular signal.

There are many ways to write the implementation part of the `Processes` module. *Programming in Modula-2* gives a single-processor implementation of `Processes` that uses coroutines to implement processes. Using coroutines has a number of consequences of which the programmer must become aware, because many Modula-2 systems provide a version of the `Processes` module that behaves the same as Wirth's version. The properties of Wirth's implementation include the following:

- A call of `StartProcess` creates a process and transfers control to it; the caller is suspended.
- A process can execute indefinitely as long as it does not perform a `WAIT` or `SEND` operation. (This includes the main program, which is treated like any other process.) For example, suppose that we call `StartProcess` twice in succession:

  ```
  StartProcess(P1, wkspSize);
  StartProcess(P2, wkspSize);
  ```

  The first call creates a process from `P1` and transfers control to it. That process executes until it performs a `WAIT` operation, at which point control returns to the original process, which then executes the second call of `StartProcess`.
- If any process terminates, the entire program halts. This property is a consequence of using coroutines to implement processes.
- A `WAIT` operation *always* suspends the current process. The next process to execute will be one of those processes that were previously suspended but are now ready to execute. The implementation given in *Programming in Modula-2* maintains a circular list of all processes; when `WAIT` suspends a process, it searches this list for the first process ready to resume executing.

- When a process performs a SEND operation on a signal `s`, the action taken depends on whether the queue associated with `s` is empty. If the queue is not empty, the process performing the SEND is suspended and the first process on the queue resumes execution. If the queue *is* empty, the SEND operation has no effect: the process that performed the SEND continues to execute, and no record is made that the SEND was ever performed. Unfortunately, another process may subsequently execute a `WAIT`, expecting the first process to perform a SEND, when in fact the first process has already performed it. One solution is to use a BOOLEAN variable to record whether a SEND was previously performed; if so, `WAIT` is not called.

EXAMPLE **Using `Processes` to Partition an Array**

To illustrate the use of the `Processes` module, we will rewrite the `Partition` module of Section 12.1, using processes rather than coroutines to partition the array. First, however, we modify the partitioning algorithm. The algorithm we presented in Section 12.1 used two "fingers," `L` and `R`, which were moved toward the middle of the array by two coroutines (represented by the procedures `MoveL` and `MoveR`). The new algorithm also moves `L` and `R` toward the middle of the array, but in a different fashion. The old method, although completely satisfactory, required that `MoveL` and `MoveR` be "tightly coupled": `MoveR` moved `R` to the left, then transferred control to `MoveL`, which moved `L` to the right, then transferred control back to `MoveR`. The contents of the array completely determined the behavior of `MoveL` and `MoveR`. With the new method, `MoveL` and `MoveR` are "loosely coupled"; `L` and `R` move independently, although they must synchronize from time to time. We can best present the new algorithm by an example.

Suppose that we begin with an array containing six numbers to sort. As before, we always select the leftmost array component as the partitioning element; however, we do not move it until partitioning is almost complete. Before partitioning, `L` points to the second array component (the one to the right of the partitioning element); `R` points to the rightmost component:

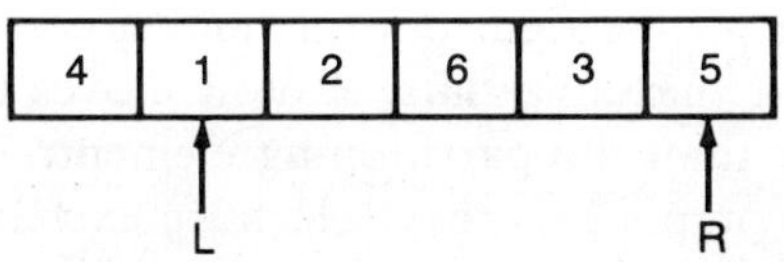

We begin moving `R` to the left until it selects an array component less than the partitioning element. At the same time, we move `L` to the right until it selects an array component greater than the partitioning element. Thus, after several steps, `L` and `R` will come to rest in the following position:

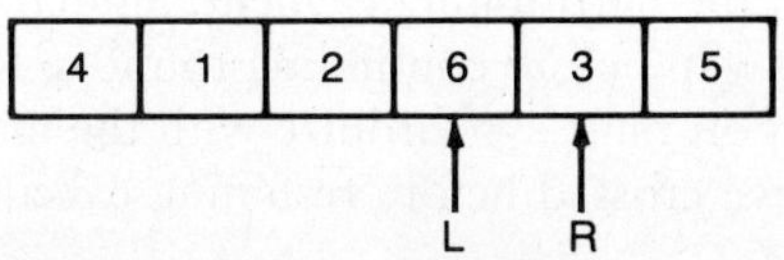

We now exchange the components selected by L and R:

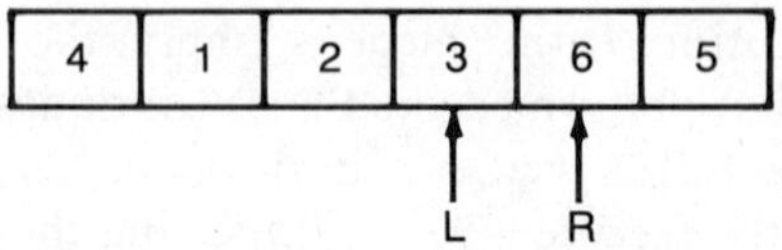

After the swap, we resume moving L and R. As before, R moves to the left until it selects a component less than the partitioning element, while L moves to the right until it selects a component greater than the partitioning element. When both L and R have stopped, we exchange the components that they select, unless L and R have crossed. In our small example, L and R do in fact cross at this point:

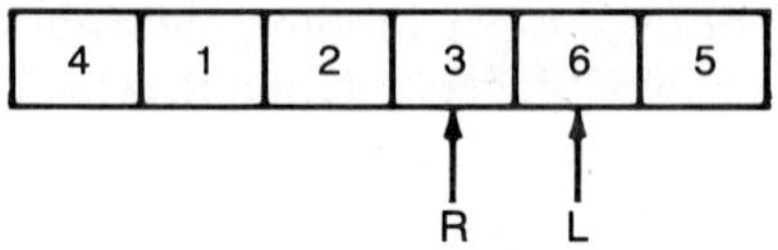

To complete the partitioning, we exchange the partitioning element (the leftmost component of the array) with the component that R selects:

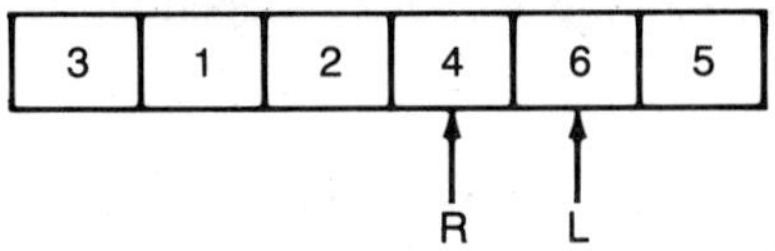

As in Section 12.1, we use two procedures, MoveL and MoveR, to move the fingers. However, this time MoveL and MoveR execute as processes rather than coroutines. MoveL moves L to the right until it finds a component greater than the partitioning element. At the same time, MoveR moves R to the left until it finds a component smaller than the partitioning element. When both L and R have stopped moving, the components they select are exchanged. It is irrelevant which process actually performs the swap; we have arbitrarily assigned this task to MoveL.

Once MoveL has found a component greater than the partitioning element, it cannot immediately swap this component with the component that R selects. MoveL must synchronize with MoveR; it must wait until MoveR has found a component that is less than the partitioning element. Similarly, MoveR must wait for MoveL to perform the swap before continuing to move R to the left. Furthermore, both MoveL and MoveR must synchronize with the main program; Split must wait until L and R have crossed before resuming execution.

MoveL has the following appearance:

```
PROCEDURE MoveL;
  (* moves L to the right *)
BEGIN
  WHILE L <= R DO
    IF array[L] > middleNumber THEN
      (* wait until MoveR is ready to swap *)
      Swap(array[L], array[R]);
      (* signal MoveR that the swap has been performed *)
    END;
    INC(L)
  END;
  (* signal Split that partitioning is complete *)
  (* terminate *)
END MoveL;
```

MoveR is similar, but does not call Swap:

```
PROCEDURE MoveR;
  (* moves R to the left *)
BEGIN
  WHILE L <= R DO
    IF middleNumber > array[R] THEN
      (* signal MoveL that MoveR is ready to swap *)
      (* wait until MoveL has performed the swap *)
    END;
    DEC(R)
  END;
  (* signal Split that partitioning is complete *)
  (* terminate *)
END MoveR;
```

Split looks like this:

```
PROCEDURE Split(lower, upper: INTEGER; VAR middle: INTEGER);
  (* partitions region of array between lower and upper so
     that all values to the left of "middle" are less than or
     equal to all values to its right *)
BEGIN
  middleNumber := array[lower];
  L := lower + 1;
  R := upper;
  (* initialize signals *)
  (* start MoveL and MoveR *)
  (* wait until partitioning is complete *)
  Swap(array[lower], array[R]);
  middle := R
END Split;
```

The order in which Split starts MoveL and MoveR is not important.

These outlines of MoveL, MoveR, and Split reveal a need for three SIGNAL variables: ReadyToSwap, SwapDone, and SplitDone. MoveL performs a WAIT operation on ReadyToSwap before swapping array[L] and array[R]; MoveR performs a SEND operation on ReadyToSwap to signal MoveL that it is ready for MoveL to perform the swap. MoveR performs a WAIT operation on SwapDone to give MoveL time to perform the swap; MoveL performs a SEND operation on SwapDone immediately after the swap. Split performs a WAIT operation on SplitDone after MoveL and MoveR begin execution; it resumes executing after either MoveL or MoveR has performed a SEND operation on SplitDone.

A closer look at MoveL and MoveR shows the need for a fourth SIGNAL variable, which we will call Terminate. We cannot afford to let MoveL or MoveR reach the end of its body, because the entire program would halt. Therefore, the last statement in both MoveL and MoveR is

```
WAIT(Terminate);
```

No SEND operation will ever be performed on Terminate, so MoveL and MoveR can never resume execution after performing the WAIT.

Using these four SIGNAL variables, our first attempt at writing MoveL might look like this:

```
PROCEDURE MoveL;
  (* moves L to the right *)
BEGIN
  WHILE L <= R DO
    IF array[L] > middleNumber THEN
      WAIT(ReadyToSwap);
      Swap(array[L], array[R]);
      SEND(SwapDone)
    END;
    INC(L)
  END;
  SEND(SplitDone);
  WAIT(Terminate)
END MoveL;
```

Unfortunately, this version of MoveL will not always behave properly. If MoveR performs a SEND on ReadyToSwap before MoveL performs its WAIT, MoveL will wait forever for a SEND that never comes. MoveR has a similar problem: If MoveL performs its SEND on SwapDone before MoveR performs its WAIT, MoveR will wait forever. We can fix the problem by introducing three BOOLEAN variables, one for each SIGNAL variable other than Terminate; we will call these readyToSwap, swapDone, and splitDone. Split initializes all three variables to FALSE. When performing a SEND, we set the corresponding BOOLEAN variable to TRUE:

```
readyToSwap := TRUE;
SEND(ReadyToSwap);
```

Before performing a WAIT on a particular signal, we first test the corresponding BOOLEAN variable. If the variable has the value FALSE, then no SEND operation has been performed, so it is safe to perform the WAIT. But if the variable is TRUE, then a SEND operation has already been performed, so we should not call WAIT. In either case, we subsequently set the BOOLEAN variable to FALSE:

```
IF NOT readyToSwap THEN
  WAIT(ReadyToSwap)
END;
readyToSwap := FALSE;
```

We now present a revised version of the Partition module that uses processes instead of coroutines to partition an array. We can test this module by using it to replace the version of Partition in the Quicksort program of Section 12.1. We need make only one change in the rest of Quicksort—it should import Processes instead of SYSTEM.

```
MODULE Partition;
  (* exports Split procedure *)

  FROM Processes IMPORT SIGNAL, StartProcess, SEND, WAIT, Init;
  IMPORT array;

  EXPORT Split;

  CONST wkspSize = 1000;

  VAR readyToSwap, swapDone, splitDone: BOOLEAN;
      ReadyToSwap, SwapDone, SplitDone, Terminate: SIGNAL;
      middleNumber: CARDINAL;
      L, R: INTEGER;

  PROCEDURE Swap(VAR i, j: CARDINAL);
    (* exchanges the contents of i and j *)
    VAR temp: CARDINAL;
  BEGIN
    temp := i;
    i := j;
    j := temp
  END Swap;
```

```
PROCEDURE MoveR;
  (* moves R to the left *)
BEGIN
  WHILE L <= R DO
    IF middleNumber > array[R] THEN
      readyToSwap := TRUE;
      SEND(ReadyToSwap);
      IF NOT swapDone THEN
        WAIT(SwapDone)
      END;
      swapDone := FALSE
    END;
    DEC(R)
  END;
  splitDone := TRUE;
  SEND(SplitDone);
  WAIT(Terminate)
END MoveR;

PROCEDURE MoveL;
  (* moves L to the right *)
BEGIN
  WHILE L <= R DO
    IF array[L] > middleNumber THEN
      IF NOT readyToSwap THEN
        WAIT(ReadyToSwap)
      END;
      readyToSwap := FALSE;
      Swap(array[L], array[R]);
      swapDone := TRUE;
      SEND(SwapDone)
    END;
    INC(L)
  END;
  splitDone := TRUE;
  SEND(SplitDone);
  WAIT(Terminate)
END MoveL;

PROCEDURE Split(lower, upper: INTEGER; VAR middle: INTEGER);
  (* partitions region of array between lower and upper so
     that all values to the left of "middle" are less than
     or equal to all values to its right *)
BEGIN
  middleNumber := array[lower];
  L := lower + 1;
  R := upper;
  readyToSwap := FALSE;
  swapDone := FALSE;
```

```
    splitDone := FALSE;
    Init(ReadyToSwap);
    Init(SwapDone);
    Init(SplitDone);
    Init(Terminate);
    StartProcess(MoveL, wkspSize);
    StartProcess(MoveR, wkspSize);
    IF NOT splitDone THEN
      WAIT(SplitDone)
    END;
    Swap(array[lower], array[R]);
    middle := R
  END Split;

END Partition;
```

12.3 An Alternative to the Processes Module

Wirth's Processes module can be difficult to use, because it provides no direct way for a process to terminate without halting the program. Another disadvantage of Processes is its reliance on signals as a method of synchronization. As we saw in Section 12.2, a SEND operation on a signal is lost if no processes are waiting on that signal. To write the Quicksort program using Processes, we needed additional BOOLEAN variables.

When Processes is not suitable, programmers can use NEWPROCESS and TRANSFER to create their own modules for process management. In this section, we present one such module, which we call ScheduledProcesses. Here is the definition part of ScheduledProcesses:

```
DEFINITION MODULE ScheduledProcesses;
  (* allows the execution of processes under the control of a
     scheduler; processes are synchronized using semaphores *)

  TYPE Semaphore;

  PROCEDURE MakeReady(proc: PROC; wkspSize: CARDINAL);
    (* prepares a process for execution *)

  PROCEDURE Scheduler;
    (* begins execution of processes that have been prepared
       by previous calls of MakeReady *)

  PROCEDURE Terminate;
    (* terminates the current process *)
```

```
  PROCEDURE InitSem(VAR sem: Semaphore; value: CARDINAL);
    (* initializes a semaphore by setting its count to "value"
       and making its queue empty *)

  PROCEDURE P(VAR sem: Semaphore);
    (* decrements semaphore count; if count is less than zero,
       current process is suspended and put on semaphore queue
    *)

  PROCEDURE V(VAR sem: Semaphore);
    (* increments semaphore count; if count is less than or
       equal to zero, enables a process on semaphore queue *)

END ScheduledProcesses.
```

A program that uses the `Processes` module must call `StartProcess` once for each process:

```
StartProcess(P1, wkspSize);
StartProcess(P2, wkspSize);
```

`StartProcess` not only creates a new process but also allows the process to begin executing immediately. When a program uses `ScheduledProcesses` instead of `Processes`, calls of `MakeReady` replace calls of `StartProcess`. `MakeReady` prepares a process to execute but, unlike `StartProcess`, does not allow the process to begin executing. After calls of `MakeReady` have created the desired number of processes, a call of the `Scheduler` procedure allows the processes to begin executing:

```
MakeReady(P1, wkspSize);
MakeReady(P2, wkspSize);
Scheduler;
```

When we call `Scheduler`, all processes that previous calls of `MakeReady` have prepared are free to begin executing; each process continues to execute until it calls `Terminate`. (If a process neglects to call `Terminate` and instead "falls off the end" of its defining procedure, the entire program terminates.)

The `Processes` module treats the main program as though it were a process itself; after calls of `StartProcess`, the main program is free to resume executing, along with the processes it created. With `ScheduledProcesses`, however, the main program does not execute as a process; after a call of `Scheduler`, the main program waits for all the created processes to terminate before it resumes executing.

For process synchronization, `ScheduledProcesses` provides *semaphores* rather than signals. Semaphores are similar to signals, but are more versatile. Instead of `WAIT` and `SEND`, `ScheduledProcesses` provides similar operations named P and V. Like a signal, each semaphore has an associated queue containing processes suspended by a P operation. Unlike a signal, however, each semaphore also has a *count*. When the count is greater than zero, a process performing a P operation is not put on the queue, but continues executing. More precisely, P performs the following actions when called:

> Decrement the semaphore count. If the count is less than 0, then suspend the current process, put it at the end of the semaphore queue, and transfer control to a process that is ready to execute.

The V operation allows a process waiting on a semaphore queue to resume execution. When called, V performs the following actions:

> Increment the semaphore count. If the count is less than or equal to 0, remove the first process from the semaphore queue and allow it to resume execution.

Each V operation increases the semaphore count. A positive count indicates the number of processes that may subsequently execute the P operation without being suspended.

We can use semaphores to solve a great many synchronization problems. Consider the problem of controlling access to several identical resources (three printers, say). Using semaphores, we can ensure that, once all the printers are in use, processes requesting a printer must wait. Initially, we create a printer semaphore and set its count to the number of resources available (three, in our example). We then require that a process wishing to use a printer must perform a P operation on the printer semaphore. We also require each process to perform a V operation on the semaphore when it has finished using the printer. The P operation ensures that at most three processes can be printing at one time; after three P operations, the semaphore count will be zero, forcing other processes to wait for a printer. The V operation increments the semaphore count and allows one waiting process (if any are waiting) to gain control of a printer.

Before we perform any P or V operations on a semaphore, we must initialize it by a call of InitSem. InitSem empties the semaphore queue and sets the semaphore count to a specified value.

Implementing the ScheduledProcesses Module

To implement ScheduledProcesses, we must maintain a queue of processes for each semaphore. In addition, we need a special queue, the *ready queue*, containing processes that are ready to execute when the processor becomes available. These queues will have type ProcessQueue. To simplify ScheduledProcesses, we will write a library module called ProcessQueues that exports ProcessQueue and procedures for manipulating process queues. The definition part of ProcessQueues has the following appearance (we leave the implementation part as an exercise):

```
DEFINITION MODULE ProcessQueues;
  (* exports type ProcessQueue and procedures for operating on
     values of this type *)

  FROM SYSTEM IMPORT ADDRESS;

  TYPE ProcessQueue;

  PROCEDURE InsertAtEnd(VAR queue: ProcessQueue;
                        process: ADDRESS);
    (* inserts a process at the end of the queue *)

  PROCEDURE DeleteFromFront(VAR queue: ProcessQueue;
                            VAR process: ADDRESS);
    (* deletes a process from the front of the queue *)

  PROCEDURE MakeQueueEmpty(VAR queue: ProcessQueue);
    (* makes the queue empty *)

  PROCEDURE IsQueueEmpty(queue: ProcessQueue): BOOLEAN;
    (* returns TRUE if the queue is empty, FALSE otherwise *)

END ProcessQueues.
```

Each call of MakeReady creates a new process (by calling NEWPROCESS), then adds it to the end of the ready queue. The Scheduler procedure selects the next process to execute. Provided that the ready queue is not empty, Scheduler removes the first process from the queue and transfers control to it. (If the queue is empty, Scheduler returns, thus terminating scheduled execution of processes.) Control returns to Scheduler for one of two reasons: either (1) a process executed a P operation on a semaphore whose count was less than or equal to zero, or (2) a process called the Terminate procedure. Scheduler uses a variable named event to distinguish between these possibilities. If the value of event is block (indicating that the current process is to be suspended as the result of a P operation), Scheduler puts the process at the end of the appropriate semaphore queue. If the value of event is terminate, Scheduler makes no attempt to save the current process on a semaphore queue or the ready queue, thus preventing subsequent scheduling of the process.

We implement a semaphore as a pointer to a record containing a count and a process queue. The InitSem procedure initializes a semaphore by allocating space for one of these records, setting the semaphore's count to the value supplied as a parameter, and making the semaphore's queue empty.

The P procedure decrements the semaphore's count; if the count becomes less than 0, P transfers control to Scheduler (by a call of TRANSFER); Scheduler puts the current process at the end of the appropriate semaphore queue and transfers control to one of the processes on the ready queue.

The V procedure increments the semaphore's count; if the count remains less than or equal to zero, V removes the first process on the semaphore queue and puts it at the end of the ready queue.

Here is the implementation part of ScheduledProcesses:

```
IMPLEMENTATION MODULE ScheduledProcesses;

  FROM SYSTEM IMPORT ADDRESS, NEWPROCESS, TRANSFER;
  FROM Storage IMPORT ALLOCATE;
  FROM ProcessQueues IMPORT ProcessQueue, InsertAtEnd,
                            DeleteFromFront, MakeQueueEmpty,
                            IsQueueEmpty;

  TYPE Semaphore = POINTER TO SemaphoreRecord;
       SemaphoreRecord = RECORD
                           count: INTEGER;
                           queue: ProcessQueue
                         END;

  VAR readyQueue: ProcessQueue;
      schedProcess, currentProcess: ADDRESS;   (* coroutines *)
      currentSemaphore: Semaphore;
      event: (block, terminate);

  PROCEDURE MakeReady(proc: PROC; wkspSize: CARDINAL);
    (* prepares a process for execution *)
    VAR wksp: ADDRESS;
        process: ADDRESS;   (* coroutine *)
  BEGIN
    ALLOCATE(wksp, wkspSize);
    NEWPROCESS(proc, wksp, wkspSize, process);
    InsertAtEnd(readyQueue, process)
  END MakeReady;

  PROCEDURE Scheduler;
    (* begins execution of processes that have been prepared
       by previous calls of MakeReady *)
  BEGIN
    WHILE NOT IsQueueEmpty(readyQueue) DO
      DeleteFromFront(readyQueue, currentProcess);
      TRANSFER(schedProcess, currentProcess);
      CASE event OF
        block:     InsertAtEnd(currentSemaphore^.queue,
                               currentProcess) |
        terminate: (* do nothing *)
```

```
        END
      END
    END Scheduler;

    PROCEDURE Terminate;
      (* terminates the current process *)
    BEGIN
      event := terminate;
      TRANSFER(currentProcess, schedProcess)
    END Terminate;

    PROCEDURE InitSem(VAR sem: Semaphore; value: CARDINAL);
      (* initializes a semaphore by setting its count to "value"
         and making its queue empty *)
    BEGIN
      ALLOCATE(sem, SIZE(SemaphoreRecord));
      sem^.count := value;
      MakeQueueEmpty(sem^.queue)
    END InitSem;

    PROCEDURE P(VAR sem: Semaphore);
      (* decrements semaphore count; if count is less than zero,
         current process is suspended and put on semaphore queue
      *)
    BEGIN
      DEC(sem^.count);
      IF sem^.count < 0 THEN
        event := block;
        currentSemaphore := sem;
        TRANSFER(currentProcess, schedProcess)
      END
    END P;

    PROCEDURE V(VAR sem: Semaphore);
      (* increments semaphore count; if count is less than or
         equal to zero, enables a process on semaphore queue *)
      VAR process: ADDRESS;    (* coroutine *)
    BEGIN
      INC(sem^.count);
      IF sem^.count <= 0 THEN
        DeleteFromFront(sem^.queue, process);
        InsertAtEnd(readyQueue, process);
      END
    END V;

  BEGIN
    MakeQueueEmpty(readyQueue)
  END ScheduledProcesses.
```

EXAMPLE **Using** ScheduledProcesses **to Partition an Array**

We can easily modify the Partition module of Section 12.2 to use ScheduledProcesses instead of Processes. The Semaphore variables ready and done replace the SIGNAL variables ReadyToSwap and SwapDone. The variable SplitDone is no longer necessary, because Scheduler makes the main program wait for both MoveL and MoveR to terminate before it can resume executing. Similarly, the Terminate procedure removes the need for the Terminate variable. We can also remove the BOOLEAN variables readyToSwap, swapDone, and splitDone; using semaphores instead of signals makes these variables unnecessary. The key changes occur in MoveL and MoveR. When MoveL locates an array component larger than middleNumber, it executes the following statements:

```
P(ready);
Swap(array[L], array[R]);
V(done);
```

By performing a P operation on the ready semaphore (whose count is 0 initially), MoveL suspends itself until MoveR performs a V operation. When MoveR locates an array component smaller than middleNumber, it performs a V operation immediately followed by a P operation:

```
V(ready);
P(done);
```

The V operation allows MoveL to resume execution; the P operation suspends MoveR until MoveL performs a V operation on the done semaphore (which it does after exchanging array[L] and array[R]).

The revised version of the Partition module follows. As in Section 12.2, we omit the rest of the Quicksort program. Outside the Partition module, Quicksort is unchanged, except that it imports ScheduledProcesses instead of Processes.

```
MODULE Partition;
  (* exports Split procedure *)

  FROM ScheduledProcesses IMPORT Semaphore, MakeReady, P, V,
                                 Scheduler, Terminate, InitSem;
  IMPORT array;

  EXPORT Split;

  CONST wkspSize = 1000;

  VAR ready, done: Semaphore;
      middleNumber: CARDINAL;
      L, R: INTEGER;
```

```
PROCEDURE Swap(VAR i, j: CARDINAL);
  (* exchanges the contents of i and j *)
  VAR temp: CARDINAL;
BEGIN
  temp := i;
  i := j;
  j := temp
END Swap;

PROCEDURE MoveR;
  (* moves R to the left *)
BEGIN
  WHILE L <= R DO
    IF middleNumber > array[R] THEN
      V(ready);
      P(done)
    END;
    DEC(R)
  END;
  Terminate
END MoveR;

PROCEDURE MoveL;
  (* moves L to the right *)
BEGIN
  WHILE L <= R DO
    IF array[L] > middleNumber THEN
      P(ready);
      Swap(array[L], array[R]);
      V(done)
    END;
    INC(L)
  END;
  Terminate
END MoveL;

PROCEDURE Split(lower, upper: INTEGER; VAR middle: INTEGER);
  (* partitions region of array between lower and upper so
     that all values to the left of "middle" are less than
     or equal to all values to its right *)
BEGIN
  middleNumber := array[lower];
  L := lower + 1;
  R := upper;
  InitSem(ready, 0);
  InitSem(done, 0);
  MakeReady(MoveL, wkspSize);
  MakeReady(MoveR, wkspSize);
  Scheduler;
  Swap(array[lower], array[R]);
```

```
      middle := R
    END Split;

  END Partition;
```

12.4 Interrupt Handling

Most single-processor systems provide a limited form of true concurrency—they allow a program to execute at the same time that input/output operations are taking place. Of course, the program must pause occasionally to allow data transfer to or from an I/O device; many computer systems provide *interrupts* for this purpose. An interrupt is a hardware signal generated when a particular event occurs (such as the completion of an I/O operation). The procedure IOTRANSFER allows programs to detect and respond to interrupts. (Although Wirth states in *Programming in Modula-2* that IOTRANSFER is specific to the PDP-11 computer, Modula-2 systems for other computers often support it. The IOTRANSFER examples in this section were tested on an IBM Personal Computer using the Logitech Modula-2/86 system.)

Using IOTRANSFER, a program can suspend a coroutine until a specified interrupt occurs. The coroutine serves as an *interrupt handler*—when control is transferred to it as the result of an interrupt, the coroutine does whatever is necessary to respond to the interrupt and then suspends itself until the next interrupt.

Three steps are involved in creating an interrupt handler. First, the program must create a coroutine (by calling NEWPROCESS) to serve as the interrupt handler. Second, the program must call TRANSFER to transfer control to the interrupt handler. After the interrupt handler has initialized its local variables (and perhaps initialized the device that it manages), it performs the third step by calling IOTRANSFER, which suspends the interrupt handler until a particular interrupt occurs. The call of IOTRANSFER must specify, by giving an *interrupt vector* number, which interrupt the handler should wait for. (Programmers can find information about these numbers in the manual for a particular computer system.) The call of IOTRANSFER must also specify what coroutine to execute after the interrupt handler is suspended.

IOTRANSFER has the following heading:

```
PROCEDURE IOTRANSFER(VAR p1, p2: ADDRESS; va: CARDINAL);
```

The variables p1 and p2 are references to coroutines, while va is an interrupt vector number. In the Second Edition of *Programming in Modula-2*, p1 and p2 were of type PROCESS; in the Third Edition, they have type ADDRESS. According to the Second Edition, if a Modula-2 system provides IOTRANSFER, the SYSTEM module must export it. The Third Edition removes this restriction, so some other module may export IOTRANSFER.

A call of IOTRANSFER suspends the current coroutine (the interrupt handler), stores a reference to this coroutine in p1, and allows the coroutine referenced by p2 to resume execution. In addition, IOTRANSFER "installs" p1 as the handler for the interrupt specified by va. When this interrupt next occurs, the following actions take place:

1. The current coroutine is suspended.
2. A reference to this coroutine is stored in p2.
3. The coroutine referenced by p1 (the interrupt handler) resumes execution.

These actions are identical to those performed for an ordinary TRANSFER; the interrupt essentially causes the insertion of a call of TRANSFER wherever the program happens to be when interrupted.

After responding to an interrupt, an interrupt handler executes IOTRANSFER to suspend itself until the next interrupt occurs and at the same time to return control to the interrupted coroutine. This call of IOTRANSFER is usually identical to the call that originally installed the interrupt handler, suggesting that we should enclose IOTRANSFER in a LOOP statement. In fact, most interrupt handlers have the following appearance:

```
PROCEDURE InterruptHandler;
  (* declarations of local variables *)
BEGIN
  (* initialize local variables *)
  LOOP
    IOTRANSFER(handler, mainProcess, interruptVector);
    (* respond to interrupt *)
  END
END InterruptHandler;
```

To initialize the interrupt handler, the main program creates a coroutine from InterruptHandler and transfers control to it:

```
NEWPROCESS(InterruptHandler, ADR(wksp), SIZE(wksp), handler);
TRANSFER(mainProcess, handler);
```

We can summarize the actions that take place from this point as follows:

1. Control is transferred to the interrupt handler.
2. The interrupt handler initializes its local variables, then calls the IOTRANSFER procedure.
3. IOTRANSFER installs the interrupt handler, then suspends it and transfers control to the main program.
4. When the specified interrupt occurs, the currently executing coroutine is suspended and assigned to the variable mainProcess; the handler resumes from the point just after the IOTRANSFER operation. When control reaches the top of the LOOP statement, the call of IOTRANSFER

reinstalls the interrupt handler (notice that this action is probably superfluous) and transfers control to the interrupted coroutine (referenced by `mainProcess`).

`IOTRANSFER` can be hard to understand because it serves two distinct purposes. The first call of `IOTRANSFER` installs the interrupt handler. Subsequent calls of `IOTRANSFER` are for the purpose of resuming an interrupted coroutine. These actions are so similar that Modula-2 combines them into one procedure.

Module Priorities

It is important to ensure that an interrupt handler is not itself interrupted by the same interrupt (or, in some cases, by other interrupts). Modula-2 allows the programmer to disable interrupts within a module by specifying a *priority* in the heading of that module. A priority is a constant expression of type `CARDINAL` enclosed in brackets (see Figure 12.2). A priority can appear in the heading of a program module, implementation module, or local module. (A definition module cannot be given a priority, because definition modules contain no statements and therefore cannot be interrupted.)

Figure 12.2 **Priority**

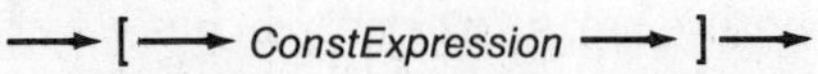

Wirth uses the term *monitor* to describe a module whose heading specifies a priority; however, this usage differs somewhat from the use of the term outside Modula-2. In operating systems terminology, a monitor is a mechanism for sharing data among several processes. The monitor hides the shared data, allowing access only through operations that it provides; in addition, the monitor permits only one process at a time to access the data (this property is called *mutual exclusion*). We can use a module whose heading contains a priority to implement a monitor, but not every such module is a monitor.

On some computers (including the PDP-11, the machine on which Modula-2 was first implemented), each interrupt has an associated priority. Modula-2 systems for such computers interpret the priority in a module heading as a command to disable interrupts of equal or lower priority. Thus, when control enters a module whose heading specifies a priority value of n, interrupts with priority n or less are disabled. When control leaves the module, the previous priority is restored. (Control enters a module when its body is executed or one of its procedures is called.)

Procedures within a module of priority n may call procedures outside the module. These procedures may be in modules of equal priority, greater priority, or no priority. (Modula-2 forbids calling a procedure in a module of lower priority.) When control enters a module for which the programmer has specified no priority, the priority level remains unchanged. (For example, if a procedure in a module with priority 5 calls a procedure in a module with no priority, interrupts of priority 5 or less remain disabled.) Calling a procedure in a module of higher priority (*m*, say) causes interrupts with priority *m* or less to be disabled temporarily; when the procedure returns, the priority returns to its old value.

On computers that do not assign priorities to interrupts, Modula-2 systems may still allow module priorities, translating them internally into a more suitable form. Some Modula-2 systems provide alternate ways to disable interrupts.

Every module that contains a call of `IOTRANSFER` must be given a priority. However, modules that have a priority should be kept small to avoid losing interrupts unnecessarily. Typically, programmers attach priorities to local modules rather than to entire compilation units, as the following example illustrates.

EXAMPLE PROGRAM

An Interrupt-driven Alarm Clock

The program `Alarm` provides a simple example of interrupt handling. `Alarm` allows the user to set an alarm to go off in a specified number of seconds. To keep track of time, the program declares a local module `Timer` that contains a handler for the timer interrupt.

After prompting the user to enter the number of seconds to wait (which it stores in the variable `waitTime`), `Alarm` calls `StartTimer` (exported by the local module). `StartTimer` installs the interrupt handler, which initializes `elapsedTime` to 0. The interrupt handler responds to all subsequent timer interrupts, incrementing the variable `elapsedTime` once a second. Meanwhile, the main program waits until `elapsedTime` reaches `waitTime`, when it writes a message and causes the terminal to beep.

The program is designed for the IBM Personal Computer, although it can easily be adapted to other machines. On the IBM PC, the number `1CH` identifies the timer interrupt. The interrupt occurs every 5/91st of a second. For accurate timing, the interrupt handler uses a variable called `ticksTimes5`, which measures elapsed time in units of 1/91st of a second. At each clock tick, the handler adds 5 to `ticksTimes5`. When `ticksTimes5` reaches or exceeds 91, another second of time has passed, so the handler increments the variable `elapsedTime` and subtracts 91 from `ticksTimes5`. In this way, any extra fraction of a second is "saved" toward the next second.

To avoid the possibility that the interrupt handler might be interrupted while it is servicing an interrupt, the heading of the `Timer` module specifies a priority of 7. Notice that it would be wrong to include a priority in the heading of `Alarm` itself, because doing so would disable the timer interrupt for the lifetime of the program. (The choice of 7 as a priority depends on the system. In the Logitech Modula-2/86 system, the highest priority is 7.)

```
MODULE Alarm;
  (* sets off an alarm in a specified number of seconds *)

  IMPORT SYSTEM;
  FROM InOut IMPORT ReadCard, Write, WriteString, WriteLn;
```

```
    CONST bel = 7C;

    VAR waitTime: CARDINAL;    (* in seconds *)

    MODULE Timer[7];
      (* exports StartTimer and elapsedTime *)

      FROM SYSTEM IMPORT WORD, ADDRESS, ADR, NEWPROCESS,
                         TRANSFER, IOTRANSFER;

      EXPORT StartTimer, elapsedTime;

      CONST timerInt = 1CH;    (* IBM PC timer interrupt *)
            wkspSize = 1000;

      VAR main, timer: ADDRESS;    (* coroutines *)
          wksp: ARRAY [1..wkspSize] OF WORD;
          elapsedTime: CARDINAL;    (* in seconds *)

      PROCEDURE InterruptHandler;
        (* handles timer interrupts; updates elapsedTime every
           second *)
        VAR ticksTimes5: CARDINAL;
      BEGIN
        elapsedTime := 0;
        ticksTimes5 := 0;
        LOOP
          IOTRANSFER(timer, main, timerInt);
          INC(ticksTimes5, 5);
          IF ticksTimes5 >= 91 THEN
            DEC(ticksTimes5, 91);
            INC(elapsedTime)
          END
        END
      END InterruptHandler;

      PROCEDURE StartTimer;
        (* installs timer interrupt handler *)
      BEGIN
        NEWPROCESS(InterruptHandler, ADR(wksp), SIZE(wksp),
                   timer);
        TRANSFER(main, timer)
      END StartTimer;

    END Timer;

  BEGIN
    WriteString("Enter time to wait (in seconds): ");
    ReadCard(waitTime);
```

```
    WriteLn;
    StartTimer;
    REPEAT
      (* wait *)
    UNTIL elapsedTime >= waitTime;
    WriteString("Time is up.");
    WriteLn;
    Write(bel)    (* sound the alarm *)
  END Alarm.
```

EXAMPLE A Driver for the IBM PC Keyboard

A common form of interrupt handler is the *device driver*, which controls the transfer of information to or from a hardware device such as a keyboard, printer, or disk drive. To illustrate how to write a device driver in Modula-2, we will develop a module, called `Keys`, that contains a keyboard driver. The driver detects characters typed at the keyboard and puts them into a buffer. The `Keys` module exports a `ReadChar` procedure for fetching a character from the buffer. `Keys` also exports a `KeyPressed` function that indicates whether any characters have been typed but not yet read (that is, `KeyPressed` returns `TRUE` if the buffer is not empty). Here is the definition part of `Keys`:

```
DEFINITION MODULE Keys;
  (* provides direct access to the keyboard *)

  PROCEDURE ReadChar(VAR ch: CHAR);
    (* reads a character typed at the keyboard; stores 0C
       into ch if there is no character to be read *)

  PROCEDURE KeyPressed(): BOOLEAN;
    (* returns TRUE if there is a character to be read, FALSE
       otherwise *)

END Keys.
```

The implementation part of `Keys` has a simple structure; unfortunately, its details are somewhat complicated. `Keys` maintains a queue of characters that have been typed but not yet read. Each time the user types a character, the module puts it at the end of this queue; each call of `ReadChar` removes the first character on the queue. For efficiency, we do not hide the structure of the queue in another module. Instead, `Keys` simply uses a one-dimensional array of characters (called `queue`), together with two variables `head` and `tail`, which mark the positions of the first and last characters in the queue, respectively. These variables "wrap around" the end of the array to make it appear as though the first character in the array immediately follows the last character.

The heart of the Keys module is the KeyboardDriver procedure, which—as a coroutine—handles keyboard interrupts. The details of KeyboardDriver depend heavily on the architecture of the IBM PC. On the PC, each time the user presses or releases a key, an interrupt occurs through vector 9H. A *scan code* indicating which key was pressed (or released) is then available, not in a memory location, but through port 60H (a *port* is a path for data transmission). On machines that use port I/O, Modula-2 systems usually provide—as part of the SYSTEM module—special procedures for performing port operations. In the Logitech Modula-2/86 system, for example, the SYSTEM module exports procedures INBYTE and OUTBYTE for receiving a byte from a port or sending a byte to a port. KeyboardDriver uses INBYTE to receive the scan code for the pressed or released key. After obtaining the scan code, KeyboardDriver must acknowledge receipt by

receiving a status byte from port 61H
setting bit 7 of the status byte
sending the status byte to port 61H
clearing bit 7 of the status byte
sending the status byte to port 61H

Fortunately, these operations are easy to perform in Modula-2 by using INBYTE, OUTBYTE, INCL, and EXCL.

After KeyboardDriver has obtained a scan code, it must determine what character the code represents, then put the character at the end of the queue. The ConvertToChar function converts a scan code to a character. The IBM PC keyboard has 83 keys; when pressed, each key produces a unique scan code (a number between 1 and 83). In addition, each key sends a scan code when released; each key's "released" scan code is equal to its "pressed" code plus 128. (For example, the left shift key sends scan code 42 when pressed and 170 when released.) Most key releases are meaningless. The only keys whose release is important are the shift, Ctrl, and Alt keys that, when pressed and held, affect the meaning of other keys. When the user presses one of the two shift keys, for example, we must translate all subsequent key presses into "shifted" characters until the user releases the shift key.

The ConvertToChar procedure depends on the variables leftShift, rightShift, shiftedKeys, and unshiftedKeys. The BOOLEAN variable leftShift is TRUE if the user has pressed but not released the left shift key; rightShift is analogous. ConvertToChar uses the strings shiftedKeys and unshiftedKeys to translate a scan code into a character; shiftedKeys[i] contains the shifted character corresponding to scan code i, and unshiftedKeys[i] contains the unshifted character corresponding to scan code i.

For simplicity, ConvertToChar recognizes only scan codes between 1 and 58. It translates the codes between 59 and 83 (generated by the function keys and the keys in the numeric keypad) into the null character. (KeyboardDriver ignores the null character and does not put it into the queue.) To further simplify ConvertToChar, we will ignore the Ctrl, PrtSc, Alt, and Caps Lock keys.

```
IMPLEMENTATION MODULE Keys[7];

  FROM SYSTEM IMPORT WORD, ADDRESS, ADR, NEWPROCESS, TRANSFER,
                     IOTRANSFER, INBYTE, OUTBYTE;

  CONST queueCapacity = 16;
        wkspSize = 1000;
        keyboardInt = 9H;
        numKeys = 58;

  VAR queueLength: [0..queueCapacity];
      head, tail: [0..queueCapacity-1];
      queue: ARRAY [0..queueCapacity-1] OF CHAR;
      wksp: ARRAY [1..wkspSize] OF WORD;
      main, driver: ADDRESS;    (* coroutines *)
      unshiftedKeys, shiftedKeys: ARRAY [0..numKeys] OF CHAR;
      leftShift, rightShift: BOOLEAN;

  PROCEDURE ReadChar(VAR ch: CHAR);
    (* reads a character typed at the keyboard; stores 0C
       into ch if there is no character to be read *)
  BEGIN
    IF queueLength > 0 THEN
      ch := queue[head];
      head := (head + 1) MOD queueCapacity;
      DEC(queueLength)
    ELSE
      ch := 0C
    END
  END ReadChar;

  PROCEDURE KeyPressed(): BOOLEAN;
    (* returns TRUE if there is a character to be read, FALSE
       otherwise *)
  BEGIN
    RETURN queueLength > 0
  END KeyPressed;

  PROCEDURE ConvertToChar(scanCode: CARDINAL): CHAR;
    (* converts a scan code into a character *)
    VAR ch: CHAR;
  BEGIN
    ch := 0C;
    IF scanCode >= 128 THEN              (* key released        *)
      IF scanCode = 170 THEN             (* left shift released *)
        leftShift := FALSE
```

```
      ELSIF scanCode = 182 THEN       (* right shift released *)
        rightShift := FALSE
      END;
    ELSIF scanCode > 58 THEN
      (* ignore *)
    ELSIF scanCode = 42 THEN          (* left shift pressed   *)
      leftShift := TRUE
    ELSIF scanCode = 54 THEN          (* right shift pressed  *)
      rightShift := TRUE;
    ELSIF leftShift OR rightShift THEN
      ch := shiftedKeys[scanCode]
    ELSE
      ch := unshiftedKeys[scanCode]
    END;
    RETURN ch
  END ConvertToChar;

  PROCEDURE KeyboardDriver;
    (* handles keyboard interrupt by fetching scan code,
       converting to character, and storing in queue *)
    CONST dataPort = 60H;
          controlPort = 61H;
    VAR scanCode: CARDINAL;
        status: BITSET;
        charRead: CHAR;
  BEGIN
    LOOP
      IOTRANSFER(driver, main, keyboardInt);
      INBYTE(dataPort, scanCode);     (* read scan code *)
      INBYTE(controlPort, status);    (* read status    *)
      INCL(status, 7);
      OUTBYTE(controlPort, status);   (* send acknowledgement  *)
      EXCL(status, 7);
      OUTBYTE(controlPort, status);   (* restore former status *)
      charRead := ConvertToChar(scanCode);
      IF (charRead # 0C) & (queueLength < queueCapacity) THEN
        queue[tail] := charRead;
        tail := (tail + 1) MOD queueCapacity;
        INC(queueLength)
      END
    END
  END KeyboardDriver;

BEGIN
  unshiftedKeys :=
" 1234567890-= qwertyuiop[] asdfghjkl;'' \zxcvbnm,./ *  ";
  unshiftedKeys[1] := 33C;    (* escape    *)
  unshiftedKeys[14] := 10C;   (* backspace *)
  unshiftedKeys[15] := 11C;   (* tab       *)
```

```
    unshiftedKeys[28] := 15C;    (* return    *)
    unshiftedKeys[29] := 0C;     (* control   *)
    unshiftedKeys[56] := 0C;     (* alt       *)
    unshiftedKeys[58] := 0C;     (* caps lock *)

    shiftedKeys :=
'  !@#$%^&*()_+  QWERTYUIOP{}  ASDFGHJKL:"~ |ZXCVBNM<>?      ';
    shiftedKeys[1]  := 33C;    (* escape       *)
    shiftedKeys[14] := 10C;    (* backspace    *)
    shiftedKeys[15] := 10C;    (* back tab     *)
    shiftedKeys[28] := 15C;    (* return       *)
    shiftedKeys[29] := 0C;     (* control      *)
    shiftedKeys[55] := 0C;     (* print screen *)
    shiftedKeys[56] := 0C;     (* alt          *)
    shiftedKeys[58] := 0C;     (* caps lock    *)

    leftShift := FALSE;
    rightShift := FALSE;
    queueLength := 0;
    head := 0;
    tail := 0;
    NEWPROCESS(KeyboardDriver, ADR(wksp), SIZE(wksp), driver);
    TRANSFER(main, driver)
  END Keys.
```

An operating system would normally supply the service that `Keys` provides. However, to run without operating system support, a program must install its own device drivers, including a keyboard driver. Even when a program does have operating system support, it can sometimes be convenient to install a custom keyboard driver. An editor, for example, may wish to assign special meanings to certain keys or key combinations. A program may also wish to provide a larger buffer than normal.

Problems with `IOTRANSFER`

Interrupt handling using `IOTRANSFER` is best reserved for programs that will run without operating system support. (Of course, operating systems themselves fall in this category.) Installing an interrupt handler on a multiuser system is not feasible because doing so would affect other users. (For this reason, `IOTRANSFER` is not a mandatory feature of Modula-2.)

Even on single-user systems, `IOTRANSFER` can be difficult to use because installing an interrupt handler causes the old interrupt handler (which most likely belongs to the operating system) to be lost. Consequently, some Modula-2 systems provide special procedures for saving an interrupt handler and later restoring it.

Another problem is that IOTRANSFER requires a relatively large amount of time. Servicing an interrupt using IOTRANSFER causes two coroutine transfers (one when the control is transferred to the interrupt handler and one when the interrupted coroutine resumes). A coroutine transfer is relatively time-consuming, as Section 12.1 noted. When interrupts occur frequently or when rapid response to an interrupt is essential, the IOTRANSFER mechanism may be too slow. Therefore, some Modula-2 systems provide ways of installing interrupt handlers so that handling an interrupt requires less overhead.

12.5 Interrupt-driven Process Scheduling

The implementations of Wirth's `Processes` module (Section 12.2) and the `ScheduledProcesses` module (Section 12.3) share a fundamental weakness. Because both implementations simulate concurrency by switching among processes, it is important to allow all processes an equitable—although not necessarily equal—amount of time to execute. Unfortunately, the implementations discussed in these sections do not guarantee that each process receives its "fair share" of processor time. The implementation of `Processes` allows a process to execute indefinitely, provided that it does not perform a `WAIT` or SEND operation. `ScheduledProcesses` is even worse: only a `P` operation (or a call of `Terminate`) can perform a process switch. Neither module will interrupt a process that is "hogging" the processor.

This weakness does not reflect an inherent problem with these modules but rather the primitive nature of the implementations given. To make the scheduling more fair, we can use the system clock. The idea is to switch processes at each clock tick: When a clock interrupt occurs, we suspend the currently executing process and transfer control to some other process that is ready to run. Thus, any process that is ready to execute will not have to wait indefinitely to use the processor.

An Interrupt-driven Implementation of the `ScheduledProcesses` Module

To modify `ScheduledProcesses` to use the clock interrupt, we need only change the implementation part of the module; the definition part remains the same. The changes to the implementation part are relatively minor. The primary difference lies in the `Scheduler` procedure. In the new `ScheduledProcesses` module, `Scheduler` is an interrupt handler. When a client module calls `Scheduler`, it performs an IOTRANSFER to install itself as a handler for the timer interrupt. When the next timer interrupt occurs, `Scheduler` resumes execution; it first puts the currently executing process at the end of the ready queue, then transfers control to the first process on the ready queue.

Control returns to Scheduler in two other cases: (1) when a process needs to be suspended because of a P operation and (2) when a process wants to terminate. Because Scheduler suspended itself by calling IOTRANSFER, it cannot be resumed until a timer interrupt occurs. Fortunately, many computers provide a "software interrupt" instruction that triggers the timer interrupt and thereby transfers control to Scheduler. The Logitech Modula-2/86 version of SYSTEM exports a procedure called SWI that executes this instruction. Writing the P and Terminate procedures is now a simple matter. When it wants to suspend the current process, P sets the variable event to block and calls the SWI procedure. When Terminate wants to invoke the scheduler, it sets event to terminate and calls SWI.

The implementation part of ScheduledProcesses is much the same as in Section 12.3:

```
IMPLEMENTATION MODULE ScheduledProcesses[7];

  FROM SYSTEM IMPORT ADDRESS, NEWPROCESS, IOTRANSFER, SWI;
  FROM Storage IMPORT ALLOCATE;
  FROM ProcessQueues IMPORT ProcessQueue, InsertAtEnd,
                            DeleteFromFront, MakeQueueEmpty,
                            IsQueueEmpty;

  CONST timerInt = 1CH;    (* IBM PC timer interrupt *)

  TYPE Semaphore = POINTER TO SemaphoreRecord;
       SemaphoreRecord = RECORD
                           count: INTEGER;
                           queue: ProcessQueue
                         END;

  VAR readyQueue: ProcessQueue;
      schedProcess, currentProcess: ADDRESS;    (* coroutines *)
      currentSemaphore: Semaphore;
      event: (block, terminate, timeout);

  PROCEDURE MakeReady(proc: PROC; wkspSize: CARDINAL);
    (* prepares a process for execution *)
    VAR wksp: ADDRESS;
        process: ADDRESS;    (* coroutine *)
  BEGIN
    ALLOCATE(wksp, wkspSize);
    NEWPROCESS(proc, wksp, wkspSize, process);
    InsertAtEnd(readyQueue, process)
  END MakeReady;

  PROCEDURE Scheduler;
    (* begins execution of processes that have been prepared
       by previous calls of MakeReady *)
```

```
BEGIN
  WHILE NOT IsQueueEmpty(readyQueue) DO
    DeleteFromFront(readyQueue, currentProcess);
    IOTRANSFER(schedProcess, currentProcess, timerInt);
    CASE event OF
      block:      InsertAtEnd(currentSemaphore^.queue,
                              currentProcess) |
      terminate: (* do nothing *) |
      timeout:   InsertAtEnd(readyQueue, currentProcess)
    END;
    event := timeout    (* restore default event *)
  END
END Scheduler;

PROCEDURE Terminate;
  (* terminates the current process *)
BEGIN
  event := terminate;
  SWI(timerInt)
END Terminate;

PROCEDURE InitSem(VAR sem: Semaphore; value: CARDINAL);
  (* initializes a semaphore by setting its count to "value"
     and making its queue empty *)
BEGIN
  ALLOCATE(sem, SIZE(SemaphoreRecord));
  sem^.count := value;
  MakeQueueEmpty(sem^.queue)
END InitSem;

PROCEDURE P(VAR sem: Semaphore);
  (* decrements semaphore count; if count is less than zero,
     current process is suspended and put on semaphore queue
  *)
BEGIN
  DEC(sem^.count);
  IF sem^.count < 0 THEN
    event := block;
    currentSemaphore := sem;
    SWI(timerInt)
  END
END P;

PROCEDURE V(VAR sem: Semaphore);
  (* increments semaphore count; if count is less than or
     equal to zero, enables a process on semaphore queue *)
  VAR process: ADDRESS;    (* coroutine *)
BEGIN
  INC(sem^.count);
```

```
    IF sem^.count <= 0 THEN
      DeleteFromFront(sem^.queue, process);
      InsertAtEnd(readyQueue, process);
    END
  END V;

BEGIN
  MakeQueueEmpty(readyQueue);
  event := timeout    (* default event *)
END ScheduledProcesses.
```

Being able to implement ScheduledProcesses does not depend on the existence of the SWI procedure. If a Modula-2 system does not provide it, we could use the CODE procedure (Section 11.2) to generate the software interrupt instruction. On a computer that provides no such instruction, we could modify ScheduledProcesses so that P and Terminate perform the job of Scheduler: Each would select the next process to execute and transfer control to it directly.

Critical Sections

The programmer must be careful when using our new version of ScheduledProcesses, because processes can be switched at each clock interrupt. Trouble can ensue if a process is interrupted in the act of modifying a data structure shared with another process. For example, suppose that two processes both want to increment a shared variable v. One process loads the value of v (say 0) into a machine register to increment it. If a timer interrupt occurs now, the state of the process is saved (including the register contents), and the other process resumes executing. It fetches the value of v (which is still 0), increments it, and stores it back into memory; the value of v is now 1. When the next timer interrupt occurs, the first process resumes executing, increments the value of v that it previously fetched, then stores it back into memory. The final value of v will be 1, when it should be 2.

A region within a process in which shared variables are accessed and/or modified is called a *critical section*. The example just described shows the importance of ensuring that only one process at a time is in a critical section. (More precisely, we must ensure that, if a process is interrupted while in a critical section, control is not transferred to any other process that is also in a critical section.) Fortunately, it is easy to do so, by using a semaphore and the P and V operations. First, we declare a semaphore:

```
VAR criticalSection: Semaphore;
```

and initialize it to 1:

```
InitSem(criticalSection, 1);
```

We then precede each critical section by a P operation on this semaphore and follow it by a V operation:

```
P(criticalSection);
(* beginning of critical section *)
        .
        .
        .
(* end of critical section *)
V(criticalSection);
```

The first process to execute the P operation reduces the semaphore's count to 0; consequently, any other process attempting to execute the P operation on `criticalSection` must wait until the first process has executed the V operation.

EXAMPLE PROGRAM

Displaying Animated Figures

The program `DisplayFigures` illustrates the critical section problem. This program does nothing but display two moving figures, each of which roughly approximates the familiar "Pac-Man" character of video arcade fame. One figure moves across the screen from left to right, while the other moves from right to left; the program terminates when the figures meet in the center of the screen. Processes created from the procedures `MoveLeftFigure` and `MoveRightFigure` draw the two figures. The variable `leftColumn` contains the current horizontal position of the left figure; `rightColumn` stores the position of the right figure. `DisplayFigures` uses the screen-handling capabilities provided by the `Screen` module (Section 11.5).

Here is a first version of `MoveLeftFigure`:

```
PROCEDURE MoveLeftFigure;
  (* moves left figure to the right until it reaches the
     right figure *)
BEGIN
  WHILE leftColumn < rightColumn DO
    GotoXY(leftColumn, middleRow);
    WriteChar('<');
    Delay(delayTime);
    WriteChar('-');
    Delay(delayTime);
    WriteChar(' ');
    INC(leftColumn)
  END;
  Terminate
END MoveLeftFigure;
```

A problem can arise if an interrupt occurs between the call of `GotoXY` and the final `WriteChar`. If the other process (the one moving the right figure) gains control during this region, it may call `GotoXY`, thus changing the cursor position, which is stored inside the `Screen` module. When `MoveLeftFigure` resumes executing, subsequent calls of `WriteChar` will write characters in the wrong place on the screen, graphically illustrating the critical section problem. The solution is to introduce a `criticalSection` semaphore, place a `P` operation before the call of `GotoXY`, and put a `V` operation at the end of the `WHILE` loop body. The `MoveRightFigure` procedure must contain a corresponding critical section. Here is the final version of `DisplayFigures`:

```
MODULE DisplayFigures;
  (* displays two animated figures, each driven by a process *)

  FROM ScheduledProcesses IMPORT Semaphore, MakeReady, P, V,
                                 Scheduler, Terminate, InitSem;
  FROM Screen IMPORT numRows, numColumns, ClearScreen, GotoXY,
                     WriteChar;

  CONST wkspSize = 1000;
        middleRow = (numRows + 1) DIV 2;
        delayTime = 2000;    (* depends on processor speed *)

  VAR leftColumn, rightColumn: CARDINAL;
      criticalSection: Semaphore;

  PROCEDURE Delay(time: CARDINAL);
    (* delays program execution by specified number of time
       units *)
  BEGIN
    WHILE timc > 0 DO
      DEC(time)
    END
  END Delay;

  PROCEDURE MoveLeftFigure;
    (* moves left figure to the right until it reaches the
       right figure *)
  BEGIN
    WHILE leftColumn < rightColumn DO
      P(criticalSection);
      GotoXY(leftColumn, middleRow);
      WriteChar('<');
      Delay(delayTime);
      WriteChar('-');
      Delay(delayTime);
      WriteChar(' ');
      INC(leftColumn);
      V(criticalSection)
    END;
    Terminate
  END MoveLeftFigure;
```

```
  PROCEDURE MoveRightFigure;
    (* moves right figure to the left until it reaches the left
      figure *)
  BEGIN
    WHILE leftColumn < rightColumn DO
      P(criticalSection);
      GotoXY(rightColumn, middleRow);
      WriteChar('>');
      Delay(delayTime);
      WriteChar('-');
      Delay(delayTime);
      WriteChar(' ');
      DEC(rightColumn);
      V(criticalSection)
    END;
    Terminate
  END MoveRightFigure;

BEGIN
  ClearScreen;
  InitSem(criticalSection, 1);
  leftColumn := 1;
  rightColumn := numColumns;
  MakeReady(MoveLeftFigure, wkspSize);
  MakeReady(MoveRightFigure, wkspSize);
  Scheduler
END DisplayFigures.
```

Other Process-scheduling Strategies

The ScheduledProcesses module provides no way to assign priorities to processes so that more important processes will be favored when a process switch occurs. A module that does allow priorities has been published by D. A. Sewry.* His module provides a different version of Wirth's StartProcess procedure:

```
PROCEDURE StartProcess(P: PROC; n: CARDINAL;
                       priority: INTEGER);
```

This procedure allows a program to assign a priority to a process at the time it is created. Like our ScheduledProcesses module, Sewry's module returns control to a scheduler at each clock interrupt. However, in order to favor processes with higher priorities, his scheduler allows a process with priority p to execute for p "time slices" before being switched.

*D. A. Sewry, "Modula-2 Process Facilities," *SIGPLAN Notices*, Vol. 19, No. 11 (November 1984), pp. 23–32.

Sewry's scheme is just one of many. Modula-2 gives the programmer the ability to create a process-scheduling module that provides exactly the right blend of simplicity and power for a particular application.

EXERCISES

Section 12.1

1. Recursive procedures can be valuable programming tools. Is there a use for a coroutine that transfers control to itself?
2. Modify the `PrintFibonacciNumbers` program so that `IncFib2` always transfers control back to the main program, which tests whether the user has typed a character. If so, the program terminates; otherwise, it transfers control back to `IncFib1` to continue Fibonacci number generation.
3. In the `Quicksort` program of Section 12.1, could `MoveL` and `MoveR` share the same coroutine variable? Could `MoveL`, `MoveR`, and `Split` share a single variable?

Section 12.2

4. The following library module hides a character buffer while exporting procedures to put a character into the buffer and fetch a character from the buffer:

```
DEFINITION MODULE Buffer;
  (* exports procedures for manipulating a hidden character
     buffer; characters are entered at end of buffer and
     retrieved from front of buffer *)

  PROCEDURE Put(ch: CHAR);
    (* puts ch into buffer; if buffer is full, waits until
       space is available *)

  PROCEDURE Get(VAR ch: CHAR);
    (* gets ch from buffer; if buffer is empty, waits until
       a character is available *)

END Buffer.
```

Write the implementation part of `Buffer`, using Wirth's `Processes` module to allow `Put` and `Get` to wait without causing the program to halt.

5. In the `Partition` module of Section 12.2, could we rewrite `MoveL` and `MoveR` to avoid the call `WAIT(Terminate)`?

Section 12.3

6. Write the implementation part of the `ProcessQueues` module.
7. Modify `ScheduledProcesses` so that the `V` procedure always performs a process switch if the ready queue is not empty.

8. Revise the implementation part of `ScheduledProcesses` to detect when the ready queue is empty but not all processes have terminated. If this condition occurs, `ScheduledProcesses` should print a message and terminate the program. (Hint: Have `ScheduledProcesses` keep a count of processes that have begun to execute but have not yet terminated.)

9. Revise the implementation part of `ScheduledProcesses` so that it deallocates the workspace of a terminating process.

10. Compare the space requirements of the versions of `Quicksort` described in Sections 12.1, 12.2, and 12.3.

Section 12.4

11. Using the `Alarm` program as a guide, write a program to display the current time in the middle of the screen in hh:mm:ss format. The program should update the time every second. Use procedures that the `Screen` module (Section 11.5) supplies for writing to the screen. When the program begins execution, prompt the user to enter the current time; use this as the starting time.

12. Extend the `Keys` module to recognize control characters (characters typed while the user presses the Ctrl key).

13. What problem might we encounter when using the `Keys` module in conjunction with interrupt-driven process switching? (Hint: What if a process is interrupted immediately after a call of `KeyPressed`?)

14. Some versions of the `SYSTEM` module export a procedure `LISTEN` that, when called in a module with a priority in its heading, temporarily lowers the priority of the module so that pending interrupts can get through. Using the `LISTEN` procedure, modify the `Keys` module so that, when `ReadChar` is called and no character is available to be read, `ReadChar` waits until the user types one.

Section 12.5

15. The implementation of `ScheduledProcesses` given in Section 12.5 relies on the fact that a "software interrupt" instruction is available. Show how to modify `ScheduledProcesses` to work without this instruction.

16. Add the following procedure to the `ScheduledProcesses` module:

```
PROCEDURE Sleep(n: CARDINAL);
  (* suspends current process for n seconds *)
```

After a process that calls `Sleep` has been suspended for the specified number of seconds, it will again be eligible to execute (along with the other processes in the ready queue).

17. Modify `ScheduledProcesses` to allow the client module to assign each process a priority at the time of creation. `ScheduledProcesses` should allow a process whose priority is p to execute for p "time slices" before switching it.

13 Wirth's Input/Output Library

Unlike many programming languages, Modula-2 provides no built-in procedures for input and output. Instead, the programmer must import these procedures from library modules that a Modula-2 system supplies. (Or programmers may choose to write their own input/output modules.) Modula-2's approach offers several advantages:

Simplicity

Omitting I/O simplifies the language and allows compilers to be smaller and more efficient.

Flexibility

A Modula-2 system is free to supply a great variety of I/O interfaces, at varying levels of sophistication. Many programs need only a simple, high-level I/O module that provides a single source of input, a single repository for output, and a few operations for reading and writing numbers and strings. Other programs may need extensive capabilities for opening and closing files, looking up file names in directories, and reading and writing data of many types. When a language provides built-in I/O, the language designer must try to compromise by providing a simple but powerful set of I/O capabilities. Unfortunately, such a compromise rarely satisfies the needs of all the language's users. Modula-2's approach requires no such compromise: if the available library modules are inappropriate for a particular application, the programmer is free to write a custom I/O module.

Support for Specialized I/O Devices

The programmer can easily add modules for specialized I/O devices. It is difficult to provide access to these devices through built-in procedures, because the devices may have widely varying I/O protocols.

Compact Object Programs

Modula-2 allows a system to divide support for I/O among a number of library modules, so programs that require few I/O operations need not be linked to an extensive I/O library. In some languages, all programs — regardless of how much I/O support they need — are linked to a standard I/O library.

At present, no standard library of I/O modules exists. The closest to a standard is the collection of modules that appears in Appendix 2 of Wirth's *Programming in Modula-2*. Wirth's library includes four I/O modules:

```
Terminal
InOut
RealInOut
FileSystem
```

`Terminal` provides a simple interface to the user's terminal; it exports a small number of procedures for simple, character-oriented input and output. `InOut` extends `Terminal` in two ways: (1) it supports both terminal and file I/O (with redirection of input and output during program execution) and (2) it provides procedures for reading and writing `INTEGER` and `CARDINAL` numbers. `RealInOut` augments `InOut` by supplying procedures for reading and writing `REAL` numbers. `FileSystem` supports file I/O in a more general fashion than `InOut`; in particular, `FileSystem` allows several files to be open simultaneously (`InOut` allows at most two files to be open simultaneously: one for input and one for output). Section 13.1 describes the `Terminal` module, Section 13.2 describes `InOut` and `RealInOut`, and Section 13.3 describes `FileSystem`. Appendix IV reproduces the original definition modules for `Terminal`, `InOut`, `RealInOut`, and `FileSystem`.

Warning: Although many Modula-2 systems supply the `Terminal`, `InOut`, `RealInOut`, and `FileSystem` modules, these modules are not part of the Modula-2 language. Modula-2 systems are free to alter them or to supply other modules instead. Alterations to these modules most often take the form of added procedures, although some systems do not supply all the procedures listed here. Furthermore, many of the procedures behave in slightly different ways from the ones described here. (The examples in this chapter were tested using the Logitech Modula-2/86 system, but the description is intended to generalize to other systems as well.) Always consult the manual for a particular system to see how its I/O modules differ from those described here.

Modula-2's lack of a standard I/O library is a serious problem when we want a program to be portable; it can be hard to transport programs written using one I/O library to a system that provides a different library. Several standard I/O libraries have been proposed or are under development; one of these may eventually become widely accepted. Until then, programmers seeking portability have two alternatives:

- They can use only the `Terminal`, `InOut`, `RealInOut`, and `FileSystem` modules, not any other I/O modules supplied with a particular system. Furthermore, they should use only the procedures this chapter describes; other procedures are not as likely to be as widely available.

- Programmers can write custom I/O library modules, basing them on the most primitive I/O modules available (`Terminal` and `FileSystem`, for example). When transporting a program to a different Modula-2 system, the programmer need modify only the custom modules, not the entire program.

13.1 The `Terminal` Module

The `Terminal` module provides procedures for reading characters typed at the user's keyboard and writing characters to the user's screen. `Terminal` has two important characteristics. First, it decouples the keyboard from the screen; characters typed at the keyboard are not automatically echoed on the screen. Second, `Terminal` supports only character (and string) I/O; it does not supply procedures for reading and writing numbers.

Programmers can use `Terminal` in programs that require direct communication with the terminal. More importantly, they can use `Terminal` as a basis for writing more sophisticated input/output modules. For example, most Modula-2 systems use `Terminal` to implement the `InOut` module.

`Terminal` exports six entities, all of which are procedures. Three of the procedures are for input:

```
Read
BusyRead
ReadAgain
```

The other three are for output:

```
Write
WriteLn
WriteString
```

The `Read` procedure reads a single character typed at the keyboard:

- `PROCEDURE Read(VAR ch: CHAR);`

If no character has been typed, `Read` waits for the user to type one. This property can be useful when we are writing a program that is to interact with the user. For example, a program can display a screenful of information, then wait until the user has typed a character before continuing. If `buffer` is an array of strings and `length` indicates the number of components in `buffer`, then the following statements print the contents of `buffer`, one screenful at a time:

```
FOR i := 1 TO length DO
  WriteString(buffer[i]);
```

```
    WriteLn;
    IF i MOD linesPerScreen = 0 THEN
      WriteString("Type any character to continue...");
      Read(ch);  (* wait until a character is typed; ignore ch *)
      WriteLn
    END
  END;
```

When a program uses Terminal, characters typed at the keyboard are not automatically echoed on the screen. If the programmer wants echoing, a call of Write should follow each call of Read:

```
Read(ch);
Write(ch);    (* echo character just read *)
```

Read performs little or no processing of the characters typed at the keyboard. On some Modula-2 systems, Read returns a special end-of-line character when the user presses the "return" or "enter" key; this character is usually the same as the EOL constant exported by InOut. Read performs no special processing for other keys. In particular, it treats the backspace character in the same way it treats any other character. If the user types

h e p <backspace> l p

Read will fetch each of these six characters, one by one, including the backspace. If a program that uses Read is going to let the user correct errors, it must handle backspaces. At the end of this section we give a procedure that reads a string while allowing the user to correct typing mistakes.

The Terminal module provides BusyRead as an alternative to Read:

- `PROCEDURE BusyRead(VAR ch: CHAR);`

Unlike Read, BusyRead does not wait if no character is available to be read. Instead, BusyRead stores the null character (0C) into ch and immediately returns. BusyRead is useful for "polling" the keyboard periodically to see if the user is typing characters. (In some versions of Terminal, BusyRead uses a different character to signal that no character is available. Other versions supply the procedure KeyPressed instead; KeyPressed returns TRUE if a character is available to be read.)

The procedure ReadAgain causes the last character that was read to be "read again" when Read is next called:

- `PROCEDURE ReadAgain;`

ReadAgain is useful when a program is using a WHILE or REPEAT loop to read characters; the character that causes the loop to terminate is not processed by the loop body and should be saved for later reading. For example, the following loop skips blanks:

```
REPEAT
  Read(ch)
UNTIL ch # ' ';
ReadAgain;
```

The last character read was not a blank, and therefore we should not skip it.

The three output procedures are straightforward:

- `PROCEDURE Write(ch: CHAR);`
- `PROCEDURE WriteLn;`
- `PROCEDURE WriteString(s: ARRAY OF CHAR);`

The `Write` procedure writes a single character to the user's screen. `WriteLn` terminates the current line of output, causing the cursor to move to the next line on the screen. `WriteString` writes a string of characters to the screen. Because `s` is a value parameter, the actual parameter may be either a string variable or a string literal. Following the usual Modula-2 convention for string termination, `WriteString` should ignore any characters following the leftmost `0C` in `s`.

EXAMPLE **Reading a String**

The following procedure, named `ReadString`, extends `Read` to read a string of characters rather than just a single character. Furthermore, `ReadString` allows the user to correct a typing mistake by pressing the backspace key and retyping the character. `ReadString` reads a string of characters from the keyboard until the user types a control character (including the end-of-line character); the procedure echoes all characters read (except for the terminating control character). Once the `str` parameter is full, `ReadString` ignores any additional characters typed.

```
PROCEDURE ReadString(VAR str: ARRAY OF CHAR);
  (* reads and echoes characters until a control character is
     typed; backspacing is allowed for correcting mistakes;
     characters typed once str is full are ignored *)
  VAR i: CARDINAL;
      ch: CHAR;
BEGIN
  i := 0;
  LOOP
    Read(ch);
    IF ch = 10C THEN                    (* backspace? *)
      IF i > 0 THEN
        DEC(i);
```

```
        Write(10C);
        Write(' ');                    (* erase previous character *)
        Write(10C);
      END
    ELSIF (ch <= 37C) OR
          (ch >= 177C) THEN            (* nonprinting? *)
      IF i <= HIGH(str) THEN
        str[i] := 0C                   (* add terminator if room *)
      END;
      EXIT
    ELSIF i <= HIGH(str) THEN          (* room left in str? *)
      str[i] := ch;
      INC(i);
      Write(ch)
    ELSE
      Write(7C)                        (* beep if str is full *)
    END
  END
END ReadString;
```

The InOut module exports a ReadString procedure that is somewhat different from our example. The InOut version skips leading blanks and then reads characters until it encounters a trailing blank or control character.

13.2 The InOut and RealInOut Modules

Of the I/O modules in Wirth's library, InOut is the most used; the services it provides suffice for a great many programs. InOut exports procedures for reading and writing three forms of data:

characters
strings
integers (of types INTEGER and CARDINAL)

Actually, all input/output performed by InOut involves characters; it even reads and writes integers in character form. The RealInOut module augments InOut by providing procedures to read and write real numbers.

InOut reads from a single input stream and writes to a single output stream. A *stream* is simply a sequential flow of input or output data. An input stream could be the characters typed by the user at the keyboard or characters read from a file; similarly, an output stream could be characters sent to the user's screen or written to a file. The procedures InOut provides do not depend on whether or not the input and output streams are files. This feature simplifies client modules, for which file I/O is the same as terminal I/O.

The most important feature InOut provides is the ability to *redirect* the input and output streams. InOut's initial input stream is the user's keyboard, and its initial output stream is the user's screen, but a program can direct either or both streams to files instead.

InOut's greatest strength—its simplicity—also serves as the source of its weaknesses:

- InOut can read only from a single input stream and write only to a single output stream. A program that needs multiple input or output streams open simultaneously would not be able to rely solely on InOut.
- InOut requires the user to enter file names during program execution; a program cannot open a file without user interaction.
- InOut supports only sequential (streamlike) file access; for example, it does not allow a program to position a file at a specified point or write in the middle of a file.
- InOut does not allow a program to write data to a file in binary form; the program can read and write integers in text form only.
- InOut allows only character and integer input/output. RealInOut provides procedures for real I/O, but these modules cannot handle input and output of other data types (records, in particular).

Programs for which InOut is insufficient must use lower-level I/O modules such as Terminal (Section 13.1) and FileSystem (Section 13.3).

Input and Output Redirection

InOut can deal with two streams simultaneously: one input stream and one output stream. A program can redirect the default input stream (normally the user's keyboard) and the default output stream (normally the user's screen) by calling OpenInput and OpenOutput:

- PROCEDURE OpenInput(defext: ARRAY OF CHAR);
- PROCEDURE OpenOutput(defext: ARRAY OF CHAR);

A call of OpenInput redirects input to come from a file, while OpenOutput redirects output to a file.

When called, OpenInput prompts the user to enter a file name and then prepares the file for reading. The defext parameter is a "default extension," not a file name. (Many operating systems allow a file name to contain an *extension*: a string of characters appended to the file name, but separated from it by a period. The extension indicates what kind of information the file contains. For example, the extension MOD in the file name PRIMES.MOD might indicate that the file contains a Modula-2 program.) When called, `OpenInput` displays a message such as

```
in>
```

on the user's screen. The user then types the name of the file to open for input. If the name typed lacks an extension, `OpenInput` appends the default extension to the file name. Thus, if the call of `OpenInput` is `OpenInput("TXT")`, then

```
in> ABC
```

makes ABC.TXT the input file. (Wirth's description of `OpenInput` states that the procedure appends the default extension if the name typed ends with a period. Some Modula-2 systems follow this rule, but others—including the Logitech system—do exactly the opposite: They append the extension if the name does *not* end with a period.)

`OpenOutput` works in exactly the same fashion as `OpenInput`, except that it displays a message such as

```
out>
```

on the screen.

`OpenInput` and `OpenOutput` have properties that Wirth's description does not mention. For example, many versions of `InOut` allow the user to retain the default stream (keyboard or screen) by pressing a particular key (usually return or escape) in response to an `in>` or `out>` prompt. Also, `OpenInput` always sends its prompt to the user's screen, even if the current output stream is a file. Similarly, `OpenOutput` always expects input from the keyboard, even if the current input stream is a file.

`InOut` exports a variable called `Done`:

- `VAR Done: BOOLEAN;`

`OpenInput` and `OpenOutput` (as well as several other procedures exported by `InOut`) affect the value of `Done`. A successful attempt to open a file gives `Done` the value `TRUE`, and a failure gives it the value `FALSE`.

A program can use the procedures `CloseInput` and `CloseOutput` to restore the original input and output streams:

- `PROCEDURE CloseInput;`
- `PROCEDURE CloseOutput;`

A call of `CloseInput` redirects the input stream to its original source; input once more comes from the keyboard. Similarly, `CloseOutput` redirects the output stream to the user's screen. A call of CloseInput can later be followed by a call of OpenInput to redirect the input stream once more; the same is true of CloseOutput. InOut does not limit the number of times a program can redirect the input and output streams. Before terminating, a program should return both streams to their original state, and should close any files that were open for input or output.

Reading and Writing Characters

The most basic input/output procedures are Read and Write, which read or write a single character:

- PROCEDURE Read(VAR ch: CHAR);
- PROCEDURE Write(ch: CHAR);

When the input stream is the user's keyboard, Read normally has the same effect as the Read procedure in Terminal. Consequently, the procedure performs little or no processing on the input characters; in particular, the user cannot backspace to correct mistakes. Also, Read does not usually echo characters it reads.

Each call of Read affects the variable Done. A successful call of Read gives Done the value TRUE. If the input stream is a file and Read detects the end of the file, it sets Done to FALSE. (In most systems, the call Read(ch) gives ch the value 0C—the ASCII null character—in this case.)

A special end-of-line character divides a stream of characters into lines. InOut supplies this character as a constant named EOL:

- CONST EOL = 36C;

(The exact value of EOL may vary, although 36C—the ASCII record separator character—is the value Wirth specifies and many Modula-2 systems adopt.) The call

```
Write(EOL);
```

writes the EOL character to the current output stream. (If the current output stream is the terminal screen, the cursor moves to the beginning of the next line.) Because this operation is so common, InOut exports a procedure that has the same effect as Write(EOL):

- PROCEDURE WriteLn;

`InOut` provides no special mechanism for detecting the end of a line when reading from a stream; a program simply tests whether the character just read is equal to `EOL`.

Reading and Writing Strings

The procedures `ReadString` and `WriteString` allow a program to read and write strings of arbitrary length:

- `PROCEDURE ReadString(VAR s: ARRAY OF CHAR);`
- `PROCEDURE WriteString(s: ARRAY OF CHAR);`

The call `WriteString(s)` writes the string `s` to the current output stream. If `s` contains a `0C` character, `WriteString` writes only the portion of `s` up to the first `0C` character.

`ReadString` is a little more complicated. When called, `ReadString` reads characters from the input stream until it finds a nonblank, then copies characters into `s` until it reads a blank or control character. It does not copy this "terminating character" into `s`, but adds a `0C` character if room remains in `s`. `ReadString` stores the terminating character in the variable `termCH`, which `InOut` exports:

- `VAR termCH: CHAR;`

If the current input stream is the terminal keyboard, then `ReadString` has another feature: It allows the user to correct mistakes by backspacing. For example, if the user types the seven characters

`h e p` <backspace> `l p` <blank>

in response to the call `ReadString(s)`, `s` receives the value `"help"` and a blank character is assigned to `termCH`.

When the input stream is the keyboard, `ReadString` normally echoes the string it reads. The Logitech version of `ReadString` echoes the characters it puts into `s`, but does not echo any leading blanks, nor does it echo the terminating character.

Reading and Writing Integers

The procedures `ReadInt` and `WriteInt` read or write a single `INTEGER` value:

- `PROCEDURE ReadInt(VAR x: INTEGER);`
- `PROCEDURE WriteInt(x: INTEGER; n: CARDINAL);`

The call ReadInt(i) skips leading blanks, reads characters until encountering a trailing blank or control character, converts the string read to the equivalent integer value, and stores the result in i. (The user can correct mistakes by backspacing.) If the string of characters read consists of decimal digits (possibly preceded by a plus or minus sign), then the conversion succeeds and the variable Done gets the value TRUE. If the conversion fails, then Done becomes FALSE (the value of i is undefined). When used to read a number typed at the keyboard, Logitech's version of ReadInt echoes the characters read except for leading blanks and the terminating character.

The call WriteInt(i, n) converts the integer i to an equivalent (base 10) string, using a minimum of n characters, and writes the string to the output stream. For example, the call WriteInt(10, 1) writes the two-character string "10", as does the call WriteInt(10, 2). However, WriteInt(10, 3) writes the three-character string "□10". The proper choice of n depends on whether i is to appear in the smallest possible amount of space, or whether blanks should precede i. When a program writes a sequence of numbers on consecutive lines to form a table, a value of 1 for n aligns the table on the left; a sufficiently large value of n aligns the table on the right. For example, the statement

```
FOR i := 1 TO 100 BY 33 DO
  WriteInt(i, 1);
  WriteLn
END;
```

produces this table:

```
1
34
67
100
```

However, the statement

```
FOR i := 1 TO 100 BY 33 DO
  WriteInt(i, 5);
  WriteLn
END;
```

produces this table:

```
□□□□1
□□□34
□□□67
□□100
```

The procedures ReadCard and WriteCard are similar to ReadInt and WriteInt, but read or write a single CARDINAL value:

- PROCEDURE ReadCard(VAR x: CARDINAL);
- PROCEDURE WriteCard(x, n: CARDINAL);

Unlike ReadInt, ReadCard will not read a number that includes a sign.

The procedures WriteOct and WriteHex allow a program to write a CARDINAL number in octal or hexadecimal:

- PROCEDURE WriteOct(x, n: CARDINAL);
- PROCEDURE WriteHex(x, n: CARDINAL);

The call WriteOct(i, n) converts i to an equivalent base 8 string of at least n characters, and then writes it to the output stream. The call WriteHex(i, n) is identical, except that it writes i in base 16. If necessary, both procedures supply leading blanks to produce n characters of output. On some systems, WriteOct and WriteHex produce a fixed-length string of digits. For example, the Logitech version of WriteOct writes a string of six octal digits, while WriteHex writes four hexadecimal digits. Thus, the statements

```
WriteCard(127, 5);
WriteLn;
WriteOct(127, 5);
WriteLn;
WriteHex(127, 5);
WriteLn;
```

produce this output:

```
□□127
000177
□007F
```

WriteOct and WriteHex are primarily useful in low-level programming, where it is often convenient to view words or bytes in octal or hex form.

EXAMPLE PROGRAM

Copying a File

The following program, which copies one file to another, illustrates the proper use of Done:

```
MODULE CopyFile;
  (* copies input file to output file *)
```

```
  FROM InOut IMPORT OpenInput, OpenOutput, CloseInput,
                    CloseOutput, Done, Read, Write;

  VAR ch: CHAR;

BEGIN
  OpenInput("TXT");
  OpenOutput("TXT");
  Read(ch);
  WHILE Done DO
    Write(ch);
    Read(ch)
  END;
  CloseInput;
  CloseOutput
END CopyFile.
```

EXAMPLE PROGRAM

Reformatting a Text File

The following program illustrates the use of EOL. Reformat copies a text file, reformatting it to divide any line longer than 80 characters into shorter lines of at most 80 characters.

```
MODULE Reformat;
  (* copies input file to output file, breaking lines
     longer than maxLength into shorter lines by inserting
     the EOL character *)

  FROM InOut IMPORT OpenInput, OpenOutput, Done, CloseInput,
                    CloseOutput, EOL, Read, Write, WriteLn;

  CONST maxLength = 80;

  VAR ch: CHAR;
      length: CARDINAL;

BEGIN
  OpenInput("TXT");
  OpenOutput("TXT");

  length := 0;
  Read(ch);
  WHILE Done DO
    INC(length);
    IF ch = EOL THEN
      length := 0
    ELSIF length > maxLength THEN
      WriteLn;
      length := 1
    END;
```

```
    Write(ch);
    Read(ch)
  END;

  CloseInput;
  CloseOutput
END Reformat.
```

The RealInOut Module

InOut does not provide procedures for reading or writing real numbers; a complementary module named RealInOut supplies these procedures.

RealInOut is separate from InOut so programs that do not need to read or write real numbers can have smaller object programs. (In many Modula-2 systems, when a program imports from a library module, all object code for the module is incorporated into the program during the linking stage. Including procedures for reading and writing real numbers in InOut would force every program importing from InOut to include the object code for these procedures.) Nevertheless, some Modula-2 systems combine InOut and RealInOut into a single module to reduce the number of library modules.

Most Modula-2 systems use InOut to implement RealInOut. As a result, RealInOut uses the input and output streams controlled by InOut. If a program redirects the input or output streams by calling procedures imported from InOut, this affects RealInOut as well.

RealInOut is a small module; it exports only three procedures (ReadReal, WriteReal, and WriteRealOct) and one variable (Done). The ReadReal procedure reads a single real number:

- `PROCEDURE ReadReal(VAR x: REAL);`

The real number format required by ReadReal differs slightly from the format of a real number in a Modula-2 program. ReadReal recognizes a real number only if it has the form shown in Figure 13.1. Although the chart in Figure 13.1 resembles the syntax chart for a real number appearing in a Modula-2 program (Figure 2.4), there are several small differences:

- A sign may precede a number read by ReadReal.
- A number read by ReadReal need not have a decimal point (allowing the user to enter real numbers in integer form); if a decimal point is present, at least one digit must follow it.
- The exponent in a number read by ReadReal may not be more than two digits long (according to Wirth's description; this limit is likely to vary from one system to another).

Figure 13.1
Real Number Syntax Required by ReadReal

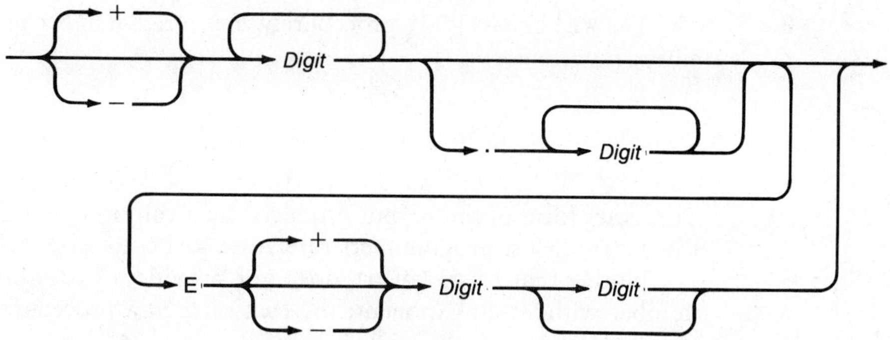

RealInOut exports a single variable, which ReadReal uses to indicate whether or not it was able to read a number:

- VAR Done: BOOLEAN;

InOut exports a variable with the same name. If a program needs to use both variables, the programmer must be careful to avoid name conflicts — for example, by qualifying Done with the name of the module to which it belongs. (See Section 2.2 for more discussion of this problem.)

The call ReadReal(x) skips blanks, and then reads characters until it encounters a blank or control character (the user can make corrections with the backspace key, however). If the string read has the form shown in Figure 13.1, ReadReal converts it to a REAL number, stores the number in the variable x, and sets the variable Done to TRUE. If the string does not represent a real number, ReadReal sets Done to FALSE. In the Logitech system, ReadReal does not echo leading blanks or the character that terminates the number.

The WriteReal procedure writes a real number in scientific notation:

- PROCEDURE WriteReal(x: REAL; n: CARDINAL);

The call WriteReal(x, n) writes x using at least n characters. If the number is less than n characters long, blanks precede it. The exact format in which WriteReal writes x depends on the system. On the Logitech system, the call

```
WriteReal(57.43, 10);
```

produces the following output:

```
□5.74E+001
```

The `WriteRealOct` procedure writes a real number in an octal form of scientific notation:

- `PROCEDURE WriteRealOct(x: REAL);`

The exact form of the output produced by a call of `WriteRealOct` depends on the system. Most programmers rarely use `WriteRealOct`.

Notice that `RealInOut` does not provide a procedure that writes a real number without an exponent; the lack of such a procedure is a shortcoming of the module.

13.3 The `FileSystem` Module

A *file* is a named collection of data located in secondary storage (magnetic disks or tapes, for example) rather than in main memory. Files have two important properties. First, they may exist independently of programs; hence, they can store information between runs of a program. Second, they can store large amounts of data. A program whose memory requirements for data storage would exceed the capacity of main memory can rely instead on one or more temporary files.

Many programming languages furnish built-in procedures for input and output using files, and some (including Pascal) provide file types. In contrast, Modula-2 provides no file type and no procedures for file manipulation. Instead, the library provided with a Modula-2 system usually includes one or more file-handling modules.

It is difficult to discuss files in Modula-2, because the language has no universally accepted library. The closest to a standard module for file-handling is Wirth's `FileSystem` module. Although not all Modula-2 systems provide the `FileSystem` module, there are at least two good reasons for studying it. First, `FileSystem` is one of the most widely available file-handling modules (although it is usually modified to some degree). Second, `FileSystem` is relatively small, yet it illustrates most of the issues that arise in the manipulation of files. The reader who understands `FileSystem` should have little difficulty transferring this knowledge to other file-handling modules.

Not every program that uses files requires the `FileSystem` module. Many programs need only to read and write character and numeric data using a single input file and a single output file; for such programs, the `InOut` and `RealInOut` modules should be adequate. Only when `InOut` and `RealInOut` do not suffice must a program use the more general—but lower-level—`FileSystem` module.

The File Type

FileSystem exports a file type, called File, that client modules can import and use to declare file variables:

```
VAR inFile, outFile, tempFile: File;
```

A program can "associate" each file variable with a single file. The association between a file variable and a file begins when the program opens the file and ends when the program closes it (after which the program may associate the variable with another file). To perform an operation on a file, a program calls the appropriate file-handling procedure, supplying the associated file variable as a parameter. For example, if the file variable inFile is currently associated with a file named INPUT.DAT, then the call

```
ReadChar(inFile, ch);
```

reads a character from INPUT.DAT. Because file-handling procedures operate on file variables, it is sometimes convenient to think of these variables as *logical* (or *internal*) files. We then call the files actually being manipulated *physical* (or *external*) files. File variables allow us to write programs that do not refer to particular file names. Instead, the user can enter names during program execution, or a program can even construct them.

Wirth's version of FileSystem defines File to be a record type. The full declaration of File appears in Appendix IV; because File tends to vary widely among Modula-2 systems, we will examine the abbreviated declaration:

```
■ TYPE File = RECORD
                 res: Response;
                 eof: BOOLEAN;
                      .
                      .
                      .
              END;
```

Procedures in the FileSystem module indicate the status of a file and signal errors by changing the values of one or more fields in the file variable (a record of type File). Because every procedure in FileSystem operates on a file variable, procedures can communicate status and error information in a uniform fashion. The fields that supply this information include res and eof.

Every file operation affects the res field. The values of res belong to the enumeration type Response:

```
■ TYPE Response = (done, ...);
```

The value of res is done after a successful operation; otherwise, res indicates what kind of error occurred. The exact list of errors and their meanings vary among systems.

The eof field has the value TRUE when the end of the file is reached; however, it does not become TRUE until an attempt to read actually fails. Consequently, programs should check the eof field after each attempt to read from a file—if eof is TRUE, the information read is not valid. A loop to read and process all the characters in a file would look like this:

```
LOOP
  ReadChar(inFile, ch);
  IF inFile.eof THEN EXIT END;
  (* process ch *)
END;
```

Most of the other fields in a File record are for internal use by the FileSystem module. We will not discuss these fields, which depend more on the details of the underlying operating system and therefore tend to vary from one Modula-2 system to another.

Opening, Closing, Creating, Deleting, and Renaming Files

Before using a file, a program must open it (if it already exists) or create it (if it does not exist). Opening a file requires associating a file variable with a physical file (specified by a file name). FileSystem provides a procedure called Lookup for this purpose:

```
■ PROCEDURE Lookup(VAR f: File; filename: ARRAY OF CHAR;
                   new: BOOLEAN);
```

If the third parameter has the value TRUE, Lookup will create the file if it does not exist. For example, the call

```
Lookup(inFile, "INPUT.DAT", FALSE);
```

will open the physical file named INPUT.DAT and associate it with the file variable inFile. Because the third parameter is FALSE, Lookup will not create the file if it does not exist. The program can detect whether INPUT.DAT was found by examining the res field of inFile, which has the value done after a successful call of Lookup.

The Create procedure allows the creation of an unnamed file for temporary use during program execution. Instead of specifying the name of the file to create, the program specifies the medium (for example, the particular disk drive) on which to create the file:

- `PROCEDURE Create(VAR f: File; mediumname: ARRAY OF CHAR);`

For example, on a personal computer, single letters often denote disk drives; to create a temporary file on drive A, a program might use the following call:

```
Create(tempFile, "A:");
```

`FileSystem` provides a procedure called `Close` for closing a file that a program no longer needs:

- `PROCEDURE Close(VAR f: File);`

For example, to close the file associated with the file variable `inFile`, we would use the call

```
Close(inFile);
```

Closing a file breaks the association between the file variable and the physical file, freeing the file variable for subsequent association with a different file. The effect on the physical file depends on whether it was temporary or permanent. Closing a temporary (nameless) file deletes the file. Closing a permanent file updates the file to reflect any changes made while it was open. Each program is responsible for closing open files before it terminates, although some systems close all open files automatically.

The `Rename` procedure allows a program to give a file a new name:

- `PROCEDURE Rename(VAR f: File; filename: ARRAY OF CHAR);`

For example, the following call gives the name `newName` to the file associated with the variable `tempFile`:

```
Rename(tempFile, newName);
```

If the second parameter to `Rename` is the empty string, then the file becomes temporary; closing the file will delete it. Conversely, `Rename` can make a temporary file permanent by assigning it a nonempty name.

File Modes

An open file must be in one of four *modes*:

read (data can be read but not written)
write (data can be appended to the file; reading is not possible)
modify (data can be both read and written)
open (the initial mode)

The *open* mode is necessary because the mode of a file is not set at the time a program opens it.

There are two ways to change the mode of a file. First, performing a read operation on a file in *open* mode implicitly changes it to *read* mode; similarly, performing a write operation on a file in *open* mode changes it to *write* mode. Second, a program can change the mode explicitly by calling one of the following procedures:

- `PROCEDURE SetRead(VAR f: File);`
- `PROCEDURE SetWrite(VAR f: File);`
- `PROCEDURE SetModify(VAR f: File);`

A program can change the mode of a file at any time. It can even restore the mode to *open*:

- `PROCEDURE SetOpen(VAR f: File);`

When called, `SetOpen` completes any changes to the file that might be pending as a consequence of prior operations; it then puts the file into *open* mode.

Each open file has an associated file position, marking the point in the file where the next operation is to take place. When a file is in *read* mode, the current position is somewhere in the middle of the file; the next read operation will fetch data stored at this position. When a file is in *write* mode, the current position is at the end of the file, where data will be written. When a file is in *modify* mode, both reading and writing can take place at the current file position; a write will overwrite the data at this position. Thus, *modify* mode, unlike *write* mode, allows the replacement of existing data.

The procedures `SetRead`, `SetWrite`, `SetModify`, and `SetOpen` do not change the current file position. A program must be able to change the position in order to, say, change a file from *write* to *read* mode and then begin reading from the beginning of the file. The procedure `Reset` makes this possible:

- `PROCEDURE Reset(VAR f: File);`

A call of Reset (1) repositions the file f to its beginning and (2) puts it in *open* mode. Thus, if tempFile is in *write* mode and we need to begin reading from it at the beginning, we could use the following statements:

```
Reset(tempFile);
SetRead(tempFile);
```

Actually, we don't need the call of SetRead; trying to read from tempFile automatically changes it from *open* to *read* mode.

Text Files Versus Binary Files

Files are classified as text files or binary files, depending on the kind of data they contain. *Text files* contain characters and therefore are human-readable. (Wirth calls these *legible* files.) Numbers written to text files must first be converted to character form. For example, suppose that we write the value of a CARDINAL variable i to a file using the procedure WriteCard from the module InOut:

```
WriteCard(i, 1);
```

WriteCard must convert the value of i to a string of one or more characters before writing it to the output file. Suppose that i has the value 4,895. Internally, 4,895 is stored as the bit pattern 0001001100011111 (assuming that CARDINAL values are represented using 16 bits). Before writing it to the output file, WriteCard first converts it to the string "4895". Thus, i is written to the file as the four bytes 00110100, 00111000 and 00111001, 00110101. The number of bytes required to write i depends on the value of i, because larger numbers require more characters.

Binary files contain binary information stored as words or bytes; consequently, binary files are not suitable for reading by humans (they are *illegible*, in Wirth's terminology). Binary files are useful for storing information that programs will share. Numbers written in binary undergo no conversion to character form. Thus, when we call a procedure to write the CARDINAL number 4,895 to a binary file, the procedure writes the number's original bit pattern (the word 0001001100011111). When written in binary, all CARDINAL numbers require the same amount of space.

We usually store data in text form if it consists exclusively of characters or if humans will need to examine it. We use binary files for data that is not human-readable (executable machine instructions, for example) or data that could be readable but is not for space reasons (a file of integers, for example). Binary files are more compact than text files (as our 4,895 example shows) and have other advantages as well: When we store numbers in a binary file and read them later, no conversion to and from character form is necessary, so we save time. Also, real numbers are best stored in binary files. (Real numbers may lose accuracy when converted from binary to text or text to binary.)

The `FileSystem` module supports both binary and text files. `FileSystem` views a binary file as a sequence of words (or bytes on some machines) and a text file as a sequence of characters; because of this similarity between binary and text files, we can use most `FileSystem` procedures with either kind of file.

Some Modula-2 systems view a text file as a sequence of *lines*, not a sequence of characters (Pascal programmers will recognize this approach). Libraries provided with these systems usually provide separate modules for text files and binary files, because this view of text files requires the procedures for manipulating text files to be different from the procedures for manipulating binary files.

Procedures for Text I/O

`FileSystem` provides two procedures for reading and writing textual data:

- `PROCEDURE ReadChar(VAR f: File; VAR ch: CHAR);`
- `PROCEDURE WriteChar(VAR f: File; ch: CHAR);`

`ReadChar` reads one character from a file; `WriteChar` writes one character. After a call of either procedure, the current file position advances by one byte.

Wirth's definition module for `FileSystem` does not specify a convention for representing the end of a line of text. The Logitech Modula-2/86 system uses the convention that the `EOL` character terminates each line of text (the Logitech `ASCII` module exports `EOL`, but it is the same as `EOL` in the `InOut` module). Therefore, a program would use the following loop to read and process each character in a line of text, leaving the current file position at the beginning of the next line:

```
LOOP
  ReadChar(inFile, ch);
  IF ch = EOL THEN EXIT END;
  (* process ch *)
END;
```

Because it may be necessary to share text files with programs that do not use this convention, `ReadChar` must make it appear that lines end with `EOL` even when they don't. The rule used by the Logitech version of `FileSystem` is that a carriage return (`15C`) or line feed (`12C`) or a carriage-return/line-feed pair will be replaced by the `EOL` character when `ReadChar` encounters it; when asked to write the EOL character, WriteChar instead writes a carriage-return/line-feed pair. (Other systems may follow different conventions, of course.)

Occasionally, a program needs to read a data item more than once (see the discussion of ReadAgain in Section 13.1). The Again procedure provides this capability:

- PROCEDURE Again(VAR f: File);

When called, Again "undoes" the effect of the previous call of ReadChar so that the next call fetches the same character as the previous call. We can also use Again to undo a call of ReadWord.

Procedures for Binary I/O

FileSystem provides two procedures for reading and writing binary data:

- PROCEDURE ReadWord(VAR f: File; VAR w: WORD);
- PROCEDURE WriteWord(VAR f: File; w: WORD);

After a call of ReadWord or WriteWord, the current file position advances by one word.

FileSystem does not provide procedures capable of reading or writing blocks of words. However, we can use ReadWord and WriteWord to write these missing procedures. Consider the problem of reading a block of words (writing a block of words is similar). A procedure for this purpose could allow a program to supply an arbitrary variable as a parameter—the procedure reads enough words to fill the variable:

```
PROCEDURE ReadBlock(VAR f: File; VAR block: ARRAY OF WORD);
  (* reads words from file f until block is full *)
  VAR i: CARDINAL;
BEGIN
  FOR i := 0 TO HIGH(block) DO
    ReadWord(f, block[i])
  END
END ReadBlock;
```

Another possibility is to supply an address and a number of words to read; the procedure reads words and stores them into memory (starting at the specified address) until it has read the specified number of words or has reached the end of the file. The procedure indicates (through a parameter) how many words it actually read.

```
PROCEDURE ReadWords(VAR f: File; addr: ADDRESS;
                    words: CARDINAL; VAR wordsRead: CARDINAL);
  (* reads words from file f, storing them at address addr;
     "words" specifies number of words to read, while wordsRead
     indicates number actually read *)
BEGIN
  wordsRead := 0;
  LOOP
    IF wordsRead = words THEN EXIT END;
    ReadWord(f, addr^);
    IF f.eof THEN EXIT END;
    INC(wordsRead);
    INC(addr, SIZE(WORD))
  END
END ReadWords;
```

This procedure is particularly useful when a file contains blocks of data of varying lengths.

We could use either procedure to read a record from a file. For example, suppose that the file variable `employeeFile` is associated with a file containing records of type `EmployeeData`. We want to read a record from this file and store it in the variable `employeeBuffer`:

```
VAR employeeBuffer: EmployeeData;
```

When calling `ReadBlock`, we supply the record variable as a parameter:

```
ReadBlock(employeeFile, employeeBuffer);
```

We would give `ReadWords` the address and size of the record:

```
ReadWords(employeeFile, ADR(employeeBuffer),
          SIZE(employeeBuffer) DIV SIZE(WORD), wordsRead);
```

We can check the value of `wordsRead` to see if enough data remained in the file to fill `employeeBuffer`.

Access Methods

There are two ways to access the information stored in a file: *sequential access* and *direct* (random) *access*. With sequential access, we read data items one by one, starting from the first item in the file; to locate information in the middle of a file, we must read all the data that precedes it. Direct access allows us to access any item in the file directly, without examining other items in the file. `FileSystem` supports both sequential and direct access.

Sequential access is the default method. Each of the procedures ReadChar, WriteChar, ReadWord, and WriteWord advances the file position. We need take no special action to access the next item in a file—it happens automatically. In order to allow direct access as well, FileSystem provides a method of representing file positions, plus procedures to calculate a file position and set a file to a desired file position.

In FileSystem, a file position is a nonnegative integer that represents the index of a byte within a file (the first byte has index 0). Using a CARDINAL value to represent a file position would be too restrictive on smaller computer systems (on a 16-bit machine, the largest CARDINAL value is 65,535). Instead, FileSystem uses a pair of CARDINAL values (called highpos and lowpos) that it treats as two halves of the same number. For example, if CARDINAL values occupy 16 bits, joining highpos and lowpos gives a 32-bit number whose value is $\text{highpos}\cdot 2^{16} + \text{lowpos}$, allowing files of up to 4,294,967,295 bytes.

FileSystem supplies two procedures for manipulating file positions:

- PROCEDURE GetPos(VAR f: File; VAR highpos, lowpos: CARDINAL);
- PROCEDURE SetPos(VAR f: File; highpos, lowpos: CARDINAL);

GetPos determines the current position of a file and returns it through the parameters highpos and lowpos. SetPos modifies the current position of a file. For example, to move to the beginning of tempFile, a program could use the call

```
SetPos(tempFile, 0, 0);
```

The Length procedure returns the length of a file (in bytes) as a pair of CARDINAL numbers:

- PROCEDURE Length(VAR f: File; VAR highpos, lowpos: CARDINAL);

A program can use the value returned by Length for positioning relative to the end of a file. For example, to move to the end of tempFile, the program could call Length, then SetPos:

```
Length(tempFile, highpos, lowpos);
SetPos(tempFile, highpos, lowpos);
```

Note: Some operating systems store a file as a collection of fixed-length blocks, forcing the length of the file to be a multiple of this block size regardless of the amount of data stored in the file. A special character marks the actual end of the file.

Implementations of `FileSystem` normally perform buffering. Each open file `f` has a buffer associated with it. The use of the buffer depends on the mode of `f`:

- If `f` is in *read* mode, the buffer acts as a "window" on `f`—it contains a portion of `f`. Attempts to read from `f` actually fetch data from the buffer; when all the data in the buffer has been read, the buffer is reloaded using the next portion of `f`.
- If `f` is in *write* mode, requests to write to `f` actually cause data to be written to the buffer; when the buffer is full, it is "flushed"—written to the physical file.
- If `f` is in *modify* mode, the buffer contains a portion of `f`. Both read and write operations are performed on the buffer until the current file position moves outside the range that the buffer represents. Then the buffer is written back to the physical file and reloaded using the new file position.

Buffering reduces the number of times that data is actually transferred to or from the disk (disk I/O is relatively slow, compared to the time required to access main memory).

Most of the time, the programmer doesn't worry about the buffer—it is normally invisible. However, when performing direct access operations on a file, a program may need some control over the buffer. `FileSystem` therefore provides the procedure `Doio`:

- `PROCEDURE Doio(VAR f: File);`

`Doio` operates on the buffer associated with the file `f`. If `f` is in *read* mode, `Doio` loads the buffer, starting at the current position of `f` (which may have just been changed using `SetPos`). If `f` is in *write* mode, `Doio` writes the buffer contents to `f` (at the old position) and assigns the buffer to the current file position (without changing the buffer contents). If `f` is in *modify* mode, `Doio` writes the buffer (at the old position) and then loads it starting from the current position in `f`.

EXAMPLE PROGRAM

Comparing Text Files

The following program, `CompareLines`, shows how to use `FileSystem` to manipulate text files. `CompareLines` compares two text files, printing any lines that differ between the files. We cannot write this program using only the `InOut` module, because it must read from two input streams at the same time.

`CompareLines` depends on the procedures `OpenFile` and `ReadLine`. `OpenFile` accepts a string typed in at the keyboard and tries to open a file with that name. If the file does not exist, `OpenFile` prompts the user for another file name; this cycle repeats until the user enters an acceptable file name. In general, a program cannot assume that a user will enter a valid file name in response to a prompt; it is always a good idea to write a procedure similar to OpenFile.

To simplify the program, we would like to be able to read two lines (one from each file) and then compare them using a procedure imported from a string-handling module. Unfortunately, FileSystem provides no procedure for reading strings, only single characters, so we must write our own procedure, called ReadLine. ReadLine reads characters from a text file—storing them into a string variable—until it reaches the end of a line or the end of the file or until the string becomes full. Notice that ReadLine checks for end of file *after* an attempt to read a character, not before.

After reading a line from each file, the program checks to see if the lines are identical. Wirth's library includes no string-handling module, so CompareLines uses the procedure Compare from the String module (Section 10.2). If the lines are not the same, CompareLines prints both lines. CompareLines terminates as soon as one of the files becomes empty.

```
MODULE CompareLines;
  (* compares two text files and prints the lines on which
     they differ *)

  FROM InOut IMPORT EOL, ReadString, WriteString, WriteLn,
                    WriteCard;
  FROM FileSystem IMPORT File, Lookup, Response, ReadChar,
                         Close;
  FROM String IMPORT CompareResult, Compare;    (* Sec. 10.2 *)

  CONST lineLen = 80;
        fileNameLen = 15;

  VAR fileName1, fileName2: ARRAY [0..fileNameLen-1] OF CHAR;
      file1, file2: File;
      lineNumber: CARDINAL;
      line1, line2: ARRAY [0..lineLen-1] OF CHAR;


  PROCEDURE OpenFile(VAR file: File;
                     VAR fileName: ARRAY OF CHAR);
    (* accepts a file name from the user, then opens file;
       repeats until file is opened successfully *)
  BEGIN
    LOOP
      ReadString(fileName);
      WriteLn;
      Lookup(file, fileName, FALSE);
      IF file.res = done THEN EXIT END;
      WriteString("Can't open file; re-enter file name: ")
    END
  END OpenFile;
```

```
    PROCEDURE ReadLine(VAR file: File; VAR str: ARRAY OF CHAR);
      (* reads characters from file and stores into str until
         end of line, end of file, or str is full; terminates
         program if str overflows *)
      VAR i: CARDINAL;
          ch: CHAR;
    BEGIN
      i := 0;
      LOOP
        ReadChar(file, ch);
        IF file.eof OR (ch = EOL) THEN
          IF i <= HIGH(str) THEN
            str[i] := 0C
          END;
          EXIT
        ELSIF i > HIGH(str) THEN
          WriteString("String overflow in ReadLine");
          WriteLn;
          HALT
        END;
        str[i] := ch;
        INC(i)
      END
    END ReadLine;

  BEGIN
    WriteString("Enter name of first file: ");
    OpenFile(file1, fileName1);
    WriteString("Enter name of second file: ");
    OpenFile(file2, fileName2);
    WriteLn;

    lineNumber := 1;
    LOOP
      ReadLine(file1, line1);
      ReadLine(file2, line2);
      IF file1.eof OR file2.eof THEN EXIT END;
      IF Compare(line1, line2) # equal THEN
        WriteString("Mismatch at line ");
        WriteCard(lineNumber, 1);
        WriteLn;
        WriteString(fileName1);
        WriteString(": ");
        WriteString(line1);
        WriteLn;
        WriteString(fileName2);
        WriteString(": ");
        WriteString(line2);
```

```
      WriteLn;
      WriteLn
    END;
    INC(lineNumber)
  END;

  IF file1.eof & NOT file2.eof THEN
    WriteString("End of file encountered while reading ");
    WriteString(fileName1);
    WriteLn
  ELSIF NOT file1.eof & file2.eof THEN
    WriteString("End of file encountered while reading ");
    WriteString(fileName2);
    WriteLn
  END;

  Close(file1);
  Close(file2)
END CompareLines.
```

EXAMPLE PROGRAM

Updating a Binary File

To illustrate the manipulation of binary files using the `FileSystem` module, we present a program named `UpdateInventory` that updates a binary file of inventory records. The file, which we assume has the name INVENT.DAT, contains records of type `Item`, each representing an item of merchandise. Each item has an identifying number between 1 and *n*, for some value of *n*; we assume that the file contains a record for every number between 1 and *n* and that the records are stored by item number. The purpose of the program is to update the `onHand` fields of certain inventory records. We assume that information for updating the inventory file is stored in the binary file UPDATE.DAT in the form of records of type `UpdateRecord`. Each update record contains the number of an item and the net change in the inventory of that item. Knowing the order of records in the inventory file, we can use the item number in each update record to directly access the inventory record that we need to update.

Because `UpdateInventory` needs to read and write records, it declares the procedures `ReadBlock` and `WriteBlock` (we presented `ReadBlock` earlier in this section). The program begins by opening the inventory file and update file, setting the former to *modify* mode (the latter is set to *read* mode by the first call of `ReadWord`). `UpdateInventory` then enters a loop in which it

1. Reads a record from the update file, terminating if it reaches the end of the file.
2. Sets the current position of the inventory file to allow access to the record selected by the number in the update file record, then calls `ReadBlock` to read the record.

3. Alters the onHand field of the inventory record to reflect the change in the number of items on hand.
4. Resets the inventory file to its position before the record was read, then writes the modified record back to the file.

To set the position of the inventory file to allow access to the record identified by `updateBuffer.number`, `UpdateInventory` uses the call

```
SetPos(inventoryFile, 0,
       (updateBuffer.number - 1) * SIZE(Item));
```

because the position of record 1 is 0, the position of record 2 is `SIZE(Item)`, and so forth.

```
MODULE UpdateInventory;
  (* updates an inventory file *)

  FROM SYSTEM IMPORT WORD;
  FROM FileSystem IMPORT File, Lookup, SetModify, ReadWord,
                         WriteWord, SetPos, Close;

  CONST inventoryFileName = "INVENT.DAT";
        updateFileName    = "UPDATE.DAT";

  TYPE StringType = ARRAY [0..19] OF CHAR;
       Item = RECORD
                number: CARDINAL;
                description: StringType;
                price: REAL;
                onHand: INTEGER
              END;
       UpdateRecord =
              RECORD
                number: CARDINAL;
                change: INTEGER
              END;

  VAR inventoryFile, updateFile: File;
      updateBuffer: UpdateRecord;
      inventoryBuffer: Item;

  PROCEDURE ReadBlock(VAR f: File; VAR block: ARRAY OF WORD);
    (* reads words from file f until block is full *)
    VAR i: CARDINAL;
  BEGIN
    FOR i := 0 TO HIGH(block) DO
      ReadWord(f, block[i])
    END
  END ReadBlock;
```

```
    PROCEDURE WriteBlock(VAR f: File; block: ARRAY OF WORD);
      (* writes a block of words to file f *)
      VAR i: CARDINAL;
    BEGIN
      FOR i := 0 TO HIGH(block) DO
        WriteWord(f, block[i])
      END
    END WriteBlock;

BEGIN
  Lookup(inventoryFile, inventoryFileName, FALSE);
  SetModify(inventoryFile);
  Lookup(updateFile, updateFileName, FALSE);

  LOOP
    ReadBlock(updateFile, updateBuffer);
    IF updateFile.eof THEN EXIT END;
    SetPos(inventoryFile, 0,
           (updateBuffer.number - 1) * SIZE(Item));
    ReadBlock(inventoryFile, inventoryBuffer);
    INC(inventoryBuffer.onHand, updateBuffer.change);
    SetPos(inventoryFile, 0,
           (updateBuffer.number - 1) * SIZE(Item));
    WriteBlock(inventoryFile, inventoryBuffer)
  END;

  Close(inventoryFile);
  Close(updateFile)
END UpdateInventory.
```

EXERCISES

Section 13.1

1. Write a program that writes a sequence of prime numbers (in order, starting at 2) to the user's terminal until the user presses the escape key. (*Hint:* After writing each number, the program should call `Terminal.BusyRead` to see if the user has typed a character.)

2. Write a `ReadCard` procedure that reads a `CARDINAL` number typed at the user's keyboard. `ReadCard` should skip leading blanks (without echoing), then read digits until it finds a nondigit. If `ReadCard` is able to read at least one digit, it should assign the value `TRUE` to a variable named `Done`; otherwise, it should set `Done` to `FALSE`. `ReadCard` need not handle backspaces, nor must it detect arithmetic overflow.

3. Generalize the `ReadString` procedure to allow the user to type tab characters. Assume that tab stops occur in positions 8, 16, ... of the string. Typing a tab character should add blanks to the string up to the next tab stop. If the next tab stop lies outside the string, `ReadString` should store blanks up to the end of the string.

Section 13.2

4. Write a program that will concatenate two files into a third file. `InOut` is sufficient for this program, because the two input files need not be open simultaneously.

5. Write a program that reads English words from an input file and copies them to an output file, writing only one word per line. Assume that the file contains only letters and whitespace characters.

6. Write a program that reads lines of text from an input file and copies them to an output file, suppressing duplicate lines. (For example, if lines 1 and 2 of the input file are the same and lines 3, 4, and 5 are the same, the program should copy only lines 1 and 3 to the output file.)

7. Write a program that prints a table showing the square and square root of each integer between 1 and 100. Each line of the table should contain a number *n*, followed by its square and square root. Align each column of the table on the right.

Section 13.3

8. In some file-handling modules, the `File` type is opaque, but in `FileSystem` it is not. What would be the advantages and disadvantages of making `File` opaque?

9. Write a program to display a file on the user's screen, pausing after each screenful until the user types a character. (Notice that `InOut` will not be sufficient, because the program must read from two input streams: the file and the user's keyboard.)

10. Modify the `ReadBlock` procedure to check for end of file. `ReadBlock` should indicate (through a variable parameter) how many words it was able to read.

11. The `CompareLines` program assumes that the `EOL` character always terminates the last line in a file. Modify `CompareLines` to work even when this assumption is false.

12. Write a program similar to `CompareLines` that compares the contents of two binary files, word by word, and prints a list of the differences between the files.

13. Write a program that makes a copy of a binary file. The program should copy the input file to the output file in blocks of 1,024 words, not word by word. (*Hint:* Use the `ReadWords` procedure.)

14. Modify the `UpdateInventory` program on the assumption that not every item number is present in the inventory file. Inventory records are still stored by item number, but some item numbers are missing. Use binary search to locate each inventory record to modify.

15. Assume that the files INVENT1.DAT and INVENT2.DAT both contain `Item` records in sorted order (as in the program `UpdateInventory`); not all items are present in both files, however. Write a program that merges the

two files into a single file, named MASTER.DAT. If a record representing an item appears in both files, the program should write a single record to MASTER.DAT representing the item; the onHand field for this record should be the sum of the onHand fields of the records in the two input files.

16. Write a program that finds the most expensive item in an inventory file (as in the `UpdateInventory` program) and changes the onHand field of the item to 0. The program should use sequential access to scan the file, then direct access to find the record it wants to modify.

17. Assume that records in a password file have the following form:

```
TYPE String10 = ARRAY [0..9] OF CHAR;
     Password = ARRAY [0..3] OF WORD; (* encoded password *)
     UserRecord = RECORD
                    userName: String10;
                    userPassword: Password
                  END;
```

    Write the following procedure:

```
PROCEDURE LookupUser(VAR passwordFile: File;
                     userName: String10;
                     VAR userPassword: Password;
                     VAR success: BOOLEAN);
  (* looks up a user name in passwordFile; if found, stores
     password into userPassword and sets success to TRUE; if
     not found, sets success to FALSE *)
```

18. Assuming that a password file contains records of the form shown in exercise 17, write the following procedure:

```
PROCEDURE AddUser(VAR passwordFile: File;
                  userName: String10;
                  userPassword: Password);
  (* adds user to passwordFile; no check is made if user is
     already present *)
```

19. Assuming that a password file contains records of the form shown in exercise 17, write the following procedure:

```
PROCEDURE ChangePassword(VAR passwordFile: File;
                         userName: String10;
                         newPassword: Password);
  (* changes user password; has no effect if user is not in
     passwordFile *)
```

20. Rewrite the `DisplayFile` program of Section 8.2 to use the `FileSystem` module. The `buffer` variable used by `DisplayFile` should no longer be necessary.

APPENDIX I

Reserved Words, Standard Identifiers, and Special Symbols

Each reserved word, standard type, and standard constant below is followed by the numbers of the sections in which it is discussed.

Reserved Words

AND 3.3
ARRAY 7.1
BEGIN 2.2
BY 4.4
CASE 4.2, 7.4
CONST 3.5, 9.1
DEFINITION 9.1
DIV 3.1
DO 4.3, 4.4, 7.3
ELSE 4.2, 7.4
ELSIF 4.2
END 2.2, 4.2, 4.3, 4.4, 7.3, 7.4, 9.1
EXIT 4.3
EXPORT 9.3
FOR 4.4
FROM 2.2
IF 4.2
IMPLEMENTATION 9.1
IMPORT 2.2
IN 7.5
LOOP 4.3
MOD 3.1
MODULE 2.2, 9.1, 9.3
NOT 3.3
OF 4.2, 7.1, 7.4, 7.5
OR 3.3
POINTER 8.1
PROCEDURE 5.1, 8.2
QUALIFIED 9.3
RECORD 7.3
REPEAT 4.3
RETURN 5.1
SET 7.5
THEN 4.2
TO 4.4, 8.1
TYPE 6.1, 9.1
UNTIL 4.3
VAR 3.5, 5.2, 8.2, 9.1
WHILE 4.3
WITH 7.3

Standard Types

BITSET 11.1
BOOLEAN 3.3
CARDINAL 3.1
CHAR 3.2
INTEGER 3.1
LONGINT 3.1
LONGREAL 3.1
PROC 8.2
REAL 3.1

Standard Constants

FALSE 3.3
NIL 8.1
TRUE 3.3

Standard Functions

	Parameter Type	*Result Type*	*Value Returned*
ABS (x)	any numeric type	same as parameter	absolute value of x
CAP (ch)	CHAR	CHAR	if ch is a lowercase letter, returns the corresponding uppercase letter; if ch is uppercase, returns ch
CHR (x)	CARDINAL	CHAR	character whose ordinal number is x
FLOAT (x)	CARDINAL	REAL	representation of x as a REAL number
HIGH (a)	any open array type	CARDINAL	length of a (in first dimension) minus 1
MAX (T)	type name	T	maximum value of type T
MIN (T)	type name	T	minimum value of type T
ODD (x)	CARDINAL, INTEGER	BOOLEAN	TRUE if x is odd; FALSE if x is even
ORD (x)	CARDINAL, INTEGER, CHAR, or enumeration	CARDINAL	ordinal number of x among values of its type
SIZE (T)	type name or variable of any type	CARDINAL	size of a variable of type T (or size of T if T is a variable)
TRUNC (x)	REAL	CARDINAL	integer part of x
VAL (T, x)	T: type name* x: CARDINAL	T	value of type T whose ordinal number is x

*T must be one of the standard identifiers CARDINAL, INTEGER, or CHAR, or the name of an enumeration type.

Standard Procedures

	Parameter Type(s)	*Action Performed*
DEC(x)	CARDINAL, INTEGER, CHAR, or enumeration	replaces x by its predecessor; if x has type CARDINAL or INTEGER, equivalent to x := x - 1
DEC(x, n)	x: CARDINAL, INTEGER, CHAR, or enumeration n: CARDINAL, INTEGER	replaces x by its nth predecessor; if x has type CARDINAL or INTEGER, equivalent to x := x - n
EXCL(s, i)	s: SET OF T (or BITSET) i: T	equivalent to s := s - T{i}
HALT	no parameters	terminates program execution
INC(x)	CARDINAL, INTEGER, CHAR, or enumeration	replaces x by its successor; if x has type CARDINAL or INTEGER, equivalent to x := x + 1
INC(x, n)	x: CARDINAL, INTEGER, CHAR, or enumeration n: CARDINAL, INTEGER	replaces x by its nth successor; if x has type CARDINAL or INTEGER, equivalent to x := x + n
INCL(s, i)	s: SET OF T (or BITSET) i: T	equivalent to s := s + T{i}

Operators and Other Symbols

+	addition, set union	OR	logical disjunction
-	subtraction, set difference	NOT ~	logical negation
*	multiplication, set intersection	=	equal
/	real division, symmetric set difference	# <>	not equal
		<	less than
DIV	integer division	<=	less than or equal to, set inclusion
MOD	modulus (remainder)		
AND &	logical conjunction	>	greater than

- `>=` greater than or equal to, set inclusion
- `IN` set membership
- `:=` assignment
- `(` starts an expression, enumeration, or parameter list
- `)` ends an expression, enumeration, or parameter list
- `{` starts a set value
- `}` ends a set value
- `[` starts a subrange specification, index list, or module priority
- `]` ends a subrange specification, index list, or module priority
- `(*` starts a comment
- `*)` ends a comment
- `^` dereferences a pointer
- `'` delimits a string literal
- `"` delimits a string literal
- `,` separates items in a list
- `;` separates statements; ends a procedure or module heading; ends a declaration or definition; separates formal parameter sections; ends an import or export list; separates field lists
- `:` separates the name of a variable, parameter, or field from its type; follows a list of case labels; separates the formal parameter list from the return type in a function heading or specification of a function type
- `|` separates cases and variants
- `.` decimal point in a real number; selects a record field; terminates a compilation unit; constructs a qualified identifier
- `..` separates a range of values in a subrange specification, list of case labels, or list of set elements

Operator Precedence

NOT ~
* / DIV MOD AND &
+ - OR
= # <> < <= > >= IN

NOT has the highest precedence; the relational operators have the lowest. Operations at the same level of precedence are performed from left to right.

APPENDIX II

EBNF Description of Modula-2's Syntax

This appendix contains a complete EBNF (Extended Backus-Naur Form) description of Modula-2's syntax. An EBNF description of a language consists of a series of *productions*. Each production defines a syntactic construct; for example, the production

Enumeration = "(" *IdentList* ")".

states that an enumeration type consists of a left parenthesis, followed by an identifier list, followed by a right parenthesis. The symbol to the left of the equals sign is called a *nonterminal*; it represents the syntactic construct being defined. The symbols to the right of the equals sign define the construct; these symbols include both nonterminals (*IdentList*, in the preceding example) and *terminals* (symbols that can actually appear in a program, including letters, digits, reserved words, and special symbols). Each production ends with a period. The equals sign and period are called *metasymbols*, because they are part of the EBNF description, not part of the language being defined. Terminals (other than reserved words) are always enclosed in quotation marks to avoid confusion with metasymbols. In addition to the equals sign and period, several other metasymbols can appear in productions.

A vertical bar | separates alternate definitions of a syntactic construct. For example, the production

Number = *Integer* | *Real*.

states that a *Number* can be either an *Integer* or a *Real*.

Square brackets [ ] surround an optional portion of a construct. The production

FormalType = [ARRAY OF] *Qualident*.

states that a *FormalType* is a *Qualident*, possibly preceded by the words ARRAY OF.

Braces {} surround a portion that we can omit or repeat as many times as we desire. The production

IdentList = *Ident* {"," *Ident*}.

states that an *IdentList* consists of one or more identifiers, separated by commas.

Parentheses () resolve ambiguities caused by the use of |. The production

Integer = *Digit* {*Digit*} |
OctalDigit {*OctalDigit*} ("B" | "C") |
Digit {*HexDigit*} "H".

shows that one alternative for an *Integer* is a sequence of octal digits followed by one of the letters B or C.

EBNF Description of Modula-2*

1 Compilation Units

1.1 *CompilationUnit* = *DefinitionModule* | [IMPLEMENTATION] *ProgramModule*.
1.2 *DefinitionModule* = DEFINITION MODULE *Ident* ";"
{*Import*} {*Definition*} END *Ident* ".".
1.3 *Definition* = CONST {*ConstantDeclaration* ";"} |
TYPE {*Ident* ["=" *Type*] ";"} |
VAR {*VariableDeclaration* ";"} |
ProcedureHeading ";".
1.4 *ProgramModule* = MODULE *Ident* [*Priority*] ";" {*Import*} *Block Ident* ".".

2 Declarations

2.1 *Declaration* = CONST {*ConstantDeclaration* ";"} |
TYPE {*TypeDeclaration* ";"} |
VAR {*VariableDeclaration* ";"} |
ProcedureDeclaration ";" |
ModuleDeclaration ";".
2.2 *ConstantDeclaration* = *Ident* "=" *ConstExpression*.
2.3 *TypeDeclaration* = *Ident* "=" *Type*.
2.4 *VariableDeclaration* = *IdentList* ":" *Type*.
2.5 *ProcedureDeclaration* = *ProcedureHeading* ";" *Block Ident*.

*The following productions have been adapted from Niklaus Wirth, *Programming in Modula-2*, 3rd ed. (New York: Springer-Verlag, 1985). Used by permission. Nonterminals have been capitalized, and productions have been reordered and renumbered.

2.6 *ProcedureHeading* = PROCEDURE *Ident* [*FormalParameters*].
2.7 *FormalParameters* = "(" [*FPSection* {";" *FPSection*}] ")" [":" *Qualident*].
2.8 *FPSection* = [VAR] *IdentList* ":" *FormalType*.
2.9 *Block* = {*Declaration*} [BEGIN *StatementSequence*] END.
2.10 *ModuleDeclaration* = MODULE *Ident* [*Priority*] ";"
{*Import*} [*Export*] *Block Ident*.
2.11 *Priority* = "[" *ConstExpression* "]".
2.12 *Import* = [FROM *Ident*] IMPORT *IdentList* ";".
2.13 *Export* = EXPORT [QUALIFIED] *IdentList* ";".

3 Types

3.1 *Type* = *SimpleType* | *ArrayType* | *RecordType* | *SetType* |
PointerType | *ProcedureType*.
3.2 *SimpleType* = *Qualident* | *Enumeration* | *SubrangeType*.
3.3 *Enumeration* = "(" *IdentList* ")".
3.4 *SubrangeType* = [*Qualident*] "[" *ConstExpression* ".." *ConstExpression* "]".
3.5 *ArrayType* = ARRAY *SimpleType* {"," *SimpleType*} OF *Type*.
3.6 *RecordType* = RECORD *FieldListSequence* END.
3.7 *FieldListSequence* = *FieldList* {";" *FieldList*}.
3.8 *FieldList* = [*IdentList* ":" *Type* |
CASE [*Ident*] ":" *Qualident* OF *Variant* {"|" *Variant*}
[ELSE *FieldListSequence*] END].
3.9 *Variant* = [*CaseLabelList* ":" *FieldListSequence*].
3.10 *SetType* = SET OF *SimpleType*.
3.11 *PointerType* = POINTER TO *Type*.
3.12 *ProcedureType* = PROCEDURE [*FormalTypeList*].
3.13 *FormalTypeList* = "(" [[VAR] *FormalType* {"," [VAR] *FormalType*}] ")"
[":" *Qualident*].
3.14 *FormalType* = [ARRAY OF] *Qualident*.

4 Statements

4.1 *StatementSequence* = *Statement* {";" *Statement*}.
4.2 *Statement* = [*Assignment* | *ProcedureCall* | *IfStatement* | *CaseStatement* |
WhileStatement | *RepeatStatement* | *LoopStatement* |
ForStatement | *WithStatement* | EXIT | RETURN [*Expression*]].
4.3 *Assignment* = *Designator* ":=" *Expression*.
4.4 *ProcedureCall* = *Designator* [*ActualParameters*].
4.5 *ActualParameters* = "(" [*ExpList*] ")".

4.6 *IfStatement* = IF *Expression* THEN *StatementSequence*
{ELSIF *Expression* THEN *StatementSequence*}
[ELSE *StatementSequence*] END.
4.7 *CaseStatement* = CASE *Expression* OF *Case* {"|" *Case*}
[ELSE *StatementSequence*] END.
4.8 *Case* = [*CaseLabelList* ":" *StatementSequence*].
4.9 *CaseLabelList* = *CaseLabels* {"," *CaseLabels*}.
4.10 *CaseLabels* = *ConstExpression* [".." *ConstExpression*].
4.11 *WhileStatement* = WHILE *Expression* DO *StatementSequence* END.
4.12 *RepeatStatement* = REPEAT *StatementSequence* UNTIL *Expression*.
4.13 *LoopStatement* = LOOP *StatementSequence* END.
4.14 *ForStatement* = FOR *Ident* ":=" *Expression* TO *Expression* [BY *ConstExpression*]
DO *StatementSequence* END.
4.15 *WithStatement* = WITH *Designator* DO *StatementSequence* END.

5 Expressions

5.1 *ConstExpression* = *Expression*.
5.2 *ExpList* = *Expression* {"," *Expression*}.
5.3 *Expression* = *SimpleExpression* [*Relation SimpleExpression*].
5.4 *Relation* = "=" | "#" | "<" | "<=" | ">" | ">=" | IN.
5.5 *SimpleExpression* = ["+" | "-"] *Term* {*AddOperator Term*}.
5.6 *AddOperator* = "+" | "-" | OR.
5.7 *Term* = *Factor* {*MulOperator Factor*}.
5.8 *MulOperator* = "*" | "/" | DIV | MOD | AND.
5.9 *Factor* = *Number* | *String* | *Set* | *Designator* [*ActualParameters*] |
"(" *Expression* ")" | NOT *Factor*.
5.10 *Set* = [*Qualident*] "{" [*Element* {"," *Element*}] "}".
5.11 *Element* = *Expression* [".." *Expression*].

6 Names

6.1 *IdentList* = *Ident* {"," *Ident*}.
6.2 *Ident* = *Letter* {*Letter* | *Digit*}.
6.3 *Qualident* = *Ident* {"." *Ident*}.
6.4 *Designator* = *Qualident* {"." *Ident* | "[" *ExpList* "]" | "^"}.

7 Literals

7.1 *Number* = *Integer* | *Real*.
7.2 *Integer* = *Digit* {*Digit*} |
OctalDigit {*OctalDigit*} ("B" | "C") |
Digit {*HexDigit*} "H".

7.3 *Digit* = *OctalDigit* | "8" | "9".
7.4 *OctalDigit* = "0" | "1" | "2" | "3" | "4" | "5" | "6" | "7".
7.5 *HexDigit* = *Digit* | "A" | "B" | "C" | "D" | "E" | "F".
7.6 *Real* = *Digit* {*Digit*} "." {*Digit*} [*ScaleFactor*].
7.7 *ScaleFactor* = "E" ["+" | "-"] *Digit* {*Digit*}.
7.8 *String* = "'" {*Character*} "'" | '"' {*Character*} '"'.

Cross-Reference Table for Nonterminals

The following table lists all the nonterminals that appear in the EBNF description of Modula-2. Following each nonterminal is the number of its defining production (in parentheses) and the numbers of the productions in which the nonterminal is referenced.

ActualParameters (4.5) 4.4, 5.9
AddOperator (5.6) 5.5
ArrayType (3.5) 3.1
Assignment (4.3) 4.2
Block (2.9) 1.4, 2.5, 2.10
Case (4.8) 4.7
CaseLabelList (4.9) 3.9, 4.8
CaseLabels (4.10) 4.9
CaseStatement (4.7) 4.2
Character 7.8
CompilationUnit (1.1)
ConstantDeclaration (2.2) 1.3, 2.1
ConstExpression (5.1) 2.2, 2.11, 3.4, 4.10, 4.14
Declaration (2.1) 2.9
Definition (1.3) 1.2
DefinitionModule (1.2) 1.1
Designator (6.4) 4.3, 4.4, 4.15, 5.9
Digit (7.3) 6.2, 7.2, 7.5, 7.6, 7.7
Element (5.11) 5.10
Enumeration (3.3) 3.2
ExpList (5.2) 4.5, 6.4
Export (2.13) 2.10
Expression (5.3) 4.2, 4.3, 4.6, 4.7, 4.11, 4.12, 4.14, 5.1, 5.2, 5.9, 5.11
Factor (5.9) 5.7, 5.9
FieldList (3.8) 3.7
FieldListSequence (3.7) 3.6, 3.8, 3.9
FormalParameters (2.7) 2.6
FormalType (3.14) 2.8, 3.13
FormalTypeList (3.13) 3.12
ForStatement (4.14) 4.2
FPSection (2.8) 2.7
HexDigit (7.5) 7.2
Ident (6.2) 1.2, 1.3, 1.4, 2.2, 2.3, 2.5, 2.6, 2.10, 2.12, 3.8, 4.14, 6.1, 6.3, 6.4
IdentList (6.1) 2.4, 2.8, 2.12, 2.13, 3.3, 3.8
IfStatement (4.6) 4.2
Import (2.12) 1.2, 1.4, 2.10
Integer (7.2) 7.1
Letter 6.2
LoopStatement (4.13) 4.2
ModuleDeclaration (2.10) 2.1
MulOperator (5.8) 5.7
Number (7.1) 5.9
OctalDigit (7.4) 7.2, 7.3
PointerType (3.11) 3.1
Priority (2.11) 1.4, 2.10
ProcedureCall (4.4) 4.2
ProcedureDeclaration (2.5) 2.1
ProcedureHeading (2.6) 1.3, 2.5
ProcedureType (3.12) 3.1
ProgramModule (1.4) 1.1
Qualident (6.3) 2.7, 3.2, 3.4, 3.8, 3.13, 3.14, 5.10, 6.4
Real (7.6) 7.1

Cross-Reference Table for Reserved Words

Cross-Reference Table for Special Symbols

APPENDIX III
Syntax Charts*

1 Compilation Units

2 Declarations

3 Types

4 Statements

---

*The syntax charts in this appendix have been adapted from Niklaus Wirth, *Programming in Modula-2*, 3rd ed. (New York: Springer-Verlag, 1985). Used by permission. Only cosmetic changes were made to the charts.

1. Compilation Units

1.1 ***CompilationUnit***

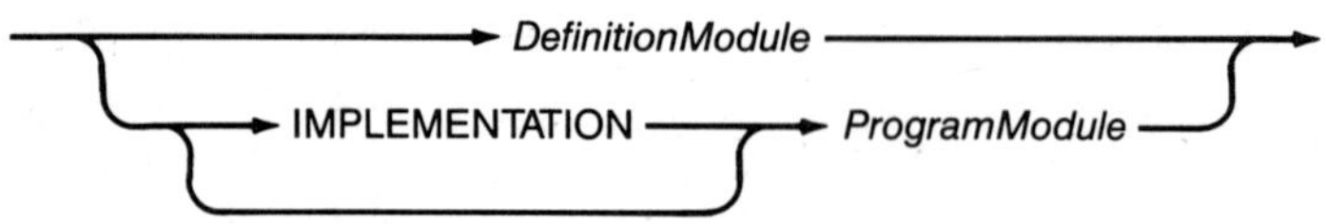

1.2 ***DefinitionModule***

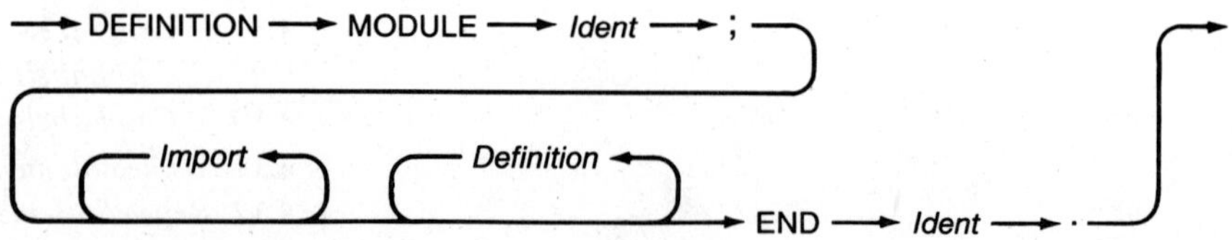

1.3 ***Definition***

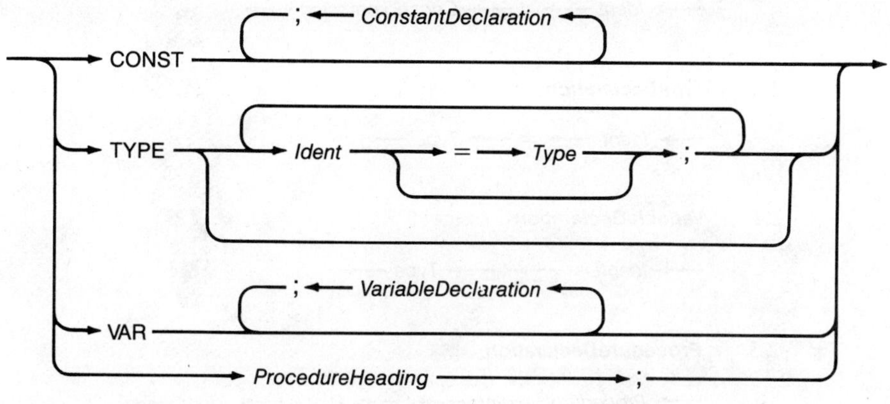

1.4 ***ProgramModule***

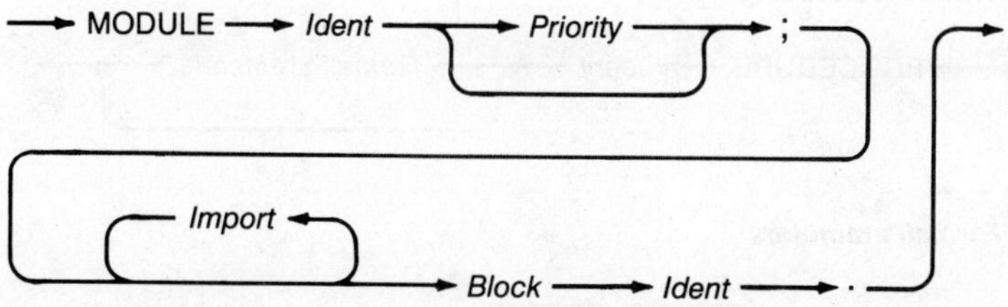

2. Declarations

2.1 ***Declaration***

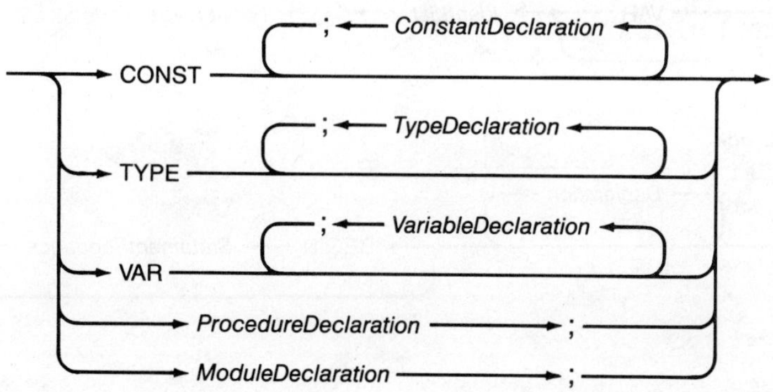

2.2 **ConstantDeclaration**

2.3 **TypeDeclaration**

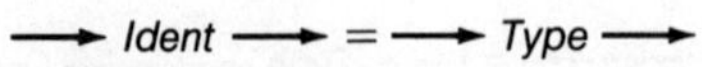

2.4 **VariableDeclaration**

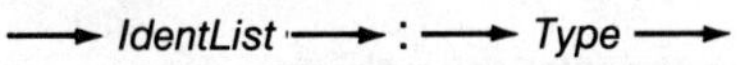

2.5 **ProcedureDeclaration**

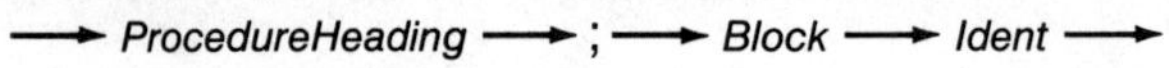

2.6 **ProcedureHeading**

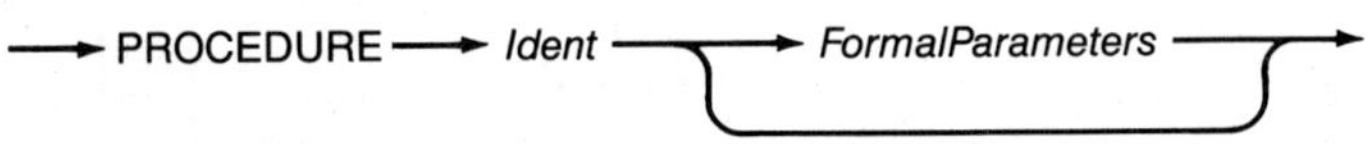

2.7 **FormalParameters**

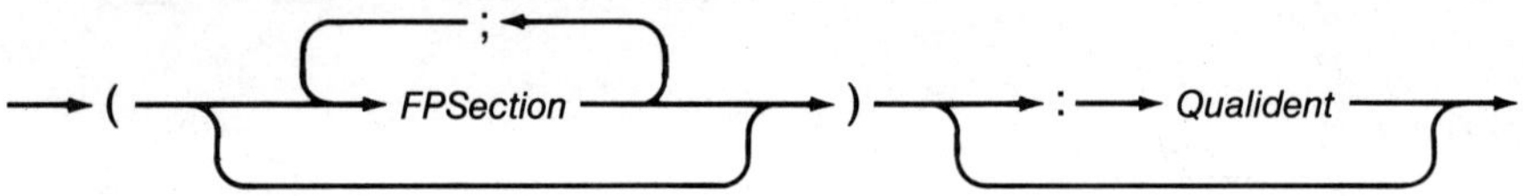

2.8 **FPSection**

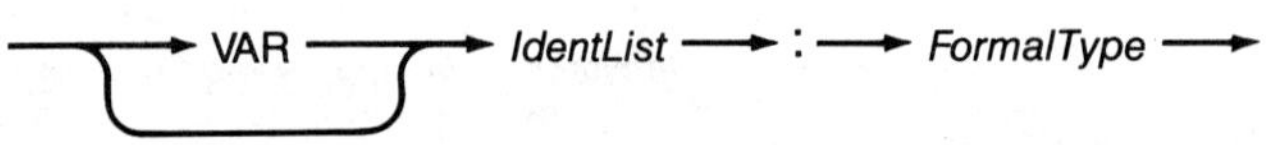

2.9 **Block**

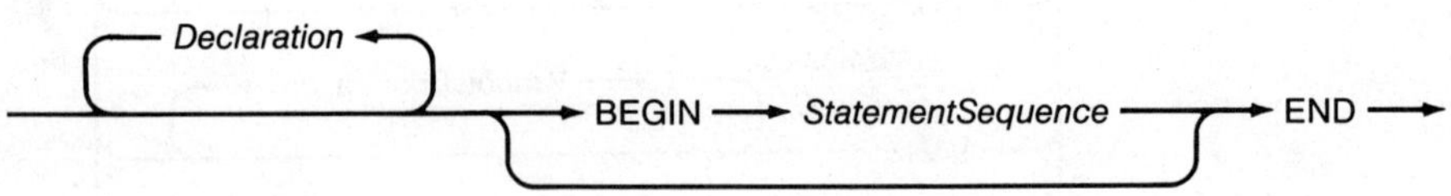

2.10 ***ModuleDeclaration***

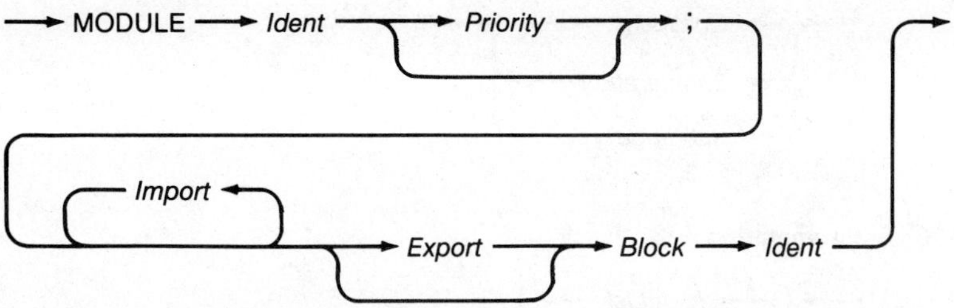

2.11 ***Priority***

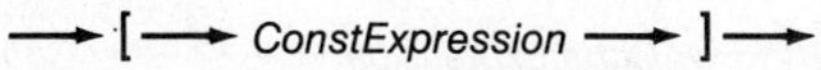

2.12 ***Import***

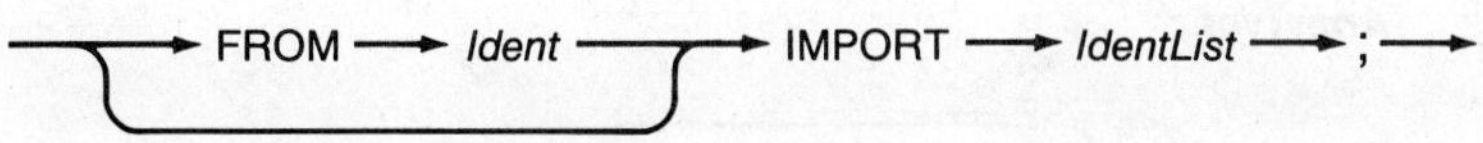

2.13 ***Export***

3. Types

3.1 ***Type***

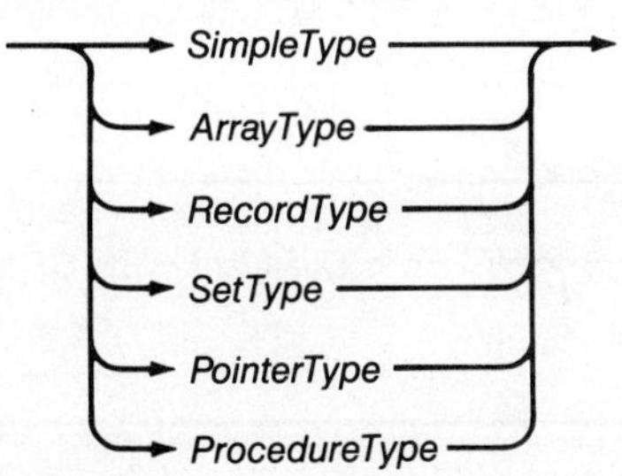

3.2 **SimpleType**

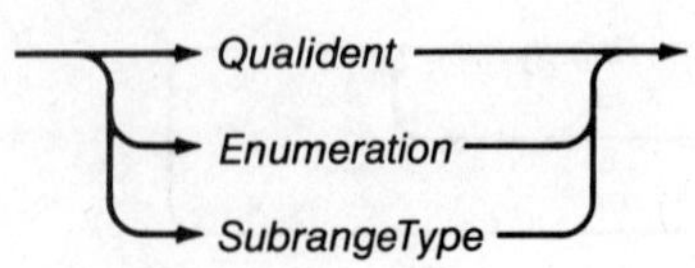

3.3 **Enumeration**

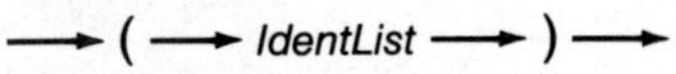

3.4 **SubrangeType**

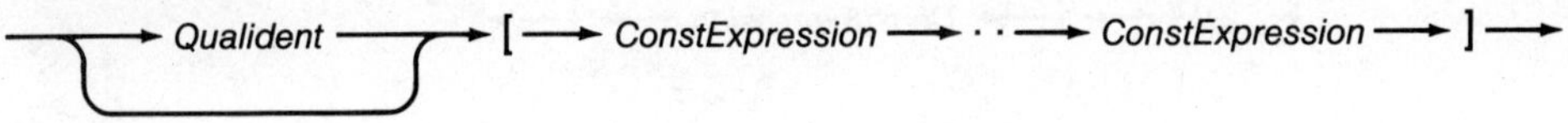

3.5 **ArrayType**

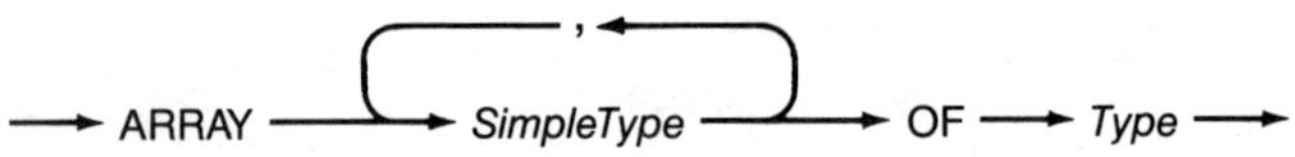

3.6 **RecordType**

3.7 **FieldListSequence**

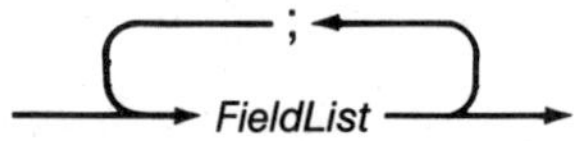

3.8 **FieldList**

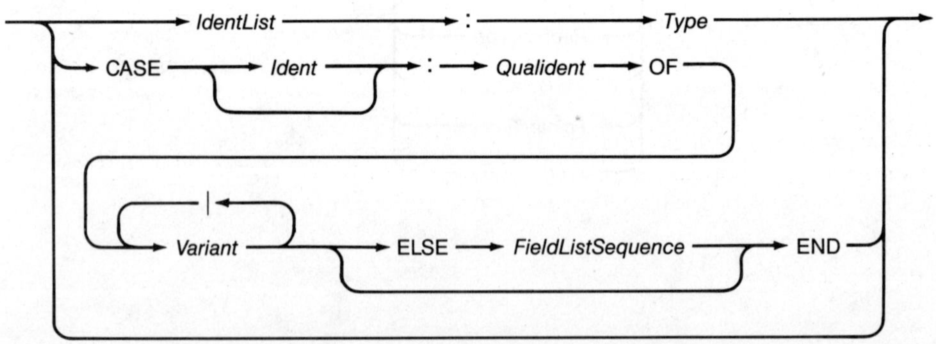

3.9 ***Variant***

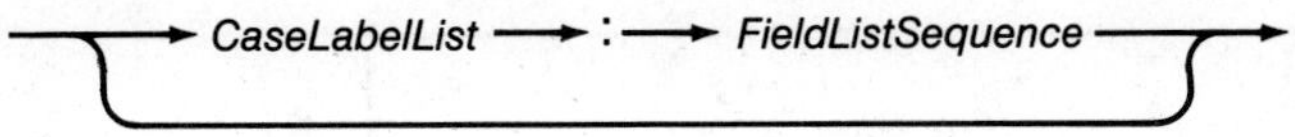

3.10 ***SetType***

3.11 ***PointerType***

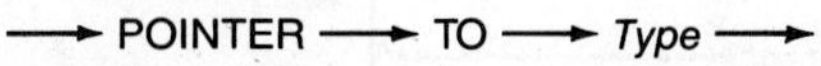

3.12 ***ProcedureType***

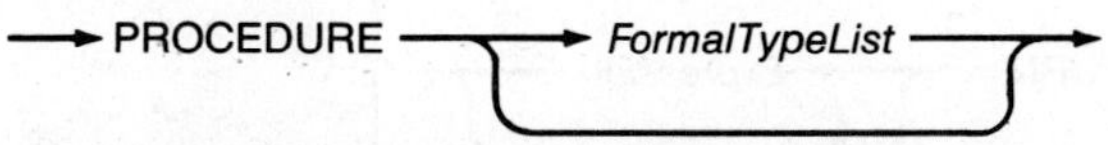

3.13 ***FormalTypeList***

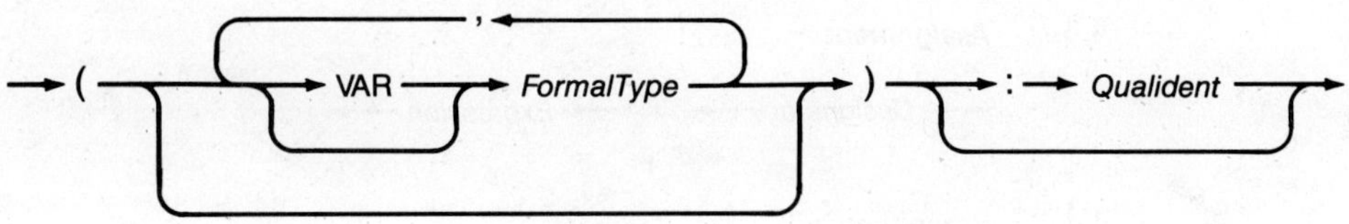

3.14 ***FormalType***

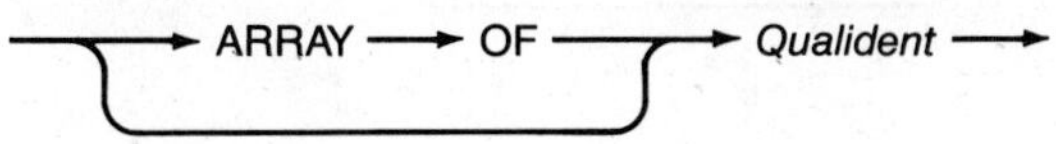

4. Statements

4.1 ***StatementSequence***

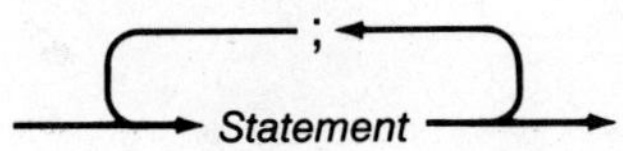

4.2 **Statement**

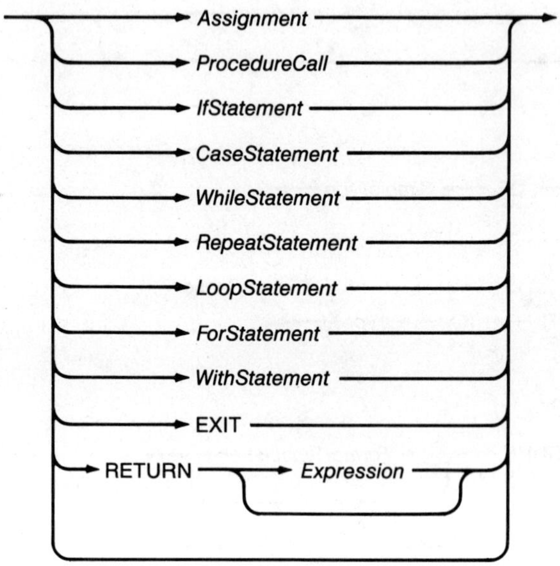

4.3 **Assignment**

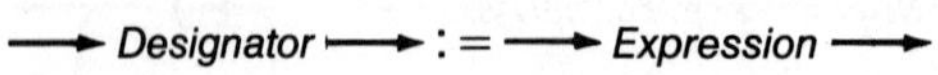

4.4 **ProcedureCall**

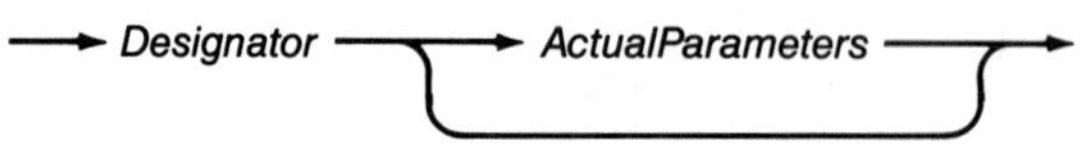

4.5 **ActualParameters**

4.6 *IfStatement*

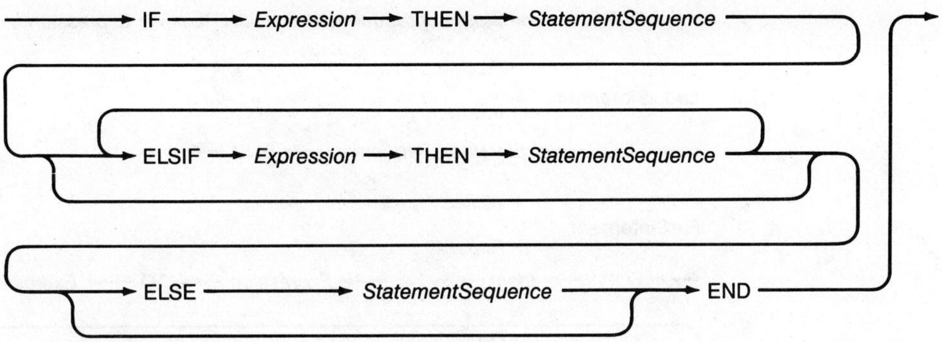

4.7 *CaseStatement*

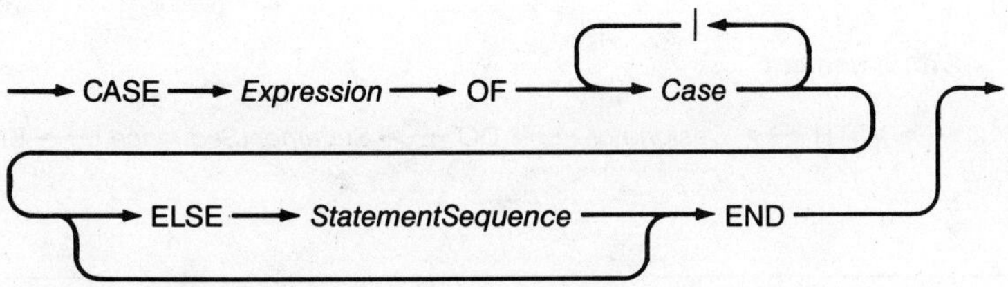

4.8 *Case*

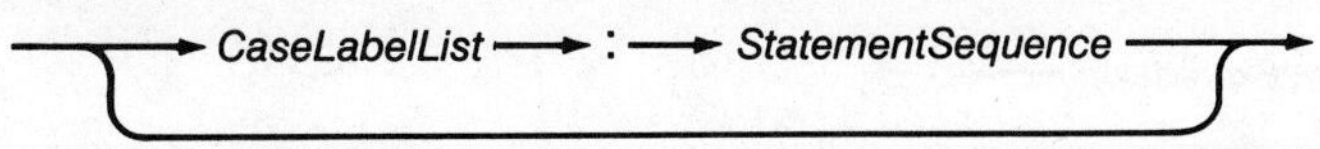

4.9 *CaseLabelList*

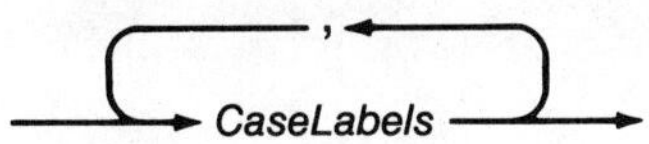

4.10 *CaseLabels*

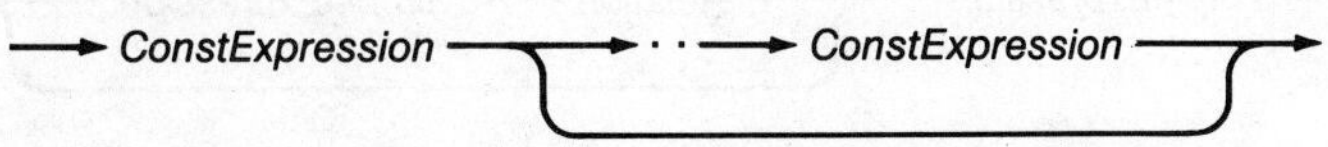

4.11 *WhileStatement*

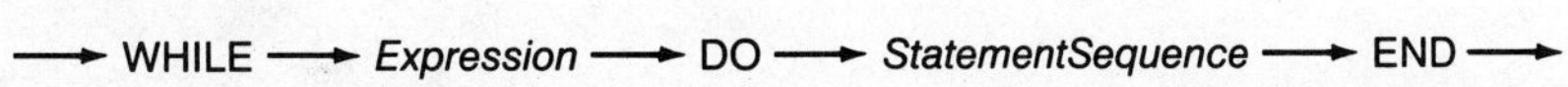

4.12 **RepeatStatement**

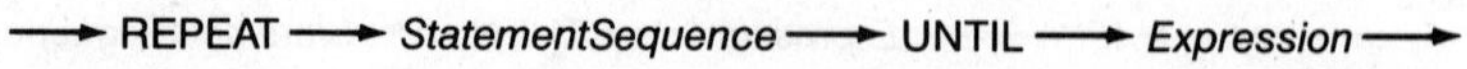

4.13 **LoopStatement**

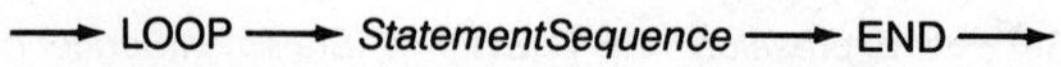

4.14 **ForStatement**

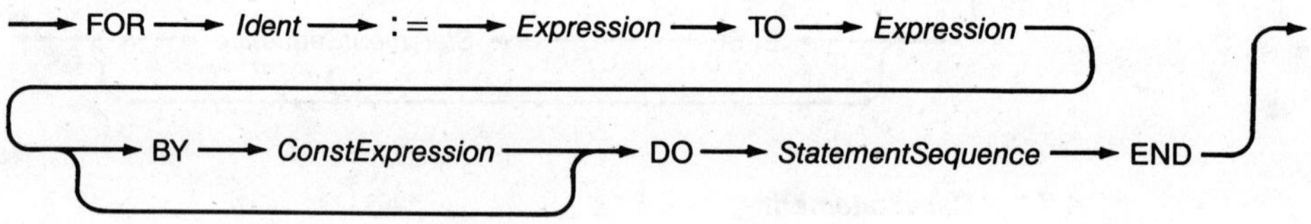

4.15 **WithStatement**

5. Expressions

5.1 **ConstExpression**

5.2 **ExpList**

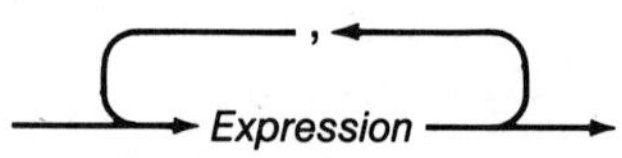

5.3 **Expression**

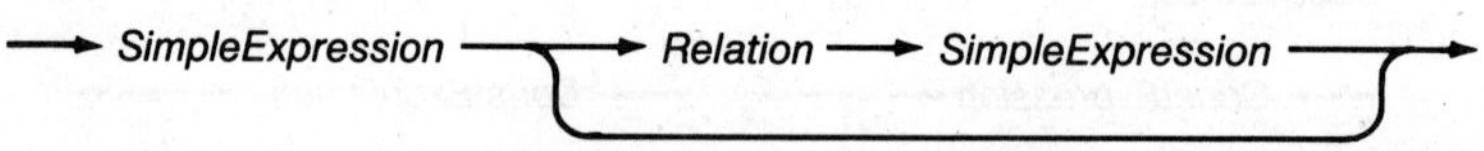

5.4 **Relation**

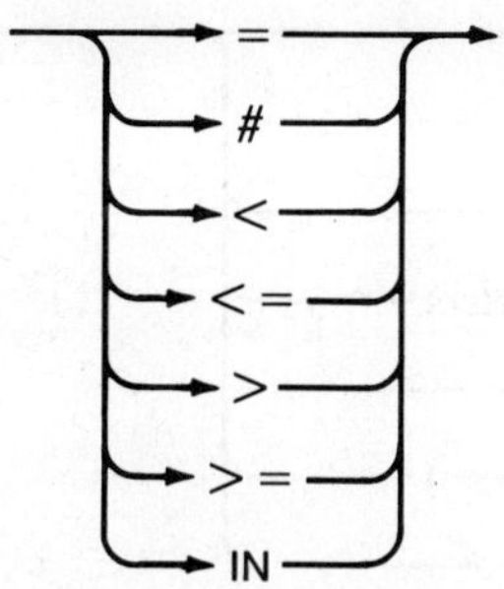

5.5 **SimpleExpression**

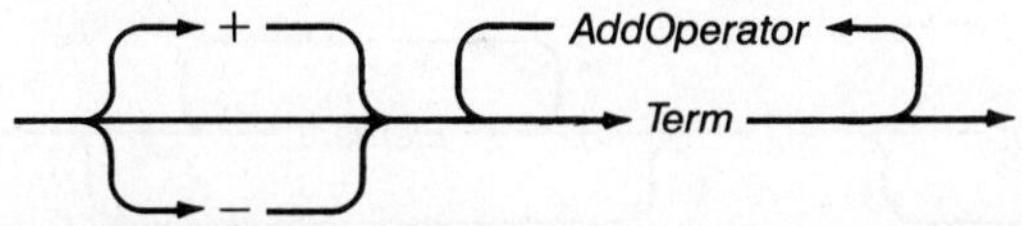

5.6 **AddOperator**

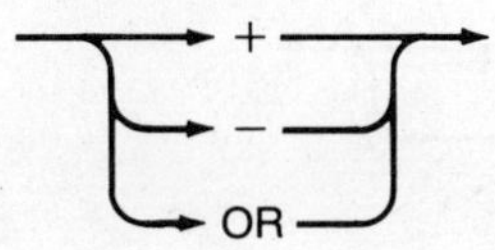

5.7 **Term**

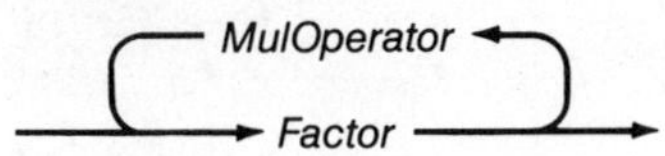

5.8 **MulOperator**

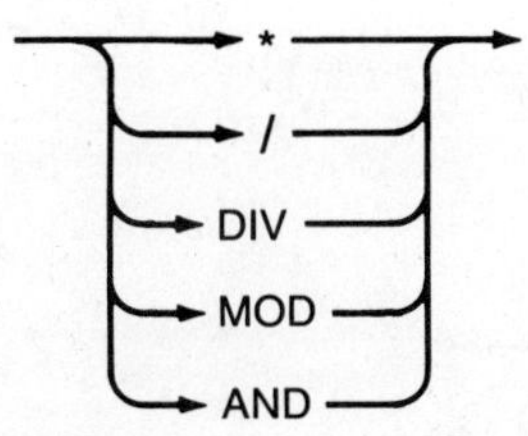

5.9 **Factor**

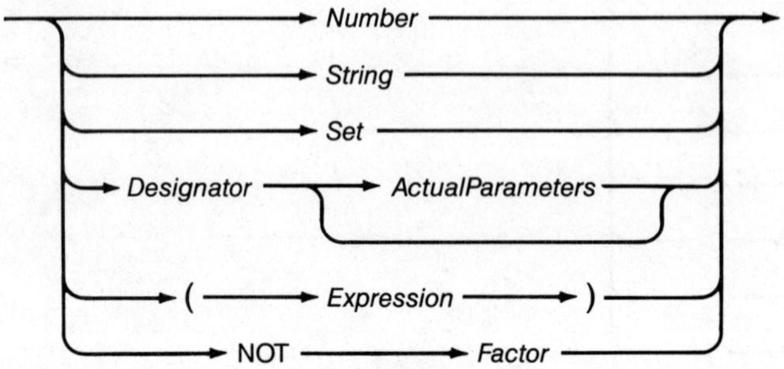

5.10 **Set**

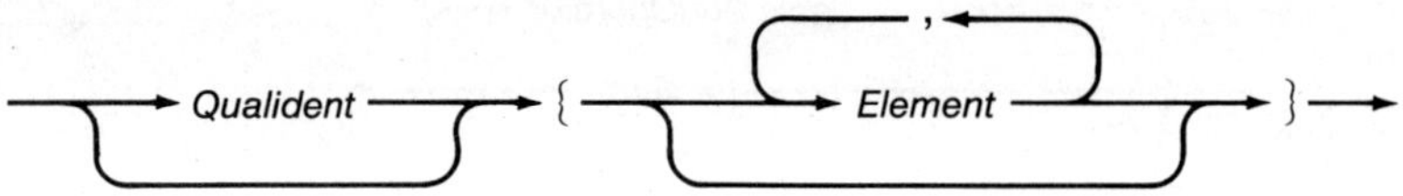

5.11 **Element**

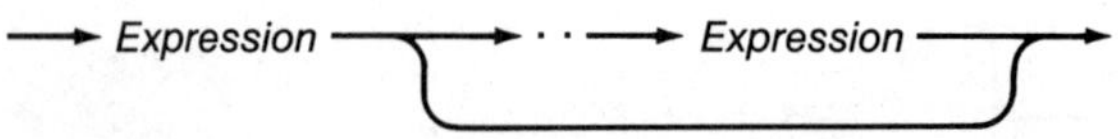

6. Names

6.1 **IdentList**

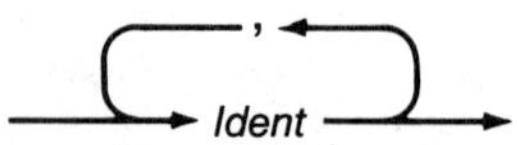

6.2 **Ident**

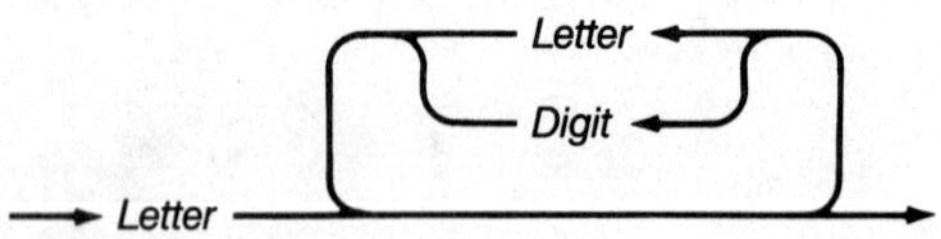

6.3 **Qualident**

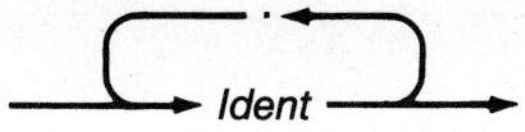

6.4 **Designator**

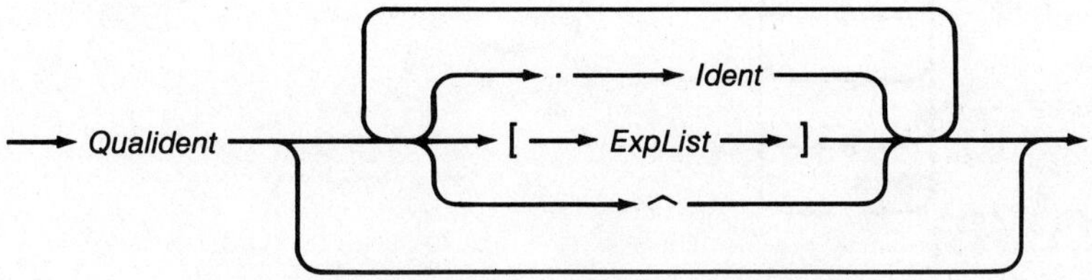

7. Literals

7.1 **Number**

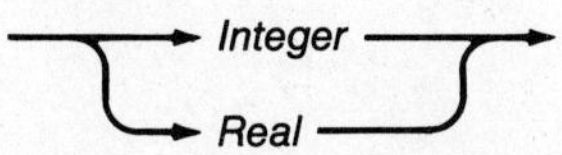

7.2 **Integer**

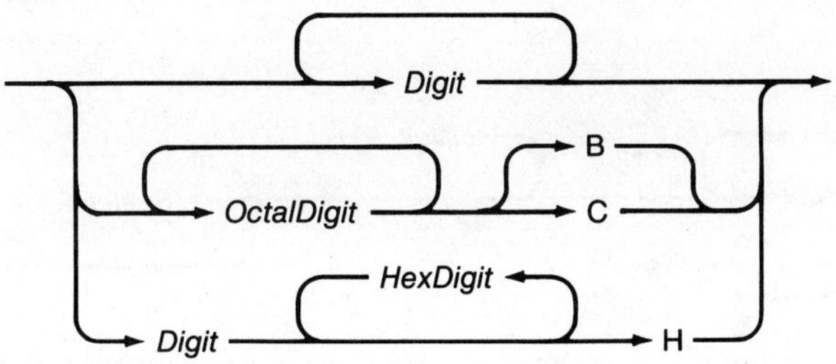

7.3 **Digit**

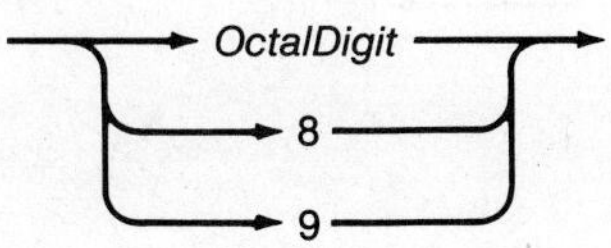

7.4 **OctalDigit**

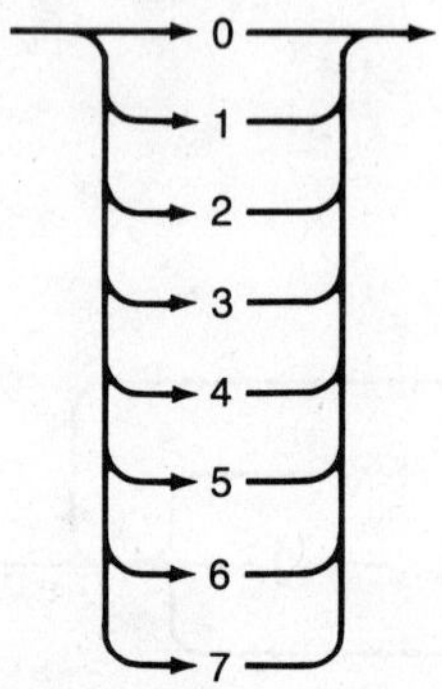

7.5 **HexDigit**

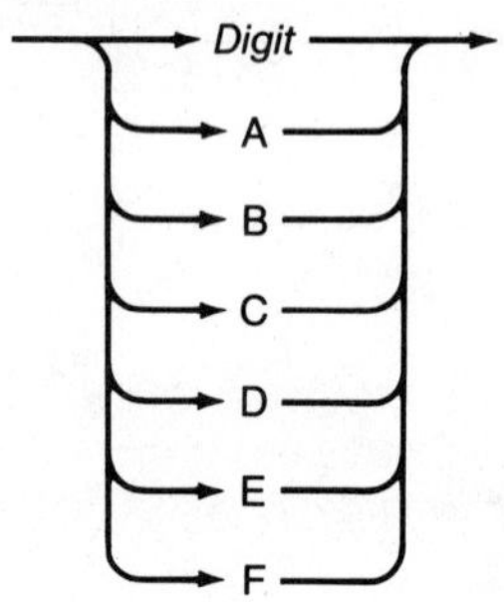

7.6 **Real**

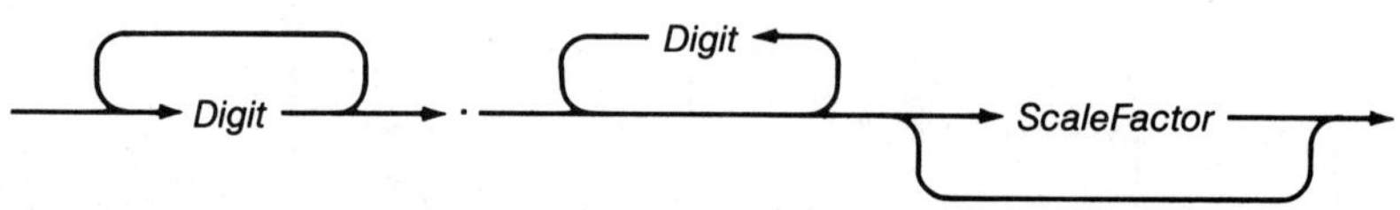

7.7 **ScaleFactor**

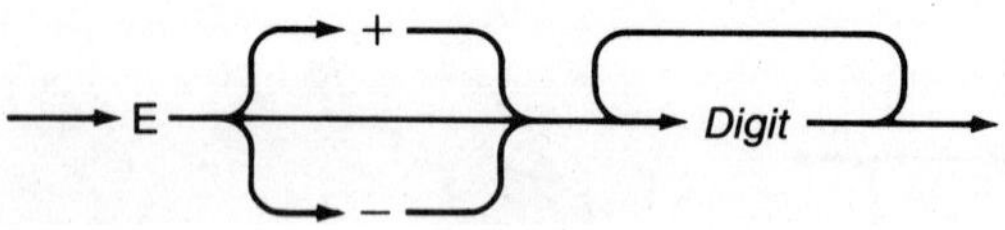

7.8 **String**

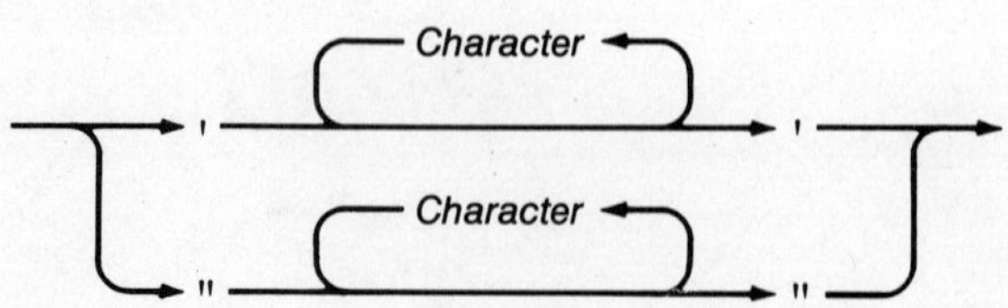

Index to Syntax Charts

APPENDIX IV

Wirth's Library

In Appendix 2 of the Third Edition of *Programming in Modula-2*, Wirth describes eleven "standard utility modules"; we will refer to these modules collectively as "Wirth's library." He emphasizes that these modules are not part of the Modula-2 language. He also acknowledges that Modula-2 systems may offer these modules in revised form or supply other modules instead.

The modules in Wirth's library can be divided into two groups. The modules in the first group provide basic operations needed by many programs:

`FileSystem`	Input/output using files
`InOut`	Input/output using standard streams
`MathLib0`	Mathematical functions
`RealInOut`	Input/output of real numbers
`Storage`	Dynamic storage allocation
`Terminal`	Input/output using a terminal

Most Modula-2 systems provide some version of these modules. The following pages contain the definition parts of these six modules, exactly as they appear in *Programming in Modula-2*, including the original comments. Spacing has been changed for consistency with the rest of this book, and typographical errors have been corrected.*

The other five modules in Wirth's library are

`CursorMouse`	Mouse input and cursor display
`GraphicWindows`	Windows containing graphics
`Menu`	"Pop-up" menus
`TextWindows`	Windows containing text
`Windows`	General window support

These modules require an environment similar to that provided by Wirth's Lilith machine, which has a mouse and a bit-mapped display. Because most Modula-2 systems do not supply these five modules, we have not included them in this appendix.

---

*These modules are reprinted from Niklaus Wirth, *Programming in Modula-2*, 3rd ed. (New York: Springer-Verlag, 1985). Used by permission.

FileSystem

The `FileSystem` module supports file input and output. Section 13.3 discusses `FileSystem`.

```
DEFINITION MODULE FileSystem;    (* S. E. Knudsen *)

  FROM SYSTEM IMPORT ADDRESS, WORD;

  TYPE Response = (done, notdone, notsupported, callerror,
                   unknownmedium, unknownfile, paramerror,
                   toomanyfiles, eom, deviceoff,
                   softparityerror, softprotected, softerror,
                   hardparityerror, hardprotected, timeout,
                   harderror);
       Command = (create, open, close, lookup, rename, setread,
                  setwrite, setmodify, setopen, doio, setpos,
                  getpos, length, setprotect, getprotect,
                  setpermanent, getpermanent, getinternal);
       Flag = (er, ef, rd, wr, ag, bytemode);
       FlagSet = SET OF Flag;
       File = RECORD
                res: Response;
                bufa, ela, ina, topa: ADDRESS;
                elodd, inodd, eof: BOOLEAN;
                flags: FlagSet;
                CASE com: Command OF
                  create, open, getinternal:
                    fileno, versionno: CARDINAL |
                  lookup:
                    new: BOOLEAN |
                  setpos, getpos, length:
                    highpos, lowpos: CARDINAL |
                  setprotect, getprotect:
                    wrprotect: BOOLEAN |
                  setpermanent, getpermanent:
                    on: BOOLEAN
                END;
              END;

  (* The routines defined by the file system can be grouped in
     routines for
     1. Opening, closing and renaming of files.
        (Create, Close, Lookup, Rename)
     2. Reading and writing of files.
        (SetRead, SetWrite, SetModify, SetOpen, Doio)
     3. Positioning of files.
        (SetPos, GetPos, Length)
```

```
   4. Streamlike handling of files.
      (Reset, Again, ReadWord, WriteWord, ReadChar,
      WriteChar) *)

PROCEDURE Create(VAR f: File; mediumname: ARRAY OF CHAR);
  (* creates a new temporary (or nameless) file f on the
     named device. *)

PROCEDURE Close(VAR f: File);
  (* terminates the operations on file f, i.e. cuts off the
     connection between variable f and the file system.
     A temporary file will hereby be destroyed whereas a
     file with a not empty name remains in the directory for
     later use. *)

PROCEDURE Lookup(VAR f: File; filename: ARRAY OF CHAR;
                 new: BOOLEAN);
  (* searches file 'filename'.  If the file does not exist
     and 'new' is TRUE, a new file with the given name will
     be created. *)

PROCEDURE Rename(VAR f: File; filename: ARRAY OF CHAR);
  (* changes the name of the file to 'filename'.  If the
     new name is empty, f is changed to be a temporary
     file. *)

PROCEDURE SetRead(VAR f: File);
  (* initializes the file for reading. *)

PROCEDURE SetWrite(VAR f: File);
  (* initializes the file for writing. *)

PROCEDURE SetModify(VAR f: File);
  (* initializes the file for modifying. *)

PROCEDURE SetOpen(VAR f: File);
  (* terminates any input- or output operations on the
     file. *)

PROCEDURE Doio(VAR f: File);
  (* is used in connection with SetRead, SetWrite, and
     SetModify in order to read, write or modify a file
     sequentially. *)

PROCEDURE SetPos(VAR f: File; highpos, lowpos: CARDINAL);
  (* sets the current position of file f to byte
     highpos * 2**16 + lowpos. *)

PROCEDURE GetPos(VAR f: File; VAR highpos, lowpos: CARDINAL);
  (* returns the current byte position of file f. *)
```

```
    PROCEDURE Length(VAR f: File; VAR highpos, lowpos: CARDINAL);
      (* returns the length of file f in highpos and lowpos. *)

    PROCEDURE Reset(VAR f: File);
      (* sets the file into state opened and the position to the
         beginning of the file. *)

    PROCEDURE Again(VAR f: File);
      (* prevents a subsequent call of ReadWord (or ReadChar)
         from reading the next value on the file.  Instead, the
         value read just before the call of Again is returned
         once more. *)

    PROCEDURE ReadWord(VAR f: File; VAR w: WORD);
      (* reads the next word on the file. *)

    PROCEDURE WriteWord(VAR f: File; w: WORD);
      (* appends word w to the file. *)

    PROCEDURE ReadChar(VAR f: File; VAR ch: CHAR);
      (* reads the next character on the file. *)

    PROCEDURE WriteChar(VAR f: File; ch: CHAR);
      (* appends character ch to the file. *)

  END FileSystem.
```

InOut

The `InOut` module provides procedures for reading and writing integers and character data. `InOut` controls a single input stream and a single output stream; these can be redirected under program control. Section 13.2 discusses `InOut`.

```
DEFINITION MODULE InOut;    (* N. Wirth *)

  CONST EOL = 36C;

  VAR Done: BOOLEAN;
      termCH: CHAR;

  PROCEDURE OpenInput(defext: ARRAY OF CHAR);
    (* request a file name and open input file "in".
       Done := "file was successfully opened".
       If open, subsequent input is read from this file.
       If name ends with ".", append extension defext *)
```

```
PROCEDURE OpenOutput(defext: ARRAY OF CHAR);
  (* request a file name and open output file "out"
     Done := "file was successfully opened".
     If open, subsequent output is written on this file *)

PROCEDURE CloseInput;
  (* closes input file; returns input to terminal *)

PROCEDURE CloseOutput;
  (* closes output file; returns output to terminal *)

PROCEDURE Read(VAR ch: CHAR);
  (* Done := NOT in.eof *)

PROCEDURE ReadString(VAR s: ARRAY OF CHAR);
  (* read string, i.e. sequence of characters not containing
     blanks nor control characters; leading blanks are
     ignored.  Input is terminated by any character <= " ";
     this character is assigned to termCH.  DEL is used for
     backspacing when input from terminal *)

PROCEDURE ReadInt(VAR x: INTEGER);
  (* read string and convert to integer.  Syntax:
     integer = ["+"|"-"] digit {digit}.
     Leading blanks are ignored.
     Done := "integer was read" *)

PROCEDURE ReadCard(VAR x: CARDINAL);
  (* read string and convert to cardinal.  Syntax:
     cardinal = digit {digit}.
     Leading blanks are ignored.
     Done := "cardinal was read" *)

PROCEDURE Write(ch: CHAR);

PROCEDURE WriteLn;
  (* terminate line *)

PROCEDURE WriteString(s: ARRAY OF CHAR);

PROCEDURE WriteInt(x: INTEGER; n: CARDINAL);
  (* write integer x with (at least) n characters on file
     "out".  If n is greater than the number of digits
     needed, blanks are added preceding the number *)

PROCEDURE WriteCard(x, n: CARDINAL);

PROCEDURE WriteOct(x, n: CARDINAL);
```

```
    PROCEDURE WriteHex(x, n: CARDINAL);
END InOut.
```

MathLib0

The MathLib0 module supplies common mathematical functions.

```
DEFINITION MODULE MathLib0;
  (* standard functions; J. Waldvogel/N. Wirth, 10.12.80 *)

    PROCEDURE sqrt(x: REAL): REAL;

    PROCEDURE exp(x: REAL): REAL;

    PROCEDURE ln(x: REAL): REAL;

    PROCEDURE sin(x: REAL): REAL;

    PROCEDURE cos(x: REAL): REAL;

    PROCEDURE arctan(x: REAL): REAL;

    PROCEDURE real(x: INTEGER): REAL;

    PROCEDURE entier(x: REAL): INTEGER;

END MathLib0.
```

The functions exported by MathLib0 perform the following actions:

sqrt	Computes the square root of a nonnegative REAL number
exp	Computes the exponential (e^x) of a REAL number
ln	Computes the natural logarithm of a positive REAL number
sin	Computes the sine of a REAL number (an angle expressed in radians)
cos	Computes the cosine of a REAL number (an angle expressed in radians)
arctan	Computes the arctangent of a REAL number; the value returned is expressed in radians
real	Converts an INTEGER value to the equivalent REAL number
entier	Converts a REAL number to type INTEGER; returns the largest INTEGER less than or equal to the REAL number

RealInOut

The RealInOut module provides procedures for reading and writing REAL numbers. RealInOut uses the input and output streams controlled by InOut. Section 13.2 discusses RealInOut.

```
DEFINITION MODULE RealInOut;    (* N. Wirth *)

  VAR Done: BOOLEAN;

  PROCEDURE ReadReal(VAR x: REAL);
    (* Read REAL number x according to syntax:

       ["+"|"-"] digit {digit} ["." digit {digit}]
       ["E" ["+"|"-"] digit [digit]]

       Done := "a number was read".
       At most 7 digits are significant, leading zeros not
       counting.  Maximum exponent is 38.  Input terminates
       with a blank or any control character.  DEL is used
       for backspacing *)

  PROCEDURE WriteReal(x: REAL; n: CARDINAL);
    (* Write x using n characters.  If fewer than n characters
       are needed, leading blanks are inserted *)

  PROCEDURE WriteRealOct(x: REAL);
    (* Write x in octal form with exponent and mantissa *)

END RealInOut.
```

Storage

The Storage module provides procedures for allocating and deallocating space during program execution. Section 8.1 discusses Storage.

```
DEFINITION MODULE Storage;    (* SEK 5.10.80 *)

  FROM SYSTEM IMPORT ADDRESS;

  PROCEDURE ALLOCATE(VAR a: ADDRESS; size: CARDINAL);
    (* ALLOCATE allocates an area of the given size and
       returns its address in a.  If no space is available,
       the calling program is killed. *)
```

```
  PROCEDURE DEALLOCATE(VAR a: ADDRESS; size: CARDINAL);
    (* DEALLOCATE frees the area at address a with the given
       size. *)

  PROCEDURE Available(size: CARDINAL): BOOLEAN;
    (* Available returns TRUE if size words could be
       allocated. *)

END Storage.
```

Terminal

The Terminal module provides procedures for character I/O using a terminal. Section 13.1 discusses Terminal.

```
DEFINITION MODULE Terminal;    (* S. E. Knudsen *)

  PROCEDURE Read(VAR ch: CHAR);

  PROCEDURE BusyRead(VAR ch: CHAR);
    (* returns 0C, if no character was typed *)

  PROCEDURE ReadAgain;
    (* causes the last character read to be returned again
       upon the next call of Read *)

  PROCEDURE Write(ch: CHAR);

  PROCEDURE WriteLn;
    (* terminate line *)

  PROCEDURE WriteString(s: ARRAY OF CHAR);

END Terminal.
```

Index to Wirth's Library

		FileSystem	InOut	MathLib0	RealInOut	Storage	Terminal
Again	procedure	■					
ALLOCATE	procedure					■	
arctan	function			■			
Available	function					■	
BusyRead	procedure						■
Close	procedure	■					
CloseInput	procedure		■				
CloseOutput	procedure		■				
Command	type	■					
cos	function			■			
Create	procedure	■					
DEALLOCATE	procedure					■	
Doio	procedure	■					
Done	variable		■		■		
entier	function			■			
EOL	constant		■				
exp	function			■			
File	type	■					
Flag	type	■					
FlagSet	type	■					
GetPos	procedure	■					
Length	procedure	■					
ln	function			■			
Lookup	procedure	■					
OpenInput	procedure		■				
OpenOutput	procedure		■				
Read	procedure		■				■
ReadAgain	procedure						■
ReadCard	procedure		■				
ReadChar	procedure	■					
ReadInt	procedure		■				
ReadReal	procedure				■		
ReadString	procedure		■				
ReadWord	procedure	■					
real	function			■			
Rename	procedure	■					
Reset	procedure	■					

		FileSystem	InOut	MathLib0	RealInOut	Storage	Terminal
`Response`	type	■					
`SetModify`	procedure	■					
`SetOpen`	procedure	■					
`SetPos`	procedure	■					
`SetRead`	procedure	■					
`SetWrite`	procedure	■					
`sin`	function			■			
`sqrt`	function			■			
`termCH`	variable		■				
`Write`	procedure		■				■
`WriteCard`	procedure		■				
`WriteChar`	procedure	■					
`WriteHex`	procedure		■				
`WriteInt`	procedure		■				
`WriteLn`	procedure		■				■
`WriteOct`	procedure		■				
`WriteReal`	procedure				■		
`WriteRealOct`	procedure				■		
`WriteString`	procedure		■				■
`WriteWord`	procedure	■					

APPENDIX V
Versions of Modula-2

The version of Modula-2 presented in this book is the one Wirth describes in *Programming in Modula-2*, Third Edition. Because some readers may have occasion to use Modula-2 compilers that conform to the Second Edition of Wirth's book, this appendix summarizes the differences between the Second Edition, which we will abbreviate *Second*, and the Third Edition, *Third*. These differences fall into four categories:

Restrictions are changes to the language definition that limit the use of existing features.

Clarifications affect the definition of Modula-2, not the language itself. The definition of Modula-2 in *Second* is sometimes incomplete or ambiguous; several of the changes in *Third* are attempts to clarify the definition of the language.

Changes consist primarily of minor modifications to the syntax of Modula-2; they do not alter the expressiveness of the language.

Extensions include both new language features and changes to existing features; extensions increase the power or flexibility of the language.

Chapter 3 Basic Types

- The standard functions MAX and MIN appear for the first time in *Third*; *Second* does not mention them. (Extension)
- The standard types LONGINT and LONGREAL appear for the first time in *Third*; *Second* does not mention them. (Extension)
- The symbol ~ (a synonym for NOT) appears for the first time in *Third*; *Second* does not mention it. (Extension)
- In *Second*, constant expressions cannot include calls of standard functions; *Third* removes this restriction. A constant expression differs from an arbitrary expression in only two respects: (1) all operands in a constant expression must be constants, and (2) it must be possible to evaluate the expression without executing the program. (Extension)

Chapter 4 Statements

- In *Second*, each case within a CASE statement must be nonempty. *Third* removes this restriction, making it possible to include extraneous | symbols without harm. (Extension)

- In *Second*, the types of the starting value and limit in a FOR statement must be *assignment-compatible* with the type of the control variable. In *Third*, the types must be *compatible*. (Restriction)

Chapter 5 Procedures

- In *Second*, the types of a variable parameter and a corresponding actual parameter must be *compatible*. In *Third*, the two types must be the *same*. (Both *Second* and *Third* allow exceptions if the formal parameter has type ADDRESS or WORD.) (Restriction)

Chapter 6 Enumeration and Subrange Types

- In *Second*, the base type of a subrange is always inferred from the type of the subrange bounds. In *Third*, an optional type name may precede the specification of a subrange to indicate the base type. This feature is useful when the base type of the subrange would be CARDINAL by default, but the programmer wants the base type to be INTEGER instead. (Extension)

Chapter 7 Array, Record, and Set Types

- In *Second*, a string literal of length 1 has type CHAR. In *Third*, a string literal of length 1 has type ARRAY [0..0] OF CHAR; a special rule states that string literals of length 1 are compatible with CHAR. These changes allow string literals of length 1 to be treated as either single characters or strings. (Extension)
- In *Second*, when the tag field is omitted in a record with a variant part, the colon that normally follows the tag field is also omitted. In *Third*, the colon remains even if there is no tag field. (Change)
- In *Second*, a variant part of a record declaration could not have empty variants. *Third* removes this restriction, allowing superfluous | symbols to be included in the variant part. (Extension)
- *Second* allows elements in set values to be constant expressions and ranges bounded by constant expressions. *Third* allows arbitrary expressions (and ranges thereof). (Extension)

Chapter 8 Pointer and Procedure Types

- In *Second*, the standard procedures NEW and DISPOSE create and destroy anonymous variables. The compiler translates each call of NEW into a call of ALLOCATE; each call of DISPOSE becomes a call of DEALLOCATE. The programmer may write ALLOCATE and DEALLOCATE or import them from a library module. In *Third*, NEW and DISPOSE are no longer standard. Instead, the programmer must import ALLOCATE and DEALLOCATE and call them directly (or provide alternate procedures for allocation and deallocation). (Change)

Chapter 9 Modules

- In *Second*, each definition module must contain an export list naming all entities to be exported. *Third* abolishes the export list; instead, all entities defined in a definition module are automatically exported. (*Third* still requires export lists for local modules that export entities.) (Change)
- In *Third*, the body of a program or implementation module `M` is not executed until the bodies of all imported modules have been initialized; furthermore, these modules are initialized in the order in which they appear in `M`'s import lists. If the import lists of two or more implementation modules form a circle, *Third* does not define the initialization order of the modules. *Second* gave no rules for the order of module initialization. (Clarification)
- *Second* did not specify the allowable operations on opaque types; *Third* allows assignment and test for equality (and inequality). (Clarification)
- *Second* allows opaque types to be pointer types or subranges of standard types; *Third* requires opaque types to be pointer types. (Restriction)
- The following sentence appears in *Second*: "If a module identifier is exported, then all identifiers occurring in that module's export list are also exported." Wirth actually intended the identifiers to be visible only when qualified by the module name. Consequently, this sentence does not appear in *Third*. (Clarification)
- The following sentences appear in *Second*: "Standard identifiers are always imported automatically. As a consequence, standard identifiers can be redeclared in procedures only, but not in modules, including the compilation unit." These sentences do not appear in *Third*. Redefinition of standard identifiers in a module is now possible; any standard identifier not redefined in a module is visible in the module. (Extension)

Chapter 11 Low-Level Programming

- *Second* requires the `ADDRESS` type to be compatible with `CARDINAL`. *Third* requires `ADDRESS` to be compatible with some arithmetic type, such as `CARDINAL`, `INTEGER`, or `LONGINT`, depending on the Modula-2 system. (Extension)
- In *Second*, the `SYSTEM` module exports the `SIZE` function. When given a variable as a parameter, `SIZE` returns a number representing the amount of storage assigned to the variable. In *Third*, `SIZE` is a standard function. Its parameter can be either a variable or the name of a type; in the latter case, `SIZE` returns a number representing the amount of storage required to store a variable of that type. (Extension)

- In *Second*, the TSIZE function (exported by the SYSTEM module) returns a value of type CARDINAL. *Third* allows the type of value returned by TSIZE to vary from one Modula-2 system to another, although it must be an arithmetic type. (Extension)

Chapter 12 Coroutines and Interrupt Handling

- In *Second*, the SYSTEM module exports a type called PROCESS; the following procedures require variables of this type:

```
PROCEDURE NEWPROCESS(P: PROC; A: ADDRESS; n: CARDINAL;
                                VAR p1: PROCESS);

PROCEDURE TRANSFER(VAR p1, p2: PROCESS);

PROCEDURE IOTRANSFER(VAR p1, p2: PROCESS; va: CARDINAL);
```

  In *Third*, the PROCESS type no longer exists, although the procedures NEWPROCESS, TRANSFER, and IOTRANSFER still do. The p1 and p2 parameters now have type ADDRESS instead of PROCESS. (Change)

- *Second* requires programs that need the NEWPROCESS, TRANSFER, and IOTRANSFER procedures to import them from SYSTEM. In *Third*, Wirth has deleted the reference to SYSTEM. Consequently, a module (or modules) other than SYSTEM may export these procedures. (Change)

APPENDIX VI

ASCII Character Set

Ordinal Number (Decimal)	Ordinal Number (Octal)	Character		Ordinal Number (Decimal)	Ordinal Number (Octal)	Character	Ordinal Number (Decimal)	Ordinal Number (Octal)	Character	Ordinal Number (Decimal)	Ordinal Number (Octal)	Character
0	000	nul		32	040		64	100	@	96	140	`
1	001	soh	(^A)	33	041	!	65	101	A	97	141	a
2	002	stx	(^B)	34	042	"	66	102	B	98	142	b
3	003	etx	(^C)	35	043	#	67	103	C	99	143	c
4	004	eot	(^D)	36	044	$	68	104	D	100	144	d
5	005	enq	(^E)	37	045	%	69	105	E	101	145	e
6	006	ack	(^F)	38	046	&	70	106	F	102	146	f
7	007	bel	(^G)	39	047	'	71	107	G	103	147	g
8	010	bs	(^H)	40	050	(	72	110	H	104	150	h
9	011	ht	(^I)	41	051	)	73	111	I	105	151	i
10	012	lf	(^J)	42	052	*	74	112	J	106	152	j
11	013	vt	(^K)	43	053	+	75	113	K	107	153	k
12	014	ff	(^L)	44	054	,	76	114	L	108	154	l
13	015	cr	(^M)	45	055	-	77	115	M	109	155	m
14	016	so	(^N)	46	056	.	78	116	N	110	156	n
15	017	si	(^O)	47	057	/	79	117	O	111	157	o
16	020	dle	(^P)	48	060	0	80	120	P	112	160	p
17	021	dc1	(^Q)	49	061	1	81	121	Q	113	161	q
18	022	dc2	(^R)	50	062	2	82	122	R	114	162	r
19	023	dc3	(^S)	51	063	3	83	123	S	115	163	s
20	024	dc4	(^T)	52	064	4	84	124	T	116	164	t
21	025	nak	(^U)	53	065	5	85	125	U	117	165	u
22	026	syn	(^V)	54	066	6	86	126	V	118	166	v
23	027	etb	(^W)	55	067	7	87	127	W	119	167	w
24	030	can	(^X)	56	070	8	88	130	X	120	170	x
25	031	em	(^Y)	57	071	9	89	131	Y	121	171	y
26	032	sub	(^Z)	58	072	:	90	132	Z	122	172	z
27	033	esc		59	073	;	91	133	[	123	173	{
28	034	fs		60	074	<	92	134	\	124	174	|
29	035	gs		61	075	=	93	135	]	125	175	}
30	036	rs		62	076	>	94	136	^	126	176	~
31	037	us		63	077	?	95	137	_	127	177	del

Nonprinting ASCII Characters

Modula-2 Symbol	*Abbreviation*	*Full Name*
0C	nul	null
1C	soh	start of heading
2C	stx	start of text
3C	etx	end of text
4C	eot	end of transmission
5C	enq	enquiry
6C	ack	acknowledge
7C	bel	bell
10C	bs	backspace
11C	ht	horizontal tabulation
12C	lf	line feed
13C	vt	vertical tabulation
14C	ff	form feed
15C	cr	carriage return
16C	so	shift out
17C	si	shift in
20C	dle	data line escape
21C	dc1	device control 1 (x-on)
22C	dc2	device control 2 (tape)
23C	dc3	device control 3 (x-off)
24C	dc4	device control 4 (tape)
25C	nak	negative acknowledge
26C	syn	synchronous idle
27C	etb	end transmission block
30C	can	cancel
31C	em	end of medium
32C	sub	substitute
33C	esc	escape
34C	fs	file separator
35C	gs	group separator
36C	rs	record separator
37C	us	unit separator
177C	del	delete

Glossary

actual parameter A variable or expression supplied to a procedure when it is called. The number of actual parameters in a procedure call must match the number of formal parameters in the heading of the procedure; each actual parameter corresponds to the formal parameter appearing in the same relative position in the procedure heading. Compare with *formal parameter*.

ADDRESS A low-level type whose values are memory addresses. The SYSTEM module exports ADDRESS; it has the standard definition

```
TYPE ADDRESS = POINTER TO WORD;
```

ADDRESS is compatible with all pointer types and some numeric type (CARDINAL, INTEGER, or LONGINT). Declaring a formal parameter to have type ADDRESS allows a corresponding actual parameter to be of any pointer type.

anonymous type A type that has no name, although its specification appears in a variable or type declaration. For example, the declaration

```
VAR str1, str2: ARRAY [0..9] OF CHAR;
```

gives the variables str1 and str2 an anonymous type. Although str1 and str2 have the same type, no other variable can be of this type.

anonymous variable A variable that has been created dynamically (typically by a call of ALLOCATE). An anonymous variable is not declared and therefore has no name; it must be referenced through a pointer variable. If p is a non-NIL pointer variable, then p^ is the anonymous variable to which p points.

arithmetic operator An operator that requires numeric operands and yields a numeric result. Modula-2 has six arithmetic operators: +, -, *, /, DIV, and MOD.

array A structured data value consisting of a fixed number of components, all of the same type; components are selected by indexing. For example, a variable A of type

```
TYPE ArrayType = ARRAY [1..10] OF INTEGER;
```

consists of ten INTEGER values; the first component of A is called A[1] and the last A[10]. The array's component type is INTEGER and its index type is [1..10] (a subrange of CARDINAL).

ASCII American Standard Code for Information Interchange, the character set this book uses. Note, however, that Modula-2 systems are free to use other character sets instead.

assignment statement A statement of the form

Designator := *Expression*

The effect of an assignment statement is to change the contents of a variable (specified by a designator) by copying the value of an expression into it. The types of the variable and expression must be assignment-compatible. (There are two exceptions: (1) a literal string can be assigned to a string variable of greater length and (2) a literal string of length 1 can be assigned to a variable of type CHAR.)

assignment-compatible A relationship between two types that holds if the types are compatible or if one is CARDINAL (or a subrange thereof) and the other is INTEGER (or a subrange thereof). Modula-2 requires assignment compatibility for

the designator and expression in an assignment statement (with the exception of the assignment of a string literal to a string variable or variable of type CHAR)

an array's index type and an expression used as an index

a value parameter and each corresponding actual parameter

the type of result to be returned by a function and the expression in a RETURN statement in the body of the function

base type A type used to create a subrange or set type. A subrange type is constructed by selecting a range of values from its base type. The base type may be implicit:

```
TYPE Months = [1..12];          (* CARDINAL is the base type *)
```

or explicit:

```
TYPE Months = INTEGER[1..12];   (* INTEGER is the base type *)
```

Each value of a set type is a set whose elements belong to the base type:

```
TYPE SetOfDays = SET OF Days;   (* Days is the base type *)
```

basic type An unstructured, standard type; either BOOLEAN, CARDINAL, CHAR, INTEGER, LONGINT, LONGREAL, or REAL.

BITSET A standard type defined as

```
TYPE BITSET = SET OF [0..W-1];
```

where W is system-dependent, but usually the number of bits in one word of memory.

block A sequence of zero or more declarations followed by a statement sequence enclosed between BEGIN and END (the statement sequence is optional; if no statement sequence is present, the word BEGIN is also omitted). The body of a procedure or module is a block.

body The body of a procedure is a block consisting of declarations (of the procedure's local variables) and statements (to be executed when the procedure is called). Program modules, implementation modules, and local modules also have bodies.

BOOLEAN A standard type whose values are denoted by the standard identifiers TRUE and FALSE.

BOOLEAN **operator** See *logical operator*.

call See *procedure call*.

CARDINAL A standard type whose values are the integers between 0 and MAX(CARDINAL).

case expression The expression that follows the word CASE in a CASE statement. The type of a case expression must be a basic type (other than REAL or LONGREAL), an enumeration type, or a subrange type.

case label A constant expression appearing in a CASE statement (representing a possible value of the case expression) or a variant part of a record (representing a possible value of the tag field). The .. symbol may separate two constant expressions to indicate a range of case labels.

case sensitivity The property (of a programming language) of distinguishing between uppercase and lowercase letters in identifiers (thus, ch, Ch, cH, and CH are different identifiers). Modula-2 is a case-sensitive language.

CASE **statement** A statement of the form

```
CASE Expression OF
  CaseLabelList : StatementSequence |
    .
    .
    .
  CaseLabelList : StatementSequence
ELSE
  StatementSequence
END
```

(the ELSE clause is optional). When a CASE statement is executed, the value of the case expression is computed and compared to the case labels. If the value of the case expression matches one of the case labels (no label may appear twice), then the statement sequence following the label is executed. If an ELSE clause is present and the value of the case expression does not match any of the case labels, then the statement sequence in the ELSE clause is executed.

CHAR A standard type whose values are the characters in a particular computer system's character set. The character set used in this book is ASCII, but this is not a requirement of Modula-2.

comment A sequence of characters enclosed between the symbols (* and *). Comments do not affect the meaning of a program. Modula-2 allows nested comments.

compatible A relationship between two types that holds if the types are the same (either denoted by the same type name or by names declared equivalent in a type declaration), if one is a subrange of the other, or if both are subranges with the same base type. Modula-2 requires compatibility for

the operands in an arithmetic expression

the operands in a relational expression

the case labels and case expression in a CASE statement

the starting value, limit, and control variable in a FOR statement

compilation unit A portion of a program that can be compiled separately from the rest of the program. Modula-2 provides three kinds of compilation units: program modules, definition modules, and implementation modules.

component A data value that is part of a larger structure (such as an array or record).

constant A value that cannot change during the execution of a program. A constant may be a literal (such as a number or string) or an identifier bound to a constant value by a constant declaration.

constant declaration A declaration of the form

CONST *Ident* = *ConstExpression* ;

The effect of a constant declaration is to associate the identifier with the value of the constant expression; the identifier may then take the place of the constant expression.

constant expression An expression whose value can be determined without executing the program in which the expression appears. The operands of a constant expression must be constants.

control variable The variable that follows the word FOR in a FOR statement. The body of the FOR statement is executed once for each value assigned to the control variable.

coroutine Similar to a procedure, but capable of suspending its operation and transferring control to another coroutine; when control returns to the coroutine, it resumes executing from where it left off. In Modula-2, a coroutine is created from a procedure by calling NEWPROCESS.

data type See *type*.

declaration A program construct that names an entity, classifies it (as a constant, type, variable, procedure, or module), and specifies its properties (for example, the declaration of a variable specifies its type). All entities that are not standard (predefined) or imported must be declared.

definition Similar to a declaration; a definition module must supply a definition for each entity it exports. A definition differs from a declaration in three ways:

A type definition may give only the name of the type (a full declaration of the type must then appear in the implementation module); the type is called an *opaque type*.

A procedure definition consists of just the procedure's heading (a full declaration of the procedure must appear in the implementation module).

Modules may be declared, but not defined.

definition module A module that begins with the words `DEFINITION MODULE`. A definition module must always have a matching implementation module of the same name; the two modules together form a library module. The definition module contains definitions of the entities that the library module exports. A definition module is a compilation unit; it can be compiled separately of other compilation units, including its matching implementation module.

dereferencing The operation of creating a name for an anonymous (dynamically allocated) variable by appending the ^ symbol (the dereferencing operator) to a pointer variable.

designator A (possibly qualified) identifier optionally followed by selectors and/or the ^ symbol. If the identifier is a variable, the selectors allow the selection of array or record components; the ^ symbol dereferences a pointer. A designator serves as a "generalized variable"; for example, a designator can appear on the left side of an assignment statement. A designator (without selectors and the ^ symbol) can also represent a constant or procedure.

dynamic allocation The allocation of space during program execution, usually for an anonymous variable. In Modula-2, a library module, such as Wirth's `Storage` module, provides procedures for dynamic allocation and deallocation.

element A value belonging to a set.

empty statement The statement consisting of no symbols. The existence of the empty statement makes the placement of semicolons less critical. For example, the body of the following REPEAT statement contains an assignment statement that has been unnecessarily terminated by a semicolon:

```
REPEAT
  ch := GetChar();     (* unnecessary semicolon *)
UNTIL ch # ' ';
```

Because of the extra semicolon, the body of the loop consists of two statements, the second of which is empty.

entity Anything that can be declared in a program and given a name. Modula-2 provides five kinds of entities: constants, types, variables, procedures, and modules.

enumeration type A type whose specification is a list of identifiers representing the values of the type. For example:

```
TYPE Days = (Sun, Mon, Tue, Wed, Thu, Fri, Sat);
```

EXIT **statement** A statement of the form

```
EXIT
```

EXIT statements may appear only inside LOOP statements; when an EXIT statement is executed, program control leaves the immediately enclosing LOOP statement.

export To make an entity visible outside the module in which it is defined.

export list A list of entities that a module exports. Export lists appear only in local modules; all entities defined in a definition module are automatically exported.

expression A sequence of operators and operands that, when evaluated, produces a single value. Modula-2 allows the construction of expressions that compute arithmetic, BOOLEAN, and set values.

field A component of a record. A field is selected for access or modification by reference to its field identifier.

field identifier An identifier used to select a field in a record.

FOR **statement** A statement of the form

FOR *Ident* := *Expression* TO *Expression* BY *ConstExpression* DO
  StatementSequence
END

The identifier is the FOR statement's *control variable*, and the three expressions are the statement's *starting value*, *limit*, and *increment*, in that order. The increment may be positive or negative; if it is omitted, the increment is 1 by default. If the increment is positive, the execution of a FOR statement proceeds as follows. The starting value is assigned to the control variable. If the control variable is less than or equal to the limit, the statement sequence is executed. The control variable is then incremented by the specified amount and again compared with the limit. The FOR statement continues to execute until the value of the control variable exceeds the limit.

formal parameter An identifier representing a variable or expression to be supplied when a procedure is called. Modula-2 provides two kinds of formal parameters: value parameters and variable parameters. Compare with *actual parameter*.

formal parameter section A portion of the list of formal parameters appearing in a procedure heading. Semicolons separate formal parameter sections; the parameters in each section share the same type and are all either value or variable parameters.

formal type A type used to declare a formal parameter. A formal type can be any Modula-2 type (standard or programmer-defined); in addition, a formal type can be an open array.

function A procedure that returns a value and therefore must be called within an expression. Compare with *proper procedure*.

function designator A designator (often just a function name) followed by a list of actual parameters, representing a call of the function. When a function with no parameters is called, a pair of empty parentheses must follow the designator. (If no parentheses are present, the designator refers to the function itself, not to a call of the function.)

function procedure See *function*.

global An entity is global to a procedure P if it is visible in P but not declared in P. Compare with *local.*

identifier A sequence of letters and digits beginning with a letter. An identifier serves as a name for a program entity (constant, type, variable, procedure, or module), a formal parameter, an enumeration value, or a record field.

IF **statement** A statement of the form

```
IF Expression THEN
   StatementSequence
ELSIF Expression THEN
   StatementSequence
   .
   .
   .
ELSE
   StatementSequence
END
```

An IF statement may have any number of ELSIF clauses (including none). The ELSE clause is optional. When an IF statement is executed, the expressions (which must be BOOLEAN) are evaluated one at a time until an expression with the value TRUE is found; the corresponding statement sequence is then executed. If all the expressions are FALSE, the statement sequence following the word ELSE (if present) is executed.

implementation module A module that begins with the words IMPLEMENTATION MODULE. An implementation module must always have a matching definition module of the same name; the two modules together form a library module. The implementation module contains full declarations of procedures and opaque types defined in the matching definition module; in addition, it may contain declarations of entities not exported, plus statements to initialize the module's variables. An implementation module is a compilation unit; it can be compiled separately from other compilation units, including its matching definition module.

import To make an entity visible inside a module. The entity must be visible in the environment that encloses the module.

import list A list of entities that a module imports. Any kind of module (program, definition, implementation, or local) may contain import lists.

index A value used to select an array component. If A is a one-dimensional array, then A[i] is the component of A selected by using the variable i as an index. The type from which the indices of A may be chosen is called the *index type* of A.

INTEGER A standard type whose values are the integers between MIN(INTEGER) and MAX(INTEGER). INTEGER includes both positive and negative integers.

interrupt A hardware signal generated when a particular event occurs (for example, the completion of an input/output operation). An interrupt causes the currently executing program to be suspended and control transferred to an interrupt handler.

interrupt handler A routine that responds to a particular interrupt. Systems that generate interrupts must provide a way to install interrupt handlers. When an interrupt occurs, control is transferred to the interrupt handler previously specified for that interrupt; once the handler has completed execution, the interrupted program can resume executing.

interrupt priority A number assigned to an interrupt to indicate its relative importance.

interrupt vector An identifying number assigned to an interrupt to distinguish it from other interrupts.

library A collection of library modules.

library module A module that provides services to other modules in a program (its *clients*). A library module has two parts: a *definition part* and an *implementation part*. The definition part specifies the services that the library module provides (the entities that the module exports); the implementation part describes how the services are implemented. Each part of a library module is itself a separate module (a *definition module* or an *implementation module*). Both parts must have the same name.

local An entity is local to the procedure or module in which it is declared. An entity is not visible outside the procedure or module to which it is local, unless it is declared in a module and exported. Compare with *global*.

local module A module declared inside a program or implementation module. Local modules are not compilation units; they cannot be compiled separately.

logical operator An operator that takes BOOLEAN operands and returns a value of type BOOLEAN. Modula-2 provides three logical operators: AND (also written &), OR, and NOT (also written ~).

LONGINT A standard type whose values are the integers between MIN(LONGINT) and MAX(LONGINT); LONGINT may include a larger range of values than the standard type INTEGER.

LONGREAL A standard type whose values are real numbers; LONGREAL may provide numbers of greater precision and magnitude than the standard type REAL.

LOOP **statement** A statement of the form

```
LOOP
   StatementSequence
END
```

The statement sequence between LOOP and END is executed indefinitely. The EXIT statement allows control to leave the immediately enclosing LOOP statement; the only other ways to leave a LOOP statement are to execute a RETURN statement or call the HALT procedure.

mixed expression An expression whose operands are of different types. In a Modula-2 expression, operands must be *compatible*; consequently, most mixed expressions are illegal.

module An entity that restricts the visibility of names in a program: entities declared in a module are not visible outside the module unless they are exported; entities visible outside the module are not visible inside it unless imported. Modula-2 provides four kinds of modules: program modules, definition modules, implementation modules, and local modules. The first three are compilation units and can be separately compiled; local modules are declared within other modules and cannot be separately compiled. Variables declared in a program module, definition module, or implementation module are *static*: they retain their values for the lifetime of the program. Variables declared in a local module have the same lifetime as variables in the enclosing procedure or module.

module body The portion of a program module, implementation module, or local module that contains the module's declarations and statements; a module body is a block. The body of an implementation module is executed before the bodies of any modules that import from its matching definition module; the body of a local module is executed before the body of the procedure or module in which it is declared.

module declaration A declaration of a local module. Module declarations may appear in program modules, implementation modules, or in local modules themselves. A module declaration may be nested inside a procedure declaration.

module priority See *priority*.

opaque export The export of an opaque type from a definition module. Clients of the module have no information about the type other than its name. Compare with *transparent export*.

opaque type A type defined in a definition module by name alone; the specification of the type does not appear. The corresponding implementation module must contain a full declaration of the type; this declaration must specify it to be a pointer type. In a client module, the only operations allowed on values of an opaque type are assignment and tests for equality and inequality. Consequently, a module that exports an opaque type normally exports procedures that operate on values of the type; such a module implements an *abstract data type*.

open array parameter A formal parameter of type ARRAY OF T, where T is a type name. A corresponding actual parameter can be an array of any length, provided that its components are of type T. The components of an open array parameter A are indexed from 0 to HIGH(A).

operator A symbol denoting an arithmetic, logical, relational, or set operation.

operator precedence Rules for determining which operation should be performed first in expressions containing more than one operator. Modula-2 has four levels of operator precedence. The operator NOT (also written ~) has the highest precedence, followed by *, /, DIV, MOD, AND (also written &), then +, -, and OR, and finally =, # (also written <>), <, <=, >, >=, and IN. Operations at the same level of precedence are performed from left to right.

ordinal number A nonnegative integer indicating the relative position of a value among all values of its type. Values of types CHAR, INTEGER, and CARDINAL have ordinal numbers, as do values of an enumeration type. The ordinal number of a value can be found by applying the standard function ORD. For example, the character 'A' occurs in position 66 of the ASCII character set; consequently, ORD('A') has the value 65 on ASCII computers (ordinal numbers begin at 0).

parameter See *actual parameter*, *formal parameter*.

pervasive The property (of an identifier) of being visible in all parts of a program (except in a module or procedure in which the identifier is redefined). All Modula-2 standard identifiers are pervasive.

pointer An address or reference to an anonymous (dynamically allocated) variable. Values of a pointer type must point to anonymous variables of a particular type. For example, a value of the type

```
TYPE String = POINTER TO StringRec;
```

would be a pointer to an anonymous variable of type StringRec. Assigning the standard constant NIL to a pointer variable indicates that it does not currently point to an anonymous variable.

precedence See *operator precedence*.

priority A value that may appear in the heading of a module to inhibit interrupts; only interrupts whose priority exceeds the priority of the module can interrupt the execution of statements within the module. A priority is a constant expression of type CARDINAL, enclosed in brackets; it may appear only in the heading of a program module, implementation module, or local module.

PROC A standard type defined as

```
TYPE PROC = PROCEDURE;
```

Values of type PROC are proper procedures with no parameters.

procedure A program entity that can be called to perform a computation. When a procedure has completed its computation, control returns to the point of the procedure call.

Modula-2 provides two kinds of procedures: *proper procedures*, whose calls are statements, and *functions*, whose calls are expressions.

procedure body The remainder of a procedure declaration following the procedure heading. A procedure body is a block.

procedure call A statement or expression that activates a procedure, consisting of a designator (often just the procedure name) and (optionally) a list of actual parameters. A call of a proper procedure is a statement; a call of a function procedure is an expression (see *function designator*).

procedure declaration A procedure heading, followed by the body of the procedure.

procedure heading The initial portion of a procedure declaration, consisting of the word PROCEDURE, an identifier (the name of the procedure), and (optionally) a list of formal parameters. In the case of a function, the list of formal parameters is followed by an identifier naming the type of value to be returned by the function.

procedure type A type whose values are procedures. The specification of a procedure type must state the type of each parameter and whether the parameter is a value parameter or variable parameter; in the case of a function, the specification must include the type of value that the function returns. For example, values of the type

```
TYPE RelationalOp = PROCEDURE (INTEGER, INTEGER): BOOLEAN;
```

are functions with two value parameters, both of type INTEGER, returning a value of type BOOLEAN.

program A Modula-2 program consists of a program module and (optionally) one or more library modules (pairs of definition and implementation modules).

program module A module that serves as a main program. A program module has the same syntax as an implementation module, but begins with the word MODULE instead of IMPLEMENTATION MODULE. A program module is a compilation unit; it can be compiled separately from other compilation units. When a program begins to execute, the bodies of all library modules are first executed, and then control is transferred to the body of the program module.

proper procedure A procedure whose call is a statement; it returns no value. Compare with *function*.

qualified export The export of entities from a module with the restriction that they must be qualified by the module name whenever they are referenced (except when they are imported using the FROM clause). Qualified export is mandatory for definition modules and optional for local modules.

qualified identifier An identifier that is preceded by the name of the module in which it is declared (the two identifiers are separated by a period). For example, if a definition module M exports a variable x, modules that import M must refer to the variable as M.x unless x is imported using the FROM clause.

qualifying identifier A module name used to qualify an identifier.

REAL A standard type whose values are real numbers.

record A structured data value consisting of a fixed number of components, possibly of different types; each component (known as a *field*) is selected by means of a name (a *field identifier*). For example, a value of the type

```
TYPE Coordinate = RECORD
                       x, y: REAL
                  END;
```

is a record with two fields of type REAL, named x and y. If position is a variable of type Coordinate, the designators position.x and position.y allow access to the fields of position.

recursive procedure A procedure that—either directly or indirectly—calls itself.

relation See *relational operator*.

relational operator An operator used to compare two operands; the result of the comparison is a BOOLEAN value. Modula-2 has seven relational operators: =, # (also written <>), <, <=, >, >=, and IN.

REPEAT **statement** A statement of the form

```
REPEAT
   StatementSequence
UNTIL Expression
```

The effect of a REPEAT statement is to repeatedly execute the statement sequence until the expression (which must be BOOLEAN) becomes TRUE. Because the expression is tested *after* each execution of the statement sequence, the latter is always executed at least once.

reserved word A sequence of letters representing a Modula-2 operator or keyword; programmers may not use reserved words as identifiers. In Modula-2, reserved words contain only capital letters. (A list of reserved words appears in Appendix I.)

RETURN **statement** A statement of the form

```
RETURN Expression
```

In a function, a RETURN statement causes the function to return; the value of the expression is the value returned by the function. In a proper procedure, a RETURN statement causes the procedure to return. In a module, a RETURN statement terminates the execution of the module body. (When a RETURN statement appears in a proper procedure or a module, it must not contain an expression.)

scale factor In a real number, the part beginning with `E` that specifies a power of 10 by which to scale the number. For example, in the REAL number `1.5E12` (representing the value 1.5×10^{12}), the scale factor is 12.

scope The region of a program in which a particular entity is visible.

selector An expression or identifier used to select a component of a structured variable. If `A` is an array variable, the index `i` in the designator `A[i]` is a selector; if `R` is a record variable, the field identifier `f` in the designator `R.f` is a selector.

separate compilation The technique by which the compilation units that comprise a program are compiled at different times, then linked before execution. Because Modula-2 systems must perform full type-checking among compilation units, the term "separate compilation" is more accurate than "independent compilation." Programming languages that provide the latter usually do not perform type-checking among compilation units.

set A structured data value consisting of an unordered collection of values (called *elements*), all of the same type (the *base type*), with no duplicates. For example, a value of type

```
TYPE SetOfDays = SET OF Days;
```

would be a collection of values chosen from the base type `Days`.

set operator An operator whose operands are sets and that yields a set value. Modula-2 provides four set operators: + (union), - (difference), * (intersection), and / (symmetric difference).

standard identifier An identifier that Modula-2 compilers recognize and that programs therefore need not declare or import. In Modula-2, standard identifiers contain only capital letters. Standard identifiers represent constants, procedures, and types. There are three standard constants (TRUE, FALSE, and NIL) and nine standard types (BITSET, BOOLEAN, CARDINAL, CHAR, INTEGER, LONGINT, LONGREAL, PROC, and REAL). A list of standard procedures appears in Appendix I.

statement A command to be performed during program execution. Modula-2 provides eleven kinds of statements: assignment, procedure call, IF, CASE, WHILE, REPEAT, LOOP, FOR, WITH, EXIT, and RETURN.

statement sequence One or more statements separated by semicolons. The statements in a statement sequence are executed from first to last.

stream An ordered collection of data values, all of the same type, that programs must access sequentially. A sequential file is a stream; so is the sequence of characters typed at a keyboard or sent to a terminal screen. Library modules such as Wirth's `InOut` module rely on the concept of a stream. `InOut` treats input as coming from a stream (and output as being sent to a stream); this view allows a program to use the same procedures to receive input from a terminal or from a file (or send output to a terminal or a file).

string A sequence of characters. Either single quotes or double quotes must enclose a string literal. A string variable must have type ARRAY [0..n] OF CHAR for some value of n.

structured type A type whose values can be divided into components. Modula-2 provides three kinds of structured types: arrays, records, and sets. Compare with *unstructured type*.

subrange type A type constructed by selecting a contiguous range of values from another type (the *base type*). For example, the values of the type

```
TYPE Months = [1..12];
```

are the integers between 1 and 12. The base type of Months is CARDINAL.

SYSTEM A module that exports system-dependent entities useful for low-level programming. SYSTEM is a *pseudomodule*, not a true library module, because it is built into each Modula-2 compiler.

tag field In a record with a variant part, a field that indicates which variant is currently active.

transfer The act of suspending the current coroutine and allowing another coroutine to resume execution.

transparent export The export of a type whose full specification appears in the definition module that exports it. Transparent export of a record type causes the names of its fields to be exported as well; similarly, transparent export of an enumeration type causes the names of the enumeration constants to be exported. Compare with *opaque export*.

type A set of values, together with a collection of operations on those values. For example, the values of type CARDINAL are the integers between 0 and MAX(CARDINAL); operations on CARDINAL values include addition, subtraction, multiplication, division, and modulus (remainder). Modula-2 provides a number of standard (predefined) types; programmers can create new types as well.

type declaration A declaration of the form

TYPE *Ident* = *Type* ;

The identifier to the left of the equals sign is the name of the new type; this identifier can appear in subsequent declarations of variables, procedures, or other types. A type specification must appear to the right of the equals sign.

type specification A description of a new type, containing enough information to determine all values of the type. For example,

```
ARRAY [1..10] OF INTEGER
```

is the specification of an array type. Type specifications may appear in type declarations and variable declarations. An anonymous type results when a type specification appears in a declaration without being given a name.

type transfer function A function that allows a value of one type to be interpreted as a value of another type. A type transfer function does not actually perform any type conversion; it is simply a way to defeat normal type-checking. Modula-2 allows the use of the name of any type (standard or programmer-defined) as a type transfer function.

unstructured type A type whose values are atomic; they cannot be divided into components. The standard types BOOLEAN, CARDINAL, CHAR, INTEGER, LONGINT, LONGREAL, and REAL are unstructured, as are all enumeration and subrange types. Compare with *structured type*.

value parameter A formal parameter that allows the transmission of data into—but not out of—a procedure. An actual parameter corresponding to a value parameter can be any expression whose type is assignment-compatible with the type of the value parameter. Assignments made to a value parameter do not affect the actual parameter. Compare with *variable parameter*.

variable An identifier representing a value that can change during program execution.

variable declaration A declaration of the form

VAR *IdentList* : *Type* ;

which declares a list of identifiers as variables of the specified type.

variable parameter A formal parameter that allows the transmission of data into and/or out of a procedure. An actual parameter corresponding to a variable parameter must be a variable (possibly a record field, array component, or anonymous variable); the types of the variable parameter and actual parameter must be the same. Compare with *value parameter*.

variant A list of case labels and fields occurring in the variant part of a record. A variant is *active* when the value of the variant part's tag field matches one of the case labels. Accessing or modifying the fields within a variant is legal only when the variant is active.

variant part A portion of a record whose structure can vary during the execution of a program. A variant part consists of a tag field (which may be omitted) and a sequence of variants. The tag field indicates which variant is currently active. Modifying the value of the tag field changes the structure of the record.

visibility An entity is visible at a particular point in a program if it is legal to reference the entity at that point. The visibility of an entity depends on where the entity is declared and where it appears in import and export lists.

WHILE **statement** A statement of the form

```
WHILE Expression DO
  StatementSequence
END
```

The effect of a WHILE statement is to repeatedly execute the statement sequence as long as the expression (which must be BOOLEAN) remains TRUE. The expression is tested *before* each execution of the statement sequence.

WITH **statement** A statement of the form

```
WITH Designator DO
  StatementSequence
END
```

The designator must specify a record variable; within the statement sequence, fields in this record may be accessed without qualification by the designator.

WORD A low-level type whose values are single words of memory. The SYSTEM module exports WORD. No operations are allowed on WORD values except assignment. However, if a procedure has a formal parameter of type WORD, a corresponding actual parameter can be of any type that requires one word of memory. A formal parameter of type ARRAY OF WORD will match an actual parameter of any type.

workspace A region of memory used to store the state of a coroutine. Typically, a workspace includes the coroutine's local variables and stack, plus enough other information about the state of the coroutine to allow it to resume executing after it has been suspended.

Bibliography

The first section of this bibliography lists books on Modula-2 and its applications. The second section contains references to articles and technical reports dealing with Modula-2. The last section lists selected publications on three related topics: Modula (the predecessor of Modula-2), Lilith, and Mesa.

I. Modula-2 Books

Adams, J. M., P. Gabrini, and B. Kurtz, *An Introduction to Computer Science with Modula-2*, D. C. Heath, Lexington, Mass., 1988.

Beidler, J., and P. Jackowitz, *Modula-2*, PWS, Boston, 1986.

Chirlian, P. M., *Introduction to Modula-2*, Matrix, Beaverton, Ore., 1984.

Christian, K., *A Guide to Modula-2*, Springer-Verlag, New York, 1986.

Ford, G., and R. Wiener, *Modula-2: A Software Development Approach*, Wiley, New York, 1985.

Gleaves, R., *Modula-2 for Pascal Programmers*, Springer-Verlag, New York, 1984.

Greenfield, S. B., *Invitation to Modula-2*, Petrocelli, Princeton, N.J., 1985.

Jones, W. C., Jr., *Modula-2: Problem Solving and Programming with Style*, Harper & Row, New York, 1987.

Joyce, E. J., *Modula-2: A Seafarer's Manual and Shipyard Guide*, Addison-Wesley, Reading, Mass., 1985.

Kaplan, I., and M. Miller, *Modula-2 Programming*, Hayden, Hasbrouck Heights, N.J., 1986.

Kelly-Bootle, S., *Modula-2 Primer*, Howard W. Sams & Company, Indianapolis, 1987.

Knepley, E., and R. Platt, *Modula-2 Programming*, Reston, Reston, Va., 1985.

McCracken, D. D., *A Second Course in Computer Science with Modula-2*, Wiley, New York, 1987.

Messer, P. A., and I. Marshall, *Modula-2: Constructive Program Development*, Blackwell Scientific Publications, Palo Alto, Calif., 1986.

Moore, J. B., and K. N. McKay, *Modula-2: Text and Reference*, Prentice-Hall, Englewood Cliffs, N.J., 1987.

Ogilvie, J. W. L., *Modula-2 Programming*, McGraw-Hill, New York, 1985.

Pinson, L., R. Sincovec, and R. Wiener, *A First Course in Computer Science with Modula-2*, Wiley, New York, 1987.

Pomberger, G., *Software Engineering and Modula-2*, Prentice-Hall, Englewood Cliffs, N.J., 1984.

Riley, D. D., *Data Abstraction and Structures: An Introduction to Computer Science 2*, Boyd & Fraser, Boston, 1987.

———, *Using Modula-2: An Introduction to Computer Science 1*, Boyd & Fraser, Boston, 1987.

Sale, A., *Modula-2: Discipline & Design*, Addison-Wesley, Sydney, Australia, 1986.

Sawyer, B., and D. Foster, *Programming Expert Systems in Modula-2*, Wiley, New York, 1986.

Schildt, H., *Modula-2 Made Easy*, Osborne McGraw-Hill, Berkeley, Calif., 1986.

———, *Advanced Modula-2*, Osborne McGraw-Hill, Berkeley, Calif., 1987.

Sincovec, R., and R. Wiener, *Data Structures with Modula-2*, Wiley, New York, 1986.

Stubbs, D. F., and N. W. Webre, *Data Structures with Abstract Data Types and Modula-2*, Brooks/Cole, Monterey, Calif., 1987.

Sutcliffe, R., *Introduction to Programming using Modula-2*, Merrill, Columbus, Ohio, 1987.

Terry, P. D., *An Introduction to Programming with Modula-2*, Addison-Wesley, Wokingham, England, 1987.

Thalmann, D., *Modula-2: An Introduction*, Springer-Verlag, New York, 1985.

Ural, S., and S. Ural, *Introduction to Programming with Modula-2*, Harper & Row, New York, 1987.

Walker, B. K., *Modula-2: Programming with Data Structures*, Wadsworth, Belmont, Calif., 1986.

Ward, T. A., *Advanced Programming Techniques in Modula-2*, Scott, Foresman, Glenview, Ill., 1987.

Wiener, R. S., *Modula-2 Wizard: A Programmer's Reference*, Wiley, New York, 1986.

Wiener, R., and R. Sincovec, *Software Engineering with Modula-2 and Ada*, Wiley, New York, 1984.

Wirth, N., *Programming in Modula-2*, 3rd ed., corrected, Springer-Verlag, New York, 1985.

———, *Algorithms & Data Structures*, Prentice-Hall, Englewood Cliffs, N.J., 1986.

II. Modula-2 Articles and Reports

History of Modula-2

Joyce, E., The making of Modula-2. *PC Magazine* **3**, 6 (April 3, 1984): 176–181.

Wirth, N., History and goals of Modula-2. *Byte* **9**, 8 (August 1984): 145–152.

———, From programming language design to computer construction. *Communications of the ACM* **28**, 2 (February 1985): 159–164.

———, Modula II, an overview: Excerpts from a talk by Niklaus Wirth. *Micro Cornucopia* 25 (August–September 1985): 76–79.

Tutorials on Modula-2

Gutknecht, J., Tutorial on Modula-2. *Byte* **9**, 8 (August 1984): 157–176.

Wirth, N., *Modula-2*, Report no. 36, Institut für Informatik, Swiss Federal Institute of Technology, Zürich, 1980.

Woteki, T., A. Freiden, D. Levy, T. Bestul, and R. Stine, Modular constructions. *PC Tech Journal* **2**, 5 (November 1984): 72–94.

Comparisons of Modula-2 with Other Languages

Bielak, R., Ada vs. Modula-2: A view from the trenches. *SIGPLAN Notices* **20**, 12 (December 1985): 13–17.

Carroll, D. W., Modula-2 versus Pascal for microcomputers: An update. *Dr. Dobb's Journal* **10**, 11 (November 1985): 28–34.

Coar, D., Pascal, Ada, and Modula-2. *Byte* **9**, 8 (August 1984): 215–232.

Djavaheri, M., and S. Osborne, Modula-2: An alternative to C for system programming. *The MODUS Quarterly* 2 (April 1985): 55–64. [Reprinted in *Journal of Pascal, Ada & Modula-2* **5**, 3 (May–June 1986): 47–52.]

Feldman, M. B., Ada vs. Modula-2: A response from the ivory tower. *SIGPLAN Notices* **21**, 5 (May 1986): 39–44.

Greenwood, J. R., Comments on "A view from the trenches"—Ada vs. Modula-2 vs. Praxis. *SIGPLAN Notices* **21**, 5 (May 1986): 45–49.

Hartel, P. H., Comparing Pascal and Modula-2 as systems programming languages. *Programming Languages and System Design*, North-Holland, New York, 1983.

Johnson, M. C., and A. Munro, Pascal's design flaws: Modula-2 solutions and Pascal patches. *Byte* **9**, 3 (March 1984): 371–388.

Joyce, E., Modula-2 for Pascal programmers. *PC Magazine* **3**, 6 (April 3, 1984): 193–197.

McAlhany, E. B., and M. D. Campbell, Modula-2 & Ada: A comparison of four features. *Journal of Pascal, Ada & Modula-2* **3**, 4 (July–August 1984): 37–48.

McClarty, H., and D. W. Smith, An introduction to Modula-2 for Pascal programmers. *Dr. Dobb's Journal* **9**, 5 (May 1984): 22–27.

McCormack, J., and R. Gleaves, Modula-2: A worthy successor to Pascal. *Byte* **8**, 4 (April 1983): 385–395.

Meng, B., Ada and Modula-2: True systems languages? *Digital Design* (August 1985): 74–79.

Moffat, D. V., UCSD Pascal vs. Modula-2: A dissenting view. *Byte* **9**, 8 (August 1984): 428–430.

Muller, H. A., Differences between Modula-2 and Pascal. *SIGPLAN Notices* **19**, 10 (October 1984): 32–39.

Ogilvie, J. W. L., Modula-to-Ada type translation. *Journal of Pascal and Ada* **3**, 1 (January–February 1984).

Paul, R. J., An introduction to Modula-2. *Byte* **9**, 8 (August 1984): 195–210.

Shammas, N., Exploring Ada and Modula-2. *Computer Language* **1**, 1 (1984): 51–60.

Stotts, P. D., Jr., A comparative survey of concurrent programming languages. *SIGPLAN Notices* **17**, 9 (September 1982): 76–87.

Sumner, R. T., and R. E. Gleaves, Modula-2 — A solution to Pascal's problems. *SIGPLAN Notices* **17**, 9 (September 1982): 28–33. [Reprinted in *Journal of Pascal and Ada* **1**, 5 (September–October 1982).]

Weisert, M., Having your Pascal and Modula, too: Excerpts from a talk at SOG IV by Mike Weisert. *Micro Cornucopia* 28 (February–March 1986): 97–99.

Modula-2: Pro and Con

Christiansen, H. P., A. Lacroix, K. Lundberg, A. McKeeman, and P. D. V. van der Stok, More or less concerns about Modula-2. *SIGPLAN Notices* **21**, 9 (September 1986): 27–31.

Cohen, D. R., Concerns of a programmer. *The MODUS Quarterly* 4 (November 1985): 6–7.

Goldberg, M., A response to "Some concerns about Modula-2." *SIGPLAN Notices* **20**, 8 (August 1985): 71–72.

Moffat, D. V., Some concerns about Modula-2. *SIGPLAN Notices* **19**, 12 (December 1984): 41–47.

Pase, D. M., System programming in Modula-2. *SIGPLAN Notices* **20**, 11 (November 1985): 49–53.

Powell, M. L., Modula-2: Good news and bad news. *Proceedings of IEEE COMPCON Spring 84* (February 1984).

Segre, L., and M. Stanton, "Some concerns about Modula-2" considered unwarranted. *SIGPLAN Notices* **20**, 5 (May 1985): 31–35.

Spector, D., Ambiguities and insecurities in Modula-2. *SIGPLAN Notices* **17**, 8 (August 1982): 43–51.

Suman, M., What's wrong with high-level languages? *Dr. Dobb's Journal of Software Tools* **12**, 2 (February 1987).

Torbett, M. A., More ambiguities and insecurities in Modula-2. *SIGPLAN Notices* **22**, 5 (May 1987): 11–17.

Implementing Modula-2 Compilers and Environments

Foster, D. G., Modula-2 compilation and beyond. *The MODUS Quarterly* 4 (November 1985): 34–46.

———, Separate compilation in a Modula-2 compiler. *Software—Practice and Experience* **16**, 2 (February 1986): 101–106.

Geissmann, L. B., *Separate Compilation in Modula-2 and the Structure of the Modula-2 Compiler on the Personal Computer Lilith*, Diss. ETH no. 7286, Swiss Federal Institute of Technology, Zürich, 1983.

Gutknecht, J., Separate compilation in Modula-2: An approach to efficient symbol files. *IEEE Software* **3**, 6 (November 1986): 29–38.

Habernoll, T., Modula-2 for VM/CMS (IBM/370). *The MODUS Quarterly* 7 (February 1987): 7–10.

Hopper, K., and W. J. Rogers, Portable language implementation project: Design and development rationale. *The MODUS Quarterly* 5 (February 1986): 24–41.

Jacobi, C., *Code Generation and the Lilith Architecture*, Diss. ETH no. 7195, Swiss Federal Institute of Technology, Zürich, 1982.

Madhavji, N. H., L. Pinsonneault, and K. Toubache, Modula-2/MUPE–2: Language and environment interactions. *IEEE Software* **3**, 6 (November 1986): 7–17.

Odegard, F. L., A programming environment for Modula-2. *The MODUS Quarterly* 6 (November 1986): 30–36.

Powell, M. L., A portable optimizing compiler for Modula-2. *Proceedings of the SIGPLAN '84 Symposium on Compiler Construction*, Montreal, June 1984. Published as *SIGPLAN Notices* **19**, 6 (June 1984): 310–318.

Sebesta, R. W., and M. A. Taylor, Fast identification of Ada and Modula-2 reserved words. *Journal of Pascal, Ada & Modula-2* **5**, 2 (March–April 1986): 36–39.

Spector, D., Lexing and parsing Modula-2. *SIGPLAN Notices* **18**, 10 (October 1983): 25–32.

Symons, J., The linking process in Modula-2. *The MODUS Quarterly* 2 (April 1985): 37–39.

Reviews of Modula-2 Systems

Anderson, B. R., Modula-2 system for Z80 CP/M. *Byte* **11**, 3 (March 1986): 225–234.

———, Review of CP/M Modula-2. *Journal of Pascal, Ada & Modula-2* **5**, 2 (March–April 1986): 33–35.

Anderson, T. L., Seven Modula-2 compilers reviewed. *Journal of Pascal, Ada & Modula-2* **3**, 2 (March–April 1984).

Bielak, R., The VMS Modula-2 compiler reviewed. *Journal of Pascal, Ada & Modula-2* **3**, 6 (November–December 1984).

Brecheen, C., and C. Bradford, Modula-2 Software Development System. *PC Tech Journal* **4**, 9 (September 1986): 187–188.

Bridger, M., ITC's Modula-2 Software Development System. *Byte* **11**, 10 (October 1986): 255–258.

Carlisle, D., Using Modula-2. *Journal of Pascal and Ada* **2**, 3 (May–June 1983): 44–48.

Cockerham, J. T., Modula-2/86 Base Language System. *PC Tech Journal* **4**, 9 (September 1986): 188–190.

———, Modular developments. *PC Tech Journal* **5**, 3 (March 1987): 114–138.

Dotzel, G., Benchmark test results for Modula-2 compiler: A benchmark test for Modula-2 implementations. *Journal of Pascal, Ada & Modula-2* **4**, 2 (March–April 1985): 28–32.

Dotzel, G., and K. Moritzen, Modula-2 and its environment. *Journal of Pascal, Ada & Modula-2* **3**, 4 (July–August 1984): 42–46.

Eldred, E., Volition Systems' Modula-2. *Byte* **9**, 6 (June 1984): 353–364.

Jacobs, C., Modula-2/86 (Logitech). *Computer Language* **1**, 1 (1984): 71–74.

———, Modula-2 (Volition Systems). *Computer Language* **1**, 2 (October 1984): 72–73.

Jewell, C., The ETH-Zürich Modula-2 compiler for the Macintosh. *The MODUS Quarterly* 5 (February 1986): 42–49.

Jones, J. P., The tale of two Modulas. *Micro Cornucopia* **34** (February–March 1987): 78–81.

Joyce, E., A $40 invitation to Modula-2. *PC Magazine* **3**, 6 (April 3, 1984): 183–186.

———, Modula-2: Son of Pascal. *Microcomputing* **VIII**, 8 (August 1984): 70–74.

———, Volition's Modula-2 on the Sage. *Byte* **9**, 10 (September 1984): 351–353.

———, Logitech's new breed of Modula-2. *Microcomputing* **VIII**, 10 (October 1984): 62–66.

Lewis, T. G., Modula-2: Language of the future. *IEEE Software* **2**, 5 (September 1985): 66–68.

Oman, P. W., Jr., Logitech Modula-2/86: Review and comparison. *IEEE Software* **3**, 3 (May 1986): 76–78.

Parker, T., Modula-2/86. *Computer Language* **3**, 6 (June 1986): 140–142.

Pitt, J., What's new with Modula-2? *PC Magazine* **3**, 6 (April 3, 1984): 187–191.

Sand, P. A., Three Modula-2 programming systems. *Byte* **12**, 1 (January 1987): 333–336.

Shammas, N. C., Modula-2 compilers for the IBM PC. *Dr. Dobb's Journal of Software Tools* **11**, 10 (October 1986): 48–63.

Shammas, N. C., and K. Magel, Microcomputer Modula-2 analysis. *Computer Language* **2**, 10 (October 1985): 83–100.

Wiener, R. S., Review of some more Modula-2 compilers. *Journal of Pascal, Ada & Modula-2* **6**, 1 (January–February 1987): 78–80.

Woteki, T., A. Freiden, D. Levy, T. Bestul, and R. Stine, Modular implementations. *PC Tech Journal* **2**, 6 (December 1984): 154–182.

Proposed Changes and Extensions to Modula-2

Anderson, T. L., The scope of imported identifiers in Modula-2. *SIGPLAN Notices* **21**, 9 (September 1986): 17–21.

Astor, E., Component control for a high-level language. *Microprocessing and Microprogramming* 9, 2 (February 1982): 85–92.

Emerson, M., Some comments on Modula-2. *The MODUS Quarterly* 2 (April 1985): 7–11.

French, C., and R. Mitchell, Opaque types in Modula-2. *The MODUS Quarterly* 2 (April 1985): 12–28.

Lovejoy, A., Extensions to Modula-2. *Journal of Pascal, Ada & Modula-2* 6, 2 (March–April 1987): 20–44.

Mohay, G. M., A simplified coroutine structure for Modula-2. *Journal of Pascal, Ada & Modula-2* 6, 1 (January–February 1987): 35–42.

Rovner, P., Extending Modula-2 to build large, integrated systems. *IEEE Software* 3, 6 (November 1986): 46–57.

Rovner, P., R. Levin, and J. Wick, *On Extending Modula-2 for Building Large, Integrated Systems*, Report no. 3, Digital Systems Research Center, Palo Alto, Calif., January 11, 1985.

Zimmer, J. A., A modest Modula wish list. *SIGPLAN Notices* 20, 11 (November 1985): 69–77.

Standardization of Modula-2

Cornelius, B., The scope problems caused by modules. *The MODUS Quarterly* 3 (July 1985): 43–59.

———, A selection of the contentious problems with the "Report on Modula-2." *The MODUS Quarterly* 3 (July 1985): 20–34.

———, Exporting a module identifier. *The MODUS Quarterly* 5 (February 1986): 2–4.

———, All about strings. *The MODUS Quarterly* 6 (November 1986): 15–20.

———, Significant changes to the language Modula-2. *The MODUS Quarterly* 6 (November 1986): 8–14.

Poulsen, O., N73: NULL-terminated strings in Modula-2. *The MODUS Quarterly* 5 (February 1986): 10–13.

Siegel, J. A., Validation of Modula-2 language implementations. *Modula-2 News* 1 (January 1985): 59–60.

Steiger, W., BSI accepted change: Multi-dimensional open arrays. *The MODUS Quarterly* 5 (February 1986): 8–9.

Welsh, J., and P. Bailes, Modula-2 standardisation: The go-betweens' tale. *The MODUS Quarterly* 7 (February 1987): 3–6.

Wichmann, B. A., Expressions in Modula-2. *The MODUS Quarterly* 3 (July 1985): 35–42.

———, Some decisions on numerical issues. *The MODUS Quarterly* 6 (November 1986): 25–26.

———, Type conversions in Modula-2. *The MODUS Quarterly* 6 (November 1986): 21–24.

Wirth's Changes to Modula-2

Wirth, N., Revisions and amendments to Modula-2. *Modula-2 News* 0 (October 1984): 2–3. [Also in *Journal of Pascal, Ada & Modula-2* 4, 1 (January–February 1985): 25–28.]

———, Letter on DIV, MOD, /, and REM. *The MODUS Quarterly* 5 (February 1986): 6–7.

———, Letter on multi-dimensional open arrays. *The MODUS Quarterly* 5 (February 1986): 5.

Modula-2 Libraries

Biagioni, E., K. Hinrichs, G. Heiser, and C. Muller, A portable operating system interface and utility library. *IEEE Software* 3, 6 (November 1986): 18–26.

Bondy, J., Draft Modula-2 library documentation to BSI. *Modula-2 News* 1 (January 1985): 38–58.

Bush, R., Modula-2 library draft. *Modula-2 News* 1 (January 1985): 22–37.

———, Modula-2 library rationale. *Modula-2 News* 1 (January 1985): 20–21.

Craig, J. M., J. M. Martel, Jr., and K. B. Richan, Design of a Modula-2 standard library. *Journal of Pascal, Ada & Modula-2* 4, 2 (March–April 1985): 33–46.

Crawford, A. L., High level input/output in Modula-2. *SIGPLAN Notices* 20, 12 (December 1985): 18–25.

Djavaheri, M., An implementation of the proposed standard library for the Unix operating system. *The MODUS Quarterly* 4 (November 1985): 26–27.

Dotzel, G., A Modula-2 I/O library proposal. *Journal of Pascal, Ada & Modula-2* 5, 2 (March–April 1986): 24–32.

Eisenbach, S., Draft BSI standard I/O library for Modula-2. *The MODUS Quarterly* 5 (February 1986): 15–23.

Hoppe, J., Some problems with the specification of standard modules. *Modula-2 News* 0 (October 1984): 4–6.

Lo, C. J., Simple patches to Modula-2 text IO. *SIGPLAN Notices* 20, 6 (June 1985): 20–25.

Nagler, R. J., and J. A. Siegel, A few modifications to a Modula standard library proposal. *The MODUS Quarterly* 4 (November 1985): 8–12.

Odersky, M., P. Sollich, and M. Weisert, Proposal for a standard library and an extension to Modula-2. *The MODUS Quarterly* 4 (November 1985): 13–25.

Peterson, B., M2 library comments. *The MODUS Quarterly* 2 (April 1985): 40–47.

Thiagarajan, R., RajaInOut: Simple, safer I/O for Logitech/MS-DOS. *The MODUS Quarterly* 3 (July 1985): 11–19.

Verhulst, E., An implementation of the standard library for PC's. *The MODUS Quarterly* 4 (November 1985): 28–33.

Abstract Data Types and Object-Oriented Design in Modula-2

Bilbe, C. R., Using the heap for Modula-2 opaque types. *Journal of Pascal, Ada & Modula-2* **4**, 6 (November–December 1985): 24–30.

Bondy, J., Uninitialized Modula-2 abstract object instances, yet again. *SIGPLAN Notices* **22**, 5 (May 1987): 58–63.

Savit, J., Uninitialized Modula-2 abstract objects, revisited. *SIGPLAN Notices* **22**, 2 (February 1987): 78–84.

Sumner, R. T., Dynamic module instantiation — Modula-2 supports classes. *The MODUS Quarterly* 2 (April 1985): 29–36.

Torbett, M. A., A note on "Protecting against uninitialized abstract objects in Modula-2." *SIGPLAN Notices* **22**, 5 (May 1987): 8–10.

Walker, B., and S. Alexander, Data abstraction with Modula-2. *Dr. Dobb's Journal* **11**, 2 (February 1986).

Wegmann, A., Object-oriented programming using Modula-2. *Journal of Pascal, Ada & Modula-2* **5**, 3 (May–June 1986): 5–17.

Wiener, R. S., Protecting against uninitialized abstract objects in Modula-2. *SIGPLAN Notices* **21**, 6 (June 1986): 63–69.

Wiener, R. S., and R. F. Sincovec, Modular software construction and object-oriented design using Modula-2. *Journal of Pascal, Ada & Modula-2* **3**, 3 (May–June 1984): 41–47.

Generics in Modula-2

Beidler, J., and P. Jackowitz, Consistent generics in Modula-2. *SIGPLAN Notices* **21**, 4 (April 1986): 32–41.

Czyzowicz, J., and M. Iglewski, Implementing generic types in Modula-2. *SIGPLAN Notices* **20**, 12 (December 1985): 26–32.

Goldsby, M. E., Concurrent use of generic types in Modula-2. *SIGPLAN Notices* **21**, 6 (June 1986): 28–34.

Gough, K. J., Writing generic utilities in Modula-2. *Journal of Pascal, Ada & Modula-2* **5**, 3 (May–June 1986): 53–62.

Leeson, J. J., and M. L. Spear, Type independent modules: The preferred approach to generic ADTs in Modula-2. *SIGPLAN Notices* **22**, 3 (March 1987): 65–70.

Shammas, N. C., Generic routines in Ada and Modula-2 and Pascal iterators. *Dr. Dobb's Journal of Software Tools* **11**, 8 (August 1986): 116–119.

Wiener, R. S., Generic sorting in Modula-2. *Journal of Pascal and Ada* **3**, 1 (January–February 1984): 33–36.

———, A generic sorting module in Modula-2. *SIGPLAN Notices* **19**, 3 (March 1984): 66–72.

Wiener, R. S., and R. F. Sincovec, Two approaches to implementing generic data structures in Modula-2. *SIGPLAN Notices* **20**, 6 (June 1985): 56–64.

Low-Level Programming in Modula-2

Albert, J. W., Practical programming in Modula-2: Controlling the video on PCs. *Micro Cornucopia* 31 (August–September 1986): 12–19.

Anderson, B. R., Bit manipulation in Modula-2. *Dr. Dobb's Journal* **10**, 11 (November 1985): 38–46.

Gutknecht, J., *System Programming in Modula-2: Mouse and Bitmap Display*, Report no. 56, Institut für Informatik, Swiss Federal Institute of Technology, Zürich, 1983.

Powell, M. L., Using Modula-2 for system programming with Unix. *USENIX Association 1984 Summer Conference Proceedings*, Salt Lake City, Utah (June 1984): 119–132.

Wiener, R. S., Interfacing assembly language to Modula-2—A case study: Creating rapid screen displays for PC's. *Journal of Pascal, Ada & Modula-2* **5**, 4 (July–August 1986): 21–26.

Other Modula-2 Programming Techniques

Craig, J. M., Elegant overlays: A scheme for organizing segmented Modula-2 programs. *Journal of Pascal, Ada & Modula-2* **5**, 1 (January–February 1986): 36–41.

Rehmer, K., Error handling using Modula-2. *SIGPLAN Notices* **22**, 3 (March 1987): 40–48.

Shammas, N. C., Modula-2: No strings attached! *Journal of Pascal, Ada & Modula-2* **3**, 2 (March–April 1984): 44–47.

———, Dynamic multidimensional arrays in Modula-2. *Computer Language* **2**, 3 (March 1985): 52–60.

———, Creating reusable modules. *Byte* **11**, 1 (January 1986): 145–150.

———, Error-handling in Ada and Modula-2, large Turbo Pascal matrices. *Dr. Dobb's Journal of Software Tools* **11**, 11 (November 1986): 120–128.

Wiener, R. S., Dynamic multidimensional arrays in Modula-2. *Journal of Pascal and Ada* **2**, 6 (November–December 1983): 43–48.

Using Modula-2 for Operating Systems and Real-Time Applications

Barrow, P., Some thoughts on Modula-2 in "real time." *The MODUS Quarterly* 3 (July 1985): 8–9.

Budgen, D., Combining MASCOT with Modula-2 to aid the engineering of real-time systems. *Software — Practice and Experience* **15**, 8 (August 1985): 767–793.

Corbeil, R. C., and A. H. Anderson, Modula-2 as a systems programming language. *Byte* **11**, 5 (May 1986): 111–120.

Crawford, A. L., Message-based synchronization in Modula. *Journal of Pascal, Ada & Modula-2* **5**, 4 (July–August 1986): 13–20.

Henry, R., Modula-2 processes — Problems and suggestions. *The MODUS Quarterly* 4 (November 1985): 47–60.

Hirschy, E., Hermes: An operating system for a Modula-2 environment. *Proceedings of the 1983 ACM Conference on Personal and Small Computers*, San Diego, December 1983. Published as *SIGPC Notes* **6**, 2 (December 1983): 163–167.

Hoppe, J., A simple nucleus written in Modula-2: A case study. *Software — Practice and Experience* **10**, 9 (September 1980): 697–706.

Justice, B., S. Osborne, and V. Wills, Building an operating system with Modula-2. *The MODUS Quarterly* 7 (February 1987): 27–53.

———, Concurrent operating system: Build it with Modula-2. *Micro Cornucopia* 34 (February–March 1987): 26–32.

Knudsen, S. E., *Medos-2: A Modula-2 Oriented Operating System for the Personal Computer Lilith*, Diss. ETH no. 7346, Swiss Federal Institute of Technology, Zürich, 1983.

Ma, F., and L. D. Wittie, Transmission Control Protocol (TCP) implementation in Modula-2. *The MODUS Quarterly* 7 (February 1987): 11–26.

Maier, G., MODEB: A real-time operating system kernel written in the high level programming language Modula-2. *Real-Time Languages and Operating Systems* **I** (1982): 61–67.

Sewry, D. A., Modula-2 and the monitor concept. *SIGPLAN Notices* **19**, 11 (November 1984): 33–41.

———, Modula-2 process facilities. *SIGPLAN Notices* **19**, 11 (November 1984): 23–32.

Terry, P. D., A Modula-2 kernel for supporting monitors. *Software — Practice and Experience* **16**, 5 (May 1986): 457–472.

Thomas, H. W., Design and performance of a simple nucleus for real-time control applications. *Software & Microsystems* **1**, 6 (October 1982): 160–166.

Wilson, C. R., Coprocessing in Modula-2. *Byte* **10**, 4 (April 1985): 113–117.

Wittie, L. D., and A. J. Frank, A portable Modula-2 operating system: SAM2S. *Proceedings of AFIPS National Computer Conference, 1984*, Las Vegas (July 1984): 282–292.

Other Applications of Modula-2

Amsterdam, J., Build a spreadsheet program. *Byte* **11**, 7 (July 1986): 96–106.

Anderson, B. R., A 68000 cross assembler. Parts 1, 2, and listings. *Dr. Dobb's Journal* **11**, 4–6 (April, May, June 1986): 52–81, 44–55, 46–62.

Bankston, J., and M. Berger, Pipeline processing with Modula-2. *Journal of Pascal, Ada & Modula-2* **5**, 5 (September–October 1986): 46–51.

Brunnschweiler, A., A SET OF CHAR module. *The MODUS Quarterly* 7 (February 1987): 55–60.

Clarke, J., A Modula-2 algorithm for the general solution of an arbitrary system of linear inequalities. *Journal of Pascal, Ada & Modula-2* **6**, 3 (May–June 1987): 32–42.

Davidson, A. H., H. B. Herrmann, and E. R. Hoffer, NewStudio: Engineering a Modula-2 application for Macintosh. *The MODUS Quarterly* 5 (February 1986): 50–60.

Dotzel, G., and K. Moritzen, LIDAS: A relational database system. *Journal of Pascal, Ada & Modula-2* **3**, 5 (September–October 1984).

Goldsby, M. E., Solving the "N <= 8 queens" problem with CSP and Modula-2. *SIGPLAN Notices* **22**, 2 (February 1987): 43–52.

Gordon, T. F., On the suitability of Modula-2 for artificial intelligence programming. *Applied Informatics* 7 (1985): 296–303.

Greenfield, S. B., An introduction to Modula-2. *Journal of Pascal, Ada & Modula-2* **3**, 3 (May–June 1984): 36–40.

Morgeson, D., Artificial intelligence using Modula-2: A simple expert system. *Journal of Pascal, Ada & Modula-2* **4**, 1 (January–February 1985): 29–38.

Muller, C., Modula-Prolog: A software development tool. *IEEE Software* **3**, 6 (November 1986): 39–45.

Ogilvie, J. W. L., Life in Modula-2. *Journal of Pascal and Ada* **2**, 4 (July–August 1983).

———, Petri net simulation using Modula-2 sets. *Journal of Pascal and Ada* **2**, 5 (September–October 1983): 35–37.

———, A pattern matcher in Modula-2. *Journal of Pascal, Ada & Modula-2* **3**, 6 (November–December 1984): 34–43.

———, Using variant records: Some basic LISP functions in Modula-2. *Journal of Pascal, Ada & Modula-2* **4**, 2 (March–April 1985): 15–20.

Park, D. J. M., Jr., A Modula-2 module which implements softkeys. *Journal of Pascal, Ada & Modula-2* **4**, 6 (November–December 1985): 41–43.

Pinson, L. J., and R. S. Wiener, Simplifying algebraic expressions. *Journal of Pascal, Ada & Modula-2* **3**, 5 (September–October 1984).

Sorensen, J. O., The usefulness of standard functions in Modula-2: An example in relation to VDI. *Journal of Pascal, Ada & Modula-2* **6**, 1 (January–February 1987): 5–9.

Ural, S., Symbolic operations on polynomials in Modula-2. *Journal of Pascal, Ada & Modula-2* **3**, 5 (September–October 1984): 40–51.

Wallach, Y., Solution of linear equations on an "Alternating Sequential/Parallel" (ASP) system using Ada and Modula-2. *Journal of Pascal, Ada & Modula-2* **6**, 2 (March–April 1987): 3–19.

Wiener, R. S., An efficient virtual hash algorithm for a spelling checker. *Journal of Pascal, Ada & Modula-2* **5**, 1 (January–February 1986): 23–29.

Modula-2 in the Curriculum

Brumfield, J. A., Teaching operating systems with Modula-2. *SIGCSE Bulletin* **18**, 1 (February 1986): 273–282.

Feldman, M. B., Modula-2 projects for an operating-systems course: Racing sorts and multiple windows. *SIGCSE Bulletin* **18**, 1 (February 1986): 283–288.

Gabrini, P. J., J. M. Adams, and B. L. Kurtz, Converting from Pascal to Modula-2 in the undergraduate curriculum. *SIGCSE Bulletin* **18**, 1 (February 1986): 50–52.

III. Selected Publications on Related Topics

Modula

Holden, J., and I. C. Wand, An assessment of Modula. *Software — Practice and Experience* **10**, 8 (August 1980): 593–621.

Hoppe, J., A comparison of Modula with other system programming languages. *Proceedings of the 5th International Computing Symposium 1977*, Liege, Belgium, April 1977, ed. E. Morlet and D. Ribbens. Elsevier North-Holland, New York, 1977: 129–134.

Smedema, C. H., P. Medema, and M. Boasson, *The Programming Languages Pascal, Modula, CHILL, and Ada*, Prentice-Hall, Englewood Cliffs, N.J., 1983.

Wand, I. C., Dynamic resource allocation and supervision with the programming language Modula. *Computer Journal* **23**, 2 (May 1980): 147–152.

Wirth, N., Design and implementation of Modula. *Software — Practice and Experience* **7**, 1 (January–February 1977): 67–84.

———, Modula: A language for modular multiprogramming. *Software — Practice and Experience* **7**, 1 (January–February 1977): 3–35.

———, The use of Modula. *Software — Practice and Experience* **7**, 1 (January–February 1977): 37–65.

———, Toward a discipline of real-time programming. *Communications of the ACM* **20**, 8 (August 1977): 577–583.

Lilith

Geissmann, L., J. Hoppe, C. Jacobi, S. E. Knudsen, W. Winiger, and N. Wirth, *Lilith Handbook — A Guide for Lilith Users and Programmers*, Institut für Informatik, Swiss Federal Institute of Technology, Zürich, 1982.

Gutknecht, J., and W. Winiger, Andra: The document preparation system of the personal workstation Lilith. *Software — Practice and Experience* **14**, 1 (January 1984): 73–100.

Ohran, R., Lilith and Modula-2. *Byte* **9**, 8 (August 1984): 181–192.

Sand, P. A., The Lilith personal computer. *Byte* **9**, 10 (September 1984): 300–311.

Schiffman, R. C., The ideal architecture for Modula-2. *Journal of Pascal and Ada* **2**, 3 (May–June 1983).

Wirth, N., *The Personal Computer Lilith*, Report no. 40, Institut für Informatik, Swiss Federal Institute of Technology, Zürich, 1981.

———, Lilith: A personal computer for the software engineer. *Proceedings of the 5th International Conference on Software Engineering*, San Diego (March 1981): 2–15.

———, Microprocessor architectures: A comparison based on code generation by compiler. *Communications of the ACM* **29**, 10 (October 1986): 978–990.

Mesa

Geschke, C. M., J. H. Morris, Jr., and E. H. Satterthwaite, Early experience with Mesa. *Communications of the ACM* **20**, 8 (August 1977): 540–553.

Lampson, B. W., and D. D. Redell, Experience with processes and monitors in Mesa. *Communications of the ACM* **23**, 2 (February 1980): 105–117.

Lauer, H. C., and E. H. Satterthwaite, The impact of Mesa on system design. *Proceedings of the 4th International Conference on Software Engineering*, Munich (September 1979): 174–182.

Mitchell, J. G., W. Maybury, and R. E. Sweet, *Mesa Language Manual*, Xerox Palo Alto Research Center Report CSL-79-3 (April 1979).

Sweet, R. E., The Mesa programming environment. *Proceedings of the ACM SIGPLAN 85 Symposium on Language Issues in Programming Environments*, Seattle, June 1985. Published as *SIGPLAN Notices* **20**, 7 (July 1985): 216–229.

Resources*

Magazines

Journal of Pascal, Ada & Modula-2

John Wiley & Sons, Inc.
Subscription Department
605 Third Avenue
New York, NY 10158

Subscription: $22 per year (six issues)

The MODUS Quarterly (Published by the Modula-2 Users Association)

North and South America:	Elsewhere:
George Symons MODUS P.O. Box 51778 Palo Alto, CA 94303 (415) 322-0547	Aline Sigrist MODUS Secretary ERDIS SA P.O. Box 35 CH-1800 Vevey 2 Switzerland
Membership: $20 per year	Membership: SFr 45 per year

Compilers

Vendor	*Machines and/or Operating Systems Supported*
ACE Associated Computer Experts bv Van Eeghenstraat 100 1071 GL Amsterdam The Netherlands 31 20 646416 Telex: 11702 Fax: 31 20 750389	Cross-compilers targeted to VAX and MC680x0, hosted on ULTRIX, BSD UNIX, Gould UTX 2.0, and VAX/VMS.
The Adesse Corporation 36 Mill Plain Road, Suite 307 Danbury, CT 06811 (203) 790-9473 Telex: 750048 Contact: Thomas Foth	IBM 370 and plug-compatible mainframes (VM/SP and VM/SP HPO)

*All information shown is subject to change.

ana-systems P.O. Box 4759 697 Saturn Court Foster City, CA 94404-0759 (415) 341-1768 ITT Telex: 49 49 940	MC68020-based computers, including Altos 3068, Apollo DOMAIN IX, Atari ST, Dual, Force, Macintosh II, Masscomp RTU, Philips Unifive, Silicon Graphics IRIS, Sun workstations, Tektronix 4400, UniPlus+; also, cross-compilers targeted to MC68020, hosted on VAX (ULTRIX, BSD UNIX, and VMS)
Technical University Berlin Informatik Rechnerbetrieb Sekr. FR 5-3 Franklinstr. 28/29 1000 Berlin 10 West Germany Contact: Thomas Habernoll	IBM 370 (VM/CMS); available free of charge to universities and research institutions
BBC Aktiengesellschaft Brown, Bovarie & Cie Abteilung ESV CH-5401 Baden Switzerland 056/75 52 52 Contact: Dr. Josef A. Muheim	PDP-11 (RSX-11 M, RSX-11 M Plus)
Digital Equipment Corporation Western Research Laboratory 100 Hamilton Avenue Palo Alto, CA 94301 (415) 853-6621 Contact: Michael Powell	VAX (UNIX or ULTRIX); available only to academic sites in the United States and Canada
Echelon, Inc. 885 N. San Antonio Road Los Altos, CA 94022 (415) 948-3820	Z80 (CP/M-80 compatible systems, including CP/M 2.2, CP/M 3.0, Z-System)
Farbware 1329 Gregory Wilmette, IL 60091 (312) 251-5310	IBM PC (MS-DOS), IBM PS/2 (OS/2), IBM AT (OS/2 and Microsoft Windows)
University of Frankfurt Lehrstuhl DBIS Box 11 19 32 D-6000 Frankfurt/Main 11 West Germany Contact: Dr. Joachim W. Schmidt	VAX (VMS)

GEFI Service 71 rue de la Victoire 75009 Paris France (1) 43 72 57 74 Contact: Chantal Fauconnet	Macintosh Plus, Macintosh SE, Macintosh II
Hochstrasser Computing AG Rebhaldenstr. 27 CH-8704 Herrliberg Switzerland 01-915 29 40	Z80 (CP/M)
Interface Technologies Corp. 3336 Richmond, Suite 200 Houston, TX 77098 (713) 523-8422 (800) 922-9049	IBM PC (MS-DOS), Amiga
University of Linz Institut für Informatik Altenbergerstrasse 69 A-4040 Linz Austria (43) 732 2468-447 Contact: G. Blaschek	IBM 370 (OS/MVS)
Logitech, Inc. 6505 Kaiser Drive Fremont, CA 94555 (415) 795-8500 (800) 231-7717 Fax: (415) 792-8901	IBM PC (MS-DOS), VAX (VMS), VAX (VMS) to 8086 cross-compiler, Lilith to 8086 cross-compiler
Masthaven Development Limited East Suite, 511 Coldhams Lane Cambridge CB1 3LN England (0223) 248844 Telex: 265871	68000 (UNIX)
Micromint, Inc. 4 Park Street Vernon, CT 06066 (800) 635-3355	SB180FX, SB180

Modula Corporation 950 North University Avenue Provo, UT 84604 (801) 375-7400 (800) LIL-ITH2	IBM PC (MS-DOS), Macintosh
ModulaWare GmbH Wilhelmstrasse 17A D-8520 Erlangen West Germany 09131 208395 Contact: Günter Dotzel	LSI-11/PDP-11 (RT-11, SHAREplus, and TSXplus)
Oxxi, Inc. P.O. Box 4000 Fullerton, CA 92634 (714) 999-6710 Fax: (714) 999-1045 Contact: John Houston	Amiga
PCollier Systems, Inc. Suite 390 7925-A North Oracle Road Tucson, AZ 85704 (800) 522-2060	IBM PC (MS-DOS)
Pecan Software Systems, Inc. 1410 39th Street Brooklyn, NY 11218 (718) 851-3100 (800) 63-PECAN	PC-DOS, MS-DOS, Amiga, Atari ST, Macintosh, Apple II and IIGS, Rainbow, Tandy, Stride, VAX, UNIX, PDP-11, others
Qudos Limited Unit 2 Cambridge Science Park Milton Road Cambridge CB4 4FD England (0223) 862333 Telex: 818114 Fax: 862946	VAX (UNIX), 68000 (BSD 4.2 UNIX or UNIX System V), 32016/32 (UNIX System V)
Queensland Institute of Technology Department of Computing Science G.P.O. Box 2434 Brisbane, Queensland Australia 4001 (07) 223 2132 Contact: Dr. K. John Gough	RT11SJ, RT11XM, TSX+

ScenicSoft, Inc. P.O. Box 909 Edmonds, WA 98020 (800) 422-2994	68000, 68010, 68020
Stony Brook Software, Inc. Forest Road Wilton, NH 03086 (603) 654-2525	8086 family
Sun Microsystems, Inc. 2550 Garcia Avenue Mountain View, CA 94043 (415) 960-1300	Sun-3 (UNIX)
Tartan Laboratories, Inc. 461 Melwood Avenue Pittsburgh, PA 15213 (412) 621-2210 Contact: Scott Wilson	VAX (UNIX), RT PC (AIX or ACIS)
TDI Software, Inc. 10410 Markison Road Dallas, TX 75238 (214) 340-4942	Amiga, Atari ST, Macintosh, 68000 (UNIX System V)
WATCOM Products, Inc. 415 Phillip Street Waterloo, Ontario Canada N2L 3X2 (519) 886-3700 Telex: 06-955458 Contact: Angie Rohrbacher	IBM 370 (VM/SP CMS)
Workman & Associates 1925 East Mountain Street Pasadena, CA 91104 (818) 791-7979	MS-DOS, Z80 (CP/M), Atari ST, XENIX

Answers to Selected Exercises

Chapter 2

1. (a) legal (b) legal (c) legal (d) illegal; contains a hyphen (e) illegal; PROCEDURE is a reserved word (f) legal (g) illegal; contains an underscore (h) legal (i) illegal; begins with a digit

2. The primary advantage of case sensitivity is that identifiers that appear to be different *are* different. Forcing the programmer to use consistent capitalization not only helps the reader of the program, but also allows compilers to detect errors caused by failure to declare an identifier. Case sensitivity also greatly enlarges the number of possible identifiers. A disadvantage of case sensitivity is that it increases the difficulty of talking about a program (the speaker must always state what letters are capitalized). Also, a programmer must be careful to capitalize properly identifiers that someone else has chosen.

3. (a) legal (b) illegal; lacks a trailing H (c) legal (d) legal (e) illegal; this is a character, not a number (f) illegal; must be preceded by 0 to make it a legal hexadecimal number (g) illegal; contains the digits 8 and 9, which may not appear in an octal number (h) legal (i) illegal; contains the letter G, which may not appear in a hexadecimal number

4. (a) legal (b) illegal; at least one digit must precede the decimal point (c) legal (d) legal (e) illegal; exponent contains a decimal point (f) illegal; the mantissa lacks a decimal point (g) legal (h) illegal; no exponent follows the letter E (i) legal

5. (a) legal (b) legal (c) illegal; begins with ' but ends with " (d) illegal; delimited by " but contains " (e) legal (f) legal (g) legal (h) illegal; delimited by ' but contains ' (i) legal

6. One advantage of Ada's method is the increased visibility of comments; with Modula-2's method, it can be difficult to find the beginning and end of a long comment or even determine whether a particular line of a program is enclosed in a comment. Ada's method also makes it easy to find all comments in a program (just use an editor to find all lines containing the symbol --). Another advantage of Ada's method is the difficulty of accidentally enclosing part of a program inside a comment (because a comment always stops at the end of a line). A disadvantage of Ada's method is that multiple-line comments require the -- symbol on each line.

7.
```
IMPORT FileSystem;
FROM FileSystem IMPORT Delete;
IMPORT Strings;
FROM Strings IMPORT Length;
```

We can refer to the other two procedures as `FileSystem.Length` and `Strings.Delete`.

8. The statement

```
if i > j then max := i; else max := j;
```

is illegal because a semicolon precedes the word `else`.

Chapter 3

1. (a) 32767 (b) 32768 (c) 32767 (d) −1

2. (a) subtracting `c1 + 2` from `1` will produce a negative result
(b) `c1` and `i1` are of different types
(c) unary minus cannot be applied to a `CARDINAL` expression
(d) `2.0` and `i1` have different types
(e) the `/` operator cannot be applied to `INTEGER` operands
(f) `-1` has type `INTEGER` and `TRUNC(r1)` has type `CARDINAL`
(g) `(r1 + r2)` has type `REAL`, while `2` is an integer
(h) Modula-2 has no `**` operator
(i) the `MOD` operator cannot be applied to `REAL` operands

3.
```
celsius := real ((fahrenheit - 32) * 5) / 9.0;
```

4. The character A can appear in a program as `'A'`, `"A"`, `101C`, `CHR(65)`, or `VAL(CHAR, 65)`. A nonprinting character can appear in the last three forms; for example, the line feed character can be written `12C`, `CHAR(10)`, or `VAL(CHAR, 10)`.

5.
```
CHR(ORD('9') - (ORD(ch) - ORD('0')))
```

6. Truth Table for AND

p	*q*	*p* AND *q*
FALSE	FALSE	FALSE
FALSE	TRUE	FALSE
FALSE	undefined	FALSE
TRUE	FALSE	FALSE
TRUE	TRUE	TRUE
TRUE	undefined	undefined
undefined	FALSE	undefined
undefined	TRUE	undefined
undefined	undefined	undefined

Truth Table for OR

p	*q*	*p* OR *q*
FALSE	FALSE	FALSE
FALSE	TRUE	TRUE
FALSE	undefined	undefined
TRUE	FALSE	TRUE
TRUE	TRUE	TRUE
TRUE	undefined	TRUE
undefined	FALSE	undefined
undefined	TRUE	undefined
undefined	undefined	undefined

7. (a) *p* and *q* are evaluated; *r* is not
   (b) *p* is evaluated; *q*, *r*, and *s* are not
   (c) *p* is evaluated; *r* is not
   (d) *p* is evaluated; *q*, *r*, and *s* are not
   (e) *p*, *q*, and *r* are evaluated
   (f) *p* and *q* are evaluated; *r* is not

8. (a) NOT *p* AND *q*
   (b) NOT *p* OR *q*
   (c) *p* AND NOT *q*
   (d) *p* OR NOT *q*
   (e) *p* AND *q* OR NOT *p* AND NOT *q*
   (f) *p* AND NOT *q* OR NOT *p* AND *q*

9. (a) 10 (b) 0 (c) .15 (d) 6.7 (e) `'1'` (f) 90 (g) TRUE (h) TRUE

10. (a) `(1.0 / (2.0 * pi)) * sqrt(k / mu)`
    (b) `(e * h / (2.0 * m)) * sqrt(l * (l + 1.0)) * B * cos(theta)`
    (c) `(1.0 / (2.0 * pi)) * sqrt(k * e * e / (m * r * r * r))`
    (d) `A * exp(-epsilon / (k * T))`

11. The constant `pi` is undefined. Also, the definition of `numGames` contains a forward reference to `numTeams`.

Chapter 4

1.
```
IF ('A' <= letter) & (letter <= 'P') THEN
  digit := (ORD(letter) - ORD('A')) DIV 3 + 2
ELSIF ('R' <= letter) & (letter <= 'Y') THEN
  digit := (ORD(letter) - ORD('A') - 1) DIV 3 + 2
ELSE
  WriteString("Error:  illegal character");
  WriteLn
END;
```

2.
```
IF CAP(command) = 'A' THEN
  WriteReal(arctan(realNum), 15)
ELSIF CAP(command) = 'C' THEN
  WriteReal(cos(realNum), 15)
ELSIF CAP(command) = 'E' THEN
  WriteReal(exp(realNum), 15)
ELSIF CAP(command) = 'L' THEN
  WriteReal(ln(realNum), 15)
ELSIF CAP(command) = 'Q' THEN
  WriteReal(sqrt(realNum), 15)
ELSIF CAP(command) = 'S' THEN
  WriteReal(sin(realNum), 15)
ELSE
  WriteString("Command not recognized.")
END;
```

3. Modula-2 provides `ELSIF` only because the language requires that each `IF` statement end with the word END. Without `ELSIF`, nested `IF` statements that test a series of conditions would require one END for each `IF`. Pascal does not have this problem, because `if` statements have no terminating symbol.

4. The dangling else problem does not exist in Modula-2. The requirement that the word END terminate every `IF` statement ensures that nested `IF` statements are unambiguous.

5.
```
INC(day);
IF (day > 31) OR
   ((month = 4) OR (month = 6) OR
    (month = 9) OR (month = 11)) & (day > 30) OR
   (month = 2) & (year MOD 4 = 0) & (day > 29) OR
   (month = 2) & (year MOD 4 # 0) & (day > 28)
THEN
  INC(month);
  day := 1
END;
IF month > 12 THEN
  INC(year);
  month := 1
END;
```

6.
```
sum := 0.0;
term := 1.0;
n := 1;
REPEAT
  sum := sum + term;
  term := term * x / FLOAT(n);
  INC(n)
UNTIL term < 0.001;
```

7.
```
LOOP
  Read(ch);
  IF ch = 12C THEN
    Read(ch);
    EXIT
  ELSIF ch = 15C THEN
    Read(ch);
    IF ch = 12C THEN
      Read(ch)
    END;
    EXIT
  END
END;
```

8. Add a BOOLEAN variable named commandOK and replace the first five statements inside the LOOP statement with the following:

```
commandOK := FALSE;
REPEAT
  WriteString("Enter a one-letter command: ");
  Read(command);
  IF command = esc THEN EXIT END;
  Write(command);
  WriteLn;
  IF (CAP(command) = 'A') OR (CAP(command) = 'C') OR
     (CAP(command) = 'E') OR (CAP(command) = 'L') OR
     (CAP(command) = 'Q') OR (CAP(command) = 'S') THEN
    commandOK := TRUE
  ELSE
    WriteString("Command not recognized; try again.");
    WriteLn
  END
UNTIL commandOK;
```

The ELSE clause in the CASE statement is no longer necessary.

9. Original WHILE statement:

```
WHILE p DO
  S
END
```

Rewritten as a REPEAT statement:

```
IF p THEN
  REPEAT
    S
  UNTIL NOT p
END
```

p is a BOOLEAN expression and *S* is a statement sequence.

10. Original WHILE statement:

```
WHILE p DO
  S
END
```

Rewritten as a LOOP statement:

```
LOOP
  IF NOT p THEN EXIT END;
  S
END
```

11. Original REPEAT statement:

```
REPEAT
  S
UNTIL p
```

Rewritten as a WHILE statement:

```
S;
WHILE NOT p DO
  S
END
```

12. Original REPEAT statement:

```
REPEAT
  S
UNTIL p
```

Rewritten as a LOOP statement:

```
LOOP
  S;
  IF p THEN EXIT END
END
```

13.

```
i := 1;
s := 1;
WHILE i <= n DO
  WriteCard(s, 1);
  s := s * 3 + 1;
  INC(i)
END;

i := 1;
s := 1;
IF i <= n THEN
  REPEAT
    WriteCard(s, 1);
    s := s * 3 + 1;
    INC(i)
  UNTIL i > n
END;

i := 1;
s := 1;
LOOP
  IF i > n THEN EXIT END;
  WriteCard(s, 1);
  s := s * 3 + 1;
  INC(i)
END;

s := 1;
FOR i := 1 TO n DO
  WriteCard(s, 1);
  s := s * 3 + 1
END;
```

14. The translation depends on whether the FOR statement has a positive increment or a negative increment.

Positive increment:	Rewritten as a LOOP statement:

FOR *v* := *l* TO *u* BY +*i* DO
  S
END
	v := *l*;
	LOOP
	  IF *v* > *u* THEN EXIT END;
	  S;
	  INC(*v*, *i*)
	END

Negative increment:	**Rewritten as a LOOP statement:**

FOR *v* := *u* TO *l* BY −*i* DO
  S
END
	v := *u*;
	LOOP
	  IF *v* < *l* THEN EXIT END;
	  S;
	  DEC(*v*, *i*)
	END

15.
```
FOR i := ORD('A') TO ORD('Z') DO
  WriteCard(i, 1);
  WriteString("   ");
  Write(CHR(i));
  WriteLn
END;
```

The original loop seems slightly preferable, because its starting value and limit ('A' and 'Z', respectively) make the intent of the loop clearer.

16. Because of the representational errors associated with REAL (and LONGREAL) numbers, a FOR statement controlled by a variable of either type could give unexpected results. In particular, the value of the control variable might never be exactly equal to the limit.

17. Several kinds of statements might change the value of the control variable. The variable could appear on the left side of an assignment, it could be supplied as an actual parameter in a procedure call, or it could be used as the control variable in another FOR statement. Use as a parameter in a procedure call changes the value of the variable only if the formal parameter is a variable parameter whose value is changed when the procedure is called (a difficult condition to test).

Chapter 5

1.
```
PROCEDURE ListPrimes(n: CARDINAL);
  VAR divisor, i, numListed: CARDINAL;
BEGIN
  numListed := 0;
  i := 2;
  WHILE numListed < n DO
    divisor := 1;
    REPEAT
      INC(divisor)
    UNTIL i MOD divisor = 0;
    IF divisor = i THEN
      WriteCard(i, 1);
      WriteLn;
      INC(numListed)
    END;
    INC(i)
  END
END ListPrimes;
```

2.
```
PROCEDURE ComplexMult(re1, im1, re2, im2: REAL;
                      VAR re3, im3: REAL);
BEGIN
  re3 := re1 * re2 - im1 * im2;
  im3 := re1 * im2 + im1 * re2
END ComplexMult;
```

3.
```
PROCEDURE ConvertToScientific(r: REAL;
                              VAR mantissa: REAL;
                              VAR exponent: INTEGER);
BEGIN
  mantissa := r;
  exponent := 0;
  WHILE mantissa < 1.0 DO
    mantissa := mantissa * 10.0;
    DEC(exponent)
  END;
  WHILE mantissa >= 10.0 DO
    mantissa := mantissa / 10.0;
    INC(exponent)
  END
END ConvertToScientific;
```

4. Modula-2 essentially requires the programmer to indicate whether or not the actual parameter should be copied (value parameters must be copied, but variable parameters need not be). Ada allows the compiler to decide—in the case of a structured parameter—whether or not the actual parameter should be copied (even `in` parameters need not be copied, since assignment to an `in` parameter is forbidden). Thus, Ada's method can be more efficient when the actual parameter is a large structure, while Modula-2's method gives the programmer more control. Ada's method has the advantage of documenting

whether the parameter serves as input to the procedure, output from the procedure, or both. Modula-2's method is not as clear: a variable parameter can serve as an input, output, or input/output parameter. On the other hand, Modula-2's method is simpler and easier to implement.

5.
```
PROCEDURE GCD(i, j: CARDINAL): CARDINAL;
  VAR temp: CARDINAL;
BEGIN
  WHILE j # 0 DO
    temp := j;
    j := i MOD j;
    i := temp
  END;
  RETURN i
END GCD;
```

6.
```
PROCEDURE Random(): REAL;
BEGIN
  randomCardinal :=
    (multiplier * randomCardinal + increment) MOD modulus;
  RETURN FLOAT(randomCardinal) / FLOAT(modulus)
END Random;
```

7.
```
PROCEDURE Reverse(n: CARDINAL): CARDINAL;
  VAR reversal: CARDINAL;
BEGIN
  reversal := 0;
  WHILE n > 0 DO
    reversal := reversal * 10 + n MOD 10;
    n := n DIV 10
  END;
  RETURN reversal
END Reverse;
```

8.
```
PROCEDURE IsFibonacci(n: CARDINAL): BOOLEAN;
  VAR current, next, temp: CARDINAL;
BEGIN
  current := 1;
  next := 2;
  WHILE current < n DO
    temp := current + next;
    current := next;
    next := temp
  END;
  RETURN current = n
END IsFibonacci;
```

9.
```
PROCEDURE CAP(ch: CHAR): CHAR;
BEGIN
  IF ('a' <= ch) & (ch <= 'z') THEN
    ch := CHR(ORD(ch) - ORD('a') + ORD('A'))
  END;
  RETURN ch
END CAP;
```

10. Modula-2's RETURN statement allows early return from a function, while removing the need for a separate assignment to the function name. An advantage of the Pascal method is that multiple assignments to the function name are possible; the function can assign one value to the function name, then later assign a different value to the name before returning. Also, Modula-2's method may require the programmer to declare a temporary variable to hold the function result.

11. When parentheses do not follow a function name, it denotes the function itself (as a procedure value), not a call of the function. A call of a proper procedure is a statement, not an expression, so it cannot possibly be confused with a reference to the procedure as a value.

12. Visible in M: P, Q, a (in M), d (in M), e
Visible in P: P, Q, a (in M), c (in P), d (in P), e
Visible in Q: P, Q, R, a (in Q), b (in Q), c (in Q), d (in M), e
Visible in R: P, Q, R, a (in Q), b (in R), c (in Q), d (in R), e, f

13. This declaration is not legal. The declaration

```
CONST TRUE = FALSE;
```

contains a forward reference to FALSE, which is (re)defined on the following line.

Chapter 6

1. The value do appears twice in the specification of the type.

2.
```
PROCEDURE NextDay(VAR day: Days);
BEGIN
  IF day = Sat THEN
    day := Sun
  ELSE
    INC(day)
  END
END NextDay;
```

3.
```
PROCEDURE ReadDay(VAR day: Days);
  VAR i: CARDINAL;
BEGIN
  WriteString("Enter 0 for Sun, 1 for Mon, etc.: ");
  LOOP
    ReadCard(i);
    WriteLn;
    IF i <= ORD(Sat) THEN EXIT END;
    WriteString("Illegal input; please re-enter: ");
  END;
  day := VAL(Days, i)
END ReadDay;
```

4. If T is any enumeration type, `succ` and `pred` have the following appearance:

```
PROCEDURE succ(x: T): T;
BEGIN
  RETURN VAL(T, ORD(x) + 1)
END succ;

PROCEDURE pred(x: T): T;
BEGIN
  RETURN VAL(T, ORD(x) - 1)
END pred;
```

5. (a) assignment-compatible (b) compatible, assignment-compatible (c) assignment-compatible (d) same, compatible, assignment-compatible (e) compatible, assignment-compatible (f) assignment-compatible (g) same, compatible, assignment-compatible (h) assignment-compatible (i) assignment-compatible (j) compatible, assignment-compatible (k) assignment-compatible (l) assignment-compatible (m) compatible, assignment-compatible (n) assignment-compatible

6. Ada's form of name equivalence has the advantage of allowing the programmer to create types that are identical but not equivalent. This ability can be useful when values of two identical types represent incompatible quantities. Consider the following Modula-2 type declaration:

```
TYPE Mass = REAL;
     Length = REAL;
```

According to Modula-2's rules for type equivalence, `Mass` and `Length` are the same (and both are equivalent to REAL). Thus, values of type `Mass` and `Length` can be mixed freely in expressions. In Ada, `Mass` and `Length` would be different types, thus preventing the accidental mixing of values of the two types.

7. Structural equivalence is harder for a compiler to check and harder to define precisely. (Are two record types the same if corresponding fields have the same type but not the same name?) Modula-2's form of name equivalence is clear and easy to check.

Chapter 7

1.
```
MODULE LetterFrequencies;
  FROM InOut IMPORT OpenInput, CloseInput, Read, Done,
                    Write, WriteString, WriteCard, WriteLn;
  VAR counts: ARRAY ['A'..'Z'] OF CARDINAL;
      ch: CHAR;
BEGIN
  FOR ch := 'A' TO 'Z' DO
    counts[ch] := 0
  END;
  WriteString("Enter name of input file.");
  WriteLn;
  OpenInput("TXT");
  Read(ch);
  WHILE Done DO
    ch := CAP(ch);
    IF ('A' <= ch) & (ch <= 'Z') THEN
      INC(counts[ch])
    END;
    Read(ch)
  END;
  CloseInput;
  FOR ch := 'A' TO 'Z' DO
    Write(ch);
    WriteCard(counts[ch], 5);
    WriteLn
  END
END LetterFrequencies.
```

2.
```
PROCEDURE SearchArray(A: SquareArray;
                      n: CARDINAL;
                      VAR i, j: CARDINAL;
                      VAR found: BOOLEAN);
  VAR i1, j1: CARDINAL;
BEGIN
  FOR i1 := 1 TO 10 DO
    FOR j1 := 1 TO 10 DO
      IF A[i1, j1] = n THEN
        i := i1;
        j := j1;
        found := TRUE;
        RETURN
      END
    END
  END;
  found := FALSE
END SearchArray;
```

3.
```
PROCEDURE SearchArray(A: SquareArray;
                      n: CARDINAL;
                      VAR i, j: CARDINAL;
                      VAR found: BOOLEAN);
BEGIN
  i := 10;
  j := 1;
  REPEAT
    IF A[i, j] = n THEN
      found := TRUE;
      RETURN
    ELSIF A[i, j] > n THEN
      DEC(i)
    ELSE
      INC(j)
    END
  UNTIL (i < 1) OR (j > 10);
  found := FALSE
END SearchArray;
```

4.
```
PROCEDURE ReverseVector(VAR A: ARRAY OF REAL);
  VAR i: CARDINAL;
      temp: REAL;
BEGIN
  FOR i := 0 TO HIGH(A) DIV 2 DO
    temp := A[i];
    A[i] := A[HIGH(A)-i];
    A[HIGH(A)-i] := temp
  END
END ReverseVector;
```

5.
```
PROCEDURE EvaluatePoly(a: ARRAY OF REAL; x: REAL): REAL;
  VAR i: CARDINAL;
      result: REAL;
BEGIN
  result := a[HIGH(a)];
  FOR i := HIGH(a) TO 1 BY -1 DO
    result := result * x + a[i-1]
  END;
  RETURN result
END EvaluatePoly;
```

6.
```
PROCEDURE FindIndexOfMax(A: ARRAY OF CARDINAL;
                         lowerBound: CARDINAL): CARDINAL;
  VAR i, maxPos: CARDINAL;
BEGIN
  maxPos := 0;
  FOR i := 1 TO HIGH(A) DO
    IF A[i] > A[maxPos] THEN
      maxPos := i
    END
  END;
  RETURN lowerBound + maxPos
END FindIndexOfMax;
```

The advantage of this approach is that the caller need not adjust the value returned by `FindIndexOfMax`. The disadvantage is that `FindIndexOf-Max` is limited to arrays with a particular index type (`CARDINAL`, in this case).

7.
```
indexOfMax := CHR(ORD('A') + FindIndexOfMax(A));
```

8.
```
PROCEDURE AssignLiteral(literal: ARRAY OF CHAR;
                        VAR str: ARRAY OF CHAR);
  VAR i: CARDINAL;
BEGIN
  FOR i := 0 TO HIGH(literal) DO
    str[i+1] := literal[i]
  END;
  str[0] := CHR(HIGH(literal)+1)
END AssignLiteral;
```

9.
```
PROCEDURE Assign(source: ARRAY OF CHAR;
                 VAR dest: ARRAY OF CHAR);
  VAR i: CARDINAL;
BEGIN
  FOR i := 0 TO ORD(source[0]) DO
    dest[i] := source[i]
  END
END Assign;
```

10.
```
PROCEDURE Length(str: ARRAY OF CHAR): CARDINAL;
BEGIN
  RETURN ORD(str[0])
END Length;
```

11. The advantages of the convention described in exercise 8 include the following: (1) String-handling procedures are faster and simpler because they have immediate access to the length of a string. (2) Strings can contain any character, including 0C. The disadvantages of this approach include: (1) Strings are limited to 255 characters. (2) Assigning a string literal to a string variable requires the overhead of a procedure call. Worse still, programmers might incorrectly use an ordinary assignment statement to assign a string literal to a

variable. (3) A formal string parameter allows actual parameters that are either string literals or string variables, but not both. The programmer must be careful not to supply a literal when a variable is required, and vice versa.

12. Using variable parameters would make the procedures execute faster, since the actual parameters would not be copied. However, the procedures would be less general, because string literals could not be supplied as actual parameters.

13.
```
PROCEDURE Replace(VAR source: ARRAY OF CHAR;
                  pattern, replacement: ARRAY OF CHAR);
  VAR index: CARDINAL;
      found, success: BOOLEAN;
BEGIN
  LOOP
    Position(pattern, source, index, found);
    IF NOT found THEN EXIT END;
    Delete(source, index, Length(pattern), success);
    Insert(replacement, source, index, success);
    IF NOT success THEN
      Error("Buffer overflow in Replace")
    END
  END
END Replace;
```

14.
```
TYPE PublicationType = (article, book);
     StringType = ARRAY [0..39] OF CHAR;
     StateType = ARRAY [0..1] OF CHAR;
     Publication =
       RECORD
         author, title: StringType;
         CASE kind: PublicationType OF
           article: magazine: StringType;
                    volume, issue: CARDINAL;
                    startPage, endPage: CARDINAL |
           book:    publisher, city: StringType;
                    state: StateType
         END;
         year: CARDINAL
       END;
```

15.
```
PROCEDURE PrintComponent(component: SystemComponent);

  PROCEDURE WriteBool(b: BOOLEAN);
  BEGIN
    IF b THEN
      WriteString("Yes")
    ELSE
      WriteString("No")
    END
  END WriteBool;
```

```
BEGIN
  WITH component DO
    WriteString("Manufacturer: ");
    WriteString(manufacturer);
    WriteLn;
    WriteString("Model: ");
    WriteString(model);
    WriteLn;
    CASE kind OF
      systemUnit: WriteString("Memory: ");
                  WriteCard(memory, 1);
                  WriteString("K");
                  WriteLn;
                  WriteString("Number of disk drives: ");
                  WriteCard(numDiskDrives, 1);
                  WriteLn;
                  WriteString("Hard disk: ");
                  WriteBool(hardDisk);
                  WriteLn |
      monitor:    WriteString("Color monitor: ");
                  WriteBool(color);
                  WriteLn;
                  WriteString("Number of lines: ");
                  WriteCard(numLines, 1);
                  WriteLn;
                  WriteString("Number of columns: ");
                  WriteCard(numColumns, 1);
                  WriteLn |
      printer:    WriteString("Mechanism: ");
                  CASE mechanism OF
                    dotMatrix:   WriteString("dot matrix") |
                    daisyWheel:  WriteString("daisy wheel") |
                    laser:       WriteString("laser")
                  END;
                  WriteLn;
                  WriteString("Speed: ");
                  WriteCard(speed, 1);
                  WriteString(" characters/second");
                  WriteLn
    END;
    WriteString("Price: ");
    WriteReal(price, 10);
    WriteLn
  END
END PrintComponent;
```

16. The knowledge of which variant is active may be implicit in the program's flow of control. For example, a program might contain a large IF statement in which one variant is active if a BOOLEAN expression is TRUE and another variant is active if the expression is FALSE. Another alternative is to store the

tag value in a single variable (separate from the records). For example, an array of variant records might have the property that the same variant is always active in each record. Including a tag field in each record would waste space, because the values of all the tag fields would be the same.

17.
```
colorSet := SetOfColors{color1, color2};

colorSet := SetOfColors{color1} + SetOfColors{color2};

colorSet := SetOfColors{};
INCL(colorSet, color1);
INCL(colorSet, color2);
```

18. Both of the following expressions compute the symmetric difference of `set1` and `set2`:

```
set1 + set2 - set1 * set2
(set1 - set2) + (set2 - set1)
```

19.
```
PROCEDURE WriteSetOfColors(s: SetOfColors);
  VAR first: BOOLEAN;

  PROCEDURE TestColor(c: Color; name: ARRAY OF CHAR);
  BEGIN
    IF c IN s THEN
      IF first THEN
        first := FALSE
      ELSE
        WriteString(", ")
      END;
      WriteString(name)
    END
  END TestColor;

BEGIN
  first := TRUE;
  WriteString("{");
  TestColor(violet, "violet");
  TestColor(blue, "blue");
  TestColor(green, "green");
  TestColor(yellow, "yellow");
  TestColor(orange, "orange");
  TestColor(red, "red");
  WriteString("}")
END WriteSetOfColors;
```

Chapter 8

1. Modula-2's restrictions are designed to increase the safety of pointer use. In languages that do not constrain pointers, the danger always exists that a reference to an invalid pointer will change an arbitrary memory location. Also, pointers can make programs hard to understand because of aliasing (multiple

names for the same variable). For example, if a pointer p points to a variable x, it may not be clear to someone reading the program that x is affected by changes made through p. The only disadvantage of Modula-2's restrictions is that they can sometimes be too confining. However, Modula-2's low-level features allow the programmer to treat pointers as addresses when absolutely necessary.

2. If p and q are equal, then p^ and q^ are *always* equal (assuming that p and q are not NIL). If p and q are unequal, then p^ and q^ are *sometimes* equal.

3.
```
PROCEDURE Insert(name, number: ARRAY OF CHAR);
  VAR current, previous, new: PhonePtr;
      compareResult: CompareResult;
      success: BOOLEAN;
BEGIN
  current := phoneList;
  previous := NIL;
  LOOP
    IF current = NIL THEN EXIT END;
    compareResult := Compare(name, current^.name);
    IF compareResult = equal THEN
      Assign(number, current^.number, success);
      RETURN
    ELSIF compareResult = less THEN
      EXIT
    END;
    previous := current;
    current := current^.next
  END;
  ALLOCATE(new, SIZE(PhoneRecord));
  Assign(name, new^.name, success);
  Assign(number, new^.number, success);
  IF previous = NIL THEN
    new^.next := phoneList;
    phoneList := new
  ELSE
    new^.next := previous^.next;
    previous^.next := new
  END
END Insert;
```

Compare and Assign are exported by the String module (Section 10.2).

4.
```
PROCEDURE Delete(prefix: ARRAY OF CHAR);
  VAR current, previous, temp: PhonePtr;
      index: CARDINAL;
      found: BOOLEAN;
BEGIN
  current := phoneList;
  previous := NIL;
  WHILE current # NIL DO
    Position(prefix, current^.name, index, found);
    IF found & (index = 0) THEN
      IF previous = NIL THEN
        phoneList := phoneList^.next
      ELSE
        previous^.next := current^.next
      END;
      temp := current;
      current := current^.next;
      DEALLOCATE(temp, SIZE(PhoneRecord))
    ELSE
      previous := current;
      current := current^.next
    END
  END
END Delete;
```

`Position` is exported by the `String` module (Section 10.2).

5.
```
PROCEDURE Print(prefix: ARRAY OF CHAR);
  VAR current: PhonePtr;
      index: CARDINAL;
      found: BOOLEAN;
BEGIN
  current := phoneList;
  WHILE current # NIL DO
    Position(prefix, current^.name, index, found);
    IF found & (index = 0) THEN
      WriteString(current^.name);
      WriteString("  ");
      WriteString(current^.number);
      WriteLn
    END;
    current := current^.next
  END
END Print;
```

`Position` is exported by the `String` module (Section 10.2).

6. A programmer cannot write NEW and DISPOSE. These procedures must allow pointer variables of all types as parameters. Although this is possible in Modula-2 by using an ADDRESS parameter (Section 11.2), another problem

arises. NEW and DISPOSE must know how much space to allocate or deallocate; this depends on the pointer variable's type, of which NEW and DISPOSE would have no knowledge.

7.
```
PROCEDURE Tabulate(f: RealFunction; start, end, inc: REAL);
  VAR x: REAL;
BEGIN
  x := start;
  WHILE x <= end DO
    WriteReal(x, 10);
    WriteString("  ");
    WriteReal(f(x), 10);
    WriteLn;
    x := x + inc
  END
END Tabulate;
```

8.
```
PROCEDURE ApplyToAll(f: RealFunction;
                     VAR v: ARRAY OF REAL);
   VAR i: CARDINAL;
BEGIN
  FOR i := 0 TO HIGH(v) DO
    v[i] := f(v[i])
  END
END ApplyToAll;
```

9.
```
PROCEDURE Reduction(f: ArithmeticOp;
                    v: ARRAY OF REAL): REAL;
  VAR result: REAL;
      i: CARDINAL;
BEGIN
  result := v[0];
  FOR i := 1 TO HIGH(v) DO
    result := f(result, v[i])
  END;
  RETURN result
END Reduction;
```

10. (a)
```
PROCEDURE Sum(x, y: REAL): REAL;
BEGIN
  RETURN x + y
END Sum;
  .
  .
  .
sum := Reduction(Sum, v);
```

(b)
```
PROCEDURE Product(x, y: REAL): REAL;
BEGIN
  RETURN x * y
END Product;
  .
  .
  .
product := Reduction(Product, v);
```

(c)
```
PROCEDURE Max(x, y: REAL): REAL;
BEGIN
  IF x > y THEN
    RETURN x
  ELSE
    RETURN y
  END
END Max;
  .
  .
  .
max := Reduction(Max, v);
```

(d)
```
PROCEDURE Min(x, y: REAL): REAL;
BEGIN
  IF x < y THEN
    RETURN x
  ELSE
    RETURN y
  END
END Min;
  .
  .
  .
min := Reduction(Min, v);
```

11.
```
PROCEDURE Sum(low, high: CARDINAL; f: Filter): CARDINAL;
  VAR i, sum: CARDINAL;
BEGIN
  sum := 0;
  FOR i := low TO high DO
    IF f(i) THEN
      sum := sum + i
    END
  END;
  RETURN sum
END Sum;
```

12. (a)

```
PROCEDURE IsOdd(n: CARDINAL): BOOLEAN;
BEGIN
  RETURN ODD(n)
END IsOdd;
  .
  .
  .
sum := Sum(1, 100, IsOdd);
```

(b)

```
PROCEDURE IsPrime(n: CARDINAL): BOOLEAN;
  VAR divisor: CARDINAL;
BEGIN
  IF (n = 0) OR (n = 1) THEN RETURN FALSE END;
  divisor := 1;
  REPEAT
    INC(divisor)
  UNTIL n MOD divisor = 0;
  RETURN divisor = n
END IsPrime;
  .
  .
  .
sum := Sum(100, 1000, IsPrime);
```

(c)

```
PROCEDURE IsPowerOf2(n: CARDINAL): BOOLEAN;
BEGIN
  WHILE n > 1 DO
    IF ODD(n) THEN RETURN FALSE END;
    n := n DIV 2
  END;
  RETURN TRUE
END IsPowerOf2;
  .
  .
  .
sum := Sum(1, 1024, IsPowerOf2);
```

13. Modula-2 prohibits the assignment of standard procedures so that compilers may replace calls of standard procedures by in-line code; a standard procedure replaced in this fashion does not have an address that can be used as a procedure value. Assignment of procedures that are local to other procedures is forbidden because of the possibility of references to nonexistent variables. Suppose that a program declares procedures P and Q, where Q is nested inside P. The body of Q may contain references to the variables of P, which exist only when P has been called but has not returned. If Modula-2 were to allow the assignment of Q to a procedure variable, P could store Q into a global variable v and then return. If the program then calls Q (through a reference to the variable v), it cannot access P's local variables, because P is not currently active.

Chapter 9

1.
```
DEFINITION MODULE ErrorMessages;

  PROCEDURE FatalError(message: ARRAY OF CHAR);
  PROCEDURE Diagnostic(message: ARRAY OF CHAR);

END ErrorMessages.

IMPLEMENTATION MODULE ErrorMessages;

  FROM InOut IMPORT WriteString, WriteLn;

  PROCEDURE FatalError(message: ARRAY OF CHAR);
  BEGIN
    WriteString("Fatal error:  ");
    WriteString(message);
    WriteLn;
    HALT
  END FatalError;

  PROCEDURE Diagnostic(message: ARRAY OF CHAR);
  BEGIN
    WriteString("Diagnostic:  ");
    WriteString(message);
    WriteLn
  END Diagnostic;

END ErrorMessages.
```

2.
```
DEFINITION MODULE ErrorMessages;

  PROCEDURE FatalError(message: ARRAY OF CHAR);
  PROCEDURE Diagnostic(message: ARRAY OF CHAR);
  PROCEDURE FetchDiagnosticCount(): CARDINAL;

END ErrorMessages.

IMPLEMENTATION MODULE ErrorMessages;

  FROM InOut IMPORT WriteString, WriteLn;

  VAR diagnosticCount: CARDINAL;

  PROCEDURE FatalError(message: ARRAY OF CHAR);
  BEGIN
    WriteString("Fatal error: ");
    WriteString(message);
    WriteLn;
    HALT
  END FatalError;
```

```
  PROCEDURE Diagnostic(message: ARRAY OF CHAR);
  BEGIN
    WriteString("Diagnostic: ");
    WriteString(message);
    WriteLn;
    INC(diagnosticCount)
  END Diagnostic;

  PROCEDURE FetchDiagnosticCount(): CARDINAL;
  BEGIN
    RETURN diagnosticCount
  END FetchDiagnosticCount;

BEGIN
  diagnosticCount := 0
END ErrorMessages.
```

3.
```
DEFINITION MODULE PolyArithmetic;

  TYPE Polynomial;

  PROCEDURE Create(coeff: ARRAY OF REAL): Polynomial;
  PROCEDURE Destroy(VAR p: Polynomial);
  PROCEDURE Equal(p1, p2: Polynomial): BOOLEAN;
  PROCEDURE Degree(p: Polynomial): CARDINAL;
  PROCEDURE ExtractCoeff(p: Polynomial; i: CARDINAL): REAL;
  PROCEDURE Evaluate(p: Polynomial; x: REAL): REAL;
  PROCEDURE Add(p1, p2: Polynomial; VAR p3: Polynomial);
  PROCEDURE Subtract(p1, p2: Polynomial;
                     VAR p3: Polynomial);
  PROCEDURE Multiply(p1, p2: Polynomial;
                     VAR p3: Polynomial);
  PROCEDURE Divide(p1, p2: Polynomial;
                   VAR quotient, remainder: Polynomial);

END PolyArithmetic.
```

4.
```
IMPLEMENTATION MODULE CharacterStacks;

  FROM Storage IMPORT ALLOCATE, DEALLOCATE;
  FROM InOut IMPORT WriteString, WriteLn;

  TYPE CharStack = POINTER TO StackRecord;
       StackRecord = RECORD
                       char: CHAR;
                       next: CharStack
                     END;
```

```
  PROCEDURE Initialize(VAR s: CharStack);
  BEGIN
    s := NIL
  END Initialize;

  PROCEDURE Push(VAR s: CharStack; ch: CHAR);
    VAR temp: CharStack;
  BEGIN
    ALLOCATE(temp, SIZE(StackRecord));
    temp^.char := ch;
    temp^.next := s;
    s := temp
  END Push;

  PROCEDURE Pop(VAR s: CharStack; VAR ch: CHAR);
    VAR temp: CharStack;
  BEGIN
    IF s = NIL THEN
      WriteString("Stack underflow in CharacterStacks.Pop");
      WriteLn;
      HALT
    END;
    ch := s^.char;
    temp := s;
    s := s^.next;
    DEALLOCATE(temp, SIZE(StackRecord))
  END Pop;

  PROCEDURE IsEmpty(s: CharStack): BOOLEAN;
  BEGIN
    RETURN s = NIL
  END IsEmpty;

END CharacterStacks.
```

5.
```
IMPLEMENTATION MODULE ComplexNumbers;

  FROM Storage IMPORT ALLOCATE;

  TYPE Complex = POINTER TO ComplexRec;
       ComplexRec = RECORD
                      realPart, imagPart: REAL
                    END;
```

```
PROCEDURE Create(realPart, imagPart: REAL): Complex;
  VAR c: Complex;
BEGIN
  ALLOCATE(c, SIZE(ComplexRec));
  c^.realPart := realPart;
  c^.imagPart := imagPart;
  RETURN c
END Create;

PROCEDURE Assign(c1: Complex; VAR c2: Complex);
BEGIN
  c2^.realPart := c1^.realPart;
  c2^.imagPart := c1^.imagPart
END Assign;

PROCEDURE Equal(c1, c2: Complex): BOOLEAN;
BEGIN
  RETURN (c1^.realPart = c2^.realPart) &
         (c1^.imagPart = c2^.imagPart)
END Equal;

PROCEDURE RealPart(c: Complex): REAL;
BEGIN
  RETURN c^.realPart
END RealPart;

PROCEDURE ImagPart(c: Complex): REAL;
BEGIN
  RETURN c^.imagPart
END ImagPart;

PROCEDURE Add(c1, c2: Complex; VAR c3: Complex);
BEGIN
  c3^.realPart := c1^.realPart + c2^.realPart;
  c3^.imagPart := c1^.imagPart + c2^.imagPart
END Add;

PROCEDURE Subtract(c1, c2: Complex; VAR c3: Complex);
BEGIN
  c3^.realPart := c1^.realPart - c2^.realPart;
  c3^.imagPart := c1^.imagPart - c2^.imagPart
END Subtract;

PROCEDURE Multiply(c1, c2: Complex; VAR c3: Complex);
BEGIN
  c3^.realPart := c1^.realPart * c2^.realPart -
                  c1^.imagPart * c2^.imagPart;
  c3^.imagPart := c1^.realPart * c2^.imagPart +
                  c1^.imagPart * c2^.realPart
END Multiply;
```

```
    PROCEDURE Divide(c1, c2: Complex; VAR c3: Complex);
      VAR denom: REAL;
    BEGIN
      denom := c2^.realPart * c2^.realPart +
               c2^.imagPart * c2^.imagPart;
      c3^.realPart := (c1^.realPart * c2^.realPart +
                       c1^.imagPart * c2^.imagPart) / denom;
      c3^.imagPart := (c1^.imagPart * c2^.realPart -
                       c1^.realPart * c2^.imagPart) / denom
    END Divide;

  END ComplexNumbers.
```

6. Writing `Add`, `Subtract`, `Multiply`, and `Divide` as functions has the advantage that client modules could combine several calls in a single expression. A disadvantage is that each call would create a new value of type `Complex`, causing a storage management problem.

7. M3.DEF, M2.DEF, M3.MOD, M4.DEF, followed by the remaining modules in any order. Alternatively, M3.DEF, M2.DEF, M4.DEF, followed by the remaining modules in any order.

8. 30

9. M4.DEF, M1.MOD, M2.MOD, M3.MOD, M4.MOD

10. The body of `M4` will be executed first, followed by the bodies of `M2`, `M3`, and `M1`.

11. No. Suppose that `M1` is the program module and `M2` is one of the library modules. If we compile all of the definition modules first, then M1.MOD and M2.MOD (and any other implementation modules) can be compiled in any order.

12. Compiling definition modules in advance saves time; when definition modules are not compiled, the compiler must read and compile a definition module whenever any of its clients is compiled. On the other hand, compiling definition modules requires more disk space (and more files) because of the symbol file that is generated during the compilation of a definition module. Not compiling definition modules simplifies the compiler, which need not read and write symbol files. Compiling definition modules makes consistency checking simpler—for example, the module key method described in Section 9.2 relies on the fact that definition modules are compiled. When definition modules are not compiled, some other means must be used to ensure consistency (for example, a Modula-2 system might maintain a central file containing version information about all modules).

13. A separate linking phase allows more rapid loading of a program. For a completed program, which will be executed many times after linking, this is an advantage. During the development of a program, however, it is a disadvan-

tage, because the program is typically executed only once after linking. Load-time linking has other advantages as well. It saves disk space; when a system requires a separate linking phase, the object code for each module becomes part of the program's code. Moreover, load-time linking guarantees that a program is always linked to the latest version of each library module; with a separate linking phase, a program may contain object code for an older version of a library module.

14. Yes. For example, `seed` might be exported by a library module, then imported into the module enclosing `RandomNumberGenerator`. Alternatively, `seed` might be exported by another local module that precedes `RandomNumberGenerator`.

15.
```
MODULE Time;

  EXPORT SetTime, AddSecond, GetTime;

  VAR hr, min, sec: CARDINAL;

  PROCEDURE SetTime(hour, minute, second: CARDINAL);
  BEGIN
    hr := hour;
    min := minute;
    sec := second
  END SetTime;

  PROCEDURE AddSecond;
  BEGIN
    INC(sec);
    IF sec = 60 THEN
      sec := 0;
      INC(min);
      IF min = 60 THEN
        min := 0;
        INC(hr);
        IF hr = 24 THEN
          hr := 0
        END
      END
    END
  END AddSecond;

  PROCEDURE GetTime(VAR hour, minute, second: CARDINAL);
  BEGIN
    hour := hr;
    minute := min;
    second := sec
  END GetTime;

END Time;
```

16. False. A local module can call HALT, for example.

17. Visible in M1: MathLib0, sqrt, a, b (in M1), P1, M3, e
    Visible in P1: MathLib0, sqrt, a, b (in M1), c (in P1), d, P1, M3, e
    Visible in M2: exp, a, c (in M2), d
    Visible in M3: b (in M1), sqrt, e
    Visible in P2: b (in P2), sqrt, e

18. The body of M5 will be executed first, followed by the bodies of M4, M3, M2, and M1.

19. The body of M3 will be executed first, followed by the body of M1. The body of M2 will be executed each time P1 is called.

Chapter 10

1.
```
IMPLEMENTATION MODULE VectorOperations;

  PROCEDURE Add(v, w: Vector; VAR sum: Vector);
  BEGIN
    sum[1] := v[1] + w[1];
    sum[2] := v[2] + w[2];
    sum[3] := v[3] + w[3]
  END Add;

  PROCEDURE Subtract(v, w: Vector; VAR difference: Vector);
  BEGIN
    difference[1] := v[1] - w[1];
    difference[2] := v[2] - w[2];
    difference[3] := v[3] - w[3]
  END Subtract;

  PROCEDURE Scale(r: REAL; v: Vector; VAR w: Vector);
  BEGIN
    w[1] := r * v[1];
    w[2] := r * v[2];
    w[3] := r * v[3]
  END Scale;

  PROCEDURE InnerProduct(v, w: Vector): REAL;
  BEGIN
    RETURN v[1] * w[1] + v[2] * w[2] + v[3] * w[3]
  END InnerProduct;

  PROCEDURE CrossProduct(v, w: Vector;
                         VAR product: Vector);
  BEGIN
    product[1] := v[2] * w[3] - v[3] * w[2];
    product[2] := v[3] * w[1] - v[1] * w[3];
    product[3] := v[1] * w[2] - v[2] * w[1]
  END CrossProduct;

END VectorOperations.
```

2. DEFINITION MODULE VectorOperations;

```
  TYPE Vector;

  PROCEDURE Create(x, y, z: REAL): Vector;
  PROCEDURE Assign(v: Vector; VAR w: Vector);
  PROCEDURE Equal(v, w: Vector): BOOLEAN;
  PROCEDURE FetchX(v: Vector): REAL;
  PROCEDURE FetchY(v: Vector): REAL;
  PROCEDURE FetchZ(v: Vector): REAL;
  PROCEDURE Add(v, w: Vector; VAR sum: Vector);
  PROCEDURE Subtract(v, w: Vector; VAR difference: Vector);
  PROCEDURE Scale(r: REAL; v: Vector; VAR w: Vector);
  PROCEDURE InnerProduct(v, w: Vector): REAL;
  PROCEDURE CrossProduct(v, w: Vector; VAR product: Vector);

END VectorOperations.
```

3. IMPLEMENTATION MODULE VectorOperations;

```
  FROM Storage IMPORT ALLOCATE;

  TYPE Vector = POINTER TO VectorRec;
       VectorRec = ARRAY [1..3] OF REAL;

  PROCEDURE Create(x, y, z: REAL): Vector;
    VAR v: Vector;
  BEGIN
    ALLOCATE(v, SIZE(VectorRec));
    v^[1] := x;
    v^[2] := y;
    v^[3] := z;
    RETURN v
  END Create;

  PROCEDURE Assign(v: Vector; VAR w: Vector);
  BEGIN
    w^ := v^
  END Assign;

  PROCEDURE Equal(v, w: Vector): BOOLEAN;
  BEGIN
    RETURN (v^[1] = w^[1]) & (v^[2] = w^[2]) &
           (v^[3] = w^[3])
  END Equal;
```

```
    PROCEDURE FetchX(v: Vector): REAL;
    BEGIN
      RETURN v^[1]
    END FetchX;

    PROCEDURE FetchY(v: Vector): REAL;
    BEGIN
      RETURN v^[2]
    END FetchY;

    PROCEDURE FetchZ(v: Vector): REAL;
    BEGIN
      RETURN v^[3]
    END FetchZ;

    PROCEDURE Add(v, w: Vector; VAR sum: Vector);
    BEGIN
      sum^[1] := v^[1] + w^[1];
      sum^[2] := v^[2] + w^[2];
      sum^[3] := v^[3] + w^[3]
    END Add;

    PROCEDURE Subtract(v, w: Vector; VAR difference: Vector);
    BEGIN
      difference^[1] := v^[1] - w^[1];
      difference^[2] := v^[2] - w^[2];
      difference^[3] := v^[3] - w^[3]
    END Subtract;

    PROCEDURE Scale(r: REAL; v: Vector; VAR w: Vector);
    BEGIN
      w^[1] := r * v^[1];
      w^[2] := r * v^[2];
      w^[3] := r * v^[3]
    END Scale;

    PROCEDURE InnerProduct(v, w: Vector): REAL;
    BEGIN
      RETURN v^[1] * w^[1] + v^[2] * w^[2] + v^[3] * w^[3]
    END InnerProduct;

    PROCEDURE CrossProduct(v, w: Vector; VAR product: Vector);
    BEGIN
      product^[1] := v^[2] * w^[3] - v^[3] * w^[2];
      product^[2] := v^[3] * w^[1] - v^[1] * w^[3];
      product^[3] := v^[1] * w^[2] - v^[2] * w^[1]
    END CrossProduct;

END VectorOperations.
```

5.
```
DEFINITION MODULE SymbolTable;

  TYPE SymTab;

  PROCEDURE Initialize(VAR table: SymTab);
  PROCEDURE EnterLabel(VAR table: SymTab;
                           label: ARRAY OF CHAR;
                           addr: CARDINAL;
                           VAR duplicate: BOOLEAN);
  PROCEDURE FindLabel(table: SymTab;
                          label: ARRAY OF CHAR;
                          VAR addr: CARDINAL;
                          VAR found: BOOLEAN);

END SymbolTable.
```

7. The original `IF` statement performs one test if `c1` is less than `c2`, two if `c1` is greater than `c2`, and three if `c1` equals `c2`. When the strings being compared are expected to have several characters in common, the `IF` statement should first test for equality between `c1` and `c2`:

```
IF c1 = c2 THEN
  IF c1 = 0C THEN RETURN equal END
ELSIF c1 < c2 THEN
  RETURN less
ELSE
  RETURN greater
END;
```

This version always performs two tests, regardless of the relationship between `c1` and `c2`.

10. The symmetric difference procedure is identical to `Union`, except that the third call of `InsertAfter` (the one following ELSE) should be removed.

11.
```
PROCEDURE Initialize(VAR s: SetOfChar; str: ARRAY OF CHAR);
  VAR i: CARDINAL;
BEGIN
  s := NIL;
  i := 0;
  WHILE (i <= HIGH(str)) & (str[i] # 0C) DO
    Include(s, str[i]);
    INC(i)
  END
END Initialize;
```

12.
```
IMPLEMENTATION MODULE CharSet;

  FROM Storage IMPORT ALLOCATE;

  TYPE SetOfChar = POINTER TO BooleanArray;
       BooleanArray = ARRAY CHAR OF BOOLEAN;
```

```
PROCEDURE Initialize(VAR s: SetOfChar);
  VAR ch: CHAR;
BEGIN
  ALLOCATE(s, SIZE(BooleanArray));
  FOR ch := MIN(CHAR) TO MAX(CHAR) DO
    s^[ch] := FALSE
  END
END Initialize;

PROCEDURE IsEmpty(s: SetOfChar): BOOLEAN;
  VAR ch: CHAR;
BEGIN
  FOR ch := MIN(CHAR) TO MAX(CHAR) DO
    IF s^[ch] THEN RETURN FALSE END
  END;
  RETURN TRUE
END IsEmpty;

PROCEDURE MakeEmpty(VAR s: SetOfChar);
  VAR ch: CHAR;
BEGIN
  FOR ch := MIN(CHAR) TO MAX(CHAR) DO
    s^[ch] := FALSE
  END
END MakeEmpty;

PROCEDURE CopySet(s1: SetOfChar; VAR s2: SetOfChar);
BEGIN
  s2^ := s1^
END CopySet;

PROCEDURE Include(VAR s: SetOfChar; ch: CHAR);
BEGIN
  s^[ch] := TRUE
END Include;

PROCEDURE Exclude(VAR s: SetOfChar; ch: CHAR);
BEGIN
  s^[ch] := FALSE
END Exclude;

PROCEDURE IsMember(s: SetOfChar; ch: CHAR): BOOLEAN;
BEGIN
  RETURN s^[ch]
END IsMember;

PROCEDURE IsEqual(s1, s2: SetOfChar): BOOLEAN;
  VAR ch: CHAR;
BEGIN
  FOR ch := MIN(CHAR) TO MAX(CHAR) DO
```

```
      IF s1^[ch] # s2^[ch] THEN RETURN FALSE END
    END;
    RETURN TRUE
  END IsEqual;

  PROCEDURE IsSubset(s1, s2: SetOfChar): BOOLEAN;
    VAR ch: CHAR;
  BEGIN
    FOR ch := MIN(CHAR) TO MAX(CHAR) DO
      IF s1^[ch] & NOT s2^[ch] THEN RETURN FALSE END
    END;
    RETURN TRUE
  END IsSubset;

  PROCEDURE Union(s1, s2: SetOfChar; VAR s3: SetOfChar);
    VAR ch: CHAR;
  BEGIN
    FOR ch := MIN(CHAR) TO MAX(CHAR) DO
      s3^[ch] := s1^[ch] OR s2^[ch]
    END
  END Union;

  PROCEDURE Intersection(s1, s2: SetOfChar;
                         VAR s3: SetOfChar);
    VAR ch: CHAR;
  BEGIN
    FOR ch := MIN(CHAR) TO MAX(CHAR) DO
      s3^[ch] := s1^[ch] & s2^[ch]
    END
  END Intersection;

  PROCEDURE Difference(s1, s2: SetOfChar;
                       VAR s3: SetOfChar);
    VAR ch: CHAR;
  BEGIN
    FOR ch := MIN(CHAR) TO MAX(CHAR) DO
      s3^[ch] := s1^[ch] & NOT s2^[ch]
    END
  END Difference;

END CharSet.
```

13. The advantage of the linked list representation is its relative efficiency—with respect to both time and space—for sets of small-to-medium size. With the linked list representation, the amount of space required to store a set is proportional to the number of elements in the set; the BOOLEAN array representation always requires the same amount of space, regardless of the size of the set. Since a BOOLEAN array requires 128 bytes of storage (assuming that a BOOLEAN value occupies one byte), a linked list is more compact except for large sets. With the BOOLEAN array representation, most of the `CharSet`

procedures perform a complete scan of the array—a relatively time-consuming operation. With the linked list representation, most procedures require time proportional to the sizes of the sets involved. The primary advantage of the `BOOLEAN` array representation is that the `Include`, `Exclude`, and `IsMember` operations are very fast, regardless of the size of the set.

16. We can use the following "do nothing" procedure to ignore a returned status value:

```
PROCEDURE IgnoreError(b: BOOLEAN);
END IgnoreError;
```

For example, suppose that `Push` returns a status value. By nesting a call of `Push` inside a call of `IgnoreError`, we can ignore the value that `Push` returns:

```
IgnoreError(Push(ch));
```

17.
```
IMPLEMENTATION MODULE CharStackModule;

  CONST stackSize = 100;

  VAR stackArray: ARRAY [1..stackSize] OF CHAR;
      topOfStack: [0..stackSize+1];
      handlerProc: ErrorHandler;

  PROCEDURE InstallErrorHandler(handler: ErrorHandler);
  BEGIN
    handlerProc := handler
  END InstallErrorHandler;

  PROCEDURE Push(ch: CHAR);
  BEGIN
    INC(topOfStack);
    IF topOfStack > stackSize THEN
      handlerProc(overflow)
    ELSE
      stackArray[topOfStack] := ch
    END
  END Push;

  PROCEDURE Pop(VAR ch: CHAR);
  BEGIN
    IF topOfStack = 0 THEN
      handlerProc(underflow)
    ELSE
      ch := stackArray[topOfStack];
      DEC(topOfStack)
    END
  END Pop;
```

```
    PROCEDURE IsEmpty(): BOOLEAN;
    BEGIN
      RETURN topOfStack = 0
    END IsEmpty;

  BEGIN
    topOfStack := 0
  END CharStackModule.
```

Chapter 11 Several answers in this section assume the existence of a constant named bits-PerWord whose value is the number of bits in one word.

1. IMPLEMENTATION MODULE CharSet;

```
    FROM Storage IMPORT ALLOCATE;

    CONST bitsPerWord = 16;
          wordsPerSet = ORD(MAX(CHAR)) DIV bitsPerWord + 1;

    TYPE SetOfChar = POINTER TO BitsetArray;
         BitsetArray = ARRAY [0..wordsPerSet-1] OF BITSET;

    PROCEDURE Initialize(VAR s: SetOfChar);
      VAR i: CARDINAL;
    BEGIN
      ALLOCATE(s, SIZE(BitsetArray));
      FOR i := 0 TO wordsPerSet - 1 DO
        s^[i] := BITSET{}
      END
    END Initialize;

    PROCEDURE IsEmpty(s: SetOfChar): BOOLEAN;
      VAR i: CARDINAL;
    BEGIN
      FOR i := 0 TO wordsPerSet - 1 DO
        IF s^[i] # BITSET{} THEN RETURN FALSE END
      END;
      RETURN TRUE
    END IsEmpty;

    PROCEDURE MakeEmpty(VAR s: SetOfChar);
      VAR i: CARDINAL;
    BEGIN
      FOR i := 0 TO wordsPerSet - 1 DO
        s^[i] := BITSET{}
      END
    END MakeEmpty;
```

```
PROCEDURE CopySet(s1: SetOfChar; VAR s2: SetOfChar);
BEGIN
  s2^ := s1^
END CopySet;

PROCEDURE Include(VAR s: SetOfChar; ch: CHAR);
BEGIN
  INCL(s^[ORD(ch) DIV bitsPerWord],
           ORD(ch) MOD bitsPerWord)
END Include;

PROCEDURE Exclude(VAR s: SetOfChar; ch: CHAR);
BEGIN
  EXCL(s^[ORD(ch) DIV bitsPerWord],
           ORD(ch) MOD bitsPerWord)
END Exclude;

PROCEDURE IsMember(s: SetOfChar; ch: CHAR): BOOLEAN;
BEGIN
  RETURN ORD(ch) MOD bitsPerWord IN
      s^[ORD(ch) DIV bitsPerWord]
END IsMember;

PROCEDURE IsEqual(s1, s2: SetOfChar): BOOLEAN;
  VAR i: CARDINAL;
BEGIN
  FOR i := 0 TO wordsPerSet - 1 DO
    IF s1^[i] # s2^[i] THEN RETURN FALSE END
  END;
  RETURN TRUE
END IsEqual;

PROCEDURE IsSubset(s1, s2: SetOfChar): BOOLEAN;
  VAR i: CARDINAL;
BEGIN
  FOR i := 0 TO wordsPerSet - 1 DO
    IF NOT (s1^[i] <= s2^[i]) THEN RETURN FALSE END
  END;
  RETURN TRUE
END IsSubset;

PROCEDURE Union(s1, s2: SetOfChar; VAR s3: SetOfChar);
  VAR i: CARDINAL;
BEGIN
  FOR i := 0 TO wordsPerSet - 1 DO
    s3^[i] := s1^[i] + s2^[i]
  END
END Union;
```

```
  PROCEDURE Intersection(s1, s2: SetOfChar;
                         VAR s3: SetOfChar);
    VAR i: CARDINAL;
  BEGIN
    FOR i := 0 TO wordsPerSet - 1 DO
      s3^[i] := s1^[i] * s2^[i]
    END
  END Intersection;

  PROCEDURE Difference(s1, s2: SetOfChar;
                       VAR s3: SetOfChar);
    VAR i: CARDINAL;
  BEGIN
    FOR i := 0 TO wordsPerSet - 1 DO
      s3^[i] := s1^[i] - s2^[i]
    END
  END Difference;

END CharSet.
```

2. The BITSET array representation is clearly superior to the BOOLEAN array representation. With a BITSET array, only eight 16-bit words are needed to store a SetOfChar value; a BOOLEAN array requires 128 bytes (64 words). The BITSET array representation offers time advantages as well, because CharSet procedures need only scan eight-word arrays rather than 64-word arrays. Only the Include, Exclude, and IsMember procedures are slower, but the time difference is small. The BITSET array representation is also superior to the linked list representation, except possibly for very small sets.

3.
```
PROCEDURE CopyWords(source: ARRAY OF WORD;
                    VAR dest: ARRAY OF WORD);
  VAR i: CARDINAL;
BEGIN
  IF HIGH(source) # HIGH(dest) THEN
    WriteString("Size error in CopyWords");
    WriteLn;
    HALT
  END;
  FOR i := 0 TO HIGH(source) DO
    dest[i] := source[i]
  END
END CopyWords;
```

4. Replace all occurrences of the CARDINAL variable card by a new REAL variable. Import ReadReal and Done from RealInOut, delete the import of ReadCard and Done from InOut, and replace both calls of ReadCard by calls of ReadReal. Import RealToGeneric, instead of CardToGeneric, from GenericTypeModule, and replace the call of CardToGeneric by a call of RealToGeneric.

5. Replace all occurrences of the CARDINAL variable card by a new REAL variable. Import ReadReal, WriteReal, and Done from RealInOut, delete the import of ReadCard, WriteCard, and Done from InOut, and replace both calls of ReadCard by calls of ReadReal. Replace the procedures LessThan and PrintCard by the following procedures:

```
PROCEDURE LessThan(addr1, addr2: ADDRESS): BOOLEAN;
  VAR r1, r2: POINTER TO REAL;
BEGIN
  r1 := addr1;
  r2 := addr2;
  RETURN r1^ < r2^
END LessThan;

PROCEDURE PrintReal(addr: ADDRESS);
  VAR r: POINTER TO REAL;
BEGIN
  r := addr;
  WriteReal(r^, 15)
END PrintReal;
```

Finally, modify the call of InitializeTree as follows:

```
InitializeTree(tree, SIZE(REAL), LessThan, PrintReal);
```

7. In the second import list, replace CharacterStacks by GenericStacks and replace CharStack by Stack. In the declaration of s, replace CharStack by Stack. In the call of Initialize, add SIZE(CHAR) as a second parameter.

9.

```
PROCEDURE LessThan(addr1, addr2: ADDRESS): BOOLEAN;
  VAR item1, item2: POINTER TO Item;
BEGIN
  item1 := addr1;
  item2 := addr2;
  RETURN item1^.number < item2^.number
END LessThan;
   .
   .
   .
GenericSort(ADR(inventory[1]), ADR(inventory[lastItem]),
            LessThan, SIZE(Item));
```

10.

```
PROCEDURE Complement(w: WORD): WORD;
BEGIN
  RETURN WORD(BITSET{0..bitsPerWord-1} - BITSET(w))
END Complement;
```

11.
```
PROCEDURE WriteBits(w: WORD);
  VAR bit: CARDINAL;
BEGIN
  FOR bit := bitsPerWord - 1 TO 0 BY -1 DO
    IF bit IN BITSET(w) THEN
      Write('1')
    ELSE
      Write('0')
    END
  END
END WriteBits;
```

12.
```
PROCEDURE ShiftRight(w: WORD; n: CARDINAL): WORD;
  VAR result: CARDINAL;
BEGIN
  result := CARDINAL(w);
  WHILE n > 0 DO
    result := result DIV 2;
    DEC(n)
  END;
  RETURN WORD(result)
END ShiftRight;
```

13.
```
PROCEDURE ShiftLeft(w: WORD; n: CARDINAL): WORD;
  VAR result: BITSET;
BEGIN
  result := BITSET(w);
  WHILE n > 0 DO
    EXCL(result, bitsPerWord-1);
    result := BITSET(CARDINAL(result) * 2);
    DEC(n)
  END;
  RETURN WORD(result)
END ShiftLeft;
```

14.
```
PROCEDURE CircularShift(w: WORD; n: CARDINAL): WORD;
  VAR result: BITSET;
BEGIN
  result := BITSET(w);
  WHILE n > 0 DO
    IF 0 IN result THEN
      result := BITSET(CARDINAL(result) DIV 2);
      INCL(result, bitsPerWord-1)
    ELSE
      result := BITSET(CARDINAL(result) DIV 2)
    END;
    DEC(n)
  END;
  RETURN WORD(result)
END CircularShift;
```

15. The call of CHR is illegal if CARDINAL(w) exceeds ORD(MAX(CHAR)).

16.
```
PROCEDURE PrintDate(date: WORD);
  CONST yearMask  = BITSET{9..15};
        yearDiv   = 512;              (* 2 ** 9 *)
        monthMask = BITSET{5..8};
        monthDiv  = 32;               (* 2 ** 5 *)
        dayMask   = BITSET{0..4};
BEGIN
  WriteCard(CARDINAL(BITSET(date) * monthMask)
           DIV monthDiv, 1);
  Write('-');
  WriteCard(CARDINAL(BITSET(date) * dayMask), 1);
  Write('-');
  WriteCard(CARDINAL(BITSET(date) * yearMask)
           DIV yearDiv + 1980, 1)
END PrintDate;
```

17.
```
PROCEDURE SetBitField(VAR w: WORD;
                      highBit, lowBit: CARDINAL;
                      newField: WORD);
  VAR bit: CARDINAL;
      result: BITSET;
BEGIN
  result := BITSET(w);
  FOR bit := lowBit TO highBit DO
    IF bit - lowBit IN BITSET(newField) THEN
      INCL(result, bit)
    ELSE
      EXCL(result, bit)
    END
  END;
  w := WORD(result)
END SetBitField;
```

18.
```
PROCEDURE LowByte(w: WORD): WORD;
BEGIN
  RETURN ShiftRight(ShiftLeft(w, 8), 8)
END LowByte;

PROCEDURE HighByte(w: WORD): WORD;
BEGIN
  RETURN ShiftRight(w, 8)
END HighByte;
```

19.
```
PROCEDURE SwapBytes(w: WORD): WORD;
  VAR temp, result: TwoBytes;
BEGIN
  temp := TwoBytes(w);
  result.lowByte := temp.highByte;
  result.highByte := temp.lowByte;
  RETURN WORD(result)
END SwapBytes;
```

20.
```
PROCEDURE WriteHex(w: WORD);
  VAR hexDigits: ARRAY [0..15] OF CHAR;
      hexString: ARRAY [0..3] OF CHAR;
      digit, n: CARDINAL;
BEGIN
  hexDigits := "0123456789ABCDEF";
  n := CARDINAL(w);
  FOR digit := 3 TO 0 BY -1 DO
    hexString[digit] := hexDigits[n MOD 16];
    n := n DIV 16
  END;
  WriteString(hexString)
END WriteHex;
```

21.
```
PROCEDURE DisplayMemory(addr: ADDRESS; numWords: CARDINAL);
  CONST numbersPerLine = 10;
  CONST numbersPerLine = 10;
        linesPerScreen = 25;
        numbersPerScreen = numbersPerLine *
                             (linesPerScreen - 1);
  VAR i: CARDINAL;
      ch: CHAR;
BEGIN
  FOR i := 1 TO numWords DO
    WriteHex(CARDINAL(addr^), 7);
    IF i MOD numbersPerLine = 0 THEN
      WriteLn
    END;
    IF i MOD numbersPerScreen = 0 THEN
      WriteString("Type any character to continue...");
      Read(ch);
      WriteLn
    END;
    INC(addr, SIZE(WORD))
  END
END DisplayMemory;
```

22. Suppose, for example, that `integer` and pointer values require the same amount of storage. The following record type allows us to perform type transfer between `integer` and `ptr` values, where `ptr` is any pointer type.

```
type variant = record
                   case boolean of
                     true:  (intval: integer);
                     false: (ptrval: ptr)
                 end;
```

Compilers normally overlay storage for the `intval` and `ptrval` fields. Thus, we can store a value into the record as an `integer` and retrieve it as a `ptr` value:

```
var i: integer;
    p: ptr;
    v: variant;
  .
  .
  .
v.intval := i;
p := v.ptrval;
```

The same record also allows transfer from `ptr` to `integer`.

Modula-2's method is better because it makes type transfer more visible; the Pascal method is a "trick" that could easily be overlooked by a person reading the program. The Modula-2 method has a second advantage: a Modula-2 compiler can check that the two types actually require the same amount of storage. If the program is transported to a machine on which the types require different amounts of storage, the compiler can detect the error. With a Pascal variant record, no such checking is possible.

23. One possibility is to require that programs perform type transfer by calling a function (the name `CAST` has been suggested) imported from the `SYSTEM` module. For example, to assign the value of an `INTEGER` variable `i` to a `BITSET` variable `s`, the programmer would write

    ```
    s := CAST(BITSET, i);
    ```

    We could identify modules that perform type transfer by checking for an import of `CAST`. Also, we could find all uses of type transfer in a module by searching for calls of `CAST`.

24.
```
IMPLEMENTATION MODULE Screen;

  FROM SYSTEM IMPORT ADR;

  CONST videoMask = BITSET{4..5};
        videoDiv = 16;

  TYPE ScreenArray =
         ARRAY [1..numRows], [1..numColumns] OF
           RECORD
             char: CHAR;
             attr: CHAR
           END;
```

```
VAR equipFlag [0:410H]: BITSET;
    monoBuffer [0B000H:0]: ScreenArray;
    colorBuffer [0B800H:0]: ScreenArray;
    screen: POINTER TO ScreenArray;
    xPos, yPos: CARDINAL;

PROCEDURE ClearScreen;
  VAR x, y: CARDINAL;
BEGIN
  FOR y := 1 TO numRows DO
    FOR x := 1 TO numColumns DO
      screen^[y, x].char := ' ';
      screen^[y, x].attr := normal
    END
  END
END ClearScreen;

PROCEDURE GotoXY(x, y: CARDINAL);
BEGIN
  xPos := x;
  yPos := y
END GotoXY;

PROCEDURE WriteChar(char: CHAR);
BEGIN
  screen^[yPos, xPos].char := char
END WriteChar;

PROCEDURE WriteAttr(attr: CHAR);
BEGIN
  screen^[yPos, xPos].attr := attr
END WriteAttr;

PROCEDURE ReadAttr(VAR attr: CHAR);
BEGIN
  attr := screen^[yPos, xPos].attr
END ReadAttr;

BEGIN
  IF CARDINAL(equipFlag * videoMask) DIV videoDiv = 2 THEN
    screen := ADR(colorBuffer)
  ELSE
    screen := ADR(monoBuffer)
  END
END Screen.
```

Chapter 12

1. When a procedure calls itself recursively, the new invocation of the procedure begins in a different state than the old invocation—the new invocation

begins executing at the beginning of the procedure body and may have different parameters than the old invocation. This difference in state makes recursion useful. A Modula-2 coroutine that transfers control to itself would serve no purpose, because the state of the coroutine after the transfer would be exactly the same as before the transfer.

2.
```
MODULE PrintFibonacciNumbers;

  FROM SYSTEM IMPORT WORD, ADDRESS, NEWPROCESS, TRANSFER,
                     ADR;
  FROM Terminal IMPORT BusyRead;
  FROM InOut IMPORT WriteCard, WriteLn;

  CONST wkspSize = 1000;

  VAR wksp1, wksp2: ARRAY [1..wkspSize] OF WORD;
      main, cor1, cor2: ADDRESS;
      fib1, fib2: CARDINAL;
      ch: CHAR;

  PROCEDURE IncFib1;
  BEGIN
    LOOP
      WriteCard(fib2, 1);
      WriteLn;
      INC(fib1, fib2);
      TRANSFER(cor1, cor2)
    END
  END IncFib1;

  PROCEDURE IncFib2;
  BEGIN
    LOOP
      WriteCard(fib1, 1);
      WriteLn;
      INC(fib2, fib1);
      TRANSFER(cor2, main)
    END
  END IncFib2;

BEGIN
  fib1 := 0;
  fib2 := 1;
  NEWPROCESS(IncFib1, ADR(wksp1), SIZE(wksp1), cor1);
  NEWPROCESS(IncFib2, ADR(wksp2), SIZE(wksp2), cor2);
  REPEAT
    TRANSFER(main, cor1);
    BusyRead(ch)
  UNTIL ch # 0C
END PrintFibonacciNumbers.
```

3. MoveL and MoveR can share a coroutine variable, but MoveL, MoveR, and Split cannot. In general, only two coroutines can share a coroutine variable. When three coroutines exist, at least two variables are necessary to store references to the two coroutines that are not currently executing.

4. The following implementation of Buffer is based on an example in Wirth's *Programming in Modula-2*.

```
IMPLEMENTATION MODULE Buffer;

  FROM Processes IMPORT SIGNAL, SEND, WAIT, Init;

  CONST bufferSize = 128;

  VAR currentSize: [0..bufferSize];
      nonfull, nonempty: SIGNAL;
      in, out: [0..bufferSize-1];
      buffer: ARRAY [0..bufferSize-1] OF CHAR;

  PROCEDURE Put(ch: CHAR);
  BEGIN
    IF currentSize = bufferSize THEN
      WAIT(nonfull)
    END;
    INC(currentSize);
    buffer[in] := ch;
    in := (in + 1) MOD bufferSize;
    SEND(nonempty)
  END Put;

  PROCEDURE Get(VAR ch: CHAR);
  BEGIN
    IF currentSize = 0 THEN
      WAIT(nonempty)
    END;
    DEC(currentSize);
    ch := buffer[out];
    out := (out + 1) MOD bufferSize;
    SEND(nonfull)
  END Get;

BEGIN
  currentSize := 0;
  in := 0;
  out := 0;
  Init(nonfull);
  Init(nonempty)
END Buffer.
```

6.
```
IMPLEMENTATION MODULE ProcessQueues;

  FROM SYSTEM IMPORT ADDRESS;
  FROM Storage IMPORT ALLOCATE, DEALLOCATE;
  FROM Terminal IMPORT WriteString, WriteLn;

  TYPE ProcessQueue = POINTER TO QueueElement;
       QueueElement = RECORD
                        next, previous: ProcessQueue;
                        process: ADDRESS
                      END;

  PROCEDURE InsertAtEnd(VAR queue: ProcessQueue;
                        process: ADDRESS);
    VAR temp: ProcessQueue;
  BEGIN
    ALLOCATE(temp, SIZE(QueueElement));
    temp^.process := process;
    IF queue = NIL THEN
      temp^.next := temp;
      temp^.previous := temp;
      queue := temp
    ELSE
      temp^.next := queue;
      temp^.previous := queue^.previous;
      queue^.previous^.next := temp;
      queue^.previous := temp
    END
  END InsertAtEnd;

  PROCEDURE DeleteFromFront(VAR queue: ProcessQueue;
                            VAR process: ADDRESS);
    VAR temp: ProcessQueue;
  BEGIN
    IF queue # NIL THEN
      process := queue^.process;
      IF queue^.next = queue THEN
        DEALLOCATE(queue, SIZE(QueueElement));
        queue := NIL
      ELSE
        temp := queue;
        queue := queue^.next;
        temp^.previous^.next := queue;
        queue^.previous := temp^.previous;
        DEALLOCATE(temp, SIZE(QueueElement))
      END
    ELSE
      WriteString("Error in ProcessQueues.DeleteFromFront");
      WriteLn;
```

```
    HALT
  END
END DeleteFromFront;

PROCEDURE MakeQueueEmpty(VAR queue: ProcessQueue);
BEGIN
  queue := NIL
END MakeQueueEmpty;

PROCEDURE IsQueueEmpty(queue: ProcessQueue): BOOLEAN;
BEGIN
  RETURN queue = NIL
END IsQueueEmpty;

END ProcessQueues.
```

7. Modify the declaration of event as follows:

```
VAR event: (block, terminate, reschedule);
```

Modify the CASE statement in the body of Scheduler as follows:

```
CASE event OF
  block:      InsertAtEnd(currentSemaphore^.queue,
                          currentProcess) |
  terminate:  (* do nothing *) |
  reschedule: InsertAtEnd(readyQueue, currentProcess)
END
```

Finally, revise the V procedure as follows:

```
PROCEDURE V(VAR sem: Semaphore);
  VAR process: ADDRESS;
BEGIN
  INC(sem^.count);
  IF sem^.count <= 0 THEN
    DeleteFromFront(sem^.queue, process);
    InsertAtEnd(readyQueue, process)
  END;
  event := reschedule;
  TRANSFER(currentProcess, schedProcess)
END V;
```

8. Modify ScheduledProcesses to import WriteString and WriteLn from Terminal. Add a declaration of a CARDINAL variable named numProcesses, and add to the body of ScheduledProcesses a statement that initializes numProcesses to 0. Add to the body of MakeReady a statement that increments numProcesses. Revise Scheduler as follows:

```
PROCEDURE Scheduler;
BEGIN
  WHILE NOT IsQueueEmpty(readyQueue) DO
```

```
    DeleteFromFront(readyQueue, currentProcess);
    TRANSFER(schedProcess, currentProcess);
    CASE event OF
      block:     InsertAtEnd(currentSemaphore^.queue,
                             currentProcess) |
      terminate: DEC(numProcesses)
    END
  END;
  IF numProcesses > 0 THEN
    WriteString("Error in ScheduledProcesses.Scheduler: ");
    WriteString("ready queue is empty but processes exist");
    WriteLn;
    HALT
  END
END Scheduler;
```

10. The version of `Quicksort` in Section 12.1 uses two static arrays as workspaces. The version in Section 12.2 requires much more space; each call of `Split` calls `StartProcess` twice, and each call of `StartProcess` allocates another workspace. The number of workspaces created depends on the number of calls of `Split`; in general, `Quicksort` will create many more than two workspaces. The version in Section 12.3 is similar: each call of `Split` calls `MakeReady` twice, and each call of `MakeReady` creates another workspace. However, if `ScheduledProcesses` were modified to deallocate the workspace of a terminating process (see exercise 9), then no more than two workspaces would exist simultaneously.

11.
```
MODULE Clock;

  IMPORT SYSTEM;
  FROM Terminal IMPORT BusyRead;
  FROM InOut IMPORT ReadCard, WriteString, WriteLn;
  FROM Screen IMPORT numRows, numColumns, ClearScreen,
                     GotoXY, WriteChar;

  CONST ypos = numRows DIV 2 + 1;
        xpos = (numColumns - 8) DIV 2 + 1;

  VAR ch: CHAR;

  MODULE Timer[7];

    FROM SYSTEM IMPORT WORD, ADDRESS, ADR, NEWPROCESS,
                       TRANSFER, IOTRANSFER;

    EXPORT StartClock, hours, minutes, seconds, timeChange;

    CONST timerInt = 1CH;
          wkspSize = 1000;
```

```
      VAR main, timer: ADDRESS;
          wksp: ARRAY [1..wkspSize] OF WORD;
          hours, minutes, seconds: CARDINAL;
          timeChange: BOOLEAN;

      PROCEDURE InterruptHandler;
        VAR ticksTimes5: CARDINAL;
      BEGIN
        ticksTimes5 := 0;
        LOOP
          IOTRANSFER(timer, main, timerInt);
          INC(ticksTimes5, 5);
          IF ticksTimes5 >= 91 THEN
            timeChange := TRUE;
            DEC(ticksTimes5, 91);
            INC(seconds);
            IF seconds = 60 THEN
              seconds := 0;
              INC(minutes);
              IF minutes = 60 THEN
                minutes := 0;
                INC(hours);
                IF hours = 24 THEN
                  hours := 0
                END
              END
            END
          END
        END
      END InterruptHandler;

      PROCEDURE StartClock;
      BEGIN
        NEWPROCESS(InterruptHandler, ADR(wksp), SIZE(wksp),
                   timer);
        TRANSFER(main, timer)
      END StartClock;

    BEGIN
      timeChange := FALSE
    END Timer;

  BEGIN
    WriteString("Enter current time.");
    WriteLn;
    WriteString("Hours: ");
    ReadCard(hours);
    WriteLn;
    WriteString("Minutes: ");
    ReadCard(minutes);
```

```
    WriteLn;
    WriteString("Seconds: ");
    ReadCard(seconds);
    WriteLn;
    StartClock;
    ClearScreen;
    REPEAT
      IF timeChange THEN
        GotoXY(xpos, ypos);
        WriteChar(CHR(ORD('0') + hours DIV 10));
        GotoXY(xpos + 1, ypos);
        WriteChar(CHR(ORD('0') + hours MOD 10));
        GotoXY(xpos + 2, ypos);
        WriteChar(':');
        GotoXY(xpos + 3, ypos);
        WriteChar(CHR(ORD('0') + minutes DIV 10));
        GotoXY(xpos + 4, ypos);
        WriteChar(CHR(ORD('0') + minutes MOD 10));
        GotoXY(xpos + 5, ypos);
        WriteChar(':');
        GotoXY(xpos + 6, ypos);
        WriteChar(CHR(ORD('0') + seconds DIV 10));
        GotoXY(xpos + 7, ypos);
        WriteChar(CHR(ORD('0') + seconds MOD 10));
        timeChange := FALSE
      END;
      BusyRead(ch)
    UNTIL ch # 0C
  END Clock.
```

13. Suppose that the queue maintained by Keys contains one character and that two processes exist. Process 1 calls KeyPressed to see if there is a character to be read; KeyPressed returns TRUE. At this point, Process 1 is interrupted by a clock interrupt and Process 2 resumes execution. Process 2 calls ReadChar, thus emptying the queue. When Process 1 resumes execution, it calls ReadChar to read a character. The queue is empty, so ReadChar fetches 0C. Because Process 1 expects a valid character, it may neglect to check the value it obtains from ReadChar, causing the program to fail.

14. Add LISTEN to the list of entities imported from SYSTEM and rewrite ReadChar as follows:

```
PROCEDURE ReadChar(VAR ch: CHAR);
BEGIN
  WHILE queueLength = 0 DO
    LISTEN
  END;
  ch := queue[head];
  head := (head + 1) MOD queueCapacity;
  DEC(queueLength)
END ReadChar;
```

16. *(Sketch)* ScheduledProcesses will maintain a *sleep queue* for processes that have called Sleep. Each process in the sleep queue has an associated timeRemaining value (a CARDINAL number). The processes in the sleep queue are sorted by timeRemaining; the process that has the least time to wait is first in the queue. The timeRemaining value for the first process, t_1, indicates the number of clock ticks that must occur before the process can resume executing. The timeRemaining value for the second process, t_2, is relative to the value for the first process; that is, the second process must wait $t_1 + t_2$ ticks before resuming execution. In general, the time-Remaining value for a process in the sleep queue is relative to the sum of the timeRemaining values for the preceding processes.

When called, Sleep inserts the current process into the sleep queue in the proper place. At each clock tick, Scheduler decrements the timeRe-maining value of the first process in the sleep queue; if the value becomes 0, Scheduler moves the process to the ready queue.

The existence of sleeping processes has some subtle consequences for the ScheduledProcesses module. In particular, Scheduler should not terminate if the ready queue is empty but the sleep queue is nonempty. Instead, it must wait until the first process on the sleep queue moves to the ready queue. Scheduler can call LISTEN (see exercise 14) to enable clock interrupts while it is waiting.

Chapter 13

1.
```
MODULE ListPrimes;

  FROM Terminal IMPORT BusyRead;
  FROM InOut IMPORT WriteCard, WriteLn;

  VAR divisor, i: CARDINAL;
      ch: CHAR;

BEGIN
  i := 2;
  REPEAT
    divisor := 1;
    REPEAT
      INC(divisor)
    UNTIL i MOD divisor = 0;
    IF divisor = i THEN
      WriteCard(i, 1);
      WriteLn
    END;
    INC(i);
    BusyRead(ch)
  UNTIL ch = 33C
END ListPrimes.
```

2.
```
PROCEDURE ReadCard(VAR i: CARDINAL);
  VAR ch: CHAR;
BEGIN
  REPEAT
    Read(ch)
  UNTIL ch # ' ';
  IF (ch < '0') OR ('9' < ch) THEN
    Done := FALSE;
    RETURN
  END;
  Done := TRUE;
  i := 0;
  REPEAT
    i := ORD(ch) - ORD('0') + 10 * i;
    Write(ch);
    Read(ch)
  UNTIL (ch < '0') OR ('9' < ch)
END ReadCard;
```

3. Add the following lines to the main IF statement immediately preceding the first ELSIF:

```
ELSIF ch = 11C THEN          (* tab? *)
  IF i > HIGH(str) THEN
    Write(7C)
  ELSE
    REPEAT
      str[i] := ' ';
      INC(i);
      Write(' ')
    UNTIL (i MOD 8 = 0) OR (i > HIGH(str))
  END
```

4.
```
MODULE ConcatenateFiles;

  FROM InOut IMPORT OpenInput, OpenOutput, CloseInput,
                    CloseOutput, Done, Read, Write,
                    WriteString, WriteLn;

  PROCEDURE CopyFile;
    VAR ch: CHAR;
  BEGIN
    OpenInput("TXT");
    Read(ch);
    WHILE Done DO
      Write(ch);
      Read(ch)
    END;
    CloseInput
  END CopyFile;
```

```
BEGIN
  WriteString("When prompted, first enter name of output ");
  WriteString("file, then names of two input files.");
  WriteLn;
  OpenOutput("TXT");
  CopyFile;
  CopyFile;
  CloseOutput
END ConcatenateFiles.
```

5.
```
MODULE SeparateWords;

  FROM InOut IMPORT OpenInput, CloseInput, OpenOutput,
                    CloseOutput, Read, Write, Done,
                    WriteString, WriteLn;

  VAR previousChar, currentChar: CHAR;

  PROCEDURE IsWhiteSpace(ch: CHAR): BOOLEAN;
  BEGIN
    RETURN ch <= ' '
  END IsWhiteSpace;

BEGIN
  WriteString("Enter name of input file.");
  WriteLn;
  OpenInput("TXT");
  WriteString("Enter name of output file.");
  WriteLn;
  OpenOutput("TXT");
  previousChar := ' ';
  Read(currentChar);
  WHILE Done DO
    IF IsWhiteSpace(currentChar) THEN
      IF NOT IsWhiteSpace(previousChar) THEN
        WriteLn
      END
    ELSE
      Write(currentChar)
    END;
    previousChar := currentChar;
    Read(currentChar)
  END;
  CloseInput;
  CloseOutput
END SeparateWords.
```

6.
```
MODULE RemoveDuplicateLines;

  FROM InOut IMPORT OpenInput, CloseInput, OpenOutput,
                    CloseOutput, Read, WriteString,
                    WriteLn, Done, EOL;

  FROM String IMPORT Compare, CompareResult;

  CONST maxLineLen = 80;

  TYPE LineBuffer = ARRAY [0..maxLineLen-1] OF CHAR;

  VAR currentLine, previousLine: LineBuffer;
      endOfFile: BOOLEAN;

  PROCEDURE ReadLine(VAR string: ARRAY OF CHAR;
                     VAR endOfFile: BOOLEAN);
    VAR pos: CARDINAL;
        ch: CHAR;
  BEGIN
    endOfFile := FALSE;
    pos := 0;
    REPEAT
      Read(ch);
      IF NOT Done THEN
        endOfFile := TRUE
      ELSIF pos > HIGH(string) THEN
        CloseInput;
        CloseOutput;
        WriteString("Buffer overflow in ReadLine");
        WriteLn;
        HALT
      ELSE
        string[pos] := ch;
        INC(pos)
      END
    UNTIL endOfFile OR (ch = EOL);
    IF pos <= HIGH(string) THEN
      string[pos] := 0C
    END
  END ReadLine;

BEGIN
  WriteString("Enter name of input file.");
  WriteLn;
  OpenInput("TXT");
  WriteString("Enter name of output file.");
```

```
    WriteLn;
    OpenOutput("TXT");
    ReadLine(previousLine, endOfFile);
    WriteString(previousLine);
    WHILE NOT endOfFile DO
      ReadLine(currentLine, endOfFile);
      IF Compare(currentLine, previousLine) # equal THEN
        WriteString(currentLine);
        previousLine := currentLine
      END
    END;
    CloseInput;
    CloseOutput
  END RemoveDuplicateLines.
```

7.
```
MODULE PrintTable;

  FROM InOut IMPORT WriteCard, WriteString, WriteLn;
  FROM RealInOut IMPORT WriteReal;
  FROM MathLib0 IMPORT sqrt;

  VAR n: CARDINAL;

BEGIN
  FOR n := 1 TO 100 DO
    WriteCard(n, 3);
    WriteCard(n * n, 7);
    WriteString("  ");
    WriteReal(sqrt(FLOAT(n)), 15);
    WriteLn
  END
END PrintTable.
```

8. The advantages of making `File` opaque are the advantages of opaque types in general. Clients would not be able to see the structure of the `File` type and hence could not become dependent on it. (Programs that rely on `FileSystem` may not be portable, because the fields of the `File` type vary from one system to another.) Also, clients could not change the fields of a `File` value accidentally (a possibility when `File` is a record type). The primary disadvantage is that clients would have to perform a procedure call to obtain status information about a file. (If `File` is a record type, clients merely access the appropriate field, avoiding the overhead of a procedure call.) Furthermore, `FileSystem` would have to export status procedures, making the module longer and more complicated.

9.
```
MODULE DisplayFile;

  FROM InOut IMPORT ReadString, WriteString, WriteLn,
                    Read, Write, EOL;
```

```
  FROM FileSystem IMPORT File, Lookup, Response, ReadChar,
                         Close;

  CONST fileNameLen = 15;
        linesPerScreen = 25;

  VAR fileName: ARRAY [0..fileNameLen-1] OF CHAR;
      file: File;
      numLines: CARDINAL;
      ch: CHAR;

BEGIN
  WriteString("Enter name of file to be displayed: ");
  LOOP
    ReadString(fileName);
    WriteLn;
    Lookup(file, fileName, FALSE);
    IF file.res = done THEN EXIT END;
    WriteString("Can't open file; re-enter file name: ")
  END;
  numLines := 0;
  LOOP
    ReadChar(file, ch);
    IF file.eof THEN EXIT END;
    Write(ch);
    IF ch = EOL THEN
      INC(numLines);
      IF numLines = linesPerScreen - 1 THEN
        WriteString("Type any character to continue...");
        Read(ch);
        WriteLn;
        numLines := 0
      END
    END
  END;
  Close(file)
END DisplayFile.
```

10.
```
PROCEDURE ReadBlock(VAR f: File; VAR block: ARRAY OF WORD;
                    VAR wordsRead: CARDINAL);
BEGIN
  wordsRead := 0;
  LOOP
    IF wordsRead > HIGH(block) THEN EXIT END;
    ReadWord(f, block[wordsRead]);
    IF f.eof THEN EXIT END;
    INC(wordsRead)
  END
END ReadBlock;
```

11. Replace the statement

```
IF file1.eof OR file2.eof THEN EXIT END;
```

with the following statement:

```
IF file1.eof & (line1[0] = 0C) OR
   file2.eof & (line2[0] = 0C) THEN EXIT END;
```

12.
```
MODULE CompareBinaryFiles;

  FROM InOut IMPORT ReadString, WriteString, WriteLn,
                    WriteCard, WriteHex;
  FROM FileSystem IMPORT File, Lookup, Response, ReadWord,
                         Close;

  CONST fileNameLen = 15;

  VAR fileName1, fileName2:
        ARRAY [0..fileNameLen-1] OF CHAR;
      file1, file2: File;
      wordNumber: CARDINAL;
      word1, word2: CARDINAL;

  PROCEDURE OpenFile(VAR file: File;
                     VAR fileName: ARRAY OF CHAR);
  BEGIN
    LOOP
      ReadString(fileName);
      WriteLn;
      Lookup(file, fileName, FALSE);
      IF file.res = done THEN EXIT END;
      WriteString("Can't open file; re-enter file name: ")
    END
  END OpenFile;

BEGIN
  WriteString("Enter name of first file: ");
  OpenFile(file1, fileName1);
  WriteString("Enter name of second file: ");
  OpenFile(file2, fileName2);
  WriteLn;

  wordNumber := 1;
  LOOP
    ReadWord(file1, word1);
    ReadWord(file2, word2);
    IF file1.eof OR file2.eof THEN EXIT END;
    IF CARDINAL(word1) # CARDINAL(word2) THEN
      WriteString("Mismatch at word ");
      WriteCard(wordNumber, 1);
      WriteLn;
```

```
          WriteString(fileName1);
          WriteString(": ");
          WriteHex(CARDINAL(word1), 1);
          WriteString("H");
          WriteLn;
          WriteString(fileName2);
          WriteString(": ");
          WriteHex(CARDINAL(word2), 1);
          WriteString("H");
          WriteLn;
          WriteLn
        END;
        INC(wordNumber)
      END;

      IF file1.eof & NOT file2.eof THEN
        WriteString("End of file encountered while reading ");
        WriteString(fileName1);
        WriteLn
      ELSIF NOT file1.eof & file2.eof THEN
        WriteString("End of file encountered while reading ");
        WriteString(fileName2);
        WriteLn
      END;

      Close(file1);
      Close(file2)
    END CompareBinaryFiles.
```

13.
```
MODULE CopyBinaryFile;

  FROM SYSTEM IMPORT WORD, ADDRESS, ADR;
  FROM InOut IMPORT ReadString, WriteString, WriteLn;
  FROM FileSystem IMPORT File, Lookup, Response, ReadWord,
                         WriteWord, Close;

  CONST bufferSize = 1024;
        fileNameLen = 15;

  VAR buffer: ARRAY [0..bufferSize-1] OF WORD;
      inputFile, outputFile: File;
      wordsRead: CARDINAL;

  PROCEDURE OpenFile(VAR file: File);
    VAR fileName: ARRAY [0..fileNameLen-1] OF CHAR;
  BEGIN
    LOOP
      ReadString(fileName);
      WriteLn;
      Lookup(file, fileName, FALSE);
```

```
      IF file.res = done THEN EXIT END;
      WriteString("Can't open file; re-enter file name: ")
    END
  END OpenFile;

  PROCEDURE ReadWords(VAR f: File; addr: ADDRESS;
                      words: CARDINAL;
                      VAR wordsRead: CARDINAL);
  BEGIN
    wordsRead := 0;
    LOOP
      IF wordsRead = words THEN EXIT END;
      ReadWord(f, addr^);
      IF f.eof THEN EXIT END;
      INC(wordsRead);
      INC(addr, SIZE(WORD))
    END
  END ReadWords;

  PROCEDURE WriteWords(VAR f: File; addr: ADDRESS;
                       words: CARDINAL);
    VAR i: CARDINAL;
  BEGIN
    FOR i := 1 TO words DO
      WriteWord(f, addr^);
      INC(addr, SIZE(WORD))
    END
  END WriteWords;

BEGIN
  WriteString("Enter name of input file: ");
  OpenFile(inputFile);
  WriteString("Enter name of output file: ");
  OpenFile(outputFile);
  LOOP
    ReadWords(inputFile, ADR(buffer), bufferSize,
              wordsRead);
    IF wordsRead = 0 THEN EXIT END;
    WriteWords(outputFile, ADR(buffer), wordsRead)
  END;
  Close(inputFile);
  Close(outputFile)
END CopyBinaryFile.
```

14. Add `Length` to the list of entities imported from `FileSystem`. Add the following declaration:

```
VAR highpos, lowpos, numRecords, low, high, mid: CARDINAL;
```

Replace the body of `UpdateInventory` with the following:

```
BEGIN
  Lookup(inventoryFile, inventoryFileName, FALSE);
  SetModify(inventoryFile);
  Length(inventoryFile, highpos, lowpos);
  numRecords := lowpos DIV SIZE(Item);
  Lookup(updateFile, updateFileName, FALSE);

  LOOP
    ReadBlock(updateFile, updateBuffer);
    IF updateFile.eof THEN EXIT END;
    low := 1;
    high := numRecords;
    REPEAT
      mid := (low + high) DIV 2;
      SetPos(inventoryFile, 0, (mid - 1) * SIZE(Item));
      ReadBlock(inventoryFile, inventoryBuffer);
      IF updateBuffer.number <= inventoryBuffer.number THEN
        high := mid - 1
      END;
      IF updateBuffer.number >= inventoryBuffer.number THEN
        low := mid + 1
      END
    UNTIL low > high;
    IF low > high + 1 THEN
      INC(inventoryBuffer.onHand, updateBuffer.change);
      SetPos(inventoryFile, 0, (mid - 1) * SIZE(Item));
      WriteBlock(inventoryFile, inventoryBuffer)
    END
  END;

  Close(inventoryFile);
  Close(updateFile)
END UpdateInventory.
```

15.
```
MODULE MergeInventoryFiles;

  FROM SYSTEM IMPORT WORD;
  FROM FileSystem IMPORT File, Lookup, ReadWord, WriteWord,
                         Close;

  CONST fileName1 = "INVENT1.DAT";
        fileName2 = "INVENT2.DAT";
        masterFileName = "MASTER.DAT";

  TYPE StringType = ARRAY [0..19] OF CHAR;
       Item = RECORD
                number: CARDINAL;
                description: StringType;
                price: REAL;
                onHand: INTEGER
              END;
```

```
  VAR file1, file2, masterFile: File;
      buffer1, buffer2: Item;

  PROCEDURE ReadBlock(VAR f: File;
                      VAR block: ARRAY OF WORD);
    VAR i: CARDINAL;
  BEGIN
    FOR i := 0 TO HIGH(block) DO
      ReadWord(f, block[i])
    END
  END ReadBlock;

  PROCEDURE WriteBlock(VAR f: File; block: ARRAY OF WORD);
    VAR i: CARDINAL;
  BEGIN
    FOR i := 0 TO HIGH(block) DO
      WriteWord(f, block[i])
    END
  END WriteBlock;

BEGIN
  Lookup(file1, fileName1, FALSE);
  Lookup(file2, fileName2, FALSE);
  Lookup(masterFile, masterFileName, TRUE);
  ReadBlock(file1, buffer1);
  ReadBlock(file2, buffer2);
  WHILE NOT file1.eof & NOT file2.eof DO
    IF buffer1.number < buffer2.number THEN
      WriteBlock(masterFile, buffer1);
      ReadBlock(file1, buffer1)
    ELSIF buffer1.number > buffer2.number THEN
      WriteBlock(masterFile, buffer2);
      ReadBlock(file2, buffer2)
    ELSE
      INC(buffer1.onHand, buffer2.onHand);
      WriteBlock(masterFile, buffer1);
      ReadBlock(file1, buffer1);
      ReadBlock(file2, buffer2)
    END
  END;
  WHILE NOT file1.eof DO
    WriteBlock(masterFile, buffer1);
    ReadBlock(file1, buffer1)
  END;
  WHILE NOT file2.eof DO
    WriteBlock(masterFile, buffer2);
    ReadBlock(file2, buffer2)
  END;
  Close(file1);
  Close(file2);
```

```
  Close(masterFile)
END MergeInventoryFiles.
```

16.
```
MODULE FindExpensiveItem;

  FROM SYSTEM IMPORT WORD;
  FROM FileSystem IMPORT File, Lookup, SetModify, ReadWord,
                         WriteWord, SetPos, Close;

  CONST inventoryFileName = "INVENT.DAT";

  TYPE StringType = ARRAY [0..19] OF CHAR;
       Item = RECORD
                number: CARDINAL;
                description: StringType;
                price: REAL;
                onHand: INTEGER
              END;

  VAR inventoryFile: File;
      inventoryBuffer: Item;
      highNumber: CARDINAL;
      highPrice: REAL;

  PROCEDURE ReadBlock(VAR f: File;
                      VAR block: ARRAY OF WORD);
    VAR i: CARDINAL;
  BEGIN
    FOR i := 0 TO HIGH(block) DO
      ReadWord(f, block[i])
    END
  END ReadBlock;

  PROCEDURE WriteBlock(VAR f: File; block: ARRAY OF WORD);
    VAR i: CARDINAL;
  BEGIN
    FOR i := 0 TO HIGH(block) DO
      WriteWord(f, block[i])
    END
  END WriteBlock;

BEGIN
  Lookup(inventoryFile, inventoryFileName, FALSE);
  SetModify(inventoryFile);
  highPrice := 0.0;
  LOOP
    ReadBlock(inventoryFile, inventoryBuffer);
    IF inventoryFile.eof THEN EXIT END;
    IF inventoryBuffer.price > highPrice THEN
      highNumber := inventoryBuffer.number;
```

```
        highPrice := inventoryBuffer.price
      END
    END;
    SetPos(inventoryFile, 0, (highNumber - 1) * SIZE(Item));
    ReadBlock(inventoryFile, inventoryBuffer);
    inventoryBuffer.onHand := 0;
    SetPos(inventoryFile, 0, (highNumber - 1) * SIZE(Item));
    WriteBlock(inventoryFile, inventoryBuffer);
    Close(inventoryFile)
  END FindExpensiveItem.
```

17.
```
PROCEDURE LookupUser(VAR passwordFile: File;
                     userName: String10;
                     VAR userPassword: Password;
                     VAR success: BOOLEAN);
  VAR buffer: UserRecord;
BEGIN
  Reset(passwordFile);
  LOOP
    ReadBlock(passwordFile, buffer);
    IF passwordFile.eof THEN EXIT END;
    IF Compare(userName, buffer.userName) = equal THEN
      userPassword := buffer.userPassword;
      success := TRUE;
      RETURN
    END
  END;
  success := FALSE
END LookupUser;
```

`ReadBlock` appears in `UpdateInventory`; `Compare` is exported by the `String` module (Section 10.2).

18.
```
PROCEDURE AddUser(VAR passwordFile: File;
                  userName: String10;
                  userPassword: Password);
  VAR buffer: UserRecord;
      highpos, lowpos: CARDINAL;
BEGIN
  SetWrite(passwordFile);
  Length(passwordFile, highpos, lowpos);
  SetPos(passwordFile, highpos, lowpos);
  buffer.userName := userName;
  buffer.userPassword := userPassword;
  WriteBlock(passwordFile, buffer);
  SetOpen(passwordFile)
END AddUser;
```

`WriteBlock` appears in `UpdateInventory`.

19.
```
PROCEDURE ChangePassword(VAR passwordFile: File;
                         userName: String10;
                         newPassword: Password);
  VAR buffer: UserRecord;
      highpos, lowpos: CARDINAL;
BEGIN
  Reset(passwordFile);
  SetModify(passwordFile);
  LOOP
    GetPos(passwordFile, highpos, lowpos);
    ReadBlock(passwordFile, buffer);
    IF passwordFile.eof THEN EXIT END;
    IF Compare(userName, buffer.userName) = equal THEN
      buffer.userPassword := newPassword;
      SetPos(passwordFile, highpos, lowpos);
      WriteBlock(passwordFile, buffer);
      EXIT
    END
  END;
  SetOpen(passwordFile)
END ChangePassword;
```

`ReadBlock` and `WriteBlock` appear in `UpdateInventory`; `Compare` is from the `String` module (Section 10.2).

20.
```
MODULE DisplayFile;

  FROM InOut IMPORT Read, Done, Write, ReadString,
                    WriteString, WriteLn, WriteCard,
                    WriteOct, WriteHex;
  FROM FileSystem IMPORT File, Lookup, Response, ReadChar,
                         Close;

  CONST fileNameLen = 15;

  TYPE WriteProcedure = PROCEDURE (CARDINAL, CARDINAL);

  VAR writeNumber: WriteProcedure;
      inputFile: File;

  PROCEDURE AskForBase(VAR writeNumber: WriteProcedure);
    VAR base: CHAR;
  BEGIN
    WriteString("Display file in decimal, hex, or octal?");
    WriteLn;
    WriteString("Enter d, h, or o: ");
    Read(base);
    Write(base);
    WriteLn;
```

```
  CASE CAP(base) OF
    'D': writeNumber := WriteCard |
    'H': writeNumber := WriteHex |
    'O': writeNumber := WriteOct
  ELSE
    WriteString("Base not recognized; using decimal.");
    WriteLn;
    writeNumber := WriteCard
  END
END AskForBase;

PROCEDURE OpenFile(VAR file: File);
  VAR fileName: ARRAY [0..fileNameLen-1] OF CHAR;
BEGIN
  WriteString("Enter name of input file: ");
  LOOP
    ReadString(fileName);
    WriteLn;
    Lookup(file, fileName, FALSE);
    IF file.res = done THEN EXIT END;
    WriteString("Can't open file; re-enter file name: ")
  END
END OpenFile;

PROCEDURE DisplayNumbers(VAR file: File;
                         writeNumber: WriteProcedure);
  CONST numbersPerLine = 10;
        linesPerScreen = 25;
        numbersPerScreen = numbersPerLine *
                             (linesPerScreen - 1);
  VAR i: CARDINAL;
      ch: CHAR;
BEGIN
  i := 0;
  LOOP
    ReadChar(file, ch);
    IF file.eof THEN EXIT END;
    writeNumber(ORD(ch), 7);
    INC(i);
    IF i MOD numbersPerLine = 0 THEN
      WriteLn
    END;
    IF i = numbersPerScreen THEN
      WriteString("Type any character to continue...");
      Read(ch);
      WriteLn;
      i := 0
    END
  END;
```

```
    Close(file)
  END DisplayNumbers;

BEGIN
  AskForBase(writeNumber);
  OpenFile(inputFile);
  DisplayNumbers(inputFile, writeNumber)
END DisplayFile.
```

Index

Structured Statements

```
CASE Expression OF
  CaseLabelList :
    StatementSequence |
  CaseLabelList :
    StatementSequence
  . . .
ELSE
  StatementSequence
END
```

```
IF Expression THEN
  StatementSequence
ELSIF Expression THEN
  StatementSequence
. . .
ELSE
  StatementSequence
END
```

```
FOR Ident := Expression TO Expression BY ConstExpression DO
  StatementSequence
END
```

```
LOOP
  StatementSequence
END
```

```
REPEAT
  StatementSequence
UNTIL Expression
```

```
WHILE Expression DO
  StatementSequence
END
```

```
WITH Designator DO
  StatementSequence
END
```

(Shaded portions are optional; constructs followed by ... may be repeated.)

Operator Precedence

```
Highest: NOT ~
         * / DIV MOD AND &
         + - OR
Lowest:  = # <> < <= > >= IN
```